ASE Test Preparation an

Covers ASE Areas A1-A8 plus A9, G1 and L1

Third Edition

James D. Halderman

**ASE Certified Master Automobile Technician
(A1–A8), plus A9, F1, G1, L1 and L3**

MW00843646

Vice President, Portfolio Management: Andrew Gilfillan

Executive Portfolio Manager: Jenifer Niles

Portfolio Management Assistant: Lara Dimmick

Senior Vice President, Marketing: David Gesell

Marketing Coordinator: Elizabeth MacKenzie-Lamb

Director, Digital Studio and Content Production: Brian Hyland

Digital Studio Producer: Allison Longley

Managing Producer: Cynthia Zonneveld

Managing Producer: Jennifer Sargunar

Content Producer: Holly Shufeldt

Content Producer: Faraz Sharique Ali

Manager, Rights Management: Johanna Burke

Operations Specialist: Deidra Headlee

Cover Design: Pearson CSC

Cover Credit: Henrik5000/Getty Images

Full-Service Management and Composition: Integra Software Service Pvt. Ltd.

Printer/Binder: LSC Communications,Inc.

Cover Printer: Phoenix Color/Hagerstown

Text Font: Helvetica Neue LT W1G-Roman

Library of Congress Cataloging-in-Publication Data
Names: Halderman, James D., author.
Title: ASE test preparation and study guide : covers ASE areas A1-A8 plus A9, G1 and L1 / James D. Halderman.
Description: Third edition. | Boston : Pearson, [2018]
Identifiers: LCCN 2018034148| ISBN 9780135232866 | ISBN 0135232864
Subjects: LCSH: Automobiles—Maintenance and repair—Examinations—Study guides. | Automobiles—Maintenance and repair—Examinations, questions, etc. | Automobile mechanics—Certification—United States. | National Institute for Automotive Service Excellence—Examinations—Study guides.
Classification: LCC TL157 .H37 2018 | DDC 629.28/72—dc23
LC record available at https://lccn.loc.gov/2018034148

4 2021

ISBN 10:   0-13-523286-4
ISBN 13: 978-0-13-523286-6

Table of Contents

(A6) Electrical/Electronic Systems   219

(A7) Heating and Air Conditioning   273

(A8) Engine Performance   315

(L1) Advanced Engine Performance Specialist Test **450**

ASE STUDY GUIDE, Third Ed.

Prepare tomorrow's automotive professionals for success on the National ASE Certification Tests with the *ASE Test Preparation and Study Guide*. This guide covers ASE areas A1-A8, and is designed to help service technicians and students of automotive technology prepare to take the National ASE Certification Tests. Written by a service technician and an automotive instructor—not a technical writer—this is the ideal supplement to all automotive technology courses.

New to this Edition

As a result of changes made to the ASE tests, many questions have been replaced with new ones, especially in the Electrical (A6) section. Many new questions were added that include reading schematics, which is difficult for beginning technicians when it involves finding a possible source of an open or shorted circuit.

Questions that involved older systems have been replaced with similar questions of newer systems, such as gasoline direct injection (GDI) and electronic throttle control (ETC) systems. The wording of the answers has also been updated to be similar to how it is on the actual ASE certification tests.

The ASE task list for each certification test has been added at the beginning of each test section. As a result of questions and concerns from technicians, a new feature in the Preface called *Test Taking Tips* has been added. This section includes the step-by-step procedure that every test taker must go through when taking the ASE tests.

Additional information about the tests has been added, including the time allowed for each test. This information is very important because often the time allowed is about equal to one minute per question. Many technicians struggle to figure out one question and can easily run out of time. The L1 (Advanced Level Engine Performance) has been updated to include questions that require the use of the Composite Vehicle Type-4 Reference Booklet. The booklet needs to be downloaded from the ASE website www.ase.com.

What Is ASE?

ASE is an abbreviation for the National Institute for Automotive Service Excellence (simply known as ASE), which was formed in 1972 to provide standardized testing of service technicians.

ASE is a nonprofit association, and its main goal is to improve the quality of vehicle service through testing and volunteer certification.

What areas of vehicle service are covered by the ASE tests?

The standard automobile test service areas include:

A1 Engine Repair
A2 Automatic Transmission/Transaxle
A3 Manual Drive Train and Axles
A4 Suspension and Steering
A5 Brakes
A6 Electrical/Electronic Systems
A7 Heating and Air Conditioning
A8 Engine Performance

- If a technician passes a test and has met the experience requirement, the technician will be awarded certification in that area.
- If a technician takes and passes all eight of the automobile tests and has achieved two or more years of work experience, ASE will award the designation of ASE Certified Master Automobile Technician.
- Check the ASE website at www.ase.com for other certification areas.

Frequently Asked Questions

How can I contact ASE?

ASE
1503 Edwards Ferry Road, NE
Suite 401

Leesburg, VA 20176
Website: www.ase.com
1-703-669-6600

When are the tests given and where?

The ASE tests are given at hundreds of test sites many times during the year. Consult the ASE website for details and locations of the test sites and the dates.

What do I have to do to register?

Register online at www.ase.com.

Telephone: 703-669-6600

Call ASE toll-free at 1-800-390-6789 or visit the website for details about cost, test locations, and dates.

How many years of work experience are needed?

ASE requires that you have two or more years of full-time, hands-on working experience either as an automobile or truck technician, except as noted below. If you have *not* previously provided work experience information, you will receive a Work Experience Report Form with your admission ticket. You *must* complete and return this form to receive a certificate.

Substitutions for work experience. You may receive credit for up to one year of the two-year work experience requirement by substituting relevant formal training in one, or a combination, of the following:

- **High School Training**: Three full years of training, either in automobile, truck, school bus repair, or in collision repair, refinishing, or damage estimating, may be substituted for one year of work experience.

- **Post-High School Training**: Two full years of post-high school training in a public or private trade school, technical institute, community or four-year college, or in an apprenticeship program may be counted as one year of work experience.

- **Short Courses**: For shorter periods of post-high school training, you may substitute two months of training for one month of work experience.

You may receive full credit for the two-year work experience requirement with the following:

- **Completion of Apprenticeship**: Satisfactory completion of either a three- or four-year bona fide apprenticeship program.

Are there any hands-on activities on the ASE test?

No. All ASE tests are written, using objective-type questions, with the correct answer selected from four possible answer choices.

Who writes the ASE questions?

All ASE test questions are written by a panel of industry experts, educators, and experienced ASE-certified service technicians. Each question is reviewed by the committee and checked for the following:

- **Technically accurate.** All test questions use the correct terms and only test for vehicle manufacturer's recommended service procedures. Slang is not used, nor are any after-market accessories included on the ASE test.

- **Manufacturer-neutral.** All efforts are made to avoid using vehicle-specific procedures that are manufacturer-specific, such as General Motors or Toyota vehicles. A service technician should feel comfortable about being able to answer the questions regardless of the type or brand of vehicle.
- **Logical answers.** All efforts are made to be sure that all answers (not just the correct answers) are probable. While this may seem to make the test tricky, it is designed to test for real knowledge of the subject.
- **Random answer.** All efforts are made to ensure the correct answers are not always the longest answer or that one letter, such as c, is not used more than any other letter.

What types of questions are asked on the ASE test?

All ASE test questions are objective. There will not be questions where you will have to write an answer. Instead, all you have to do is select one of the four possible answers and place a mark in the correct place on the score sheet.

- **Multiple-choice questions**

This type of question has one correct (or mostly correct) answer (called the key) and three incorrect answers (called distracters).

A multiple-choice question example:

What part of an automotive engine does not move?

    a. Piston
    b. Connecting rod
    c. Block
    d. Valve

The correct answer is c (block). This type of question asks for a specific answer. Answer a (piston), b (connecting rod), and d (valve) all move during normal engine operation. The best answer is c (block) because even though it may vibrate, it does not move as the other parts do.

- **Technician A and Technician B questions**

This type of question is generally considered to be the most difficult according to service technicians who take the ASE test. This type of question is basically two true and false questions. A situation or condition is usually stated and two technicians (A and B) say what they think could be the correct answer and you must decide which technician is correct.

    a. A only
    b. B only
    c. Both A and B
    d. Neither A nor B

The best way to answer this type of question is to carefully read the question and consider each Technician A and Technician B answers to be solutions to a true or false question. Then, answer the question based on either one technician or both technicians are correct or not correct.

Example:

Two technicians are discussing an engine that has lower-than specified fuel pressure. Technician A says that the fuel pump could be the cause. Technician B says that the fuel-pressure regulator could be the cause. Which technician is correct?

    a. A only
    b. B only
    c. Both A and B
    d. Neither A nor B

Analysis:

Is Technician A correct? The answer is yes, because if the fuel pump was defective, the pump pressure could be lower than specified by the vehicle manufacturer. Is Technician B correct? The answer is yes, because a stuck open or a regulator with a weak spring could be the cause of lower-than-specified fuel pressure. The correct answer is therefore c (Both Technicians A and B are correct).

- **Most-likely-type questions**

This type of question asks which of the four possible items listed is the most likely to cause the problem or symptom. This type of question is often considered to be difficult because recent experience may lead you to answer the question incorrectly. Even though it is possible, it is not the "most likely" answer.

Example:

Which of the items below is the most likely to cause blue exhaust at engine start?

  a. Valve stem seals
  b. Piston rings
  c. Clogged PCV valve
  d. A stuck oil pump regulator valve

Analysis:

The correct answer is a because valve stem seals are the most likely to cause this problem. Answer b is not correct because even though worn piston rings can cause the engine to burn oil and produce blue exhaust smoke, it is not the most likely cause of blue smoke at engine start. Answers c and d are not correct because even though these items could contribute to the engine burning oil and producing blue exhaust smoke, they are not the most likely.

- **Except-type questions**

ASE will sometimes use a question that includes answers that are all correct except one. You have to determine which of the four questions is not correct.

Example:

A radiator is being pressure-tested using a hand-operated tester. This test will check for leaks in all except:

  a. Radiator
  b. Heater core
  c. Water pump
  d. Evaporator

Analysis:

The correct answer is d because the evaporator is not included in the cooling system and will not be pressurized during this test. Answers a (radiator), b (heater core), and c (water pump) are all being tested under pressure exerted on the cooling system by the pressure tester.

- **Least-likely-type questions**

Another type of question asked on many ASE tests is a question that asks which of the following is least likely to be the cause of a problem or symptom. In other words, all of the answers are possible, but it is up to the reader to determine which answer is the least likely to be correct.

Example:

Which of the following is the least likely cause of low oil pressure?

  a. Clogged oil pump screen
  b. Worn main bearing
  c. Worn camshaft bearing
  d. Worn oil pump

Analysis:

The correct answer is c because even though worn camshaft bearings can cause low oil pressure, the other answers are more likely to be the cause.

Should I guess if I don't know the answer?

Yes. ASE tests simply record the correct answers, and by guessing, you will have at least a 25% (1 out of 4) chance. If you leave the answer blank, it will be scored as being incorrect. Instead of guessing entirely, try to eliminate as many of the answers as possible as not being very likely. If you can eliminate two out of the four, you have increased your chance of guessing to 50% (two out of four).

HINT: Never change an answer. Some research has shown that your first answer is most likely to be correct. It is human nature to read too much into the question rather than accept the question as it was written.

Is each test the same every time I take it?

No. ASE writes many questions for each area and selects from this "test bank" for each test session. You may see some of the same questions if you take the same test in the spring and again in the fall, but you will also see many different questions.

Can I skip questions I don't know and come back to answer later?

Yes. You may skip a question if you wish, and the program will remind you that you skipped a question. It is often recommended to answer the question or guess, and go on with the test so that you do not run out of time to go back over the questions.

How much time do I have to take the tests?

TEST	TEST NAME	NUMBER OF QUESTIONS	TESTING TIME (MINUTES)
A1	Engine Repair	60	75
A2	Automatic Transmission/Transaxle	60	75
A3	Manual Drive Train and Axles	50	60
A4	Suspension and Steering	50	60
A5	Brakes	55	75
A6	Electrical/Electronic Systems	60	90
A7	Heating and Air Conditioning	60	75
A8	Engine Performance	60	75
A9	Light Vehicle Diesel Engines	60	75
G1	Auto Maintenance and Light Repair	55	90
L1	Advanced Engine Performance Specialist	60	150

Note: Additional questions may be included for research and will not count in the grading, but every question should be answered as these are not labeled as not counting. Recertification tests have about half of the number of questions and reduced time limit to reflect the shorter number of questions. Check the ASE website at www.ase.com for additional information.

Will I have to know specifications and gauge readings?

Yes and no. You will be asked the correct range for a particular component or operation and you must know about what the specification should be. Otherwise, the questions will state that the value is less than or greater than the allowable specification. The question will deal with how the service technician should proceed or what action should be taken.

Can I take a break during the test?

Yes, you may use the restroom, but you must sign out when leaving the test room and sign in when re-entering the room.

How are the tests scored?

The ASE tests are scored immediately and you will know if you passed or failed, as soon as it is submitted.

What percentage do I need to achieve to pass the ASE test?

While there is no exact number of questions that must be answered correctly in each area, an analysis of the test results indicates that the percentage needed to pass is about 65% to 70%. Therefore, in order to pass the Engine Repair (A1) ASE certification test, you will have to answer about 39 questions correct out of 60. In other words, you can miss about 21 questions and still pass.

What happens if I do not pass?

If you fail to achieve a passing score on any ASE test, you can take the test again at the next testing session.

Do I have to pay another registration fee if I already paid it once?

Yes. The registration fee is due at every test session, whether you select to take one or more ASE tests. Therefore, it is wise to take as many tests as you can at each test session.

Are the questions in this study guide actual ASE test questions?

No. The test questions on the actual ASE certification tests are copyrighted and cannot be used by others. The test questions in this study guide cover the same technical information and the question format is similar to the style used on the actual test.

What happens when I arrive at the testing center?

STEP 1 Arrive at the test site prepared to take the test. Bring a photo ID and your test registration paper.

STEP 2 Before being assigned a computer on which you will take the test, the following will be performed:

- A locker will be assigned in which to put everything including keys, cell phone, books, coats, and wallet, except for the government-issued photo ID.

- When entering the test area, you will be asked to turn all of your pockets inside out to verify that there is nothing left in your pockets.

- Then, you will be asked to stand on a line with your arms outstretched and a sensor wand will be used to check for anything on your body. You will be asked to turn around, and again, the wand will be used to check your other side.

- You will also be asked to lift up your pants so the inspector can see your socks and verify there is nothing hidden in them.

- If glasses are being worn, these must be taken off and inspected for any possible recording device that may be used to capture a copy of the questions on the screen.

STEP 3   After being checked, you will be given your photo ID and the key to the locker.

STEP 4   You will receive scratch paper and pencils, and if taking an advanced test, such as the L1 Advanced level test, a Composite Vehicle Reference booklet.

STEP 5   The inspector will ask you to sign in and wait while he/she starts the computer that you will use for your test.

Note: The testing area is under video surveillance at all times.

STEP 6   After the testing computer has been set up, you will be escorted to the computer cubical and instructed to place your photo ID on a holder, and the key to your locker on the desk in front of you.

STEP 7   At this time, you click on the screen and read through a short tutorial of what you can expect with the test. The tutorial will show you how to flag and unflag questions for review at the end of the test. You can even change the language to Spanish. When the tutorial is finished, the test is ready. Click start and the questions are displayed. Each test has a time limit and the time remaining is displayed on the upper left corner. The number of the test questions is shown at the upper right corner of the screen, such as 17/50.

HINT: *If you are spending too much time on one question, flag it and go on to keep on task. The program will display and allow you to go back and answer the question you skipped if there is time remaining at the end.*

STEP 8   After the last question has been displayed and answered, you will be shown a screen displaying any flagged questions. Once all questions are answered, you can click to exit and you have completed the test. Exit the test area.

STEP 9   When you exit the testing area, you will be asked to sign out and show your photo ID. Your test score will be printed out, stamped, and signed, and given to you before you retrieve your belongings, and then, you are free to leave the testing center.

Start Now

Even if you have been working on vehicles for a long time, taking an ASE certification test can be difficult. The questions will not include how things work or other "textbook" knowledge. The questions are based on "real world" diagnosis and service. The tests may seem tricky to some because the "distracters" (the wrong answers) are designed to be similar to the correct answer. If this is your first time taking the test or you are going to recertify, start now to prepare. Allocate time each day to study.

Practice Is Important

Many service technicians do not like taking tests. As a result, many technicians rush through the test to get it over with quickly. Also, many service technicians have lots of experiences on many different vehicles. This is what makes them good at what they do, but when an everyday problem is put into a question format (multiple choice), the answer may not be as clear as your experience has taught you.

Keys to Success

The key to successful test-taking includes:

- Practice answering similar-type questions.
- Carefully read each question two times to make sure you understand the question.
- Read each answer.
- Pick the best answer.
- Avoid reading too much into each question.
- Do not change an answer unless you are sure that the answer is definitely wrong.
- Look over the glossary of automotive terms for words that are not familiar to you.

The best preparation is practice, practice, and more practice. This is where using the ASE Test Prep practice tests can help.

Engine Repair (A1)

ENGINE REPAIR TEST CONTENT AREAS

This ASE study guide for Engine Repair (A1) is divided into the sub-content areas that correlate to the actual ASE certification test as follows:

CONTENT AREA	NUMBER OF QUESTIONS IN TEST	NUMBER OF STUDY GUIDE QUESTIONS
A. General Engine Diagnosis	15	32 (1–32)
B. Cylinder Head and Valve Train Diagnosis and Repair	10	43 (33–75)
C. Engine Block Diagnosis and Repair	10	43 (76–118)
D. Lubrication and Cooling Systems Diagnosis and Repair	8	17 (119–135)
E. Fuel, Electrical, Ignition, and Exhaust Systems Inspection and Service	7	18 (136–153
TOTAL	**50**	**153**

TIME ALLOWED TO TAKE THE TEST

The allocated time to take the Engine Repair Certification test is 75 minutes. ASE adds 10 additional questions to the test for re-search purposes. These questions do not count toward your score, but they are embedded within the test and there is no way of knowing which ones do not count. As a result, the technician needs to answer 60 questions in 75 minutes, or about one question per minute.

If taking the recertification A1 test, there are just 25 questions with no additional research questions included. The time allocated to take the recertification test is 30 minutes, which means about one minute per question.

BEFORE USING THIS STUDY GUIDE

Before trying to answer the questions and looking at the explanations, look over the following list of the content that ASE states will be covered in the certification test. For best results using this study guide, check service information or consult an automotive textbook for details on any of the content areas that are not familiar before trying to answer the questions. For additional information about the ASE test, visit the website at **www.ase.com**.

ENGINE REPAIR (A1) CERTIFICATION TEST

A. GENERAL ENGINE DIAGNOSIS (15 QUESTIONS)

1. Verify the driver's complaint and/or road-test the vehicle; determine needed action.
2. Determine if the no-crank, no-start, or hard starting condition is an ignition system, cranking system, fuel system, or engine mechanical problem.
3. Inspect the engine assembly for fuel, oil, coolant, and other leaks; determine necessary action.
4. Listen to engine noises; determine needed action.
5. Diagnose the cause of excessive oil consumption, coolant consumption, unusual engine exhaust color, odor, and sound; determine needed action.
6. Perform engine vacuum tests; determine needed action.
7. Perform cylinder power balance tests; determine needed action.
8. Perform cylinder compression tests; determine needed action.
9. Perform cylinder leakage tests; determine needed action.

B. CYLINDER HEAD AND VALVE TRAIN DIAGNOSIS AND REPAIR (10 QUESTIONS)

1. Remove cylinder heads, disassemble, clean, and prepare for inspection.
2. Visually inspect cylinder heads for cracks, warpage, corrosion, leakage, and the condition of passages; determine needed repairs.
3. Inspect and repair damaged threads where allowed; install core and gallery plugs.
4. Inspect, test, and verify valve springs for squareness, pressure, and free height comparison; replace as necessary.
5. Inspect valve spring retainers, rotators, locks/keepers, and lock grooves.
6. Replace valve stem seals.
7. Inspect valve guides for wear; check valve stem-to-guide clearance; determine needed repairs.
8. Inspect valves and valve seats; determine needed repairs.
9. Check valve spring installed (assembled) height and valve stem height; determined needed repairs.
10. Inspect pushrods, rocker arms, rocker arm pivots, and shafts for wear, bending, cracks, looseness, and blocked oil passages; repair or replace as required.
11. Inspect and replace hydraulic or mechanical lifters/lash adjusters.
12. Adjust valves on engines with mechanical or hydraulic lifters.
13. Inspect and replace camshaft(s) (includes checking drive gear wear and backlash, end play, sprocket and chain wear, overhead cam drive sprocket(s), drive belt(s), belt tension, tensioners, camshaft reluctor ring/tone-wheel, and variable valve timing components).
14. Inspect and measure camshaft journals and lobes; measure camshaft lift.
15. Inspect and measure camshaft bore for wear, damage, out-of-round, and alignment; determine needed repairs.
16. Inspect valve timing; time camshaft(s) to crankshaft.
17. Inspect cylinder head mating surface condition and finish; reassemble and install gasket(s) and cylinder head(s); replace/torque bolts according to manufacturers' procedures.

C. ENGINE BLOCK DIAGNOSIS AND REPAIR (10 QUESTIONS)

1. Disassemble engine block and clean and prepare components for inspection.
2. Visually inspect engine block for cracks, corrosion, passage condition, core and gallery plug holes, and surface warpage; determine needed action.
3. Inspect and repair damaged threads where allowed; install core and gallery plugs.
4. Inspect and measure cylinder walls; remove cylinder wall ridges; hone and clean cylinder walls; determine need for further action.
5. Visually inspect crankshaft for surface cracks and journal damage; check oil passage condition; measure journal wear; check crankshaft sensor reluctor ring (where applicable); determine needed action.
6. Inspect and measure main bearing bores and cap alignment and fit.
7. Install main bearings and crankshaft; check bearing clearances and end play; replace/retorque bolts according to manufacturers' procedures.
8. Inspect camshaft bearings for unusual wear; remove and replace camshaft bearings; install camshaft, timing chain, and gears; check end play.
9. Inspect auxiliary (balance, intermediate, idler, counterbalance, or silencer) shaft(s) and support bearings for damage and wear; determine needed action.
10. Inspect, measure, service, repair, or replace pistons, piston pins, and pin bushings; identify piston and bearing wear patterns that indicate connecting rod alignment problems; determine needed action.
11. Inspect connecting rods for damage, alignment, bore condition, and pin fit; determine needed action.
12. Inspect, measure, and install or replace piston rings; assemble piston and connecting rod; install piston/rod assembly; check bearing clearance and sideplay; replace/retorque fasteners according to manufacturers' procedures.
13. Inspect, reinstall, or replace crankshaft vibration damper (harmonic balancer).
14. Inspect crankshaft flange and flywheel mating surfaces; inspect and replace crankshaft pilot bearing/bushing (if applicable); inspect flywheel/flexplate for cracks and wear (includes flywheel ring gear); measure flywheel runout; determine needed action.
15. Inspect and replace pans, covers, gaskets, and seals.
16. Assemble engine parts using formed-in-place (tube-applied) sealants or gaskets, according to manufacturers' specifications; reinstall engine.

D. LUBRICATION AND COOLING SYSTEMS DIAGNOSIS AND REPAIR (8 QUESTIONS)

1. Diagnose engine lubrication system problems; perform oil pressure tests; determine needed action.
2. Disassemble and inspect oil pump (includes gears, rotors, housing, and pick-up assembly); measure oil pump clearance; inspect pressure relief devices and pump drive; determine needed action.
3. Inspect, test, and replace internal and external engine oil coolers.
4. Fill crankcase with oil and install engine oil filter.
5. Perform cooling system pressure tests; perform coolant dye test; determine necessary action.
6. Inspect and test radiator, heater core, pressure cap, and coolant recovery system; replace as required.
7. Inspect, replace, and adjust drive belt(s), tensioner(s), and pulleys.
8. Inspect and replace engine cooling system and heater system hoses, pipes and fittings.
9. Inspect, test, and replace thermostat, coolant bypass, and thermostat housing.
10. Inspect and test coolant; drain, flush, and refill cooling system with recommended coolant; bleed air as required.
11. Inspect and replace water pump.
12. Inspect and test fan (both electrical and mechanical), fan clutch, fan shroud, air dams, and cooling fan electrical circuits; repair or replace as required.
13. Verify proper operation of engine-related warning indicators.

E. FUEL, ELECTRICAL, IGNITION, AND EXHAUST SYSTEMS INSPECTION AND SERVICE (7 QUESTIONS)

1. Inspect, clean, or replace fuel injection system components, intake manifold, and gaskets.
2. Inspect, service, or replace air filters, filter housings, and intake ductwork.
3. Inspect turbocharger/supercharger; determine needed action.
4. Test engine cranking system; determine needed repairs.
5. Inspect and replace crankcase ventilation system components.
6. Inspect and install ignition system components; adjust timing.
7. Inspect and diagnose exhaust system; determine needed repairs.

ENGINE REPAIR (A1)

CATEGORY: GENERAL ENGINE DIAGNOSIS

1. Technician A says that oil should be squirted into all of the cylinders before taking a compression test. Technician B says that if the compression greatly increases when some oil is squirted into the cylinders, it indicates defective or worn piston rings. Which technician is correct?

   a. A only
   b. B only
   c. Both A and B
   d. Neither A nor B

2. Two technicians are discussing oil leaks. Technician A says that an oil leak can be found using a fluorescent dye in the oil with a black light to check for leaks. Technician B says that a white spray powder can be used to locate oil leaks. Which technician is correct?

   a. A only
   b. B only
   c. Both A and B
   d. Neither A nor B

3. Technician A says that a worn (stretched) timing chain and worn gears will cause the valve timing to be retarded. Technician B says that if the timing chain slack is over ½ inch (13 mm), the timing chain and gears should be replaced. Which technician is correct?

   a. A only
   b. B only
   c. Both A and B
   d. Neither A nor B

4. Leaking antifreeze can be what color?

   a. Green
   b. Orange
   c. Red
   d. Any of the above

5. An increase in oil viscosity can be due to _____.

   a. wear metals in the oil
   b. fuel dilution of the oil
   c. a clogged air filter
   d. any of the above

6. Oil is discovered inside the air cleaner assembly. Technician A says that the cause could be excessive blowby past the piston rings. Technician B says that the cause could be a clogged PCV valve, hose, or passage. Which technician is correct?

   a. Technician A
   b. Technician B
   c. Both A and B
   d. Neither A nor B

7. Two technicians are discussing the cause of low oil pressure. Technician A says that a worn oil pump could be the cause. Technician B says that worn main or rod bearings could be the cause. Which technician is correct?

   a. A only
   b. B only
   c. Both A and B
   d. Neither A nor B

8. A noisy valve train is being diagnosed. Technician A says that the rocker arm may be adjusted too tightly. Technician B says that the rocker arm may be adjusted too loosely or may be worn. Which technician is correct?

   a. A only
   b. B only
   c. Both A and B
   d. Neither A nor B

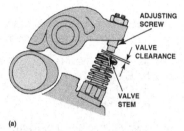

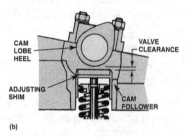

9. Two technicians are diagnosing a problem with an OHV V-8 with flat-bottom lifters. The valve covers have been removed and the engine is running. One pushrod is not rotating. Technician A says that the camshaft is worn and must be replaced. Technician B says that the lifter is worn and must be replaced. Which technician is correct?

   a. A only
   b. B only
   c. Both A and B
   d. Neither A nor B

10. A head gasket failure is being diagnosed. Technician A says that an exhaust analyzer can be used to check for HC when the tester probe is held above the radiator coolant. Technician B says that a combustion tester liquid changes color in the presence of combustion gases. Which technician is correct?

   a. A only
   b. B only
   c. Both A and B
   d. Neither A nor B

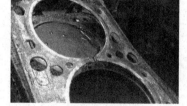

11. Excessive exhaust system back pressure has been measured. Technician A says that the catalytic converter may be clogged. Technician B says that the muffler may be clogged. Which technician is correct?

   a. A only
   b. B only
   c. Both A and B
   d. Neither A nor B

12. Technician A says that black exhaust smoke is an indication of a too-rich air-fuel mixture. Technician B says that white smoke (steam) is an indication of coolant being burned in the engine. Which technician is correct?

   a. A only
   b. B only
   c. Both A and B
   d. Neither A nor B

13. Technician A says that cranking vacuum should be the same as idle vacuum. Technician B says that a sticking valve is indicated by a floating valve gauge needle reading. Which technician is correct?

   a. A only
   b. B only
   c. Both A and B
   d. Neither A nor B

14. Two technicians are discussing a cylinder power balance test. Technician A says the more the engine RPM drops, the weaker the cylinder. Technician B says that all cylinder RPM drops should be within 50 RPM of each other. Which technician is correct?

   a. A only
   b. B only
   c. Both A and B
   d. Neither A nor B

15. A cylinder leakage (leak-down) test indicates 30% leakage, and air is heard coming out of the air inlet. Technician A says that this is a normal reading for a slightly worn engine. Technician B says that one or more intake valves are defective. Which technician is correct?

   a. A only
   b. B only
   c. Both A and B
   d. Neither A nor B

16. During a cylinder leakage (leak-down) test, air is noticed coming out of the oil fill opening. Technician A says that the oil filter may be clogged. Technician B says that the piston rings may be worn or defective. Which technician is correct?

   a. A only
   b. B only
   c. Both A and B
   d. Neither A nor B

17. The low oil pressure warning light usually comes on _____.

   a. whenever an oil change is required
   b. whenever oil pressure drops dangerously low (3 to 7 psi)
   c. whenever the oil filter bypass valve opens
   d. whenever the oil filter anti-drain-back valve opens

18. Two technicians are discussing a compression test. Technician A says that the engine should be cranked over with the pressure gauge installed for "3 puffs." Technician B says that the maximum difference between the highest-reading cylinder and the lowest-reading cylinder should be 20%. Which technician is correct?

    a. A only
    b. B only
    c. Both A and B
    d. Neither A nor B

19. A compression test gave the following results:
    cylinder #1 = 155, cylinder #2 = 140, cylinder #3 = 110, cylinder #4 = 105. Technician A says that a defective (burned) valve is the most likely cause. Technician B says that a leaking head gasket could be the cause. Which technician is correct?

    a. A only
    b. B only
    c. Both A and B
    d. Neither A nor B

20. An engine noise is being diagnosed. Technician A says that a double knock is likely to be due to a worn rod bearing. Technician B says that a knock only when the engine is cold is usually due to a worn piston pin. Which technician is correct?

    a. A only
    b. B only
    c. Both A and B
    d. Neither A nor B

21. Two technicians are discussing how to perform a road test to verify the customer's concerns about noise from the engine. Technician A says that the owner should drive and the technician ride along to verify the problem. Technician B says that the vehicle should be driven next to a building to better hear engine noise as it bounces off the walls. Which technician is correct?

    a. A only
    b. B only
    c. Both A and B
    d. Neither A nor B

22. An engine equipped with a turbocharger is burning oil (blue exhaust smoke all the time). Technician A says that a defective wastegate could be the cause. Technician B says that a plugged PCV system could be the cause. Which technician is correct?

    a. A only
    b. B only
    c. Both A and B
    d. Neither A nor B

23. An engine cranks rapidly but does not start. Technician A says that a defective coil on a waste-spark-type ignition could be the cause. Technician B says that a broken timing belt could be the cause. Which technician is correct?

    a. A only
    b. B only
    c. Both A and B
    d. Neither A nor B

24. An engine uses an excessive amount of oil. Technician A says that clogged oil drain-back holes in the cylinder head could be the cause. Technician B says that worn piston rings could be the cause. Which technician is correct?

    a. A only
    b. B only
    c. Both A and B
    d. Neither A nor B

25. Two technicians are discussing engine and transmission/transaxle mounts. Technician A says that a defective (collapsed) mount can cause an engine or driveline vibration. Technician B says that some mounts are fluid filled and should be checked for leakage. Which technician is correct?

    a. A only
    b. B only
    c. Both A and B
    d. Neither A nor B

26. An engine is misfiring. A power balance test indicates that when the spark to cylinder #4 is grounded, there is no change in the engine speed. Technician A says that a burned valve is a possible cause. Technician B says that a defective cylinder #4 injector or spark plug wire could be the cause. Which technician is correct?

    a. A only
    b. B only
    c. Both A and B
    d. Neither A nor B

27. Technician A says that white exhaust can be caused by a defective cylinder head gasket allowing coolant to enter the combustion chamber. Technician B says a leaking fuel injector can be the cause of white exhaust smoke. Which technician is correct?

    a. A only
    b. B only
    c. Both A and B
    d. Neither A nor B

28. Cranking vacuum should be _____.

    a. 2.5 inches Hg or higher
    b. over 25 inches Hg
    c. 17 to 21 inches Hg
    d. 6 to 16 inches Hg

29. Technician A says that during a power balance test, the cylinder that causes the biggest RPM drop is the weak cylinder. Technician B says that if one spark plug wire is grounded out and the engine speed does not drop, a weak or dead cylinder is indicated. Which technician is correct?

    a. A only
    b. B only
    c. Both A and B
    d. Neither A nor B

30. A good reading for a cylinder leakage test would be _____.

    a. within 20% among cylinders
    b. all cylinders below 20% leakage
    c. all cylinders above 20% leakage
    d. all cylinders above 70% leakage and within 7% of each other

31. A smoothly operating engine depends on _____.

   a. high compression on most cylinders
   b. equal compression among cylinders
   c. cylinder compression levels above 100 psi (700 kPa) and within 70 psi (500 kPa) of each other
   d. compression levels below 100 psi (700 kPa) on most cylinders

32. Technician A says that the paper test shown could detect a burned valve. Technician B says that a grayish-white stain could be a coolant leak. Which technician is correct?

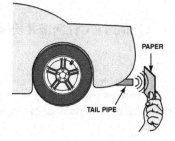

   a. A only
   b. B only
   c. Both A and B
   d. Neither A nor B

ENGINE REPAIR (A1)

CATEGORY: CYLINDER HEAD AND VALVE TRAIN DIAGNOSIS AND REPAIR

33. Two technicians are discussing torquing cylinder head bolts. Technician A says that many engine manufacturers recommend replacing the head bolts after their first use. Technician B says that many manufacturers recommend tightening the head bolts to a specific torque, then turning the bolts an additional number of degrees. Which technician is correct?

    a. A only
    b. B only
    c. Both A and B
    d. Neither A nor B

34. Two technicians are discussing timing the camshaft to the crankshaft. Technician A says that marks are often provided on the cam and crank gears or pulley so that the engine can be properly timed. Technician B says that some engines use a camshaft sprocket or gear that is not keyed to the camshaft. Which technician is correct?

    a. A only
    b. B only
    c. Both A and B
    d. Neither A nor B

35. The setup shown is being used to check _____.

    a. valve spring installed height
    b. valve stem height
    c. valve spring squareness and free height
    d. valve spring tension

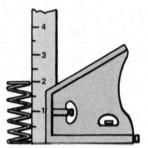

36. Cleaning chemicals are usually either a alkaline (caustic) material or an acid material. Which of the following statements is true?

    a. Both alkaline and acids have a pH of 7 if rated according to distilled water.
    b. An acid is lower than 7 and a alkaline is higher than 7 on the pH scale.
    c. An acid is higher than 7 and a alkaline is lower than 7 on the pH scale.
    d. Pure water is a 1 and a strong acid is a 14 on the pH scale.

37. Many cleaning methods involve chemicals that are hazardous to use and expensive to dispose of after use. The least hazardous method is generally considered to be the _____.

    a. pyrolytic oven
    b. hot vapor tank
    c. hot soak tank
    d. cold soak tank

38. Magnetic crack detection _____.

    a. uses a red dye to detect cracks in aluminum
    b. uses equal compression among cylinders
    c. uses a fine iron powder to detect cracks in iron parts
    d. uses a magnet to remove cracks from iron parts

39. Technician A says that engine parts should be cleaned before a thorough test can be done to detect cracks. Technician B says that pressure testing can be used to find cracks in blocks or cylinder heads. Which technician is correct?

    a. A only
    b. B only
    c. Both A and B
    d. Neither A nor B

40. A cylinder head should be removed by loosening the head bolts in which order?

    a. Any order as long as all bolts are removed
    b. In the same order as the tightening sequence
    c. In the reverse order of the tightening sequence
    d. Loosen each a quarter of a turn and then one-half a turn in the same order as the tightening sequence

41. Technician A says that damaged threads in a hole of a cylinder head can be repaired using a die. Technician B says that an insert may be required to restore a damaged thread. Which technician is correct?

    a. A only
    b. B only
    c. Both A and B
    d. Neither A nor B

42. Pushrods should be checked for _____.

    a. weight
    b. straightness
    c. diameter
    d. All of the above

43. A 0.015 inch feeler gauge is able to be inserted between the straight edge and the cylinder head. What should the service technician do?

    a. Reinstall on the engine if a copper gasket is used
    b. Resurface or replace the cylinder head
    c. Grind the valves and seats and reinstall the cylinder head on the engine
    d. Clean the head surface with brake cleaner and sandpaper to remove any dirt and reinstall on the engine.

44. The typical valve stem-to-valve guide clearance is _____.

    a. 0.030 to 0.045 inches (0.8 to 0.10 millimeters)
    b. 0.015 to 0.020 inches (0.4 to 0.5 millimeters)
    c. 0.005 to 0.010 inches (0.13 to 0.25 millimeters)
    d. 0.001 to 0.003 inches (0.03 to 0.08 millimeters)

45. Which statement is true about surface finish?

    a. Cast-iron surfaces should be smoother than aluminum surfaces.
    b. The rougher the surface is, the higher the micro inch finish measurement.
    c. The smoother the surface is, the higher the micro inch finish measurement.
    d. A cylinder head should be a lot smoother than a crankshaft journal.

46. A valve should be discarded if the margin is less than _____ after refacing.

    a. 0.001 inch
    b. 0.006 inch
    c. 0.030 inch
    d. 0.060 inch

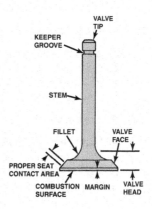

47. To lower and narrow a valve seat that has been cut at a 45° angle, use a cutter or stone of what angle?

   a. 60°
   b. 45°
   c. 30°
   d. 15°

48. Valve spring inserts (shims) are designed to _____.

   a. increase installed height of the valve
   b. decrease stem height of the valve
   c. adjust the correct installed height
   d. decrease valve spring pressure to compensate for decreased installed height

49. When aligning the timing marks on an overhead valve (cam-in-block) engine, what is the most likely method?

   a. The timing mark on the camshaft should be at the 12 o'clock position and the mark on the crankshaft should be at the 6 o'clock position.
   b. The timing mark on the camshaft should be at the 12 o'clock position and the mark on the crankshaft should be at the 12 o'clock position.
   c. The timing mark on the camshaft should be at the 6 o'clock position and the mark on the crankshaft should be at the 12 o'clock position.
   d. The timing mark on the camshaft should be at the 6 o'clock position and the mark on the crankshaft should be at the 6 o'clock position.

50. Umbrella-type valve stem seals _____.

   a. fit tightly onto the valve guide
   b. fit on the valve face to prevent combustion leaks
   c. fit tightly onto the valve stem
   d. lock under the valve retainer

51. Many technicians always use new hollow pushrods because:

   a. It is less expensive to buy than clean
   b. All of the dirt cannot be cleaned out from the hollow center
   c. Pushrods wear at both ends
   d. Pushrods shrink in length if removed from an engine

52. The cylinder head bolts should be tightened (torqued) in what general sequence?

   a. The four outside bolts first, then from the center out
   b. From the outside bolts to the inside bolts
   c. From the inside bolts to the outside bolts
   d. From the front of the engine and torquing bolts from front to rear

53. Most bolt torque specifications are for _____.

   a. clean threads only
   b. clean and lubricated threads
   c. dirty threads
   d. new bolts with dry threads

54. Before the valves are removed from the cylinder head, what operation is NOT needed to be done?

   a. Remove valve locks (keepers)
   b. Remove cylinder head(s) from the engine
   c. Remove burrs from the stem of the valve(s)
   d. Remove the valve stem seals

55. Technician A says that all valve train parts that are to be reused should be kept together. Technician B says that before testing valve springs for tension, the damper spring should be removed if used. Which technician is correct?

    a. A only
    b. B only
    c. Both A and B
    d. Neither A nor B
       Incorrect

56. What is this technician doing?

    a. Tightening the camshaft sprocket retaining bolt
    b. Adjusting the cam timing
    c. Adjusting the timing chain tension
    d. Adjusting the camshaft end play

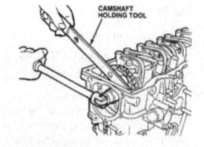

57. An aluminum cylinder head is checked for warpage using a straight-edge and a feeler (thickness) gauge. The amount of warpage on a V-8 cylinder head was 0.002 inch (0.05 millimeter). Technician A says that the cylinder head should be resurfaced. Technician B says that the cylinder head should be replaced. Which technician is correct?

    a. A only
    b. B only
    c. Both A and B
    d. Neither A nor B

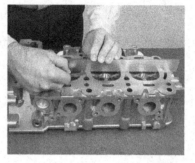

58. Technician A says the valve guide should be reconditioned or replaced *before* the valve seats are reconditioned. Technician B says the valve seats should be replaced before replacing or reconditioning the valve guides. Which technician is correct?

    a. A only
    b. B only
    c. Both A and B
    d. Neither A nor B

59. Technician A says that a dial indicator (gauge) is often used to measure valve guide wear by measuring the amount by which the valve head is able to move in the guide. Technician B says that a ball gauge can be used to measure the valve guide. Which technician is correct?

    a. A only
    b. B only
    c. Both A and B
    d. Neither A nor B

60. Technician A says that a worn valve guide can be reamed and a valve with an oversize stem can be used. Technician B says that a worn valve guide can be replaced with a bronze insert to restore the cylinder head to useful service. Which technician is correct?

    a. A only
    b. B only
    c. Both A and B
    d. Neither A nor B

61. Technician A says that worn integral guides can be repaired. Technician B says that worn integral guides can be replaced. Which technician is correct?

    a. A only
    b. B only
    c. Both A and B
    d. Neither A nor B

62. Valve-to-valve guide is measured using a _____.

   a. micrometer
   b. feeler gauge
   c. dial indicator
   d. plastigage

63. Before a valve spring is reused, it should be checked for _____.

   a. squareness
   b. free height
   c. tension
   d. All of the above

64. Many manufacturers recommend that valves be ground with an interference angle. This angle is the difference between the _____.

   a. valve margin and valve face angles
   b. valve face and valve seat angles
   c. valve guide and valve face angles
   d. valve head and margin angles

65. Technician A says that cooling system plugs in a cylinder head are usually driven in using a driver and a hammer. Technician B says that the cooling system plugs are usually threaded into the cylinder head. Which technician is correct?

   a. A only
   b. B only
   c. Both A and B
   d. Neither A nor B

66. Coolant passages in the cylinder head should be inspected for _____.

   a. corrosion
   b. restrictions (blockages)
   c. leakage
   d. All of the above

67. Technician A says that valve stem height and installed height mean the same thing. Technician B says the installed height can be corrected by grinding the stem of the valve. Which technician is correct?

   a. A only
   b. B only
   c. Both A and B
   d. Neither A nor B

68. Technician A says that valve stem seals of the O-ring type are installed on top of the valve locks (keepers). Technician B says that a vacuum pump can be used to determine if the valve stem seal is correctly seated. Which technician is correct?

   a. A only
   b. B only
   c. Both A and B
   d. Neither A nor B

69. Before the valves are removed from the cylinder head, what operations need to be completed?

   a. Remove valve keepers (locks)
   b. Remove cylinder head(s) from the engine
   c. Remove burrs from the stem of the valve(s)
   d. All of the above

70. Technician A says that the fluorescent penetrant test method can be used to detect cracks in iron, steel, or aluminum parts. Technician B says that the dye penetrant test can only be used with aluminum parts. Which technician is correct?

   a. A only
   b. B only
   c. Both A and B
   d. Neither A nor B

71. What is this technician doing?

   a. Measuring the camshaft bearing clearance
   b. Checking the camshaft end play
   c. Measuring camshaft for runout
   d. Positioning the camshaft sprocket onto the camshaft in the specified location

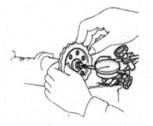

72. The camshaft bore should be inspected on which type(s) of engines?

   a. Single overhead camshaft engines
   b. Dual overhead camshaft engines
   c. Cam-in block engines
   d. All of the above

73. What is this technician installing?

   a. A valve spring insert
   b. A valve spring seat
   c. A valve stem seal
   d. A valve guide

74. What other engine component may have to be machined if the cylinder heads are machined on a V-type engine?

   a. Exhaust manifold
   b. Intake manifold
   c. Block deck
   d. Distributor mount (if the vehicle is so equipped)

75. What is this technician doing?

   a. Removing the pushrod
   b. Determining zero lash
   c. Adjusting the pushrod length
   d. Adjusting the ratio of the rocker arm

ENGINE REPAIR (A1)

CATEGORY: ENGINE BLOCK DIAGNOSIS AND REPAIR

76. A cylinder head is being installed. Technician A says to use a form-in-place sealant between the block and the head. Technician B says that the "front" on a head gasket indicates that it should be installed toward the auxiliary drive belt end of the engine. Which technician is correct.

   a. A only
   b. B only
   c. Both A and B
   d. Neither A nor B

77. The torque-angle method involves _____.

   a. turning all bolts the same number of turns
   b. torquing to specifications and loosening by a specified number of degrees
   c. torquing to one-half specifications, then to three-quarter torque, then to full torque
   d. turning bolts a specified number of degrees after initial torque

78. The feeler gauge shown is thinner than specification. Technician A says that the cylinder should be honed until the piston ring end gap is within specifications. Technician B says the piston ring should be replaced with an oversize ring. Which technician is correct?

   a. A only
   b. B only
   c. Both A and B
   d. Neither A nor B

79. Piston ring end gap can be *increased* by _____.

   a. filing the ring to make the gap larger
   b. installing oversize rings
   c. sleeving the cylinder
   d. knurling the piston

80. What is this technician measuring?

   a. Piston ring back spacing
   b. Piston ring end gap
   c. Piston ring side clearance
   d. Piston groove surface finish

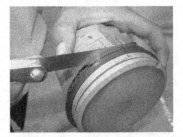

81. What is being measured with this tool setup?

   a. Checking the runout of the crankshaft
   b. Measuring the front bearing oil clearance
   c. Locating top dead center
   d. Measuring crankshaft end play

82. The most common cause of premature bearing failure is _____.

   a. misassembly
   b. dirt
   c. lack of lubrication
   d. overloading

83. Technician A says the main bearing cap is being de-burred proper to assembly. Technician B says that the bearing cap is being cleaned. Which technician is correct?

   a. A only
   b. B only
   c. Both A and B
   d. Neither A nor B

84. To check a crankshaft journal for taper and out-of-round, the journal should be measured in at least how many locations?

   a. One
   b. Two
   c. Four
   d. Six

85. Piston ring end gap should only be measured _____.

   a. after all cylinder work has been performed
   b. after installing the piston in the cylinder
   c. after installing the rings on the piston
   d. Both a and c

86. Piston ring side clearance is a measure taken between the _____ and the _____.

   a. piston (side skirt); cylinder wall
   b. piston pin; piston pin retainer (clip)
   c. piston ring; piston ring land
   d. compression ring; oil control ring

87. Before the timing chain on an OHV engine can be inspected and removed, the following component(s) must be removed:

   a. Valve cover (rocker arm cover)
   b. Vibration damper
   c. Cylinder head(s)
   d. Intake manifold (V-type engines only)

88. Technician A says the part on the top of the photo is a thread chaser. Technician B says the part at the bottom of the photo is a tap. Which technician is correct?

   a. A only
   b. B only
   c. Both A and B
   d. Neither A nor B

89. Lower than normal oil pressure could be caused by _____.

   a. a worn oil pump
   b. worn rod bearings
   c. worn main bearing
   d. any of the above

90. The ridge at the top of the cylinder _____.

   a. is caused by wear at the top of the cylinder by the rings
   b. represents a failure of the top piston ring to correctly seal against the cylinder wall
   c. should not be removed before removing pistons except when reboring the cylinders
   d. means that a crankshaft with an incorrect stroke was installed in the engine

91. Technician A says that the dye penetrant test method can be used to detect cracks in iron, steel, or aluminum parts. Technician B says that the dye penetrant test can only be used with aluminum parts. Which technician is correct?

   a. A only
   b. B only
   c. Both A and B
   d. Neither A nor B

92. Connecting rod caps should be marked (if they were not marked at the factory) before the piston and connecting rod assembly is removed from the engine_____.

   a. because they are balanced together
   b. because they are machined together
   c. to make certain that the heavier rod is matched to the heavier piston
   d. to make certain that the lighter rod is matched to the lighter piston

93. Protective covers should be placed over the connecting rod threads to help prevent damage to the

   _____.

   a. connecting rod
   b. crankshaft
   c. cylinder wall
   d. camshaft

94. A misaligned connecting rod causes what type of engine wear?

   a. Cylinder taper
   b. Barrel-shaped cylinders
   c. Ridge wear
   d. Angle wear on the piston skirt

95. Piston damage as shown is most likely to be caused by _____.

   a. valves hitting the piston head
   b. abnormal combustion
   c. lugging the engine during operation
   d. high engine speeds that can break piston heads

96. The diameter of the piston is measured _____.

   a. across the top (head) of the piston
   b. across the piston pin
   c. across the thrust surface
   d. between the top and second piston ring

97. A worn piston pin causes what type of problem?

   a. Engine burns an excessive amount of oil (blue smoke)
   b. Engine produces a knocking noise that will disappear if the cylinder is grounded out
   c. Engine produces a double knocking noise that will not disappear if the cylinder is grounded out
   d. Engine knock when warm only

98. Two technicians are discussing removing and installing a crankshaft vibration damper (harmonic balancer). Technician A says that a puller is often needed to remove a vibration damper. Technician B says that an installation tool is often needed to install a vibration damper. Which technician is correct?

 a. A only
 b. B only
 c. Both A and B
 d. Neither A nor B

99. The typical journal-to-bearing clearance is _____.

 a. 0.00015 to 0.00018 inch
 b. 0.0005 to 0.0025 inch
 c. 0.150 to 0.250 inch
 d. 0.020 to 0.035 inch

100. Camshaft bearings in a cam-in block engine are being discussed. Technician A says that Plastigage should be used to check for proper bearing clearance. Technician B says that a special tool is required to install cam bearings in a cam-in-block engine. Which technician is correct?

 a. A only
 b. B only
 c. Both A and B
 d. Neither A nor B

101. Typical piston-to-cylinder clearance is _____.

 a. 0.001 to 0.003 inch
 b. 0.010 to 0.023 inch
 c. 0.100 to 0.150 inch
 d. 0.180 to 0.230 inch

102. What is this technician doing?

 a. Deglazing the cylinder bore
 b. Measuring the cylinder bore for out-of-round and taper
 c. Honing the cylinder
 d. Measuring the surface finish of the cylinder wall

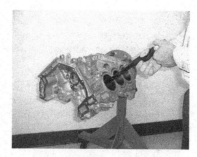

103. If the gauging plastic strip (Plastigage®) is wider than specified after the bearings are tightened, this results _____.

 a. in excessive oil clearance
 b. from using old, dried Plastigage
 c. insufficient oil clearance
 d. in a small side (thrust) clearance

104. What is this technician measuring?

 a. Rod bearing oil clearance
 b. Connecting rod side clearance
 c. Crankshaft end play
 d. Thrust bearing clearance

105. Typical thrust bearing clearance is:

    a. 0.001 to 0.003 inch
    b. 0.002 to 0.012 inch
    c. 0.025 to 0.035 inch
    d. 0.050 to 0.100 inch

106. A 0.010 inch feeler gauge is able to slide between the straight edge and the main bearing bore (saddle bore) as shown. Technician A says that the block should be replaced. Technician B says that oversize main bearings should be used. Which technician is correct?

    a. A only
    b. B only
    c. Both A and B
    d. Neither A nor B

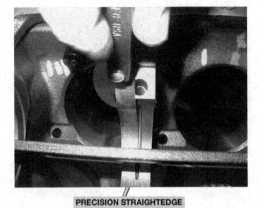

PRECISION STRAIGHTEDGE

107. If the bell housing is not properly torqued to the engine block, _____.

    a. the bell housing will distort
    b. the engine block will crack
    c. the rear cylinder can be distorted (become out-of-round)
    d. the crankshaft will crack

108. If the bore of an engine is increased without any other changes except for the change to proper-size replacement pistons, the displacement will _____ and the compression ratio will

    _____.

    a. increase; increase
    b. increase; decrease
    c. decrease; increase
    d. decrease; decrease

109. Technician A says that pistons should be removed from the crankshaft side (bottom) of the cylinder when disassembling an engine to prevent possible piston or cylinder damage. Technician B says that the rod assembly should be marked before disassembly. Which technician is correct?

    a. A only
    b. B only
    c. Both A and B
    d. Neither A nor B

110. The micrometer reading is _____.

    a. 0.252 inch
    b. 0.025 inch
    c. 0.00252 inch
    d. 2.52 inch

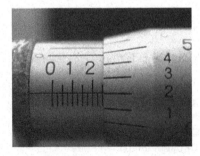

111. A cylinder is 0.004 inch out-of-round. Technician A says that the block should be bored and oversize pistons installed. Technician B says that oversize piston rings should be used. Which technician is correct?

    a. A only
    b. B only
    c. Both A and B
    d. Neither A nor B

112. Technician A says that the tool shown is used to dress (restore) a grinder wheel. Technician B says that it is used to determine the thread pitch of metric fasteners. Which technician is correct?

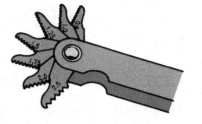

   a. A only
   b. B only
   c. Both A and B
   d. Neither A nor B

113. After the engine block has been machined, the block should be cleaned with _____.

   a. a stiff brush and soap and water
   b. a clean cloth and engine oil
   c. WD-40
   d. spray solvent washer

114. Technician A says that piston rings should be installed with the dot or mark up (toward the cylinder head). Technician B says that the mark on the piston rings is used to identify the position (groove) in which the ring should be installed. Which technician is correct?

   a. A only
   b. B only
   c. Both A and B
   d. Neither A nor B

115. Two technicians are discussing ring gap. Technician A says that the ring should be checked in the same cylinder in which it is to be installed. Technician B says that the ends of the piston ring can be filed if the clearance is too small. Which technician is correct?

   a. A only
   b. B only
   c. Both A and B
   d. Neither A nor B

116. Two technicians are discussing bearing clearance measurement. Technician A says that the main and rod bearing clearance can be measured with plastic gauging material (Plastigage). Technician B says that the engine crankshaft should be rotated for two complete revolutions when Plastigage is used between the crankshaft and the main or rod bearings. Which technician is correct?

   a. A only
   b. B only
   c. Both A and B
   d. Neither A nor B

117. When pistons are installed in the block, the notch or arrow on the piston should be facing _____.

   a. toward the lifter side of the block
   b. toward the front of the engine
   c. toward the rear of the engine
   d. away from the lifter side of the block

118. A bearing shell is being installed in a connecting rod. The end of the bearing is slightly above the parting line. Technician A says that this is normal. Technician B says that the bearing is too big. Which technician is correct?

   a. A only
   b. B only
   c. Both A and B
   d. Neither A nor B

ENGINE REPAIR (A1)

CATEGORY: LUBRICATION AND COOLING SYSTEMS DIAGNOSIS AND REPAIR

119. A water pump has been replaced three times in three months on a rear-wheel-drive vehicle. Technician A says that the drive belt(s) may be installed too tightly. Technician B says that a cooling fan may be bent or out of balance. Which technician is correct?

    a. A only
    b. B only
    c. Both A and B
    d. Neither A nor B

120. As the percentage of antifreeze in the coolant increases, _____.

    a. the freeze point decreases (up to a point)
    b. the boiling point decreases
    c. the heat transfer increases
    d. all of the above

121. The procedure that should be used when refilling an empty cooling system includes the following: _____.

    a. determine capacity, and then fill the cooling system half with antifreeze and the rest of the way with water.
    b. fill completely with antifreeze, but mix a 50/50 solution for the overflow bottle.
    c. fill the block and one half of the radiator with 100% pure antifreeze and fill the rest of the radiator with water.
    d. fill the radiator with antifreeze, start the engine, drain the radiator, and refill with a 50/50 mixture of antifreeze and water.

122. Which statement is *true* about thermostats?

    a. The temperature marked on the thermostat is the temperature at which the thermostat should be fully open
    b. Thermostats often cause overheating
    c. The temperature marked on the thermostat is the temperature at which the thermostat should start to open
    d. Both a and b

123. Technician A says that the radiator should always be inspected for leaks and proper flow before installing a rebuilt engine. Technician B says that overheating during slow city driving can be due to a defective electric cooling fan. Which technician is correct?

    a. A only
    b. B only
    c. Both A and B
    d. Neither A nor B

124. Technician A says the positive crankcase ventilation (PCV) system uses a valve located between the intake manifold and the valve cover (cylinder head cover). Technician B says that about 20% of the air needed by the engine at idle speed flows through the PCV system. Which technician is correct?

    a. A only
    b. B only
    c. Both A and B
    d. Neither A nor B

125. Turning the oil pump before starting the engine should be done
_____.

    a. to lubricate engine bearings
    b. to lubricate valve train components
    c. to supply oil to the camshaft
    d. All of the above

126. An engine oil cooler should be inspected for _____.

    a. engine oil leaks
    b. coolant leaks
    c. air leaks
    d. Both a and b

127. Which antifreeze coolant should be used if the manufacturer specifies coolant that is both silicate and phosphate free?

    a. Organic acid technology (OAT), e.g., DEX-COOL (orange)
    b. Ethylene glycol (green)
    c. Asian red
    d. European pink

128. The "hot" light on the dash is being discussed by two technicians. Technician A says that the light comes on if the cooling system temperature is too high for safe operation of the engine. Technician B says that the light comes on whenever there is a decrease (drop) in cooling system pressure. Which technician is correct?

    a. A only
    b. B only
    c. Both A and B
    d. Neither A nor B

129. Technician A says that an electric cooling fan should come on at the same temperature that the thermostat opens. Technician B says that a defective electric fan can cause overheating, especially in city driving. Which technician is correct?

    a. A only
    b. B only
    c. Both A and B
    d. Neither A nor B

130. A customer complains that the heater works sometimes, but sometimes only cold air comes out while driving. Technician A says that the water pump is defective. Technician B says that the cooling system could be low on coolant. Which technician is correct?

    a. A only
    b. B only
    c. Both A and B
    d. Neither A nor B

131. Normal operating temperature is reached when _____.

    a. the radiator cap releases coolant into the overflow
    b. the upper radiator hose is hot and pressurized
    c. the electric cooling fan has cycled at least once (if the vehicle is so equipped)
    d. either b or c occur

132. For best results, the oil should be drained when the engine is_____?

    a. at normal operating temperature
    b. at room temperature
    c. cold—not yet started
    d. run for 30 seconds, then turned off before draining the oil

133. Two technicians are discussing engine oil. Technician A says that the higher the viscosity, the better. Technician B says that a SAE 20W-50 will work better in a new vehicle instead of the specified SAE 5W-20. Which technician is correct?

a. A only
b. B only
c. Both A and B
d. Neither A nor B

134. Normal oil pump pressure in an engine is _____.

a. 3 to 7 psi
b. 10 to 60 psi
c. 100 to 150 psi
d. 180 to 210 psi

135. In typical engine lubrication systems, what components are the last to receive oil?

a. Main bearings
b. Rod bearings
c. Valve trains
d. Oil filters

CATEGORY: FUEL, ELECTRICAL, IGNITION, AND EXHAUST SYSTEMS INSPECTION AND SERVICE

136. An engine cranks but will not start. No spark is available at the end of a spark plug wire with a spark tester connected and the engine cranked. Technician A says that a defective crankshaft position (CKP) sensor could be the cause. Technician B says that a defective ignition module could be the cause. Which technician is correct?

    a. A only
    b. B only
    c. Both A and B
    d. Neither A nor B

137. Two technicians are discussing a waste spark-type of ignition system. Technician A says that a defective coil can cause a crank, but no-start condition. Technician B says that a defective coil could affect the spark output to two spark plugs. Which technician is correct?

    a. A only
    b. B only
    c. Both A and B
    d. Neither A nor B

138. Battery voltage during cranking is below specifications. Technician A says that a defect in the engine may be the cause. Technician B says that the starter motor may be defective. Which technician is correct?

    a. A only
    b. B only
    c. Both A and B
    d. Neither A nor B

139. Technician A says that a leaking intake manifold gasket can cause a vacuum leak. Technician B says that a clogged air filter can cause a low power concern. Which technician is correct?

    a. A only
    b. B only
    c. Both A and B
    d. Neither A nor B

140. A starter motor cranks the engine too slowly to start. Technician A says that the cause could be a weak or defective battery. Technician B says that the cause could be loose or corroded battery cable connections. Which technician is correct?

    a. A only
    b. B only
    c. Both A and B
    d. Neither A nor B

141. Technician A says that a clogged port fuel injector can cause a misfire. Technician B says that a leaking injector lower O-ring can cause a vacuum leak. Which technician is correct?

    a. A only
    b. B only
    c. Both A and B
    d. Neither A nor B

142. Which computer sensor may have to be replaced if the engine had been found to have a defective head gasket or cracked head?

    a. Throttle position sensor
    b. Oxygen sensor
    c. Manifold absolute pressure sensor
    d. Engine coolant temperature sensor

143. Technician A says that a defective PCV valve could cause a rough idle. Technician B says that an EGR valve stuck open could cause a rough idle. Which technician is correct?

    a. A only
    b. B only
    c. Both A and B
    d. Neither A nor B

144. Technician A says the catalytic converter must be replaced if it rattles when tapped. Technician B says a catalytic converter can be defective and not working yet not be clogged. Which technician is correct?

    a. A only
    b. B only
    c. Both A and B
    d. Neither A nor B

145. A supercharged engine lacks power. What is *not* a possible cause?

    a. Clogged air filter
    b. Restricted intercooler
    c. Clogged condenser
    d. Restricted exhaust

146. Technician A says that a defective one-way exhaust check valve could cause the air pump to fail. Technician B says that the air should stop flowing to the exhaust manifold when the engine is warm and operating in closed loop. Which technician is correct?

    a. A only
    b. B only
    c. Both A and B
    d. Neither A nor B

147. Two technicians are discussing positive crankcase ventilation (PCV) valves. Technician A says that if the valve rattles, it is good. Technician B says the PCV valve may still require replacement even if it rattles. Which technician is correct?

    a. A only
    b. B only
    c. Both A and B
    d. Neither A nor B

148. A spark plug has dry, black fluffy deposits. Technician A says this is caused by the engine burning oil. Technician B says that the engine may be operating with a rich air-fuel mixture. Which technician is correct?

    a. A only
    b. B only
    c. Both A and B
    d. Neither A nor B

149. A 2-foot-long spark plug wire is being tested using an ohmmeter. The wire measures 7.86 kΩ (7,860 ohms). Technician A says the wire is okay. Technician B says that the wire resistance is higher than the specification for most vehicles. Which technician is correct?

    a. A only
    b. B only
    c. Both A and B
    d. Neither A nor B

150. Technician A says that moving the position of the crankshaft position (CKP) sensor can be used to adjust the ignition timing on an engine equipped with coil-on-plug (COP)-type ignition. Technician B says that a misfire can be caused by a defective coil on a COP system. Which technician is correct?

    a. A only
    b. B only
    c. Both A and B
    d. Neither A nor B

151. A turbocharged engine is burning oil. Technician A says that a defective turbocharger could be the cause. Technician B says that a clogged PCV system could be the cause. Which technician is correct?

    a. A only
    b. B only
    c. Both A and B
    d. Neither A nor B

152. Technician A says that low fuel pressure can cause the engine to produce low power. Technician B says that all fuel pumps should be able to pump at least 2 pints (1 liter) per minute. Which technician is correct?

    a. A only
    b. B only
    c. Both A and B
    d. Neither A nor B
       Incorrect

153. An engine misfire is being diagnosed. One spark plug wire measured "OL" on a digital ohmmeter set to the auto range scale. Technician A says that the spark plug wire should be replaced. Technician B says that the spark plug wire is okay. Which technician is correct?

    a. A only
    b. B only
    c. Both A and B
    d. Neither A nor B

ENGINE REPAIR (A1)

CATEGORY: GENERAL ENGINE DIAGNOSIS

1. **The correct answer is b.** Technician B is correct that if the compression reading is greatly increased with a couple of squirts of oil in the cylinder, then when the compression test is first performed without the oil, the piston rings are worn or broken. Technician A is not correct because oil should only be squirted into those cylinders that achieved a lower than normal compression test reading to help determine the reason for the low compression. Answers c and d are not correct because only Technician B is correct.

2. **The correct answer is c.** Both technicians are correct. Technician A is correct that a fluorescent dye can be added to the engine oil and allowed to circulate. A black light is then turned on and any leaks will show as a bright yellow-green area. This is the preferred method for locating fluid leaks. Technician B is correct because a white powder spray (such as foot spray) will show the location of leaks by turning dark where the liquid contacts the white powder. Answers a, b, and d are not correct because both technicians are correct.

3. **The correct answer is c.** Both technicians are correct. Technician A is correct because as the timing chain stretches, the camshaft will lag behind the rotation of the crankshaft (retarded). Technician B is correct because the timing chain and gears should all be replaced as a set if the slack is greater than factory specifications (usually less than ½ in.). Answers a, b, and d are not correct because both technicians are correct.

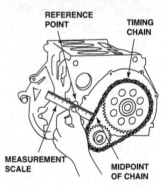

4. **The correct answer is d.** Antifreeze can be green (older IAT-type or phosphate organic acid technology, which is a dark green), as well as orange (DEX-COOL), or red (Asian red). Answers a, b, and c are not correct because any of the colors could indicate a coolant (antifreeze) leak.

5. **The correct answer is a.** Small particles of steel, cast iron, and other metals in an engine can react chemically to increase the viscosity (thickness) of the oil. Answer b is not correct because if fuel were added to oil, it would become thinner (lower viscosity). Answer c is not correct because a clogged air filter does not have a direct effect on the viscosity of the oil. It is true that dirt could get into the oil, which will make the oil thicker but this is not a direct result of the air filter itself. Answer d is not correct because it includes b and c, which are not correct.

6. **The correct answer is c.** Both technicians are correct. Technician A is correct because if the piston rings are worn or defective, blowby gases will force oil fumes out of the PCV system inlet and into the air cleaner assembly. Technician B is correct because if the PCV valve or hose is clogged, all crankcase vapors have only one place to go and that is through the PCV system inlet hose that gets its fresh air from the air cleaner assembly. Answers a, b, and d are not correct because both technicians are correct.

7. **The correct answer is c.** Both technicians are correct. Technician A is correct because a worn oil pump can cause low oil pressure. An oil pump wears because it is the only engine part that operates on unfiltered oil. Technician B is correct because worn bearings allow an excessive amount of oil to escape and return to the oil pan resulting in a drop in oil pressure. Answers a, b, and d are not correct because both technicians are correct.

8. **The correct answer is b.** Technician B is correct because noise is created by the rocker arm pounding onto the end of the valve when the clearance (lash) is greater than specified by the vehicle manufacturer. Technician A is not correct because the engine will not create noise if the valve clearance is too tight. The valves may not close all the way if the clearance is too tight which could lead to a burned valve. Answers c and d are not correct because only Technician B is correct.

9. **The correct answer is c.** Both technicians are correct. Technician A is correct because it is the slight angle on the cam lobe that helps create a rotating force on flat-bottomed lifters. If the lobe is worn, the lifter and the pushrod will not rotate. Technician B is also correct because the bottom of a lifter is slightly convex which helps rotate the lifter as it rides over the cam lobe. If the bottom of the lifter is worn, it will not rotate. Answers a, b, and d are not correct because both technicians are correct.

10. **The correct answer is c.** Both technicians are correct. Technician A is correct because if exhaust gases are escaping from the combustion chamber and into the coolant past a defective head gasket, HC (hydrocarbons) or CO (carbon monoxide) emissions will be able to be measured above the coolant with the engine running. Technician B is correct because combustion tester liquid that changes color when exposed to exhaust gases can also be used to verify a defective head gasket. Answers a, b, and d are not correct because both technicians are correct.

11. **The correct answer is c.** Both technicians are correct. Technician A is correct because a clogged catalytic converter can be the cause of an exhaust system restriction. Technician B is correct because a clogged (or damaged) muffler can cause an exhaust system restriction. A muffler can be clogged by parts broken from the internal baffles. If the catalytic converter is replaced and the exhaust is still restricted, a clogged muffler (or resonator) could be the cause. Answers a, b, and d are not correct because both technicians are correct.

12. **The correct answer is c.** Both technicians are correct. White smoke or steam is an indication that coolant is getting into the combustion chamber and is being vaporized by the heat of combustion. Technician A is correct because an excessively rich air-fuel mixture will create black exhaust smoke. A slightly rich engine may not emit black smoke because the catalytic converter will usually oxidize the unburned fuel (hydrocarbons) into H_2O (water) and CO_2 (carbon dioxide). Answers a, b, and d are not correct because both technicians are correct.

13. **The correct answer is d.** Neither technician is correct. Technician A is not correct because the specification for cranking vacuum is greater than 2.5 in. Hg. Even though a sound engine with a completely closed throttle may be able to produce 17 in. Hg to 21 in. Hg vacuum (at sea level) during cranking, it is not the specification for cranking vacuum. Technician B is not correct because a floating vacuum gauge needle is an indication of an overly rich or lean air-fuel mixture, not a sticking valve. A sticking valve will cause the vacuum gauge needle to move rapidly up and down. Answer c is not correct because neither technician is correct.

14. **The correct answer is b.** Technician B only is correct. All cylinders should drop the same (within 50 RPM) when they are canceled or grounded out. This indicates that each cylinder was contributing an equal amount of the operation of the engine. If a cylinder drops the RPM less than others, the cylinder is weak. Technician A is not correct because the more the engine RPM drops when a cylinder is canceled, the more that cylinder is contributing to the operation of the engine. Answers c and d are not correct because only Technician B is correct.

15. **The correct answer is b.** A leakage of 30% is excessive and if air is heard escaping from the engine air inlet, then one or more intake valves must be leaking. It is also possible that the cylinder being tested is not at TDC on the compression stroke. If the cylinder were at TDC of the exhaust stroke, both intake and exhaust valves would be open and air would also be heard coming from the tailpipe. Technician A is not correct because 30% leakage is too much for a slightly worn engine. Leakage should not exceed 20%. Answers c and d are not correct because only Technician B is correct.

16. **The correct answer is b.** Technician B is correct because if the piston rings were worn (or broken), compressed air could escape past the rings and flow into the crankcase. The air would then escape from the engine through the oil drain-back holes and other openings in the block and eventually be heard at the oil fill opening. Technician A is not correct because the oil filter is not being tested and the compressed air entering the combustion chamber could not get into or past the oil filter. Answers c and d are not correct because only Technician B is correct.

17. **The correct answer is b.** The oil pressure light comes on whenever the pressure drops to between 3 and 7 psi. Answer a is not correct because the oil pressure light is not the same as the amber "change oil soon" light. Answer c is not correct because there is no indication when the bypass valve opens, which often occurs when the oil is cold or the oil filter is dirty and creates a restriction. Answer d is not correct because this valve simply keeps oil from draining back into the oil pan after the engine stops running.

18. **The correct answer is b.** Technician B is correct because the maximum difference, as specified by most vehicle manufacturers, is 20%. If the highest reading is 160 psi, then the lowest cylinder compression should be greater than 128 psi (160 × 20% = 32 psi. 160 psi – 32 psi = 128 psi). Technician A is not correct because the engine should be cranked through at least four compression events or 4 to 5 "puffs" (not 3 "puffs"). Answers c and d are not correct because only Technician B is correct.

19. **The correct answer is b.** Technician B is correct because if the head gasket were leaking between cylinder number 3 and 4, the compression on these cylinders would be lower than normal. The defective gasket would allow compression to escape to the adjacent cylinders. Technician A is not correct because a burned valve would only affect one cylinder. It would be very rare that two cylinders side-by-side would both have a burned valve and is, therefore, not a "likely" cause. Answers c and d are not correct because only Technician B is correct.

20. **The correct answer is d.** Neither technician is correct. Technician A is not correct because a double knock is usually caused by a worn piston pin, which causes one click when the piston stops at TDC and another as the crankshaft pulls the piston downward after reaching TDC. Technician B is not correct because a worn piston pin will make noise at all temperatures and not change when the cylinder is grounded out. Answers a, b, and c are not correct because neither technician is correct.

21. **The correct answer is c.** The correct answer is that both Technicians A and B are correct. Technician A is correct because the customer can more easily drive the vehicle under the exact conditions, such as speed and throttle position, to create the noise concern. The technician can also concentrate on listening for the noise without having to worry about traffic conditions. Technician B is also correct because noise from the vehicle would tend to bounce off walls or buildings making engine noise easier to hear. Answers a, b, and d are not correct because both technicians are correct.

22. **The correct answer is b.** Technician B is correct because if the PCV system were clogged, crankcase pressure would increase and force oil into the combustion chamber through the air cleaner assembly where the PCV system normally receives fresh air. The increased crankcase pressure can also cause oil to be forced from the turbocharger bearing (bushing) area into the intake or exhaust side of the turbocharger. Technician A is not correct because the wastegate simply directs the exhaust through the turbocharger or into the exhaust manifold bypassing the turbocharger. If the wastegate were to fail, it could cause a lack of turbo boost or the possibility of over boost. An over boost condition *could* cause excessive oil consumption (it would not be a direct cause). Answers a, c, and d are not correct because only Technician B is correct.

23. **The correct answer is b.** Technician B only is correct because the engine is cranking rapidly, which means that the engine lacks compression. A broken timing belt would allow many of the valves to be either closed all the time or partially open all the time. Answer a is not correct because even though a defective coil on a waste spark-type ignition system could cause a misfire, it would not likely cause a no-start condition. Answers c and d are not correct because only Technician B is correct.

24. **Both technicians are correct.** Technician A is correct because if the oil drain-back holes were clogged, oil would eventually cover the valves and oil would be drawn into the combustion chamber past the valve guides. Technician B is correct because oil can be drawn into the combustion chamber past the worn piston rings during the intake stroke. Answers a, b, and d are not correct because both technicians are correct.

25. **The correct answer is c.** Technician A is correct because a defective engine mount can cause the engine to be out of position in the vehicle causing a vibration. Technician B is correct because some mounts are filled with fluid and should be inspected for leakage. Answers a, b, and d are not correct because both technicians are correct.

26. **The correct answer is c.** Both technicians are correct. Technician A is correct because a burned valve will cause the cylinder to produce less than normal power. Technician B is correct because a fault in either the injector or the spark plug wire can cause the cylinder to misfire. Answers a, b, and d are not correct because both technicians are correct.

27. **The correct answer is a.** Technician A only is the correct answer. When coolant enters into the combustion chamber past a defective head gasket, the water turns to steam during the combustion process. This steam is then seen as white exhaust smoke when it exits the tail pipe. Answer b is not correct because a leaking fuel injector would cause a rich air-fuel mixture, which would cause black or gray exhaust smoke and not white smoke. Answers c and d are not correct because only technician A is correct.

28. **The correct answer is a.** Vacuum measured during cranking should be *at least* 2.5 in. Hg. Obviously, the higher the cranking vacuum, the better the engine cylinder is sealed. Answer b is not correct because the only time that vacuum in an engine can be near 25 in. Hg. is during deceleration. Answer c is not correct because even though it is possible for some engines to produce 17–21 in. Hg. during cranking, it should not be considered the specification for cranking vacuum. Answer d is not correct for the same reason as given for answer c.

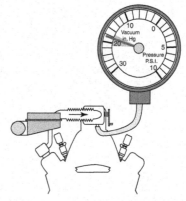

29. **The correct answer is b.** Technician B only is correct. If the engine speed (RPM) drops when a cylinder is canceled (spark plug wire is grounded), the cylinder is producing power and contributing to the engine speed at idle. Answer a is not correct because the biggest drop in engine RPM is created by the strongest cylinder, not the weakest. Answers c and d are not correct because only Technician B is correct.

30. **The correct answer is b.** A good mechanically sound engine should measure less than 20% leakage. The lower the amount of leakage, the better the engine. Answer a is not correct because all cylinders should be *less than* 20%, not within 20% of each other. Answer c is not correct because the leakage should be *less than* 20%, not *more* than 20%. Answer d is not correct because the leakage should be very low. A 70% leakage rate means that 70% of the air entering the cylinder is escaping past the piston rings or valves.

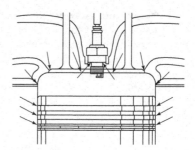

31. **The correct answer is b.** A good mechanically sound engine should measure less than 20% leakage. The lower the amount of leakage, the better the engine. Answer a is not correct because all cylinders should be *less than* 20%, not within 20% of each other. Answer c is not correct because the leakage should be *less than* 20%, not *more* than 20%. Answer d is not correct because the leakage should be very low. A 70% leakage rate means that 70% of the air entering the cylinder is escaping past the piston rings or valves.

32. **The correct answer is c.** Both technicians are correct. Technician A is correct because any misfire will cause paper held at the tailpipe to "puff." A burned valve will cause one cylinder to not produce as strong an exhaust stream as the others creating the uneven exhaust detected by holding the paper at the tailpipe. Technician B is correct because antifreeze tends to leave a gray/white stain on the engine where coolant has leaked and then evaporated by the engine heat. Answers a, b, and d are not correct because both technicians are correct.

ENGINE REPAIR (A1)

CATEGORY: CYLINDER HEAD AND VALVE TRAIN DIAGNOSIS AND REPAIR

33. **The correct answer is c.** Both technicians are correct. Technician A is correct because many vehicle manufacturers recommend replacing the head bolts after use because they are stretched during use and cannot be reused. Technician B is correct because many vehicle manufacturers recommend an initial torque setting, and then turning the fasteners additional degrees. This is called torque-angle or torque-to-yield method. Answers a, b, and d are not correct because both technicians are correct.

34. **The correct answer is c.** Both technicians are correct. Technician A is correct because most cam and crank gears or pulleys are equipped with a mark used to correctly time the camshaft/crankshaft timing. Technician B is also correct because some camshaft sprockets or gears are not keyed to the camshaft but are tightened in position. These types of camshafts require a special tool to properly position the camshaft before the retaining bolt is tightened. Answers a, b, and d are not correct because both technicians are correct.

35. **The correct answer is c.** All valve springs must be checked that they are square and of equal height. Answer a is not correct because the installed height of a spring is measured from the bottom of the retainer and locks in place to the valve seat. Answer b is not correct because stem height is a measurement of the valve itself from the spring seat, not a measure of the spring. Answer d is not correct because the setup shown is not placing a load on the spring and, therefore, cannot be used to measure spring tension.

36. **The correct answer is b.** Pure water is a 7 on the pH scale with acids represented by numbers lower than 7 and caustic materials (bases) represented by numbers higher than 7. Answers a, c, and d are not correct because these statements do not correctly represent the pH scale.

37. **The correct answer is a.** The pyrolytic oven is the least hazardous method of cleaning. Answers b, c, and d are not correct because the chemicals used in these cleaning methods represent hazards to the service technician during their use and may also create a hazardous waste problem.

38. **The correct answer is c.** Magnetic lines of force tend to get stronger at edges and, therefore, a fine powder can be used to locate cracks in iron parts. Answer a is not correct because aluminum parts cannot be checked using a magnetic field. Answer b is not correct because a magnetic method can be used on iron, but not on aluminum parts. Answer d is not correct because the answer states that the magnet removes the cracks rather than simply detecting the cracks.

39. **The correct answer is c.** Both technicians are correct. Technician A is correct because the parts must be clean to be able to see small cracks or faults. Technician B is correct because pressure testing using air will detect cracks in engine parts that are under water by observing bubbles from the fault area. Answers a, b, and d are not correct because both technicians are correct.

40. **The correct answer is c.** The correct answer is that all engine part fasteners should be removed in the reverse order of the tightening sequence. This method helps reline any built-up stress in the part and helps reduce the possibility of warpage when the part is removed. Answers a, c, and d are not correct because any of these methods could result in warpage when the part is removed.

41. **The correct answer is b.** Technician B only is correct. Damaged threads in a cylinder head may require that a thread repair insert be installed to allow a bolt to be used again in the threaded hole. Answer a is not correct because a die is used to make or repair threads on a rod and cannot be used to repair threads in a hole in the cylinder head. Answers c and d are not correct because only Technician B is correct.

42. **The correct answer is b.** Most vehicle manufacturers specify that warpage and out of straightness of less than 0.002 in. The best way to determine if the pushrods are straight is to roll them on a flat surface and check for any light under the pushrod as it is rolled. Answer a is not correct because the length would be affected if bent and are different length for different cylinders or valves in some engines. Answer c is not correct because the diameter is determined by the vehicle manufacturer and does not change with use. Answer d is not correct because only answer b is correct.

43. **The correct answer is b.** The cylinder head surface should be machined or the cylinder head replaced because the head is warped beyond the normal maximum allowed. Normal maximum warpage is less than 0.004 in. for a V-8 cylinder head. Answer a is not correct because the cylinder head is distorted beyond specifications. Answer c is not correct because even though the valves and the seats can be ground, the cylinder head must still be resurfaced before it is installed on the engine. Answer d is not correct because using sandpaper will not straighten a warped cylinder head and may even cause waviness in the head after it has been properly resurfaced.

44. **The correct answer is d.** Typical valve guide clearance is between one and three thousandths of an inch (0.001 to 0.003 in.). Answers a, b, and c are not correct because these figures represent a much greater clearance than is generally accepted.

45. **The correct answer is b.** The higher the micro inch finish measurement, the rougher the surface. For example, a surface finish of 90 micro-inches (m in.) is rougher than a surface that measures 30 m in. Answer a is not correct because an aluminum surface should be slightly smoother than a cast iron surface although the specifications are often close. Answer c is not correct because a smooth surface has a lower micro-inch finish measurement. Answer d is not correct because a crankshaft journal is smoother than a cylinder head surface.

46. **The correct answer is c.** Most vehicle manufacturers recommend that the margin be at least 0.030 in. Answers a and b are too small and could cause the valve to burn if used in an engine. Answer d is not correct because even though 0.060 in. could be used without harm in an engine, 0.060 in. is not the discard dimension.

47. **The correct answer is c.** A 30° stone will remove material from the top part of the valve seat, which will narrow and lower the seat. Answer a is not correct because a 60° stone will cut the bottom of the seat and while it too will narrow the seat, the seat will be raised as the 60° angle is being cut. Answer b is not correct because a 45° angle will simply widen the seat because it is the same angle as the seat. Answer d is not correct because it would narrow and lower the seat, but the low angle would remove more material around the seat than desirable.

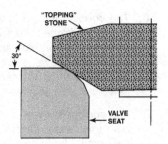

48. **The correct answer is c.** Valve spring inserts (shims) placed under the valve springs restore the original spring height that was lengthened when the valves were ground and the valves moved upward in the head. Answer a is not correct because when installing a valve spring insert, the installed height of the spring would be decreased (compressing the spring more) rather than increased (compressing the spring less). Answer b is not correct because the valve spring insert will not change the location of the tip (stem height) of the valve. Answer d is not correct because the valve spring insert would increase (not decrease) valve spring pressure to compensate for an increased (not decreased) installed height.

49. **The correct answer is c.** The crankshaft/camshaft relationship on most overhead valve engines involve aligning the two timing marks together with the camshaft mark at the 6 o'clock position and the crankshaft mark at the 12 o'clock position. Answers a, b and d are not correct because they do not represent the usual position of the timing marks for an OHV engine.

50. **The correct answer is c.** An umbrella-type valve stem seal fits snugly on the stem of the valve and moves up and down with the valve. Answer a is not correct because umbrella seals are not attached to the guides like positive-type seals. Answer b is not correct because the valve seals are used on the stem of the valve, not on the head or a valve. Answer d is not correct because the O-ring-type valve stem seals are locked into place under the retainer, not umbrella-type seals.

51. **The correct answer is b.** It is almost impossible to remove all of the dirt or varnish from inside the hollow pushrods. If reused in a new or rebuilt engine, the trapped dirt or varnish may become dislodged and cause wear or damage to the engine parts. Answer a is not correct because the cleaning time or cost of replacement pushrods is not the reason why most engine rebuilders recommend the replacement rather than the cleaning of hollow pushrods. Answer c is not correct because even though they do wear, this is not the primary reason why they are replaced. Answer d is not correct because pushrods do not change length when removed from the engine.

52. **The correct answer is c.** All fasteners should be tightened from the center of the component toward the outside to prevent stress buildup that could cause a cylinder head or other component being tightened to crack. Answers a, b, and d are not correct because they do not include tightening from the center outward.

53. **The correct answer is b.** The torque specification for engine bolts prescribes that the threads are clean and lubricated with engine oil. Answer a is not correct because even though threads must be clean, they must also be lightly oiled. Answer c is not correct because dirty threads would interfere with proper rotating torque and result in less clamp force. Answer d is not correct because new bolts are not necessary for all engines and the threads should be lubricated, not dry.

54. **The correct answer is d.** The valve stem seals do not need to be removed to remove the valves from the cylinder head. Answer **a** is not correct because the keepers have to be removed before the valves will be released from the retainer. Answer b is not correct because the cylinder head from the block before the valves can be removed from the head. Answer **c** is not correct because the burrs should be remove from the stem of the valve to avoid damaging the guide.

55. **The correct answer is c.** Both technicians are correct. Technician A is correct because parts wear together and they should be kept together to avoid creating additional wear to the parts that contact each other. Technician B is correct because the valve spring tension specifications are for the valve spring only. Answers a, b, and d are not correct because both technicians are correct.

56. **The correct answer is a.** The camshaft is being held to keep it from rotating as the retaining bolt is being tightened. Answer b is not correct because cam timing is achieved by using offset keys or other devices on the camshaft sprocket that varies the relationship between the camshaft and the crankshaft. Answer c is not correct because the chain tension is determined by the tensioner and is not adjustable at the camshaft sprocket. Answer d is not correct because a replacement camshaft bearing or shim is needed to change the end play.

57. **The correct answer is d.** Neither technician is correct. Technician A is not correct because 0.002 in. out-of-flatness is generally considered to be within factory specifications and, therefore, even though the cylinder head *could* be resurfaced, it would not be *required*. Technician B is not correct because replacement is not necessary if the cylinder head is within factory specifications. Answer c is not correct because neither technician is correct.

58. **The correct answer is a.** Technician A only is correct because the valve guide must be straight and true because the guide is used to control the cutter for the seats. Technician B is not correct because the valve guide(s) should be serviced first since the tools used for seat conditioning are installed in the valve guide. Answers c and d are not correct because only Technician A is correct.

59. **The correct answer is c.** Both technicians are correct. Technician A is correct because some vehicle manufacturers specify that the valve be opened a certain distance and the play in the guide be measured at the edge of the head of the valve using a dial indicator. Technician B is correct because a ball gauge (small hole gauge) can be used to measure the inside diameter of the guide. The ball gauge is then measured with a micrometer. Answers a, b, and d are not correct because both technicians are correct.

60. **The correct answer is c.** Both technicians are correct. Technician A is correct because many vehicle manufacturers recommend that the old guide be reamed oversize and that oversize stem valves be used to restore the cylinder head to useful service. Technician B is correct because a bronze insert can be used to restore the guide and allow the use of the stock valves. Answers a, b, and d are not correct because both technicians are correct.

61. **The correct answer is c.** Both technicians are correct. Technician A is correct because worn integral guides to useful service by an automotive machine shop. Technician B is correct because replacement guides can be inserted in the cylinder head that has integral guides after the guides have been reamed to the proper size for the replacement guide. Answers a, b, and d are not correct because both technicians are correct.

62. **The correct answer is a.** The valve-to-guide clearance between is measured using a micrometer to measure the diameter of the valve stem and to measure the inside diameter of the valve guide that is determined using a small ball gauge. The difference between these two is the valve-to-guide clearance. Answers b, c, and d are not correct because they cannot be used to measure the clearance between the valve stem and the valve guide.

63. **The correct answer is d.** A valve spring should be checked for squareness, proper free height, and tension. The tension should be checked at the designated height and without the dampener spring installed, if equipped. Answers a, b, and c are not correct because all three are correct, so the best answer is d.

64. **The correct answer is b.** The difference between the valve face angle and the valve seat angle is called the interference angle and it is usually specified as being 1°. Answer a is not correct because the margin in the area above the valve face and this angle is not the interference angle. Answers c and d are also not correct because they do not describe the interference angle.

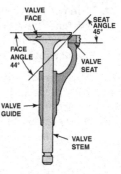

65. **The correct answer is a.** Technician A only is correct. Plugs that are installed to cover the cooling passage opening, where the core sand was removed during production, are usually driven into the opening using a hammer and a driver. Answer b is not correct because the cooling passage openings are not threaded. Answers c and d are not correct because only Technician A is correct.

66. **The correct answer is d.** The correct answer is all of the above. The coolant passages in the cylinder head should be inspected for corrosion, restriction, blocking, or signs of leakage. Answers a, b, and c are not correct because all of the items listed should be checked.

67. **The correct answer is d.** Neither technician is correct. Technician A is not correct because valve stem height is the distance from the spring seat to the top of the valve stem, whereas installed height is the distance from the valve seat to the bottom part of the valve spring retainer. Technician B is not correct because the valve stem height can be changed by grinding the stem, but not the installed height. Answers a, b, and c are not correct because neither technician is correct.

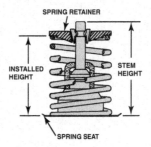

68. **The correct answer is b.** Technician B only is correct. O-ring-type valve stem seals can be checked using a hand-operated vacuum pump and a sealing cup to check whether the seal has been correctly installed. Technician A is not correct because the O-ring is installed under the keeper, not on top of the keeper. Answers a, c, and d are not correct because only Technician B is correct.

69. **The correct answer is d.** All of the answers are correct. Before valves can be removed, the keepers have to be removed and the cylinder head has to be off of the block. To avoid damage to the grinder, any burrs on the valve stems should be removed before removing the valve from the head. Answers a, b, and c are not correct because all are correct and, therefore, answer d is the best answer.

70. **The correct answer is a.** Technician A only is correct because fluorescent dye can be used on aluminum or iron parts to check for cracks. Technician B is not correct because even though it is commonly used to check aluminum parts, dye penetrant testing can also be used on iron parts. Answers c and d are not correct because only Technician A is correct.

71. **The correct answer is b.** The dial indicator is positioned to read movement of the camshaft, which is the end play. Answer a is not correct because a micrometer or Plastigage® is required to measure the camshaft bearing clearance. Answer c is not correct because the dial indicator is not positioned correctly to read runout. Answer d is not correct because a dial indicator is not used to properly locate the camshaft sprocket.

72. **The correct answer is d.** The camshaft bore should be inspected on all types of engines regardless of design. Answers a, b, and c are not correct because the camshaft bores on all types of engines should be inspected.

73. **The correct answer is b.** A steel spring seat is being installed on this aluminum head to protect the surface of the head from damage that the valve spring could cause during normal engine operation. Some engines use a combination of spring seat and valve stem seal. Answer a is not correct because even though they look similar, a valve spring insert is used to restore the proper valve spring installed height. Answer c is not correct because the part does not include a seal. Answer d is not correct because the seat is being installed around the valve guide.

74. **The correct answer is b.** The intake manifold may require machining to fit onto the cylinder heads after they have been machined. A formula is used to determine the amount that needs to be removed to allow the intake manifold to align properly with the parts in the head. Answers a, c, and d are not correct because these surfaces do not have to be machined when the cylinder heads are machined.

75. **The correct answer is b.** Zero lash is being determined by tightening the rocker arm adjusting nut until the pushrod cannot be rotated. Answer a is not correct because even though the technician is turning the adjusting nut, the rocker arm would have to be moved in order to remove the pushrod. Answer c is not correct because pushrod length is not adjustable. Answer d is not correct because the ratio of the rocker arm is not adjustable.

ENGINE REPAIR (A1)

CATEGORY: ENGINE BLOCK DIAGNOSIS AND REPAIR

76. **The correct answer is b.** Technician B only is correct. A head gasket is labeled "front" if it has to be placed on the block correctly to avoid blocking coolant passages. The word "front" does mean toward the front of the engine, which is the accessory drive belt end. Answer a is not correct because form-in-place sealant is only used to seal parts that experience low pressure and are not designed to take the place of a cylinder head gasket. Answers c and d are not correct because only Technician B is correct.

77. **The correct answer is d.** The torque-angle method of tightening involves torquing the fasteners to a specified torque and then turning them a specified number of degrees. Answer a is not correct because even though all bolts should be turned the same number of degrees (not turns), this answer does not include a specified initial torque as a starting point. Answer b is not correct because this answer includes loosening the fasteners after torquing instead of tightening after the initial torquing. Answer c is the usual method to tighten a fastener using a torque wrench instead of using the torque-angle method as specified in the question.

78. **The correct answer is d.** Neither technician is correct. Technician A is not correct because the proper method is to file the ends of the ring to achieve the proper end gap. Technician B is not correct because an oversize ring would make the gap smaller, not larger. Answers a, b, and c are not correct because neither technician is correct.

79. **The correct answer is a.** The piston ring end gap can be increased by filing the ends of the piston ring. Answer b is not correct because oversize rings would decrease the piston ring end gap. Answer c is not correct because a sleeve is used to restore the cylinder and while a slightly larger bore would cause the piston ring end gap to increase, the installation of a sleeve by itself would not necessarily increase piston ring end gap. Answer d is not correct because knurling the piston would increase the diameter of the piston skirt and would not increase the piston ring end gap.

80. **The correct answer is c.** The feeler gauge is being used to measure the clearance between the piston ring and the piston ring groove. Normal clearance is usually between 0.001 in. and 0.003 in. Answer a is not correct because back spacing is determined by measuring the depth of the piston ring groove, not the width. Answer b is not correct because piston ring end gap is measured with a feeler gauge with the ring installed in the cylinder bore. Answer d is not correct because the surface finish is not measured using a feeler gauge.

81. **The correct answer is d.** The dial indicator is positioned to show the amount of movement that the crankshaft moves as it is pried forward and rearward. This movement is called the crankshaft end play or thrust bearing clearance. Answer a is not correct because the dial indicator is not in the right position to measure runout. It has to be 90° (right angle) to the crankshaft to measure runout. Answer b is not correct because a dial indicator is not used to check main bearing oil clearance. Oil clearance is measured using a micrometer or Plastigage. Answer c is not correct because the dial indicator needs to be touching the piston or valve lifter to determine top dead center.

82. **The correct answer is b.** According to engine bearing manufacturers, the most common cause of premature bearing failure is dirt. Answers a, c, and d are each a possible cause of premature engine bearing failure, but they are not the most common cause.

83. **The correct answer is a.** Technician A only is correct. If the block was machined, such as aligned honed, the bearing caps need to be de-burred proper to assembly to ensure that the parts fit correctly to the block without interference or gaps. Technician b is not correct because cleaning does not require that a file be used on parts. Answers c and d are not correct because only Technician A is correct.

84. **The correct answer is d.** To check for taper, the crankshaft journal has to be measured at a minimum of six locations. Answers a, b, and c are not correct because when measuring taper, there must be at least two measurements so the difference (taper) can be determined and this does not allow enough measurements to determine out-of-round. To be able to determine accurately whether or not a crankshaft journal is out-of-round or tapered, at least six measurements must be taken 120° apart.

85. **The correct answer is a.** The cylinder should be bored and/or honed and thoroughly cleaned before the piston ring end gap is checked. Answers b, c, and d are not correct because the ring gap cannot be checked after the piston has been installed in the cylinder.

86. **The correct answer is c.** The side clearance is between the piston ring and piston ring groove. This clearance allows the piston ring to twist during engine operation. Answer a is not correct because this is the piston-to-cylinder wall clearance, not the piston ring side clearance. Answers b and d are not correct because they do not represent the difference between the piston ring and the piston ring groove.

87. **The correct answer is b.** The vibration damper (harmonic balancer) has to be removed on an OHV engine to gain access to the timing gear and chain. Answers a, c, and d are not correct because removing the valve cover, cylinder head, or intake manifold will not allow access to the timing chain.

88. **The correct answer is c.** Both technicians are correct. Technician A is correct because a thread chaser will not remove any material from the metal, but will simply clean the threads. Technician B is correct because the bottom photo shows a tap. Answers a, b, and d are not correct because both technicians are correct.

89. **The correct answer is d.** Answer a is correct because lower than normal oil pressure can be caused by a worn oil pump because it may not be able to supply enough oil to keep the bearing clearance filled with oil. Answers b and c are correct because if the rod bearings were worn, an excessive amount of engine oil can escape from between the bearing and the crankshaft journal, thereby reducing oil pressure.

90. **The correct answer is a.** The ridge is the untouched area (original diameter of the cylinder) above where the piston rings contact the sides of the cylinder. Answer b is not correct because the top piston ring has been contacting the cylinder wall. Answer c is not correct because the ridge should be removed before removing the piston to avoid damage to the pistons. Answer d is not correct because the ridge is normal wear due to the piston ring and does not indicate that the stroke of the crankshaft is not correct.

91. **The correct answer is a.** Technician A only is correct. Dye penetrant is primarily used to check pistons and other nonmagnetic materials for cracks, but it can be used to check iron and steel parts. Answer b is not correct because even though these are other methods that can be used to check iron and steel parts for cracks, the dye penetrant method can be used on other materials besides aluminum. Answers c and d are not correct because they do not state that Technician A only is correct.

92. **The correct answer is b.** The rod and cap are machined together, and then separated. They should always be kept together and the cap reattached in the proper direction. Answer a (balanced together) is a true statement, but the weight would not be the same if the cap was reinstalled backward. It is for this reason that the two are machined together. Answers c and d are not correct because the rod cap and rod itself are being discussed, not the rod piston assembly.

93. **The correct answer is b.** While the protective caps would protect all parts of the engine, the most likely part to be damaged is the crankshaft as the piston-rod assembly is being installed into the engine. Answers a, c, and d are not correct because b is the best answer.

94. **The correct answer is d.** If the connecting rod is bent or misaligned, it creates an angled force applied to the piston as it moves up and down in the cylinder creating angled wear. Answer a is not correct because a tapered cylinder is caused by normal wear of the piston rings against the cylinder wall. Answer b is not correct because crankshaft journals can wear in a barrel shape, but not cylinders. Answer c is not correct because a ridge is normally created in a high-mileage engine due to wear created by the piston rings.

95. **The correct answer is b.** Abnormal combustion (ping, preignition, spark knock, or detonation) raises the temperature and the pressure inside the combustion chamber, which can cause pistons to melt and even blow holes through the top of the pistons. Answer a, while this could occur, would only be a factor if there were a failure of the timing belt or chain. Answer c is not correct because lugging can cause harm to connecting rod bearings, not pistons. Answer d is not correct because high speeds can most stretch connecting rods and damage main bearings, not break pistons, except indirectly.

96. **The correct answer is c.** The diameter of a piston is measured 90° from the piston pin across the thrust surface. Answer a is not correct because the head of the piston is smaller in diameter than the lower part of the piston to allow for heat expansion. Answers b and d are not correct.

97. **The correct answer is c.** A worn piston pin will cause a double knock sound. The first sound occurs when the piston stops at top dead center and the second sound occurs as the piston is pulled downward by the connecting rod after top dead center. Answer a is not correct because piston rings and valve stem seals are used to control oil consumption. Answer b is not correct because unlike a rod bearing, the noise of a piston pin does not stop when the cylinder is grounded out. Answer d is not correct because it often occurs when the engine is cold.

98. **The correct answer is c.** Both technicians are correct. Many crankshaft vibration dampeners (harmonic balancers) are a light press fit on the end of the crankshaft, which requires the use of a puller to safely remove, and an installation tool to safely install, to prevent causing damage to the balancer. Answers a, b, and d are not correct because both technicians are correct.

99. **The correct answer is b.** Most bearing oil clearance specifications are usually close to 0.001″ to 0.003″ and 0.0005″ (one-half thousandth) to 0.0025″ (two and a half thousandth) is a typical clearance specification. Answer a is too small a clearance and answers c and d represent too much clearance.

100. **The correct answer is b.** Technician B only is correct. The cam bearings used in a cam-in-block engine requires the use of a long tool that holds the cam bearing so it can be properly placed and then driven into location. Answer a is not correct because the cam bearings used in a cam-in-block engine are full round and are not two sections where Plastigage can be used. Bearing clearance is determined by measuring the inside diameter of the bearing and subtracting the outside diameter of the camshaft bearing journal. Answers c and d are not correct because Technician B only is correct.

101. **The correct answer is a.** Typical piston-to-cylinder clearance is one to three thousandth of an inch (0.001″ to 0.003″), which is the best answer. Answers b, c, and d are too great a clearance.

102. **The correct answer is b.** A dial bore gauge is being used to measure the difference in the cylinder at various places to determine the amount of cylinder taper and to determine if it is out-of-round. Answer a is not correct because a dial bore gauge is being shown and this tool is used to measure the cylinder bore only. It is not a tool equipped with an abrasive which is needed to be used to remove the cylinder wall glaze. A dial bore gauge is used to measure the difference within a cylinder bore. Answer c is not correct because a dial bore gauge is not used to remove material from the cylinder. Answer d is not correct because a dial bore gauge is being used and this tool does not measure the surface finish.

103. **The correct answer is c.** If the Plastigage strip has been squeezed so that it is wider than specified, the oil clearance is insufficient. Answer a is not correct because a large oil clearance will not squeeze the plastic strip as much and the clearance will be larger than specified. Answer b is not correct because, even though this could cause an inaccurate reading, the best answer is still c. Answer d is not correct because side clearance is not measured using Plastigage.

104. **The correct answer is b.** The connecting rod side clearance is the distance between the connecting rods and the sides (check) of the crankshaft journal. Answer a is not correct because oil clearance is between the bearing and the rod journal, not between the check of the rod journal and the connecting rod. Answers c and d are not correct because the feeler gauge is measuring between the connecting rods and not the thrust bearing clearance.

105. **The correct answer is b.** Most engine manufacturers specify a crankshaft thrust bearing clearance between two and twelve thousandth of an inch (0.002 in. to 0.012 in.). Answer a is not correct because this clearance is too small. Answers c and d are not correct because they are too great and usually outside of the specified measurements for thrust bearing clearance.

106. **The correct answer is d.** Neither technician is correct. Technician A is not correct because the block can be restored to useful service if it is line bored or honed. Technician B is not correct because oversize bearings will not restore the alignment of the main bearing bores. Answers a, b, and c are not correct because neither technician is correct.

107. **The correct answer is c.** The rear cylinder(s) can become distorted if the bell housing bolts are not properly torqued. Answer a is not correct because, even though it may be possible to distort the bell housing, the most correct and most important reason for torquing the bell housing is to prevent distortion of the block. Answer b is not correct because while cracking the block may be possible, it is very unlikely to occur. Answer d is not correct because the crankshaft is not affected when the bell housing is being attached to the back of the engine block.

108. **The correct answer is a.** Both the compression and the displacement will be increased if the cylinder bore is increased. When the cylinder bore is increased, the volume of the cylinder is increased when the piston is at bottom dead center, yet the combustion chamber volume has not been increased, so the larger cylinder volume is being compressed into the same volume when the piston is at top dead center. Answer b is not correct because while the displacement will increase, the compression rate will be increased instead of being decreased. Answer c is not correct because the displacement is increased when the bore (cylinder diameter) is increased. Answer d is not correct because both are increased, not decreased.

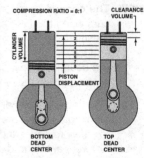

109. **The correct answer is b.** Technician B is correct because the connecting rod and cap should be marked for proper reassembly if they are not marked at the factory. Technician A is not correct because while it may be possible to do this on some engines, damage to the piston could still occur as it passes the lower part of the cylinder that may be rusted or corroded. Answers c and d are not correct because Technician B is correct.

110. **The correct answer is a.** The correct answer is 0.252 in. because the number 2 (0.200 of an inch) is showing as well as two vertical lines each representing 0.025 of an inch (0.200 + 0.025 + 0.025 = .250 in.) plus another 2 on the barrel equals 0.252 in. Answers b, c, and d are not correct answers.

111. **The correct answer is a.** Technician A is correct. It is wise to bore the cylinder to an oversize and use an oversize piston in any engine that has a cylinder that is out-of-round by 0.004 in. Most factory specifications call for a maximum out-of-round of 0.0015 in. or less. All cylinders should have the same bore, so all cylinders should be bored to the same size. Technician B is not correct because the out-of-round of the cylinder is excessive according to most vehicle manufacturer's specifications. Answers c and d are not correct because Technician A is correct.

112. **The correct answer is b.** Technician B is correct because the part shown is a metric thread pitch gage. The numbers represent the measurement in millimeters (mm) between the threads. Technician A is not correct because the tool used to dress the grinder stones uses a wheel rather than individual blades. Answers c and d are not correct because only Technician B is correct.

113. **The correct answer is a.** Soap (or detergent) and water should be used to clean a block after machining because the soapsuds will lift any grit remaining in the machined grooves. Answer b is not correct because while a clean cloth and engine oil can be used to prepare an engine block for assembly, it will not remove the grit from the small grooves left from the machining or grinding operation. Answer c is not correct because WD-40 will help prevent rust from forming but it will not clean as well as soap and water. Answer d is not correct because it requires the soap or detergent and water rather than a solvent (oil-based product) to lift the grit from the block surfaces.

114. **The correct answer is c.** Both technicians are correct. Technician A is correct because the mark on the piston rings usually indicates the upward direction so the ring will twist correctly in the groove during engine operation. Technician B is correct because the mark may be different between the top and the second ring. Answers a, b, and d are not correct because both technicians are correct.

115. **The correct answer is c.** Both technicians are correct. Technician A is correct because the cylinder bore diameter can vary slightly and the end gap of the piston ring should always be checked in the cylinder in which it is to be installed to make sure that the gap is within factory specifications. Technician B is correct because the end gap can be increased by filing the ends of the ring using a hand file or a rotary ring gap filing tool. Answers a, b, and d are not correct because both technicians are correct.

116. **The correct answer is a.** Technician A only is correct. The oil bearing clearance can be checked using plastic gauge material (Plastigage). While some vehicle manufacturers recommend that direct measurement of the bearings as installed be subtracted from the diameter of the bearing journal to determine the oil clearance, it is possible to use Plastigage. Answer b is not correct because the crankshaft should not be moved (rotated) when the Plastigage is being used. Answers c and d are not correct because Technician A only is correct.

117. **The correct answer is b.** The notch, arrow, or other mark on a piston should be installed facing toward the front (accessory drive belt end) of the engine. The piston pin is offset on many pistons and this ensures that the piston is correctly installed. Answer a is not correct because the piston mark cannot be pointed toward the side of the engine. Answer c is not correct as explained for answer b. Answer d is not correct because the arrow should face the front of the engine.

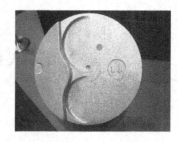

118. **A only is correct.** The insert bearing should extend slightly above the bearing cap to provide the necessary crush when assembled to keep the bearing from spinning during engine operation. Answer b is not correct because the bearing size is determined by the thickness of the insert and the difference between a standard and a 0.010 in. undersize bearing (thicker shell) insert may not be visible. Answers c and d are not correct because they do not indicate that Technician A only is correct.

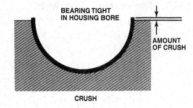

BEARING TIGHT
IN HOUSING BORE

AMOUNT
OF CRUSH

CRUSH

ENGINE REPAIR (A1)

CATEGORY: LUBRICATION AND COOLING SYSTEMS DIAGNOSIS AND REPAIR

119. **The correct answer is c.** Both technicians are correct. Technician A is correct because the drive belt(s) could have been installed and tightened too tightly creating an excessive force on the water pump bearing. Technician B is also correct because the cooling fan blade(s) may be bent causing a vibration, which could also damage the water pump bearing. Answers a, b, and d are not correct because both technicians are correct.

120. **The correct answer is a.** The freezing point of the coolant decreases as the percentage of antifreeze increases up to a point (about 70%) and then it starts to increase. Antifreeze by itself freezes at about 0°F (-18°C). Answer b is not correct because the boiling point increases rather than decreases as the percentage of antifreeze is increased. Answer c is not correct because the heat transferability of the coolant is decreased as the percentage of antifreeze is increased in the coolant. Answer d is not correct because answers b and c are not correct.

121. **The correct answer is a.** Most vehicle manufacturers recommend that a 50/50 mix of antifreeze and water be used for the cooling system. Filling half the system with 100% antifreeze and the rest with water will result in a 50/50 mix. Answers b and c are not correct because these methods will not result in a 50/50 antifreeze to water mix. Answer d will result in a 50/50 mix if all of the coolant can be drained from the system before refilling it with the 50/50 mix. However, this method uses more antifreeze coolant than is necessary and, therefore, is not the recommended method and not the best answer to this question.

122. **The correct answer is c.** The temperature on the thermostat is the temperature that it starts to open and is fully opened about 20° higher. Answer a is not correct because the temperature on the thermostat is when it starts to open not when it is fully open. Answer b is not correct because even though thermostats can cause overheating, they most often fail in the open position causing the engine to not reach operating temperature. Answer d is not correct because it involves both answers a and b which were not correct.

123. **The correct answer is c.** Both technicians are correct. Technician A is correct because the radiator should always be checked for proper operation before using it in a vehicle with a new or rebuilt engine. Technician B is correct because an inoperative electric cooling fan can cause overheating during slow, city driving. Answers a, b, and d are not correct because both technicians are correct.

124. **The correct answer is c.** Both technicians are correct. Technician A is correct because the PCV valve is located between the intake manifold and the valve (cylinder head) cover. Technician B is correct because about 20% of the air needed by the engine at idle speed flows through the PCV valve. Answers a, b, and d are not correct because both technicians are correct.

125. **The correct answer is d.** Answer a is correct because the oil pump should be rotated before starting the engine after a rebuild to lubricate the bearings as well as the valve train components (answer b) including the camshaft (answer c).

126. **The correct answer is d.** Both answers a and b are correct. Answer a is correct because an engine oil cooler has engine oil circulated through the passages and these passages should not leak oil. Answer b is correct because most engine oil coolers use engine coolant to cool as well as warm the engine coil. Coolant should not leak from the cooler or any of the lines or fittings. Answer c is not correct because air is not used in most engine oil coolers and if so, would be just passing through the cooling fins and an air leak is not a factor.

127. **The correct answer is a.** Coolant that uses organic acid technology such as DEX-COOL does not contain any silicates or phosphates. Answers b, c, and d all contain either silicates or phosphates.

128. **The correct answer is a.** Technician A is correct because the HOT light (engine coolant temperature warning lamp) will come on about 258°F (125°C) to warn the driver that the engine coolant temperature is too high for safe engine operation. Technician B is not correct because the warning light does not react to cooling system pressure, just temperature. Answers c and d are not correct because only Technician A is correct.

129. **The correct answer is b.** Technician B only is correct. The purpose and function of the electric cooling fan is to provide airflow through the radiator at low vehicle speeds. When the vehicle exceeds about 35 mph (56 km/h), there is enough airflow to keep the engine cool and the electric cooling fan shuts off. If the electric cooling fan is not operating, the engine could overheat during slow city-type driving conditions. Answer a is not correct because the thermostat opens about 20° lower than the temperature that is fully open and the cooling fan will come on at a higher than the fully open temperature of the thermostat. Answer c and d are not correct because only Technician B is correct.

130. **The correct answer is b.** Technician B is correct because the heater will have coolant flowing through the core when the water pump is operating slowly such as during engine idle. However, when the engine speed increases, the coolant will be taking the path of lower resistance and bypass the heater core unless the coolant level is properly filled. Technician A is not correct because even though the water pump could have worn the impeller blades, the most likely cause is low coolant level. Answers c and d are not correct because only Technician B is correct.

131. **The correct answer is d.** Answer d is correct because normal operating temperature causes the upper hose to become hot and pressurized and will cause the cooling fans to cycle on and off. Answer a is not correct because the radiator cap will only release coolant to the overflow if the pressure exceeds the rating of the cap and does not represent what normally occurs when the engine reaches normal operating temperature. Answers b and c are not correct alone because either can be an indication of when normal operating temperature has been achieved and, therefore, answer d is the best answer.

132. **The correct answer is a.** The engine oil flows best when it is warm and also is able to hold dirt in suspension best at normal operating temperature. Answers b and c are not correct because the oil can hold more dirt and flow best if the oil is at normal operating temperature. Answer d is not correct because this procedure will not ensure that the oil is at normal operating temperature.

133. **The correct answer is d.** Neither technician is correct. The thickness (viscosity) is the measure of the resistance to flow and is not an indicator of quality. The API rating indicates quality. Technician A is not correct because even though a thicker oil (higher viscosity) may cause an increase in oil pressure, the thickness of the oil is not an indication of quality. The higher viscosity could keep vital engine parts from receiving oil at start up, especially in cold weather. Technician B is not correct because a higher viscosity oil would decrease fuel economy and is not recommended by the vehicle manufacturers in most cases. Answer c is not correct because both technicians are wrong.

134. **The correct answer is b.** Normal oil pressure is generally 10 psi per 1000 RPM and, therefore, oil pressure between 10 psi and 60 psi would be the best answer. Answer a is not correct because the pressure is too low and represents the oil pressure that could turn on the oil pressure warning light but is not high enough to be considered normal. Answers c and d are both too high for normal oil pressure.

135. **The correct answer is c.** The valves components are the last to receive oil from the oil pump. The oil first flows to bearings (cam, main, and rod), and then to the rocker arms. Answer a is not correct because the main bearings are usually one of the first components to receive oil after it leaves the oil pump. Answer b is not correct because the rod bearings receive engine oil from the main bearings and are one of the first locations in the engine to receive oil. Answer d is not correct because the oil filter is the first place the oil is pumped when leaving the oil pump.

CATEGORY: FUEL, ELECTRICAL, IGNITION, AND EXHAUST SYSTEMS INSPECTION AND SERVICE

136. **The correct answer is c.** Both technicians are correct. Technician A is correct because a defective crankshaft position (CKP) sensor will prevent the necessary signal to the ignition module to trigger the ignition coil, which would cause a no spark condition. Technician B is also correct because a defective ignition module can cause a no spark condition. Answers a, b, and d are not correct because both technicians are correct.

137. **The correct answer is b.** Technician B is correct because each coil fires two spark plugs at the same time. If the coil is defective and not capable of supplying a spark, both spark plugs attached to the coil will not fire. Answer a is not correct because even if two spark plugs will not fire, most engines will still start and run, even though the engine will not produce normal power. Answers c and d are not correct because Technician B only is correct.

138. **The correct answer is c.** Both technicians are correct. Technician A is correct because a fault in the engine itself such as worn bearings or other mechanical fault can cause the engine to require a greater force to rotate. Technician B is also correct because a defective starter motor will often draw an excessive amount of current from the battery thereby reducing the battery voltage during cranking. Answers a, b, and d are not correct because they do not include that both technicians are correct.

139. **The correct answer is c.** Both technicians are correct. Technician A is correct because air can enter through a gap in the intake manifold, which is called a vacuum leak. Technician B is correct because a reduction in the amount of air entering the engine is similar to what occurs if the throttle plate is not opened. Answers a, b, and d are not correct because both technicians are correct.

140. **The correct answer is c.** Both technicians are correct. Technician A is correct because a weak or defective battery will cause a starter to rotate slower than normal. Technician B is also correct because a loose or corroded battery cable will cause a voltage drop in the cranking circuit, which will reduce the current flow to the starter. Answers a, b, and d are not correct because they do not include that both technicians are correct.

141. **The correct answer is c.** Both technicians are correct. Technician A is correct because a clogged port fuel injector can cause a lack of fuel to one cylinder, which would cause a misfire condition. Technician B is correct because a leaking lower injector O-ring will cause outside air to enter the intake manifold. Air leaking into the intake manifold is commonly called a vacuum leak. Answers a, b, and d are not correct because both technicians are correct.

142. **The correct answer is b.** The oxygen sensor should be replaced if the engine has a blown head gasket. Additives in conventional coolant such as silicates and phosphates can coat the oxygen sensor causing the sensor to incorrectly sense the oxygen content in the exhaust. Answer a is not correct because the throttle position sensor would not be directly related to a fault with the head gasket nor be affected by the condition, as would the oxygen sensor.

    Answer c is not correct because a blown head gasket would not affect the MAP sensor directly. While it is possible for some coolant to get into the sensor through the intake system, this would be very unlikely. Answer d is not correct because a blown head gasket would not affect the ECT sensor since it is already exposed to coolant normally. A defective ECT sensor could be the cause of the blown head gasket if it had not accurately measured engine coolant temperature.

143. **The correct answer is c.** Both technicians are correct. Technician A is correct because up to 20% of the air needed by the engine at idle speed flows though the PCV valve. If the flow is not correct, the engine idle will be affected. Technician B is also correct because if the EGR valve was stuck partially open at idle, the exhaust gases would dilute the air-fuel mixtures by displacing oxygen. The engine idle would be unstable because of the incorrect mixture. Answer c and d are not correct because both Technicians A and B are correct.

144. **The correct answer is c.** Both technicians are correct. Technician A is correct because if the catalytic converter rattles when tapped, the substrate is broken and the converter should be replaced. Technician B is also correct because the converter can be poisoned by lead or other chemicals and the active material rendered unable to start the chemical reactions as designed, but yet not be physically clogged. Answers c and d are not correct because both Technicians A and B are correct.

145. **The correct answer is c.** A clogged condenser would affect the operation of the air conditioning system and could increase the coolant temperature by restricting airflow through the radiator, but would not cause a reduction in engine power. Answers a, b, and d are not correct because each of these could cause a reduction in engine power. A clogged air filter would reduce the amount of air entering the engine. A restricted intercooler would also reduce the amount of air entering the engine. A restricted exhaust would reduce the amount of exhaust exiting the engine and create higher than normal backpressure, thereby reducing engine power.

146. **The correct answer is c.** Both technicians are correct. Technician A is correct because the exhaust could travel up through the defective one-way check valve and damage the air pump as well as the switching valves and hoses. Technician B is also correct because the airflow from the air pump should be switched from the exhaust manifold to the catalytic converter when the engine is operating in closed loop. If the air were to continue to flow to the exhaust manifold, the oxygen sensor would read the air from the air injection reaction (AIR) pump as being caused by a lean air-fuel mixture; then the vehicle computer would try to incorrectly enrich the mixture. Answers c and d are not correct because both Technicians A and B are correct.

147. **The correct answer is b.** Technician B only is correct. The spring inside the PCV valve can lose tension due to heating and cooling cycles during normal engine operation. If the valve does not rattle, then it is defective and should be replaced, but this does not mean that it is serviceable just because it does rattle when shaken. Technician A is not correct saying because the valve rattles, the valve is good. The valve should be replaced when it does not rattle when shaken or whenever recommended to be replaced by the vehicle manufacture interval. Answers c and d are not correct because Technician B only is correct.

148. **The correct answer is b.** Technician B only is correct. Dry, fluffy deposits on spark plugs are usually an indication of a rich air-fuel mixture. Technician A is not correct because the deposits are usually wet when the engine is burning oil because oil does not burn very well. Answers c and d are not correct because they do not indicate that Technician B only is correct.

149. **The correct answer is a.** Technician A only is correct. The spark plug wire should measure less than 10,000 ohms per foot of length and a reading of 7.86k ohms (7,860 ohms) is well below the maximum allowable 20,000 ohms (two feet times 10,000 = 20,000 ohms). Technician B is not correct because the resistance is within the specifications for most vehicle manufacturers. Answers c and d are not correct because Technician A only is correct.

150. **The correct answer is b.** Technician B only is correct. Technician B is correct because a coil-on-plug ignition system uses a coil for each spark plug and if it fails, a misfire will occur. Technician A is not correct because adjusting the crankshaft position (CKP) sensor just adjusts the air gap and does not affect when the signal occurs. Ignition timing is not adjustable on an engine equipped with a waste-spark or COP-type ignition. Answers c and d are not correct because only Technician B is correct.

151. **The correct answer is c.** Both technicians are correct. Technician A is correct because if the bushings are worn in the turbocharger, engine oil can get past and be drawn into the turbocharger where the oil will then flow into the cylinder and be consumed. Technician B is correct because a clogged positive crankcase ventilation (PCV) system can cause crankcase pressure to increase, which can cause engine oil to be forced into the intake manifold. Answers a, b, and d are not correct because both technicians are correct.

152. **The correct answer is c.** Both technicians are correct. Technician A is correct because an engine will produce less than normal torque and power if not supplied with an adequate amount of fuel under the pressure. Technician B is also correct because most vehicle specifications require that the fuel pump be capable of supplying one-half pint of fuel in 15 seconds or two pints (1 liter) every minute (60 seconds). Answers a, b, and d are not correct because both technicians are correct.

153. **The correct answer is a.** Technician A only is correct. The reading on the ohmmeter (OL, or over limit) indicates that the spark plug wire is electrically open and lacks continuity. The wire should be replaced. Technician B is not correct because a good spark plug wire should measure less than 10,000 ohms per foot or less than 30,000 ohms for most spark plug wires. The wire being tested did not register any continuity and is, therefore, electrically open and should be replaced. Answers b, c, and d are not correct because only Technician A is correct.

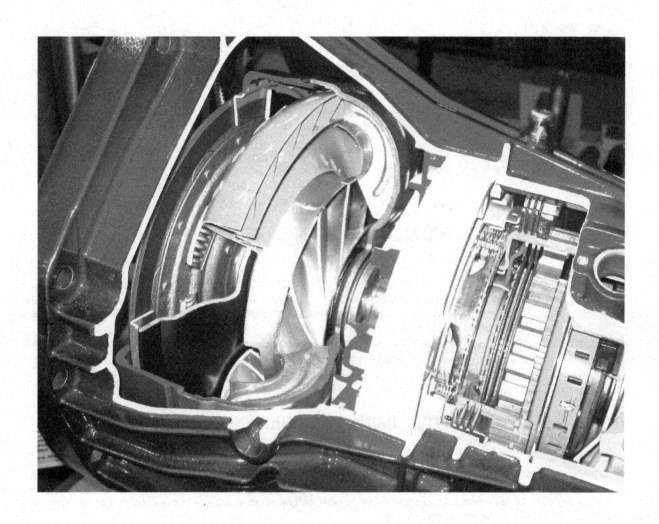

AUTOMATIC TRANSMISSION/TRANSAXLE CONTENT AREA

This ASE study guide for Automatic Transmission/Transaxle (A2) is divided into the sub-content areas that correlate to the actual ASE certification test as follows:

CONTENT AREA	QUESTIONS IN TEST	NUMBER OF STUDY GUIDE QUESTIONS
A. General Transmission/Transaxle Diagnosis	25	57 (1–57)
1. Mechanical/Hydraulic Systems (11)		
2. Electronic Systems (14)		
B. In-Vehicle Transmission/Transaxle Repair	12	29 (58–86)
C. Off-Vehicle Transmission/Transaxle Repair	13	24 (87–110)
1. Removal and Installation (4)		
2. Disassembly and Assembly (5)		
3. Friction and Reaction Units (4)		
TOTAL	**50**	**110**

TIME ALLOWED TO TAKE THE TEST

The allocated time to take the Automatic Transmission/Transaxle certification test is 75 minutes. ASE adds 10 additional questions to the test for research purposes for a total of 60 questions. These questions do not count toward your score, but they are embedded within the test and there is no way of knowing which ones do not count. As a result, the technician needs to answer 60 questions in 75 minutes, or about one question per minute.

If taking the recertification A2 test, there are just 25 questions with no additional research questions included. The time allocated to take the recertification test is 30 minutes, which means about one minute per question.

BEFORE USING THIS STUDY GUIDE

Before trying to answer the questions and looking at the explanations, look over the following list of the content that ASE states will be covered in the certification test. For best results using this study guide, check service information or consult an automotive textbook for details on any of the content areas that are not familiar before trying to answer the questions. For additional information about the ASE test, visit the website at **www.ase.com**.

AUTOMATIC TRANSMISSION/TRANSAXLE (A2) CONTENT AREA

A. GENERAL TRANSMISSION/TRANSAXLE DIAGNOSIS (25 QUESTIONS)

1. Mechanical/Hydraulic Systems (11 questions)

1. Road test the vehicle to verify mechanical/hydraulic system problems based on driver's concern; determine necessary action.
2. Diagnose noise, vibration, harshness, and shift quality problems; determine necessary action.
3. Diagnose fluid loss, type, level, and condition problems; determine necessary action.
4. Perform pressure tests; determine necessary action.
5. Perform stall tests; determine necessary action.
6. Perform torque converter clutch (lock-up converter) mechanical/hydraulic system tests; determine necessary action.

2. Electronic Systems (14 questions)

1. Road test the vehicle to verify electronic system problems based on driver's concern; determine necessary action.
2. Perform pressure tests on transmissions equipped with electronic pressure control; determine necessary action.
3. Perform torque converter clutch (lock up converter) electronic system tests; determine necessary action.
4. Diagnose electronic transmission control systems using appropriate test equipment, service information, technical service bulletins, and schematics; diagnose shorts, grounds, opens, and resistance problems in electrical/electronic circuits; determine necessary action.
5. Verify proper operation of charging system; check battery, connections, and power/ground circuits.
6. Differentiate between engine performance, or other vehicle systems, and transmission/transaxle related problems; determine necessary action.
7. Diagnose shift quality concerns resulting from problems in the electronic transmission control system; determine necessary action.

B. IN-VEHICLE TRANSMISSION/TRANSAXLE MAINTENANCE AND REPAIR (12 QUESTIONS)

1. Inspect, adjust, and replace manual valve shift linkage, transmission range sensor/switch, and park/neutral position switch (inhibitor/neutral safety switch).
2. Inspect, adjust, and replace cables or linkages for the throttle valve (TV) and accelerator pedal.
3. Inspect and replace external seals and gaskets.
4. Inspect and replace driveshaft yoke, drive axle joints, and bushings, and seals.
5. Check condition and operation of engine cooling system; inspect transmission cooler, lines and fittings.
6. Inspect valve body mating surfaces, bores, valves, springs, sleeves, retainers, brackets, check balls, screens, spacer plates, and gaskets; replace as necessary.
7. Torque valve body fasteners to specification.
8. Inspect accumulator and servo bores, pistons, seals, pins/pin bores, springs, and retainers; repair or replace as necessary.

9. Inspect, test, adjust, repair, or replace electrical/electronic components and circuits including control modules, solenoids, sensors, relays, terminals, connectors, switches, and harnesses.

10. Inspect, replace, and/or align power train mounts.

11. Replace fluid and filter(s); verify proper fluid level and type (for transmissions with, or without, a dipstick).

C. OFF-VEHICLE TRANSMISSION/TRANSAXLE REPAIR (13 QUESTIONS)

1. Removal and Installation (4 questions)

1. Remove and install transmission/transaxle; inspect engine core plugs, rear crankshaft seal, transmission dowel pins, dowel pin holes, and mating surfaces.

2. Inspect converter flex (drive) plate, converter attaching bolts, converter pilot, crankshaft pilot bore, converter pump drive surfaces.

3. Install torque converter and establish correct converter-to-pump engagement; inspect converter free movement for pilot engagement during transmission installation.

4. Inspect, test, flush or replace transmission fluid cooler.

5. Inspect brackets, wiring harnesses, fuel lines, heat shields, inspection covers, and related components for proper routing and installation.

6. Perform module coding and/or programming (including adaptive learning reset); road test to confirm proper operation.

2. Disassembly and Assembly (5 questions)

1. Disassemble, clean, and inspect transmission case, sub-assemblies, mating surfaces, and thread condition.

2. Inspect and measure fluid pump components; replace as necessary.

3. Check bearing preload; determine needed service.

4. Check end play; inspect, measure, and replace thrust washers and bearings as needed.

5. Inspect shafts; replace as necessary.

6. Inspect fluid delivery circuit, including seal rings, ring grooves, sealing surface areas, feed pipes, orifices, and encapsulated check valves (balls).

7. Inspect bushings; replace as necessary.

8. Inspect and measure components of the planetary gear assembly; replace as necessary.

9. Inspect case bores, passages, bushings, vents, mating surfaces, and dowel pins; repair or replace as necessary.

10. Inspect valve body mating surfaces, bores, valves, solenoids, springs, sleeves, retainers, brackets, check balls, screens, spacer plates, and gaskets; replace as necessary.

11. Inspect transaxle drive chains, sprockets, gears, bearings, and bushings; replace as necessary.

12. Inspect and measure transaxle final drive components; repair, replace and/or adjust as necessary.

13. Assemble after repair.

3. Friction and Reaction Units (4 questions)

1. Inspect components of the hydraulic clutch pack assembly; replace as necessary.

2. Measure clutch pack clearance; adjust as necessary.

3. Air test the operation of clutch and servo assemblies.

4. Inspect components of one way clutch assemblies; replace as necessary.

5. Inspect bands and drums (housings/cylinders); replace and/or adjust as necessary.

AUTOMATIC TRANSMISSION/TRANSAXLE (A2)

CATEGORY: GENERAL TRANSMISSION AND TRANSAXLE DIAGNOSIS

1. An hydraulically controlled automatic transmission shifts erratically (sometimes too soon, sometimes too late, and often shifts harshly). Technician A says that a misadjusted TV cable could be the cause if equipped. Technician B says that a defective TP sensor could be the cause if the transmission is electronically shifted. Which technician is correct?

   a. A only
   b. B only
   c. Both A and B
   d. Neither A nor B

2. One automatic transmission cooler line became pinched in a minor accident. Technician A says that the transmission may overheat. Technician B says that premature wear may occur due to the lack of lube oil being returned from the cooler. Which technician is correct?

   a. A only
   b. B only
   c. Both A and B
   d. Neither A nor B

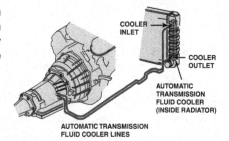

COOLER INLET

COOLER OUTLET

AUTOMATIC TRANSMISSION FLUID COOLER (INSIDE RADIATOR)

AUTOMATIC TRANSMISSION FLUID COOLER LINES

3. Two technicians are discussing what could be wrong with a hydraulically controlled automatic transmission/transaxle that does not shift out of first gear regardless of vehicle speed. Technician A says that a defective governor could be the cause. Technician B says that a weak pump could be the cause. Which technician is correct?

   a. A only
   b. B only
   c. Both A and B
   d. Neither A nor B

4. Two technicians are discussing an electronically controlled automatic transmission that will not go into any forward gear or reverse. Technician A says that a defective computer could be the cause. Technician B says that an excessively worn torque converter clutch could be the cause. Which technician is correct?

   a. A only
   b. B only
   c. Both A and B
   d. Neither A nor B

5. A vehicle equipped with an electronically controlled transaxle stalls whenever slowing to a stop after being driven over 20 miles (32 km). Technician A says that one of the shift solenoids could be defective. Technician B says that a torque converter clutch solenoid is likely to be defective. Which technician is correct?

   a. A only
   b. B only
   c. Both A and B
   d. Neither A nor B

6. An electronically controlled automatic transmission operates normally in reverse but the vehicle does not shift at all when moving forward. Technician A says that a defective torque converter is the likely cause. Technician B says that a defective computer could be the cause. Which technician is correct?

   a. A only
   b. B only
   c. Both A and B
   d. Neither A nor B

7. An electronically controlled overdrive automatic transmission is equipped with a transmission fluid temperature sensor. Technician A says that the shift points may be changed if the fluid temperature is too low. Technician B says that overdrive may be disabled if the transmission fluid temperature is too high. Which technician is correct?

   a. A only
   b. B only
   c. Both A and B
   d. Neither A nor B

8. An automatic overdrive transmission does not shift into overdrive. It functions normally in all other gear ranges. Technician A says that the gear selector display (PRNDL) or manual linkage may not be properly adjusted. Technician B says the governor may be defective. Which technician is correct?

   a. A only
   b. B only
   c. Both A and B
   d. Neither A nor B

9. A customer complains that her front-wheel-drive SUV seems to accelerate slower than normal from a stop but performs normally at higher speeds. The customer stated that the engine was tested and found to be operating properly. What is the *most likely* cause?

   a. Low fluid level
   b. A defective torque converter
   c. A worn pump
   d. Excessive end play in the planetary gearset pinions

10. An automatic transmission is not shifting correctly. A check of the fluid level indicates that the fluid is full of air bubbles. Technician A says that the fluid level may be too high (overfilled). Technician B says that the fluid level may be too low. Which technician is correct?

    a. A only
    b. B only
    c. Both A and B
    d. Neither A nor B

11. A rear-wheel-drive vehicle equipped with an automatic transmission shudders during hard accelera-tion from a stop. Technician A says that the transmission mounts may be collapsed causing a change in the drive shaft angle. Technician B says that a slipping direct (forward) clutch is a possible cause. Which technician is correct?

    a. A only
    b. B only
    c. Both A and B
    d. Neither A nor B

12. An automatic transmission slips when cold only, yet performs normally when warm. Which of the fol-lowing could be the cause?

    a. Lower than normal line pressure
    b. A shorted slow/reverse pressure switch
    c. A defective torque converter
    d. A worn planetary gear set

13. An electronically controlled automatic transaxle starts in second gear and does not shift out of sec-ond gear. Which is the *most likely* cause?

    a. A defective vehicle speed sensor
    b. An electrically open shift solenoid
    c. A defective pressure control solenoid
    d. A faulty computer

14. Two technicians are discussing the diagnosis of an automatic transmission that is not shifting correctly. Technician A says that the mainline pressure should be checked. Technician B says that the governor pressure should be checked if a pressure tap is available. Which technician is correct?

   a. A only
   b. B only
   c. Both A and B
   d. Neither A nor B

15. All of the following service operations should be performed during a routine troubleshooting procedure of an automatic transmission/transaxle fault except:

   a. checking the fluid level
   b. adjusting the TP sensor
   c. checking the line pressure
   d. a thorough test drive

16. An automatic transaxle upshifts harshly during normal acceleration. What failed part is the *most likely* cause?

   a. Oxygen (O_2) sensor
   b. Throttle position (TP) sensor
   c. Intake air temperature (IAT) sensor
   d. Idle air control (IAC) valve

17. ATF is observed leaking out of the bell housing area of an automatic transmission. Technician A says that the fluid may have been overfilled and it is leaking out of the vent pipe. Technician B says that the front seal may require replacement. Which technician is correct?

   a. A only
   b. B only
   c. Both A and B
   d. Neither A nor B

18. A vehicle equipped with an electronically controlled automatic transmission has a defective throttle position (TP) sensor. Technician A says that the transmission will default to second or third gear and will not upshift regardless of how fast the vehicle is driven. Technician B says that the transmission may or may not shift differently depending on the vehicle. Which technician is correct?

   a. A only
   b. B only
   c. Both A and B
   d. Neither A nor B

19. Two technicians are discussing an electronically controlled automatic transmission that does not shift correctly. Technician A says that a shift valve may be stuck. Technician B says that the transmission range switch may be out of adjustment. Which technician is correct?

   a. A only
   b. B only
   c. Both A and B
   d. Neither A nor B

20. An electronically controlled automatic transmission shifts harshly. Technician A says that the electronic pressure control (EPC) solenoid may be defective. Technician B says that the torque converter clutch solenoid may be defective. Which technician is correct?

   a. A only
   b. B only
   c. Both A and B
   d. Neither A nor B

21. During a stall test, the engine speed is lower than specifications. Technician A says that the clutch inside the torque converter may be defective. Technician B says that the engine may have a drivability problem, which would cause it to produce less than normal power. Which technician is correct?

   a. A only
   b. B only
   c. Both A and B
   d. Neither A nor B

22. A vehicle is slow to accelerate at low vehicle speed only yet shifts at the proper speeds. Technician A says that the torque converter may be defective. Technician B says that the torque converter clutch may be slipping. Which technician is correct?

   a. A only
   b. B only
   c. Both A and B
   d. Neither A nor B

23. A customer complained of poor fuel economy. Technician A says that the torque converter clutch may be defective. Technician B says that the automatic transmission/transaxle may not be shifting into overdrive. Which technician is correct?

   a. A only
   b. B only
   c. Both A and B
   d. Neither A nor B

24. Technician A says that a defective brake switch can prevent the operation of the torque converter clutch. Technician B says that a fault in the engine operation can be felt as a transmission fault by many drivers. Which technician is correct?

   a. A only
   b. B only
   c. Both A and B
   d. Neither A nor B

25. Two technicians are discussing pressure gauge readings. Technician A says that if the pressure is too low, a clogged filter or an internal leak could be the cause. Technician B says that if the pressure is too high at the wrong time, such as at gear changes, an internal leak at a servo or clutch seal is likely. Which technician is correct?

   a. A only
   b. B only
   c. Both A and B
   d. Neither A nor B

26. After an overhaul, an electronically controlled transaxle shifts too harshly. Technician A says that the electrical connector(s) at the transaxle may not be properly attached. Technician B says that the wrong type of ATF may be the cause. Which technician is correct?

   a. A only
   b. B only
   c. Both A and B
   d. Neither A nor B

27. A transmission cooler becomes partially restricted. What is the *most likely* result?

   a. Slipping clutches (bands)
   b. Excessive gear noise
   c. The torque converter slipping due to lack of fluid
   d. Excessive wear to bushings

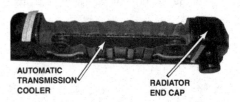

AUTOMATIC TRANSMISSION COOLER

RADIATOR END CAP

28. A hydraulically controlled automatic transmission is found to be low on fluid. Which is the *least likely* cause?

   a. A defective clutch piston seal
   b. A leaking oil pan gasket
   c. A defective front seal
   d. A defective modulator valve

29. What should be performed to pinpoint an oil pressure leak with the transmission/transaxle pan removed?

   a. Pressure test with regulated air pressure
   b. Look for leakage at the pickup tube seal
   c. Check the line (mainline) pressure
   d. Remove and visually check the valve body

30. Two technicians are discussing the use of the overdrive (OD) button as shown. Technician A says that overdrive should be switched off if towing or to prevent constant shifting while in city traffic. Technician B says that the torque converter clutch (lockup converter) should also be switched off when the "OD" button is pushed so fuel economy would be reduced while driving at slow speeds. Which technician is correct?

   a. A only
   b. B only
   c. Both A and B
   d. Neither A nor B

31. A pressure test is being performed with the engine running and the gear selector in park except where stated. All of the following test results are within standard parameters *except:*

   a. Mainline pressure is 50 psi
   b. Governor pressure is 50 psi
   c. Cooler line pressure is 50 psi
   d. Low/reverse is 150 psi (in reverse)

32. A stall test is being performed with the results shown. The specification for this vehicle is 1850–1950 RPM. What is the *most likely* cause?

   a. A weak or excessively worn engine
   b. A slipping forward clutch
   c. A defective torque converter clutch
   d. A defective or out-of-adjustment manual valve

33. What is this technician doing?

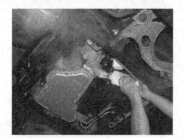

   a. Coating the housing to prevent corrosion
   b. Leak checking a transaxle
   c. Coating the transaxle mount to prevent squeaks
   d. Applying stop leak to the pan gasket

34. Pressure gauges are attached to the transmission and the vehicle is being test-driven. The pressures are all within specifications until the vehicle is accelerated rapidly and the mainline pressure decreases. Which is the *most likely* cause?

   a. A slipping forward clutch
   b. A defective (slipping) torque converter clutch
   c. A stuck shift valve
   d. A clogged filter

35. A vibration is being diagnosed on a rear wheel drive vehicle. The torque converter was separated from the flexplate and the vibration was eliminated. Which is the *most likely* cause?

   a. A worn or damaged pump assembly
   b. A defective torque converter
   c. A defective U-joint(s)
   d. A worn extension housing bushing

36. An OBD II-equipped vehicle has many stored transmission-related diagnostic trouble codes (DTCs). What is the preferred method of clearing the codes after the repairs are completed?

   a. Using a scan tool
   b. Disconnecting the negative battery cable for 10 minutes, then reattach
   c. Disconnect the TCM with the ignition off
   d. Remove the PCM/TCM fuse for 10 seconds and then reinstall

37. During a pressure test of an electronically controlled automatic transmission, the mainline pressure did not increase as the vehicle speed increased. Technician A says that a defective pressure control solenoid could be the cause. Technician B says that a defective shift solenoid could be the cause. Which technician is correct?

   a. A only
   b. B only
   c. Both A and B
   d. Neither A nor B

38. A check engine light is being diagnosed. A scan tool indicates that the electronically controlled automatic transmission is shifting correctly, yet a diagnostic trouble code (DTC) for excessive slippage is indicated. What is the *most likely* cause?

   a. A worn or defective torque converter clutch
   b. A slipping forward clutch
   c. A defective pressure control solenoid
   d. Low on fluid

39. A customer concern involves excessive "creeping" when stopped. What is the *most likely* cause?

   a. Fluid level too high
   b. Fluid level too low
   c. Incorrect engine idle speed
   d. Forward clutch slippage

40. A vehicle equipped with a torque converter clutch slips in reverse only. Technician A says that a worn torque converter clutch could be the cause. Technician B says that the transmission fluid level may be too high. Which technician is correct?

   a. A only
   b. B only
   c. Both A and B
   d. Neither A nor B

41. The shift points are higher than normal on an electronically controlled automatic transaxle and yet there are no stored diagnostic trouble codes. Which is the *most likely* cause?

   a. A defective input shaft speed sensor
   b. A misadjusted TP sensor
   c. An Incorrect ATF level
   d. Misadjusted manual valve linkage

42. An automatic transmission has an engine speed flare between all shifts. Technician A says that low fluid level could be the cause. Technician B says that a faulty shift solenoid could be the cause. Which technician is correct?

   a. A only
   b. B only
   c. Both A and B
   d. Neither A nor B

43. A clunk sound is heard during a 2–3 shift. Which is the *most likely* cause?

   a. A slipping torque converter clutch
   b. Misadjusted manual valve linkage
   c. A defective accumulator
   d. A worn pump assembly

44. A vehicle fails to move in either forward or reverse. Technician A says that the filter screen could be clogged. Technician B says that the pump may be defective. Which technician is correct?

   a. A only
   b. B only
   c. Both A and B
   d. Neither A nor B

45. A vehicle is slow to accelerate, yet seems to perform normally at highway speeds. Which is the *most likely* cause?

   a. Low on fluid
   b. A defective stator in the torque converter
   c. A shorted pressure control solenoid
   d. A clogged oil screen

46. An excessive slippage diagnostic trouble code (DTC) is being discussed. Technician A says that a defective torque converter clutch could be the cause. Technician B says that an open shift solenoid could be the cause. Which technician is correct?

   a. A only
   b. B only
   c. Both A and B
   d. Neither A nor B

47. An automatic transmission is hard to fill with ATF because the fluid keeps blowing back out of the fill tube. What is the *most likely* cause?

   a. A clogged or restricted cooler line
   b. A worn pressure regulator valve bore
   c. A clogged or restricted filter
   d. A clogged breather vent

48. A transmission slips when it shifts. Which is the *most likely* cause?

   a. A defective torque converter
   b. A defective one-way clutch
   c. Worn planetary gears
   d. An open shift solenoid

49. A vehicle owner complains that the electronically controlled transmission does not downshift from highway speed during rapid wide-open-throttle (WOT) operation. Technician A says that a defective TP sensor could be the cause. Technician B says that a defective or worn torque converter clutch could be the cause. Which technician is correct?

   a. A only
   b. B only
   c. Both A and B
   d. Neither A nor B

50. The ATF is dark brown/black and rancid smelling. Technician A says that a restricted or partially clogged cooler could be the cause. Technician B says that a slipping clutch pack could be the cause. Which technician is correct?

   a. A only
   b. B only
   c. Both A and B
   d. Neither A nor B

51. A poor fuel economy concern is being diagnosed. A scan tool check indicates that the torque converter clutch is not being commanded on at highway speeds. Which is the *most likely* cause?

   a. Low ATF level
   b. Stuck open cooling system thermostat
   c. ATF level too high
   d. A defective torque converter

52. A shudder during shifting occurs after a transmission fluid and filter change. Technician A says that the most likely cause is the use of the wrong type of filter. Technician B says that the wrong type of ATF could be the cause. Which technician is correct?

   a. A only
   b. B only
   c. Both A and B
   d. Neither A nor B

53. The engine speed (RPM) is lower than specified during a stall test. Technician A says that the transmission/transaxle may be low on fluid. Technician B says that the torque converter clutch may be slipping. Which technician is correct?

   a. A only
   b. B only
   c. Both A and B
   d. Neither A nor B

54. Automatic transmission fluid is found to be pink and milky. What is the *most likely* cause?

   a. Overheating of the fluid
   b. Aeration of the fluid due to being overfilled
   c. Engine oil is mixing with the fluid
   d. Engine coolant is mixing with the fluid

55. Which is the *most likely* cause for an electronically controlled automatic transmission/transaxle to stay in second gear and not shift?

   a. A bad computer
   b. A defective torque converter clutch
   c. An excessively worn clutch
   d. Overfilled automatic transmission fluid (ATF)

56. An automatic transaxle does not hold when in the PARK. What is the *most likely* cause?

   a. A roller clutch installed backward
   b. A broken ring gear on the flexplate
   c. Misadjusted shift linkage
   d. Worn pump

57. A transmission fluid temperature (TFT) sensor wire was broken during an accident. Which is the *most likely* result?

   a. The transmission/transaxle will start in second gear and shift normally after that
   b. The overdrive and the torque converter clutch may be inoperative
   c. No symptoms or change in shifting will be noticed
   d. The transmission/transaxle will not engage in drive or reverse

AUTOMATIC TRANSMISSION/TRANSAXLE (A2)

CATEGORY: IN-VEHICLE TRANSMISSION/TRANSAXLE MAINTENANCE AND REPAIR

58. The intermediate (kickdown) band is found to be out of adjustment. What is the *most likely* cause?

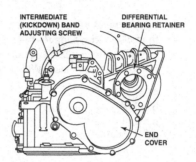

   a. A worn band
   b. A worn drum
   c. A low fluid level
   d. A defective pressure regulator

59. A technician performed an automatic transmission fluid service and refilled the unit with the incorrect automatic transmission fluid (friction modified instead of highly friction modified). Technician A says that the transmission will slip. Technician B says that shudder or harsher than normal shifts are likely to occur. Which technician is correct?

   a. A only
   b. B only
   c. Both A and B
   d. Neither A nor B

60. Two technicians are discussing the adjustment of the band shown. Technician A says that the locknut should be loosened and the adjustment screw torqued to factory specifications, and then the locknut tightened. Technician B says that the adjustment screw is used to adjust the clearance between the drum and the band. Which technician is correct?

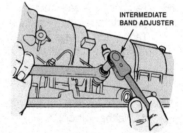

   a. A only
   b. B only
   c. Both A and B
   d. Neither A nor B

61. When checking for excessive voltage drop of the battery ground connection, what meter selection should be used?

   a. DCV
   b. ACV
   c. Hz
   d. A

62. Technician A says that the manual linkage may get out of adjustment if an engine or transmission mount were to fail. Technician B says that the shift selector (PRNDL) should be adjusted so it matches the manual valve detents. Which technician is correct?

   a. A only
   b. B only
   c. Both A and B
   d. Neither A nor B

63. Technician A says that the method shown is the correct way to remove an automatic transmission pan. Technician B says that all the pan bolts should be removed first and the pan dropped straight down to avoid the possibility of spilling ATF. Which technician is correct?

   a. A only
   b. B only
   c. Both A and B
   d. Neither A nor B

64. Technician A says that the filter shown should be replaced rather than cleaned whenever the transmission/transaxle is being serviced. Technician B says that the filter should be soaked in ATF before being installed. Which technician is correct?

   a. A only
   b. B only
   c. Both A and B
   d. Neither A nor B

65. An automatic transmission/transaxle is being refilled with ATF after a filter replacement. Technician A says to add the amount of ATF that the factory specifies as the capacity for the unit. Technician B says to use the exact type of fluid recommended to avoid possible shifting problems. Which technician is correct?

   a. A only
   b. B only
   c. Both A and B
   d. Neither A nor B

66. Technician A says that this style of transmission/transaxle pan uses room temperature vulcanization (RTV) sealant and not a gasket. Technician B says that a contact adhesive can be applied to hold the gasket in place. Which technician is correct?

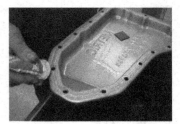

   a. A only
   b. B only
   c. Both A and B
   d. Neither A nor B

67. What is the usual method to tighten the retaining bolts for the pan on automatic transmission/transaxles?

   a. Start by hand to avoid cross-threading
   b. Tighten gradually
   c. A torque wrench should be used to achieve the final torque
   d. All of the above

68. A hydraulically controlled automatic transmission is not shifting correctly. Which service operation should the technician perform first?

   a. Perform a pressure test
   b. Adjust the bands
   c. Check the transmission fluid
   d. Check for proper engine vacuum

69. An electronically controlled automatic transmission is not shifting correctly. All of the following should be performed to locate the cause *except* _____.

   a. check the transmission fluid
   b. check scan tool data (PID)
   c. retrieve stored diagnostic trouble codes (DTCs)
   d. reflash the computer

70. Proper operation of electronically controlled automatic transmission/transaxles depends on proper charging voltage. The proper charging voltage should be _____.

    a. 5 volts
    b. 10–12 volts
    c. 13–15 volts
    d. 16 volts or higher

71. A TV cable breaks on a hydraulically controlled automatic transmission. Technician A says that the shifts may be too harsh. Technician B says that the shifts may occur at too low a speed (shifts too early). Which technician is correct?

    a. A only
    b. B only
    c. Both A and B
    d. Neither A nor B

72. Technician A says that the cooler should always be flushed whenever replacing an automatic transmission/transaxle. Technician B says that aqueous (water-based) solvent should be used to flush a cooler. Which technician is correct?

    a. A only
    b. B only
    c. Both A and B
    d. Neither A nor B

73. An automatic transmission/transaxle pump volume test is being performed. Technician A says that a good pump should be able to pump about 2 quarts (2 liters) in 30 seconds through the cooler. Technician B says that the engine should be operated at about 1000 RPM during the cooler flow test. Which technician is correct?

    a. A only
    b. B only
    c. Both A and B
    d. Neither A nor B

74. Two technicians are discussing an automatic transmission fluid leak from the rear seal of the extension housing on a rear-wheel-drive automatic transmission. Technician A says that the drive shaft has to be removed to replace the seal. Technician B says that the bushing in the extension housing may also need to be replaced. Which technician is correct?

    a. A only
    b. B only
    c. Both A and B
    d. Neither A nor B

75. Corrosion is discovered in the electrical connector on the unit shown. Technician A says that the transmission/transaxle may not be in the correct range as selected by the driver. Technician B says that the backup lights may not work correctly. Which technician is correct?

    a. A only
    b. B only
    c. Both A and B
    d. Neither A nor B

76. This technician is servicing an automatic transaxle that is not shifting correctly. What is this technician checking?

a. The output speed sensor (OSS) for wear or damage
b. A shift solenoid for damage
c. The throttle valve for wear or damage
d. The valve body connector for wear or damage

77. Too much automatic transmission shaft end play could be caused by any of the following worn parts *except* _____.

a. planetary carrier
b. selective washer
c. clutch
d. transmission case

78. The transmission oil pan has been removed to check for the location of a pressure leak. Which procedure should be performed?

a. Air pressure test
b. Check the mainline pressure
c. Remove and check the valve body
d. Measure the pump pressure

79. A transmission fluid leak is discovered at the rear of the unit. Which is the *most likely* cause?

a. The ATF level is too high
b. Excessive output shaft endplay
c. A worn extension housing bushing
d. A worn slip yoke

80. The torque converter clutch solenoid (shown) is being replaced on an automatic transaxle. Technician A says that the battery must be disconnected before the old solenoid is removed to prevent causing damage to the valve body. Technician B says that the torque converter has to be removed to replace the torque converter clutch solenoid. Which technician is correct?

a. A only
b. B only
c. Both A and B
d. Neither A nor B

81. Two technicians are discussing the unit shown. Technician A says that it attaches to the extension housing area of the automatic transmission. Technician B says that it is attached near the front of the transmission, near the torque converter. Which technician is correct?

a. A only
b. B only
c. Both A and B
d. Neither A nor B

82. Technician A says that some bands can be adjusted externally using a torque wrench. Technician B says that some bands are adjusted by tightening the adjusting screw, and then loosening the adjustment a specified number of rotations (turns). Which technician is correct?

a. A only
b. B only
c. Both A and B
d. Neither A nor B

83. Two technicians are discussing how best to check for proper voltage and current to the automatic transmission. Technician A says that a voltmeter reading of above 12 volts means that the unit power source is okay. Technician B says that a headlight should be used in the circuit to make sure that the power feed circuit is capable of supplying enough current to make the headlight shine bright. Which technician is correct?

   a. A only
   b. B only
   c. Both A and B
   d. Neither A nor B

84. The pan has been removed from an automatic transmission and nonmetallic material is discovered on the bottom. Technician A says that it is normal to have some friction material in the bottom of the pan. Technician B says that the transmission should be disassembled to find the exact location of where the wear has occurred. Which technician is correct?

   a. A only
   b. B only
   c. Both A and B
   d. Neither A nor B

85. The automatic transmission fluid is being changed and the old fluid is dark brown and has a rancid smell. Technician A says that the cooler should be flushed and checked for proper flow. Technician B says that using the incorrect fluid may be the cause. Which technician is correct?

   a. A only
   b. B only
   c. Both A and B
   d. Neither A nor B

86. All of the following are correct service procedures *except* _____.

   a. the correct type and amount of fluid should always be used.
   b. all wiring should be carefully inspected for possible heat damage.
   c. the valve body fastener should always be tightened to the specified torque using a torque wrench.
   d. the filters should be thoroughly cleaned.

AUTOMATIC TRANSMISSION/TRANSAXLE (A2)

CATEGORY: OFF-VEHICLE TRANSMISSION/TRANSAXLE REPAIR

87. The clutch pack clearance is less than specifications. Technician A says that too many friction discs may have been installed. Technician B says that too thin a clutch pack pressure plate may have been installed. Which technician is correct?

    a. A only
    b. B only
    c. Both A and B
    d. Neither A nor B

88. The tool shown is being used to install the _____.

    a. pump bushing
    b. pump seal
    c. stator support
    d. stator seal

89. What part(s) should be marked before removal?

    a. Pump gears
    b. The direction the steels are installed in the clutch packs
    c. The snap rings
    d. The planetary gears

90. Two technicians are discussing removal of an automatic transmission from a rear-wheel-drive vehicle. Technician A says that the cooler lines have to be removed before the drive shaft is removed. Technician B says that the engine should be supported before removing the transmission. Which technician is correct?

    a. A only
    b. B only
    c. Both A and B
    d. Neither A nor B

91. Two technicians are discussing overhauling an automatic transmission/transaxle. Technician A says that all rubber seals and the friction discs should be replaced. Technician B says that all the steel discs should also be replaced as part of an overhaul. Which technician is correct?

    a. A only
    b. B only
    c. Both A and B
    d. Neither A nor B

92. Technician A says that all clutch packs should be air-checked before being installed into the automatic transmission/transaxle. Technician B says that the clutch pack clearance can be checked with a dial indicator. Which technician is correct?

    a. A only
    b. B only
    c. Both A and B
    d. Neither A nor B

93. Two technicians are discussing air-checking a clutch pack. Technician A says that the pressure should be at least 100 psi (690 kPa). Technician B says that a dull thud or clunk should be heard when the clutch plates are engaged using air pressure. Which technician is correct?

   a. A only
   b. B only
   c. Both A and B
   d. Neither A nor B

94. Technician A says that selective thickness snap rings or pressure or retaining plates are used to obtain the proper clutch pack clearance. Technician B says that air-checking a clutch pack will determine whether or not the clutch pack clearance is okay. Which technician is correct?

   a. A only
   b. B only
   c. Both A and B
   d. Neither A nor B

95. Technician A says that friction discs should be soaked in ATF before being assembled in a clutch pack. Technician B says that the seals and O-rings should be soaked for several hours before being installed in a clutch pack. Which technician is correct?

   a. A only
   b. B only
   c. Both A and B
   d. Neither A nor B

96. Proper assembly of an automatic transmission/transaxle can be verified by performing each of the following *except* _____.

   a. end play measurements
   b. clutch pack measurements
   c. vacuum testing the regulator valve
   d. air pressure checks

97. Technician A says that assembly lube can be used on all seals and O-rings during assembly of an automatic transmission/transaxle. Technician B says that automatic transmission fluid can be used to lubricate seals and O-rings during the assembly of an automatic transmission/transaxle. Which technician is correct?

   a. A only
   b. B only
   c. Both A and B
   d. Neither A nor B

98. Technician A says that pulse-width-modulated solenoids have higher resistance than shift solenoids that are simply pulsed on and off. Technician B says that all solenoids should be checked for proper resistance before the automatic transmission/transaxle is installed in the vehicle. Which technician is correct?

   a. A only
   b. B only
   c. Both A and B
   d. Neither A nor B

99. Technician A says that all friction and steel plates in a clutch pack should be replaced during an overhaul. Technician B says that the automatic transmission fluid cooler should always be flushed when a unit is rebuilt or replaced. Which technician is correct?

   a. A only
   b. B only
   c. Both A and B
   d. Neither A nor B

100. A technician left out the wavy spring from a clutch pack. Technician A says that the shift may be too soft. Technician B says that the shift may be too harsh. Which technician is correct?

    a. A only
    b. B only
    c. Both A and B
    d. Neither A nor B

101. The shift valves in a valve body are being tested for proper operation. Technician A says that all valves should be tested by moving the valves in their bores using a nonmetallic prying tool. Technician B says that the valves can be removed and cleaned using crocus cloth. Which technician is correct?

    a. A only
    b. B only
    c. Both A and B
    d. Neither A nor B

102. A valve body is being serviced. Technician A says that the sharp edges on the valves should be rounded to help the valve move in the valve body bore. Technician B says that gasket sealer should be used between the valve body and the separator plate to prevent fluid leaks between these surfaces. Which technician is correct?

    a. A only
    b. B only
    c. Both A and B
    d. Neither A nor B

103. Technician A says that bands can be adjusted on some automatic transmissions from the outside of the case. Technician B says that some bands are only adjusted by the use of selective length rods. Which technician is correct?

    a. A only
    b. B only
    c. Both A and B
    d. Neither A nor B

104. Two technicians are discussing reinstalling an automatic transmission/transaxle back in a vehicle. Technician A says that the torque converter should be attached to the flex plate (drive plate) before installing the transmission/transaxle. Technician B says that the torque converter should be attached to the transmission/transaxle before installing the assembly in the vehicle. Which technician is correct?

    a. A only
    b. B only
    c. Both A and B
    d. Neither A nor B

105. What is being measured by the dial indicator?

    a. Pump runout
    b. Input shaft endplay
    c. Bell housing runout
    d. Input shaft runout

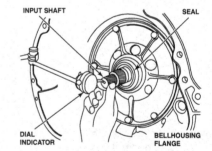

106. What is being measured with the feeler gauge?

    a. Snap ring depth
    b. Clutch housing clearance
    c. Clutch pack clearance
    d. Input shaft endplay

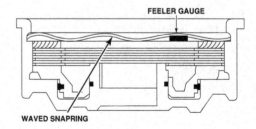

107. The measurement being taken exceeds factory specifications. Technician A says that the inner and outer gears should be replaced. Technician B says that the entire pump assembly should be replaced. Which technician is correct?

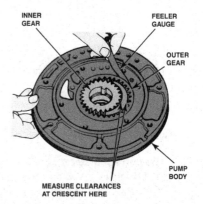

a. A only
b. B only
c. Both A and B
d. Neither A nor B

108. Technician A says that the clutch drum should be carefully inspected for cracks or wear. Technician B says that the piston seals should be replaced whenever the clutch assembly is removed or disassembled. Which technician is correct?

a. A only
b. B only
c. Both A and B
d. Neither A nor B

109. What is this technician doing?

a. Installing a bushing
b. Compressing an accumulator piston
c. Compressing a clutch pack
d. Adjusting a band

110. The contact surface between the drive axle shaft and the final drive is discovered to have metal transfers as shown. Technician A says that this can occur if the driver was spinning the drive wheels for a long time on snow or mud. Technician B says that it could be caused by a lack of lubrication. Which technician is correct?

a. A only
b. B only
c. Both A and B
d. Neither A nor B

AUTOMATIC TRANSMISSION/TRANSAXLE (A2)

CATEGORY: GENERAL TRANSMISSION AND TRANSAXLE DIAGNOSIS

1. **The correct answer is c.** Both technicians are correct. Technician A is correct because a misadjusted or sticking TV cable can cause shifting related problems because the calibration between the position of the throttle and shift points and line pressure is critical for the proper operation of the transmission. Technician B is correct because the throttle position sensor is a major sensor used by the powertrain control module (PCM) in determining proper shift points. If the TP sensor is sticking or misadjusted or defective, the signal to the PCM can be erratic causing the PCM to make erratic shifts. Answers a, b, and d are not correct because both technicians are correct.

2. **The correct answer is c.** Both technicians are correct. Technician A is correct because a restricted cooler line would prevent the flow of ATF through the cooler and thereby increase the temperature of the fluid, which could cause the transmission to operate hotter than designed. Technician B is correct because a restricted cooler line will reduce the flow of ATF from the cooler to the transmission where it is used to lubricate the bushings and bearings. Answers a, b, and d are not correct because both technicians are correct.

3. **The correct answer is a.** Technician A only is correct because governor pressure is used to control the shift points based on vehicle speed. If the governor is not functioning, the transmission will not shift out of first gear. Technician B is not correct because while a weak pump can cause shifting problems, it is unlikely to cause the transmission to not upshift. Answers c and d are not correct because Technician A only is correct.

4. **The correct answer is d.** Neither technician is correct. Technician A is not correct because a faulty computer will usually cause the transmission to default to second or third gear only and reverse. While the shift solenoid and the pressure control solenoid will not work, the transmission will still partially function. Technician B is not correct because the torque converter clutch does not affect the shifting of the transmission in forward or reverse. Answers a, b, and c are not correct because neither technician is correct.

5. **The correct answer is b.** Technician B only is correct because if the torque converter clutch solenoid were to become stuck in the applied position, the engine would stall because the torque converter clutch would provide a mechanical link between the engine and the drive wheels. When the drive wheels are stopped by the brakes, the engine speed is also stopped. Often the engine will restart immediately because when the engine stalls, the transmission line pressure drops to zero and the torque converter clutch is released. Technician A is not correct because a defective shift solenoid will cause incorrect shifting but cannot cause the engine to stall. Answers c and d are not correct because Technician B only is correct.

6. **The correct answer is b.** Technician B only is correct because if the computer fails, the transmission defaults to either second or third gear to allow the vehicle to keep moving, but will not shift. Technician A is not correct because a defective torque converter would affect transmission operation in both forward and reverse and not just in forward.

7. **The correct answer is c.** Both technicians are correct. Technician A is correct because when the transmission fluid temperature is low, the computer will usually command that the shifts be slightly delayed to help the engine achieve normal operating temperature as soon as possible for the lowest possible exhaust emissions. Technician B is correct because the computer will prevent the operation of overdrive and may apply the torque converter clutch in all gears except first in an attempt to reduce the temperature of the automatic transmission fluid. Answers a, b, and d are not correct because both technicians are correct.

8. **The correct answer is a.** Technician A only is correct because if the gear selector was incorrectly placed in drive 3 (third gear), the transmission would shift correctly but would not shift into overdrive because the gear selector and manual valve are in a position that blocks the shift into overdrive. Technician B is not correct because a defective governor would likely cause shifting problems in all gears and would be unlikely to prevent the lack of overdrive. Answers c and d are not correct because Technician A only is correct.

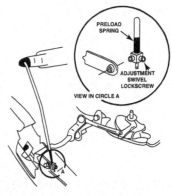

9. **The correct answer is b.** If the stator one-way clutch inside the torque converter is not locking, the torque converter will not be able to multiply engine torque. As result, this would cause a loss of torque applied to the transaxle and slower than normal acceleration especially at lower speed. Answer a is not correct because low automatic transmission fluid level would not likely cause a lack of acceleration at low vehicle speed even though it may cause a delay in applying clutches when the transaxle is first shifted into a drive gear. Answer c is not correct because while a worn pump could cause lower-than-normal fluid pressure and maybe cause some shifting problems, it is unlikely to cause a lack of acceleration only at lower vehicle speeds. Answer d is not correct because a worn planetary gear set, while it could cause nose, it is unlikely to be the cause of the slower-than-normal acceleration only at lower vehicle speeds.

10. **The correct answer is c.** Both technicians are correct. Technician A is correct because if the transmission fluid is overfilled, the rotation of the planetary gears can force air into the fluid. This aerated fluid can foam and cause a lack of proper lubrication and can cause clutches and servos to not function correctly. Technician B is correct because if the fluid level is too low, air will be drawn into the pump along with fluid creating foam or fluid filled with bubbles. Answers a, b, and d are not correct because both technicians are correct.

11. **The correct answer is c.** Both technicians are correct. Technician A is correct because a "launch shudder" occurs if the two U-joints are not within about 0.5° of each other, which could be caused by a collapsed transmission mount. Technician B is correct because maximum torque is being applied to the direct (forward) clutch during rapid acceleration from a start. If the clutch discs are worn, or if the clutch pack piston seal is torn or leaking, the vehicle could shudder during acceleration. Answers a, b, and d are not correct because both technicians are correct.

12. **The correct answer is a.** If the line pressure is lower than normal, it can cause the clutches to slip. The lower-than-normal line pressure could be due to low fluid level or a weak pump. Then when the transmission warms up, the fluid expands and the slippage could stop. Answer b is not correct because a shorted low/reverse pressure switch would affect the transmission operation at all temperatures, not just when cold. Answer c is not correct because a defective torque converter would not cause the transmission to slip even though it could be the cause of slower-than-normal acceleration. Answer d is not correct because a worn planetary gear set, while it could cause noise (usually a whine), it is unlikely to cause the transmission to slip when cold only.

13. **The correct answer is d.** The computer controls the shift solenoids and if the computer were to fail, the solenoids would be off and the transaxle would default to one gear (usually second gear) to allow the vehicle limited use until it can be repaired. Answer a (vehicle speed sensor) is not likely to cause the transmission to start in second gear and not shift even though it could offset when shifts occur. Answer b (electrically open shifted solenoid) would cause shifting problems but is unlikely to cause the transaxle to default to second gear and not shift. Answer c (defective pressure control solenoid) will cause shifting problems but is unlikely to cause the transaxle to default to second gear.

14. **The correct answer is c.** Both technicians are correct. Technician A is correct because a fault with the mainline pressure indicates that there could be a fluid pump or regulator problem, which would have a direct connection to the rest of the hydraulic system causing shifting problems. Technician B is correct because governor pressure should increase with vehicle speed and the pressure should correspond to published specifications from the vehicle manufacturer. A fault with the governor or governor hydraulic circuit would cause shifting problems. Answers a, b, and d are not correct because both technicians are correct.

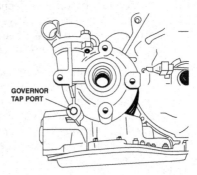

15. **The correct answer is b.** The adjustment of the throttle position (TP) sensor is not included in the procedure that should be followed during a routine analysis of a transmission/transaxle fault because even though it could cause shifting problems, an adjustment is unlikely to be necessary or possible on most vehicles. Answers a (fluid level check), c (line pressure check), and d (test drive) are not correct because all three should be done as part of a thorough automatic transmission/transaxle diagnosis.

16. **The correct answer is b.** If the throttle position (TP) sensor were to fail, the PCM/TCM would not be able to determine the accelerator pedal position. To help protect the transaxle, the PCM/TCM would then command a firm shift to help avoid slipping the clutches to help prevent heat build-up or wear. This firm shifting strategy would be noticed by the driver as a harsh shift. Answer a is not correct because a failed oxygen sensor would not likely cause a change in the shifting of the transaxle, but may affect fuel economy and exhaust emission instead. Answer c is not correct because a defective intake air temperature (IAT) sensor is likely to affect the air-fuel mixture but not likely to be the cause of a harsh shifting transaxle. Answer d is not correct because a defective IAC is likely to cause idle-related engine problem but not contribute to or cause the transaxle to upshift harshly.

17. **The correct answer is b.** Technician B is only correct because fluid leaking from the front seal will drip downward from the bell housing area. Technician A is not correct because most vents are located at the top of the transmission and any leakage would be forced rearward by normal airflow during vehicle operation. Therefore, an overfilled transmission would show fluid leakage down both sides and all over the rear of the case, instead of from the bell housing area. Answers c and d are not correct because Technician B only is correct.

18. **The correct answer is b.** Technician B only is correct because a failed throttle position sensor is likely to cause a hesitation during acceleration and may affect some drivability, but it is unlikely to cause a transmission fault because the computer will use a substituted value for the failed throttle position sensor. If the sensor were giving a false high or low reading, the shifting and shift points of the transmission would be affected. Technician A is not correct because the throttle position is just one of many sensors used to determine the shifting of an electronically shifted transmission and a fault in one sensor is seldom enough to cause the unit to default to second or third gear start and not shift. Answers c and d are not correct because Technician B only is correct.

19. **The correct answer is c.** Both technicians are correct. Technician A is correct because a stuck shift valve will often cause the transmission to not shift and/or skip a gear depending on which shift valve is stuck and in which position. Technician B is correct because if the transmission range switch is not adjusted correctly, the transmission may not be starting off in the correct gear or may not upshift depending on the which gear was actually selected. Answers a, b, and d are not correct because both technicians are correct.

20. **The correct answer is a.** Technician A is only correct because a faulty pressure control solenoid will often cause maximum pressure to be applied to the clutches resulting in a harsh shift. Technician B is not correct because a torque converter clutch (TCC) does not affect shifting even though it may feel as if a shift is occurring when the TCC applies. Answers c and d are not correct because Technician A only is correct.

21. **The correct answer is b.** Technician B only is correct because an engine fault could prevent the engine from being able to achieve the specified engine speed (RPM) during a torque converter stall test. Technician A is not correct because the torque converter clutch is not tested or applied during a stall test. Answers c and d are not correct because Technician B only is correct.

22. **The correct answer is a.** Technician A only is correct because a bad stator inside the torque converter would prevent normal torque multiplication to occur and reduced vehicle performance during acceleration. Technician B is not correct because a slipping torque converter clutch would increase torque multiplication (not decrease) thereby increasing performance during acceleration rather than decreasing performance. The TCC is also not often applied during acceleration and would therefore not affect acceleration. Answers c and d are not correct because Technician A only is correct.

23. **The correct answer is c.** Both technicians are correct. Technician A is correct because a loss of fuel economy will occur if the torque converter clutch fails to apply. At cruise speed, slippage of 150–250 RPM is normal if the TCC is not applied, thereby reducing fuel economy. Technician B is correct because if the transmission/transaxle fails to shift into overdrive for whatever reason, the result is a decrease in fuel economy because the engine is rotating faster than normal resulting in reduced fuel economy at highway speeds. Answers a, b, and d are not correct because both technicians are correct.

24. **The correct answer is c.** Both technicians are correct. Technician A is correct because if the brake switch failed in the on position (brake applied position), the torque converter clutch is disabled. It is normal operation to shut off electrical current to the torque converter clutch when the brakes are applied. Technician B is correct because a surging or engine miss is often thought to be a transmission fault by many drivers and should be investigated by the technician as a possible cause of a shifting concern during diagnosis. Answers a, b, and d are not correct because both technicians are correct.

25. **The correct answer is a.** Technician A only is correct because a clogged transmission fluid filter would restrict the flow of fluid and could cause a decrease in pressure. An internal leak could also cause a decrease in pressure because the fluid could flow through the leak faster than the pump could supply the necessary fluid in order to build normal pressure. Technician B is not correct because the pressure would drop, rather than increase, during a shift change, if there were an internal leak at a clutch pack piston seal or accumulator, rather than increase. Answers c and d are not correct because Technician A only is correct.

26. **The correct answer is b.** Technician B only is correct because the use of a nonfriction-modified or a friction-modified fluid instead of the specified highly-friction-modified fluid will cause the transaxle to shift harsher than normal. The highly-friction-modified fluid is designed to allow some slippage to occur whereas a non-friction-modified fluid allows the clutch to engage faster resulting in a harsh shift complaint. Technician A is not correct because even though the case wiring connection can affect the operation of the transaxle, it is unlikely to cause a harsh shift. Answers c and d are not correct because Technician B only is correct.

27. **The correct answer is d.** The most likely problem due to a restricted cooler line is wear to the bushings because the fluid leaves the torque converter and flows to the cooler. Then the fluid returns to the transmission as lube oil to lubricate the bushings before flowing downward back into the pan. Answer a is not correct because even though the flow of fluid is restricted, it is unlikely to cause a slipping clutch or band because the pump is still able to pick up and pressurize fluid from the pan. Answer b is not correct because even though the lack of lubricating fluid may cause wear and gear noise, it is unlikely to cause wear to the planetary gears because they are lubricated by fluid that is splashed onto the parts during normal operation. Answer c is not correct because the flow of fluid is from the torque converter to the cooler instead of from the cooler to the torque converter. A partially restricted cooler is unlikely to cause slippage to occur in the torque converter.

28. **The correct answer is a.** The least likely cause of low fluid in an automatic transmission is a defective clutch piston seal because the resulting leak would cause the fluid to flow back into the pan and not outside the unit. While this fault would cause shifting problems, the fluid level would not be low as a result of this leak. Answers b and c are not correct because a leaking oil pan gasket or front seal will cause the fluid to be lower than normal as the fluid leaks onto the ground. Answer d is not correct because a defective modulator valve will cause ATF to be drawn into the engine by the engine vacuum.

29. **The correct answer is a.** Using regulated air pressure applied to the circuits is the best way to pinpoint an oil pressure leak when the pan has been removed. Answer b is not correct because checking for leakage at the pick-up tube which is on the suction side of the pump would not be a place to check for a pressure leak. Answer c is not correct because checking for line pressure is not possible with the transmission pan removed and would not be a method used to find the source of a pressure leak. Answer d is not correct because while a defective separator plate gasket or other fault may be found using visual inspection, it usually not the preferred method to use to find the location of a fluid pressure leak with the transmission pan removed.

30. **The correct answer is a.** Technician A only is correct because while overdrive reduces engine torque while improving fuel economy, it could cause the transmission to overheat while towing, or constantly engage and disengage during city driving. In overdrive, the torque converter clutch will often disengage when the vehicle is under a heavy load such as occurs during towing. The torque converter then generates a lot of heat as the engine attempts to power the vehicle through an overdrive ratio in the transmission. For this reason, it is wise to tow a vehicle in direct drive (1:1 ratio) with the torque converter clutch engaged to avoid overheating the transmission. Technician B is not correct because the torque converter clutch is not disengaged when the overdrive is turned off, just the shift into overdrive. Answers c and d are not correct because Technician A only is correct.

31. **The correct answer is b.** The governor pressure should not be about 50 psi with the engine running and the gear selector in park. While the exact specification for each model transmission/transaxle varies, the governor pressure should increase as vehicle speed increases and 50 psi should not be achieved until the vehicle travels at about 50 MPH. Answers a, c, and d are not correct because they represent typical pressures.

32. **The correct answer is b.** The tachometer indicates that the stall speed is about 2300 RPM, which is higher than the stated specification of 1850–1950 RPM. This higher-than-normal stall speed could be caused by a slipping forward clutch because the drive wheels are not rotating (speedometer indicator zero), which means that something inside the transmission is slipping and the most likely part is the forward clutch because it is applied in all forward gears. Answer a is not correct because an excessively worn engine would not produce normal power, which would most likely cause the stall speed to be lower (not higher) than specifications. Answer c is not correct because the torque converter clutch is not applied at zero vehicle speed and would not affect the stall test results. Answer d is not correct because the transmission is in a drive gear and even if it were in second, this would not offset the stall speed.

33. **The correct answer is b.** The technician is applying powder to the area that is being checked for leaks. The powder will become dark when it absorbs automatic transmission fluid and the location of the leak can be more easily located. Answer a is not correct because a coating is not needed to prevent corrosion of an aluminum alloy housing. Answer c is not correct because the powder is not being applied to the transaxle mount and mounts do not require a coating to prevent squeaks. Answer d is not correct because a powder cannot be used to stop a leak. If there is a leak, the gasket should be replaced instead of using stop leak materials.

34. **The correct answer is d.** A partially clogged filter can cause the mainline pressure to drop during rapid acceleration due to the increased volume of fluid being drawn by the pump, which cannot maintain pressure. Answer a is not correct because while a slipping forward clutch could be the cause of slippage during rapid acceleration, it is most likely to cause a drop in the mainline pressure. Answer b is not correct because the torque converter clutch usually disengages during rapid acceleration and it is unlikely to cause a drop in the mainline pressure. Answer c is not correct because while a stuck shift valve can cause shifting problems, it is unlikely to cause a decrease in mainline pressure during rapid acceleration.

35. **The correct answer is b.** A defective, out-of-balance torque converter is the most likely cause of a vibration that occurs until the torque converter is separated from the engine. The torque converter is large and has enough weight (mass) to create a vibration unless it is properly balanced. When the torque converter was separated from the engine flexplate, the torque converter no longer is being rotated with the engine, which means that an engine fault is not a possible cause. Answer a is not correct because the pump is relatively small and is unlikely to cause a vibration if the rotating parts are out-of-balance. Answers c and d are not correct because while defective U-joints or a worn extension housing or bushing could cause vibrations, the vehicle would have to be moving for this to become a possible cause.

36. **The correct answer is a.** The preferred method of clearing OBD II DTCs is to use a scan tool. This will also clear all of the adaptive and learned values without causing harm or the loss of other vehicle functions such as the operation of the radio or power accessories. Answer b is not correct because disconnecting the battery while it may work, is not the preferred (best practices) method to use to clear transmission codes. Disconnecting the negative battery cable can also cause drivability and emissions-related concerns for the vehicle owner as well as some accessories such as auto up power windows and radio preset stations. Answer c is not correct because disconnecting the TCM is not the preferred method as recommended by vehicle manufacturers. Answer d is not correct because disconnecting the PCM/TCM fuse is not the preferred method as recommended by vehicle manufacturers.

37. **The correct answer is a.** Technician A only is correct because the mainline pressure should increase as the vehicle speed increases and it is the job of the pressure control solenoid to control this pressure. Often when the pressure control solenoid fails, the default is a constant high pressure, which could cause harsher than normal shifts. Technician B is not correct because a shift solenoid does not control mainline pressure and is used to control fluid flow for shifts to occur. Answers c and d are not correct because Technician A only is correct.

38. **The correct answer is a.** A worn or defective torque converter clutch will cause excessive slippage and will trigger a diagnostic trouble code because the input and output speed sensors indicate a speed difference, which is out of range for the particular transmission. Answer b is not correct because, while a slipping forward clutch could cause an excessive slippage DTC, it is less likely than the torque converter clutch because the transmission is shifting correctly. A worn or slipping forward clutch would cause shifting problems in all forward gears. Answer c is not correct because a defective pressure control solenoid is more likely to cause shifting problems and less likely to cause excessive slippage problems. Answer d is not correct because a low fluid level is more likely to cause shifting problems and less likely to cause excessive slippage problems.

39. **The correct answer is c.** It is normal for the vehicle to move forward slightly (creep) when the engine is at idle and the brakes are released with the gear selector in drive. If the idle speed is too high, the vehicle will tend to move forward or creep excessively. Answers a and b are not correct because too high or too low a fluid level will not cause the vehicle to creep excessively although it can cause the fluid to become aerated (filled with air bubbles), which could affect the shifting of the transmission. Answer d is not correct because if the forward clutch was slipping, the vehicle would tend to creep less than normal, not more than normal.

40. **The correct answer is d.** Neither technician is correct. Technician A is not correct because a worn torque converter clutch would slip in both forward and reverse. Technician B is not correct because, even though the transmission fluid may become aerated (full of air bubbles) if overfilled, it is unlikely to cause a problem in reverse only. Answers a, b, and c are not correct because neither technician is correct.

41. **The correct answer is b.** A misadjusted throttle position (TP) sensor that is producing a higher-than-normal reading during acceleration will cause the powertrain control module (PCM) to delay the shifts as if the vehicle were being accelerated at a faster rate than intended. Answer a is not correct because a defective input shaft speed sensor would not likely cause a delayed shift and would likely trigger a diagnostic trouble code. Answer c is not correct because incorrect automatic transmission fluid level is unlikely to cause a delayed shift although it could cause harsh or slow shifts. Answer d is not correct because the manual valve is used to select the gear selector and is unlikely to cause delayed shifts.

42. **The correct answer is a.** Technician A only is correct because low fluid level can create a lack of fluid needed to activate the clutches or bands resulting in a slow apply and an engine speed increase until the shift has been completed. Technician B is not correct because, even though a defective shift solenoid could cause an engine flare, it is unlikely to affect all gear changes. Answers c and d are not correct because Technician A only is correct.

43. **The correct answer is c.** A defective accumulator for the 2 to 3 shift is the most likely cause of a clunk sound to be heard during the shift. The accumulator should soften the engagement of the clutch or band during a shift and if the accumulator is stuck or the spring is broken, a loud clunk and a harsher than normal shift is the most likely cause. Answer a is not correct because a slipping torque converter clutch would not cause a noise and would most likely slip during acceleration in all gears and not just during a 2 to 3 shift. Answer b is not correct because a misadjusted manual valve, while it could affect which gears are selected, is unlikely to cause a clunk during a 2 to 3 shift. Answer d is not correct because a worn pump assembly could cause problems with shifting in all gears and is unlikely to cause a clunk sound during a 2 to 3 shift.

44. **The correct answer is c.** Both technicians are correct. Technician A is correct because if the filter screen were clogged, fluid flow could be restricted enough to prevent the clutches and/or bands from applying thereby preventing the transmission from shifting into forward or reverse ranges. Technician B is correct because a defective pump may not be able to supply the amount of flow and pressure necessary to apply the clutches/bands needed for drive and reverse. Answers a, b, and d are not correct because both technicians are correct.

45. **The correct answer is b.** A defective stator inside the torque converter could cause a lack of torque multiplication resulting in sluggish acceleration. During acceleration, the stator has to be locked in one direction thereby allowing fluid to be redirected inside the torque converter to create an increase in torque. If the one-way clutch on the stator were to fail, torque multiplication will not occur and acceleration will be sluggish. Answer a (low fluid) is not correct because while it could cause aeration and shifting problems, it is unlikely to cause slow acceleration. Answer c (shorted pressure control solenoid) is not correct  because this fault would affect shifting and is unlikely to cause slow acceleration, yet allows the vehicle to perform normally at highway speeds. Answer d (clogged filter screen) is unlikely to cause sluggish acceleration although it could cause shifting or engagement problems.

46. **The correct answer is a.** Technician A is only correct because a slipping torque converter clutch will cause slippage as determined by signals received from the ignition system (engine speed) and the vehicle speed (VS) sensor located on the output shaft. The computer compares these readings to what they should be for each gear and triggers a diagnostic trouble code (DTC) if the difference exceeds specifications. Technician B is not correct because an open shift solenoid would not function and therefore, would prevent proper shifting but is unlikely to cause a slippage to occur that would trigger a DTC. Answers c and d are not correct because Technician A only is correct.

47. **The correct answer is d.** The most likely cause of ATF being forced out of the fill tube is a clogged vent port, which would prevent air from escaping as fluid is added to the unit. The vent port allows air to escape as the fluid expands due to heat and air to enter when the fluid cools. Answer a is not correct because while a restricted or clogged cooler line can cause the transmission to overheat and increase wear, it could not cause fluid to back up in the fill tube. Answer b is not correct because even though a worn pressure regulator valve bore can cause pressure and shifting problems, it will not prevent the fluid from entering the fill tube correctly. Answer c is not correct because a restricted or clogged filter will reduce the flow of fluid to the clutches or bands, but will not prevent fluid from entering the fill tube.

48. **The correct answer is b.** A defective one-way clutch can cause the transmission to slip because the clutch must lock in one direction and free wheel in the opposite direction. If the clutch fails to lock, the transmission will act as if it is slipping and not transmitting engine torque correctly to the drive wheels. Answer a is not correct because a defective torque converter cannot cause slippage during shifts although it can cause a lack of power during acceleration, which may be thought to be slippage to a driver. Answer c is not correct because worn planetary gears will make noise but will not cause the transmission to slip. Answer d is not correct because an open shift solenoid would prevent shifts from occurring and will not cause the transmission to slip when it shifts.

49. **The correct answer is a.** Technician A only is correct because the throttle position (TP) sensor is the major input to the PCM to determine shift points and a fault with this sensor could prevent the transmission from downshifting during rapid acceleration. Technician B is not correct because a worn or defective torque converter clutch would not prevent the transmission from downshifting although it could prevent the operation of the TCC, which feels like a shift to many drivers. Answers c and d are not correct because Technician A only is correct.

50. **The correct answer is c.** Both technicians are correct. Technician A is correct because a restricted or partially clogged cooler would cause the ATF to reach higher than normal temperatures, which causes the fluid to combine with the oxygen in the air (oxidize) creating the dark brown and rancid smelling fluid. Technician B is correct because a slipping clutch pack will cause excessive heat beyond what is normally created in the torque converter and other components, which could cause the fluid to oxidize and change color. Answers a, b, and d are not correct because both technicians are correct.

51. **The correct answer is b.** When the temperature of the engine is cold, the computer prevents the operation of the torque converter clutch to allow the engine and the transmission to reach operating temperature as soon as possible. An engine thermostat that is stuck open would prevent the engine from reaching normal operating temperature especially in cold weather, and the computer would prevent the operation of the torque converter clutch, which improves fuel economy. Answers a and c are not correct because even though an incorrect level of ATF can cause transmission problems, it cannot cause the computer to not command the torque converter clutch to engage at highway speeds. Answer d is not correct because even though the torque converter could be faulty, it would not cause the computer to not command the application of the torque converter clutch at highway speeds.

52. **The correct answer is b.** Technician B only is correct because the wrong type of fluid, which does not contain the proper amount of friction modifiers that are recommended, can cause the clutch to grab and release very quickly during engagement creating a shudder or vibration. Technician A is not correct because even though the use of the wrong type of filter could affect the life of the fluid and/or the transmission, it is unlikely to cause a friction-related shudder during shifts. Answers c and d are not correct because Technician B only is correct.

53. **The correct answer is d.** Neither technician is correct. Technician A is not correct because low fluid level, while it could affect the results of a stall test, would most likely cause the engine speed to be higher, rather than lower due to the lack of the proper amount of fluid in the system. Technician B is not correct because the torque converter clutch is not engaged during a stall test (zero vehicle speed). Answers a, b, and c are not correct because neither technician is correct.

54. **The correct answer is d.** When engine coolant mixes with automatic transmission fluid (ATF), the result looks like a strawberry milkshake (pink and milky). A leak between the cooler and the radiator is the most likely cause. Answer a is not correct because overheated fluid usually turns brown rather than pink. Answer b is not correct because while aerated fluid may look foamy, it will not turn to the color pink nor be milky. Answer c is not correct because brown or black engine oil mixing with red automatic transmission fluid would cause the ATF to turn brown rather than pink.

55. **The correct answer is a.** A defective computer would not command the shift solenoids, so the unit would operate in the default gear, which is usually second gear (both shift solenoids off position). Answer b is not correct because it cannot cause the transmission itself to remain in second gear and not shift. Answer c is not correct because even though worn clutches can cause a shifting problem, it is unlikely to cause the transmission to stay in second gear only and not shift. Answer d is not correct because even though a transmission that is overfilled with ATF may not shift correctly, it is unlikely to cause the transmission to start in second gear and not shift.

56. **The correct answer is c.** If the shift linkage was not adjusted correctly, the parking pawl may not be fully engaging the teeth of the holding element. Answer a is not correct because the roller clutch is not connected to the output shaft of the transaxle and is not used to hold the vehicle stationary when the gear selector is placed in PARK. Answer b is not correct because the ring gear on the flexplate is used by the starter to rotate the engine and would not have any effect on where or not the vehicle is held when the gear selector is placed into PARK. Answer d is not correct because a worn pump could cause lower-then-normal fluid pressure and volume but this would not have any effect on the operation of the gear selector linkage and the parking pawl operation.

57. **The correct answer is b.** An open transmission fluid temperature (TFT) sensor wire would be interpreted by the computer as very cold fluid temperature. The computer often delays the operation of overdrive and the torque converter clutch until the transmission fluid reaches a certain predetermined value in an attempt to get the fluid up to normal operating temperature as soon as possible. Answer a is not correct because the fluid temperature sensor fault is not major enough to cause the computer to command a default gear selection, such as second gear only. Answer c is not correct because even though no symptoms may be noticed by the average driver, the computer will usually attempt to raise the very low fluid temperature by delaying the application of the torque converter clutch and overdrive in many cases. Answer d is not correct because the transmission systems are still intact enough to allow almost normal operation of the automatic transmission.

CATEGORY: IN-VEHICLE TRANSMISSION/TRANSAXLE MAINTENANCE AND REPAIR

58. **The correct answer is a.** A worn band is the most likely cause for the band adjustment to be incorrect. Answer b is not correct because the drum is steel and is less likely to wear than the friction surface of the band. Answer c is not correct even though low fluid level could be the root cause of the worn band. The most likely cause for the adjustment being needed is due to wear on the band. Answer d is not correct because, while a defective pressure regulator could cause the band to wear prematurely, it is the wear on the band itself that makes the adjustment necessary.

59. **The correct answer is b.** Technician B only is correct because the transmission is designed for fluid that is high-friction modified and if conventional-friction modified fluid is used, it will cause the clutches to lock-up more rapidly than normal resulting in a harsh shift. Often the clutches grab and release rapidly until the clutches are fully engaged resulting in a shudder or vibration during shifts if the incorrect fluid is used. Technician A is not correct because using friction modified instead of highly friction modified fluid will create an increase in friction in the clutch plates rather than a decrease in friction and is unlikely to cause slippage. Answers c and d are not correct because Technician B only is correct.

60. **The correct answer is b.** Technician B only is correct because the band adjustment is made to be sure that the specified clearance exists between the drum and the band for proper operation of the servo that is used to apply the band. Technician A is not correct because loosening the lock nut and torquing the adjusting screw is only the first step of the adjustment procedure. The adjusting screw should also be loosened a specified number of turns to achieve the proper clearance between the band and the drum. Answers c and d are not correct because Technician B only is correct.

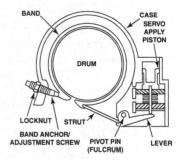

61. **The correct answer is a.** The correct answer is direct current volts (DCV). Battery and system voltage is direct current and a voltage drop should not exceed 0.2 volt at each connection while the circuit is under load. Answers b, c, and d are not correct because voltage drop is measured in units of DC volts.

62. **The correct answer is c.** Both technicians are correct. Technician A is correct because the manual linkage may need adjustment if the engine or transmission is moved out of location, such as can occur if an engine or transmission mount were to fail (collapse). The proper repair procedure would be to replace the failed mounts before adjusting the linkage. Technician B is correct because the dash indicator (PRNDL) must match the positions on the manual valve for proper selection by the driver. Answers a, b, and d are not correct because both technicians are correct.

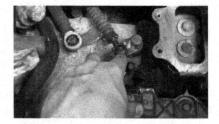

63. **The correct answer is a.** Technician A only is correct because the photo does show the correct way to remove an automatic transmission pan by allowing only one end to drop in order to control the flow of fluid. This method helps prevent spills or the possibility of hot automatic transmission fluid burning the service technician. Technician B is not correct because even though this method can be performed, it is not the recommended method because ATF will still flow from around the pan and spillage is more likely to occur than if the fluid is directed to one end only. Answers c and d are not correct because Technician A only is correct.

64. **The correct answer is a.** Technician A only is correct because a paper or fiber filter cannot be cleaned but rather should be replaced. If a screen is used, it can often be cleaned rather than re-placed, but many experts recommend that the screen also be replaced to be sure that any trapped debris does not flow through the transmission parts and valve body where it could cause wear or sticking moving parts. Technician B is not correct because a filter, unlike clutch friction discs, does not need to be soaked in ATF prior to use. Answers c and d are not correct because Technician A only is correct.

65. **The correct answer is b.** Technician B only is correct because the exact type of fluid must be used to provide the proper clutch and/or band engagement without slippage, shudder, or harshness. Technician A is not correct because the specifications for the capacity of the system includes the torque converter, cooler, and cooler lines, as well as the amount of any fluid trapped in accumulators and clutch packs and should not be used to determine the amount of fluid needed to refill after a rou-tine service. Answers c and d are not correct because Technician B only is correct.

66. **The correct answer is b.** Technician B only is correct because the ridge in the middle of the pan rail is used to squeeze a gasket and using a contact adhesive is a good method to use to make sure that the gasket remains in the proper position during installation. Technician A is not correct be-cause the ridge in the middle of the pan rail indicates that a gasket should be used rather than RTV sealant. Pan rails that use RTV are usually flat. Answers c and d are not correct because Technician B only is correct.

67. **The correct answer is d.** All of the above are correct. Answer a is correct because starting bolts by hand reduces the chances of cross threading, which can damage the transmission case. Answer b is correct because tightening the bolts gradually helps assure that the pan will be evenly tightened and that none of the bolts will be in a bind, which can cause the bolt to be tight, yet not properly clamp the pan to the case. Answer c is correct because a torque wrench should be used not only to achieve the specified torque but also to achieve even tightening of all of the fasteners.

68. **The correct answer is c.** The most important diagnostic step that should be performed concerning a shifting problem is to check the condition and level of the fluid. Answer a is not correct even though a pressure test should be performed to help diagnose shifting problems. It is not the first step that should be performed when diagnosing a shifting problem. Answer b is not correct because while the bands may need to be adjusted, this operation should not be performed before checking the fluid. Answer d is not correct because even though a low vacuum from the engine can cause shift timing concerns, the checking of the vacuum should not be done before checking the fluid.

69. **The correct answer is d.** Reflashing of the computer may be necessary to cure a particular prob-lem, but it is not one of the steps that should be followed during diagnosis. Answer a is not correct because the fluid should be checked as part of the diagnosis of a shifting problem. Answer b is not correct because checking scan tool data (PID) is one of the steps that should be performed while diagnosing a shifting problem with an electronically shifted automatic transmission. Answer c is not correct because retrieving stored diagnostic trouble codes (DTCs) is one of the steps that should be followed when diagnosing a faulty transmission.

70. **The correct answer is c.** The charging voltage of most vehicles falls into the range of 13 to 15 volts. Answers a, b, and d are not correct because these answers do not include the typical range for the charging system voltage.

71. **The correct answer is c.** Both technicians are correct. Technician A is correct because if the TV cable breaks, some transmissions have a fail-safe check ball in the valve body that increases the throttle pressure in the event of TV cable failure. Technician B is correct because a broken throttle valve (TV) cable would prevent the transmission from delaying the shift due to throttle position and would shift as if the throttle were not being depressed. This can cause the shifts to occur too early. Answers a, b, and d are not correct because both technicians are correct.

72. **The correct answer is a.** Technician A only is correct because trapped debris in the cooler could be drawn into the new automatic transmission/transaxle where it could cause excessive wear or sticking of valves and other faults if the cooler and cooler lines are not thoroughly cleaned. Technician B is not correct because some remaining water-based solvent may remain trapped in the cooler where it can cause severe damage to the friction discs if allowed to circulate through the automatic transmission/transaxle. Most friction material uses water-soluble glue to hold the friction material to the steel back-ing plate, and any water in the system can cause the friction material to separate from the backing and travel through the system causing valves to stick and causing other faults. Answers c and d are not correct because Technician A only is correct.

73. The correct answer is c. Both technicians are correct. Technician A is correct because most coolers should be able to flow about one gallon per minute or at least 2 quarts (liters) in 30 seconds. If less than 2 quarts of fluid is measured flowing through the cooler, then the cooler or cooler line(s) are restricted or clogged and should be cleaned or replaced. Technician B is correct because the engine and the pump should be operated at about 1000 RPM (fast idle) during the cooler flow test. If the engine speed is too slow, the transmission/transaxle pump may not be able to supply the specified volume of fluid and the results would indicate a restricted cooler. Answers a, b, and d are not correct because both technicians are correct.

74. The correct answer is c. Both technicians are correct. Technician A is correct because the drive shaft slip yoke attaches to the output shaft of the transmission and has to be removed to replace the seal. Technician B is correct because a worn bushing can cause the slip yoke to wear or damage the seal. Failure to replace the bushing in the extension housing can cause premature failure of the replacement seal. Answers a, b, and d are not correct because both technicians are correct.

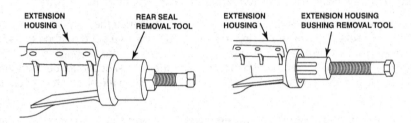

75. The correct answer is c. Both technicians are correct. Technician A is correct because in many transmission range switches, each gear position has a known resistance through which a voltage signal is sent. If there is corrosion in the connector, the resistance may not match the gear selected by the driver. Technician B is correct because the connector usually controls the operation of the backup (reverse) lights and the corrosion could cause enough of a voltage drop (resistance) to prevent the proper operation of the backup lights. Answers a, b, and d are not correct because both technicians are correct.

76. The correct answer is a. The photo shows an output speed sensor (OSS) being checked for damage. Plus, because it is a magnetic sensor, the tip should be free of metal particles which could indicate a mechanical problem inside the unit. Answers b and c are not correct because the parts shown are not a shift solenoid or throttle valve. Answer d is not correct because the part is not an electrical connector that attaches to the valve body.

77. The correct answer is c. A worn clutch would NOT affect the shaft endplay measurement even though it could affect the internal clearances inside the clutch itself. Answers a, b, and d are not correct because any of these could affect the transmission shaft end play.

78. The correct answer is a. To check for the location of a pressure leak, the best method is to perform an air pressure test where regulator air pressure (25–30 psi) is applied to the various fluid passages and observe or listen for the proper application of the clutches and bands. Answer b is not correct because the mainline pressure, while it should be checked, cannot be measured in this case because the oil pan has been removed and the engine should not be started. Answer c is not correct because inspecting the valve body will not identify the location of a pressure leak. Answer d is not correct because the pump pressure cannot be measured with the pan removed.

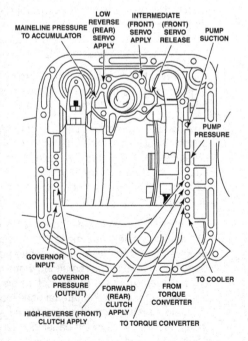

79. The correct answer is c. A worn extension housing bushing can cause excessive movement of the slip yoke to occur leading to leakage between the yoke and the rear seal. Answer a is not correct because even though too high level of automatic transmission fluid (ATF) can cause problems, it is unlikely to be the cause of a leak from the rear seal. Answer b is not correct because endplay occurs in the longitudinal axis of the output shaft and is unlikely to cause the rear seal to leak fluid. Answer d is not correct because a slipping yoke can wear on the inside (splines) and on the outside due to dirt wearing the outer surface, but is unlikely to wear enough to cause a leak.

80. **The correct answer is d.** Neither technician is correct. Technician A is not correct because the shift solenoids can be safely removed without causing harm without disconnecting the battery as long as the ignition switch is off. A voltage spike could occur, which could cause damage to the vehicle computer (not the valve body) if a solenoid is disconnected with current flowing through the windings of the solenoid. Technician B is not correct because the torque converter clutch solenoid is usually located in the valve body area and the torque converter does not need to be removed to replace the torque converter clutch solenoid. Answer c is not correct because neither technician is correct.

81. **The correct answer is a.** Technician A only is correct because the unit shown is the vehicle speed sensor, also known as the output shaft speed sensor, and is usually located in the extension housing. The signals from this sensor are often used by the vehicle computer for speedometer and cruise control as a shift control and slippage fault detection. Technician B is not correct because the unit shown is a vehicle speed sensor and not a turbine or input speed sensor, which would be installed toward the front or input end of the transmission. Answers c and d are not correct because Technician A only is correct.

82. **The correct answer is c.** Both technicians are correct. Technician A is correct because a typical band adjustment procedure specifies that the lock nut be loosened and the adjusting screw tightened to a specified torque using a torque wrench. Technician B is correct because the band adjustment procedure usually includes loosening the adjustment screw a specified number of times after it has been tightened to a specified torque. Answers a, b, and d are not correct because both technicians are correct.

83. **The correct answer is b.** Technician B only is correct because a headlight requires that enough current (amperes) be available to cause the light to be bright. If the headlight is dim, there is resistance in the circuit, which is reducing the amount of current that is available. Answer a is not correct because even if 12 volts is measured, this does not mean that there is a lack of resistance in the circuit because resistance is only effective when current flows. Answers c and d are not correct because only Technician B is correct.

84. **The correct answer is a.** Technician A only is correct because it is normal for some friction material to be found in the pan during a transmission service and does not indicate that the unit must be repaired or parts replaced. If there were metallic particles in the pan, then this would indicate that some metallic (hard part) has worn and the cause of this type of sediment in the bottom of the pan should be investigated. Technician B is not correct because some friction material (nonmetallic) sediments are considered normal and unless there is a large quantity of material or metallic material in the pan, further investigation is usually not necessary. Answers c and d are not correct because Technician A only is correct.

85. **The correct answer is a.** Technician A only is correct because dark brown and rancid smelling fluid indicates that the fluid has been overheated. A thorough inspection and testing of the cooler and cooler lines should be performed and any faults corrected before refitting the automatic transmission with fresh fluid. Technician B is not correct because even though using the wrong fluid can cause shifting problems, it is unlikely to cause the extreme temperature needed to oxidize the fluid enough to cause it to turn dark brown and have a rancid smell. Answers c and d are not correct because Technician A only is correct.

86. **The correct answer is d.** Answer d is correct because filters should be replaced rather than cleaned. Answers a, b, and c are not correct because all are correct service procedures.

AUTOMATIC TRANSMISSION/TRANSAXLE (A2)

CATEGORY: OFF-VEHICLE TRANSMISSION/TRANSAXLE REPAIR

87. **The correct answer is a.** Technician A only is correct because any extra friction discs in a clutch pack would decrease the clutch pack clearance. Technician B is not correct because too thin of a selective clutch pack pressure plate would cause the clearance to be greater than, rather than less than this specification. Answers c and d are not correct because Technician A only is correct.

88. **The correct answer is a.** The seal driver is being used to seat the pump seal. Answers a, c, and d are not correct because the seal driver is not being used to install the pump bushing (answer a), nor the stator support (answer c), nor the stator seal (answer d).

89. **The correct answer is a.** The fluid pump gears should be marked if they are not marked from the factory so that they can be reinstalled in the proper location because the gear teeth have worn together and they should be kept together. Answer b is not correct because it does not matter if the steels used in clutch packs are kept in their original location or not because they press against friction discs, which are replaced during an overhaul. Answer c is not correct because snap rings usually are manufactured with an angle cut at the open end and therefore, do not have to be marked as to direction. Answer d is not correct because planetary gears are usually replaced as an assembly and are not disassembled so they do not need to be marked.

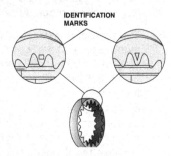

90. **The correct answer is b.** Technician B only is correct because the transmission and transmission mount help support the engine and, therefore, the engine should be supported before the transmission is removed to ensure that the engine mounts are not damaged and that the engine remains in its original installed position. Technician A is not correct because the cooler lines, while they should be disconnected before removing the transmission, do not have to be disconnected before removing the drive shaft. Answers c and d are not correct because Technician B only is correct.

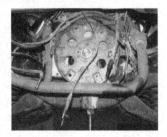

91. **The correct answer is a.** Technician A only is correct because all soft parts including rubber seals and O-rings, as well as the friction discs, should be replaced as part of an automatic transmission/transaxle overhaul. Technician B is not correct because even though the steel discs can be replaced, they do not need to be replaced unless they have been overheated and distorted or worn. Answers c and d are not correct because Technician A only is correct.

92. **The correct answer is c.** Both technicians are correct. Technician A is correct because the operation of the clutch pack can be verified by applying regulated compressed air into the clutch pack apply passage. Technician B is correct because the clearance in a clutch pack cannot be easily determined in many units without using a dial indicator and compressed air to operate the clutch pack and not only check for proper operation, but also to check that the clutch pack has the specified clearance. Answers a, b, and d are not correct because both technicians are correct.

93. **The correct answer is b.** Technician B only is correct because a correctly functioning clutch pack should produce a dull thud or clunk when regulated air pressure is applied to the clutch pack. This noise results from the compression of the friction and steel discs by the apply piston by the compressed air overcoming the return spring pressure. Technician A is not correct because the air pressure should be regulated to 25–30 psi to avoid causing damage to the piston seals, which may result if a higher pressure is applied to the clutch pack. Answers c and d are not correct because Technician B only is correct.

94. **The correct answer is a.** Technician A only is correct because depending on the unit, a selective thickness snap ring or clutch pack pressure or retaining plate is used to achieve the specified clutch pack clearance. If the clearance is too small, then a thinner snap ring or plate should be installed to achieve the specified clearance. Technician B is not correct because even though using regulated compressed air can indicate by the sound that the clutch pack clearance may be okay, it cannot be used by itself without using a dial indicator to measure the actual movement of the apply piston. Answers c and d are not correct because Technician A only is correct.

95. **The correct answer is a.** Technician A only is correct because the fiber friction discs will absorb automatic transmission fluid and should be soaked for as long as possible before installation in the unit to help ensure proper clearances are achieved and proper operation of the unit. Technician B is not correct because even though all rubber parts should be coated with fluid or assembly lube prior to assembly, it is not necessary to soak these parts in automatic transmission fluid because they will not absorb ATF. Answers c and d are not correct because Technician A only is correct.

96. **The correct answer is c.** Answer c is correct because the regulator valve in the pump usually cannot be checked by vacuum testing. Answers a, b, and d are not correct because all are checks that should be performed on an automatic transmission/transaxle to verify proper assembly before installing the unit in the vehicle.

97. **The correct answer is c.** Technician A is correct because assembly lube is miscible (can be mixed) with ATF and is used by many technicians to hold and lubricate parts during assembly. The low melting point of assembly lube helps ensure that the lube will mix with the fluid and not cause clogs or other possible problems. Technician B is correct because automatic transmission fluid (ATF) can be used to lubricate rubber seals and O-rings because it is the same fluid that these components are exposed to during normal operation. Answers a, b, and d are not correct because both technicians are correct.

98. The correct answer is b. Technician B only is correct because all solenoids including shift solenoids, the torque connector clutch solenoid, and the pressure control solenoid should be carefully inspected and checked that each has the specified electrical resistance, which indicates that the windings are neither shorted nor electrically open. Technician A is not correct because pulse-width modulated solenoids should have about one-half of the resistance of a solenoid that is simply turned on and off. The lower resistance allows the solenoid to react quicker to small voltage changes than is possible to achieve with higher resistance solenoids. The resistance should always be checked because the solenoids often look identical and the only way to determine the type of solenoid is to measure the resistance of the windings. Answers c and d are not correct because Technician B only is correct.

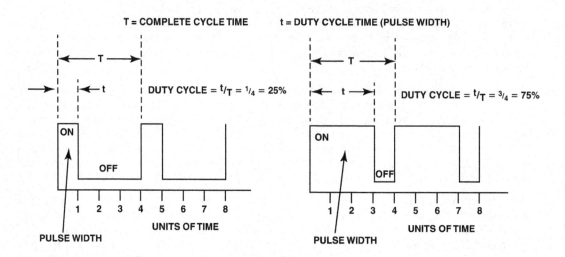

99. The correct answer is b. Technician B only is correct because the transmission cooler should always be flushed and checked for proper flow whenever the automatic transmission/transaxle is rebuilt or replaced to insure that the fluid is cooled properly to prevent harm from occurring. Technician A is not correct because although the friction discs should be replaced, the steel plates (discs) do not necessarily need to be replaced. Answers c and d are not correct because Technician B only is correct.

100. The correct answer is b. Technician B only is correct because the purpose and function of the wavy washer is to help cushion the clutch apply and without this spring, the shifts will be harsher than normal. Technician A is not correct because the wavy spring is used to soften the shift and without it, the shifts will be harsher than normal. Answers c and d are not correct because Technician B only is correct.

101. The correct answer is c. Both technicians are correct. Technician A is correct because a plastic tool should be used to move the valves against the springs to be sure that they move smoothly without binding or sticking. Technician B is correct because crocus cloth is very fine and while it will remove varnish that can cause the valve to stick, it is not abrasive enough to reduce the size of the valve, which could cause fluid leakage. Answers a, b, and d are not correct because both technicians are correct.

102. The correct answer is d. Neither technician is correct. Technician A is not correct because the valves should have sharp edges to be able to cut through any varnish that may start to accumulate and to provide a flat surface for the fluid to act against. Rounding the sharp edges can lead to many shift-related problems. Technician B is not correct because gasket sealer should never be used on a separator plate gasket because it can dislodge and cause valves to stick in the bore of the valve body. Answers a, b, and c are not correct because neither technician is correct.

103. The correct answer is c. Both technicians are correct. Technician A is correct because the bands can be adjusted without having to remove the unit from the vehicle or to remove the pan because the adjusting screw can be adjusted on the outside of the case. Technician B is correct because in some units, the only adjustment for the band is the use of a selective rod, which is determined by taking clearance measurements of the assembled components. Answers a, b, and d are not correct because both technicians are correct.

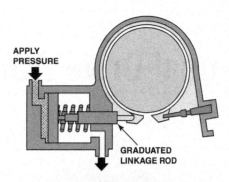

APPLY
PRESSURE

GRADUATED
LINKAGE ROD

104. The correct answer is b. Technician B only is correct because the torque converter has to be aligned with the input shaft as well as the stator support shaft and this is best achieved by installing the torque converter on the front of the transmission/transaxle, then installing the unit in the vehicle. Technician A is not correct because installing the torque converter onto the flexplate before installing the transmission is likely to prevent the proper engagement of the splines of the input shaft. Answers c and d are not correct because Technician B only is correct.

105. The correct answer is b. The dial indicator is located on the end of the input shaft and the technician is moving the shaft inward and outward to measure the input shaft endplay. Answer a (pump runout) is not correct because the dial indicator is placed to measure in and out rather than runout. Answer c (bell housing runout) is not correct because the dial indicator is attached to and is measuring the amount that the input shaft can move inward and outward. Answer d (input shaft runout) is not correct because the tip of the dial indicator is touching the end of the input shaft and not the side of the shaft, which it would have to do to measure runout.

106. The correct answer is c. The feeler gauge is measuring the clutch pack clearance because it is located between the clutches and the snap ring, which in this case is a wavy snap ring. Answer a (snap ring depth) is not correct because the measurement is not a necessary measurement and simply indicates how much cushioning the wavy snap ring is able to provide. Answer b is not correct because the feeler gauge is not in a position to measure the clearance between the clutch pack housing and the case. Answer d is not correct because the feeler gauge is not touching the input shaft and the clutch pack clearance does not affect input shaft endplay.

107. The correct answer is b. Technician B only is correct because the pump housing itself is worn and the only solution is to replace the entire pump assembly. Technician A is not correct because the dimension that exceeds factory specifications is between the outer gear and the pump housing and replacing the inner and outer gears would not change this measurement. Answers c and d are not correct because Technician B only is correct.

108. The correct answer is c. Both technicians are correct. Technician A is correct because any faults in the clutch drum can cause shifting and wear problems. Technician B is correct because all rubber parts including all seals should be replaced anytime the automatic transmission/transaxle is overhauled or disassembled for any reason to ensure proper operation of all clutches and drums. Answers a, b, and d are not correct because both technicians are correct.

109. The correct answer is b. The technician is compressing an accumulator piston using an engine valve spring compressor. Answer a is not correct because a driver is used to install a bushing rather than a C-clamp-type tool as shown. Answer c is not correct because the compressor is applying pressure to a unit in the case rather than to a clutch pack. Answer d is not correct because a C-clamp-type tool is not used to adjust a band.

110. The correct answer is c. Both technicians are correct. Technician A is correct because when one drive wheel is spinning on ice, snow, or mud, the other drive wheel is stationary. The resulting rotation of the final drive unit against the stationary drive axle shaft can result in overheating and metal transfer to occur as shown. Technician B is correct because the final drive unit should be lubricated with automatic transmission fluid enough to prevent wear from occurring during most normal driving conditions. If there were a lack of lubrication, the metal transfer could occur during normal driving conditions. Answers a, b, and d are not correct because both technicians are correct.

MANUAL DRIVE TRAIN AND AXLES CONTENT AREA

This ASE study guide for Manual Drive Train and Axles (A3) is divided into the sub-content areas that correlate to the actual ASE certification test as follows:

CONTENT AREA	QUESTIONS IN TEST	NUMBER OF STUDY GUIDE QUESTIONS
A. Clutch Diagnosis and Repair	6	36 (1–36)
B. Transmission Diagnosis and Repair	7	16 (37–52)
C. Transaxle Diagnosis and Repair	7	13 (53–65)
D. Drive Shaft/Half Shaft and Universal Joint/Constant Velocity (CV) Joint Diagnosis and Repair (Front and Rear Wheel Drive)	5	21 (66–86)
E. Drive Axle Diagnosis and Repair	7	19 (87–105)
1. Ring and Pinion Gears (3)		
2. Differential Case Assembly (2)		
3. Limited Slip Differential (1)		
4. Axle Shafts (1)		
F. Four-Wheel Drive/All-Wheel Drive Component Diagnosis and Repair	8	11 (106–116)
TOTAL	**40**	**116**

TIME ALLOWED TO TAKE THE TEST

The allocated time to take the Manual Drive Train and Axles Certification test is 60 minutes. ASE adds 10 additional questions to the test for research purposes for a total of 50 questions. These questions do not count toward your score, but they are embedded within the test and there is no way of knowing which ones do not count. As a result, the technician needs to answer 50 questions in 60 minutes, or about 1 question per minute.

If taking the recertification A3 test, there are just 20 questions with no additional research questions included. The time allocated to take the recertification test is 30 minutes, which means about one minute per question.

BEFORE USING THIS STUDY GUIDE

Before trying to answer the questions and looking at the explanations, look over the following list of the content that ASE states will be covered in the certification test. For best results using this study guide, check service information or consult an automotive textbook for details on any of the content areas that are not familiar before trying to answer the questions. For additional information about the ASE test, visit the website at **www.ase.com**.

MANUAL DRIVE TRAIN AND AXLES (A3) CERTIFICATION TEST

A. CLUTCH DIAGNOSIS AND REPAIR (6 QUESTIONS)

1. Diagnose clutch noise, binding, slippage, pulsation, chatter, pedal feel/effort, and release problems; determine needed repairs.
2. Inspect, adjust, and replace clutch pedal linkage, cables and automatic adjuster mechanisms, brackets, bushings, pivots, and springs.
3. Inspect, adjust, replace, and bleed hydraulic clutch slave and master cylinders, lines, and hoses.
4. Inspect, adjust, and replace release (throw-out) bearing, lever, and pivot.
5. Inspect and replace clutch disc and pressure plate assembly.
6. Inspect and replace pilot bearing.
7. Inspect and measure flywheel and ring gear; repair or replace as necessary.
8. Inspect engine block, clutch (bell) housing, and transmission case mating surfaces; determine needed repairs.
9. Measure flywheel-to-block runout and crankshaft end play; determine needed repairs.
10. Inspect, replace, and align powertrain mounts.

B. TRANSMISSION DIAGNOSIS AND REPAIR (6 QUESTIONS)

1. Diagnose transmission noise, hard shifting, jumping out of gear, and fluid leakage problems; determine needed repairs.
2. Inspect, adjust, and replace transmission external shifter assembly, shift linkages, brackets, bushings/grommets, pivots, and levers.
3. Inspect and replace transmission gaskets, sealants, seals, and fasteners; inspect sealing surfaces.
4. Remove and replace transmission; inspect transmission.
5. Disassemble and clean transmission components; reassemble transmission.
6. Inspect, repair, and/or replace transmission shift cover and internal shift forks, bushings, levers, shafts, sleeves, detent mechanisms, interlocks, and springs.
7. Inspect and replace input (clutch) shaft, bearings, and retainers.
8. Inspect and replace main shaft, gears, thrust washers, bearings, and retainers/snaprings.
9. Inspect and replace synchronizer hub, sleeve, keys (inserts), springs, and blocking (synchronizing) rings; measure blocking ring clearance.
10. Inspect and replace counter (cluster) gear, shaft, bearings, thrust washers, and retainers/snap rings.
11. Inspect and replace reverse idler gear, shaft, bearings, thrust washers, and retainers/snap rings.
12. Measure and adjust shaft, gear, and synchronizer end play.
13. Measure and adjust bearing preload.
14. Inspect, repair, and replace extension housing and transmission case mating surfaces, bores, bushings, and vents.
15. Inspect and replace speedometer drive gear, driven gear, and retainers.
16. Inspect, test, and replace transmission sensors and switches.
17. Inspect lubrication devices; check fluid level, and refill with proper fluid.

C. TRANSAXLE DIAGNOSIS AND REPAIR (8 QUESTIONS)

1. Diagnose transaxle noise, hard shifting, jumping out of gear, and fluid leakage problems; determine needed repairs.
2. Inspect, adjust, and replace transaxle external shift assemblies, linkages, brackets, bushings/grommets, cables, pivots, and levers.
3. Inspect and replace transaxle gaskets, sealants, seals, and fasteners; inspect sealing surfaces.
4. Remove and replace transaxle; inspect, replace, and align transaxle mounts.
5. Disassemble and clean transaxle components; reassemble transaxle.
6. Inspect, repair, and/or replace transaxle shift cover and internal shift forks, levers, bushings, shafts, sleeves, detent mechanisms, interlocks, and springs.
7. Inspect and replace input shaft, bearings, and retainers.
8. Inspect and replace output shaft, gears, thrust washers, bearings, and retainers/snap rings.
9. Inspect and replace synchronizer hub, sleeve, keys (inserts), springs, and blocking (synchronizing) rings; measure blocking ring clearance.
10. Inspect and replace reverse idler gear, shaft, bearings, thrust washers, and retainers/snap rings.
11. Inspect, repair, and replace transaxle case mating surfaces, bores, bushings, and vents.
12. Inspect and replace speedometer drive gear, driven gear, and retainers.
13. Inspect, test, and replace transaxle sensors and switches.
14. Diagnose differential assembly noise and vibration problems; determine needed repairs.
15. Remove and replace differential assembly.
16. Inspect, measure, adjust, and replace differential pinion gears (spiders), shaft, side gears, thrust washers, and case.
17. Inspect and replace differential side bearings.
18. Measure shaft end play/preload (shim/spacer selection procedure).
19. Inspect lubrication devices; check fluid level and refill with proper fluid.

D. DRIVE SHAFT/HALF SHAFT AND UNIVERSAL JOINT/CONSTANT VELOCITY (CV) JOINT DIAGNOSIS AND REPAIR (FRONT AND REAR WHEEL DRIVE) (6 QUESTIONS)

1. Diagnose shaft and universal/CV joint noise and vibration problems; determine needed repairs.
2. Inspect, service, and replace shafts, yokes, boots, and universal/CV joints.
3. Inspect, service, and replace shaft center support bearings.
4. Check and correct propeller shaft balance.
5. Measure shaft runout.
6. Measure and adjust shaft angles.
7. Diagnose, inspect, service, and replace wheel bearings, seals, and hubs.

E. REAR WHEEL DRIVE AXLE DIAGNOSIS AND REPAIR (7 QUESTIONS)

1. Ring and Pinion Gears (3 questions)

1. Diagnose noise, vibration, and fluid leakage problems; determine needed repairs.
2. Inspect and replace companion flange and pinion seal; measure companion flange runout.
3. Measure ring gear runout; determine needed repairs.
4. Inspect and replace ring and pinion gear set, collapsible spacers, sleeves (shims), and bearings.
5. Measure and adjust drive pinion depth.
6. Measure and adjust drive pinion bearing preload (collapsible spacer or shim type).
7. Measure and adjust differential (side) bearing preload, and ring and pinion backlash (threaded cup or shim type).
8. Perform ring and pinion tooth contact pattern checks; determine needed adjustments.

2. **Differential Case Assembly (2 questions)**

   1. Diagnose differential assembly noise and vibration problems; determine needed repairs.
   2. Remove and replace differential assembly.
   3. Inspect, measure, adjust, and replace differential pinion gears (spiders), shaft, side gears, thrust washers, and case.
   4. Inspect and replace differential side bearings.
   5. Measure differential case runout; determine needed repairs.

3. **Limited Slip Differential (1 question)**

   1. Diagnose limited slip differential noise, slippage, and chatter problems; determine needed repairs.
   2. Inspect, flush, and refill with correct lubricant.
   3. Inspect, adjust, and replace clutch (cone/plate) pack.

4. **Axle Shafts (1 question)**

   1. Diagnose rear axle shaft noise, vibration, and fluid leakage problems; determine needed repairs.
   2. Inspect and replace rear axle shaft wheel studs.
   3. Remove, inspect, and replace rear axle shafts, seals, bearings, and retainers.
   4. Measure rear axle flange runout and shaft end play; determine needed repairs.
   5. Inspect axle housing and vent.

F. FOUR-WHEEL DRIVE COMPONENT DIAGNOSIS AND REPAIR (7 QUESTIONS)

1. Diagnose drive assembly noise, vibration, leakage and steering problems; determine needed repairs.
2. Inspect, adjust, and repair transfer case manual shifting mechanisms, bushings, mounts, levers, and brackets.
3. Remove and replace transfer case.
4. Disassemble transfer case; clean and inspect internal transfer case components; determine needed repairs.
5. Reassemble transfer case.
6. Check transfer case fluid level; drain and refill with proper fluid.
7. Inspect, service, and replace drive/propeller shaft and universal/CV joints.
8. Inspect, service, and replace drive axle universal/CV joints and drive/half-shafts.
9. Inspect, service, and replace wheel bearings, seals, and hubs.
10. Check transfer case and axle seals and all vents.
11. Diagnose drive system actuation and engagement concerns; repair or replace components as necessary (including: viscous, hydraulic, magnetic, mechanical, vacuum, and electrical /electronic).
12. Inspect tires for condition and matching circumference; verify proper size for vehicle application.

MANUAL DRIVE TRAIN AND AXLES (A3)

CATEGORY: CLUTCH DIAGNOSIS AND REPAIR

1. A clutch is slipping. What could be the cause?

    a. A weak pressure plate
    b. An oil-soaked clutch disc
    c. A sticking clutch cable
    d. All of the above

2. Technician A says that too much clutch pedal free play can cause the clutch to shudder during rapid acceleration. Technician B says that too little clutch pedal free play can cause the clutch to slip. Which technician is correct?

    a. A only
    b. B only
    c. Both A and B
    d. Neither A nor B

3. A clutch is chattering when engaged. Technician A says that too much clutch free play is the cause. Technician B says that oil or grease may be on the friction disc. Which technician is correct?

    a. A only
    b. B only
    c. Both A and B
    d. Neither A nor B

4. A manual transmission has gear grinding and is difficult to shift or get into gear, especially reverse. Technician A says that the clutch may not be fully releasing. Technician B says that too much clutch pedal free play could be the cause. Which technician is correct?

    a. A only
    b. B only
    c. Both A and B
    d. Neither A nor B

5. Two technicians are discussing bleeding a hydraulic clutch. Technician A says to open the bleeder and allow the fluid to gravity bleed. Technician B says to have an assistant slowly depress the clutch pedal as the bleeder valve is opened at the slave cylinder to bleed the air out of the system. Which technician is correct?

    a. A only
    b. B only
    c. Both A and B
    d. Neither A nor B

6. Two technicians are discussing a transmission that is difficult to shift into gear. Technician A says that the clutch may not be fully releasing. Technician B says that the synchronizer rings (blocking rings) may be worn. Which technician is correct?

    a. A only
    b. B only
    c. Both A and B
    d. Neither A nor B

7. A new clutch has been installed and adjusted. This technician is attempting to rotate the output shaft while an assistant depresses the clutch pedal with the transmission in fourth gear (direct 1:1 gear in most units). What is the technician checking?

   a. That the clutch linkage is adjusted correctly to allow the input shaft to rotate
   b. The pressure plate holding force
   c. The pilot bearing
   d. The release (throw-out) bearing

8. A vehicle equipped with a manual 5-speed transmission is difficult to shift especially into first gear and reverse. Technician A says that the input shaft of the transmission may be partially seized to the pilot bearing. Technician B says that the throw-out bearing may be worn. Which technician is correct?

   a. A only
   b. B only
   c. Both A and B
   d. Neither A nor B

9. A customer complained that a grinding noise is heard and a vibration is felt when the driver's foot lightly depresses the clutch pedal. Technician A says that a defective input shaft bearing in the transmission/transaxle is the most likely cause. Technician B says the pilot bearing is the most likely cause. Which technician is correct?

   a. A only
   b. B only
   c. Both A and B
   d. Neither A nor B

10. The owner of a manual transmission vehicle stated that the transmission shifts normally but the engine speed does not drop after an upshift has been completed and the clutch has been released. Technician A says that the clutch may be slipping. Technician B says that the cause may be due to a defective throw-out (release) bearing. Which technician is correct?

   a. A only
   b. B only
   c. Both A and B
   d. Neither A nor B

11. Technician A says that the flywheel should be resurfaced whenever the clutch friction disc and pressure plate are replaced. Technician B says that it may be necessary to install a shim between the crankshaft and the flywheel if the flywheel is machined. Which technician is correct?

   a. A only
   b. B only
   c. Both A and B
   d. Neither A nor B

12. A scored transmission input shaft bearing retainer (quill) was discovered when the transmission was removed to replace a worn and slipping clutch. Technician A says that the front transmission bearing should be replaced. Technician B says that the bearing retainer should be replaced to provide the proper operation of the throw-out (release) bearing. Which technician is correct?

   a. A only
   b. B only
   c. Both A and B
   d. Neither A nor B

13. A clutch on a pickup truck equipped with a hydraulic clutch does not disengage. Technician A says that the hydraulic clutch may need to be properly bled. Technician B says that the clutch master cylinder may be defective. Which technician is correct?

   a. A only
   b. B only
   c. Both A and B
   d. Neither A nor B

14. An owner of a manual transmission vehicle complained that the clutch slipped during hard acceleration. Technician A says that the clutch linkage may need adjustment. Technician B says the clutch may require replacement. Which technician is correct?

   a. A only
   b. B only
   c. Both A and B
   d. Neither A nor B

15. A clutch engages close to the floor and will often not disengage. What is the *most likely* cause?

   a. Worn clutch disc
   b. Misadjusted clutch linkage
   c. Weak pressure plate
   d. Worn flywheel

16. An owner of a vehicle equipped with a manual transmission and a cable-operated clutch complained that the transmission is difficult to shift without grinding the gears. Which is the *least likely* cause?

   a. Incorrect gear lube in the transmission
   b. Bulkhead (firewall) flex
   c. Incorrect clutch adjustment
   d. Misadjusted clutch switch

17. A loud squeak is heard every time the clutch pedal is depressed or released. What is the *most likely* cause?

   a. A defective release (throw-out) bearing
   b. A defective input shaft bearing
   c. A cracked diaphragm spring on the pressure plate
   d. The clutch pedal linkage needs lubrication

18. A clutch is chattering when it is engaged. What is the *most likely* cause?

   a. Oil or grease on the friction surface(s)
   b. A worn release (throw-out) bearing
   c. A worn clutch fork
   d. A defective pilot bearing (bushing)

19. The starter motor spins but the engine does not crank. What is the *most likely* cause?

   a. A slipping clutch
   b. A broken ring gear
   c. A seized pilot bearing
   d. An open clutch safety switch

20. Two technicians are discussing clutch linkage adjustment. Technician A says that most hydraulic clutches are self-adjusting and that no adjustment is needed. Technician B says that many cable-operated clutches are self-adjusting and that no adjustment is needed. Which technician is correct?

   a. A only
   b. B only
   c. Both A and B
   d. Neither A nor B

21. Which is the *least likely* location for the clutch linkage adjuster (clutch free-play adjustment)?

    a. The bell housing area at the fork pivot
    b. The adjuster at the clutch fork
    c. Near the bulkhead (firewall)
    d. Near the flywheel at the pilot bearing

22. A replacement clutch is being installed and the flywheel has blue hard spot areas and has many surface cracks. Technician A says that the flywheel should be replaced. Technician B says that the flywheel should be resurfaced. Which technician is correct?

    a. A only
    b. B only
    c. Both A and B
    d. Neither A nor B

23. The fluid level in the reservoir of a hydraulic clutch master cylinder was found to be low. Technician A says that DOT 3 brake fluid should be used to restore the level to the indicated mark. Technician B says that the clutch slave cylinder may be leaking. Which technician is correct?

    a. A only
    b. B only
    c. Both A and B
    d. Neither A nor B

24. What is this technician doing?

    a. Removing the pilot bearing
    b. Removing the flywheel
    c. Centering the release (throw-out) bearing
    d. Aligning the clutch (input) shaft with the pilot bearing

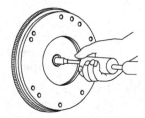

25. What is being measured?

    a. Flywheel radial runout
    b. Pressure plate shim height
    c. Release (throw-out) bearing clearance
    d. Flywheel lateral runout

26. A replacement clutch is being installed in a rear-wheel-drive vehicle. Technician A says that an alignment tool should be used to align the clutch disc with the pilot bearing. Technician B says that the pressure plate should be compressed before installation. Which technician is correct?

    a. A only
    b. B only
    c. Both A and B
    d. Neither A nor B

27. A squealing sound is heard and the sound changes when the driver exerts force on the clutch pedal. Technician A says that the pilot bearing is defective. Technician B says that the input shaft bearing is defective. Which technician is correct?

    a. A only
    b. B only
    c. Both A and B
    d. Neither A nor B

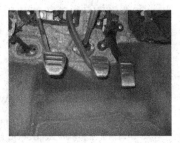

28. A clutch is being replaced. Technician A says that the clutch cover bolts should be loosened one turn at a time to avoid warping the clutch cover. Technician B says that the retaining bolts should be tightened one turn at a time to avoid warping the clutch cover. Which technician is correct?

    a. A only
    b. B only
    c. Both A and B
    d. Neither A nor B

29. A clutch is being removed to get access to replace a leaking block expansion plug. Technician A says that the pressure plate should be marked so it can be reinstalled in the same location on the flywheel just in case the vehicle uses a clutch/flywheel that is balanced as an assembly. Technician B says that the clutch disc should be marked so it can be installed on the input shaft in the same location. Which technician is correct?

    a. A only
    b. B only
    c. Both A and B
    d. Neither A nor B

30. What is this technician doing?

    a. Aligning the clutch disc with the pilot bearing
    b. Removing the pilot bearing using a puller
    c. Adjusting the alignment of the pressure plate
    d. Using a depth measurement tool to adjust the fingers of the pressure plate

31. Two technicians are discussing the clutch part shown. Technician A says that the pressure plate should be replaced. Technician B says that the release (throw-out) bearing should be replaced. Which technician is correct?

    a. A only
    b. B only
    c. Both A and B
    d. Neither A nor B

32. This clutch part is being discussed. Technician A says that it can be cleaned, lubricated, and reused. Technician B says that it should be replaced every time the clutch is replaced. Which technician is correct?

    a. A only
    b. B only
    c. Both A and B
    d. Neither A nor B

33. What is a clutch aligning tool used to align?

    a. Throw-out (release) bearing with the pressure plate
    b. Clutch disc with the pilot bearing (bushing)
    c. Pressure plate with the clutch disc
    d. Clutch disc with the throw-out (release) bearing

34. A growling sound is heard when the engine is running and the transmission/transaxle is in neutral with the clutch engaged (foot off of the clutch pedal). The noise stops when the clutch pedal is depressed. What is the *most likely* cause?

    a. A release (throw-out) bearing
    b. Lack of lubrication at the fork and pivot
    c. An input shaft bearing
    d. A pilot bearing

35. The clutch master cylinder was replaced and now the clutch pedal feels mushy and the transmission cannot be shifted in gear. Technician A says that the slave cylinder may have to be removed from the bell housing and positioned so that all of the trapped air can be properly bled from the system. Technician B says that the clutch itself should be replaced. Which technician is correct?

    a. A only
    b. B only
    c. Both A and B
    d. Neither A nor B

36. A pickup truck equipped with a diesel engine has been towed to the shop. The engine speed increases when the driver depresses the accelerator pedal and releases the clutch pedal, but the vehicle does not move. Technician A says that the clutch may be defective. Technician B says that the dual-mass flywheel may be defective. Which technician is correct?

    a. A only
    b. B only
    c. Both A and B
    d. Neither A nor B

CATEGORY: TRANSMISSION DIAGNOSIS AND REPAIR

37. Which component *cannot* be removed before removing the transmission/transaxle from the vehicle?

    a. Vehicle speed sensor
    b. Reverse (backup) light connector
    c. Front bearing retainer (quill)
    d. Drive axle shaft(s)

38. A manual transmission is difficult to shift into all gears but only when the outside temperature is below freezing (32°F or 0°C). Technician A says that the brass blocking ring could be defective. Technician B says that incorrect gear lubricant could be the cause. Which technician is correct?

    a. A only
    b. B only
    c. Both A and B
    d. Neither A nor B

39. Various lubricants are used in a manual transmission *except* _____.

    a. Automatic transmission fluid (ATF)
    b. high temperature chassis grease
    c. SAE 80W-90 gear lube
    d. engine oil

40. The bearing shown is defective. What other part should be replaced?

    a. The bearing retainer (or bearing cup)
    b. The synchronizer assembly
    c. The main shaft thrust washer
    d. The input shaft

41. A manual 5-speed transmission in a rear-wheel-drive vehicle is noisy in all gears except fourth. Technician A says that the main shaft bearing(s) is likely to be defective. Technician B says that the countershaft bearing(s) is likely to be defective. Which technician is correct?

    a. A only
    b. B only
    c. Both A and B
    d. Neither A nor B

42. Technician A says that a cracked or worn shift fork can cause incomplete shifts. Technician B says that excessive input shaft or main shaft end play can cause incomplete shifts. Which technician is correct?

    a. A only
    b. B only
    c. Both A and B
    d. Neither A nor B

43. What is this technician doing?

    a. Repacking a transmission thrust washer
    b. Reassembling a synchronizer assembly
    c. Adjusting the shift fork clearance
    d. Aligning the hub with the speed gear

44. A customer complained of hard shifting particularly into first gear and reverse. Technician A says that the blocking ring may be worn. Technician B says that the clutch may be defective or out of adjustment. Which technician is correct?

   a. A only
   b. B only
   c. Both A and B
   d. Neither A nor B

45. A 5-speed manual transmission jumps out of fifth gear while driving. What is the *most likely* cause?

   a. A worn input shaft bearing
   b. A worn shift lever
   c. Low on lubricating oil
   d. A cracked synchronizer ring

46. A snap ring is being reinstalled on a manual transmission as shown. Technician A says that the sharp edges (points) at the ends of the snap ring should be installed up toward the technician. Technician B says that the snap ring can be installed in either direction as long as it fits correctly into the groove. Which technician is correct?

   a. A only
   b. B only
   c. Both A and B
   d. Neither A nor B

47. What procedure is being set up?

   a. Aligning the synchronizer hub
   b. Measuring the main shaft endplay
   c. Pressing a speed gear onto the main shaft
   d. Using a bearing splitter to press a gear and/or bearing from a shaft

48. What does this switch or sensor control?

   a. Reverse lights
   b. Neutral safety switch
   c. Clutch safety switch
   d. Vehicle speed sensor

49. These plastic gears are different colors. Technician A says that these gears should be changed if a different differential axle ratio is installed in the vehicle. Technician B says that these gears press onto the input shaft. Which technician is correct?

   a. A only
   b. B only
   c. Both A and B
   d. Neither A nor B

50. If this part (rubber hose with white cap) was to become plugged with mud, what is the *most likely* result?

   a. Hard shifting
   b. Gear (growling) noise
   c. Vibration at highway speeds
   d. Seal leakage

51. A transmission is low on lubricant. Which component is the *least likely* to fail?

   a. Synchronizer assembly
   b. Speed gear bearing(s)
   c. Input shaft bearing
   d. Shift forks

52. What is the *most likely* cause of the damaged gear?

   a. Speed shifting
   b. Shifting using the clutch
   c. Rapid clutch engagement while on dry pavement
   d. Spinning the rear drive wheels

MANUAL DRIVE TRAIN AND AXLES (A3)

CATEGORY: TRANSAXLE DIAGNOSIS AND REPAIR

53. The owner of a vehicle equipped with a manual transaxle complained that gear clash was heard whenever shifting. Which is the *least likely* to be the cause?

    a. Worn blocking ring
    b. Misadjusted clutch linkage
    c. Defective output shaft bearing
    d. Defective pilot bearing

54. Technician A says that the clearance between the synchronizer ring (blocking ring) and the speed gear should be measured with a feeler (thickness) gauge. Technician B says that a worn synchronizer ring (blocking ring) can cause gear clash when shifting. Which technician is correct?

    a. A only
    b. B only
    c. Both A and B
    d. Neither A nor B

55. The owner of a front-wheel-drive vehicle complains that the shift lever is difficult to move in all positions. Which is the *most likely* cause?

    a. A seized pilot bearing
    b. A misadjusted clutch
    c. A worn release (throw-out) bearing
    d. Dirty/corroded shift linkage

56. A growling sound is heard with the engine running and the transaxle is in neutral with the clutch engaged (foot off of the clutch pedal). What is the *most likely* cause?

    a. Excessive main shaft endplay
    b. An input shaft bearing
    c. An output bearing
    d. A pilot bearing

57. Two technicians are discussing the reassembly of a transaxle as shown. Technician A says that the shim is used to control input shaft endplay. Technician B says that the shim is used under the bearing cup to provide bearing preload. Which technician is correct?

    a. A only
    b. B only
    c. Both A and B
    d. Neither A nor B

58. A transaxle is being reassembled as shown. Technician A says that a gap between the halves is normal and will be closed when the retaining bolts are tightened to factory specifications. Technician B says that RTV silicone sealer should be used to fill the gap. Which technician is correct?

    a. A only
    b. B only
    c. Both A and B
    d. Neither A nor B

59. Which type of lubricant is usually *not* used in a manual transaxle?

    a. Automatic transmission fluid (ATF)
    b. Hydraulic oil
    c. SAE 80W-90 gear lube
    d. Engine oil

60. What operation is being performed on this transaxle case?

    a. Straightening a warped case
    b. Installing the countershaft
    c. Installing the bearing cup into the bearing pocket
    d. Pressure lubricating the bearing

61. What is this technician doing?

    a. Removing the gears from the shaft
    b. Adjusting the free play of the synchronizer ring
    c. Checking the clearance between the speed gears
    d. Removing a snap ring

62. What is being measured in the figure?

    a. Synchronizer clearance
    b. Gear thrust clearance
    c. Output shaft runout
    d. Selective snap ring thickness

63. This transaxle has been overheated. What is the *most likely* cause?

    a. The driver was slipping the clutch
    b. Worn synchronizer sleeve(s)
    c. A lack of or low on lubricating oil
    d. Defective input shaft bearings

64. A 5-speed manual transaxle is noisy in all gears. Which is the *least likely* cause?

    a. A pilot bearing
    b. An input shaft bearing
    c. An output shaft bearing
    d. Final drive side (differential) bearings

65. The photo shows a paper blocker ring used in a manual transaxle. What type of lubricant will harm this type of blocker ring?

    a. SAE 80W-90 gear lube
    b. ATF
    c. Engine oil
    d. Manual transmission fluid

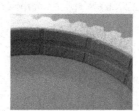

CATEGORY: DRIVE SHAFT/HALF SHAFT AND UNIVERSAL JOINT/CV JOINT DIAGNOSIS AND REPAIR

66. A clunk is heard and felt when a pickup truck first accelerates from a stop. Technician A says that yoke splines may need to be lubricated with grease. Technician B says that the center support bearing (carrier or hanger bearing) could be defective. Which technician is correct?

   a. A only
   b. B only
   c. Both A and B
   d. Neither A nor B

67. A rear-wheel-drive vehicle shutters or vibrates when first accelerating from a stop. The vibration is less noticeable at higher speeds. What is the *most likely* cause?

   a. Drive shaft unbalance
   b. Excessive U-joint working angles
   c. Unequal U-joint working angles
   d. Brinelling of the U-joint

68. A defective outer CV joint will usually make a _____.

   a. rumbling noise
   b. growling noise
   c. clicking noise
   d. clunking noise

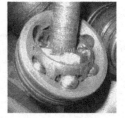

69. The last step before installing the drive axle shaft into the vehicle after replacing the CV joint boot is to _____.

   a. "Burp the boot" and tighten the clamp
   b. lubricate the CV joint with chassis grease
   c. mark the location of the boot on the drive axle shaft
   d. separate the CV joint before installation

70. The splines of the drive shaft yoke should be lubricated to prevent _____.

   a. a vibration
   b. spline bind
   c. rust
   d. transmission fluid leaks from the extension housing

71. A rear axle uses a C-clip-type axle retainer. The rear-axle bearing is noisy and requires replacement. Technician A says that the axle itself may also require replacement. Technician B says that the rear-axle seal should also be replaced. Which technician is correct?

   a. A only
   b. B only
   c. Both A and B
   d. Neither A nor B

72. Two technicians are discussing CV joints on a front-wheel-drive vehicle. Technician A says that the drive axle shaft has to be removed from the hub bearing before it can be removed from the vehicle. Technician B says that most CV joints are bolted onto the drive axle shaft. Which technician is correct?

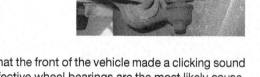

   a. A only
   b. B only
   c. Both A and B
   d. Neither A nor B

73. An owner of a front-wheel-drive minivan complained that the front of the vehicle made a clicking sound whenever turning a corner. Technician A says that defective wheel bearings are the most likely cause. Technician B says that defective inner CV joint(s) may be the cause. Which technician is correct?

   a. A only
   b. B only
   c. Both A and B
   d. Neither A nor B

74. A CV joint boot is discovered torn and grease has covered the inside of the wheel. Technician A says that the boot should be replaced. Technician B says that the joint may be worn and require replacement. Which technician is correct?

   a. A only
   b. B only
   c. Both A and B
   d. Neither A nor B

75. Technician A says that CV joints are packed with special grease that comes with the replacement boot kit or joint assembly. Technician B says that chassis grease is suitable for use in a CV joint. Which technician is correct?

   a. A only
   b. B only
   c. Both A and B
   d. Neither A nor B

76. Incorrect or unequal U-joint working angles are *most likely* to be caused by _____.

   a. a bent drive shaft
   b. a collapsed engine or transmission mount
   c. a dry output shaft spline
   d. defective or damaged U-joints

77. A vehicle owner complained that a severe vibration was felt throughout the entire vehicle at highway speeds. What is the *least likely* cause?

   a. Excessive drive shaft working angles
   b. A bent drive shaft
   c. Worn CV joints
   d. A defective rear tire(s)

78. Two technicians are discussing the drive axle shaft shown. Technician A says that the weight in the center should be transferred to the new replacement axle shaft. Technician B says that the weight is necessary for proper balance and if not positioned correctly can cause the vehicle to vibrate at highway speeds. Which technician is correct?

   a. A only
   b. B only
   c. Both A and B
   d. Neither A nor B

79. What is the technician doing with a wooden dowel rod?

    a. Rotating the bearing in the housing so it can be removed
    b. Packing grease into the CV joint
    c. Checking for free play in the CV joint
    d. Aligning the hub with the spline

80. Technician A says that some CV joint boot clamps must be torqued to factory specifications using a torque wrench. Technician B says that a split-type CV joint boot should be used to replace a torn boot. Which technician is correct?

    a. A only
    b. B only
    c. Both A and B
    d. Neither A nor B

81. What is being performed?

    a. The hub bearing is being pressed onto the end of the drive axle shaft
    b. Removing the drive axle from the hub
    c. The outer CV joint is being removed from the drive axle shaft
    d. The CV joint boot is being installed over the CV joint

82. Hose clamps have been installed around a composite drive shaft (propeller shaft). Technician A says that this is a safety precaution to help keep the shaft from twisting. Technician B says that the drive shaft is being balanced using the hose clamps. Which technician is correct?

    a. A only
    b. B only
    c. Both A and B
    d. Neither A nor B

83. A dented drive shaft is found during a visual inspection. Technician A says that the dent is simply cosmetic and that no repair is necessary. Technician B says that the drive shaft should be replaced. Which technician is correct?

    a. A only
    b. B only
    c. Both A and B
    d. Neither A nor B

84. Two technicians are discussing drive shaft (propeller shaft) angles. Technician A says that a vibration can occur if the front and rear U-joint angles are not within 0.5 degrees of each other. Technician B says that a collapsed transmission mount can cause the drive shaft angles to be unequal. Which technician is correct?

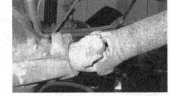

    a. A only
    b. B only
    c. Both A and B
    d. Neither A nor B

85. Drive shaft U-joint working angles can be changed by _____.

    a. replacing the U-joints
    b. using shims or wedges under the transmission or rear axle
    c. rotating the position of the drive shaft on the yoke
    d. tightening the differential pinion nut

86. Two technicians are discussing U-joints. Technician A says that a defective U-joint could cause a loud "clunk" noise when the transmission is shifted between drive and reverse. Technician B says that a worn U-joint can cause a clicking or squeaking sound when driving the vehicle in reverse, but not while moving forward. Which technician is correct?

    a. A only
    b. B only
    c. Both A and B
    d. Neither A nor B

CATEGORY: DRIVE AXLE DIAGNOSIS AND REPAIR

87. A service technician removed the inspection/fill plug from the differential of a rear-wheel drive vehicle and gear lube started to flow out. Technician A says that the technician should quickly replace the plug to prevent any more loss of gear lube. Technician B says to catch the fluid and allow the fluid to continue to drain. Which technician is correct?

    a. A only
    b. B only
    c. Both A and B
    d. Neither A nor B

88. The drive pinion gear is positioned with a shim that is too thick. This will cause contact with the ring gear teeth too close to the _____ on the drive side.

    a. face
    b. heel
    c. flank
    d. toe

89. The backlash exceeds specifications. The technician should _____.

    a. position the ring gear closer to the drive pinion gear
    b. position the ring gear farther from the drive pinion gear
    c. install shims behind the side gears
    d. remove a shim from the pinion gear

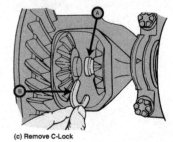

90. What is this technician doing?

    a. Removing/installing the ring gear
    b. Removing/installing the axle shaft
    c. Removing/installing the side gears
    d. Removing/installing the pinion drive gear

(c) Remove C-Lock

91. A growling sound is heard from the rear of a rear-wheel-drive vehicle while turning left only. Technician A says that defective rear axle bearings may be the cause. Technician B says that defective side bearings may be the cause. Which technician is correct?

    a. A only
    b. B only
    c. Both A and B
    d. Neither A nor B

92. Technician A says that if the backlash is okay, then the side bearing preload is also okay. Technician B says that a ring gear tooth pattern check will indicate if the drive pinion depth is correct. Which technician is correct?

    a. A only
    b. B only
    c. Both A and B
    d. Neither A nor B

93. Two technicians are discussing which lubricants are used in a limited-slip differential. Technician A says to use SAE 80W-140. Technician B says that most vehicle manufacturers usually specify SAE 80W-90 be used with or without special limited-slip additives. Which technician is correct?

    a. A only
    b. B only
    c. Both A and B
    d. Neither A nor B

94. A defective wheel bearing usually sounds like _____.

    a. marbles in a tin can
    b. a clicking sound like a ball-point pen
    c. a baby rattle
    d. a noisy tire

95. A ring gear and pinion setup is being analyzed using marking grease. Technician A says that the pattern on the ring gear will indicate whether the pinion depth is correct. Technician B says that the pattern will indicate whether the backlash is correct. Which technician is correct?

    a. A only
    b. B only
    c. Both A and B
    d. Neither A nor B

96. Two technicians are discussing the pinion depth adjustment in a differential. Technician A says that the pinion depth is adjusted using a shim. Technician B says that the pinion depth is adjusted by adjusting the pinion nut. Which technician is correct?

    a. A only
    b. B only
    c. Both A and B
    d. Neither A nor B

97. A differential pinion seal is leaking. What should be used to remove the pinion nut?

    a. Air impact wrench
    b. Torque wrench
    c. Socket and wrench while companion flange is being held with a holding tool
    d. Gear puller

98. A ring gear and pinion are being replaced. Which part(s) usually *requires* replacement?

    a. Ring gear bolts
    b. Differential side bearings
    c. Axle seals
    d. Pinion bearings

99. A technician says that differential side bearings must be _____.

    a. slightly loose to allow for expansion
    b. preloaded to a specified amount
    c. torqued to specification
    d. checked using bore gauge

100. A vehicle is equipped with different-size tires on the same drive axle (P205/75R x 15 on the left rear and P215/75R x 15 on the right rear). What part may wear due to this tire-size mismatch?

    a. Drive pinion bearings
    b. Side gear bearings
    c. Rear axle bearings
    d. Pinion gear thrust washers

101. Water was found in both the front and rear differential housings of the drive axles of a four-wheel-drive vehicle. Technician A says that driving in water up to the center of the axles can usually cause water to get into the differential housing. Technician B says that the vehicle was likely under water. Which technician is correct?

   a. A only
   b. B only
   c. Both A and B
   d. Neither A nor B

102. To remove a C-clip axle, what step does *not* need to be done?

   a. Remove the differential cover
   b. Remove the axle flange bolts/nuts
   c. Remove the differential pinion shaft
   d. Remove the differential pinion shaft lock pin

103. What is this technician doing?

   a. Installing the pinion nut
   b. Checking for specified backlash between the ring gear and pinion
   c. Checking pinion shaft rotating torque
   d. Seating the pinion seal

104. The pinion seal is leaking as shown. All of the service operations should be performed *except* _____.

   a. drive shaft removed and replaced
   b. drive flange removed and replaced
   c. pinion seal removed and replaced
   d. pinion gear removed and replaced

105. Technician A says that this setup is used to check the differential ring gear backlash. Technician B says that it is being used to check ring gear runout. Which technician is correct?

   a. A only
   b. B only
   c. Both A and B
   d. Neither A nor B

MANUAL DRIVE TRAIN AND AXLES (A3)

CATEGORY: FOUR-WHEEL DRIVE/ALL-WHEEL DRIVE COMPONENT DIAGNOSIS AND REPAIR

106. Technician A says that automatic-locking front hubs must be driven in reverse to get them to start working before driving in forward. Technician B says that manual hubs will often not lock the front axles to the drive train until the vehicle has been driven several feet. Which technician is correct?

    a. A only
    b. B only
    c. Both A and B
    d. Neither A nor B

107. The owner of a full-size four-wheel-drive pickup truck complains that whenever turning sharply and accelerating rapidly, a severe vibration is felt. Technician A says that the transfer case may be defective. Technician B says that this is normal if conventional Cardan U-joints are used to drive the front wheels. Which technician is correct?

    a. A only
    b. B only
    c. Both A and B
    d. Neither A nor B

108. A transfer case is difficult to shift from four-wheel low to four-wheel high (range shift). Technician A says that the shift linkage or shift fork may be worn, damaged, or misadjusted. Technician B says that incorrect lubricant could be the cause. Which technician is correct?

    a. A only
    b. B only
    c. Both A and B
    d. Neither A nor B

109. Technician A says that a four-wheel-drive vehicle can be safely towed with all four wheels on the ground as long as the transfer case is in the neutral position. Technician B says that most vehicle manufacturers recommend that four-wheel-drive vehicles be towed on a flat-bed trailer to help prevent damage to the four-wheel drive components. Which technician is correct?

    a. A only
    b. B only
    c. Both A and B
    d. Neither A nor B

110. Transfer cases use what lubricant?

    a. Automatic transmission fluid (ATF)
    b. Special fluid
    c. SAE 80W-90 gear lube
    d. Any of the above depending on application

111. A transfer case is extremely noisy in all selections except in two-wheel drive and neutral (N) whenever the vehicle is moving. Technician A says that the drive chain may be stretched causing the noise as it hits the inside of the case. Technician B says that one or more of the transfer case bearings could be defective. Which technician is correct?

    a. A only
    b. B only
    c. Both A and B
    d. Neither A nor B

112. A four-wheel-drive vehicle will not go into four-wheel drive (the shift lever moves, but the front wheels are not being powered). Technician A says that the front axle coupler may not be working correctly. Technician B says that the viscous coupling between the transfer case and the rear axle could be defective. Which technician is correct?

   a. A only
   b. B only
   c. Both A and B
   d. Neither A nor B

113. A grinding sound is heard when the driver attempts to shift into four-wheel low range from four-wheel high range while traveling about 20 MPH (32 km/hr). Technician A says that the drive chain could be slipping on the sprockets and cause this sound. Technician B says that a center differential inside the transfer case could be the cause. Which technician is correct?

   a. A only
   b. B only
   c. Both A and B
   d. Neither A nor B

114. The owner of an all-wheel drive sport utility vehicle (SUV) complained that the vehicle tends to vibrate and hop when turning a corner. A visual inspection showed that the viscous coupling on the rear drive shaft was blue and looked as if it had been overheated. Which is the *most likely* cause?

   a. Mismatched tire sizes
   b. Worn output shaft bearings
   c. Frozen U-joints on the front or rear drive shaft
   d. Excessive slack in the transfer case chain

115. A four-wheel-drive vehicle is noisy in four-wheel low, but not in four-wheel high or two-wheel drive. Which is the *most likely* cause?

   a. Excessive axial play in the planetary gears
   b. A loose drive chain
   c. A defective input bearing
   d. A defective rear output bearing

116. A vehicle equipped with all-wheel drive with 20,000 miles on new tires has a blowout on the left front due to road debris. Technician A says to replace the left front tire only. Technician B says to replace both front tires. Which technician is correct?

   a. A only
   b. B only
   c. Both A and B
   d. Neither A nor B

MANUAL DRIVE TRAIN AND AXLES (A3)

CATEGORY: CLUTCH DIAGNOSIS AND REPAIR

1. **The correct answer is d.** All of the three options are correct. A weak pressure plate (answer a) can cause the clutch to slip as well as an oil-soaked clutch (friction) disc (answer b) and a sticking clutch cable (answer c), which could prevent the clutch from fully engaging.

2. **The correct answer is b.** Technician B only is correct because a lack of free play at the clutch pedal will cause the clutch to slip because it could be partially released. Technician A is not correct because excessive clutch pedal free play will not cause the clutch to shudder because while it may not fully disengage making shifting difficult, a shudder is usually caused by a fault with the clutch disc causing it to grab and release causing the shudder. Answers c and d are not correct because only Technician B is correct.

3. **The correct answer is b.** Technician B only is correct because oil or grease on the friction surface(s) of a friction disc will cause the clutch to chatter when engaged. Technician A is not correct because even though too much clutch free play could cause hard shifting due to the clutch not fully disengaging, a chattering is not likely to occur. Answers c and d are not correct because Technician B only is correct.

4. **The correct answer is c.** Both technicians are correct. Technician A is correct because if the clutch is not being fully released, some torque is being transmitted through the clutch and into the transmission making shifting difficult. Technician B is correct because too much clutch pedal free play is likely to prevent the clutch from fully disengaging creating a hard-to-shift condition. Answers a, b, and d are not correct because both technicians are correct.

5. **The correct answer is c.** Both technicians are correct. Technician A is correct because a hydraulic clutch can often be bled by simply allowing the brake fluid to flow out of the bleeder valve on the slave cylinder, which would push out any trapped air. Technician B is correct because trapped air can often be bled from the hydraulic brake system by depressing the brake pedal as the bleeder valve on the slave cylinder is opened. Answers a, b, and d are not correct because both technicians are correct.

6. **The correct answer is c.** Both technicians are correct. Technician A is correct because if the clutch is not being fully released, shifting will be difficult because engine torque is being applied to the transmission. Technician B is correct because worn synchronizer rings will often not be able to slow the faster gear enough to enable a smooth, easy shift to occur. Answers a, b, and d are not correct because both technicians are correct.

7. **The correct answer is a.** The technician should be able to rotate the output shaft when the transmission is in gear with the clutch depressed if the clutch linkage is properly adjusted. If the output shaft cannot be rotated, then the clutch should be checked before completing the installation. Answer b is not correct because the clutch is disengaged (clutch pedal depressed) during this test. Answer c is not correct because the procedure is being used to check that the clutch is properly adjusted even though a seized pilot bearing could also be detected. Answer d is not correct because the release (throw-out) bearing cannot be tested by simply checking that it can properly depress the pressure plate, but should be tested with the engine running.

8. **The correct answer is a.** Technician A only is correct because a seized pilot bearing will transfer engine torque to the input shaft of the transmission just the same as if the clutch was not disengaged making it very difficult to shift, especially in first gear or reverse. Technician B is not correct because a worn release (throw-out) bearing will likely cause noise rather than create a condition that would allow engine torque to be applied to the transmission when the clutch pedal is depressed. Answers c and d are not correct because Technician A only is correct.

9. **The correct answer is d.** Neither technician is correct. Technician A is not correct because the input bearing will usually make noise when the clutch is engaged (clutch pedal up) and not as the pedal is being depressed. The most likely cause is a defective release (throw-out) bearing. Technician B is not correct because a pilot bearing usually makes a squealing noise that will change as the clutch is depressed, but is unlikely to cause a grinding sound when the clutch pedal is lightly depressed. Answers a, b, and c are not correct because neither technician is correct.

10. **The correct answer is a.** Technician A only is correct because if the clutch is working correctly, the engine speed (RPM) should drop after a higher gear has been selected and the clutch released. Because the engine speed remains high, the clutch must be slipping. Technician B is not correct because a defective throw-out (release) bearing will make the transmission hard to shift but it would not cause the clutch to slip or the engine speed to remain high after an upshift. Answers c and d are not correct because Technician A only is correct.

11. **The correct answer is c.** Both technicians are correct. Technician A is correct because most vehicle manufacturers recommend that the flywheel be resurfaced whenever a clutch is replaced to make certain that the new friction disc will have the proper surface finish for best performance. Technician B is correct because when material is removed from the surface of the flywheel, the geometry of the release fork and release (throw-out) bearing is changed. A shim equal in thickness to the amount of material removed from the flywheel should be installed between the crankshaft and the flywheel to restore the proper clutch component geometry. Answers a, b, and d are not correct because both technicians are correct.

12. **The correct answer is b.** Technician B only is correct because the front bearing retainer, also called a quill, should be replaced so that the release (throw-out) bearing will have a smooth surface over which to move so that the proper clutch operation will be restored. Technician A is not correct because even though the bearing retainer should be replaced, this does not mean that the front bearing needs to be replaced unless defective. Answers c and d are not correct because Technician B only is correct.

13. **The correct answer is c.** Both technicians are correct. Technician A is correct because air trapped in the hydraulic clutch circuit would be compressed and would not transfer the force necessary to disengage the clutch. Technician B is correct because if the clutch master cylinder was not functioning correctly, it could not create the pressure needed to disengage the clutch. Answers a, b, and d are not correct because both technicians are correct.

14. **The correct answer is c.** Both technicians are correct. Technician A is correct because if the clutch linkage is not properly adjusted, the clutch may not be fully engaged resulting in slippage. Technician B is correct because a worn clutch or weak pressure plate can cause the clutch to slip. Answers a, b, and d are not correct because both technicians are correct.

15. **The correct answer is b.** A misadjusted clutch linkage is the most likely cause of the clutch engaging too close to the floor and not disengaging fully at times. Less free play would allow the clutch to operate as designed. Answer a is not correct because as a clutch disc wears, the free play is decreased (not increased) making it unlikely to cause the problem of engagement too close to the floor. Answers c and d are not correct because a weak pressure plate or a worn flywheel could cause the clutch to slip but will not cause the clutch to grab too close to the floor.

16. **The correct answer is d.** A misadjusted clutch switch is the least likely cause of hard shifting even though it could cause the vehicle to be able to be started without the clutch fully disengaged. Answers a, b, and c are not correct because all of them could cause difficulty shifting and are therefore not the *least likely* cause.

17. **The correct answer is d.** A squeaking sound will be heard when the clutch pedal is depressed or released if the linkage needs to be lubricated. Answer a is not correct because a release (throw-out) bearing will usually make noise as the clutch pedal is being depressed and it causes a growling sound rather than a squeaking sound. Answer b is not correct because an input shaft bearing will make noise when the clutch is engaged (foot off the pedal) and not when the clutch is depressed or released. Answer c is not correct because a cracked diaphragm spring will usually reduce the clamping force on the clutch disc and may or may not cause a growling sound when the clutch is disengaged, rather than a squeaking sound.

18. **The correct answer is a.** Oil or grease on the friction surfaces of a clutch will cause it to chatter when it is engaged (clutch pedal up). Some slippage then grip can occur creating a rapid on and off action, which causes the chatter. Answer b is not correct because a worn release (throw-out) bearing will cause a growling noise when the clutch is being disengaged (clutch pedal moving downward), but will not cause the clutch to chatter when it is engaged. Answer c is not correct because a worn clutch fork can cause the clutch pedal to grab at the wrong height but is unlikely to cause the clutch to chatter. Answer d is not correct because while a defective pilot bearing can make it difficult to shift, it will not cause the clutch to chatter.

19. **The correct answer is b.** A broken flywheel ring gear would cause the starter motor to turn but would not rotate the engine. Answer a is not correct because a slipping clutch would not affect the cranking of the engine because the clutch is disengaged (clutch pedal down) during engine cranking. Answer c is not correct because even though a seized pilot bearing could cause starter motor torque to be applied to the input shaft of the transmission even if the clutch pedal is depressed, it would not cause the starter motor to spin and not crank the engine. Answer d is not correct because an open (broken circuit) in the clutch safety switch would prevent the starter from engaging at all and could not cause the starter to spin.

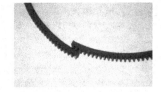

20. **The correct answer is c.** Both technicians are correct. Technician A is correct because the fluid in the hydraulic clutch assembly is able to provide the same travel as the clutch disc wears. Technician B is correct because many cable-operated clutches have mechanical mechanisms that ratchet and readjust the clutch linkage when the clutch disc wears. (Some clutches are designed so that the clutch pedal has to be pulled upward to adjust.) Answers a, b, and d are not correct because both technicians are correct.

21. **The correct answer is d.** The least likely location for clutch adjustment is near the pilot bearing. Answers a, b, and c are all not correct because they mention locations where clutch linkage (free play) adjustments can be achieved.

22. **The correct answer is a.** Technician A only is correct because a flywheel that has been overheated and contains heat cracks should be replaced because the depth of the cracks are unknown and the blue hard spots will return even if ground because the heat has changed the metallurgy of the cast iron. Technician B is not correct because the hard spots will return even if ground and the depth of the heat cracks is often deeper than could be safely removed from the friction surface of the flywheel. Answers c and d are not correct because Technician A only is correct.

23. **The correct answer is c.** Both technicians are correct. Technician A is correct because most hydraulic clutch systems are designed to use DOT 3 brake fluid. Technician B is correct because a leak anywhere in the system will cause the fluid level to drop in the hydraulic clutch master cylinder reservoir. Answers a, b, and d are not correct because both technicians are correct.

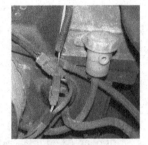

24. **The correct answer is a.** A slide hammer is being used to remove the pilot bearing from the end of the crankshaft or flywheel. Answer b is not correct because the flywheel is bolted to the crankshaft of the engine and a slide hammer is not used for removal. Answer c is not correct because a release (throw-out) bearing does not need to be centered because it is already in the center of the crankshaft or flywheel. Answer d is not correct because a slide hammer is not used to align the input shaft. An align tool is used through the clutch disc for this purpose.

25. **The correct answer is d.** The dial indicator is being used to check the lateral runout of the flywheel because the plunger of the dial indicator is pressed against the surface of the flywheel. Answer a is not correct because to measure radial runout, the dial indicator must be located on the outer edge of the flywheel instead of against the clutch friction surface. Answer b is not correct because the shim thickness needed is determined by the amount of material machined from the flywheel and is not checked using a dial indicator. Answer c is not correct because the clearance for the release (throw-out) bearing is determined after the entire clutch assembly has been installed.

26. **The correct answer is a.** Technician A is correct because the clutch friction disc must be properly aligned to allow the input shaft of the transmission to slide through the slots of the friction disc and into the pilot bearing. Technician B is not correct because the pressure plate is simply bolted to the flywheel, where the springs are compressed by the friction disc, as the bolts are tightened. Answers c and d are not correct because Technician A only is correct.

27. **The correct answer is a.** Technician A only is correct because a pilot bearing will make noise with the clutch disengaged (pedal down) and change in tone as the clutch pedal is being depressed. Technician B is not correct because an input bearing noise would be heard with the clutch engaged (foot off the clutch pedal). Answers c and d are not correct because Technician A only is correct.

28. **The correct answer is c.** Both technicians are correct. Technician A is correct because the pressure plate (clutch cover) can be warped if the retaining bolts are not loosened one turn at a time due to the forces exerted by the cover spring(s). Technician B is correct because the clutch cover (pressure plate) can become warped if the retaining bolts are not tightened one turn at a time. Answers a, b, and d are not correct because both technicians are correct.

29. **The correct answer is a.** Technician A is correct because clutch pressure plates (clutch covers) should be reinstalled in the same location as the flywheel to maintain the original balance of the pressure plate/flywheel assembly in case the assembly was balanced as an assembly. Technician B is not correct because the clutch disc is not attached to the flywheel but instead rotates with the input shaft of the transmission and therefore does not need to be marked. Answers c and d are not correct because Technician A only is correct.

30. **The correct answer is a.** The technician is using a plastic clutch disc aligning tool to center the clutch disc with the pilot bearing before the pressure plate (clutch cover) is bolted to the flywheel. Answer b is not correct because a slide hammer is often used to remove a pilot bearing. Answer c is not correct because the clutch (friction) disc is what needs to be aligned with the pilot bearing, not the pressure plate, which bolts to the flywheel. Answer d is not correct because the tool being used is not designed to measure the depth of the pressure plate spring fingers.

31. **The correct answer is c.** Both technicians are correct. Technician A is correct because several fingers are broken off of the diaphragm spring of the pressure plate, which cannot be repaired and therefore, the assembly must be replaced. Technician B is correct because the release (throw-out) bearing rides on the fingers of the diaphragm spring and would be damaged by the broken spring. Answers a, b, and d are not correct because both technicians are correct.

32. **The correct answer is a.** Technician A only is correct because a clutch fork can be reused if it is not cracked or excessively worn or damaged. Technician B is not correct because even though a clutch fork could be replaced, it is usually not necessary until it is bent or damaged. Answers c and d are not correct because Technician A only is correct.

33. **The correct answer is b.** The clutch aligning tool is used to make sure that the splines in the center of the clutch disc are aligned with the pilot bearing or bushing. Then, when the transmission is installed, the input shaft can be easily inserted through the clutch disc and into the pilot bearing. Answer a is not correct because while these two parts (throw-out bearing and pressure plate) are in line, an aligning tool is not needed for the installation of the transmission. Answer c is not correct because the clutch disc needs to be aligned with the pilot bearing, whereas the pressure plate is then installed using the bolts in the flywheel and this cannot be changed. Answer d is not correct because the throw-out bearing is around the input shaft of the transmission and rests on the fingers of the pressure plate, but it is not necessary for these two to be aligned as is the clutch disc with the pilot bearing.

34. **The correct answer is c.** An input shaft bearing will usually make a growling sound when the clutch pedal is up and the engine is running. Answer a is not correct because a release (throw-out) bearing will usually make noise when the clutch pedal is being depressed rather than when the clutch pedal is up. Answer b is not correct because a squeaking sound (not a growling sound) is often heard at the clutch fork and pivot points with the engine running and the clutch engaged (clutch pedal up) if the pivot points are not lubricated. Answer d is not correct because a pilot bearing will cause a squealing sound as the clutch pedal is being depressed.

35. **The correct answer is a.** Technician A only is correct because air can be trapped in the slave cylinder making it very difficult to bleed all of the air out of the hydraulic clutch system unless it is repositioned to allow the air to escape. Technician B is not correct because even though the clutch may need to be replaced, the most common problem is air trapped in the system when the clutch master cylinder was replaced.

36. **The correct answer is c.** Both technicians are correct. Technician A is correct because a defective or excessively worn clutch can cause the engine to increase in speed and not power the vehicle when the clutch is engaged (pedal up). Technician B is correct because a dual-mass flywheel consists of a primary section attached to the engine and the secondary section, which is attached to the clutch separated by springs and dampers. If these dampening devices fail, torque is not transferred from the engine to the clutch. Answers a, b, and d are not correct because both technicians are correct.

MANUAL DRIVE TRAIN AND AXLES (A3)

CATEGORY: TRANSMISSION DIAGNOSIS AND REPAIR

37. **The correct answer is c.** The front bearing retainer (quill) cannot be removed without first removing the transmission/transaxle from the vehicle. Answers a, b, and d are not correct because the vehicle speed sensor, reverse light connector, and the drive axle shafts can all usually be removed without having to remove the unit from the vehicle.

38. **The correct answer is b.** Technician B only is correct because too thick a lubricant can cause difficult shifting into all gears especially when cold. Technician A is not correct because a worn brass blocking-ring, while it could cause difficult shifting, would not cause a shifting problem in all gears, but rather just the gear that uses the worn blocking ring. Answers c and d are not correct because Technician B only is correct.

39. **The correct answer is b.** High-temperature grease is the only lubricant listed that is not used in a manual transmission/transaxle. Answers a, c, and d are not correct because depending on the vehicle manufacturer and year, manual transmissions and transaxles may use ATF, SAE 80W-90 gear lube, or engine oil (usually SAE 5W-30).

40. **The correct answer is a.** The front bearing retainer (quill) should be replaced because it also contains the outer race for the bearing or replace the outer bearing cup if replaceable. Answer b is not correct because the bearing can be replaced as a separate unit and the synchronizer assembly does not need to be replaced unless damaged. Answer c is not correct because the thrust washer, while it may have to be replaced to achieve the specified clearance, is not a necessary part that has to be replaced when the bearing is replaced. Answer d is not correct because the bearing can usually be replaced as a separate item without requiring the replacement of the entire input shaft assembly.

41. **The correct answer is b.** Technician B only is correct because engine torque is applied through the countershaft in all forward gears except fourth, where it goes straight through the main shaft. Technician A is not correct because main shaft bearings or speed gear bearings would be noisy in all gears. Answers c and d are not correct because Technician B only is correct.

42. **The correct answer is c.** Both technicians are correct. Technician A is correct because a cracked or worn shift fork will make it difficult to shift into the gear selected because it will not apply the correct force on the synchronizer sleeve or may not move it enough to complete the shift. Technician B is correct because if the speed gears can move on the main shaft, the synchronizer sleeve may not be able to move far enough to complete the shift. Answers a, b, and d are not correct because both technicians are correct.

43. **The correct answer is b.** The technician is installing the synchronizer keys and springs between the hub and the sleeve. Answer a is not correct because a thrust washer is a flat piece that is lubricated by the lube in the transmission. Answer c is not correct because while a shift fork does operate (move) the synchronizer sleeve, it is not being adjusted for clearance. Answer d is not correct because the hub and the sleeve are being assembled and not the speed gear.

44. **The correct answer is b.** Technician B only is correct because if the clutch is not fully released, engine torque is being applied to the transmission making shifting difficult or impossible. Technician A is not correct because a blocking ring would affect the shifting into one gear only. Answers c and d are not correct because Technician B only is correct.

45. **The correct answer is d.** A cracked synchronizer (blocking) ring can cause the transmission to jump out of fifth gear because the backward cut taper on the sleeve would not be able to keep the ring engaged during acceleration and deceleration. Answer a is not correct because, while a worn input shaft bearing could cause noise, it is unlikely to cause the transmission to jump out of fifth gear. Answer b is not correct because even though a worn shift lever could cause incomplete shifting, it is unlikely to cause the transmission to jump out of fifth gear. Answer c is not correct because low lubricating oil level can cause excessive wear, but is unlikely to cause the transmission to jump out of fifth gear.

46. **The correct answer is a.** Technician A only is correct because the sharp tips of the snap ring must be installed up so that snap-ring pliers can grasp the ends of the ring for removal in the future. Technician B is not correct because if the snap ring were to be installed upside down, it is very difficult for the snap-ring pliers to grasp the ends without slipping. Answers c and d are not correct because Technician A only is correct.

47. **The correct answer is d.** A bearing splitter is being used to press gears and/or bearings off the shaft. Answers a, b, and c are not correct because they do not correctly identify the use and purpose of a bearing splitter.

48. **The correct answer is a.** This is a reverse (backup) light switch, which makes contact when the shifter is moved to the reverse position. Answer b is not correct because a neutral safety switch is not used on manual transmission vehicles. Answer c is not correct because the clutch safety switch is usually located on the clutch linkage and not on the transmission. Answer d is not correct because the switch is located near the shifter at the top of the transmission instead of near the output shaft.

49. **The correct answer is a.** Technician A only is correct because the speedometer gear(s) must be changed to provide the proper speedometer reading if the rear axle ratio has been changed. Technician B is not correct because the gears attach to the output shaft and are either a press fit requiring that the plastic gears be heated in water before installation or are a slip fit and retained by a clip. Answers c and d are not correct because Technician A only is correct.

50. **The correct answer is d.** If the vent hose became clogged with mud, the movement of the gears through the lubricating oil could cause an increase in pressure, and the pressure is likely to force the oil past the seals creating a transmission fluid leak. Answers a, b, and c are not correct because a clogged transmission vent is unlikely to cause hard shifting (answer a), gear noise (answer b), or a vibration (answer c).

51. **The correct answer is a.** The synchronizer assembly is the component inside the manual transmission that is the least likely to fail due to lack of lubrication because there is very little movement between the components and they do not transfer any engine torque. Answers b and c are not correct because the bearings must be able to support and operate under the forces of the engine and drivetrain and will likely overheat and fail due to lack of lubrication. Answer d is not correct because the shift fork is stationary but it can rub against the synchronizer sleeve creating heat and wear if not properly lubricated.

52. **The correct answer is c.** The most likely cause for the breakup of a gear inside a manual transmission is a shock load that can occur if the clutch were engaged with the engine at high RPM (high torque) with the drive wheels on dry pavement. Answer a is not correct because even though speed shifting can cause damage, it is not likely to break a speed gear, which requires a shock load and maximum traction or resistance in the drivetrain. Answers b and d are not correct because the engine torque is not being applied to the gears under high traction conditions.

MANUAL DRIVE TRAIN AND AXLES (A3)

CATEGORY: TRANSAXLE DIAGNOSIS AND REPAIR

53. **The correct answer is c.** A defective output shaft bearing(s) is not likely to cause gear clash even though it could cause noise while driving. Answer a is not correct because a worn blocking ring can cause gear clash when shifting into the gear with the worn ring. Answer b is not correct because a misadjusted clutch linkage could cause the clutch to not fully disengage thereby causing gear clash whenever shifting into any gear. Answer d is not correct because a defective pilot bearing could keep the input shaft turning even when the clutch has been depressed causing gear clash whenever shafting into any gear.

54. **The correct answer is c.** Both technicians are correct. Technician A is correct because a feeler gauge is used to measure how far the ring travels up onto the ramp of the speed gear. If the measurement is less than specified, the blocking ring should be replaced. Technician B is correct because the blocking ring forces the speed gear to rotate at the same speed as the previous gear thereby allowing a smooth shift. If the blocking ring is worn, a gear clash can result when shifting. Answers a, b, and d are not correct because both technicians are correct.

55. **The correct answer is d.** Dirty or corroded shift linkage is the most likely cause for a complaint of excessive force needed to move the shifter. Answer a is not correct even though a seized pilot bearing can make it difficult to get the transmission into gear especially first and reverse, but it could not cause the linkage to be difficult to move. Answers b and c are not correct because even though a misadjusted clutch or worn release bearing could cause difficulty getting into a gear, they would not cause the linkage to be difficult to move.

56. **The correct answer is b.** A defective input shaft bearing will make a growling sound with the engine running and the clutch engaged. Answer a is not correct because even though excessive main shaft endplay may cause shifting problems, it will not cause a growling noise. Answer c is not correct because a defective output bearing will cause a growling sound as the vehicle is being driven and not when the transaxle is in neutral. Answer d is not correct because not only do few transaxles use a pilot bearing but if it did, it would make a squealing sound, which would change as the clutch pedal is depressed.

57. **The correct answer is c.** Both technicians are correct. Technician A is correct because the shim would affect input shaft endplay. Technician B is correct because the shim is used to provide the proper bearing preload and is determined by following the manufacturer's recommended procedures. The thicker the shim is behind the bearing cup, the greater the bearing preload. Answers a, b, and d are not correct because both technicians are correct.

58. **The correct answer is d.** Neither technician is correct. Technician A is not correct because the case halves should not be closed by tightening the retaining bolts. The bolts are used to simply keep the two halves of the transaxle case together. Technician B is not correct because even though RTV silicone is often used as the seal between the case halves of a transaxle, the gap is excessive. The reason for the gap must be determined and corrected before installing the retaining bolts so as to provide the proper shaft endplay and bearing preload measurements. Answers a, b, and c are not correct because neither technician is correct.

59. **The correct answer is b.** Hydraulic oil is not used in manual transaxles nor recommended by vehicle manufacturers. Answers a, c, and d are not correct because these may be specified for use by vehicle manufacturers in manual transaxles.

60. **The correct answer is c.** The driver is being used to seat the bearing cup into the bearing pocket of a transaxle. Answer a is not correct because if the case is warped, it must be replaced and the tool being used would not, or could not, be used to straighten a transaxle case. Answer b is not correct because the countershaft meshes with the main shaft and is installed as an assembly into the case of the transaxle. Answer d is not correct because the bearings are usually lubricated by splashed oil and the tool is not a lubricating tool.

61. **The correct answer is a.** The two screwdrivers are being used to slide the speed gear and synchronizer off of the shaft. A press is sometimes needed to perform this operation and a press should be used to reinstall the gears onto the shaft. Answer b is not correct because the free play in the synchronizer is not adjustable and can only be checked for wear by using a feeler gauge. Answer c is not correct because the clearance is determined by using a feeler gauge instead of two screwdrivers. Answer d is not correct because most snap rings are removed using snap-ring pliers. If two screwdrivers are used to remove a snap ring, they would have to be close together to grab the opening of the snap ring and not opposite each other as shown.

62. **The correct answer is b.** A feeler gauge is being used to check the gear thrust clearance to determine the correct thickness of selective snap ring to use to permit the specified clearance. Answer a is not correct because the feeler gauge is not being inserted between the blocking ring and the speed gear. Answer c is not correct because output shaft runout is determined by using a dial indicator on the shaft as it is revolved between two V-blocks. Answer d is not correct because a micrometer is used to measure the thickness of snap rings.

63. **The correct answer is c.** A lack of lubricating oil is the most likely cause for this transaxle to overheat and cause the excessive wear to the gears. Answer a is not correct because even though slipping the clutch can cause excessive heat to be generated, it is unlikely that enough heat would be transferred to the transaxle to cause the damage shown. Answer b is not correct because worn synchronizer sleeve(s) would cause the transaxle to be difficult to shift but would not cause it to overheat. Answer d is not correct because a defective bearing will usually cause noise and while it could create excessive heat, not enough heat to damage the gears if the proper amount of lubricating oil was installed in the transaxle.

64. **The correct answer is a.** A defective pilot bearing is the least likely to cause noise in all gears because most transaxles do not use a pilot bearing and if it did, it would make a squealing noise that changes when the clutch is depressed and not in every gear as the vehicle is being driven. Answers b, c, and d are not correct because all of the bearings could be the cause of excessive noise in all gears if defective.

65. **The correct answer is a.** Paper friction material works best with automatic transmission fluid and may not work correctly if SAE 80W-90 gear lube is used. Answers b, c, and d are not correct because many transaxles use engine oil or automatic transmission fluid and these are compatible with paper-type blocker rings.

CATEGORY: DRIVE SHAFT/HALF SHAFT AND UNIVERSAL JOINT/CV JOINT DIAGNOSIS AND REPAIR

66. **The correct answer is c.** Both technicians are correct. Technician A is correct because the drive shaft yoke can bind on the output shaft when the vehicle stops and then accelerates. The movement of the rear end (downward when stopped and upward when accelerating) creates the bind if the splines are not lubricated. Technician B is correct because the rubber surrounding mount, which is part of the center support bearing assembly, can fail which would cause a clunk sound during rapid acceleration. Answers a, b, and d are not correct because both technicians are correct.

67. **The correct answer is c.** Unequal U-joint working angles will cause a launch shutter, which is felt mostly during rapid acceleration from a stop. Answer a is not correct because an out-of-balance drive shaft will be most noticeable at highway speeds. Answer b is not correct because excessive U-joint working angles will usually cause a vibration that increases as the vehicle speed increases and not when first accelerating. Answer d is not correct because a brinelled U-joint may cause a noise when a drive gear is selected and may squeak but is not likely to cause the vehicle to shutter when first being accelerated.

68. **The correct answer is c.** A worn or defective outer CV joint will make a clicking sound especially when the vehicle is turning a corner at low speed. Answers a and b are not correct because a wheel bearing usually makes a rumbling or growling sound. Answer d is not correct because a clunking noise is often heard from a defective inner (not outer) CV joint.

69. **The correct answer is a.** The last step before installing the drive axle shaft into the vehicle after replacing the CV joint boot is to burp out any trapped air from within the boot and then tighten the retaining clamp. Answer b is not correct because chassis grease should not be used to lubricate CV joints. Answers c and d are not correct because these operations should be performed during disassembly and not reassembly.

70. **The correct answer is b.** Spline bind is prevented by lubricating the drive shaft slip yoke. This prevents noise when accelerating from a stop when the drive shaft angle changes slightly due to the torque of the engine being applied to the rear end. Answer a is not correct because while it will stop a clunking sound when first accelerating, it will not eliminate or cause a vibration. Answer c is not correct because even though the spline may rust if not lubricated, the primary purpose of the grease is to prevent the splines from binding. Answer d is not correct because the transmission fluid is sealed between the outer surface of the yoke and the extension housing and not on the inside of the output shaft.

71. **The correct answer is c.** Both technicians are correct. Technician A is correct because the inner race of the bearing is the axle shaft itself and if this surface is worn by the bearing, the entire axle must be replaced. Technician B is correct because the rear axle seal should be replaced when the bearing is replaced to prevent rear axle fluid leaks. Answers a, b, and d are not correct because both technicians are correct.

72. **The correct answer is a.** Technician A only is correct because the splines of the drive axle shaft mesh with the splines of the hub bearing assembly, which transfers engine torque to the drive wheels. The drive axle shaft must be separated from the hub bearing or the hub bearing removed from the drive axle shaft before the CV joint can be replaced. Technician B is not correct because the outer CV joint is not bolted to the drive axle shaft but is splined to the shaft. Answers c and d are not correct because only Technician A is correct.

73. **The correct answer is d.** Neither technician is correct. Technician A is not correct because defective wheel bearings usually make a growling or rumbling sound. Technician B is not correct because a defective inner CV joint usually makes a clunking sound but not usually when cornering. Answer c is not correct because neither technician is correct.

74. **The correct answer is c.** Both technicians are correct. Technician A is correct because the boot will definitely need to be replaced. Technician B is correct because depending on how long the boot has been torn and how much wear has occurred to the CV joint due to a lack of lubrication, the joint or the entire drive axle shaft may need to be replaced. Answer d is not correct because both technicians are correct.

75. **The correct answer is a.** Technician A only is correct because the grease that is supplied with the boot kit or CV joint assembly is the only grease that should be used because it is formulated to provide the maximum protection based on the exact application. Technician B is not correct because chassis grease does not contain the additive necessary to protect the CV joint and may not be compatible with the CV joint boot material. Answers c and d are not correct because Technician A only is correct.

76. **The correct answer is b.** A collapsed engine or transmission mount is the most likely cause of unequal drive shaft U-joint angles. Answer a is not correct because a bent drive shaft will cause a vibration but cannot cause the working angles of the U-joints to change. Answer c is not correct because even though a dry (non-lubricated) shaft spline can cause noise during acceleration from a stop, it cannot cause unequal U-joint angles. Answer d is not correct because defective or damaged U-joints will not cause the working angles to change.

77. **The correct answer is c.** Worn CV-joints are not likely to cause a vibration at highway speeds even though they could cause noise. Answers a, b, and d can all create a vibration at highway speeds.

78. **The correct answer is d.** Neither technician is correct. Technician A is not correct because the weight is used to dampen certain frequencies that may be created under certain conditions. The weight may or may not be needed on the replacement drive axle shaft because the design of the replacement may be different enough as to not need the weight. The weight should not be transferred to the replacement shaft if the replacement does not come with the damper weight. Technician B is not correct because the weight is not used to balance the drive axle shaft but to simply dampen vibration. Answers a, b, and c are not correct because neither technician is correct.

79. **The correct answer is a.** A wooden dowel rod is being used to rotate the inner bearing race so the balls can be removed for cleaning and inspection. Answer b is not correct because grease does not have to be pressed into the bearings with force in a CV joint. Answer c is not correct because clearances are too close to measure and this is why CV joints are serviced as an assembly rather than as separate replaceable parts. Answer d is not correct because the splines will be aligned okay when the joint is assembled and no alignment is necessary.

80. **The correct answer is a.** Technician A only is correct because a torque wrench must be used to properly crimp the retaining clamps on CV joints that use hard plastic boots. Technician B is not correct because most vehicle manufacturers recommend that the CV joint be disassembled, thoroughly cleaned and inspected before replacing the boot. A split-type boot is used when the CV joint does not have to be removed. But it is very difficult if not impossible to thoroughly clean and inspect the joints without removing it from the vehicle. Answers c and d are not correct because Technician A only is correct.

81. **The correct answer is b.** A special tool is being used to push the drive axle from the splines of the hub bearing assembly. Answer a is not correct because the hub bearing is not a press fit onto the splines of the axle shaft. Answer c is not correct because the outer CV joint cannot be removed until the drive axle shaft has been removed from the hub bearing assembly. Answer d is not correct because the CV joint boot has to be installed before the drive axle shaft is installed. The tool is being used to remove the drive axle shaft and is not being used to install a CV joint boot.

82. **The correct answer is b.** Technician B only is correct because the weight of the screw mechanism on the hose clamp(s) is often enough to bring an out-of-balance drive shaft into balance. Technician A is not correct because composite drive shafts do not need extra support. Answers c and d are not correct because Technician B only is correct.

83. **The correct answer is b.** Technician B only is correct because the torque is transferred through the hollow drive shaft on the surface and any dent on this surface can cause it to collapse if enough engine torque is applied. Technician A is not correct because a dented drive shaft must be replaced to avoid its failure. Answers c and d are not correct because Technician B only is correct.

84. **The correct answer is c.** Both technicians are correct. Technician A is correct because to prevent driveline vibration, the front and rear U-joint working angles must be within 0.5 degree of each other. Technician B is correct because a collapsed transmission mount can cause the angles to change possibly causing a vibration felt at highway speeds. Answers a, b, and d are not correct because both technicians are correct.

85. **The correct answer is b.** Shims under the transmission mount or a wedge under the leaf springs at the rear of the vehicle can be used to correct or adjust drive shaft U-joint working angles. Answer a is not correct because the working angle of a U-joint is not changed if the U-joint itself is replaced. Answer c is not correct because the relationship between the front and the rear U-joints remain the same even if the slip yoke is changed at the output shaft of the transmission. Answer d is not correct because tightening the differential pinion nut will not change the working angles of the U-joints.

86. **The correct answer is c.** Both technicians are correct. Technician A is correct because a worn U-joint can make a clunk sound when the excessive clearance is taken up when the transmission is shifted to drive or reverse or from reverse to drive. Technician B is correct because a worn U-joint would often make a squeaking sound in reverse because the rollers are being moved in a direction which is opposite where most of the wear has occurred. Answers a, b, and d are not correct because both technicians are correct.

CATEGORY: DRIVE AXLE DIAGNOSIS AND REPAIR

87. **The correct answer is b.** Technician B only is correct because the level of the gear lube should be at the bottom of the fill hole and if filled higher could cause the fluid to be aerated (filled with air) thereby reducing the efficiency of the lubricant. Technician A is not correct because the rear end is overfilled and this can cause the fluid to be filled with air caused by the gears spinning inside the housing leading to a decrease in lubrication effectiveness. Answers c and d are not correct because Technician B only is correct.

88. **The correct answer is d.** As the thickness of the shim increases, the pinion gear moves toward the rear and closer to the ring gear thereby closer to the toe. Answer a is not correct because the pattern will be more toward the toe rather than the face of the drive side of the ring gear. Answer b is not correct because the pattern will be more toward the toe rather than the heel of the drive side of the ring gear. Answer c is not correct because the pattern will be toward the toe rather than the flank of the drive side of the ring gear.

89. **The correct answer is a.** The backlash is reduced if the ring gear is moved closer to the pinion drive gear. Answer b is not correct because the backlash would increase (rather than decrease) if the ring gear were farther from the pinion drive gear. Answer c is not correct even though shims are often used to move the position of the ring gear, because adding shims of equal thickness behind the side gears would simply increase bearing preload and not change the relationship between the ring gear and pinion drive gear. Answer d is not correct because removing a shim from the pinion gear would tend to increase rather than decrease backlash.

90. **The correct answer is b.** The C-clip, which retains the drive axle, is either being removed or installed. Answers a, c, and d are not correct because even though the axles have to be removed to remove or install the ring gear, side bearing, and pinion gear, the best answer is that the axle is being removed or installed.

91. **The correct answer is a.** Technician A only is correct because as a vehicle turns a corner, vehicle weight is shifted placing a greater load on the axle bearing on the right side as the vehicle turns to the left. Technician B is not correct because side bearings are close to the center of the vehicle and do not support the weight of the vehicle and therefore would not be likely to be affected during cornering. Answers c and d are not correct because Technician A only is correct.

92. **The correct answer is b.** Technician B only is correct because the gear teeth pattern can detect incorrect pinion depth. Technician A is not correct because backlash and side bearing preload are two different issues that the service technician must address whenever adjusting a differential. It is normal operating procedure to achieve the proper backlash first, then add equal shims (or rotate the adjuster) on both side bearings to achieve the proper bearing preload. Answers c and d are not correct because Technician B only is correct.

93. **The correct answer is b.** Technician B only is correct because most vehicle manufacturers recommend the use of SAE 80W-90 gear lube with or without an additional limited-slip additive. Technician A is not correct because except for very few exceptions, SAE 80W-140 is not used in passenger vehicles or light truck applications because it is too thick (high viscosity) to achieve acceptable fuel economy. Answers c and d are not correct because Technician B only is correct.

94. **The correct answer is d.** The sound of a defective wheel or axle bearing is a rumble or growling sound that is often very similar to the sound of a winter tire with an aggressive tread design. Answers a, b, and c are not correct because the sound is a growling or rumble sound.

95. The correct answer is c. Both technicians are correct. Technician A is correct because the pattern will detect if the pinion depth is correct. Technician B is correct because backlash will be indicated on the tooth pattern even though it should also be checked using a dial indicator. Answers a, b, and d are not correct because both technicians are correct.

96. The correct answer is a. Technician A only is correct because pinion depth is determined by how far the pinion gear extends into the housing and this is adjusted by using various thickness of shims between the pinion gear and the pinion bearing. Technician B is not correct because the pinion depth is not adjusted using the drive pinion nut. The drive pinion nut is used to provide the correct amount of preload to the pinion bearing. Answers c and d are not correct because Technician A only is correct.

97. The correct answer is c. All vehicle manufacturers recommend the use of a long-handled holding tool and hand tools to remove and install the drive pinion nut. Answer a is not correct because using an air impact can cause damage to the drive pinion bearing and/or seat. Answer b is not correct because a torque wrench should not be used to remove fasteners. Answer d is not correct because the pinion nut is a treaded fastener and a gear puller will cannot be used to remove the pinion nut.

98. The correct answer is a. The ring gear bolts are usually specified to be replaced when the ring gear and pinion are replaced because of the tremendous forces that are exerted on these hardened fasteners. Answer b is not correct because the side bearings may need to be replaced and many service technicians do replace all differential bearings when major service work is being performed, but it is not required that they be replaced. Answer c is not correct because even though many service technicians recommend that all seals be replaced, it is not required. Answer d is not correct because even though the pinion bearing is often replaced when the ring gear and pinion are replaced, it is not required.

99. The correct answer is b. Answer b is correct because side gears must be preloaded to help because torque tends to move the ring gear and the preload will maintain the proper fit between the ring gear and pinion. The lubricant helps keep heat and expansion under control. Answer a is not correct because if the bearings were loose, the proper wear pattern between the ring gear pinions could not be maintained. Answer c is not correct because while the bearing caps have to be torqued to factory specification, the bearing preload is determined by checking the backlash. Answer d is not correct because a bore gauge is not used to check for bearing preload as it can only check that a cylinder or bore is round.

100. The correct answer is d. The pinion (spider) gears thrust washers will wear because the different tire sizes will cause the differential case to rotate. The pinions will be spinning and wear will occur on the thrust washers underneath the pinion gears. Answer a is not correct because the drive pinion bearing attaches to the drive shaft and rotates the same as the drive shaft regardless of tire size or other factors that occur. Answer b is not correct because the side bearings are splined to the axles and while they will be rotating at slightly different speeds, this difference is taken up by the rotation of the pinion (spider) gears. Answer c is not correct because the rear axle bearings are not affected by the different size tires.

101. The correct answer is b. Technician B only is correct because the differential housing vent tubes of most four-wheel-drive vehicles are located higher than the differential housing to prevent water getting into the vents if driving through high water. Rubber hoses usually extend from the differential housing or axle housing upward above the level of the top of the tires. Technician A is not correct because the rear axle seals would not only prevent the loss of rear end lubricant, but would also prevent water from entering into the rear end components. Answers c and d are not correct because Technician B only is correct.

102. The correct answer is b. To remove a C-clip-type axle, the retaining bolts do not have to be removed because this type of axle does not use a retainer. Answers a, c, and d are not correct because the differential cover (answer a), differential pinion shaft (answer c), and the differential pinion shaft lock pin (answer d) must all be removed to remove the axle.

103. **The correct answer is c.** The pinion shaft rotating torque is being measured using an inch-pound torque wrench. The pinion nut should be tightened until the specified rotating torque is achieved assuring that the pinion bearing has the correct preload. Answer a is not correct because the pinion nut requires a lot more torque than can be achieved using an inch-pound torque wrench. Answer b is not correct because a dial indicator attached to the ring gear is used to check for proper backlash. Answer d is not correct because the pinion seal is installed before the driver flange.

104. **The correct answer is d.** The pinion gear does not have to be removed to replace a pinion seal. Answers a, b, and c are not correct because the drive shaft (answer a), drive flange (answer b), and pinion seal (answer c) all have to be removed before a replacement seal can be installed

105. **The correct answer is a.** Technician A only is correct because the dial indicator is pressing against a gear tooth and the technician is rotating the ring gear checking for the amount of free play or backlash that exists between the ring gear and pinion. Technician B is not correct because to check for ring gear runout, the tip of the dial indicator has to be touching the side of the ring gear and not a gear tooth. Answers c and d are not correct because Technician A only is correct.

CATEGORY: FOUR-WHEEL DRIVE/ALL-WHEEL DRIVE COMPONENT DIAGNOSIS AND REPAIR

106. **The correct answer is b.** Technician B only is correct because manually locking front hubs may not lock until the vehicle has been driven several feet. This can be an issue if the vehicle gets stuck before the selector is placed in four wheel drive because the front hubs may not engage because the vehicle cannot be driven far enough (usually one revolution of the tires) to engage the hubs to transmit engine torque to the front wheels. Technician A is not correct because automatic locking hubs do not require the vehicle to be driven in reverse to disengage. Answers c and d are not correct because Technician B only is correct.

107. **The correct answer is b.** Technician B only is correct because conventional Cardan U-joints will cause a vibration if the front wheels are turned to an angle where the joint will cause the tire to speed up and slow down as it rotates creating a vibration. This is normal and no harm is done. Four-wheel drive should be selected when slippery conditions are present and the tires could slip, easily avoiding the severe vibration. Technician A is not correct because this type of fault is usually associated with drive shaft joints. Answers c and d are not correct because Technician B only is correct.

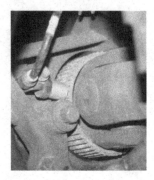

108. **The correct answer is c.** Both technicians are correct. Technician A is correct because a misadjusted, damaged, or worn shift linkage can cause the transfer case to be difficult to shift from one range to another range. Technician B is correct because if the incorrect lubricant were used in the transfer case, the range shift could be difficult. Answers a, b, and d are not correct because both technicians are correct.

109. **The correct answer is c.** Both technicians are correct. Technician A is correct because some vehicle manufacturers state that the vehicle can be towed with all four wheels on the ground if the transfer case is in neutral (if equipped). Technician B is correct because most vehicle manufacturers recommend that all four-wheel-drive vehicles be transported on a flat-bed trailer or towed with dollies so that all four wheels are off the ground. Answers a, b, and d are not correct because both technicians are correct.

110. **The correct answer is d.** Any of the above is correct depending on the application. Answer a is correct because most transfer cases require automatic transmission fluid (ATF). Answer b is also correct because some transfer cases require a specified fluid. Answer c is correct because some older units use SAE 80W-90 gear lube.

111. **The correct answer is c.** Both technicians are correct. Technician A is correct because a stretched drive chain could cause noise because engine torque is applied through the chain when in four-wheel-drive mode. Technician B is correct because defective bearings could cause transfer case noise, especially when high torque loads are applied to the transfer case. Answers a, b, and d are not correct because both technicians are correct.

112. **The correct answer is a.** Technician A only is correct because if the front-drive axle shaft coupler is not engaged, the front wheels will not be powered even though the transfer case was properly shifted into four-wheel drive. Technician B is not correct because if the viscous coupling were defective, it would become disconnected and not transfer engine torque to the rear drive wheels. Answers c and d are not correct because Technician A only is correct.

113. **The correct answer is d.** Neither technician is correct. Technician A is not correct because this condition is normal and most transfer cases should not be shifted into low range without either stopping completely or traveling at a very low speed. Technician B is not correct because even though the drive chain could be slipping over the teeth of the sprockets, it is more likely to be normal for the noise to occur if a shift into four-wheel drive low range is attempted while driving. The noise is created by the teeth of the range hub attempting to mesh with the internal splines of the gear set as shown. Answers a, b, and c are not correct because neither technician is correct.

114. **The correct answer is a.** Mismatched tires will create a condition where the front and rear drive axles could be rotating at different speeds. It is the purpose and function of the viscous coupling to allow for a slight amount of slippage to occur but it will quickly become overheated if the difference in speeds continues. Answer b is not correct because worn bearings would create excessive noise but will not cause the rear drive shaft to rotate at a different speed than the front drive shaft, thereby creating the condition, which will cause the viscous coupling to overheat. Answer c is not correct because even though frozen U-joints could cause drive train vibration, they will not affect the operation of the viscous coupling. Answer d is not correct because a worn transfer case drive chain will usually cause noise but will not create unequal rotation speeds of the front and rear drive shafts that would cause the viscous coupling to overheat.

115. **The correct answer is a.** Excessive axial play in the planetary gear set is the most likely cause because engine torque is applied through the gears when in low range, whereas the entire planetary gear set rotates as an assembly when in four wheel drive high. Answer b is not correct because a loose drive chain would tend to be noisy in both four-wheel high and four-wheel low position. Answer c is not correct because a defective input bearing would tend to be noisy in all gears not just four-wheel drive low. Answer d is not correct because a defective rear output bearing would tend to be noisy in all gear positions rather than just in four-wheel drive low.

116. **The correct answer is d.** Neither technician is correct. Technician A is not correct because the tire size should be within 0.5 percent or about 1/16 in. tread depth difference according to vehicle manufacturer's specifications to avoid problems with a four-wheel drive system. Technician B is not correct because the rear tires should also be replaced to keep all four tires within the specified rolling circumference. Answers a, b, and c are not correct because neither technician is correct.

SUSPENSION AND STEERING TEST CONTENT AREAS

This ASE study guide for Suspension and Steering (A4) is divided into the sub-content areas that correlate to the actual ASE certification test as follows:

CONTENT AREA	QUESTIONS IN TEST	NUMBER OF STUDY GUIDE QUESTIONS
A. Steering Systems Diagnosis and Repair	10	28 (1–28)
1. Steering Columns and Manual Steering Gears (3)		
2. Power-Assisted Steering Units (4)		
3. Steering Linkage (3)		
B. Suspension Systems Diagnosis and Repair	11	30 (29–58)
1. Front Suspensions (6)		
2. Rear Suspensions (5)		
C. Related Suspension and Steering Service	2	4 (59–62)
D. Wheel Alignment Diagnosis, Adjustment, and Repair	12	33 (63–95)
E. Wheel and Tire Diagnosis and Repair	5	15 (96–110)
TOTAL	**40**	**110**

TIME ALLOWED TO TAKE THE TEST

The allocated time to take the Suspension and Steering (A4) Certification test is 60 minutes. ASE adds 10 additional questions to the test for research purposes for a total of 50 questions. These questions do not count toward your score, but they are embedded within the test and there is no way of knowing which ones do not count. As a result, the technician needs to answer 50 questions in 60 minutes, or about one question per minute.

If taking the recertification A4 test, there are just 20 questions with no additional research questions included. The time allocated to take the recertification test is 30 minutes, which means about one minute per question.

BEFORE USING THIS STUDY GUIDE

Before trying to answer the questions and looking at the explanations, look over the following list of the content that ASE states will be covered in the certification test. For best results using this study guide, check service information or consult an automotive textbook for details on any of the content areas that are not familiar before trying to answer the questions. For additional information about the ASE test, visit the website at **www.ase.com**.

SUSPENSION AND STEERING (A4) CERTIFICATION TEST

A. STEERING SYSTEMS DIAGNOSIS AND REPAIR (10 QUESTIONS)

1. Steering Columns and Manual Steering Gears (3 questions)

1. Diagnose steering column noises and steering effort concerns (including manual and electronic tilt and telescoping mechanisms); determine needed repairs.
2. Diagnose manual steering gear (non-rack and pinion type) noises, binding, vibration, freeplay, steering effort, and lubricant leakage concerns; determine needed repairs.
3. Diagnose manual rack and pinion steering gear noises, binding, vibration, freeplay, steering effort, and lubricant leakage concerns; determine needed repairs.
4. Inspect and replace steering column, steering shaft U-joint(s), flexible coupling(s), collapsible columns, steering wheels (includes steering wheels with air bags and/or other steering wheel mounted controls and components).
5. Remove and replace manual steering gear (non-rack and pinion type) (includes vehicles equipped with air bags and/or other steering wheel mounted controls and components).
6. Adjust manual steering gear (non-rack and pinion type) worm bearing preload and sector lash.
7. Remove and replace manual rack and pinion steering gear (includes vehicles equipped with air bags and/or other steering wheel mounted controls and components).
8. Adjust manual rack and pinion steering gear.
9. Inspect and replace manual rack and pinion steering gear inner tie rod ends (sockets) and bellows boots.
10. Inspect and replace manual rack and pinion steering gear mounting bushings and brackets.

2. Power-Assisted Steering Units (4 questions)

1. Diagnose power steering gear (non-rack and pinion type) noises, binding, vibration, freeplay, steering effort, steering pull (lead), and fluid leakage concerns; determine needed repairs
2. Diagnose power rack and pinion steering gear noises, binding, vibration, freeplay, steering effort, steering pull (lead), and fluid leakage concerns; determine needed repairs.
3. Inspect power steering fluid level and condition; adjust level in accordance with vehicle manufacturers' recommendations.
4. Inspect, adjust, align, and replace power steering pump belt(s) and tensioners.
5. Diagnose power steering pump noises, vibration, and fluid leakage; determine needed repairs.
6. Remove and replace power steering pump; inspect pump mounting and attaching brackets.
7. Inspect and replace power steering pump seals, gaskets, reservoir, and valves.
8. Inspect and replace power steering pump pulley.
9. Perform power steering system pressure and flow tests; determine needed repairs.
10. Inspect and replace power steering hoses, fittings, O-rings, and coolers.
11. Remove and replace power steering gear (non-rack and pinion type) (includes vehicles equipped with air bags and/or other steering wheel mounted controls and components).
12. Remove and replace power rack and pinion steering gear; inspect and replace mounting bushings and brackets (includes vehicles equipped with air bags and/or other steering wheel mounted controls and components).
13. Adjust power steering gear (non-rack and pinion type) worm bearing preload and sector lash
14. Inspect and replace power steering gear (non-rack and pinion type) seals and gaskets.
15. Adjust power rack and pinion steering gear.
16. Inspect and replace power rack and pinion steering gear inner tie rod ends (sockets), and bellows boots.

17. Flush, fill, and bleed power steering system.

18. Diagnose, inspect, repair, or replace components of variable-assist steering systems.

19. Diagnose, inspect, repair, or replace components of power steering idle speed compensation systems.

3. Steering Linkage (3 questions)

1. Inspect and adjust (where applicable) front and rear steering linkage geometry (including parallelism and vehicle ride height).

2. Inspect and replace pitman arm.

3. Inspect and replace center link (relay rod/drag link/intermediate rod).

4. Inspect, adjust (where applicable), and replace idler arm and mountings.

5. Inspect, replace, and adjust tie rods, tie rod sleeves, clamps, and tie rod ends (sockets).

6. Inspect and replace steering linkage damper.

B. SUSPENSION SYSTEMS DIAGNOSIS AND REPAIR (13 QUESTIONS)

1. Front Suspensions (6 questions)

1. Diagnose front suspension system noises, body sway/roll, and ride height concerns; determine needed repairs.

2. Inspect and replace upper and lower control arms, bushings, shafts, rebound and jounce bumpers.

3. Inspect, adjust, and replace strut rods/radius arms (compression/tension), and bushings.

4. Inspect and replace upper and lower ball joints (with or without wear indicators).

5. Inspect and replace kingpins, bearings, and bushings.

6. Inspect and replace steering knuckle/spindle assemblies and steering arms.

7. Inspect and replace front suspension system coil springs and spring insulators (silencers).

8. Inspect and replace front suspension system leaf spring(s), leaf spring insulators (silencers), shackles, brackets, bushings, and mounts.

9. Inspect, replace, and adjust front suspension system torsion bars and mounts.

10. Inspect and replace stabilizer bar (sway bar) bushings, brackets, and links.

11. Inspect and replace strut cartridge or assembly.

12. Inspect and replace strut bearing and mount.

2. Rear Suspensions (5 questions)

1. Diagnose rear suspension system noises, body sway/roll, and ride height concerns; determine needed repairs.

2. Inspect and replace rear suspension system coil springs and spring insulators(silencers).

3. Inspect and replace rear suspension system lateral links/arms (track bars), control (trailing) arms, stabilizer bars (sway bars), bushings, and mounts.

4. Inspect and replace rear suspension system leaf spring(s), leaf spring insulators(silencers), shackles, brackets, bushings, and mounts.

5. Inspect and replace rear strut cartridge or assembly, and upper mount assembly.

6. Inspect nonindependent rear axle assembly for bending, warpage, and misalignment.

7. Inspect and replace rear ball joints and tie rod/toe link assemblies.

8. Inspect and replace knuckle/spindle assembly.

3. Miscellaneous Service (2 questions)

1. Inspect and replace shock absorbers, mounts, and bushings.

2. Inspect and replace air shock absorbers, lines, and fittings.

3. Diagnose and service front and/or rear wheel bearings.

4. Diagnose, inspect, adjust, repair, or replace components of electronically controlled suspension systems (including primary and supplemental air suspension and ride control systems).

5. Inspect and repair front and/or rear cradle (crossmember/subframe) mountings, bushings, brackets, and bolts.

C. WHEEL ALIGNMENT DIAGNOSIS, ADJUSTMENT, AND REPAIR (12 QUESTIONS)

1. Diagnose vehicle wander, drift, pull, hard steering, bump steer (toe curve), memory steer, torque steer, and steering return concerns; determine needed repairs.
2. Measure vehicle ride height; determine needed repairs.
3. Check and adjust front and rear wheel camber on suspension systems with a camber adjustment.
4. Check front and rear wheel camber on non-adjustable suspension systems; determine needed repairs.
5. Check and adjust caster on suspension systems with a caster adjustment.
6. Check caster on non-adjustable suspension systems; determine needed repairs.
7. Check and adjust front wheel toe.
8. Center steering wheel.
9. Check toe-out-on-turns (turning radius/angle); determine needed repairs.
10. Check SAI/KPI (steering axis inclination/king pin inclination); determine needed repairs.
11. Check included angle; determine needed repairs.
12. Check rear wheel toe; determine needed repairs or adjustments.
13. Check rear wheel thrust angle; determine needed repairs or adjustments.
14. Check front wheel setback; determine needed repairs or adjustments.
15. Check front cradle (crossmember/subframe) alignment; determine needed repairs or adjustments.

D. WHEEL AND TIRE DIAGNOSIS AND REPAIR (5 QUESTIONS)

1. Diagnose tire wear patterns; determine needed repairs.
2. Check tire condition, tread pattern, and size; check and adjust air pressure.
3. Diagnose wheel/tire vibration, shimmy, and noise concerns; determine needed repairs.
4. Rotate tires/wheels and torque fasteners according to manufacturers' recommendations.
5. Measure wheel, tire, axle flange, and hub runout (radial and lateral); determine needed repairs.
6. Diagnose tire pull (lead) problems; determine corrective actions.
7. Dismount and mount tire on wheel.
8. Balance wheel and tire assembly (static and/or dynamic).

SUSPENSION AND STEERING (A4)

CATEGORY: STEERING SYSTEMS DIAGNOSIS AND REPAIR

1. All of the following components can cause excessive play in the steering wheel *except* _____.

   a. a worn U-joint between the steering gear and the steering column shaft
   b. a worn outer tie rod end
   c. loosened steering gear attachment bolts
   d. overtightened center link retaining nuts

2. A "dry park" test to determine the condition of the steering components and joints should be performed with the vehicle _____.

   a. on level ground
   b. on turn plates that allow the front wheels to move
   c. on a frame contact lift with the wheels off the ground
   d. lifted off the ground about 2 inches (5 cm)

3. A power steering pressure test is being performed; the pressure is higher than specifications with the engine running and the steering wheel is stationary in the straight-ahead position. Technician A says that a restricted high-pressure line could be the cause. Technician B says that the internal leakage inside the steering gear or rack-and-pinion unit could be the cause. Which technician is correct?

   a. A only
   b. B only
   c. Both A and B
   d. Neither A nor B

4. Two technicians are discussing the replacement of an inner tie rod end (ball-socket assembly) of a rack-and-pinion steering gear. Technician A says that the inner and outer tie rod ends are part of the rack and cannot be replaced separately. Technician B says that the steering gear unit should be removed from the vehicle before the inner tie rod end can be removed. Which technician is correct?

   a. A only
   b. B only
   c. Both A and B
   d. Neither A nor B

5. Two technicians are discussing installation of a tie rod end to the steering knuckle. Technician A says to tighten the nut to specifications if a prevailing torque nut. Technician B says to tighten a cotter key-type nut to specifications and then tighter if necessary if the cotter keyhole does not line up. Which technician is correct?

   a. A only
   b. B only
   c. Both A and B
   d. Neither A nor B

6. What is adjustable with the adjustment slots for the idler arm?

   a. Play in the steering wheel
   b. Steering effort
   c. Steering wheel return after cornering
   d. Level steering linkage to prevent bump steer

   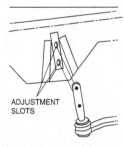

   ADJUSTMENT
   SLOTS

7. Excessive steering wheel free-play is being discussed. Technician A says that a worn steering flexible coupler could be the cause. Technician B says that a worn groove in the housing around the control valve could be the cause. Which technician is correct?

   a. A only
   b. B only
   c. Both A and B
   d. Neither A nor B

8. Two technicians are discussing replacement of the pitman shaft seal on an integral power steering gear. Technician A says that the pitman shaft must be removed before the old seal can be removed. Technician B says that the steering gear unit should be removed from the vehicle before the seal can be removed. Which technician is correct?

   a. A only
   b. B only
   c. Both A and B
   d. Neither A nor B

9. A customer complains that the steering lacks power assist only when cold. Technician A says that the power steering fluid may be low. Technician B says that a worn housing around the rotary (spool) valve is the most likely cause. Which technician is correct?

   a. A only
   b. B only
   c. Both A and B
   d. Neither A nor B

10. What tool should a technician use to disconnect an outer tie rod end from an aluminum steering knuckle after the retaining nut has been removed?

   a. A brass hammer
   b. An aluminum tapered tool ("pickle fork")
   c. A puller
   d. A torch using a rosebud tip

11. A driver complains that the vehicle darts when traveling over rises or dips in the road. Technician A says that bump steer caused by an unlevel steering linkage could be the cause. Technician B says that worn rack bushings could be the cause. Which technician is correct?

   a. A only
   b. B only
   c. Both A and B
   d. Neither A nor B

12. The adjustment procedure for a typical integral power steering gear is _____.

   a. over-center adjustment, then worm thrust bearing preload
   b. worm thrust bearing preload, then the over-center adjustment
   c. torque pitman arm retaining bolt, then the over-center adjustment
   d. tie rod end, then worm thrust bearing preload

13. Technician A says that the tie rod sleeve clamps should be positioned as shown on the left. Technician B says that they should be installed as shown on the right. Which technician is correct?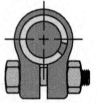

   a. A only
   b. B only
   c. Both A and B
   d. Neither A nor B

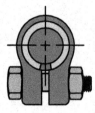

14. Two technicians are discussing the proper procedure for bleeding air from a power steering system. Technician A says that the front wheels of the vehicle should be lifted off the ground before bleeding. Technician B says that the steering wheel should be turned left and right during the procedure. Which technician is correct?

   a. A only
   b. B only
   c. Both A and B
   d. Neither A nor B

15. A power steering pressure gauge is being used to help diagnose the cause of hard steering. Technician A says that the pressure should be greater than 200 psi with the wheels straight ahead. Technician B says that pressure reaches its maximum reading when the wheels are turned against the stops. Which technician is correct?

   a. A only
   b. B only
   c. Both A and B
   d. Neither A nor B

16. A customer complains that power steering assist stops when driving in the rain. What is the *most likely* cause?

   a. The steering linkage tie rod ends are getting wet causing a bind
   b. Water is getting into the power steering fluid through the high-pressure hose
   c. Moisture is getting into the steering gears displacing the lubricant
   d. The power steering pump drive belt is loose or defective

17. A tie rod end is being replaced. Technician A says the steering wheel may be crooked when driving straight and excessive tire wear can occur if an alignment is not performed. Technician B says that the power steering system should be bled after the tie rod is installed. Which technician is correct?

   a. A only
   b. B only
   c. Both A and B
   d. Neither A nor B

18. A power steering pump is being tested using a pressure gauge. The pressure increases to the specified value when the valve is closed restricting the flow of fluid to the steering gear. The pressure only rises a little when the steering wheel is turned all the way to the left or right with the valve open. Technician A says that the pump is weak and should be replaced. Technician B says that the steering gear is defective and should be replaced. Which technician is correct?

   a. A only
   b. B only
   c. Both A and B
   d. Neither A nor B

19. Which of the following is *least likely* to cause loose steering?

   a. A loose pitman arm retaining nut
   b. A worn idler arm
   c. A worn center link
   d. A loose tie rod end

20. Power steering fluid is observed dripping out of the boots of the power rack-and-pinion steering gear assembly. What is the *most likely* cause?

   a. A loose or worn inner tie rod end (ball-socket assembly)
   b. Leaking control valve seals
   c. A leaking inner rack seal
   d. A loose stub U-joint

21. Two technicians are discussing airbags. Technician A says that the airbag should be disabled when service work is going to be performed on the steering column or related components. Technician B says that the connector(s) for the airbags are yellow. Which technician is correct?

   a. A only
   b. B only
   c. Both A and B
   d. Neither A nor B

22. A customer complains that the steering on a vehicle equipped with a conventional power steering gear is hard to steer at times. Which is the *least likely* cause?

   a. A loose power steering belt
   b. A defective intermediate shaft U-joint
   c. Loose tie rod ends
   d. A defective ball joint(s)

23. How is the rack support usually adjusted on a rack-and-pinion steering gear?

   a. No adjustment necessary—just thread into the rack assembly
   b. Torque to 80–100 lb-ft
   c. Tighten and back off about 60°
   d. Tighten until all steering wheel free-play is eliminated

24. A vehicle owner complains of a binding in the steering when turning and noise when driving over bumps in the road. What is the *most likely* cause?

   a. Worn outer tie rod ends
   b. Low power steering fluid level
   c. Defective upper strut mount
   d. Worn power steering pump drive belt

25. The power steering fluid is being checked on a vehicle equipped with a rack-and-pinion steering. The fluid is silver/black in color. Technician A says that this is normal for a vehicle equipped with rack-and-pinion steering. Technician B says that the rack and pinion gear teeth must be worn because the silver color is likely a result of the wear metals. Which technician is correct?

   a. A only
   b. B only
   c. Both A and B
   d. Neither A nor B

26. What is being measured in the illustration?

   a. The tie rod bending strength
   b. Tightness of the inner ball-socket assembly
   c. Toe-in
   d. The play in the tie rod

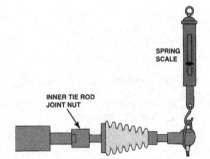

27. Two technicians are discussing bump steer. Technician A says that an unlevel steering linkage can be the cause. Technician B says that if the steering wheel moves when the vehicle is bounced up and down, then the steering linkage may be bent. Which technician is correct?

   a. A only
   b. B only
   c. Both A and B
   d. Neither A nor B

SUSPENSION AND STEERING (A4)

CATEGORY: SUSPENSION SYSTEMS DIAGNOSIS AND REPAIR

28. If this part were to fail, what would be the *most likely* symptom?

    a. Hard, stiff steering
    b. Excessive free-play in the steering wheel
    c. Shimmy-type vibration in the steering wheel at highway speeds
    d. Wandering when driving straight

29. A noise is heard from the front end of the vehicle while traveling over bumpy sections of road. Technician A says that worn or deteriorated control arm bushings could be the cause. Technician B says that worn or deteriorated strut rod bushings could be the cause. Which technician is correct?

    a. A only
    b. B only
    c. Both A and B
    d. Neither A nor B

30. Two technicians are discussing the inspection of load-carrying ball joints. Technician A says that the vehicle should be on the ground with the ball joints *loaded*, then checked for free-play movement. Technician B says that the ball joints should be *unloaded* before checking for free-play in the ball joints. Which technician is correct?

    a. A only
    b. B only
    c. Both A and B
    d. Neither A nor B

31. A light film of oil is observed on the upper area of a shock absorber. Technician A says that this condition should be considered normal. Technician B says that a rod seal may bleed fluid during cold weather causing the oil film. Which technician is correct?

    a. A only
    b. B only
    c. Both A and B
    d. Neither A nor B

32. A vehicle equipped with coil-spring front suspension and a leaf-spring rear suspension "dog tracks" while driving on a straight, level road. Technician A says that a broken center bolt could be the cause. Technician B says that defective upper control arm bushings on the front could be the cause. Which technician is correct?

    a. A only
    b. B only
    c. Both A and B
    d. Neither A nor B

33. What part *must* be replaced when servicing the outer wheel bearing on a non-drive wheel?

    a. The bearing cup
    b. The grease seal
    c. The cotter key
    d. The retainer washer

34. A defective wheel bearing usually sounds like _____.

    a. marbles in a tin can
    b. a noisy tire
    c. a baby rattle
    d. a clicking sound—like a ballpoint pen

35. Two technicians are discussing a vehicle that is sagging at the rear. Technician A says that new shock absorbers will restore the vehicle to proper ride height. Technician B says that the rear springs should be replaced. Which technician is correct?

    a. A only
    b. B only
    c. Both A and B
    d. Neither A nor B

36. A wear indicator-type ball joint is shown. Technician A says that the ball joint is worn and should be replaced. Technician B says that the ball joint is serviceable. Which technician is correct?

    a. A only
    b. B only
    c. Both A and B
    d. Neither A nor B

37. A fleet vehicle was found to have damaged suspension-limiting rubber bump stops (jounce bumpers). Technician A says that sagging springs could be the cause. Technician B says that defective or worn shock absorbers could be the cause. Which technician is correct?

    a. A only
    b. B only
    c. Both A and B
    d. Neither A nor B

38. The preferred method to use to separate tapered chassis parts is to use a _____.

    a. pickle fork tool
    b. torch to heat the joint until it separates
    c. puller tool
    d. drill to drill out the tapered part

39. Before the strut cartridge can be removed from a typical MacPherson strut assembly, which operation is necessary to prevent possible personal injury?

    a. The brake caliper and/or brake hose should be removed from the strut housing
    b. The coil spring should be compressed
    c. The upper strut mounting bolts should be removed
    d. The lower attaching bolts should be removed

40. Two technicians are discussing wheel bearings that were discovered to have dents in the outer race (brinelling). Technician A says that the vehicle may have been overloaded. Technician B says that the bearing may have been overtightened. Which technician is correct?

    a. A only
    b. B only
    c. Both A and B
    d. Neither A nor B

41. Wear indicator ball joints should be checked _____.

    a. loaded with the weight of the vehicle on the ground to observe the wear indicator
    b. unloaded
    c. with a floor jack placed under the lower control arm
    d. using a dial indicator

42. What is being done in the drawing?

    a. Replacing a control arm bushing
    b. Adjusting a ball joint
    c. Replacing a ball joint
    d. Straightening a bent or damaged control arm

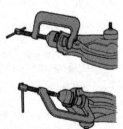

43. The axial play in a lower load-carrying ball joint is measured and it is 0.150 in. (3.8 mm) (specification is 0.090 in.). Technician A says that the ball joint should be replaced. Technician B says that the lower ball joint on the other side of the vehicle should also be replaced. Which technician is correct?

    a. A only
    b. B only
    c. Both A and B
    d. Neither A nor B

44. A rear-wheel-drive vehicle equipped with front coil springs and rear leaf springs is sagging down at the right rear and the left front is higher than the right front. Which is the *most likely* cause?

    a. A broken stabilizer bar link in the left front
    b. A broken rear track rod
    c. A broken leaf spring on the right rear
    d. A broken left front shock absorber

45. A pull toward one side during braking is one symptom of defective or worn _____.

    a. stabilizer bar links
    b. strut rod bushings
    c. rear leaf springs
    d. track (panhard) rod

46. Two technicians are discussing the installation of a replacement strut unit in a conventional MacPherson strut in a front suspension. Technician A says that the coil spring should be compressed before loosening the retaining nut. Technician B says that the replacement strut has to be filled with oil before being installed. Which technician is correct?

    a. A only
    b. B only
    c. Both A and B
    d. Neither A nor B

47. If the rear track rod (panhard rod) is bent, what problem is *most likely* to occur?

    a. The vehicle will sway when rounding curves
    b. The rear axle will be out of alignment with the front wheels
    c. A loud knocking noise will be heard during turns
    d. The vehicle pulls to one side during braking

48. One of the holes in the lower control arms is covered by the coil spring. Technician A says that the spring is installed correctly. Technician B says that the spring may be installed upside down. Which technician is correct?

    a. A only
    b. B only
    c. Both A and B
    d. Neither A nor B

49. A vehicle wanders when traveling at highway speeds and the driver has to make constant corrections to the steering wheel to maintain control. Which is *least likely* to cause this problem?

    a. Worn control arm bushings
    b. Worn ball joints
    c. Leaking shock absorbers/struts
    d. Worn strut rod bushings

50. The rear of a sport utility vehicle is sagging. Which is the *least likely* cause?

    a. Excessive load in the rear of the vehicle
    b. Incorrect Springs
    c. Broken spring seats
    d. Leaking shock absorbers

51. One rear leaf spring is broken on a rear-wheel-drive vehicle. Technician A says that both rear springs should be replaced. Technician B says that rear shock absorbers may have to be replaced to restore proper ride height. Which technician is correct?

   a. A only
   b. B only
   c. Both A and B
   d. Neither A nor B

52. What is the *most likely* cause of this condition on the rear of this front-wheel-drive vehicle?

   a. Excessively worn stabilizer bar bushings
   b. A broken rear track rod
   c. A broken rear control arm or ball joint
   d. A broken shock absorber

53. A vehicle makes a loud clunking sound only when the brakes are applied. Which is the *most likely* cause?

   a. A worn or defective strut rod (compression/tension) bushing
   b. A worn shock absorber
   c. Sagging springs
   d. A loose wheel bearing

54. A noisy rear suspension is being diagnosed. Technician A says that sagging rear springs could be the cause. Technician B says that damaged or missing spring insulators could be the cause. Which technician is correct?

   a. A only
   b. B only
   c. Both A and B
   d. Neither A nor B

55. A vehicle has ride (trim) height lower on the left side than on the right side. Which is the *most likely* cause?

   a. Worn ball joints on the left side
   b. A worn or leaking shock absorber on the right side
   c. A weak or leaking shock absorber on the left side
   d. Sagging springs on the left side

56. A rear-wheel-drive vehicle has been hoisted on a frame-type lift and the rear shock absorbers are being replaced. Technician A says that the rear axle should be supported to prevent it from falling when the rear shocks are removed. Technician B says that the rear springs should be compressed before the shocks are removed. Which technician is correct?

   a. A only
   b. B only
   c. Both A and B
   d. Neither A nor B

57. New front coil springs are being installed to correct a sag condition. Technician A says that the springs are often marked left and right and should be replaced on the specified side of the vehicle. Technician B says that the springs must be installed right side up to be sure that they fit correctly in the spring seats. Which technician is correct?

   a. A only
   b. B only
   c. Both A and B
   d. Neither A nor B

58. The ball joints are being checked for wear. Technician A says the vehicle should be raised using a jack at location "X". Technician B says the vehicle should be raised using a jack at location "Y". Which technician is correct?

   a. A only
   b. B only
   c. Both A and B
   d. Neither A nor B

SUSPENSION AND STEERING (A4)

CATEGORY: RELATED SUSPENSION AND STEERING SERVICE

59. A technician unbolts the lateral acceleration sensor and turns it on its side while looking at a scan tool date display. Technician A says that the sensor should display 1 "G" when the sensor is turned on its side with the ignition key on. Technician B says that the sensor value should remain the same regardless of its position. Which technician is correct?

    a. A only
    b. B only
    c. Both A and B
    d. Neither A nor B

60. A vibration at highway speed could be due to _____.

    a. excessive hub runout
    b. broken stabilizer bar link
    c. worn shocks
    d. any of the above

61. Two technicians are discussing a vehicle that is equipped with electronically controlled shock absorbers. Technician A says that if the connector is unplugged, the shock is set to its most firm setting. Technician B says that the shock actuator usually uses compressed air to adjust the firmness of the shock. Which technician is correct?

    a. A only
    b. B only
    c. Both A and B
    d. Neither A nor B

62. A "loaded strut" is a strut that is _____.

    a. an insert designed to fit into the original housing
    b. a strut that is gas-charged
    c. a strut assembly that includes the strut, spring, and upper bearing assembly in one unit
    d. a strut that is spring loaded

SUSPENSION AND STEERING (A4)

CATEGORY: WHEEL ALIGNMENT DIAGNOSIS, ADJUSTMENT, AND REPAIR

63. Technician A says that a vehicle will pull (or the lead) to the side with the most camber (or least negative camber) if the difference exceeds factory specifications. Technician B says that a vehicle will pull (or lead) to the side with the most front toe. Which technician is correct?

    a. A only
    b. B only
    c. Both A and B
    d. Neither A nor B

64. Which angle will be changed by adjusting strut rods (if applicable)?

    a. Toe
    b. Camber
    c. Caster
    d. Toe-out on turns

65. A front-wheel-drive vehicle with independent rear suspension pulls or steers to the right. Technician A says that the right rear could be toed in more than the left rear. Technician B says that the incorrect front toe could be the cause. Which technician is correct?

    a. A only
    b. B only
    c. Both A and B
    d. Neither A nor B

66. If metal shims are used for alignment adjustment in the front as shown, they adjust _____.

    a. camber
    b. caster
    c. toe
    d. camber and caster

67. A pickup truck was aligned and then the owner installed a heavy camper. Technician A says that the extra weight will change the camber and caster on the front wheels. Technician B says that the weight will cause the toe to change. Which technician is correct?

    a. A only
    b. B only
    c. Both A and B
    d. Neither A nor B

68. The vehicle above will _____.

a. pull toward the right and feather edge both tires
b. pull toward the left
c. wear the outside of the left tire and the inside of the right tire
d. wear the inside of both front tires and pull to the left

Specifications:		Min.	Preferred	Max.
Camber		0°	1.0°	1.4°
Caster		.8°	1.5°	2.1°
Toe		0.10°	0.06°	0.15°

Results:	L	R		
Camber	−0.1°	0.6°		
Caster	1.8°	1.6°		
Toe	−0.3°	+0.12°		

69. The vehicle above will _____.

a. pull toward the left
b. pull toward the right
c. wander
d. lead to the left slightly

Specifications:		Min.	Preferred	Max.
Camber		−0.25°	+0.5°	1°
Caster		0°	+2°	+4°
Toe		0°	0.1°	0.2°

Results:	L	R		
Camber	−0.2°	+0.1°		
Caster	3.6°	1.8°		
Toe	−0.16°	+0.32°		

70. The vehicle above will _____.

a. wander
b. wear tires, but will not pull
c. will pull, but not wear tires
d. pull toward the left and cause feather-edge tire wear

Specifications:		Min.	Preferred	Max.
Camber		−0.25°	+0.5°	1°
Caster		0°	+2°	+4°
Toe		0°	0.1°	0.2°

Results:	L	R		
Camber	−0.2°	+0.1°		
Caster	3.6°	1.8°		
Toe	−0.16°	+0.32°		

71. The right front tire is worn on the outside and the vehicle pulls toward the right. Technician A says that the camber on the right front may need to be adjusted. Technician B says that the caster on the right front may need to be adjusted. Which technician is correct?

a. A only
b. B only
c. Both A and B
d. Neither A nor B

72. Which alignment angle is most likely to need correction and cause the most tire wear?

    a. Toe
    b. Camber
    c. Caster
    d. SAI

73. A front-wheel-drive vehicle pulls toward the right during rapid acceleration from a stop. The most *likely cause* is _____.

    a. worn or defective tires
    b. leaking or defective shock absorbers
    c. normal torque steer
    d. a defective power steering rack-and-pinion steering assembly

74. A vehicle is pulling to the right. Technician A says that more camber on the right than the left could be the cause. Technician B says that more toe-in on the left than on the right could be the cause. Which technician is correct?

    a. A only
    b. B only
    c. Both A and B
    d. Neither A nor B

75. A vehicle pulls to the right after turning a right turn and pulls to the left after turning a left turn. Technician A says that the upper strut bearing could be the cause. Technician B says that excessive positive caster on both front wheels could be the problem. Which technician is correct?

    a. A only
    b. B only
    c. Both A and B
    d. Neither A nor B

76. An owner wants to install larger wheels and tires on his sport utility vehicle (SUV). Technician A says that the camber and toe angles will change. Technician B says that the SAI and included angle will be changed if larger wheels and tires are installed. Which technician is correct?

    a. A only
    b. B only
    c. Both A and B
    d. Neither A nor B

77. If the turning radius (toe-out on turns or Ackerman angle as shown) is out of specification, what should be replaced?

    a. The outer tie rod ends
    b. The inner tie rod ends
    c. The idler arm
    d. The steering knuckle

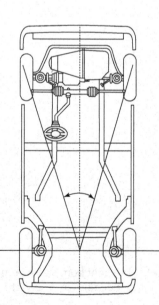

78. The thrust angle is being corrected. The alignment technician should adjust which angle to reduce thrust angle?

    a. Rear camber
    b. Front SAI or included angle and camber
    c. Rear toe
    d. Rear caster

79. A four-wheel alignment is being performed on a front-wheel-drive vehicle. The first angle corrected should be the _____.

    a. front camber
    b. front caster
    c. rear toe
    d. front toe

80. Adding a wedge as shown will change what angle in the rear of this front-wheel-drive vehicle?

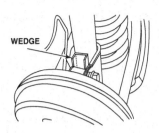

WEDGE

    a. Rear camber
    b. Rear toe
    c. Rear caster
    d. Rear SAI

81. Technician A says that the present alignment will cause excessive tire wear to the inside of both front tires. Technician B says that the rear of the vehicle will dog track because of the difference in the rear toe. Which technician is correct?

    a. A only
    b. B only
    c. Both A and B
    d. Neither A nor B

Specifications:

front camber	$0.5° \pm 0.3°$
front caster	3.5° to 4.5°
toe	$0° \pm 0.1°$
rear camber	$0° \pm 0.5°$
rear toe	−0.1° to 0.1°

Alignment angles:

front camber left	0.5°	total toe	0.0°
front camber right	−0.1°	rear camber left	0.15°
front caster left	3.8°	rear camber right	−0.11°
front caster right	4.5°	rear toe left	−0.04°
front toe left	−0.2°	rear toe right	0.08°
front toe right	+0.2°		

82. Technician A says that the present alignment will cause excessive tire wear to the rear tires. Technician B says that the total front toe being set to zero will not cause any tire wear or handling concerns. Which technician is correct?

    a. A only
    b. B only
    c. Both A and B
    d. Neither A nor B

Specifications:

front camber	$0.5° \pm 0.3°$
front caster	3.5° to 4.5°
toe	$0° \pm 0.1°$
rear camber	$0° \pm 0.5°$
rear toe	−0.1° to 0.1°

Alignment angles:

front camber left	0.5°	total toe	0.0°
front camber right	−0.1°	rear camber left	0.15°
front caster left	3.8°	rear camber right	−0.11°
front caster right	4.5°	rear toe left	−0.04°
front toe left	−0.2°	rear toe right	0.08°
front toe right	+0.2°		

83. With the present alignment, the vehicle could _____.

    a. pull toward the right
    b. go straight
    c. pull toward the left
    d. wander

Specifications:

front camber	0.5° ± 0.3°
front caster	3.5° to 4.5°
toe	0° ± 0.1°
rear camber	0° ± 0.5°
rear toe	−0.1° to 0.1°

Alignment angles:

front camber left	0.5°	total toe	0.0°
front camber right	−0.1°	rear camber left	0.15°
front caster left	3.8°	rear camber right	−0.11°
front caster right	4.5°	rear toe left	−0.04°
front toe left	−0.2°	rear toe right	0.08°
front toe right	+0.2°		

84. Two technicians are discussing what could be causing a rear-wheel-drive vehicle to wander while driving straight on a level, straight road. Technician A says that low or unequal tire pressure could be the cause. Technician B says that loose or worn steering linkage could be the cause. Which technician is correct?

    a. A only
    b. B only
    c. Both A and B
    d. Neither A nor B

85. A steering wheel is not straight when the vehicle is traveling on a straight highway. Which adjustment or procedure should the technician perform?

    a. Remove the steering wheel and reattach in the straight-ahead position
    b. Adjust the camber angle
    c. Adjust the tie rod sleeves (toe angle)
    d. Adjust the caster angle

86. A front-wheel-drive vehicle is being checked for proper alignment. The SAI is okay, but the camber and included angle are less than specifications. What is the *most likely* cause?

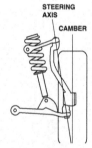

    a. No problem—this is normal for a front-wheel-drive vehicle
    b. A worn ball joint(s)
    c. Worn tie rod ends
    d. A bent strut

87. A vehicle owner complains that the front tires squeal when turning a corner even at very low speeds. Which is the *most likely* cause?

    a. A bent center link
    b. A bent steering arm
    c. A loose idler arm
    d. Worn ball joints

88. A front-wheel-drive vehicle equipped with a MacPherson-type front suspension is being aligned. The left camber is −1.0° and the right camber is +1.0°. Technician A says that the engine cradle could be shifted to the left. Technician B says that a leaking strut could be the cause. Which technician is correct?

    a. A only
    b. B only
    c. Both A and B
    d. Neither A nor B

89. A front-wheel-drive vehicle with an independent rear suspension steers to the right. Technician A says that unequal front toe could be the cause. Technician B says that unequal rear toe could be the cause. Which technician is correct?

    a. A only
    b. B only
    c. Both A and B
    d. Neither A nor B

90. A customer is experiencing steering wheel up and down (tramp) vibration at highway speeds. Technician A says that the front wheel camber could be out of specifications. Technician B says that the front toe may be out of specifications. Which technician is correct?

    a. A only
    b. B only
    c. Both A and B
    d. Neither A nor B

91. Rotating the cam bolts will change _____.

    a. camber only
    b. caster only
    c. both camber and caster
    d. SAI

92. The shim is being used on the rear of this front-wheel-drive vehicle and will change what angle(s)?

    a. Rear camber and toe
    b. Rear camber only
    c. Rear toe only
    d. Caster

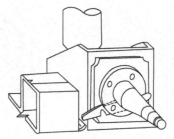

93. The eccentric cam is being rotated on the strut as shown, which will change what angle(s)?

    a. Caster
    b. Toe
    c. Camber
    d. SAI and caster

94. The camber needs to be increased (more positive) on the suspension shown without affecting the caster angle. Which of the following should be performed?

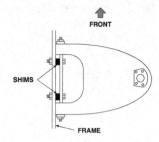

    a. Add shims to the front only
    b. Add equal shims to the front and rear
    c. Move shim(s) from the front to the rear
    d. Remove equal shims from the front and rear

95. Adjustment made at the exploded view component as shown would change which angle?

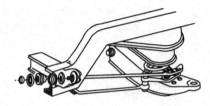

    a. Camber
    b. Caster
    c. Toe
    d. Toe-out on turns (TOOT)

SUSPENSION AND STEERING (A4)

CATEGORY: WHEEL AND TIRE DIAGNOSIS AND SERVICE

96. A tire has excessive radial runout. Technician A says that it should be broken down on a tire-changing machine and the tire rotated 180° on the wheel and retested. Technician B says that the tire should be replaced. Which technician is correct?

    a. A only
    b. B only
    c. Both A and B
    d. Neither A nor B

97. Using the modified X tire rotation method on a front-wheel-drive vehicle would place the right front tire on the _____.

    a. left front
    b. left rear
    c. right rear
    d. right front

98. A tire is worn excessively on both edges. The most likely cause of this type of tire wear is _____.

    a. overinflation
    b. underinflation
    c. excessive radial runout
    d. excessive lateral runout

99. When seating a bead of a tire, never exceed _____.

    a. 30 psi
    b. 40 psi
    c. 50 psi
    d. 60 psi

100. Which type of clip-on wheel weight should a technician use on aluminum (alloy) wheels?

    a. Lead or steel weights
    b. Coated (painted) weights
    c. Uncoated lead or steel weights with longer than normal clips
    d. Aluminum weights

101. Technician A says that lug nuts should be tightened in a star pattern. Technician B says that a torque wrench should be used to be assured that all of the lug nuts are uniformly tightened to a specified torque. Which technician is correct?

    a. A only
    b. B only
    c. Both A and B
    d. Neither A nor B

102. Two technicians are discussing mounting a tire on a wheel. Technician A says that for the best balance, the tire should be match mounted. Technician B says that silicone spray should be used to lubricate the tire bead. Which technician is correct?

    a. A only
    b. B only
    c. Both A and B
    d. Neither A nor B

103. Most manufacturers of passenger vehicles specify a lug nut (wheel nut) tightening torque specification of about _____.

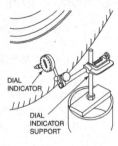

    a. 80–100 lb-ft
    b. 110–125 lb-ft
    c. 130–150 lb-ft
    d. 160–175 lb-ft

104. Two technicians are discussing a vehicle that has excessive lateral runout. Technician A says that the rim could be bent. Technician B says that the hub could have excessive runout. Which technician is correct?

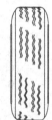

    a. A only
    b. B only
    c. Both A and B
    d. Neither A nor B

105. What is the *most likely* cause of this type of tire wear on the left rear of a front-wheel-drive vehicle?

    a. Incorrect rear toe
    b. Incorrect rear camber
    c. Overinflation
    d. Underinflation

106. The owner of a full-size sport utility vehicle (SUV) complained that the tire pressure monitoring system (TPMS) warning lamp was on (not flashing) yet all four tires were properly inflated according to the driver's side door placard. On this vehicle, the dash does not include information on individual inflation pressures but instream just a warming lamp and message. What is the *most likely* cause?

    a. Incorrect inflation pressure
    b. A full-size spare tire that is underinflated
    c. A defective tire pressure sensor
    d. A fault with the tire pressure monitoring system (TPMS) controller

107. A rear-wheel-drive vehicle has a vibration that is felt in the steering wheel at highway speeds. Technician A says that the drive shaft (prop shaft) may be bent or out of balance. Technician B says that the front tires could be out of balance. Which technician is correct?

    a. A only
    b. B only
    c. Both A and B
    d. Neither A nor B

108. A low tire warning lamp is on. The technician checked and all four tires were properly inflated to the specification found on the driver's door placard. Technician A says that the full-size spare could be low. Technician B says to overinflate the tires to put out the warning lamp. Which technician is correct?

    a. A only
    b. B only
    c. Both A and B
    d. Neither A nor B

109. A TPMS dash warning is flashing. Technician A says that this means that a low tire has been detected. Technician B says that this means that the system has detected a fault such as a wheel sensor that is not broadcasting data. Which technician is correct?

   a. A only
   b. B only
   c. Both A and B
   d. Neither A nor B

110. What may be required to learn a new tire pressure monitor wheel sensor?

   a. A scan tool
   b. A TPMS tool
   c. A magnet
   d. All of the above

SUSPENSION AND STEERING (A4)

CATEGORY: STEERING SYSTEMS DIAGNOSIS AND REPAIR

1. **The correct answer is d.** An overtightened center link retaining nut is unlikely to cause excessive steering wheel play. Answers a, b, and c are all likely to cause excessive play in the steering wheel.

2. **The correct answer is a.** The vehicle must be on level ground when conducting a dry park test; with the vehicle weight on the front wheels, resistance is applied to the steering linkage. Answers b, c, and d are not correct because these methods will allow the front wheels to move and not apply a load on the steering linkage.

3. **The correct answer is a.** Technician A only is correct because an abnormal restriction in the high pressure line will cause an increase in pressure. Technician B is not correct because the pressure would be lower (not higher) if there was an internal leakage in the steering gear because normal restriction is being bypassed. Answers c and d are not correct because only Technician A is correct.

4. **The correct answer is d.** Neither technician is correct. Technician A is not correct because the inner tie-rod ends are separate components and can be replaced separately in most vehicles. Technician B is not correct because the inner tie-rod end can usually be replaced without requiring that the rack and pinion steering gear unit be removed. Answer c is not correct because neither technician is correct.

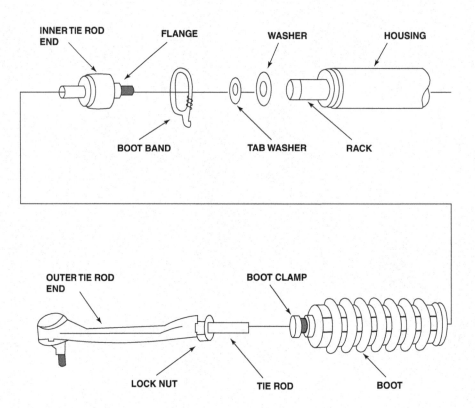

5. **The correct answer is c.** Both technicians are correct. Technician A is correct because a torque prevailing nut must be new and torqued to factory specifications. Technician B is correct because the nut retaining a tapered stud should never be loosened, but rather tightened further to align the cotter keyhole to prevent the joint from loosening. Answers a, b, and d are not correct because both technicians are correct.

6. **The correct answer is d.** Bump steer is caused by unlevel steering linkage, which causes a force to be applied to the steering linkage when the suspension moves up and down during normal driving. To achieve level steering linkage, some vehicles are equipped with adjustable slots that allow the idler arm to be moved up or down. Answers a, b, and c are not correct because the slots are used to adjust the idler arm to prevent bump steer and no other purpose.

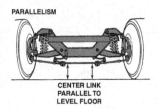

PARALLELISM

CENTER LINK
PARALLEL TO
LEVEL FLOOR

7. **The correct answer is a.** Technician A only is correct because a worn flexible coupler located on the intermediate shaft of the steering column between the steering wheel and the steering gear can cause excessive steering wheel free play. Technician B is not correct because a worn groove in the control valve housing will not cause excessive steering wheel free play although it could cause hard steering when the vehicle is cold. Answers c and d are not correct because Technician A only is correct.

8. **The correct answer is d.** Neither technician is correct. Technician A is not correct because the pitman shaft seal can be replaced without removing the pitman shaft by removing the pitman arm retaining nut, pitman arm, and pitman seal retaining snap ring. Technician B is not correct because the steering gear does not *have* to be removed to replace the pitman seal. Answer c is not correct because neither technician is correct.

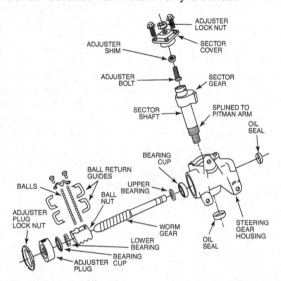

9. **The correct answer is b.** Technician B only is correct because a worn control valve housing in the steering gear would allow power steering fluid to leak past the seals and result in hard steering until the fluid warms allowing the Teflon seals to become pliable and begin to seal the fluid. Technician A is not correct because low power steering fluid is unlikely to cause a lack of power assist when cold even though it could cause excessive noise due to aeration of the fluid. Answers c and d are not correct because Technician B only is correct.

10. **The correct answer is c.** A puller is the correct tool, which is used to separate a tapered steering tie rod end from an aluminum steering knuckle without doing any harm to either the outer tie rod end or the aluminum steering knuckle. Answer a is not correct because a brass hammer can cause harm to the aluminum steering knuckle. Answer b is not correct because a tapered separator tool, commonly referred to as a "pickle fork" because it is shaped like a pickle fork, can damage the rubber grease seal of the tie rod end as well as possibly damage or deform the aluminum steering knuckle. Answer d is not correct because using a torch will cause damage to the rubber grease seal of the tie rod end as well as cause damage to or deform the aluminum steering knuckle.

11. **The correct answer is c.** Both technicians are correct. Technician A is correct because if the steering linkage is not level, it will cause a force that steers the front wheels when the suspension moves up and down. Technician B is correct because worn or damaged rack bushings can cause the steering rack to be un-level creating a bump steer condition. Answers a, b, and d are not correct because both technicians are correct.

12. **The correct answer is b.** The proper procedure to adjust a typical integral power steering gear is to adjust the worm gear thrust bearing preload, and then the over-center adjustment. Answers a, c, and d are not correct because they do not specify the correct adjustment procedure.

13. **The correct answer is a.** Technician A only is correct because the clamp should cover the split on the tire rod adjusting sleeve. Technician B is not correct because the clamp and sleeve openings are aligned, which could reduce the clamping force on the sleeve. Answers c and d are not correct because only Technician A is correct.

14. **The correct answer is c.** Both technicians are correct. Technician A is correct because keeping the front wheels off the ground helps prevent any trapped air from dispersing into small bubbles or foam due to the resistance forces created by the weight of the vehicle on the ground. Technician B is correct because the steering wheel must be turned all the way to the left and all the way to the right to allow fluid to flow through the power steering system to allow any trapped air to escape. Answers a, b, and d are not correct because both technicians are correct.

15. **The correct answer is b.** Technician B is correct because the steering gear provides a restriction to the flow of the power steering fluid when the steering wheel is turned all the way against the stop either to the left or to the right. Technician A is not correct because the steering gear presents little restriction with the wheels in the straight ahead position and should have less than 150 psi in the power steering system unless there is an unwanted restriction in the system. Answers c and d are not correct because only Technician B is correct.

16. **The correct answer is d.** A loose or worn power steering pump drive belt could cause a lack of power assist if covered with water, reducing the ability of the belt to apply engine torque to the power steering pump. Answer a is not correct because water could not cause the tie rod to bind. Answer b is not likely because the power steering system is sealed and is unlikely to cause a lack of power assist if some water did get into the power steering pump reservoir. Answer c is not correct because the steering gear uses power steering fluid as a lubricant and as stated in answer b, is not likely to cause a lack of power assist.

17. **The correct answer is a.** Technician A only is correct because replacing the tie rod end can affect the toe setting and cause the steering wheel to be crooked if an alignment is not performed after the repair. Excessive tire wear can also occur if the toe is not correct. Technician B is not correct because replacing the tie rod end would generally not cause air to get into the power steering hydraulic system. Answers c and d are not correct because only Technician A is correct.

18. **The correct answer is b.** Technician B only is correct because the steering gear should restrict the flow of power steering fluid causing the pressure to increase as the front wheels are turned left and right. The pressure did increase when the valve was closed indicating that the pump is capable of supplying the necessary pressure, but the steering gear is leaking internally and requires repair or replacement. Technician A is not correct because the pump was capable of supplying the specified pressure when the valve was closed and is, therefore, not at fault. Answers c and d are not correct because Technician B only is correct.

19. **The correct answer is a.** A loose pitman arm retaining nut is not likely to cause loose steering (excessive play in the steering wheel) because the pitman arm is splined to the pitman (sector) shaft and the nut is simply provided to keep the arm from falling off of the shaft. Answers b, c, and d are not correct because each can cause excessive play in the steering if worn.

20. **The correct answer is c.** A leaking inner rack seal will allow power steering fluid to leak into the rack housing and eventually drip from around the dust boots, which are designed to keep water and dirt from getting into the rack housing and are not designed to seal power steering fluid. Answer a is not correct because a loose or worn inner tie rod end boot will not cause a power steering fluid leak because the power steering fluid should be sealed by the inner and outer rack seals. Answer b is not correct because a leaking control valve seal will cause hard steering, especially when the vehicle is cold, but will not cause an external leak. Answer d is not correct because a loose stub shaft retaining nut could cause fluid leakage out of the top of a "hat" portion of the steering gear and not out of the boots.

21. **The correct answer is c.** Both technicians are correct. Technician A is correct because the airbags should be temporarily disabled when service work is being performed on or near the steering column to avoid the possibility of accidental deployment. Technician B is correct because all airbags (supplemental inflatable restraints) use yellow electrical connectors for easy identification. Answers a, b, and d are not correct because both technicians are correct.

22. **The correct answer is c.** Loose tie rod ends would be the least likely cause for the steering to bind at times because the steering would feel loose and have excessive play. Answer a is not correct because a loose power steering belt can cause the power steering pump to work some times and not work at other times creating a feeling that the steering is normal one instant and not working or binding another time. Answer b is not correct because a defective intermediate shaft U-joint can bind at times depending on the angle of the U-joint and how fast the steering wheel is turned. Answer d is not correct because a defective ball joint can cause a bind if the internal parts rub without proper lubrication causing the front wheels to bind when being turned.

23. **The correct answer is c.** The rack support is usually tightened and then backed off (rotated counterclockwise) 60° on one flat of the hex-shaped adjusting nut. Answer a is not correct because if the adjustment is too tight, the steering wheel will be difficult to turn and if too loose, excessive play in the steering wheel can occur. Answers b and d are not correct because they do not correctly state the tightening procedure.

24. **The correct answer is c.** The most likely cause of these two issues occurring means that the fault is likely in the upper strut mount area. A defective upper strut mount can cause binding in the steering as the mount often causes excessive friction which resists the turning of the front wheels. A defective or worn upper strut mount can also cause noise when driving over rough roads or bumps due to the excessive clearance in the upper bearing assembly. Answer a is not correct because while worn outer tie rods ends can cause excessive play in the steering, it is unlikely to cause the steering to bind nor to cause noise. Answer b is not correct because while low power steering fluid may cause a feeling in the steering that a customer could think was binding in the steering, it would not likely cause noise when driving over bumps. Answer d is not correct because while a worn power steering pump drive belt may cause a feeling in the steering wheel that a customer could think was binding in the steering, it would not likely cause noise when driving over bumps.

25. **The correct answer is d.** Neither technician is correct. The silver/black power steering fluid indicates that aluminum was worn from the control valve area of the rack-and-pinion steering assembly. The Teflon sealing rings can wear grooves in the housing. Technician A is not correct because power steering fluid should be amber or red (if automatic transmission fluid is used) and not silver or black. Technician B is not correct because the gear teeth are not exposed to the power steering fluid in a power rack-and-pinion steering gear assembly. The-rack-and pinion gear teeth are lubricated by grease that is installed during manufacture and is designed to last the life of the vehicle. Answer c is not correct because neither technician is correct.

26. **The correct answer is b.** The spring scale is being used to check the force necessary to move the tie rod while it is attached to the inner ball-socket assembly of a rack-and-pinion steering gear. Too little force indicates a worn joint and too much force could indicate a binding joint. Answers a, c, and d are not correct because they do not indicate the testing of the force needed to move the tie rod for proper ball-socket assembly operation.

27. **The correct answer is c.** Technician A is correct because unlevel steering linkage will cause a turning force to be applied to the front wheels when they move up and down during normal suspension movement. Technician B is correct because the steering linkage must be parallel to the suspension and move together to prevent suspension movement from affecting the steering. If the steering wheel moves when the vehicle is bounced (jounced), then this means that the steering linkage is not level. Answers a, b, and d are not correct because both technicians are correct.

SUSPENSION AND STEERING (A4)

CATEGORY: SUSPENSION SYSTEMS DIAGNOSIS AND REPAIR

28. **The correct answer is c.** The steering damper is used to reduce steering linkage movement, which can result in a steering wheel shimmy while driving over various types of road surfaces. Answer a is not correct even though the steering could be difficult to turn if the dampener were to become seized but this is not likely. Answers b and d are not correct because the dampener does not affect the play in the steering because it is mounted in parallel with the linkage and is not part of the linkage itself.

29. **The correct answer is c.** Both technicians are correct. Technician A is correct because noise will be heard from the front suspension if the control arm bushings are worn or deteriorated. The noise may be a squeaking sound or a loud clunking sound if the bushings are partially or completely missing. Technician B is correct because worn or deteriorated strut rod bushings can cause noise when driving over rough roads or during braking or accelerating. Answers a, b, and d are not correct because both technicians are correct.

30. **The correct answer is b.** Technician B only is correct because the weight of the vehicle must be removed (unloaded) from the ball joint to be able to check for excessive free play in the joint itself. Technician A is not correct because if the joint has the weight of the vehicle applied, it is impossible to check for free play in the joint because the weight of the vehicle is being applied to keep the joint together. However, wear indicator-type ball joints must be checked with the weight being applied to the joint, but the question asks how to check for free play and in this case the ball joint has to be unloaded. Answers c and d are not correct because only Technician B is correct.

31. **The correct answer is c.** Both technicians are correct. Technician A is correct because it is normal for a thin film of oil to be seen at the top of a shock absorber near the seal. If liquid is observed dripping from the shock absorber, then this is a fault and the shock absorber should be replaced. Technician B is correct because cold temperatures can cause the rod seal to bleed a thin layer of fluid and this condition is considered normal. Answers a, b, and d are not correct because both technicians are correct.

32. **The correct answer is a.** Technician A only is correct because a broken rear leaf spring center bolt would allow the rear axle to move forward or rearward on one side of the vehicle creating a dog tracking condition. Technician B is not correct because defective upper control arm bushings on the front of the vehicle would not cause the rear of the vehicle to run out of align with the front wheels. Answers c and d are not correct because only Technician A is correct.

33. **The correct answer is c.** The cotter key *must* be replaced when it is removed because the metal fatigue can cause the end of the cotter key to break off if it is straightened and then bent over a second time. This broken part of the cotter key can become wedged in the wheel bearing, which could cause the wheel to lock leading to a possible collision and personal injury. Answer a is not correct because the bearing cup is usually replaced with the bearing and is not replaced as a part of routine service. Answer b is not correct even though it should be replaced if the front inner bearings are being serviced. Notice that the question involves servicing just the outer wheel bearings; otherwise, both the seal and the cotter key should be replaced. Answer d is not correct because the retainer washer does not wear and its replacement is not necessary.

34. **The correct answer is b.** A defective wheel bearing (brinelled or worn) will cause a hum, rumbling, or growling noise, which increases with vehicle speed similar to the noise of winter tires with an aggressive tread design. Answers a, c, and d are not correct because these sounds indicate other faults but are not typical of the noise made by a defective wheel bearing.

35. **The correct answer is b.** Technician B only is correct because the springs support the weight of the vehicle and if they sag, then replacement springs are needed to restore the proper vehicle height. Technician A is not correct because shock absorbers are designed to dampen the action of the springs and do not support any of the vehicle weight unless special load-lifting-type shock absorbers are installed. Answers c and d are not correct because only Technician B is correct.

36. **The correct answer is b.** Technician B is correct. The wear indicator on the ball joint is still visible above the grease fitting. When the ball joint has worn enough to require replacement, the indicator is flush with the base of the joint as shown. Technician A is not correct because the wear indicator does not show that the ball joint is excessively worn. Answers c and d are not correct because only Technician B is correct.

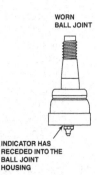

WORN
BALL JOINT

INDICATOR HAS
RECEDED INTO THE
BALL JOINT
HOUSING

37. **The correct answer is c.** Both technicians are correct. Technician A is correct because sagging springs would cause the vehicle to ride at a lower than normal height, thereby close to the bump stop. Technician B is also correct because worn shock absorbers can cause the rapid compression of the springs when the vehicle hits a bump in the road causing the suspension to travel farther upward faster than normal. Answers a, b, and d are not correct because both technicians are correct.

38. **The correct answer is c.** A tie rod separating tool should be used to separate tapered chassis parts without doing any harm. Answer a is not correct because a pickle fork tool often damages the rubber grease seal and should only be used if the joint is to be replaced. Answer b is not correct because a torch will not separate a tapered joint and the heat could reduce the strength of the steel parts plus destroying the rubber grease seal. Answer d is not correct because a shock or force is required to separate a tapered joint and a drilled hole would ruin the part.

39. **The correct answer is b.** The coil spring *must* be compressed before the strut retaining nut is removed because the spring tension needs to be removed from exerting force on the upper bearing assembly. Failure to compress the spring could result in possible personal injury when the upper retaining nut is removed and the spring expands upward. Answer a is not correct because even though the brake caliper and/or brake hose has to be removed on most vehicles in order to remove the strut from the vehicle, it is not necessary to prevent personal injury and may not be needed to be performed on many vehicles. Answers c and d are not correct because the upper strut mounting bolts and the lower attaching bolt, while often necessary to be removed to replace the strut cartridge, are not necessary to prevent personal injury.

40. **The correct answer is c.** Both technicians are correct. Technician A is correct because an overloaded vehicle can cause the rollers of the bearing to be forced into the outer race (cup) creating dents and causing the bearing to be noisy as the rollers pass over the dents during vehicle travel. Technician B is correct because the rollers could be forced into the outer race causing a dent if the bearings were overtightened, especially if the wheels were not being rotated during the bearing adjustment procedures. Answers a, b, and d are not correct because both technicians are correct.

41. **The correct answer is a.** Answer a is correct because the weight of the vehicle must be applied to the ball joint to force the indicator into its wear position where it can be observed by the technician. Answer b is not correct because while the free play of the load-carrying ball joints must be checked with the load removed, an indicator-type ball joint is checked with the load of the vehicle on the ball joints. Answer c is not correct because placing a jack under the lower control arm would tend to unload the ball joint. Answer d is not correct because the wear indicator itself is used to determine the amount of wear without a need to use a dial indicator to measure it.

42. **The correct answer is a.** The drawing shows a large clamp-type tool being used to press a new bushing into the control arm. Answer b is not correct because ball joints are not adjustable. Answer c is not correct because the drawing shows the control arm bushing area of the control arm rather than the ball joint section, even though a similar operation could be used to replace press-fit-type ball joints. Answer d is not correct because control arms are to be replaced rather than straightened if damaged or bent.

43. **The correct answer is c.** Both technicians are correct. Technician A is correct because 0.150 in. (150 thousandth of an inch) is greater than the maximum allowable specifications for most vehicles of 0.050 in. (50 thousandth of an inch). Technician B is correct because ball joints should always be replaced as a pair to maintain handling and steering. Answers a, b, and d are not correct because both technicians are correct.

44. **The correct answer is c.** Defective rear leaf springs can cause the rear of the vehicle to sag, thereby causing the left front to rise. Answer a is not correct because a broken stabilizer bar link will cause noise from the front and can cause the vehicle to lean excessively when cornering but it is not a load-carrying component so it could not cause the vehicle to sag down in the rear or rise up in the front. Answer b is not correct because the track rod keeps the rear wheels tracking properly behind the front wheels and could not cause the described problem. Answer d is not correct because a standard shock absorber does not support the vehicle weight and could not cause the problem even though a broken shock absorber could have contributed to the breaking of the rear leaf spring.

45. **The correct answer is b.** A defective strut rod bushing (also called a tension/compression rod bushing) can cause a pull during braking because the lower control arm is able to move toward the rear of the vehicle reducing the caster angle on that side. Answer a is not correct because worn or defective stabilizer bar links would cause noise while driving and excessive body lean during cornering, but they would not affect braking because the links do not keep the lower control arm in position. Answer c is not correct because even though defective rear leaf springs can cause the vehicle to sag, they are not likely to cause a pull to one side during braking. Answer d is not correct because a track rod keeps the rear axle centered under the vehicle and is not likely to cause a pull during braking.

46. **The correct answer is a.** Technician A only is correct because before removing the strut retainer nut, the coil spring has to be compressed to prevent personal injury. After the spring has been compressed, the retaining nut can be removed. The bearing and retainer are then removed. Answer b is not correct because the strut cartridge is a sealed unit and cannot be opened or serviced. Answers c and d are not correct because Technician A only is correct.

47. **The correct answer is b.** The rear axle is kept centered under the body by the track rod (panhard rod). If the track rod is bent, the rear axle will be shifted to one side causing it to be out of alignment with the front. Answer a is not correct because a rear track bar is not designed to keep the vehicle from swaying when cornering but rather is designed to keep the rear axle centered over the body and acts as one of the major suspension members. Answer c is not correct because a track bar would not cause any noise during cornering if bent. Answer d is not correct because the track rod is in the rear and would not have a major influence on braking even though it could cause some weird handling.

48. **The correct answer is a.** Technician A is correct because if the coil spring is correctly installed,one of the holes in the lower control arm should be completely covered and the other hole either open or only partially covered. Technician B is not correct because if the coil spring were installed upside down, both holes would be covered. Answers c and d are not correct because only technician A is correct.

49. **The correct answer is c.** Leaking shock absorbers are the least likely cause of vehicle wander when driving on a straight level road. Leaking shock absorbers could cause excessive body movement when traveling over bumps or dips in the road and could cause a harsh ride. Answers a, b, and d are not correct because all of these components could cause the vehicle to wander due to looseness in the suspension components that allow the front wheels to move left and right as the vehicle is traveling straight.

50. **The correct answer is d.** The least likely cause of a vehicle to sag in the rear would be leaking shock absorbers because even though this condition can cause the vehicle to ride roughly or cause the body to bounce over bumps in the road, the shock absorbers are not a load-carrying component. Answers a, b, and c are not correct because all of these could cause the rear of the vehicle to sag.

51. **The correct answer is a.** Technician A only is correct because if one rear spring is replaced, the other spring on the same axle should also be replaced to maintain the proper ride height and spring rate. Technician B is not correct because, even though replacing shock absorbers would be wise when the springs are installed, they do not contribute to the load-carrying capacity of the suspension system and would not be needed to restore the proper ride height unless special load-carrying shock absorbers are used. The springs support the vehicle weight and the shocks control the action of the springs. Answers c and d are not correct because Technician A only is correct.

52. **The correct answer is c.** A broken rear control arm or ball joint can cause the top of the left rear wheel to become angled inward at the top because the control arm locates the wheel and allows for up and down movement. Answer a is not correct because a worn stabilizer bushing can cause noise during suspension travel and the stabilizer bar is used to control body lean in corners. A fault with a bushing would not cause the wheel to be angled in at the top. Answer b is not correct because a broken rear track rod would allow the entire rear suspension to move sideways and would not cause one wheel to be angled inward. Answer d is not correct because a shock absorber is not a structural part of the suspension but rather is used to control the movement of the springs.

53. **The correct answer is a.** Worn or defective strut rod bushings will cause a loud clunking sound when the brakes are applied because the strut rods are used to keep the front wheels from moving forward or rearward. When the brakes are applied, the braking force causes the front wheels to move toward the rear. If the bushing is excessively worn or missing, the strut rod contacts the frame creating the loud noise. Answers b, c, and d are not correct although they would make some noise if defective. They cannot cause a loud clunk when braking.

54. **The correct answer is b.** Technician B only is correct because the spring seat insulators isolate the suspension from the body of the vehicle. If one of these spring insulators is damaged or missing, road and suspension noise will be transferred to the body. Technician A is not correct because sagging springs will not cause noise even though the suspension height is not correct. Answers c and d are not correct because only Technician B is correct.

55. **The correct answer is d.** Sagging springs will cause the vehicle to be lower than normal. If a heavy load has been carried in the vehicle on the left side, the left side springs could have sagged and remained lower than normal even though the load had been removed. Sagging springs require replacement. Answers a, b, and c are not correct because they do not support the weight of the vehicle and cannot be the cause of the problem.

56. **The correct answer is a.** Technician A only is correct because the shock absorbers themselves limit the rear axle travel. If the shocks were removed, the rear axle could drop and cause damage to the brake lines or control arm bushings. Technician B is not correct because the rear springs are attached to the rear axle and while they could fall if the rear axle is lowered, they do not have to be compressed when replacing the rear shock absorbers. Answers c and d are not correct because only Technician A is correct.

57. **The correct answer is c.** Both technicians are correct. Technician A is correct because all factory and most replacement springs are marked left and right because they are slightly different ratings to compensate for the weight of the driver.
Technician B is correct because most springs have to be installed with the correct end facing up to match the spring seats in the frame and on the lower control arm. Answers a, b, and d are not correct because both technicians are correct.

58. **The correct answer is b.** Technician B only is correct. The weight of the vehicle needs to be removed from the ball joint so any free play can be seen. By placing the jack under the lower control arm and lifting the vehicle, the coil spring is compressed allowing any free-play in the load-carrying lower ball to be measured. Technician A is not correct because if the vehicle were raised using the jack point under the frame, would cause the coil spring to exert a force on the ball joint keeping it compressed so any free-paly could not be measured. Answers c and d are not correct because only technician B is correct.

SUSPENSION AND STEERING (A4)

CATEGORY: RELATED SUSPENSION AND STEERING SERVICE

59. **The correct answer is a.** Technician A only is correct because a lateral acceleration sensor is used to detect cornering forces and the output as read on a scan tool is read in G's. When the sensor is un-bolted and turned on its side, the sensor should indicate 1 G, which is the force of gravity. Technician B (answer b) is not correct because the sensor should respond to the force of gravity. Answers c and d are not correct because Technician A only is correct.

60. **The correct answer is a.** The correct answer is excessive hub runout. If the bearing hub runout is excessive, the wheel which is attached to the hub will wobble as it rotates. It is this wobble that will be felt as a vibration. Hub runout can be measured using a dial indicator and should not exceed vehicle manufacturer's specifications. Answer b is not correct because a brake stabilizer bar link may cause noise or excessive body lean while cornering. It will not cause a vibration at highway speed. Answer c is not correct because worn shocks would allow more suspension movement than normal, but would not be the cause for a vibration. Answer d is not correct because just answer a is correct.

61. **The correct answer is a.** Technician A only is correct because the default setting for adjustable shock absorbers is a firm setting for safety reasons. If there were a fault in the system, the suspension would be able to respond to rapid changes which would help maintain vehicle stability. The only dis-advantage is a harsh ride that the driver or passengers may notice. Technician B (answer b) is not cor-rect because adjustable shock absorbers use a solenoid or motor to control the shocks. Compressed air is used in air shocks to control ride height at the rear. Answers c and d are not correct because Technician A only is correct.

62. **The correct answer is c.** A loaded strut is an assembly that includes the strut housing containing the strut hydraulic cylinder plus the coil spring and an upper mount. Using a loaded strut is a repair option that allows the technician to replace all of the strut components with one part number. Answer a is not correct because the insert is just one component of a strut assembly. Answer b is not correct because being gas-charged is just one specification of the strut and it does not mean that it contains all of the other parts that are included with a loaded strut. Answer d is not correct because a strut spring is compressed or loaded when it is installed onto the strut but this is not the same as a loaded strut, which is one part number for a complete assembled component.

SUSPENSION AND STEERING (A4)

CATEGORY: WHEEL ALIGNMENT DIAGNOSIS, ADJUSTMENT, AND REPAIR

63. **The correct answer is a.** Technician A only is correct because camber is a pulling angle if both front wheels are not within 0.5°. Technician B is not correct because while incorrect front toe can cause vehicle handling problems, it is not a pulling angle and, therefore, would not cause a pull. Answers c and d are not correct because only Technician A is correct.

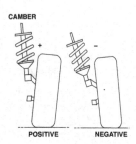

64. **The correct answer is c.** The strut rods adjust caster if they are adjustable. Rotating the adjusting nuts on the strut rod moves the lower control arm forward or rearward, thereby moving the lower ball joint and the caster angle. Answers a and b are not correct because moving the lower ball joint forward or rearward does not change any other angle *directly* except for caster even though camber and toe are somewhat affected by the changes in caster. Answer d is not correct because toe-out on turns is determined by the angle of the steering arm and would not change at all if the strut rod is adjusted.

65. **The correct answer is a.** Technician A only is correct because a vehicle equipped with an independent front suspension will steer (pull) in the direction of the greatest rear toe angle if the rear toe angles are not equal or close to being equal. The rear toe of a vehicle acts like a rudder of a boat and will cause the vehicle to steer in the opposite direction the rear wheels are pointing. Technician B is not correct because incorrect front toe cannot cause pull. Answers c and d are not correct because only Technician A is correct.

66. **The correct answer is d.** The shims adjust both camber and caster because if shims of equal thickness were removed or added, the camber is changed. If a shim was added or removed from either the front or the rear location, then caster and camber would be changed because the upper ball joint would be moved. If a shim is removed from the front and placed in the rear, this caster only is changed while maintaining the same camber. Answers a and b are not correct because both angles are adjusted. Answer c is not correct because even though the toe angle will change, it is not directly changed by adding or removing shims.

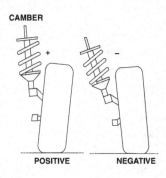 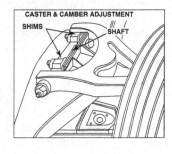

67. **The correct answer is c.** Both technicians are correct. Technician A is correct because the extra weight of the camper will cause the springs to compress, which usually changes the camber and caster. Technician B is correct because the extra weight of the camper will cause the front toe angle to change as the camber changes when the springs compress. The truck should be aligned with the camper installed to avoid handling or tire wear problems. Answers a, b, and d are not correct because both technicians are correct.

68. **The correct answer is a.** The vehicle will pull to the right because the right front camber is greater than the left front camber by 0.7°. Both front tires will feather edge because the toe is not within specifications. Answer b is not correct because the vehicle will pull to the side with the most camber (right). Answer c is not correct because the tire wear will occur on the inside edges of both front tires due to the excessive toe-out. Answer d is not correct because even though the vehicle will wear the inside of both front tires, it could pull to the right, not to the left.

69. **The correct answer is b.** The vehicle will pull toward the right because the caster is unequal by 1.8° and will pull toward the side with the least amount of caster. Answer a is not correct because the difference in the caster angle will cause the vehicle to pull toward the right. Answer c is not correct because the vehicle will pull rather than be unstable, which would cause wandering. Answer d is not correct because the vehicle could pull toward the right due to the caster difference rather than to the left.

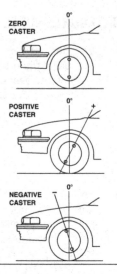

70. **The correct answer is c.** The alignment will cause the vehicle to pull toward the right due to the difference in the caster angles (pulls toward the side with the least caster) and not cause tire wear. Answer a (wander) is not correct because a vehicle cannot wander if it is pulling to one side. Wander is usually caused by a toe-out condition and this vehicle has the specified (within range) toe-in. Answer b is not correct because the two tire wearing angles, camber and toe, are within factory-specified limits and, therefore, excessive tire wear should not be a concern. The vehicle will pull due to the difference in the front caster angles. Answer d is not correct because the vehicle will pull to the right, not to the left, and will not feather-edge the tires because front toe is within factory specifications.

71. **The correct answer is a.** Technician A only is correct because the tire wear and pulling are consistent with the symptoms that would be created if the camber on the right front was excessively positive. This situation could occur if the vehicle had struck a curb and had bent the lower control arm. Technician B is not correct because incorrectly adjusted caster angles will not cause tire wear on one edge only. Answers c and d are not correct because only Technician A is correct.

72. **The correct answer is a.** Toe is the alignment angle that most often requires adjustment and will wear the tires if not within factory specifications. Answer b is not correct because even though incorrect camber can cause tire wear, it is not as important as toe and is less often in need of adjustment. Answer c is not correct because caster does not directly affect tire wear especially compared to incorrect toe setting. Answer d is not correct because SAI (steering axis inclination) is not an adjustable angle in most cases and has little effect on tire wear even though it can affect vehicle handling if it is not within factory specifications.

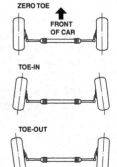

73. **The correct answer is c.** Torque steer occurs when engine torque is applied unequally to the front drive wheels, thereby creating a pull that is noticeable during rapid acceleration. Answers a, b, and d are not correct because even though these components can cause a pull, they are not likely to cause a pull only during acceleration.

74. **The correct answer is a.** Technician A only is correct because a vehicle will pull to the side with the most camber (the highest positive camber or the lowest negative camber angles). Technician B is not correct because even if there is unequal toe between the left and the right side, the toe angle splits when the vehicle is being driven and the steering wheel is forced crooked as the front wheels align themselves. Answers c and d are not correct because only Technician A is correct.

75. **The correct answer is a.** Technician A only is correct because this condition (often called memory steer) occurs when there is a binding in the steering that creates a force to be applied to the steering linkage and results in a pull that can change from one direction to the other. A binding upper strut mount can cause memory steer. Technician B is not correct because excessive positive caster creates a force on the suspension that tends to force the steering wheel to a straight ahead position rather than to one direction or the other. Answers c and d are not correct because only Technician A is correct.

76. **The correct answer is d.** Neither technician is correct. Technician A is not correct because the alignment angles are not changed when tires/wheels are installed even though the wheel offset difference could cause some handling concerns for the driver. Technician B is not correct because the suspension angles are not changed when different size wheels and tires are installed even though the handling may be changed as a result. Answers a, b, and c are not correct because neither technician is correct.

77. **The correct answer is d.** The angle of the steering knuckle (arm) determines the amount of toe-out-on-turns (TOOT), also called the Ackerman effect, and, therefore, if this measurement is not within factory specifications, the steering arm is likely damaged in a collision. Answers a, b, and c are not correct because these items do not affect the toe-out-on-turn angles(s).

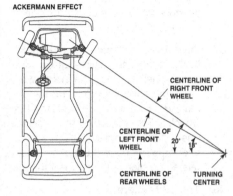

ACKERMANN EFFECT

CENTERLINE OF RIGHT FRONT WHEEL

CENTERLINE OF LEFT FRONT WHEEL

20° 18°

CENTERLINE OF REAR WHEELS

TURNING CENTER

78. **The correct answer is c.** The rear toe angle determines the thrust angle. The rear toe is similar to a rudder on a boat and affects the direction of vehicle travel. Answer a is not correct because the thrust angle is the total of both rear wheels, not the camber angle. Answer b is not correct because the front angles do not affect the rear thrust angle. Answer d is not correct because rear caster is not measured or adjustable on the rear and would not affect the rear thrust angle.

79. **The correct answer is c.** The rear toe should be the first angle adjusted if needed because the front wheels (toe) are then set parallel to the rear to achieve the proper vehicle tracking. Answers a, b, and d are not correct because even though the angles should be adjusted if out of factory specification, they are not the first angle that should be adjusted.

80. **The correct answer is a.** The wedge will move the axle hub outward at the top, thereby increasing camber. Answer b is not correct because the wedge is being installed vertically and would move the top of the wheel outward. To change toe, the wedge would have to be installed toward the front or rear of the vehicle. Answer c is not correct because rear caster is not changeable and if it were, the pivot point of the lower control arm would need to be moved forward or rearward. Answer d is not correct because rear SAI is not measured or corrected.

81. **The correct answer is d.** Neither technician is correct. Technician A is not correct because front camber and toe are within specifications. It would require negative camber or a toe-out condition to cause tire wear on the inside edges of the front tires. Technician B is not correct because the rear toe is within specifications. Answers a, b, and c are not correct because neither technician is correct.

82. **The correct answer is b.** Technician B only is correct because zero is an acceptable reading for toe, which indicates that both front wheels are traveling straight. Technician A is not correct because the total rear toe is within factory specifications and will not cause a dog tracking condition. Answers c and d are not correct because only Technician B is correct.

83. **The correct answer is c.** The present alignment is not perfect but the vehicle would most likely track left. The caster difference (0.7°) would indicate a slight tendency to pull to the left and the camber difference (0.6°) also would cause a pull to the left. Answers a and b are not correct because the vehicle could pull to the left. Answer d is not correct because a wander is usually caused by a lack of directional control and in this situation, the vehicle could pull to the left.

84. **The correct answer is c.** Both technicians are correct. Technician A is correct because low tire pressures can cause the vehicle to wander due to the lack of sidewall support of the tires. Technician B is correct because loose steering linkage can cause the vehicle to travel first in one direction, then the other, causing the vehicle to wander. Answers a, b, and d are not correct because both technicians are correct.

85. **The correct answer is c.** To straighten the steering wheel, the technician should adjust the toe by rotating the tie rod sleeves or adjusters with the steering wheel in the straight ahead position. Answer a is not correct because this method would not allow the steering gear to be centered, thereby creating a concern especially if the vehicle is equipped with a variable ratio steering gear. Answer b is not correct because adjusting the camber will not straighten the steering wheel. Answer d is not correct because adjusting the caster angle will not straighten the steering wheel.

86. The correct answer is d. A bent strut is the most likely cause because the SAI is the angle of the upper strut mount and the lower pivot (ball joint). The camber is under specifications, as well as the included angle (camber plus SAI), which indicates that there is a bent strut. Answer a is not correct because the camber and included angle should be close to equal and within factory specifications. Answers b and c are not correct because worn ball joints or tie rod ends will not cause the camber and the included angle to be out of specifications.

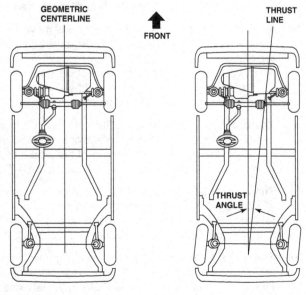

87. The correct answer is b. The angle of the steering arms determines the Ackerman angle (toe-out-on-turns) or the amount that the wheels rotate when turning. The inside wheel turns at a greater angle than the outside wheel to allow for the greater distance the outside wheel must travel. If the steering arm (steering knuckle) is bent, the front wheel(s) will not turn to the proper angle and the tire(s) will squeal due to the slipping of the tread across the pavement. Answers a, c, and d are not correct because even though this can cause steering-related problems, they are not the most likely to cause this particular problem of slow speed tire squeal.

88. The correct answer is a. Technician A only is correct because if the engine cradle was shifted to the left, the lower control for the left side would be moved toward the outside, which would decrease the camber reading on the left and increase the camber reading on the right. Technician B is not correct because even though a leaking strut could cause a handling problem, it cannot cause the camber angle to decrease on the left and increase on the right. Answers c and d are not correct because only Technician A is correct.

89. The correct answer is b. Technician B only is correct because the difference in the rear toe will cause the vehicle to steer toward the side that has the greatest amount of toe just as a rudder is used to steer a boat. Technician A is not correct because unlike the rear wheels, the front wheels are tied together with tie rods and this causes the toe to split equally as the vehicle is driven. Answers c and d are not correct because only Technician B is correct.

90. The correct answer is d. Neither technician is correct. Technician A is not correct because incorrect camber cannot cause a tramp-type vibration even though it can cause excessive tire wear and/or a pulling condition if not corrected. Technician B is not correct because incorrect toe can cause excessive tire wear and an off center steering wheel, but it cannot cause a tramp-type vibration. Only a fault with a wheel or tire can cause a tramp-type vibration. Answer c is not correct because neither technician is correct.

91. The correct answer is c. The cam bolts are able to change camber if both are rotated the same direction by the same amount. Caster is adjusted by rotating one cam only or both in opposite directions to maintain the same camber. Answers a, b, and d are not correct because camber and caster can be adjusted.

92. The correct answer is a. Answer a is correct because the shim is positioned so that the camber will be changed (outward at the bottom to decrease camber) plus some toe because the shim is also toward the front will change the toe setting. Answer b is not correct because to change camber only, the shim would need to be placed at the top or bottom of the hub. Answer c is not correct because the shim would need to be placed at the front or rear of the hub to change the toe only. Answer d is not correct because caster cannot be changed using a shim and is not adjusted on the rear of a vehicle.

93. **The correct answer is c.** The camber will be adjusted by rotating the eccentric cam at the base of the strut. Answer a is not correct because caster will not be changed. Answer b is not correct because even though the toe will change slightly when the eccentric is rotated, the toe change is due to the change in the camber. Answer d is not correct because neither the SAI nor the caster is changed when the eccentric is rotated.

94. **The correct answer is b.** When shims are added to both the front and rear positions, the control arm will be moved toward the right, thereby increasing positive camber. Answer a is not correct because adding shims to the front position will increase camber but it will also increase caster by moving the ball joint rearward. Answer c is not correct because moving shim(s) from the front to the rear will decrease caster and keep the camber about the same. Answer d is not correct because removing shims will decrease camber, not increase camber.

95. **The correct answer is b.** By adjusting the strut rod, the lower control arm is moved forward or rearward, thereby changing the caster angle. Answer a is not correct because even though the camber angle may change as the strut rod is adjusted, it is the result of the change in the caster angle that caused the change in the camber. Answer c is not correct because even though the toe will change, it is a result of the change in the caster angle. Answer d is not correct because toe-out-on-turns are not adjustable but rather are built into the angle of the steering arms.

SUSPENSION AND STEERING (A4)

CATEGORY: WHEEL AND TIRE DIAGNOSIS AND SERVICE

96. **The correct answer is a.** Technician A only is correct because all tires and wheels are not perfectly round and some minor differences may have caused the excessive radial runout (out of round). By rotating the tire on the rim, the high spot of the tire may be aligned with the low spot of the wheel, which could reduce the total amount of runout. Technician B is not correct because even though the tires could be defective and require replacement, the tires should be rotated on the rim and then checked again for excessive runout before replacement. Answers c and d are not correct because only Technician A is correct.

97. **The correct answer is c.** Using the modified X tire rotation method, the driven wheels are moved straight forward or rearward and the non-drive wheels are crossed as they are moved forward or rearward. In a front-wheel-drive vehicle, the front wheels are moved straight back so the right front would be placed on the right rear. Answers a, b, and d are not correct because they do not place the wheel in the correct position using the modified X tire rotation method.

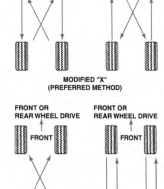

98. **The correct answer is b.** Underinflated tires will cause the tires to wear excessively on both the inside and outside edges. Answer a is not correct because overinflation rather than underinflation will cause excessive tire wear in the center of the tread. Answer c is not correct because excessive radial runout will cause a tramp-type vibration, but is unlikely to cause tire wear on both edges. Answer d is not correct because excessive lateral runout will cause a shimmy-type vibration, but is unlikely to cause tire wear on both edges.

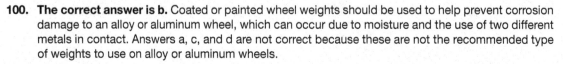

99. **The correct answer is b.** Never exceed 40 psi when seating the bead of the tire during installation, as a rim or bead damage can occur, which could cause personal injury. After the tire bead has been seated, the specified amount of air pressure can be used. Answers a, c, and d are not correct because they do not state the industry standard for maximum pressure during tire installation.

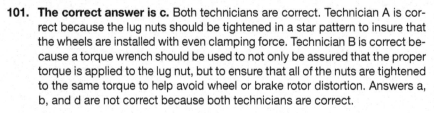

100. **The correct answer is b.** Coated or painted wheel weights should be used to help prevent corrosion damage to an alloy or aluminum wheel, which can occur due to moisture and the use of two different metals in contact. Answers a, c, and d are not correct because these are not the recommended type of weights to use on alloy or aluminum wheels.

101. **The correct answer is c.** Both technicians are correct. Technician A is correct because the lug nuts should be tightened in a star pattern to insure that the wheels are installed with even clamping force. Technician B is correct because a torque wrench should be used to not only be assured that the proper torque is applied to the lug nut, but to ensure that all of the nuts are tightened to the same torque to help avoid wheel or brake rotor distortion. Answers a, b, and d are not correct because both technicians are correct.

TORQUE SEQUENCE

102. **The correct answer is a.** Technician A only is correct because when match mounting, the highest portion of the tire (usually at or near the major splice) is aligned with the valve core, which is usually drilled at the smallest diameter of the wheel, resulting in a smoother ride and less weight needed to balance the tire/wheel assembly. Technician B is not correct because only a material that is approved for tire mounting should be used. The use of silicone spray lubricant could cause the tire to rotate on the rim during braking. Answers c and d are not correct because only Technician A is correct.

103. **The correct answer is a.** Most vehicle manufacturers specify a wheel tightening torque of about 80–100 lb-ft and even though some may be less than 80 lb-ft or greater than 100 lb-ft, this is the best answer. Answers b, c, and d are not correct because they are higher than the usual specified wheel lug nut torque for passenger vehicles.

104. **The correct answer is c.** Both technicians are correct. Technician A is correct because if the wheel is bent, the lateral runout could be excessive. The excessive lateral runout could occur if the vehicle hit or slid into a curb. Technician B is correct because the mounting hub could have excessive lateral runout, which would be transferred and the amount amplified at the outer diameter of the wheel. Hub or spindle replacement may be necessary to correct the excessive runout. Answers c and d are not correct because both technicians are correct.

105. **The correct answer is a.** Diagonal tire wear is shown and is a result of incorrect toe setting on the rear of a front-wheel-drive vehicle. The wear pattern is created by the tire being dragged sideways as it rotates. Answer b is not correct because incorrect camber will cause excessive tire wear on one side of the tread. Answer c is not correct because an overinflated tire will be worn more in the center of the tread compared to the outside edges. Answer d is not correct because an underinflated tire will cause excessive wear on both the inside and outside edges of the tread.

106. **The correct answer is b.** Many full-size SUVs are equipped with a full-size spare tire that includes its own TPMS sensor. When the pressure drops below the threshold pressure of 25%, that is below the specified inflation pressure, the warning lamp will be triggered. Answer a is not correct because the correct inflation pressure is what is specified on the driver's door placard. Answer c is not correct because if a TPMS sensor were defective, the warning lamp would be flashing and/or a warning message would be displayed indicating that system fault has been detected. Answer c is not correct because if a TPMS control module (controller) were defective, the warning lamp would be flashing and/or a warning message would be displayed indicating that system fault has been detected.

107. **The correct answer is b.** Technician B only is correct because an out-of-balance front tire will cause a vibration that is felt in the steering wheel at highway speeds. Answer a is not correct because while an out-of-balance driveshaft (prop shaft) will cause a vibration, it will be felt throughout the vehicle and in the seat rather than in the steering wheel. Answers c and d are not correct because only Technician B is correct.

108. **The correct answer is a.** Technician A only is correct because many vehicles equipped with a full-size spare tire use a pressure sensor in the spare. If the inflation pressure drops below 25% of the placard pressure, the warning lamp will come on. Technician B is not correct because overinflating the tires can also trigger the warning light. Answers c and d are not correct because only Technician A is correct.

109. **The correct answer is b.** Technician B only is correct because a flashing TPMS dash warning light indicates that the system has detected a fault in the system. The most likely reason is that the system has detected that one or more of the wheel sensors is not broadcasting tire pressure information to the TPMS controller. Technician A (answer a) is not correct because the warning lamp would be on, but not flashing if a low tire was detected. Answers c and d are not correct because Technician B only is correct.

110. **The correct answer is d.** Depending on the year, make, and model of vehicle, a new tire pressure sensor may be learned by just driving the vehicle, but others may require the use of a scan tool, such as a special TPMS tester or a magnet. Answers a, b, and c are not correct because any one of these may be required depending on the exact vehicle.

BRAKES TEST CONTENT AREAS

This ASE study guide for Brakes (A5) is divided into the sub-content areas that correlate to the actual ASE certification test as follows:

CONTENT AREA	QUESTIONS IN TEST	NUMBER OF STUDY GUIDE QUESTIONS
A. Hydraulic System Diagnosis and Repair	12	57 (1–57)
1. Master Cylinders (3)		
2. Lines and Hoses (3)		
3. Valves and Switches (3)		
4. Bleeding, Flushing, and Leak Testing (3)		
B. Drum Brake Diagnosis and Repair	5	37 (58–94)
C. Disc Brake Diagnosis and Repair	10	35 (95–129)
D. Electronic Brake Control Systems— Antilock Brake Systems (ABS), Traction Control Systems (TCS), and Electronic Stability Control System (ESC)— Diagnosis and Repair	7	17 (130–146)
TOTAL	**45**	**146**

TIME ALLOWED TO TAKE THE TEST

The allocated time to take the Brakes Certification test is 75 minutes. ASE adds 10 additional questions to the test for research purposes for a total of 55 questions. These questions do not count toward your score, but they are embedded within the test and there is no way of knowing which ones do not count. As a result, the technician needs to answer 55 questions in 75 minutes, or about one question per minute.

If taking the recertification A5 test, there are just 23 questions with no additional research questions included. The time allocated to take the recertification test is 30 minutes, which means about one minute per question.

BEFORE USING THIS STUDY GUIDE

Before trying to answer the questions and looking at the explanations, look over the following list of the content that ASE states will be covered in the certification test. For best results using this study guide, check service information or consult an automotive textbook for details on any of the content areas that are not familiar before trying to answer the questions. For additional information about the ASE test, visit the website at **www.ase.com**.

BRAKES (A5) CERTIFICATION TEST

A. HYDRAULIC SYSTEM DIAGNOSIS AND REPAIR (14 QUESTIONS)

1. Master Cylinders (non-ABS) (3 questions)

1. Diagnose poor stopping or dragging caused by problems in the master cylinder; determine needed repairs.
2. Diagnose poor stopping, dragging, high or low pedal, or hard pedal caused by problems in the step bore master cylinder and internal valves (e.g., volume control devices, quick take-up valve, fast-fill valve, pressure regulating valve); determine needed repairs.
3. Measure and adjust master cylinder pushrod length.
4. Check master cylinder for defects by depressing brake pedal; determine needed repairs.
5. Diagnose the cause of master cylinder external fluid leakage.
6. Remove master cylinder from vehicle; install master cylinder; test operation of the hydraulic system.
7. Bench bleed (check for function and remove air) all non-ABS master cylinders.

2. Fluids, Lines, and Hoses (3 questions)

1. Diagnose poor stopping, pulling, or dragging caused by problems in the brake fluid, lines, and hoses; determine needed repairs.
2. Inspect brake lines and fittings for leaks, dents, kinks, rust, cracks, or wear; tighten loose fittings and supports.
3. Inspect flexible brake hoses for leaks, kinks, cracks, bulging, or wear; tighten loose fittings and supports.
4. Fabricate and/or replace brake lines (double flare and ISO types), hoses, fittings, and supports.
5. Select, handle, store, and install proper brake fluids (including silicone fluids).
6. Inspect brake lines and hoses for proper routing.

3. Valves and Switches (Non-ABS) (4 questions)

1. Diagnose poor stopping, pulling, or dragging caused by problems in the hydraulic system valve(s); determine needed repairs.
2. Inspect, test, and replace metering, proportioning, pressure differential, and combination valves.
3. Inspect, test, replace, and adjust load or height sensing-type proportioning valve(s).
4. Inspect, test, and replace brake warning light, switch, and wiring.

4. Bleeding, Flushing, and Leak Testing (Non-ABS) (4 questions)

1. Bleed (manual, pressure, vacuum, or surge method) and/or flush hydraulic system.
2. Pressure test brake hydraulic system.

B. DRUM BRAKE DIAGNOSIS AND REPAIR (6 QUESTIONS)

1. Diagnose poor stopping, pulling, or dragging caused by drum brake hydraulic problems; determine needed repairs.
2. Diagnose poor stopping, noise, pulling, grabbing, dragging, or pedal pulsation caused by drum brake mechanical problems; determine needed repairs.
3. Remove, clean, inspect, and measure brake drums; follow manufacturers' recommendations in determining need to machine or replace.
4. Machine drums according to manufacturers' procedures and specifications.

5. Using proper safety procedures, remove, clean, and inspect brake shoes/linings, springs, pins, self-adjusters, levers, clips, brake backing (support) plates and other related brake hardware; determine needed repairs.

6. Lubricate brake shoe support pads on backing (support) plate, self-adjuster mechanisms, and other brake hardware.

7. Install brake shoes and related hardware.

8. Pre-adjust brake shoes and parking brake before installing brake drums or drum/hub assemblies and wheel bearings.

9. Reinstall wheel, torque lug nuts, and make final checks and adjustments.

C. DISC BRAKE DIAGNOSIS AND REPAIR (13 QUESTIONS)

1. Diagnose poor stopping, pulling, or dragging caused by disc brake hydraulic problems; determine needed repairs.

2. Diagnose poor stopping, noise, pulling, grabbing, dragging, pedal pulsation, or pedal travel caused by disc brake mechanical problems; determine needed repairs.

3. Retract integral parking brake caliper piston(s) according to manufacturers' recommendations.

4. Remove caliper assembly from mountings; clean and inspect for leaks and damage to caliper housing.

5. Clean, inspect, and measure caliper mountings and slides for wear and damage.

6. Remove, clean, and inspect pads and retaining hardware; determine needed repairs, adjustments, and replacements.

7. Disassemble and clean caliper assembly; inspect parts for wear, rust, scoring, and damage; replace all seals, boots, and any damaged or worn parts.

8. Reassemble caliper.

9. Clean, inspect, and measure rotor with a dial indicator and a micrometer; follow manufacturers' recommendations in determining need to machine or replace.

10. Remove and replace rotor.

11. Machine rotor, using on-car or off-car method, according to manufacturers' procedures and specifications.

12. Install pads, calipers, and related attaching hardware; bleed system.

13. Adjust calipers with integrated parking brakes according to manufacturers' recommendations.

14. Fill master cylinder to proper level with recommended fluid; inspect caliper for leaks.

15. Reinstall wheel, torque lug nuts, and make final checks and adjustments.

D. POWER ASSIST UNITS DIAGNOSIS AND REPAIR (4 QUESTIONS)

1. Test pedal free travel with and without engine running to check power booster operation.

2. Check vacuum supply (manifold or auxiliary pump) to vacuum-type power booster.

3. Inspect the vacuum-type power booster unit for vacuum leaks and proper operation; inspect the check valve for proper operation; repair, adjust, or replace parts as necessary.

4. Inspect and test hydro-boost system and accumulator for leaks and proper operation; repair, adjust, or replace parts as necessary.

E. MISCELLANEOUS SYSTEMS (WHEEL BEARINGS, PARKING BRAKES, ELECTRICAL, ETC.) DIAGNOSIS AND REPAIR (7 QUESTIONS)

1. Diagnose wheel bearing noises, wheel shimmy and vibration problems; determine needed repairs.

2. Remove, clean, inspect, repack wheel bearings, or replace wheel bearings and races; replace seals; adjust wheel bearings according to manufacturers' specifications.

3. Check parking brake system; inspect cables and parts for wear, rusting, and corrosion; clean or replace parts as necessary; lubricate assembly.

4. Adjust parking brake assembly; check operation.

5. Test the service and parking brake indicator and warning light(s), switch(es), and wiring.

6. Test, adjust, repair, or replace brake stop light switch, lamps, and related circuits.

F. ANTI-LOCK BRAKE SYSTEM (ABS) DIAGNOSIS AND REPAIR (11 QUESTIONS)

1. Follow accepted service and safety precautions when inspecting, testing, and servicing of ABS hydraulic, electrical, and mechanical components.

2. Diagnose poor stopping, wheel lock up, pedal feel and travel, pedal pulsation, and noise problems caused by the ABS; determine needed repairs.

3. Observe ABS warning light(s) at startup and during road test; determine if further diagnosis is needed.

4. Diagnose ABS electronic control(s), components, and circuits using self diagnosis and/or recommended test equipment; determine needed repairs.

5. Depressurize integral (high pressure) components of the ABS following manufacturers' recommended safety procedures.

6. Fill the ABS master cylinder with recommended fluid to proper level following manufacturers' procedures; inspect system for leaks.

7. Bleed the ABS hydraulic circuits following manufacturers' procedures.

8. Perform a fluid pressure (hydraulic boost) diagnosis on integral (high pressure) ABS; determine needed repairs.

9. Remove and install ABS components following manufacturers' procedures and specifications; observe proper placement of components and routing of wiring harness.

10. Diagnose, service, and adjust ABS speed sensors and circuits following manufacturers' recommended procedures (includes voltage output, resistance, shorts to voltage/ground, and frequency data).

11. Diagnose ABS braking problems caused by vehicle modifications (tire size, curb height, final drive ratio, etc.) and other vehicle mechanical and electrical/electronic modifications (communication, security, radio, etc.).

12. Repair wiring harness and connectors following manufacturers' procedures.

BRAKES (A5)

CATEGORY: HYDRAULIC, POWER ASSIST, AND PARKING BRAKE SYSTEMS DIAGNOSIS AND REPAIR

1. What is the switch in the center of this cutaway hydraulic brake component?

   a. Metering valve
   b. Pressure differential switch
   c. Proportioning valve
   d. Master cylinder check valve

2. Two technicians are discussing master cylinders. Technician A says that it is normal to see fluid movement in the reservoir when the brake pedal is depressed. Technician B says a defective master cylinder can cause the brake pedal to slowly sink to the floor when depressed. Which technician is correct?

   a. A only
   b. B only
   c. Both A and B
   d. Neither A nor B

3. The primary brake circuit fails due to a leak in the lines leaving the rear section of a dual-split master cylinder. Technician A says that the driver will notice a lower-than-normal brake pedal and some reduced braking power. Technician B says that the brake pedal will "grab" higher than normal. Which technician is correct?

   a. A only
   b. B only
   c. Both A and B
   d. Neither A nor B

4. Two technicians are discussing a problem where the brake pedal travels too far before the vehicle starts to slow. Technician A says that the brake pedal linkage may be out of adjustment. Technician B says that one circuit from the master cylinder may be leaking or defective. Which technician is correct?

   a. A only
   b. B only
   c. Both A and B
   d. Neither A nor B

5. The rear brakes lock up during a regular brake application. Technician A says a stuck open metering valve could be the cause. Technician B says that stuck front disc brake calipers could be the cause. Which technician is correct?

   a. A only
   b. B only
   c. Both A and B
   d. Neither A nor B

6. A lower-than-normal and spongy brake pedal is being diagnosed. Technician A says that air in the hydraulic system could be the cause. Technician B says a defective pressure differential switch could be the cause. Which technician is correct?

   a. A only
   b. B only
   c. Both A and B
   d. Neither A nor B

7. The button on the _____ valve should be depressed or held out when pressure bleeding the brakes.

   a. metering
   b. proportioning
   c. pressure differential
   d. residual check

8. Most vehicle manufacturers specify brake fluid that meets what specification?

   a. DOT 3
   b. DOT 4
   c. DOT 5
   d. Either a or b

9. Two technicians are discussing the reason that the brake fluid level in the master cylinder drops after several months of driving. Technician A says that it may be normal due to the wear of the disc brake pads. Technician B says that a low brake fluid level may indicate a hydraulic leak somewhere in the system. Which technician is correct?

   a. A only
   b. B only
   c. Both A and B
   d. Neither A nor B

10. Two technicians are discussing brake fluid. Technician A says that brake fluid should only be used from a sealed container because it absorbs moisture from the air. Technician B says that brake fluid should be handled with care because it can remove paint from the vehicle if spilled. Which technician is correct?

    a. A only
    b. B only
    c. Both A and B
    d. Neither A nor B

11. If automatic transmission fluid or power steering fluid gets into a master cylinder, all of the rubber parts must be replaced because _____.

    a. the rubber seals will shrink in size and cause internal leaks
    b. the rubber seals will become hardened and cause external leaks
    c. the rubber seals will melt and dissolve causing brake failure
    d. the rubber seals will swell and cause brake failure

12. Two technicians are discussing brake lines. Technician A says that a double lap flare end can be used when replacing a line that came from the factory with an ISO flare. Technician B says that a replacement line with an ISO flare can be used to replace a line that came from the factory with a double lap flare end. Which technician is correct?

    a. A only
    b. B only
    c. Both A and B
    d. Neither A nor B

13. The brake bleeding procedure usually specified for most rear-wheel-drive vehicles with a dual split master cylinder is usually _____.

    a. RR, LR, RF, LF
    b. LF, RF, LR, RR
    c. RF, LR, LF, RR
    d. LR, RR, LF, RF

14. What should be used to replace a leaking brake line?

    a. Double-wrapped steel brake line
    b. Copper line
    c. Copper-nickel brake line
    d. Either a or c

15. Most manufacturers recommend that disassembled brake parts should be cleaned with _____.

    a. throttle body cleaner
    b. denatured alcohol
    c. stoddard solvent
    d. detergent and water

16. A customer complains that the brake pedal is lower than normal. Technician A says that the vacuum power brake booster may be defective. Technician B says that air in the hydraulic system could be the cause. Which technician is correct?

    a. A only
    b. B only
    c. Both A and B
    d. Neither A nor B

17. The rubber used in most brake system components will swell if exposed to _____.

    a. engine oil or ATF
    b. moisture in the air
    c. DOT 5 brake fluid
    d. water

18. Technician A says brake fluid should be filled to the top of the reservoir to be assured of proper brake pressure when the brakes are applied. Technician B says that the brake fluid level should be filled only to the maximum-level line to allow for expansion when the brake fluid gets hot during normal operation. Which technician is correct?

    a. A only
    b. B only
    c. Both A and B
    d. Neither A nor B

19. Self-apply of the brakes can occur if _____.

    a. the master cylinder is leaking at the rear seal (secondary seal of the primary piston)
    b. the vent port (compensating port) is clogged or covered
    c. the replenishing port inlet is clogged or covered
    d. the vacuum booster vacuum hose is restricted

20. Technician A says that the brake pedal height should be checked as part of a thorough visual inspection of the brake system. Technician B says the pedal free play and pedal reserve should be checked. Which technician is correct?

    a. A only
    b. B only
    c. Both A and B
    d. Neither A nor B

21. Technician A says the red brake warning lamp on the dash will light if there is a hydraulic failure or low brake fluid level. Technician B says the red brake warning lamp on the dash will light if the parking brake is on. Which technician is correct?

   a. A only
   b. B only
   c. Both A and B
   d. Neither A nor B

22. A vehicle tends to lock up the front wheels when being driven on slippery road surfaces. Technician A says that the metering valve may be defective. Technician B says the proportioning valve may be stuck open. Which technician is correct?

   a. A only
   b. B only
   c. Both A and B
   d. Neither A nor B

23. Two technicians are discussing bleeding air from the brake hydraulic system. Technician A says to depress the brake pedal slowly and not allow pedal to go to the floor to prevent possible seal damage inside the master cylinder. Technician B says to wait 15 seconds between strokes of the brake pedal. Which technician is correct?

   a. A only
   b. B only
   c. Both A and B
   d. Neither A nor B

24. The brakes were found to be dragging on the right front on a rear-wheel drive vehicle equipped with front disc brakes and drum rear brakes. What is the most likely cause?

   a. Open brake (stop) light switch
   b. A leaking vacuum booster
   c. Air in the line
   d. Stuck caliper slides

25. Technician A says that the bleeder valve should be opened before pushing the caliper piston back into the caliper during disc brake service. Technician B says to use a brake hose clamp on the brake line as the piston is pushed into the caliper during disc brake service. Which technician is correct?

   a. A only
   b. B only
   c. Both A and B
   d. Neither A nor B

26. An import vehicle is in the shop for a brake fluid replacement as recommended by the manufacturer. Technician A says that all that is required is to suction the old fluid out of the master cylinder reservoir and replace with new fluid. Technician B says that all of the bleeders should be opened and the brake fluid bled until only fresh fluid is seen. Which technician is correct?

   a. A only
   b. B only
   c. Both A and B
   d. Neither A nor B

27. Two technicians are discussing the installation of a new master cylinder. Technician A says that the master cylinder should be bled on the bench before being installed on the vehicle. Technician B says that a new or rebuilt master cylinder is already fitted with brake fluid and ready to install on the vehicle. Which technician is correct?

   a. A only
   b. B only
   c. Both A and B
   d. Neither A nor B

28. The special tool shown is used to _____.

   a. depress the proportioning valve
   b. hold the metering valve open
   c. center the pressure differential switch
   d. clamp off the brake hose to the front calipers

29. A replacement vacuum brake booster and master cylinder was installed and then during a test drive, the brakes self-applied after about 10 minutes of driving. Technician A says that the brake pedal linkage may be incorrectly adjusted or the wrong parts were installed that has caused the vent port (compensating port) to be blocked. Technician B says the master cylinder reservoir may have been overfilled. Which technician is correct?

   a. A only
   b. B only
   c. Both A and B
   d. Neither A nor B

30. Which of the following conditions can cause the red brake warning lamp to light?

   a. Low brake fluid level in the master cylinder reservoir
   b. Parking brake applied
   c. A leak in either the front or rear brake line
   d. All of the above

31. The front of the vehicle dips downward in the front during light braking. Which of the following is the *most likely* cause?

   a. An internally leaking master cylinder
   b. A defective metering valve
   c. A stuck open proportioning valve
   d. Air in the lines

32. Brake fluid is observed leaking from the rear of the master cylinder and flowing down the front of the vacuum brake booster assembly. Which fault is the *most likely*?

   a. The vacuum booster has a hole, which is drawing the brake fluid from the master cylinder
   b. A leaking master cylinder cover seal
   c. A bent master cylinder push rod
   d. A leaking secondary seal on the primary piston of the master cylinder

33. The owner of a sport utility vehicle (SUV) complains that the brake pedal drops when the brake pedal is depressed while stopped at a traffic light. The brakes seem to operate normally and no external fluid leaks can be seen. Technician A says that the metering or proportioning valve may be defective. Technician B says that the master cylinder may be leaking internally due to a failed seal(s). Which technician is correct?

   a. A only
   b. B only
   c. Both A and B
   d. Neither A nor B

34. What is the purpose of the two units that are located under this front-wheel-drive vehicle?

   a. Front metering valves to prevent front wheel lockup
   b. Hydraulic brake line connectors to the rear brakes
   c. Brake fluid filters
   d. Rear proportioning valves to limit rear wheel lockup

35. The brake lines from the master cylinder are being replaced because they were damaged in a collision. Technician A says that the replacement lines should be coiled like the factory original to help increase brake pressure to the rear brakes. Technician B says the coils are to help reduce vibration and to allow the brake line to move slightly as the body moves on the frame. Which technician is correct?

    a. A only
    b. B only
    c. Both A and B
    d. Neither A nor B

36. What is this brake hydraulic component?

    a. A master cylinder
    b. A proportioning valve
    c. A metering valve
    d. A combination valve

37. What is the *most likely* service being performed?

    a. Adding fresh brake fluid through the caliper
    b. Checking the caliper for water
    c. Installing a new flexible brake line
    d. Bleeding the air from the disc brake caliper and line

38. Brake fluid is discovered on the sidewall of the rear tire as shown. What is the *most likely* cause?

    a. A hole in the brake drum
    b. Leaking rear wheel cylinder
    c. A leaking rear proportioning valve
    d. A leaking rear flexible brake hose

39. Two technicians are discussing the system in the illustration. Technician A says that this valve helps reduce rear wheel lockup during hard braking. Technician B says that the lever should be disconnected to bleed the rear brakes. Which technician is correct?

    a. A only
    b. B only
    c. Both A and B
    d. Neither A nor B

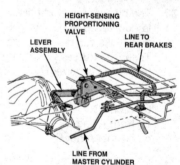

40. Two technicians are discussing using the equipment shown. Technician A says that the pressure exerted on the master cylinder should be less than about 20 psi (138 kPa). Technician B says that a button on the metering valve may need to be opened to allow bleeding of the front brakes. Which technician is correct?

    a. A only
    b. B only
    c. Both A and B
    d. Neither A nor B

41. The right front wheel brake line on a front-wheel-drive vehicle is cut by road debris. Which other wheel brake may be affected?

    a. The left front
    b. All of the brakes, except the parking brake, will be affected
    c. The right rear
    d. The left rear

42. Two technicians are discussing manual brake bleeding. Technician A says that an assistant should apply as much force as possible on the brake pedal to force the air and the brake fluid out of the bleeder valves. Technician B says that the assistant should pump the brake pedal rapidly before bleeding to force the air toward the bleeder valves. Which technician is correct?

    a. A only
    b. B only
    c. Both A and B
    d. Neither A nor B

43. Two technicians are discussing gravity bleeding. Technician A says that gravity bleeding of disc brakes can be achieved by opening the bleeder valve(s) and waiting until clear brake fluid without bubbles is observed flowing out of the valve, then closing the valve. Technician B says that if the bleeder valve is opened, air will get into the brake system unless the brake pedal is depressed. Which technician is correct?

    a. A only
    b. B only
    c. Both A and B
    d. Neither A nor B

44. Technician A says a pull to the right during braking could be caused by a defective metering valve. Technician B says a pull to the left could be caused by a defective proportioning valve. Which technician is correct?

    a. A only
    b. B only
    c. Both A and B
    d. Neither A nor B

45. The rear brake lights do not work when the brake pedal is depressed. Technician A says that low brake fluid in the master cylinder can be the cause. Technician B says that an open in the wiring to the brake lights could be the cause. Which technician is correct?

    a. A only
    b. B only
    c. Both A and B
    d. Neither A nor B

46. The red brake warning light on the dash is on and the parking brake is fully released. Technician A says that the brake fluid may be low in the master cylinder. Technician B says that the rear brake linings may be worn to the limit where replacement is necessary. Which technician is correct?

    a. A only
    b. B only
    c. Both A and B
    d. Neither A nor B

47. Technician A says that a restricted flexible brake hose can cause a low brake pedal. Technician B says air in the brake lines can cause a low brake pedal. Which technician is correct?

    a. A only
    b. B only
    c. Both A and B
    d. Neither A nor B

48. A driver has to "pump up" the brakes (depress the brake pedal several times) before the vehicle starts to slow down. Technician A says that the rear drum brakes may need replacing or adjusting. Technician B says that loose front wheel bearings could be the cause. Which technician is correct?

   a. A only
   b. B only
   c. Both A and B
   d. Neither A nor B

49. A Hydro-Boost hydraulic brake booster is being diagnosed. Technician A says that if the accumulator is loose and can be moved by hand with the engine off, then it has lost its charge and must be replaced. Technician B says it is normal to lose power-assisted brakes as soon as the engine stops on a vehicle equipped with Hydro-Boost. Which technician is correct?

   a. A only
   b. B only
   c. Both A and B
   d. Neither A nor B

50. A vehicle equipped with a vacuum brake booster has no power assist until the engine has run for a minute or two, then the power assist works normally. What is the *most likely* cause?

   a. Worn front disc brake pads
   b. Brake pedal push rod adjusted too short
   c. Engine needs a tune-up to produce a higher vacuum at idle speed
   d. A defective check valve

51. Technician A says that a defective vacuum brake booster can cause a lower-than-normal brake pedal during normal braking. Technician B says that worn or misadjusted rear drum brakes can cause a lower-than-normal brake pedal during normal braking. Which technician is correct?

   a. A only
   b. B only
   c. Both A and B
   d. Neither A nor B

52. A brake pedal pulsation complaint is being diagnosed on a vehicle equipped with a Hydro-Boost brake-assist system. Technician A says the pulsation could be caused by a loose power steering pump belt. Technician B says that a defective (warped) front disc brake rotor could be the cause. Which technician is correct?

   a. A only
   b. B only
   c. Both A and B
   d. Neither A nor B

53. The first step in diagnosing a Hydro-Boost problem is _____.

   a. a pressure test of the pump
   b. a volume test of the pump
   c. to tighten the power steering drive belt
   d. a thorough visual inspection

54. A brake pedal feels spongy when depressed. Technician A says that a defective hydraulic brake booster could be the cause. Technician B says that a defective vacuum brake booster could be the cause. Which technician is correct?

   a. A only
   b. B only
   c. Both A and B
   d. Neither A nor B

55. A defective vacuum brake booster will cause a _____.

    a. hard brake pedal
    b. soft (spongy) brake pedal
    c. low brake pedal
    d. slight hissing noise when the brake pedal is depressed

56. Two technicians are discussing the testing of a vacuum brake booster. Technician A says to check the operation of a vacuum brake booster, the brake pedal should be depressed until the assist is depleted and then the engine should be started and then checked for a high brake pedal. Technician B says the booster should be depleted and the brake pedal should drop when the engine starts if the booster is okay. Which technician is correct?

    a. A only
    b. B only
    c. Both A and B
    d. Neither A nor B

57. Two technicians are discussing vacuum brake boosters. Technician A says a low, soft brake pedal is an indication of a defective booster. Technician B says that there should be at least two power-assisted brake applications if the engine stops running. Which technician is correct?

    a. A only
    b. B only
    c. Both A and B
    d. Neither A nor B

BRAKES (A5)

CATEGORY: DRUM BRAKE DIAGNOSIS AND REPAIR

58. Technician A says that the backing plate should be lubricated with chassis grease on the shoe pads. Technician B says that the brakes will squeak when applied if the shoe pads are not lubricated. Which technician is correct?

   a. A only
   b. B only
   c. Both A and B
   d. Neither A nor B

59. Technician A says that most experts recommend that the springs be inspected and replaced if necessary every time the brake linings are replaced. Technician B says that the star wheel adjuster must be cleaned and lubricated to ensure proper operation. Which technician is correct?

   a. A only
   b. B only
   c. Both A and B
   d. Neither A nor B

60. A star wheel adjuster is installed on the wrong side of the vehicle. Technician A says that the adjuster will cause the brake to lock up if installed on the wrong side. Technician B says the adjuster would cause the clearance to increase rather than decrease when activated. Which technician is correct?

   a. A only
   b. B only
   c. Both A and B
   d. Neither A nor B

61. What is this technician doing?

   a. Removing the inner lip on the outside edge of the drum
   b. Checking the surface finish of the drum
   c. Resurfacing the inside wear surface of the drum
   d. Using a drum micrometer

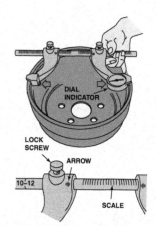

62. The surface of a brake drum is heat checked as shown. What is the preferred procedure that should be followed?

   a. Replace the drum
   b. Weld the cracks and machine to the original inside dimension
   c. Use a carbide cutter to remove the cracks
   d. Use a grinding stone attachment to remove the cracks

63. Technician A says the drum brake shown is a left side brake assembly. Technician B says that it is a leading-trailing type brake assembly. Which technician is correct?

   a. A only
   b. B only
   c. Both A and B
   d. Neither A nor B

64. A brake drum is being measured with a drum micrometer. What is the micrometer reading?

   a. .123
   b. .153
   c. .553
   d. .578

65. A brake pedal pulsation concern is being discussed. Technician A says that if the pulsation occurs when the parking brake is applied, the rear brakes are the usual cause. Technician B says that an out-of-round brake drum can be the cause. Which technician is correct?

   a. A only
   b. B only
   c. Both A and B
   d. Neither A nor B

66. New rear brake shoes were replaced on a rear-wheel-drive vehicle equipped with front disc brakes and rear drum brakes. During the test drive, smoke was observed coming from both rear wheels. Technician A says that this is normal because the new linings always smoke when first heated due to the resins in the lining. Technician B says that the parking brake cable may not have been fully released causing the brakes to drag. Which technician is correct?

   a. A only
   b. B only
   c. Both A and B
   d. Neither A nor B

67. After performing a brake job on a rear-wheel-drive vehicle equipped with front disc and rear drum brakes, the rear brakes tend to grab and the rear tires squeal at times during normal braking. What is the least likely cause?

   a. Oil or grease on the rear linings
   b. Stuck front disc brake calipers
   c. A defective proportioning valve
   d. A stuck open metering valve

68. The rear drum brakes are being replaced on a rear-wheel-drive vehicle. Two brake drums stamped MAX ID 9.56 in. are being measured. The left drum is 9.506 in. and the right drum is 9.559 in. Technician A says to machine the left drum and to replace the right drum. Technician B says to machine both drums. Which technician is correct?

   a. A only
   b. B only
   c. Both A and B
   d. Neither A nor B

69. Two technicians are discussing the measuring and machining of brake drums. Technician A says that the drums should be measured at four places around the drum to check for out-of-roundness. Technician B says that about 0.015 in. should be allowed for wear less than the discard dimension. Which technician is correct?

   a. A only
   b. B only
   c. Both A and B
   d. Neither A nor B

70. Which is the most likely cause of chatter marks on the friction surface of a brake drum during machining?

    a. Machining the drum at too fast a speed
    b. Using the wrong cutter
    c. Dirt or grease buildup on the inside of the drum
    d. Lack of a vibration dampener

71. During a rear drum brake inspection, it was discovered that both front-facing linings were excessively worn, whereas the rearward-facing linings were slightly worn. What is the most likely cause?

    a. A stuck wheel cylinder piston
    b. A stuck parking brake cable in the applied position
    c. Weak hold-down springs
    d. Lack of proper lubrication of the backing plate

72. What operation is being performed?

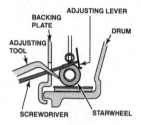

    a. Adjusting the brake shoes inward away from the drum
    b. Adjusting the brake shoes outward against the drum
    c. Adjusting the backing plate clearance
    d. Assembling the self-adjuster

73. What is this technician doing?

    a. Measuring the inside diameter (ID) of the brake drum
    b. Checking the brake drum for taper
    c. Measuring the brake drum for out-of-round
    d. Setting the shoe setting caliper to adjust the drum brakes

74. The shoe contact pads on the backing plate should be lubricated with _____.

    a. chassis grease
    b. wheel bearing grease
    c. vaseline (petroleum jelly)
    d. high-temperature brake grease

75. Technician A says the part shown has to be installed with the socket toward the secondary brake shoe. Technician B says that the part shown is constructed for left and right side application so be careful not to mix them. Which technician is correct?

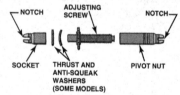

    a. A only
    b. B only
    c. Both A and B
    d. Neither A nor B

76. A drum brake wheel cylinder is being inspected. Technician A says that any dampness at all around the wheel cylinder indicates that it has been leaking and should be replaced. Technician B says that if brake fluid drips from the dust boot, the wheel cylinder should be replaced. Which technician is correct?

    a. A only
    b. B only
    c. Both A and B
    d. Neither A nor B

77. New wheel cylinders are being installed. Which operation is not required?

    a. The wheel cylinder should be bled of any trapped air
    b. The retainer fastener should be torqued to factory specifications
    c. The brake line should be attached
    d. Compressing the pistons before installing the wheel cylinder on the backing plate

78. A low brake pedal can be caused by any of the following *except* _____.

    a. a clogged vacuum hose to vacuum brake booster
    b. misadjusted rear drum brakes
    c. air in the line
    d. misadjusted push rod between the brake pedal and the master cylinder

79. Technician A says that the Tinnerman nuts (speed nuts) used to hold the brake drum on should be reinstalled when the drum is replaced. Technician B says that a drum should be removed inside a sealed vacuum enclosure or wetted with water or solvent to prevent the possible release of asbestos dust into the air. Which technician is correct?

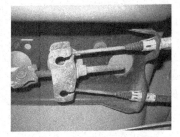

    a. A only
    b. B only
    c. Both A and B
    d. Neither A nor B

80. The owner of a vehicle equipped with front disc brakes and rear drum brakes complains that a squeaking sound is heard every time the brake pedal is depressed, even when the vehicle is stopped. Technician A says that the front caliper guide pin O-rings are worn and should be replaced. Technician B says that the shoe pads (ledges) on the rear brake backing plate may need to be lubricated. Which technician is correct?

    a. A only
    b. B only
    c. Both A and B
    d. Neither A nor B

81. Most brake experts and vehicle manufacturers recommend replacing brake lining when the lining thickness is worn to _____.

    a. 0.030 in. (0.8 mm)
    b. 0.040 in. (1.0 mm)
    c. 0.050 in. (1.3 mm)
    d. 0.060 in. (1.5 mm)

82. Technician A says that star-wheel adjusters use different threads (left- and right-handed) for the left and right side of the vehicle. Technician B says that the threads and end caps of the adjusters should be lubricated with brake grease before being installed. Which technician is correct?

    a. A only
    b. B only
    c. Both A and B
    d. Neither A nor B

83. Technician A says the parking brake cable adjustment should be performed after adjusting the rear brakes. Technician B says the parking brake cable should require two to seven clicks of the parking brake lever to apply the parking brake. Which technician is correct?

    a. A only
    b. B only
    c. Both A and B
    d. Neither A nor B

84. A parking brake requires 15 clicks to apply and does not hold the vehicle from moving on a slight grade. Technician A says the rear linings need to be adjusted. Technician B says the rear linings need to be replaced. Which technician is correct?

   a. A only
   b. B only
   c. Both A and B
   d. Neither A nor B

85. Technician A says that the parking brake hand lever can turn on the red brake warning lamp. Technician B says that a foot-operated parking brake can turn on the red brake warning lamp. Which technician is correct?

   a. A only
   b. B only
   c. Both A and B
   d. Neither A nor B

86. After assembling a drum brake, it is discovered that the brake drum will not fit over the new brake shoes. Technician A says that the parking brake cable may not have been fully released. Technician B says to check to see if both shoes are contacting the anchor pin. Which technician is correct?

   a. A only
   b. B only
   c. Both A and B
   d. Neither A nor B

87. Technician A says that hard spots in a brake drum should be removed using a carbide-tip machining tool. Technician B says the drum should be replaced if hard spots are discovered. Which technician is correct?

   a. A only
   b. B only
   c. Both A and B
   d. Neither A nor B

88. The letters EF on the edge of a brake lining mean _____.

   a. wear resistance codes
   b. relative noise level codes
   c. coefficient of friction codes
   d. brake lining composition

89. Many experts recommend that brake drums should be cleaned after machining with _____.

   a. spray brake cleaner
   b. denatured alcohol
   c. a shop cloth
   d. soap or detergent and water

90. Technician A says to use masking tape temporarily over the lining material to help prevent getting grease on the lining. Technician B says that grease on the brake lining can cause the brakes to grab. Which technician is correct?

   a. A only
   b. B only
   c. Both A and B
   d. Neither A nor B

91. A rear drum brake is being inspected. The primary shoe is not contacting the anchor pin at the top. Technician A says that this is normal. Technician B says that the parking brake cable may be adjusted too tight or is stuck. Which technician is correct?

   a. A only
   b. B only
   c. Both A and B
   d. Neither A nor B

92. Technician A says that brake drums on the same axle should be close to the same inside diameter for best brake balance. Technician B says that a brake drum may be cracked if it rings like a bell when tapped with a light steel hammer. Which technician is correct?

   a. A only
   b. B only
   c. Both A and B
   d. Neither A nor B

93. Technician A says that linings with asbestos can be identified by the dark gray color. Technician B says that all brake pads and linings should be treated as if they do contain asbestos. Which technician is correct?

   a. A only
   b. B only
   c. Both A and B
   d. Neither A nor B

94. Technician A says that brake drums should be labeled left and right before being removed from the vehicle so that they can be reinstalled in the same location. Technician B says that the shoes may have to be adjusted inward to remove a worn brake drum. Which technician is correct?

   a. A only
   b. B only
   c. Both A and B
   d. Neither A nor B

BRAKES (A5)

CATEGORY: DISC BRAKE DIAGNOSIS AND REPAIR

95. A defective wheel bearing usually sounds like _____.

    a. marbles in a tin can
    b. a noisy tire
    c. a baby rattle
    d. a clicking sound like a ball-point pen

96. After a disc brake pad replacement, the brake pedal went to the floor the first time the brake pedal was depressed. After several brake applications, the brake pedal returned to normal. The most likely cause was _____.

    a. air in the lines
    b. improper disc brake pad installation
    c. lack of proper lubrication of the caliper slides
    d. normal operation

97. Two technicians are discussing rotor finish. Technician A says to use a sandpaper block on both sides of the rotor while being rotated on the lathe for one minute to achieve the proper surface finish after the rotor has been machined. Technician B says that the rotor should have a nondirectional finish. Which technician is correct?

    a. A only
    b. B only
    c. Both A and B
    d. Neither A nor B

98. Two technicians are discussing hard spots in brake rotors. Technician A says the rotor should be replaced. Technician B says the hard spots are caused by using riveted, rather than bonded brake pads. Which technician is correct?

    a. A only
    b. B only
    c. Both A and B
    d. Neither A nor B

99. A service technician is replacing the two front disc brake calipers. Technician A says that the brake pedal should be held down about 1 in. (2.5 cm) to prevent the loss of brake fluid from the lines when the calipers are removed. Technician B says that some front disc brake calipers have to be installed on the correct side to position the bleeder valve toward the top. Which technician is correct?

    a. A only
    b. B only
    c. Both A and B
    d. Neither A nor B

100. Two technicians are discussing machining brake rotors. Technician A says that the rotor finish is Ra (roughness average) measured in micro inches. Technician B says that the higher the number, the smoother the rotor. Which technician is correct?

    a. A only
    b. B only
    c. Both A and B
    d. Neither A nor B

101. Technician A says that some vehicle manufacturers recommend that front disc brake rotors be machined on the vehicle. Technician B says that some vehicle manufacturers recommend that brake rotors not be machined unless there is excessive rust or a brake pedal pulsation complaint. Which technician is correct?

- **a.** A only
- **b.** B only
- **c.** Both A and B
- **d.** Neither A nor B

102. What procedure is being performed?

- **a.** Checking for proper caliper clearance
- **b.** Retracting the caliper piston
- **c.** Bleeding a disc brake caliper
- **d.** Removing the caliper assembly

103. A clicking sound from the front wheels is heard every time the brakes are applied either when traveling forward or in reverse. It only occurs once per brake application. What is the *most likely* cause?

- **a.** Worn caliper piston(s)
- **b.** A restricted front brake hose
- **c.** Loose front wheel bearings
- **d.** Worn caliper slides (ways)

104. Disc brake pads are being replaced on a vehicle equipped with an electric parking brake (EPB). Technician A says that a scan tool should be used to retract the caliper piston so that the rear pads can be changed. Technician B says that a scan tool should be used to reset the pads after the pads have been replaced the caliper reattached. Which technician is correct?

- **a.** A only
- **b.** B only
- **c.** Both A and B
- **d.** Neither A nor B

105. Which brake lubricant should be used on the rubber O-rings on the caliper slide bushings?

- **a.** Vaseline (petroleum jelly)
- **b.** Silicone grease
- **c.** Anti-seize compound
- **d.** Disc brake wheel bearing grease

106. A front disc brake rotor has excessive rotor lateral runout (see figure). Technician A says that the rotor should be machined or replaced. Technician B says that this condition can cause the steering wheel to shake or shimmy during braking. Which technician is correct?

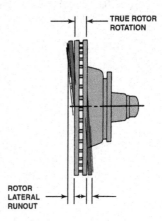

- **a.** A only
- **b.** B only
- **c.** Both A and B
- **d.** Neither A nor B

107. A front disc brake rotor is being checked for excessive thickness variation. Technician A says to use a straight edge and a feeler gauge to check for this condition. Technician B says that the rotor should be measured in four to eight locations using a micrometer to determine if the rotor is within specifications. Which technician is correct?

   a. A only
   b. B only
   c. Both A and B
   d. Neither A nor B

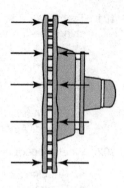

THICKNESS VARIATION AT DIFFERENT POINTS AROUND THE ROTOR

108. A technician is cleaning the caliper mounts to prevent what fault(s)?

   a. Sticking calipers
   b. Uneven disc brake pad wear
   c. Noise during brake application
   d. All of the above

109. Technician A says that all metal-to-metal contact areas of the disc brake system should be lubricated with special brake grease for proper operation. Technician B says that the lubrication helps reduce brake noise (squeal). Which technician is correct?

   a. A only
   b. B only
   c. Both A and B
   d. Neither A nor B

110. Technician A says that disc brake pads are marked for left and right side of the vehicle. Technician B says that the outboard pad should be installed before installing the inboard pad. Which technician is correct?

   a. A only
   b. B only
   c. Both A and B
   d. Neither A nor B

111. Typical maximum rotor lateral runout specifications are _____.

   a. 0.0003 to 0.0005 in. (0.008 to 0.013 mm)
   b. 0.003 to 0.005 in. (0.08 to 0.13 mm)
   c. 0.030 to 0.050 in. (0.8 to 1.3 mm)
   d. 0.300 to 0.500 in. (8.0 to 13 mm)

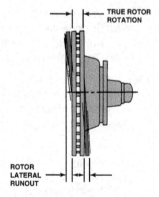

TRUE ROTOR ROTATION

ROTOR LATERAL RUNOUT

112. A disc brake rotor is being installed on a lathe for machining. During the setup, a scratch test is performed. The scratch extended all the way around the rotor. Technician A says that the rotor should be loosened, rotated 180°, and retightened. Technician B says that the rotor is not warped. Which technician is correct?

   a. A only
   b. B only
   c. Both A and B
   d. Neither A nor B

113. The wrong replacement rear disc brake pads were installed on a vehicle that used an integral parking brake. The inboard pad did not have a pin that fits into a notch on the caliper piston. Technician A says that the brakes will likely over adjust. Technician B says that the parking brake will not work. Which technician is correct?

   a. A only
   b. B only
   c. Both A and B
   d. Neither A nor B

114. Technician A says that disc brake rotors should be cleaned with brake cleaner after machining. Technician B says that rotors should be cleaned with soap and water after machining. Which technician is correct?

   a. A only
   b. B only
   c. Both A and B
   d. Neither A nor B

115. Technician A says that a lack of lubrication on the back of the disc brake pads can cause brake noise. Technician B says that pads that are not correctly crimped to the caliper housing can cause brake noise. Which technician is correct?

   a. A only
   b. B only
   c. Both A and B
   d. Neither A nor B

116. A typical disc brake "loaded caliper" usually includes what parts?

   a. New or rebuilt (remanufactured) caliper assembly
   b. Replacement caliper guide pins
   c. Any needed shims and hardware
   d. All of the above

117. Technician A says that all disc brakes should be handled as if they contain asbestos. Technician B says to remove brake pads inside a vacuum unit or wetted to help prevent asbestos dust from being inhaled. Which technician is correct?

   a. A only
   b. B only
   c. Both A and B
   d. Neither A nor B

118. What part must be replaced when servicing an outer wheel bearing on a non-drive wheel?

   a. The bearing cup
   b. The grease seal
   c. The cotter key
   d. The retainer washer
   e. Miscellaneous Diagnosis and Repair

119. Technician A says that rotor thickness variation is a major cause of a pulsating brake pedal. Technician B says that at least 0.015 in. (0.4 mm) should be left on a rotor after machining to allow for wear if the specification was stated as the minimum thickness. Which technician is correct?

   a. A only
   b. B only
   c. Both A and B
   d. Neither A nor B

120. The letters DE on the edge of a disc brake pad indicate _____.

   a. wear resistance codes
   b. relative noise level codes
   c. coefficient of friction codes
   d. thickness codes

121. Typical maximum rotor thickness variation (parallelism) specifications are _____.

    a. 0.0003 to 0.0005 in. (0.008 to 0.013 mm)
    b. 0.003 to 0.005 in. (0.08 to 0.13 mm)
    c. 0.030 to 0.050 in. (0.8 to 1.3 mm)
    d. 0.300 to 0.500 in. (8.0 to 13 mm)

122. Two technicians are discussing a caliper that is leaking brake fluid. Technician A says that the caliper should be replaced. Technician B says that the caliper on the other side of the vehicle should also be replaced. Which technician is correct?

    a. A only
    b. B only
    c. Both A and B
    d. Neither A nor B

123. Technician A says that disc brake pads should be replaced if they are worn down to the thickness of the steel backing. Technician B says the pads should be removed and inspected whenever there is a brake performance complaint. Which technician is correct?

    a. A only
    b. B only
    c. Both A and B
    d. Neither A nor B

124. A "chirping" noise is heard while the vehicle is moving forward but it stops when the brakes are applied. Technician A says that the noise is likely caused by the disc brake pad wear sensors. Technician B says the noise is likely a wheel bearing because the noise stops when the brakes are applied. Which technician is correct?

    a. A only
    b. B only
    c. Both A and B
    d. Neither A nor B

125. Uneven disc brake pad wear is being discussed. Technician A says a single piston floating caliper type brake may be stuck. Technician B says the caliper may be stuck on the slides and unable to "float." Which technician is correct?

    a. A only
    b. B only
    c. Both A and B
    d. Neither A nor B

126. Two technicians are discussing wheel bearing replacement. Technician A says that the outer race should be replaced when the bearing is replaced. Technician B says that a driver is recommended to install a bearing race. Which technician is correct?

    a. A only
    b. B only
    c. Both A and B
    d. Neither A nor B

127. A C-clamp is being used on a disc brake caliper. Technician A says that the clamp is used to hold the caliper while the pads are removed. Technician B says the clamp is being used to compress the caliper piston in the bore. Which technician is correct?

    a. A only
    b. B only
    c. Both A and B
    d. Neither A nor B

128. A wheel bearing is being repacked with grease. Technician A says to remove all of the old grease by forcing new grease into the bearing. Technician B says that the bearing should be cleaned and dried before applying grease to the bearing. Which technician is correct?

    a. A only
    b. B only
    c. Both A and B
    d. Neither A nor B

129. Two technicians are discussing front wheel bearings that are used on the front of most front-wheel-drive vehicles. Technician A says that they are sealed units and that they cannot be lubricated or adjusted. Technician B says that they look as if they are sealed but can be adjusted and should be lubricated when the brakes are replaced. Which technician is correct?

    a. A only
    b. B only
    c. Both A and B
    d. Neither A nor B

BRAKES (A5)

CATEGORY: ELECTRONIC BRAKE CONTROL SYSTEMS—ABS, TCS, ESC—DIAGNOSIS AND REPAIR

130. A vehicle equipped with four-wheel ABS pulls to the right during hard braking. What is the *most likely* cause?

   a. A stuck left front caliper piston
   b. A defective left front wheel speed sensor
   c. A defective right front wheel speed sensor
   d. A defective ABS control solenoid for the right rear wheel brake

131. An owner of a vehicle equipped with ABS brakes complained that whenever he tried to stop on icy or slippery roads, the brake pedal would pulse up and down rapidly. Technician A says that this is normal for many ABS units. Technician B says that the ABS unit is malfunctioning. Which technician is correct?

   a. A only
   b. B only
   c. Both A and B
   d. Neither A nor B

132. Technician A says a scan tool may be necessary to bleed some ABS hydraulic units. Technician B says that only DOT 3 or DOT 4 (not DOT 5) brake fluid should be used with ABS. Which technician is correct?

   a. A only
   b. B only
   c. Both A and B
   d. Neither A nor B

133. The red brake warning lamp is on and the amber ABS lamp is off. Technician A says that a wheel speed sensor may be defective. Technician B says that the red brake warning lamp can be turned on by low brake fluid level. Which technician is correct?

   a. A only
   b. B only
   c. Both A and B
   d. Neither A nor B

134. A vehicle equipped with antilock brakes (ABS) and electronic stability control (ESC) is being driven through a curve on a wet highway. What might the driver experience?

   a. A vibration as the system tries to control the vehicle
   b. A flashing traction control (TC) amber warning light in the dash
   c. A pulsating brake pedal if the driver has a foot on the brake
   d. All of the above

135. Technician A says that the amber ABS dash light could indicate a fault in the wheel speed sensor. Technician B says that the amber ABS dash light should not light or flash at any time unless there is a fault detected by the ABS controller. Which technician is correct?

   a. A only
   b. B only
   c. Both A and B
   d. Neither A nor B

136. Technician A says that it may be normal for the hydraulic pump and solenoids to operate after the vehicle starts to move after a start. Technician B says that the ABS is disabled (does not function) below about 5 mph (8 km/h). Which technician is correct?

   a. A only
   b. B only
   c. Both A and B
   d. Neither A nor B

137. A customer wanted the ABS checked because of a rapid tire chirping noise during hard braking. Technician A says that the speed sensors may be defective. Technician B says that tire chirp is normal during an ABS stop on dry pavement. Which technician is correct?

   a. A only
   b. B only
   c. Both A and B
   d. Neither A nor B

138. The owner of an SUV equipped with larger wheels and tires (24 in. diameter wheels instead of the factory 19 in. diameter) arrived at a shop complaining that the brakes do not seem to be working properly. The customer stated that the brakes worked properly before the new wheels were installed. What could be the cause?

   a. Too much clearance between the wheels and the disc brake calipers
   b. A faulty wheel speed sensor
   c. The wheel speed sensors need to be calibrated to the new wheel diameter
   d. Normal operation when larger diameter wheels and tires are installed.

139. Technician A says that ABS is usually disabled if the amber ABS dash warning lamp is on. Technician B says that normal base brakes should still function normally even if the amber ABS warning lamp is on. Which technician is correct?

   a. A only
   b. B only
   c. Both A and B
   d. Neither A nor B

140. Which is the least likely to cause the amber ABS warning lamp to light?

   a. A leaking accumulator
   b. Using the small spare tire on one wheel
   c. A cracked wheel speed sensor tone ring
   d. A stuck ABS control solenoid

141. Technician A says that ABS brakes should be bled in the same sequence as used for non-ABS equipped vehicles. Technician B says that some ABS units must be pressure bled. Which technician is correct?

   a. A only
   b. B only
   c. Both A and B
   d. Neither A nor B

142. A vehicle equipped with ABS has the amber ABS light on and a stored diagnostic trouble code (DTC) for a right front wheel speed sensor. Which is the *least likely* cause?

   a. Sensor wiring too close to spark plug wires
   b. A defective wheel speed sensor
   c. A loose wheel bearing
   d. Low brake fluid level in the master cylinder reservoir

143. An analog wheel speed sensor is being diagnosed using a digital multimeter. All of the following meter settings can be used to check the sensor for proper operation *except* _____.

a. Hz
b. ACV
c. DCV
d. DCA

144. The brake (stop light) switch is _____.

a. An input to the ABS control module
b. An input to the stop signal relay
c. Connects directly to the rear brake lights
d. Both a and b

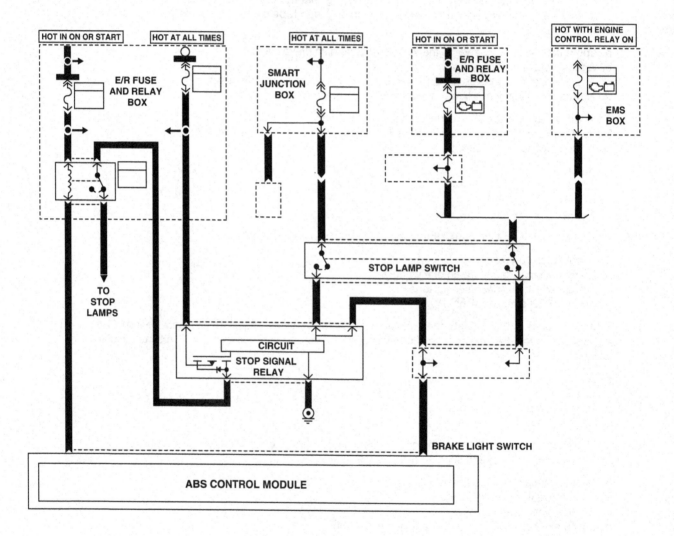

145. Looking at the wiring diagram, what is the most likely the purpose of the neutral switch as an input to the electric parking brake module?

   a. Used to release the parking brakes on both rear wheels when the gear selector is moved into the neutral position.

   b. Used to apply the parking brake when the gear selector is moved into the neutral position.

   c. Used to apply the parking brake on one side only and release the other side at the same time to allow the vehicle to roll forward or rearward when the gear selector is moved to the neutral position.

   d. To light the "N" in the PRNDL display on the dash or center console.

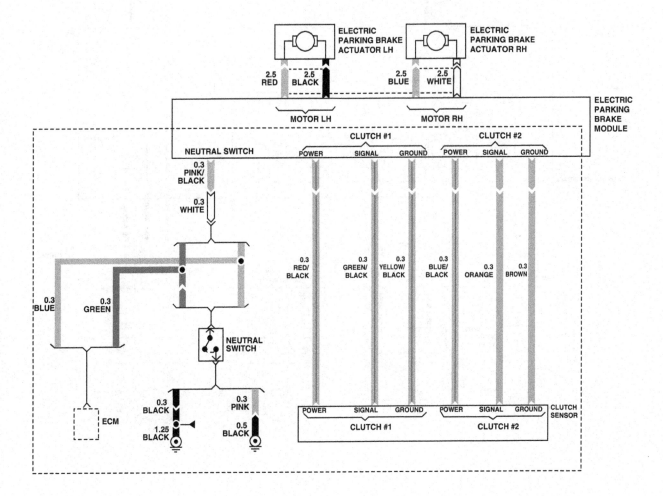

146. What is true about the antilock system shown in the figure?

    a. It uses four wheel speed sensors

    b. The hydraulic pump motor is controlled by the ABS hydraulic unit

    c. The ABS system is a three-channel system

    d. All of the above

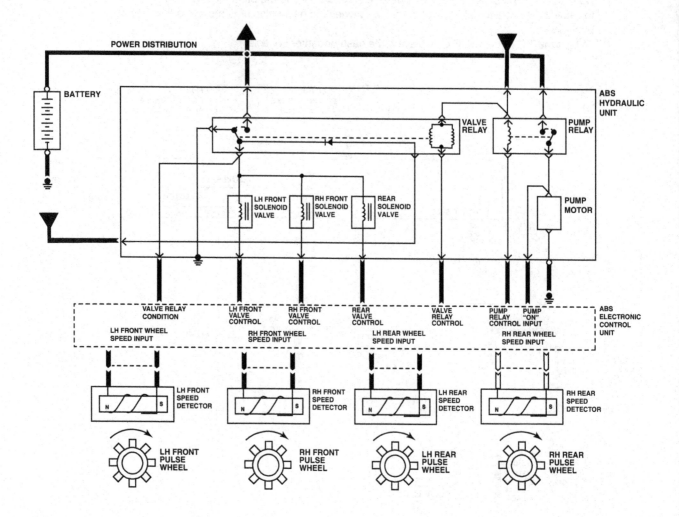

BRAKES (A5)

CATEGORY: HYDRAULIC, POWER ASSIST, AND PARKING BRAKE SYSTEMS DIAGNOSIS AND REPAIR

1. **The correct answer is b.** The switch is the pressure differential switch, which completes the electrical path to ground to light the red brake warning lamp in the event that there is a difference in pressure between the two brake circuits. Answers a, c, and d are not correct because they are not the switch shown.

2. **The correct answer is c.** Both technicians are correct. Technician A is correct because fluid movement in the reservoir occurs when the primary seals on the master cylinder pistons move forward past the vent (compensating) ports. Technician B is correct because if the primary seals are leaking, the brake pedal will slowly sink toward the floor under steady brake pedal force. Answers a, b, and d are not correct because both technicians are correct.

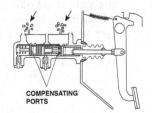

COMPENSATING PORTS

3. **The correct answer is a.** Technician A is correct because when a hydraulic leak occurs, the fluid for the affected brake circuit cannot be pressurized. The rearward piston usually pressurizes the brake fluid in the front of the sealing cup, which is used to only apply the brakes for that section, but also applies pressure to the forward master cylinder piston. If a leak occurs in the rear portion brake circuit, the primary piston is still able to push on the forward piston by making actual physical contact. The entire distance the primary piston (rearward piston) has to travel to control the forward piston is translated into a lower-than-normal brake pedal and lower braking power due to half of the brakes not working as designed. Technician B is not correct because the brake pedal will be lower than normal and not higher than normal. Answers c and d are not correct because only Technician A is correct.

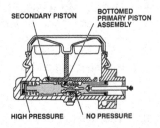

SECONDARY PISTON — BOTTOMED PRIMARY PISTON ASSEMBLY

HIGH PRESSURE — NO PRESSURE

4. **The correct answer is c.** Both technicians are correct. Technician A is correct because if there is excessive clearance in the brake pedal linkage, the brake pedal must travel further to push on the master cylinder piston resulting in a lower-than-normal brake pedal. Technician B is correct because if the hydraulic line or component is leaking from one circuit of the master cylinder, the brake pedal has to be depressed further to apply the remaining pressure-building piston and seal, which operates the other hydraulic circuit. Answers a, b, and d are not correct because both technicians are correct.

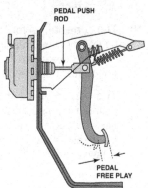

PEDAL PUSH ROD

PEDAL FREE PLAY

5. **The correct answer is b.** Technician B is correct because if the front disc brake caliper were stuck, a higher than normal force would be needed on the brake pedal to slow the vehicle. This greater force on the brake pedal will cause the rear brakes to apply before the front brakes creating a rear brake lockup condition. Technician A is not correct because a stuck open metering valve is unlikely to cause this problem because fluid pressure would be delivered to the front brakes without being delayed until the pressure reaches over about 300 psi. Answers c and d are not correct because only Technician B is correct.

6. **The correct answer is a.** Technician A is correct because air is compressible and brake pedal force when exerted on a closed hydraulic system that contains air will compress the air. The air in the system will cause the brake pedal to feel soft or spongy rather than normal hard or firm and will cause the pedal to travel further before braking occurs. Technician B is not correct because the pressure differential switch is used to turn on the red brake warning lamp in the event of unequal pressure between the two separate hydraulic circuits. Answers c and d are not correct because only Technician A is correct.

7. **The correct answer is a.** The metering valve must be bypassed by pushing in or pulling out on the button depending on vehicle when pressure bleeding. The metering valve closes off the passage to the front brakes at low pressures and does not allow brake fluid to pass during bleeding. The metering valve allows normal brake fluid flow above 70 to 300 psi to allow for normal braking after the rear brakes have applied. Answer b is not correct because the proportioning valve limits the pressure to the rear brakes. Answer c is not correct because the pressure differential is used to turn on the red brake warning lamp if there is a hydraulic failure. Answer d is not correct because the residual check valve is used to keep a slight amount of pressure applied to the drum brakes to help keep the sealing cups from collapsing inward when the brake pedal is released.

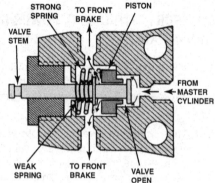

8. **The correct answer is d.** Answer d is correct because either DOT 3 or DOT 4 depending on the make and model of vehicle. Answer a is not correct: while DOT 3 brake fluid recommended by most domestic and Asian vehicle manufacturers, the best answer is d because most European and some domestic vehicles specify the use of DOT4 brake fluid. Answer b is not correct; even though DOT 4 is the recommend fluid to use in many European vehicles, it is not recommended for use in many domestic or Asian vehicles. Answer c is not correct because DOT 5 is silicone based and does not mix with polyglycol-based DOT 3 or DOT 4 brake fluid and is not recommended.

9. **The correct answer is c.** Both technicians are correct. Technician A is correct because as the disc brake pads wear, the caliper piston moves closer to the rotor, which requires that additional brake fluid in the caliper would reduce the level in the master cylinder reservoir. Technician B is correct because a leak anywhere in the hydraulic system would cause the brake fluid level in the master cylinder reservoir to drop. Answers a, b, and d are not correct because both technicians are correct.

10. **The correct answer is c.** Both technicians are correct. Technician A is correct because brake fluid is hygroscopic and readily absorbs moisture from the air reducing its boiling point. Technician B is correct because brake fluid will remove paint if spilled on the finish of a vehicle. Answers a, b, and d are not correct because both technicians are correct.

11. **The correct answer is d.** The rubber seals will swell, which can close off the ports in the master cylinder leading to complete brake system failure. Answer a is not correct because the rubber seals will swell (become larger), not shrink in size. Answer b is not correct because the rubber seals will swell and not become hardened and external fluid leaks would not usually occur. Answer c is not correct because the seals will not melt but will simply become larger (swell in size).

12. **The correct answer is d.** Neither technician is correct. Technician A is not correct because a double lap flare end will not fit properly in fittings designed for ISO flare, sometimes referred to as a ball or bubble flare. Technician B is not correct because a line equipped with and ISO flare cannot be used to replace a line with a double lap flare because the angles and shape of the fittings would not allow proper sealing and should never be interchanged. Answers a, b, and c are not correct because neither technician is correct.

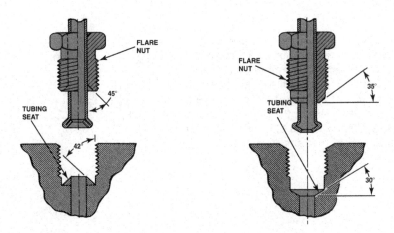

13. **The correct answer is a.** The brake bleeding sequence that is most often recommended for a rear-wheel-drive vehicle is right rear (RR), left rear (LR), then the right front (RF) and left front (LF). This sequence starts the bleeding sequence farthest from the master cylinder and works toward the master cylinder. Answers b, c, and d are not correct because they are not the sequences that are most often recommended for a rear-wheel-drive vehicle.

14. **The correct answer is d.** Answer a is correct because most brake line is constructed of double-wall brake tubing. Answer c is also correct because many European-brand vehicles use copper-nickel brake line that is more corrosion resistant than steel brake line. Answer b is not correct because copper line does not have the strength to withstand brake system pressures.

15. **The correct answer is b.** Denatured alcohol (ethyl alcohol with an additive that makes it poisonous to drink) should be used to clean brake parts because it evaporates easily and does not leave a film. Answer a (throttle-body cleaner) is not correct because even though it is often used to clean brake parts, it is not the recommended solvent to use because it may leave a film that could be harmful to brake components. Answer c (Stoddard solvent) should not be used because it is a petroleum-based material and therefore it could cause seal swelling and it leaves a film when dried. Answer d (detergent and water) is not recommended to use on brake parts because any remaining moisture would combine with the brake fluid causing contaminates.

16. **The correct answer is b.** Technician B is correct because air is compressible, and when the driver depresses the brake pedal, the air in the hydraulic system is compressed causing the brake pedal to travel further than if there was no air in the system. Technician A is not correct because a defective power brake booster causes a hard brake pedal (lack of assist), not a low brake pedal. Answers c and d are not correct because only Technician B is correct.

17. **The correct answer is a.** Engine oil or ATF will cause rubber seals and O-rings to swell. Answer b is not correct because moisture, while harmful to brake fluid, will not cause rubber brake components to swell in size. Answer c is not correct because while DOT 5 brake fluid is not miscible (able to be mixed) with DOT 3, it would not cause the rubber seals to swell even though it could cause other brake system faults. Answer d is not correct because water will not cause rubber brake components to swell even though water in the brake system can cause the brake fluid to become contaminated and reduce its boiling point temperature.

18. **The correct answer is b.** Technician B is correct because brake fluid gets hot and expands as the heat from the brake pads and shoes is transferred to the brake fluid. Technician A is not correct because the brakes could self-apply when the brake fluid gets hot and expands if the brake fluid level were above the MAX line. The pressure in the hydraulic system is created by the pistons in the master cylinder and is not affected by the level of the brake fluid unless the reservoir is empty. Answers c and d are not correct because Technician B only is correct.

19. **The correct answer is b.** If the vent (compensating) port is clogged, the brake fluid cannot flow back into the reservoir when it becomes hot. As a result, the fluid pressure increases and the brakes can be applied due to the increased fluid pressure. Answer a is not correct because a leaking seal at the master cylinder cannot cause a buildup of hydraulic pressure necessary to apply the brakes. Answer c is not correct because a clogged replenishing (inlet) port could cause a low brake pedal but is not likely to cause a pressure buildup in the hydraulic system. Answer d is not correct because a restricted vacuum brake booster would not cause an increase in pressure in the hydraulic system, although it could cause a hard brake pedal due to the lack of power assist.

20. **The correct answer is c.** Both technicians are correct. Technician A is correct because the brake pedal height has to be correct for the proper functioning of the master cylinder and the entire braking system. Technician B is correct because the free play and pedal reserve are necessary for the proper operation of the braking system. Answers a, b, and d are not correct because both technicians are correct.

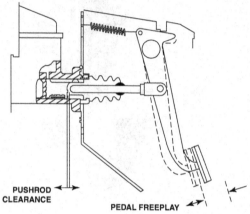

PUSHROD CLEARANCE

PEDAL FREEPLAY

21. **The correct answer is c.** Both technicians are correct. Technician A is correct if there is a hydraulic failure that causes a difference in pressure between the two split systems, the red brake warning lamp comes on. The brake fluid level also can trigger the red brake warning lamp. Technician B is correct because the same red brake warning lamp is used to notify the driver that the parking brake is applied. Answers a, b, and d are not correct because both technicians are correct.

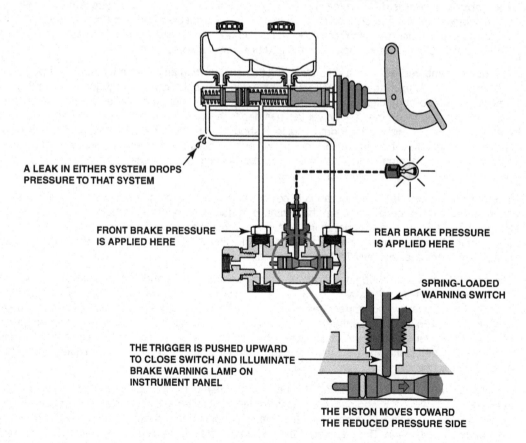

A LEAK IN EITHER SYSTEM DROPS PRESSURE TO THAT SYSTEM

FRONT BRAKE PRESSURE IS APPLIED HERE

REAR BRAKE PRESSURE IS APPLIED HERE

SPRING-LOADED WARNING SWITCH

THE TRIGGER IS PUSHED UPWARD TO CLOSE SWITCH AND ILLUMINATE BRAKE WARNING LAMP ON INSTRUMENT PANEL

THE PISTON MOVES TOWARD THE REDUCED PRESSURE SIDE

22. **The correct answer is a.** Technician A is correct because the metering valve closes off the passage(s) to the front brakes until 70 to 300 psi is applied to the hydraulic system to allow the rear brake to be applied before the brake fluid pressure is applied to the front disc brakes. If the metering valve were to fail in the open position, hydraulic brake fluid pressure would be applied to the front brakes as soon as the brake pedal is depressed, which could cause the vehicle to nose dive or the front wheels to lock up if on a slippery surface. Technician B is not correct because the proportioning valve only controls (limits) the flow of brake fluid to the rear brakes during hard braking and would not cause the problem of front wheel lockup on slippery surfaces during light braking. Answers c and d are not correct because only Technician A is correct.

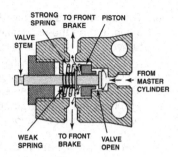

23. **The correct answer is c.** Both technicians are correct. Technician A is correct because any trapped air bubble can be turned into foam if the brake pedal is depressed rapidly during the brake bleeding procedure. Technician B is correct because most vehicle manufacturers recommend a 15-second delay period between brake pedal applications to allow time for the trapped air to bubbles to combine, which makes it easier to bleed from the system. Answers a, b, and d are not correct because both technicians are correct.

24. **The correct answer is d.** Answer d is correct because a stuck caliper can cause the brakes to drag. Answer b is not correct because a leaking vacuum brake booster would cause a hard brake pedal, but would not the cause of a dragging brake at one wheel. Answer c is not correct because air in the line would cause a spongy brake pedal and not cause a disc brake to drag (stuck applied).

25. **The correct answer is a.** Technician A is correct because the piston will force the old brake fluid out of the bleeder valve and therefore, help prevent it from being forced upward into the ABS hydraulic control unit or the master cylinder where the dirty fluid could cause harm. Technician B is not correct because most vehicle manufacturers do not recommend clamping a flexible brake hose because it can damage the inner liner of the hose. Answers c and d are not correct because only Technician A is correct.

26. **The correct answer is b.** Technician B is correct because all bleeder valves must be opened to allow all of the old brake fluid to be purged from the system as new fresh brake fluid is added to the master cylinder reservoir. Technician A is not correct because even though it is wise to remove most of the old fluid from the master cylinder, the procedure would not replace all of the old fluid from the system. Answers c and d are not correct because only Technician B is correct.

27. **The correct answer is a.** Technician A is correct because air trapped in the passages of the master cylinder is difficult, if not impossible, to remove if not bled before installing the master cylinder on the vehicle. Technician B is not correct because master cylinders must be filled and bled of any trapped air before installation on the vehicle. Brake fluid is hygroscopic and absorbs moisture from the air unless stored in a sealed container. The brake fluid would quickly become contaminated if stored or shipped unsealed in a master cylinder. Answers c and d are not correct because only Technician A is correct.

28. **The correct answer is b.** The tool is used to hold open the metering valve to allow manual bleeding of the front brakes. Answers a, c, and d are not correct because they do not correctly identify the special tool.

29. **The correct answer is c.** Both technicians are correct. Technician A is correct because a blocked vent (compensating) port will cause the brakes to self-apply as the brake fluid gets hot and expands due to normal braking. If the vent port were blocked by the blocked by an improper adjusted master cylinder pushrod, the expanding fluid, the expanding fluid cannot return to the master cylinder reservoir and instead causes the pressure in the brake line to increase creating a self-apply condition. Technician B is correct because the hot brake fluid expands and applies the brakes if the brake fluid could not expand in the reservoir. Answers a, b, and d are not correct because both technicians are correct.

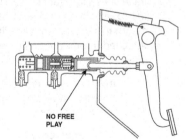

30. **The correct answer is d.** All of the items listed in answers a, b, and c can turn on the red brake warning lamp. The warning lamp can be turned on by the input from the brake fluid reservoir level sensor. The parking brake lever switch can also turn on the red brake warning lamp. If there is unequal brake fluid pressure between the two sections of the system, the pressure differential switch will turn on the red brake warning lamp. Answers a, b, and c are not correct because all of the items are correct making d the best answer.

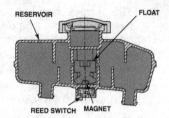

31. **The correct answer is b.** A faulty (stuck open) metering valve will cause hydraulic pressure to be applied to the front disc brakes before the brake fluid pressure has overcome the return spring pressure on the rear brakes, causing the vehicle to dip down at the front during light braking. Answer a is not correct because a leaking master cylinder would not cause the front brakes to be applied before the rear brakes. Answer c is not correct because the proportioning valve limits the maximum brake fluid pressure that is sent to the rear wheel brakes during hard braking and would not cause the front to dip during light brake applications. Answer d is not correct because even though air in the lines can cause a problem, it is unlikely to cause the front brakes to apply first during a light braking causing the front of the vehicle to dip.

32. **The correct answer is d.** The secondary (rear) seal on the primary piston (rear most) will cause visible brake fluid leakage if defective. Answer a is not correct because a hole in the vacuum booster cannot draw brake fluid from the master cylinder unless the rear seal of the master cylinder is leaking. Answer b is not correct because a leaking cover seal will likely show as leakage all around the master cylinder and not just at the rear as stated in the question. Answer c is not correct because a bent master cylinder push rod would cause a low brake pedal but is not likely to cause a leak.

33. **The correct answer is b.** Technician B is correct because the brake pedal will sink if the master cylinder piston seals are leaking internally. Technician A is not correct because the metering and proportioning valves are used to control and limit brake fluid pressure to the front (metering valve) and rear (proportioning valve) and will not cause the brake pedal to sink if defective unless there is an external fluid leak, which was not found during a visual inspection. Answers c and d are not correct because only Technician B is correct.

34. **The correct answer is d.** The photo shows two proportioning valves that are used to limit the maximum pressure sent to the rear brakes during hard braking. Two proportioning valves are needed on this front-wheel-drive vehicle because it uses a diagonal split braking system. Answer a is not correct because metering valves are usually not used on front-wheel-drive vehicles. Answer b is not correct because even though they may look like large line connectors, they are actually proportioning valves. Answer c is not correct because braking systems do not use filters since they are a sealed system and dirt and debris rarely are a concern in a hydraulic brake system.

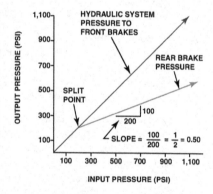

35. **The correct answer is b.** Technician B is correct because the coils are necessary to help prevent brake line breakage and metal fatigue. The master cylinder attaches to the body of the vehicle and the brake lines are attached to the frame of the vehicle. The movement between these two components due to deflection of the rubber mounts can cause the brake lines to crack unless they are coiled to absorb this movement and vibration. Technician A is not correct because even though the lines should be coiled, it does not increase the pressure of the brake fluid. Answers c and d are not correct because only Technician B is correct.

36. **The correct answer is d.** The photo shows a combination valve; a combination of the proportioning valve, metering valve, and pressure differential switch. Answers a, b, and c are not correct because the photo shows a combination valve and not a master cylinder, proportioning valve, or metering valve only.

37. **The correct answer is d.** A plastic line attached to the bleeder valve and flowing to a container filled with clean brake fluid is the manual method for bleeding the trapped air from the hydraulic brake system. Answer a is not correct even though the fresh brake fluid would be drawn into the caliper when the brake pedal is released; the primary purpose is to bleed the air out of the system. Answer b is not correct because any water in the system would be absorbed by the brake fluid. Answer c is not correct even though bleeding the system is usually necessary after a flexible brake hose is replaced.

38. **The correct answer is b.** A leaking wheel cylinder is the most likely cause for this brake fluid leak because the fluid is under pressure during a brake application, which can cause the brake fluid to be thrown outward and onto the inside of the rear tire. Answer a is not correct because even though a hole in the brake drum could cause water to get onto the brakes, there has to be a failure of the hydraulic system to cause brake fluid to be thrown onto the sidewall of a tire. Answer c is not correct because a proportioning valve is usually not located near the rear wheels and a leak would not cause brake fluid to be thrown against the tires. Answer d is not correct because the flexible brake hose for the rear brakes is usually located in the center of the vehicle or to one side and is unlikely to cause brake fluid to splash onto a tire if the hose leaked.

39. **The correct answer is a.** Technician A is correct because the unit shown is a height sensing proportioning valve that limits the maximum brake fluid pressure to the rear brakes during hard braking based on the height of the rear suspension. If the suspension height is low (vehicle loaded), a high pressure can be applied to the rear brakes. If the rear suspension height is high indicating a lightly loaded vehicle, the brake fluid pressure is reduced to help prevent rear wheel lockup. Technician B is not correct because brake fluid will flow freely through the proportioning valve at the lower pressure used for bleeding so the linkage does not need to be removed. Answer c and d are not correct because Technician A only is correct.

40. **The correct answer is c.** Both technicians are correct. Technician A is correct because pressure bleeding should be limited to about 20 psi (138 kPa) according to most vehicle manufacturer's recommendations. Technician B is correct because the metering valve needs to be kept in the open position because it is normally closed at the pressure valve used for pressure bleeding. Otherwise, the front brakes can be bled. Answers a, b, and d are not correct because both technicians are correct.

41. **The correct answer is d.** Front-wheel-drive vehicles use a diagonal split braking system, which ties the right front with the left rear on a separate circuit from the left front/right rear brakes. Answers a, b, and c are not correct because the right front and the left rear are operated off the same circuit or portion of the master cylinder.

42. **The correct answer is d.** Neither technician is correct. Technician A is not correct because it does not require much force to push brake fluid through an open bleeder valve. Technician B is not correct because rapid pumping of the brake pedal will not force the air toward the bleeder valve and could cause any trapped air to turn to foam making it more difficult to bleed the air out of the hydraulic system. Answers a, b, and c are not correct because neither technician is correct.

43. **The correct answer is a.** Technician A is correct because brake fluid along with any trapped air will normally flow downward and out of an open bleeder valve. Technician B is not correct because gravity will force the brake fluid out of the open bleeder and air will not be drawn into the system. Answers c and d are not correct because Technician A only is correct.

44. **The correct answer is d.** Neither technician is correct. Technician A is not correct because the metering valve controls brake fluid pressure to both front wheel brakes and could not cause a pull if defective. Technician B is not correct because the proportioning valve controls brake fluid pressure to the rear wheel brakes and could not cause a pull if defective. Answers a, b, and c are not correct because neither technician is correct.

45. **The correct answer is b.** Technician B is correct because an open circuit means that there is a break in the wiring or a defective component that prevents electrical current to flow from the brake switch to the rear brake lights. Technician A is not correct because low brake fluid may trigger the red brake warning lamp on the dash, but is unlikely to cause the rear brake light to fail. Answers c and d are not correct because Technician B only is correct.

46. **The correct answer is a.** Technician A is correct because many vehicles are equipped with a brake fluid reservoir sensor that will turn on the red brake warning lamp if the brake fluid level drops below a safe level. Technician B is not correct because even though rear brakes that need to be replaced may cause other problems or noises, they will not cause the red brake warning lamp to come on unless there is a hydraulic failure. Answers c and d are not correct because Technician A only is correct.

47. **The correct answer is b.** Technician B is correct because air is compressible and greater brake pedal travel is necessary before braking action starts if there is air trapped in the hydraulic brake system. Technician A is not correct because even though a restricted flexible brake hose could cause the brakes to drag and be slow to release, it is unlikely to cause a low brake pedal. Answers c and d are not correct because Technician B only is correct.

48. **The correct answer is c.** Both technicians are correct. Technician A is correct because each stroke of the master cylinder delivers about one teaspoon full of brake fluid into the hydraulic brake system. If the rear brakes had a large clearance between the linings and the drum, several brake pedal applications may be necessary to extend the wheel cylinder piston enough to start to slow the vehicle. Technician B is correct because loose wheel bearings can cause the rotor to move away from the caliper piston requiring a greater amount of brake fluid before the brake pads actually touch the rotor. Answers a, b, and d are not correct because both technicians are correct.

49. **The correct answer is a.** Technician A is correct because the accumulator should be solidly mounted to the Hydro-Boost unit if it is properly charged. Technician B is not correct because it is the purpose and function of the accumulator to provide several power-assisted stops in the event that the engine stalls as a safety measure. Answers c and d are not correct because Technician A only is correct.

50. **The correct answer is d.** A defective vacuum check valve can cause the vacuum to be lost when the engine is off. This would explain why the power assist would function normally after the engine ran for a minute or two. Answer a is not correct because worn front disc brake pads cannot cause a lack of power assist and should not affect the brake pedal height unless there was a fault in the caliper(s) that prevented the movement of the piston outward as the brake pads wore. Answer b is not correct because a shorter-than-normal pushrod would cause a low brake pedal and could not be returned to normal operation by operating the engine for a minute or two. Answer c is not correct because even though the engine may not be producing normal vacuum, this would not explain why the power assist was lost when the engine was turned off.

51. **The correct answer is b.** Technician B is correct because worn or misadjusted brake shoes can cause a lower-than-normal brake pedal because the lining has to travel further before controlling the brake drum requiring more brake fluid from the master cylinder. Technician A is not correct because a defective vacuum brake booster will cause a hard brake pedal and not a lower-than-normal brake pedal. Answers c and d are not correct because Technician B only is correct.

52. **The correct answer is b.** Technician B is correct because a warped disc brake rotor will cause the brake pedal to pulsate during braking. Technician A is not correct because even though the flow of power steering fluid may not be as steady as when the power steering pump belt is tight, the Hydro-Boost should not be affected because the accumulator is used to supply temporary assist pressure when the power steering pump is not functioning. Answers c and d are not correct because Technician B only is correct.

53. **The correct answer is d.** A thorough visual inspection should be the first step in any diagnostic procedure. Answers a, b, and c are not correct because even though these are to be performed as part of diagnosing a Hydro-Boost problem, they are not the first step that the service technician should perform.

54. **The correct answer is d.** Neither technician is correct. Technician A is not correct because a hard brake pedal is the symptom of a failed hydraulic brake booster, not a soft spongy brake pedal. Technician B is not correct because a hard brake pedal is the symptom of a failed vacuum brake booster rather than a soft or spongy brake pedal. Answer c is not correct because neither technician is correct.

55. **The correct answer is a.** A defective vacuum brake booster will cause a hard brake pedal because of the lack of assist. Answer b is not correct because a soft (spongy) brake pedal is usually caused by air trapped in the hydraulic system. Answer c is not correct because a low brake pedal is usually caused by worn or misadjusted rear drum brakes or air trapped in the hydraulic system. Answer d is not correct because a slight hissing noise is normal for a vacuum brake booster because outside air enters the rear chamber of the booster from the interior of the vehicle.

56. **The correct answer is b.** Technician B is correct because the brake pedal should drop when the engine starts if the vacuum booster has been previously discharged. Technician A is not correct because the brake pedal should drop when the engine starts and not be a high brake pedal. Answers c and d are not correct because only Technician B is correct.

57. **The correct answer is b.** Technician B is correct because all power-assisted brakes are designed to be able to provide two or more assisted brake applications even if the engine stalls as a safety consideration. Technician A is not correct because a defective vacuum brake booster will cause a hard brake pedal (lack of power assist). Answers c and d are not correct because only Technician B is correct.

BRAKES (A5)

CATEGORY: DRUM BRAKE DIAGNOSIS AND REPAIR

58. **The correct answer is b.** Technician B is correct because the edges of the brake shoes contacting the backing plate may cause a squeaking sound when the brakes are applied if lubricant is not applied to the shoe pads (ledges). Technician A is not correct because only high-temperature brake grease or silicone grease should be used to lubricate the backing plate. Answers c and d are not correct because only Technician B is correct.

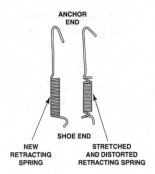

59. **The correct answer is c.** Both technicians are correct. Technician A is correct because the return springs as well as the hold-down and connecting springs can lose their tension during normal braking due to heating and cooling cycles. Technician B is correct because the star wheel adjuster cannot function correctly unless it is free to move and the lubrication will help eliminate rust and corrosion. Answers a, b, and d are not correct because both technicians are correct.

60. **The correct answer is b.** Technician B is correct because star-wheel adjusters use right-hand and left-hand threads and are labeled left and right. If they are installed on the wrong side of the vehicle, the adjusting lever will rotate the threads inward, rather than outward, thereby increasing the clearance between the brake shoe and the drum. Technician A is not correct because the adjuster will be rotated the opposite direction and the over-ride spring will prevent any harm. Answers c and d are not correct because only Technician B is right.

61. **The correct answer is d.** A drum micrometer should be rotated slightly in the brake drum to be sure to get an accurate measurement. Answer a is not correct because a brake lathe is needed to remove the lip created by the brake shoes. Answer b is not correct because a surface-measuring instrument is an electronic instrument and the tool shown is not electronic. Answer c is not correct because resurfacing of the drum is performed using a drum lathe.

62. **The correct answer is a.** A heat checked brake drum should be replaced because the deep cracks are non-repairable. Answers b, c, and d are not correct because repairing a heat checked brake drum is not recommended by vehicle manufacturers.

63. **The correct answer is a.** Technician A is correct because the self-adjuster works off the rear (secondary) brake shoe as the vehicle is stopped while traveling in reverse and the adjuster is on the right indicating that this is a left side drum brake. Technician B is not correct because this brake is a servo brake with the shorter primary lining on the left and the longer secondary lining on the right. A leading-trailing brake system uses lining that are usually the same length. Answers c and d are not correct because only Technician A is correct.

64. **The correct answer is c.** The micrometer reading is a 5, meaning 0.500 in., plus two lines each of which indicates 0.025 in. for a total of 0.050 in. plus three lines on the thimble for a total reading of 0.553 in. Answers a, b, and c are not correct because they do not state the actual micrometer reading.

65. **The correct answer is c.** Both technicians are correct. Technician A is correct because the parking brake operates the rear brakes only, so if the pulsation is felt using the parking brake, then the rear drums or shoes have to be the cause. Technician B is correct because an out-of-round brake drum can cause a brake pedal pulsation because the brake shoes are forced to move in and out slightly, which is transferred to the brake pedal through the movement of brake fluid at the wheel cylinder through to the master cylinder. Answers a, b, and d are not correct because both technicians are correct.

66. **The correct answer is b.** Technician B is correct because the parking brake may not be fully released or the parking brake cable may have been adjusted with the old worn brake linings. The brakes rubbing against the drum created heat and the smoke was observed by the customer. Technician A is not correct because while it is often recommended that new brakes be properly bedded in before returning the vehicle to the customer, smoke should not be visible if everything had been properly assembled. Answers c and d are not correct because only Technician B is correct.

67. **The correct answer is d.** A stuck open metering valve would not be a likely cause of rear wheel lockup because the metering valve simply delays the operation of the front brakes on a front disc, rear drum brake system. Answers a, b, and c are not correct because all three items can cause brakes to grab and are therefore not the least likely to create the condition.

68. **The correct answer is a.** Technician A is correct because the right drum has to be replaced because it is only one-thousandth of an inch smaller than the maximum allowable inside dimension (9.560 minus 9.559 = 0.001 in.). The left side can be machined because it is about 50-thousandth of an inch from needing replacement (9.560 minus 9.506 = 0.054 in.). Technician B is not correct because the right drum cannot be machined. Answers c and d are not correct because Technician A only is correct.

69. **The correct answer is c.** Both technicians are correct. Technician A is correct because when accurately measuring a brake drum for out-of-round, it should be measured at four or more locations around the drum. Technician B is correct because most vehicle manufacturers recommend that at least 15-thousandth of an inch (0.015 in.) be allowed for wear when machining a brake drum. Answers a, b, and d are not correct because both technicians are correct.

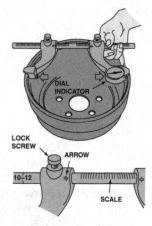

70. **The correct answer is d.** Chatter marks are caused by vibration during the machining of a brake drum and can be greatly reduced or eliminated by using a vibration dampener over the drum before machining. Answer a is not correct even though operating a brake lathe faster than specified could contribute to the chatter marks, it is not the most likely. Answers b and c can also contribute to the formation of the chatter marks but they are not the most likely cause.

71. **The correct answer is b.** During parking brake operation, the strut pushes the primary shoe against the brake drum. If the cable were to become stuck in this applied position, excessive wear will occur to the brakes, especially the primary (forward facing) shoe. Answer a is not correct because even though a stuck wheel cylinder piston could cause this condition, it is not the most likely cause. Answer c is not correct because weak hold-down springs can cause the shoes to bind and wear unevenly, but it is not the most likely cause of excessive wear to the primary shoe. Answer d is not correct even though a lack of proper lubrication of the backing plate could contribute to excessive brake shoe wear, it is not the most likely cause.

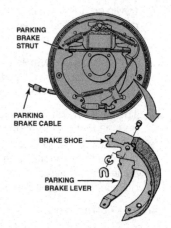

72. **The correct answer is a.** The illustration shows a screwdriver being used to push the adjusting lever away from the star-wheel adjuster and a brake spoon being used to rotate the adjuster inward. Answer b is not correct because the adjusting lever would not need to be moved away from the star wheel to adjust the brakes outward. Answer c is not correct because the star-wheel adjuster does not affect the clearance between the shoes and the backing plate. Answer d is not correct because the star-wheel adjuster is assembled and installed on the drum brake and is simply being adjusted.

73. **The correct answer is d.** A brake shoe clearance gauge (shoe setting caliper) is being used to set the inside dimension of the brake drum. The other side of the gauge is then placed over the brake shoes and the star-wheel adjuster is rotated until the gauge can slide over the shoes. This gauge is designed to provide about 20-thousandth of an inch (0.020 in.) clearance between the shoes and the drum. Answer a is not correct because the gauge does not actually measure the drum, but rather is set to the size of the drum so the shoes can be adjusted to fit the drum. Answers b and c are not correct because the gauge is used to adjust the shoes to the drum and is not used to measure the drum.

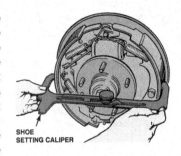

SHOE SETTING CALIPER

74. **The correct answer is d.** Only high-temperature grease designed for use on braking systems should be used to lubricate the backing plate. Answers a, b, and c are not correct because all of these products may not be able to withstand the temperature of a braking system and could melt or evaporate allowing metal-to-metal contact and wear to occur between the brake shoes and the backing plate ledges (pads).

75. **The correct answer is c.** Both technicians are correct. Technician A is correct because the part shown is a star-wheel adjuster and the star-wheel end is installed toward the rear or secondary brake shoe. Technician B is correct because star-wheel adjusters use different threads for left side and right side brakes and will not function correctly if installed on the wrong side of the vehicle. Answers a, b, and d are not correct because both technicians are correct.

76. **The correct answer is b.** Technician B is correct because if the brake fluid drips from the dust boot, the sealing cup(s) inside the wheel cylinder have failed. Technician A is not correct because some dampness may be observed around the dust boots of a wheel cylinder and should be considered normal according to most vehicle manufacturers. Answers c and d are not correct because only Technician B is correct.

77. **The correct answer is d.** The pistons in a wheel cylinder do not need to be compressed when installing new wheel cylinders. The pistons are free to move and a light spring between the two pistons is easily compressed by the brake shoes as they are installed onto the backing plate. Answers a, b, and c are not correct because these operations must be performed and are, therefore, not one of the operations that need not be performed.

78. **The correct answer is a.** A clogged vacuum hose to the vacuum brake booster would cause a lack of power assist and a hard brake pedal, but not a low brake pedal. Answers b, c, and d are all possible causes of a low brake pedal.

79. **The correct answer is b.** Technician B is correct because precautions must be taken to prevent the possibility of releasing brake dust into the air as the brake drum is being removed. Technician A is not correct because the Tinnerman nuts are used to keep the brake drums from falling off during vehicle assembly and they serve no other purpose and can be discarded. Answers c and d are not correct because Technician B only is correct.

80. **The correct answer is b.** Technician B is correct because the brake shoes could make noise if the backing plate ledges or pads under the brake shoes are not lubricated with high-temperature brake grease. Technician A is not correct because worn disc brake caliper guide pin O-rings are not likely to cause a squeaking sound every time the brakes are depressed even though they can cause some noise when the brakes are applied when the vehicle is moving.

81. **The correct answer is a.** Most vehicle manufacturers specify that brake lining be replaced when the lining thickness has been worn to 30-thousandth of an inch (0.030 in.) (3/32 in.) or less. Answers b, c, and d are not correct because even though some vehicle manufacturers recommend that the brakes be replaced when the lining thickness is less than the amount in the answer, most manufacturers state 0.030 in. as the minimum allowable lining thickness.

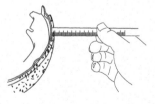

82. **The correct answer is c.** Both technicians are correct. Technician A is correct because self-adjusters are designed for left and right side brakes and they will not work correctly if switched to the opposite side of the vehicle because the threads are reversed. Technician B is correct because the end caps and the threads of the adjusters should be thoroughly cleaned and lubricated when rear drum brakes are serviced to permit proper operation. Answers a, b, and d are not correct because both technicians are correct.

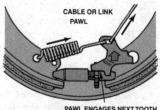

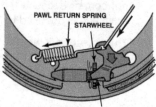

83. **The correct answer is c.** Both technicians are correct. Technician A is correct because most vehicle manufacturers recommend that the rear drum brakes be checked for proper lining-to-drum clearance before adjusting the parking brake cable. Technician B is correct because most vehicle manufacturers specify that the parking brake cable is properly adjusted if it requires about two to seven clicks when fully engaged, and always less than 10. If over 10 clicks, either the rear brakes or the parking brake cable need adjustment. Answers a, b, and d are not correct because both technicians are correct.

84. **The correct answer is a.** Technician A is correct because a normally operating parking brake should be able to hold the vehicle on a slight grade using just two to seven clicks. The high number of clicks indicates that the rear brake shoes are farther than normal from the brake drum. This could be due to worn brake linings and/or a lack of proper adjustment of the rear brakes or parking brake cable. Technician B is not correct because the fact that the parking brake will not hold the vehicle steady on a slight incline does not necessarily mean that the rear brakes need to be replaced. Answers c and d are not correct because Technician A only is correct.

85. **The correct answer is c.** Both technicians are correct. Technician A is correct because the hand-operated parking brake will turn on the same red brake warning lamp as is used to warn the driver of a hydraulic base brake problem. Technician B is correct because the foot-operated parking brake will turn on the red brake warning lamp on the dash if it is in the applied position. Answers a, b, and d are not correct because both technicians are correct.

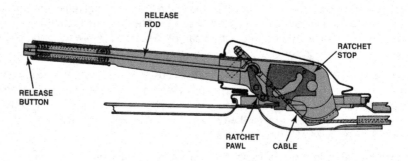

86. **The correct answer is c.** Both technicians are correct. Technician A is correct because if the parking brake cable has been adjusted with the worn brake shoes or is applied or stuck, the drum will often not fit over the shoes because the primary (forward) shoe is being pushed outward by the parking brake lever. Technician B is correct because both brake shoes should contact the anchor pin if the parking brake is fully released. Answers a, b, and d are not correct because both technicians are correct.

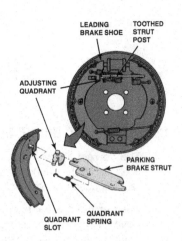

87. **The correct answer is b.** Technician B is correct because the drum should be replaced if hard spots are found on the friction surface of a brake drum. Technician A is not correct because even though the hard spots may be able to be ground flush using with the machined friction surface of the drum using a stone, the hard spots are still present and will cause uneven wear to occur to the brake lining. Most vehicle manufacturers recommend replacing brake drums that have hard spots. Answers c and d are not correct because only Technician B is correct.

88. **The correct answer is c.** The edge code letters represent the coefficient of friction codes; the first letter indicates when the lining is cold and the second when the lining is hot. Answer a is not correct because the edge codes do not indicate wear factors. Answer b is not correct because edge codes do not indicate noise factors. Answer d is not correct because even though parts of the code identify the manufacturer, they do not indicate the composition of the lining material.

89. **The correct answer is d.** Machined brake drums should be cleaned using soap or detergent and water to float any particles that could be trapped in the small grooves of the drum. Conventional cleaners cannot float out these particles. Answers a, b, and c are not correct because they will not lift particles out of the grooves on the drum.

90. **The correct answer is c.** Both technicians are correct. Technician A is correct because using masking tape over the friction surface of the brake linings is an excellent method to use to prevent the possibility of getting grease on the linings. Technician B is correct because grease or brake lining can cause the brake to grab. Answers a, b, and d are not correct because both technicians are correct.

91. **The correct answer is b.** Technician B is correct because the parking brake lever will force the primary shoe away from the anchor pin if the parking brake is applied. Technician A is not correct because it is not normal for the primary shoe to not contact the anchor pin at the top if everything is adjusted properly. Answers c and d are not correct because only Technician B is correct.

92. **The correct answer is a.** Technician A is correct because unequal thickness drums will heat and expand differently, which could cause a brake pull under certain situations. Most vehicle manufacturers recommend that the drums on the same axle be within 0.020 in. inside diameter of each other. Technician B is not correct because the drum should ring when lightly tapped with a hammer if it is not cracked. A cracked drum will not ring when hit. Answers c and d are not correct because only Technician A is correct.

93. **The correct answer is b.** Technician B is correct because even though asbestos use has been reduced, all brake linings should be handled as if they contain asbestos and take the necessary steps to ensure that brake dust does not become airborne. Technician A is not correct because brake lining color is not an indication of whether or not the lining material contains asbestos. Answers c and d are not correct because only Technician B is correct.

94. **The correct answer is c.** Both technicians are correct. Technician A is correct because many vehicle manufacturers recommend that the brake drums be machined to the axle flange to insure proper wheel balance after the brake service work has been performed. Technician B is correct because the brake shoes can wear into the brake drum creating a ridge, which prevents the drum from being removed unless the linings are adjusted inward. Answers a, b, and d are not correct because both technicians are correct.

BRAKES (A5)

CATEGORY: DISC BRAKE DIAGNOSIS AND REPAIR

95. **The correct answer is b.** A defective wheel bearing often creates a growling or rumbling sound that is similar to the sound made by aggressive tread, winter-type tires. Answers a, c, and d are not correct because these do not produce a rumbling or growling-type noise.

96. **The correct answer is d.** It is normal for the brake pedal to go to the floor after disc brake pads have been replaced because the pistons have been retracted into the caliper bore and brake fluid from the master cylinder has to be restored before hydraulic pressure can be created. It often requires several brake applications to restore proper brake pedal operation. Answers a, b, and c are not correct because the condition is considered to be normal and no other fault is indicated.

97. **The correct answer is c.** Both technicians are correct. Technician A is correct because using sandpaper (150 grit aluminum oxide) for one minute on each side of the rotor will smooth the rotor to an acceptable finish. Technician B is correct because a non-directional surface finish is necessary to prevent the disc brake pads from moving during a brake application, which helps prevent brake squeal. Using sandpaper for one minute will not only provide the correct surface finish but will also produce a nondirectional surface. Answers a, b, and d are not correct because both technicians are correct.

98. **The correct answer is a.** Technician A is correct because even though hard spots on a rotor may be able to be ground smooth, the areas will remain and can cause brake noise and a pulsating brake pedal. Most vehicle manufacturers recommend replacing any rotor that has hard spots. Technician B is not correct because hard spots are caused by excessive heat, which changes the metallurgy of the cast iron, creating the hard spots, and is not caused by using riveted instead of bonded brake pads. Answers c and d are not correct because Technician A only is correct.

99. **The correct answer is c.** Both technicians are correct. Technician A is correct because depressing and holding the pedal down about 1 in. will cause the pistons inside the master cylinder to close off the fluid from the reservoir and stop the loss of brake fluid when the brake line is disconnected. Technician B is correct because many calipers are constructed so that they will fit on either side of the vehicle but the air cannot be successfully bled unless the bleeder screw is at the top of the caliper. Answers a, b, and d are not correct because both technicians are correct.

100. **The correct answer is a.** Technician A is correct because rotor finish is measured in Ra (roughness average) in a unit called micro inches, which represent roughness of the surface. The higher the number is, the rougher the surface. Most vehicle manufacturers recommend a rotor finish smoother than 40 in. for best braking performance as well as a nondirectional surface. Technician B is not correct because the higher the surface finish number, the rougher (not the smoother) the surface. A 40 in. surface is smoother than an 80 in. surface.

101. **The correct answer is c.** Both technicians are correct. Technician A is correct because many vehicle manufacturers do recommend that front disc brake rotors be machined on the vehicle to be sure that the rotors are being machined as they will be operating on the vehicle. Technician B is correct because many vehicle manufacturers recommend that rotors only be machined if there is a brake pedal pulsation complaint or if there is excessive rust on the friction surface. Machining a rotor reduces its heat storage capability. Answers a, b, and d are not correct because both technicians are correct.

102. **The correct answer is b.** The caliper piston is being pushed into the caliper bore with the bleeder valve open to allow brake fluid to escape and not be forced back up into the electronic brake hydraulic (ABS) unit or the master cylinder. This operation is needed to be performed to remove the caliper so that the disc brake pads can be replaced. Answer a is not correct because the pliers are being used to force the piston inward and not used to check for proper clearance. Answer c is not correct because, even though the bleeder valve is open, it is used to remove the brake fluid form the caliper and is not used to bleed air from the caliper. Answer d is not correct because the caliper piston is being pushed inward and is not being used to remove the caliper itself.

103. **The correct answer is d.** Worn caliper slides (ways) can cause a noise when the caliper hits the caliper mount when the brakes are first applied. Answer a is not correct because caliper pistons do not actually contact the caliper bore, but rather ride on the square-cut O-ring seal so noise is not possible. Answer b is not correct because a restricted front brake hose could affect the operation of the brake but would not cause a clicking sound every time the brakes are applied. Answer c is not correct because loose wheel bearings would make a growling or rumbling sound and are unlikely to create a clicking sound when the brakes are applied.

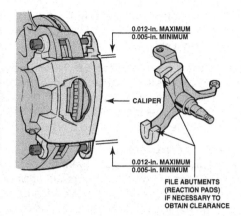

0.012-in. MAXIMUM
0.005-in. MINIMUM

CALIPER

0.012-in. MAXIMUM
0.005-in. MINIMUM

FILE ABUTMENTS
(REACTION PADS)
IF NECESSARY TO
OBTAIN CLEARANCE

104. **The correct answer is c.** Both technicians are correct. Technician A is correct because a scan tool can be sure to command the rear caliper piston to retract to allow clearance for the removal and replacement of the rear disc brake pads. Technician B is correct because a scan tool can be used to command the rear caliper piston to apply then release to provide the correct running clearance between the rotor and the rear disc brake pads. Answers a, b, and d are not correct because both technicians are correct.

105. **The correct answer is b.** Silicone grease is the type of lubricant recommended by vehicle manufacturers for use on rubber brake components. The use of the lubricant such as those listed in answers a, c, and d would either melt easily due to normal brake temperatures (Vaseline) or interact with the rubber and cause swelling, which could cause brake failure.

106. **The correct answer is c.** Both technicians are correct. Technician A is correct because the lateral runout exceeds factory specifications. The rotor must be restored to proper dimensional accuracy either by machining or replacement. Technician B is correct because the runout will usually cause a vibration in the steering wheel (front disc brake rotor) or a pulsating brake pedal because the rotor is applying an uneven force to the caliper pistons as it rotates. This uneven force is then transferred through the hydraulic brake system to the brake pedal and is felt by the driver as a pulsation. Answers a, b, and d are not correct because both technicians are correct.

107. **The correct answer is b.** Technician B is correct because a micrometer must be used and the rotor should be measured at four to eight locations around the rotor to determine the maximum difference in rotor thickness. Technician A is not correct because a micrometer must be used because the maximum allowable difference in thickness is less than one-half of one-thousandth of an inch, which could not be measured using a straight edge on one side of a rotor. Answers c and d are not correct because Technician B only is correct.

108. **The correct answer is d.** All of the above are correct. Clean, rust-free caliper mounts are necessary to help prevent of the calipers from sticking (answer a), as well as preventing unequal disc brake pad wear (answer b) and help prevent noise during brake applications (answer c). Answers a, b, and c are not correct because all are correct.

109. **The correct answer is c.** Both technicians are correct. Technician A is correct because all metal-to-metal contact points between the disc brake pad backing and the caliper should be lubricated with silicone or synthetic grease to allow freedom of movement for proper disc brake operation. Technician B is correct because metal-to-metal contact can create noise as the movement occurs between the caliper and pad during normal braking. Lubrication of these points of contact helps eliminate the noise. Answers a, b, and d are not correct because both technicians are correct.

110. **The correct answer is d.** Neither technician is correct. Technician A is not correct because even though the outboard pad and inboard pad are often a different size and shape, there is no difference in the right- and left-hand disc brake pads. Technician B is not correct because the disc brake pads can usually be installed in any order and it is not necessary to install the outboard pad before the inboard pad. Answers a, b, and c are not correct because neither technician is correct.

111. **The correct answer is b.** Typical brake rotor runout specifications range from three- to five-thousandth of an inch (0.003 to 0.005 in.). Answers a, c, and d are not correct because they are not the usual runout specifications.

112. **The correct answer is b.** Technician B is correct because the scratch test indicates that the rotor is not warped; otherwise, the scratch would have occurred over only part of the rotor face. Technician A is not correct because the rotor should be rotated 180°, if the scratch is made on one-half of the rotor face to check if the rotor has been installed correctly on the brake lathe. Answers c and d are not correct because Technician B only is correct.

113. **The correct answer is b.** Technician B is correct because the pin is necessary to lock the disc brake piston to the pad to prevent the piston from rotating as the parking brake is applied. Without the pin, the piston would simply rotate against the back of the pad and the parking brake would not apply. Technician A is not correct because the caliper piston would simply rotate against the back of the piston instead of pushing the piston and the pads toward the rotor. Answers c and d are not correct because Technician B only is correct.

114. **The correct answer is b.** Technician B is correct because soap (or detergent) and water will float particles from grooves in the surface. Technician A is not correct because brake cleaner may clean the surface but will not float out any particles that could cause excessive brake wear. Answers c and d are not correct because Technician B only is correct.

115. **The correct answer is c.** Both technicians are correct. Technician A is correct because brake noise is created by movement and sound is actually moving air. Lubricant on the backside of the disc brake pads helps prevent brake noise by preventing metal-to-metal contact between the steel backing of the pad and the disc brake caliper and piston. Technician B is correct because by properly crimping the pads to the caliper, movement between the two is reduced thereby reducing noise. Answers a, b, and d are not correct because both technicians are correct.

116. **The correct answer is d.** All of the above are include with a loaded caliper assembly. A typical loaded caliper includes a new or rebuilt (remanufactured) caliper assembly (a) plus any needed guides pins (b) and shims and hardware (c). Answers a, b, and c are not correct because these parts or components are not part of a typical loaded caliper even though these parts may be available.

117. **The correct answer is c.** Both technicians are correct. Technician A is correct because most vehicle manufacturers recommend that the disc pads be handled as if they do contain asbestos and to take the necessary precautions to avoid allowing brake dust from becoming airborne. Technician B is correct because in order to help prevent brake dust from becoming airborne, the brakes should be wetted or disassembled in a vacuum chamber. Answers a, b, and d are not correct because both technicians are correct.

118. **The correct answer is c.** The cotter key must be replaced when it is removed because if a part breaks off, it can get into the wheel bearing possibly causing the wheel to lock, leading to a possible collision and personal injury. Answer a is not correct because while the bearing cup should be replaced when the bearing is replaced, it is not necessary to replace it when repacking a bearing or removing the wheel bearing for other service work. Answer b is not correct because even though most experts recommend replacing the grease seal, it would not be necessary if just the outer wheel bearing is being serviced. The best answer is still the cotter key because failure to replace the part could result in a serious accident. Answer d is not correct because the retaining washer is not a wearing or critical part.

119. **The correct answer is c.** Both technicians are correct. Technician A is correct because rotor thickness variation is the major cause of a pulsating brake pedal. As the brake pad travels over the uneven surface, the pad(s) move in and out of the caliper bore. This movement of the piston moves the brake fluid in the caliper and transfers movement back to the master cylinder and eventually to the driver's foot through the brake pedal. Technician B is correct because rotors should not be machined to the minimum thickness, but at least 15-thousandth of an inch (0.015 in.) should be left to allow for wear if the specification stated minimum thickness. If the specification was stated as a machine, then the extra thickness for wear is already factored into the dimension. Answers a, b, and d are not correct because both technicians are correct.

120. **The correct answer is c.** The brake lining edge codes indicate the coefficient of friction using two letters. The first letter represents the coefficient of friction when the lining is cold and the second when the lining is hot. Answers a, b, and d are not correct because the letters refer to the coefficient of friction and not other information.

121. **The correct answer is a.** The maximum allowable thickness variation specified by most vehicle manufacturers is one-half of a thousandth of an inch or 0.0005 in.; therefore, the answer 0.0003 to 0.0005 in. is the closest to this specification. Answers b, c, and d are not correct because all are too great.

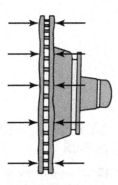

**THICKNESS VARIATION
AT DIFFERENT POINTS
AROUND THE ROTOR**

122. **The correct answer is c.** Both technicians are correct. Technician A is correct because a leaking caliper means that the seals are leaking and the brake caliper is not able to function as designed. Technician B is correct because the other side caliper has been working under that same conditions and as a result may also fail shortly. Replacing both calipers on the same axle (either front or both rear) will help insure proper brake balance and restore the brake system to like new performance. Answers a, b, and d are not correct because both technicians are correct.

123. **The correct answer is c.** Both technicians are correct. Technician A is correct because most vehicle manufacturers recommend that the disc brake pads be replaced if worn down to about the thickness of the steel backing plate which makes a convenient gauge to use. Technician B is correct because most vehicle manufacturers recommend that the pads be removed and inspected for cracks or delamination which is something that cannot be checked unless the pads are removed. Answers a, b, and d are not correct because both technicians are correct.

124. **The correct answer is a.** Technician A is correct because the disc brake pad sensor rubs against the rotor and makes a noise. The noise generally stops when the brakes are applied. The braking forces cause the soft metal wear sensor to deflect and dampen, so the chirping sound is not heard when the brakes are applied. Technician B is not correct because a wheel bearing seldom makes a chirping sound and would not stop when the brakes are applied. Answers c and d are not correct because Technician A only is correct.

125. **The correct answer is b.** Technician B is correct because if the caliper slides are stuck and unable to slide, then one pad will wear more than the other during braking. All of the braking is provided by the pad moving against the piston and because the caliper cannot move, little if any braking force is being applied to the rotor by the outboard pad. Technician A is not correct because a seized piston will not allow the brakes to be applied at all and no wear will occur. Answers c and d are not correct because only Technician B is correct.

126. **The correct answer is c.** Both technicians are correct. Technician A is correct because the outer race (cup) should always be replaced when the bearing is replaced because any indentation or fault in the outer race will be transferred to the new bearing possibly causing it to fail prematurely. Technician B is correct because the outer race (cup) should be installed using a driver according to the recommended service procedures of most vehicle manufacturers. Answer a, b, and d are not correct because both technicians are correct.

127. **The correct answer is b.** Technician B is correct because the C-clamp is a commonly used tool used to compress caliper pistons back into the bore. Technician A is not correct because the pistons do not need to be held to remove the disc brake pads. Answers c and d are not correct because Technician B only is correct.

128. **The correct answer is b.** Technician B is correct because the bearing should be thoroughly cleaned and carefully inspected before applying new grease. The bearing cannot be thoroughly inspected if it is not cleaned and the new grease may not be compatible with the old grease. Technician A is not correct because vehicle manufacturers specify that the bearing should be thoroughly cleaned and inspected before applying new grease. Answers c and d are not correct because Technician B only is correct.

129. **The correct answer is a.** Technician A is correct because most front-wheel-drive vehicles with front wheel bearings are sealed units that must be replaced as an assembly. Technician B is not correct because even though they do contain ball bearings or in some cases two rows of tapered roller bearings, the unit is sealed and cannot be serviced except for replacement. Answers c and d are not correct because Technician A only is correct.

BRAKES (A5)

CATEGORY: ELECTRONIC BRAKE CONTROL SYSTEMS—ABS, TCS, ESC—DIAGNOSIS AND REPAIR

130. **The correct answer is a.** A stuck left front caliper piston will prevent the proper operation of the left front brake creating a pull to the right during braking because only the right front brake is working. Answers b and c are not correct because wheel speed sensor faults cannot cause the vehicle to pull. A fault in a wheel speed sensor will usually trigger a diagnostic trouble code and the ABS controller may limit antilock braking and will turn on the amber ABS warning lamp. Answer d is not correct because control solenoids are normally open to allow for normal braking and a fault would not cause a brake pull to the right even if stuck in the closed (no right brakes) position.

131. **The correct answer is a.** Technician A is correct because the brake pedal pulsates up and down rapidly as the hydraulic control unit pulses the vehicles brakes on and off during an ABS stop and is considered to be normal operation. Technician B is not correct because no fault of the ABS is indicated by this occurrence. Answers c and d are not correct because Technician A only is correct.

132. **The correct answer is c.** Both technicians are correct. Technician A is correct because a scan tool is needed to bleed some ABS hydraulic units. The scan tool is used to open and close valves or solenoids to allow any trapped air to escape and be bled out of the system. Technician B is correct because most vehicle manufacturers recommend that only DOT 3 (most domestic and Asian) or DOT 4 (most European) brake fluid be used in the antilock braking system and never use DOT 5 as it tends to foam when used in an antilock system caused by the pulsating solenoid valves. Answers a, b, and d are not correct because both technicians are correct.

133. **The correct answer is b.** Technician B is correct because low brake fluid level is a major base brake fault requiring that the red brake warning lamp comes on to warn the driver. Technician A is not correct because a wheel speed sensor fault could cause the amber ABS warning lamp to be turned on by the controller but not the red brake warning lamp. Answers c and d are not correct because Technician B only is correct.

134. **The correct answer is d.** All of the answers are correct. Answer a is correct because the electronic stability control system pulses the wheel brakes to restore the vehicle to the proper path and pulsation of the brakes can be heard and felt as a vibration or pulsing sound. Answer b is correct when the system is functioning and trying to restore traction, the traction control of electronic stability control amber light will flash when it is actively trying to control the vehicle. Answer c is correct because the system pulses individual wheel brakes and a pulsating brake pedal is often felt if the drive is depressing the brake pedal. Answers a, b, and c are not correct because all are correct.

135. **The correct answer is a.** Technician A is correct because wheel speed sensors are included in the items monitored by the ABS controller and if a problem is detected in a sensor, the amber ABS warning lamp will light. Technician B is not correct because it is normal for the amber ABS warning lamp to flash as part of a self-test when the vehicle is first started. Answers c and d are not correct because Technician A only is correct.

136. **The correct answer is c.** Both technicians are correct. Technician A is correct because most antilock braking system controllers perform a self-test and these often involve operating the pump motor plus the solenoids and/or valves as soon as the vehicle reaches 3 to 5 mph. Technician B is correct because most antilock braking systems stop attempting to keep the tires from locking up when the vehicle speed is less than about 5 mph. The accuracy of wheel speed sensors is limited at such low speeds and a locked tire at this speed does not threaten vehicle stability. Answers a, b, and d are not correct because both technicians are correct.

137. **The correct answer is b.** Technician B is correct because most antilock braking systems (ABS) allow a certain amount of slip during hard braking and this slippage is heard as tire chirps as the brakes are alternately applied, held, and released. Technician A is not correct because the tire noise was heard under hard braking conditions where the antilock function is likely to occur and does not indicate a fault is present. Answers c and d are not correct because Technician B only is correct.

138. **The correct answer is d.** The larger wheels and tires cause an increased load on the brakes because the wheel revolves slower and weigh more than the stock wheels and tires. The only solution requires replacement wheels and tires so that the outside diameter (O.D.) of the wheel/tire assembly is with 3% of the factory tires to insure proper brake operation. Answer a is not correct because the distance between the wheels and the caliper does not affect how the brakes perform. Answer b is not correct because a faulty wheel speed sensor would likely cause a diagnostic trouble code to set but not likely to reduce braking performance. Answer c is not correct because the wheel speed sensors use a tone wheel attached to the wheel hub and not the wheel so the calibration can't be changed.

139. **The correct answer is c.** Both technicians are correct. Technician A is correct because the amber dash warning lamp indicates that a fault in the antilock braking system (ABS) has been detected and the controller will usually disable the antilock function as long as the fault is present. Technician B is correct because the amber ABS warning lamp only indicates a fault in the antilock braking system and not in the base brake components so normal braking should be available. Answers a, b, and d are not correct because both technicians are correct.

140. **The correct answer is b.** Most vehicle manufacturers program the ABS controller to be able to tolerate the difference in tire size when the smaller spare tire is used on one wheel. The smaller tire will cause the wheel to rotate faster than the others and while it could trigger a diagnostic trouble code on some vehicles, it is unlikely on most ABS equipped vehicles. Answers a, c, and d are all very likely to set a diagnostic trouble code and turn on the amber ABS warning lamp.

141. **The correct answer is b.** Technician B is correct because even though most vehicles equipped with antilock brakes can be bled manually, some do require pressure bleeding to get all of the trapped air out of the system. Technician A is not correct because many vehicles use a different brake bleeding sequence for ABS equipped vehicles from the sequence for the same vehicle that is not so equipped. Answers c and d are not correct because Technician B only is correct.

142. **The correct answer is d.** Low brake fluid in the master cylinder reservoir is not likely to cause an ABS fault even though it could cause the red brake warning lamp to light if the fluid level is too low for safe operation of the base brakes. Answers a, b, and c are all likely causes for the ABS controller to set a wheel speed sensor diagnostic trouble code and turn on the amber ABS warning lamp.

143. **The correct answer is d.** The setting for DC amperes (DCA) is not used to check for the proper operation of an analog wheel speed sensor. Answer a (hertz or Hz) is used to check the frequency output of wheel speed sensors. Answer b (AC volts) is used to check for proper output voltage. Answer c (DC volts) is often used to check the bias voltage that the ABS controller applies to the wheel speed sensor.

144. **The correct answer is d.** Both answers a and b are correct. Answer a is correct because the stop lamp switch completes the circuit the circuit between the smart junction box and the stop signal relay and then as an input to the ABS control module. Answer b is correct because when the stop lamp switch is closed, the output from the switch is sent to the stop signal relay. Answer c is not correct because the voltage to the rear stop lamps is through the E/R Fuse and Relay box and not directly form the stop lamp switch.

145. **The correct answer is b.** For safety, the electric parking brake module will apply the parking brakes to both rear wheel if the gear selector is placed in the neutral, position to prevent the vehicle from moving. If the driver wants the vehicle to move (roll), then the driver can release the parking brake manually using the button or control on the dash or center console. Answer a is not correct because by releasing the parking brake when the transmission is moved into the neutral position will cause the vehicle to move if it is an incline creating a potential safety issue. Answer c is not correct because by releasing the parking brake on only side of then vehicle.

146. **The correct answer is d.** All of the above are correct. Answer a is correct because the wiring diagram shows that there is a spend sensor (detector) at each of the four wheels. Answer b is correct because the solid box around surrounding the ABS hydraulic unit means that whatever is inside the box is a part of the unit itself. The pump motor and pump relay are both inside the hydraulic unit. Answer c is correct because inside the hydraulic unit are three solenoid valves, one for each front wheel brake and one that is used to control both rear brakes making this a three-channel-type system.

ELECTRICAL/ELECTRONIC SYSTEMS CONTENT AREAS

This ASE study guide for Electrical/Electronic Systems (A6) is divided into the sub-content areas that correlate to the actual ASE certification test as follows:

CONTENT AREA	QUESTIONS IN TEST	NUMBER OF STUDY GUIDE QUESTIONS
A. General Electrical/Electronic System Diagnosis	13	30 (1-30)
B. Battery and Starting System Diagnosis and Repair	9	29 (31-59)
C. Charging System Diagnosis and Repair	5	12 (60-71)
D. Lighting Systems Diagnosis and Repair	6	15 (72-86)
E. Instrument Cluster and Driver Information Systems Diagnosis and Repair	6	9 (87-95)
F. Body Electrical Systems Diagnosis and Repair	11	26 (96-122)
TOTAL	**50**	**122**

TIME ALLOWED TO TAKE THE TEST

The allocated time to take the Engine Repair Certification test is 75 minutes. ASE adds 10 additional questions to the test for research purposes for a total of 60 questions. These questions do not count toward your score, but they are embedded within the test and there is no way of knowing which ones do not count. As a result, the technician needs to answer 60 questions in 75 minutes, or about one question per minute.

If taking the recertification A6 test, there are just 25 questions with no additional research questions included. The time allocated to take the recertification test is 45 minutes, which means more than one minute per question is allowed due to the number of schematics that need to be studied in this certification test.

BEFORE USING THIS STUDY GUIDE

Before trying to answer the questions and looking at the explanations, look over the following list of the content that ASE states will be covered in the certification test. For best results using this study guide, check service information or consult an automotive textbook for details on any of the content areas that are not familiar before trying to answers the questions. For additional information about the ASE test, visit the website at **www.ase.com**.

ELECTRICAL/ELECTRONIC SYSTEMS (A6) CERTIFICATION TEST

A. GENERAL ELECTRICAL/ELECTRONIC SYSTEM DIAGNOSIS (13 QUESTIONS)

1. Check voltages and voltage drops in electrical/electronic circuits; interpret readings and determine needed repairs.
2. Check current flow in electrical/electronic circuits; interpret readings and determine needed repairs.
3. Check continuity and resistances in electrical/electronic circuits and components; interpret readings and determine needed repairs.
4. Check electronic circuit waveforms; interpret readings and determine needed repairs.
5. Use scan tool data, bidirectional controls, and/or diagnostic trouble codes (DTCs) to diagnose electronic systems; interpret readings and determine necessary action.
6. Find shorts, grounds, opens, and resistance problems in electrical/electronic circuits; determine needed repairs.
7. Measure and diagnose the cause(s) of abnormal key-off battery drain (parasitic draw); determine needed repairs.
8. Inspect, test, and replace fusible links, circuit breakers, fuses, diodes, and current limiting devices.
9. Read and interpret electrical schematic diagrams and symbols.
10. Research applicable vehicle and service information, such as vehicle service history, service precautions, technical service bulletins, and service campaigns/recalls.
11. Diagnose failures in the data bus communications network; determine needed repairs.
12. Remove and replace control modules; program, reprogram, code, initialize, and/or configure as needed.

B. BATTERY AND STARTING SYSTEM DIAGNOSIS AND REPAIR (9 QUESTIONS)

1. Perform battery state-of-charge test; determine needed service.
2. Perform battery tests (load and capacitance); determine needed service.
3. Follow manufacturer's procedure to restore (or maintain if applicable) electronic memory functions.
4. Perform battery charge in accordance with manufacturer's recommendations.
5. Inspect, clean, repair, and/or replace battery(ies), battery cables, connectors, clamps, hold-downs, trays, and vent tubes.
6. Jump-start a vehicle using jumper cables, a booster battery, or auxiliary power supply.
7. Perform starter current draw test; determine needed repairs.
8. Perform starter circuit voltage drop tests; determine needed repairs.
9. Inspect, test, repair, and/or replace starter, relays, solenoids, modules, switches, connectors, and wires of starter circuits.
10. Differentiate between electrical and engine mechanical problems that cause a slow crank, no-crank, extended cranking, or a cranking noise condition.

C. CHARGING SYSTEM DIAGNOSIS AND REPAIR (5 QUESTIONS)

1. Diagnose charging system problems that cause a no-charge, a low charge, or an overcharge condition; determine needed repairs.
2. Inspect, reinstall, and/or replace pulleys, tensioners, and drive belts; adjust belts and check alignment.
3. Perform charging system voltage output test; determine needed repairs.
4. Perform charging system current output test; determine needed repairs.
5. Inspect and test generator (alternator) control components including sensors, regulators, and modules; determine needed repairs.
6. Perform charging circuit voltage drop tests; determine needed repairs.
7. Inspect, test, repair, and/or replace connectors, terminals, and wires of charging system circuits.
8. Remove, inspect, and replace generator (alternator).

D. LIGHTING SYSTEMS DIAGNOSIS AND REPAIR (6 QUESTIONS)

1. Diagnose the cause of brighter-than-normal, intermittent, dim, continuous, or no operation of exterior lighting; determine needed repairs.
2. Inspect, replace, aim, and/or level headlight assemblies and auxiliary light assemblies (fog lights/driving lights), including high-intensity discharge (HID) and LED systems.
3. Inspect, test, repair, and/or replace switches, relays, bulbs, LEDs, sockets, connectors, terminals, wires, and control modules of exterior lighting.
4. Diagnose the cause of turn signal and/or hazard light system malfunctions; determine needed repairs.
5. Inspect, test, repair, and/or replace switches, flasher units, bulbs, sockets, connectors, terminals, wires, and control modules of turn signal and hazard light circuits.
6. Diagnose the cause of intermittent, dim, continuous, or no operation of interior lighting circuits (such as courtesy, dome, map, vanity, glove box, cargo, trunk, hood, instrument, and accent lighting); determine needed repairs.
7. Inspect, test, repair, and/or replace switches, relays, bulbs, sockets, connectors, terminals, wires, and control modules of interior lighting circuits (such as courtesy, dome, map, vanity, glove box, cargo, trunk, hood, instrument, and accent lighting).
8. Inspect, test, repair, and/or replace trailer wiring harness, relays, connectors, and control modules (including brake control).

E. INSTRUMENT CLUSTER AND DRIVER INFORMATION SYSTEMS DIAGNOSIS AND REPAIR (6 QUESTIONS)

1. Diagnose the cause of intermittent, dim, no lights, continuous operation, or no brightness control of instrument lighting circuits; determine needed repairs.
2. Inspect, test, repair, and/or replace switches, relays, bulbs, LEDs, sockets, connectors, terminals, wires, and control modules of instrument lighting circuits.
3. Diagnose the cause of high, low, intermittent, or no readings on electronic instrument cluster gauges; determine needed repairs.
4. Diagnose the cause of constant, intermittent, or no operation of warning lights, indicator lights, audible warning devices, and other driver information systems; determine needed repairs.
5. Inspect, test, repair, and/or replace bulbs, sockets, connectors, terminals, switches, relays, sensors, timers, wires, gauges, sending units, electronic components, and control modules of electronic instrument clusters and driver information system circuits.

F. BODY ELECTRICAL SYSTEMS DIAGNOSIS AND REPAIR (11 QUESTIONS)

1. Diagnose operation of comfort and convenience accessories and related circuits (such as power windows, power seats, adjustable pedal height, power locks, trunk locks, remote start, moon roof, sunroof, sun shade, keyless entry, voice activation, phone pairing technology, wireless connectivity, steering wheel controls, camera systems, park assist, cruise control, and automated exterior lighting); determine needed repairs.

2. Inspect, test, repair, and/or replace components, connectors, terminals, and wiring of comfort and convenience accessories.

3. Diagnose operation of heated and cooled accessories and related circuits (such as heated/cooled seats, heated steering wheel, heated mirror, heated glass, and heated/cooled cup holders); determine needed repairs.

4. Inspect, test, repair, and/or replace components, connectors, terminals, and wiring of heated and cooled accessories.

5. Diagnose operation of security/anti-theft systems and related circuits (such as theft deterrent, door locks, keyless entry, remote start, and starter/fuel disable); determine needed repairs.

6. Inspect, test, repair, and/or replace components, connectors, terminals, and wiring of security/anti-theft systems.

7. Diagnose operation of entertainment/infotainment and related circuits (such as radio, DVD, navigation, amplifiers, speakers, antennas, and voice-activated accessories); determine needed repairs.

8. Inspect, test, repair, and/or replace components, connectors, terminals, and wiring of entertainment/infotainment systems.

9. Diagnose operation of safety systems and related circuits (such as supplemental restraint systems, wipers, washers, horn, speed control, collision avoidance, telematics, heads-up display, park assist, and camera systems); determine needed repairs.

10. Inspect, test, repair, and/or replace components, connectors, terminals, and wiring of safety systems.

ELECTRICAL/ELECTRONIC SYSTEMS (A6)

CATEGORY: GENERAL ELECTRICAL/ELECTRONIC SYSTEM DIAGNOSIS

1. Technician A says a short-to-voltage may or may not blow a fuse and may or may not affect more than one circuit. Technician B says that a short-to-ground (grounded) will usually cause a decrease in circuit resistance and an increase in current flow causing the fuse to blow. Which technician is correct?

   a. A only
   b. B only
   c. Both A and B
   d. Neither A nor B

2. Why is it important to verify the reported electrical symptom?

   a. The problem may be intermittent
   b. There may be related symptoms not reported by the customer
   c. The service advisor may have misunderstood the problem
   d. All of the above are correct

3. How would you tell if a fusible link is blown?

   a. Cut the insulation open and inspect the wire
   b. Replace the fusible link and see if current flows
   c. Pull both ends to see if the link stretches
   d. Cut the link in the middle and make sure that both ends are intact

4. What meter reading represents 10 ohms?

   a. 0.010 Ω
   b. 0.010 kΩ
   c. 0.10 MΩ
   d. 10.0 kΩ

5. A fuse keeps blowing. Technician A says that a test light can be used in place of the fuse and unplug components in the circuit until the test light goes out. Technician B says that a circuit breaker can be used in the place of the fuse. Which technician is correct?

   a. A only
   b. B only
   c. Both A and B
   d. Neither A nor B

6. What is the meter measuring?

   a. Resistance (ohms)
   b. Current (amperes)
   c. Voltage drop
   d. Available voltage

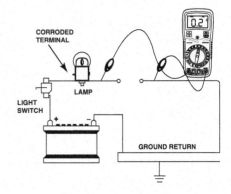

7. Technician A says that a low or zero reading on an ohmmeter indicates continuity. Technician B says that an ohmmeter set on the highest scale and reading infinity means no continuity. Which technician is correct?

   a. A only
   b. B only
   c. Both A and B
   d. Neither A nor B

8. A DMM set to read KΩ reads OL on the display. This means that the component or circuit being measured _____.

   a. is open
   b. is shorted
   c. is okay—normal reading
   d. has low resistance

9. If a digital meter face shows 0.93 when set to read K ohm scale, the reading means _____.

   a. 93 ohms
   b. 930 ohms
   c. 9300 ohms
   d. 93,000 ohms

10. A reading of 432 shows on the face of the meter set to the millivolt scale. The reading means _____.

   a. 0.432 volts
   b. 4.32 volts
   c. 43.2 volts
   d. 4320 volts

11. If a component such as a dome light has power (voltage) on both the power side and the ground side of the bulb, this indicates _____.

   a. a defective (open) bulb
   b. a short-to-ground
   c. a corroded bulb socket
   d. an open ground-side circuit

12. A circuit that has a relay does not work but the relay can be heard to click when activated. Technician A says the coil of the relay could be open. Technician B says that the coil of the relay could be shorted. Which technician is correct?

   a. A only
   b. B only
   c. Both A and B
   d. Neither A nor B

13. The voltage is being checked at several locations as shown in the figure. Technician A says that the circuit is okay. Technician B says that there is a fault with lamps A and B because the voltage is lower after the current flows through the two lamps. Which technician is correct?

   a. A only
   b. B only
   c. Both A and B
   d. Neither A nor B

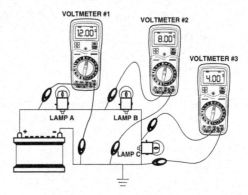

14. The blower motor only runs at high speed. The blower motor does not operate at all when the other speeds are selected. The possible cause can be:

   a. a short-to-ground at X
   b. an open at W
   c. an open at Y
   d. a short-to-ground at Z

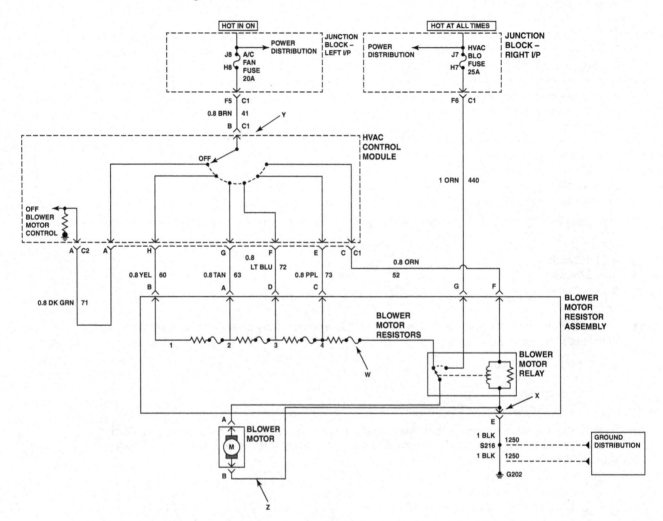

15. One fog light is out. The technician is checking to see if electrical power is available at the socket. Which position on the digital multimeter (DMM) should the technician select?

   a. DC V
   b. DC A
   c. Ω
   d. AC V

16. The motor circuit shown is being tested by measuring the voltage at several locations in the circuit. Voltmeter #1 = 12.62 Voltmeter #2 = 12.62 Voltmeter #3 = 6.82

What is the *most likely* cause?

   a. Normal operation—no fault
   b. High resistance in the motor
   c. A shorted ignition switch
   d. High resistance in the motor switch

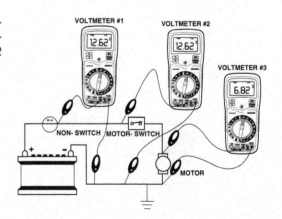

17. A convertible top will not operate either up or down. The relay(s) does not click when the switch is depressed. Technician A says that the switch could be defective. Technician B says that the electric pump motor for the power convertible top could be defective and not cause the relays to click when the switch is moved. Which technician is correct?

    a. A only
    b. B only
    c. Both A and B
    d. Neither A nor B

18. The circuit shown is being tested at various points using a voltmeter. Technician A says that the battery voltage is 4.0 volts. Technician B says that there must be a poor ground connection or loose connection on the battery. Which technician is correct?

    a. A only
    b. B only
    c. Both A and B
    d. Neither A nor B

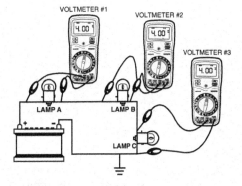

19. The fuse to the cigarette lighter keeps blowing. What is the *most likely* cause?

    a. High resistance in the heater element of the lighter
    b. Corrosion on the electrical connector to the lights
    c. A short-to-ground
    d. Poor lighter socket ground

20. What is this meter measuring?

    a. Resistance of the ECT sensor
    b. Voltage signal of the ECT sensor
    c. Voltage output from the PCM
    d. Resistance of the electrical connector

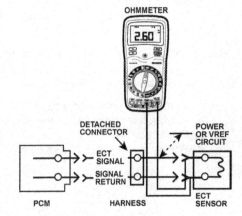

21. The windshield wiper operates too slowly at times even when set to the high-speed position. This fault can be caused by all of the following *except* _____.

    a. high resistance in the wiper circuit
    b. a blown fuse
    c. excessive voltage drop in the power side of the circuit
    d. a poor electrical ground connector

22. The meter shown reads OL. Technician A says that this means that the meter leads are defective. Technician B says that this means that the resistance between the test leads is greater than the meter can measure. Which technician is correct?

a. A only
b. B only
c. Both A and B
d. Neither A nor B

23. To test the voltage at the bulb that does not work, where should the technician connect the voltmeter leads?

a. The positive (red) lead to point A and the negative (–) lead to point B
b. The positive (red) lead to point B and the negative (–) lead to ground
c. The positive (red) lead to point B and the negative (–) lead to point A
d. The positive (red) lead to ground and the negative (–) lead to point A

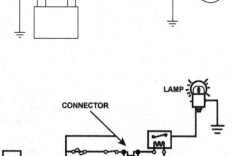

24. The electrical connector is being tested in the circuit shown. The meter indicates 00.00 volts on the display. What is the most likely cause?

a. Normal for a good connector
b. Corroded terminals inside the connector
c. Open circuit
d. Battery is completely discharged

25. A relay is being checked out of the vehicle using a DMM. Technician A says that the coil winding can be checked by selecting the DC volt setting. Technician B says that the coil should measure OL on the meter if the relay is okay. Which technician is correct?

a. A only
b. B only
c. Both A and B
d. Neither A nor B

26. A light circuit containing a relay as shown is being tested using two voltmeters. Technician A says the relay diode must be blown open. Technician B says the relay contacts must be electrically open. Which technician is correct?

   a. A only
   b. B only
   c. Both A and B
   d. Neither A nor B

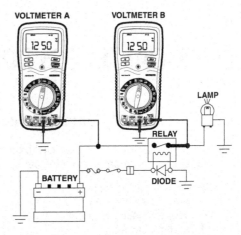

27. One rear taillight does not work and a test light is being used to check for voltage at a taillight socket. Technician A says that the alligator clip on the test light should be attached to a good ground before testing. Technician B says that the lights should be turned on before testing the socket terminal. Which technician is correct?

   a. A only
   b. B only
   c. Both A and B
   d. Neither A nor B

28. A circuit containing a relay, switch, and lamp is being checked. If the coil of the relay is electrically open, what would be the result?

   a. Normal operation
   b. The light will not light (relay will not work)
   c. The relay will click but the lightbulb will not light
   d. A blown fuse

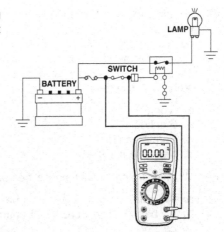

29. Two technicians are discussing performing a wire repair to a broken wire under the hood. Technician A says that the wire should be soldered and the splice covered with electrical tape. Technician B says that the wire should be soldered and covered with a heat-shrink tubing that contains an adhesive inside to seal against the weather. Which technician is correct?

   a. A only
   b. B only
   c. Both A and B
   d. Neither A nor B

30. A jumper is being used to bypass a switch to check the operation of the accessory lights as shown. Technician A says that the jumper wire should be fused for extra protection to avoid the possibility of doing harm to the circuit wiring. Technician B says that a jumper wire should not be used to bypass a switch during testing to prevent overheating the wires. Which technician is correct?

   a. A only
   b. B only
   c. Both A and B
   d. Neither A nor B

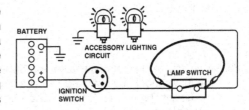

CATEGORY: BATTERY AND STARTING SYSTEM DIAGNOSIS AND REPAIR

31. The starter solenoid makes a clicking noise when the ignition key is turned to the start position. A probable cause is _____.

    a. low battery voltage
    b. a defective hold-in coil in the solenoid
    c. poor connections at the battery
    d. all of the above

32. Whenever jump-starting a disabled vehicle with another vehicle, what procedure should be followed?

    a. The last connection should be the positive (+) post of the dead battery
    b. The last connection should be the engine block of the disabled vehicle
    c. The alternator must be disconnected on both vehicles
    d. The ignition on both vehicles should be in the on (run) position

33. A battery high-rate discharge (load capacity) test is being performed on a 12-volt battery. Technician A says that a good battery should have a voltage reading of higher than 9.6 volts while under load at the end of the 15-second test. Technician B says that the battery should be discharged (loaded to two times its CCA rating). Which technician is correct?

    a. A only
    b. B only
    c. Both A and B
    d. Neither A nor B

34. When charging a maintenance-free battery _____.

    a. the initial charging rate should be about 35 amperes for 30 minutes
    b. the battery may not accept a charge for several hours, yet may still be a good (serviceable) battery
    c. the battery temperature should not exceed 125°F (hot to the touch)
    d. all of the above

35. Normal key-off battery drain (parasitic draw) on a vehicle with many computer and electronic circuits is _____.

    a. 20–30 milliamperes
    b. 2–3 amperes
    c. 0.20–0.40 A
    d. 150–300 milliamperes

36. A vehicle being tested has a key-off battery drain that exceeds specifications. Technician A says that the fuses should be removed one at a time until the excessive drain is eliminated, thereby pinpointing the circuit. Technician B says a short finder should be used to locate the source of the draw. Which technician is correct?

    a. A only
    b. B only
    c. Both A and B
    d. Neither A nor B

37. Technician A says that disconnecting a battery can cause drivability problems on some vehicles after the battery has been reconnected. Technician B says that disconnecting a battery can cause radio station presets to be lost. Which technician is correct?

    a. A only
    b. B only
    c. Both A and B
    d. Neither A nor B

38. A customer arrives at a shop and his battery voltage is measured to be 13.6 volts with the engine off. What is the *most likely* result?

    a. The alternator is overcharging the battery
    b. The alternator is undercharging the battery
    c. Normal surface charge
    d. The battery is sulfated

39. An absorbed glass mat (AGM) battery is being charged. Technician A says that it should be charged at the highest rate to overcome the high internal resistance of the battery. Technician B says that a battery charger designed to charge an AGM battery should be used. Which technician is correct?

    a. A only
    b. B only
    c. Both A and B
    d. Neither A nor B

40. The owner of a vehicle has a habit of leaving the lights on when parked at work requiring that the battery be jump-started every evening. Technician A says that this deep cycling of the battery could reduce the life of a battery. Technician B says that this practice can cause harm to the alternator. Which technician is correct?

    a. A only
    b. B only
    c. Both A and B
    d. Neither A nor B

41. Technician A says that a battery should not be stored on a concrete floor. Technician B says that a battery will not be able to be fully charged if placed on a concrete floor when being charged. Which technician is correct?

    a. A only
    b. B only
    c. Both A and B
    d. Neither A nor B

42. A customer states that the starter will not crank the engine on Monday after the vehicle has remained parked since Friday evening. Technician A says that key-off battery drain (parasitic draw) test should be performed. Technician B says the battery should be charged and load tested. Which technician is correct?

    a. A only
    b. B only
    c. Both A and B
    d. Neither A nor B

43. A new battery is being installed in a vehicle. The technician noticed that a large spark occurred between the battery post and the cable end as the last connection was being completed. Technician A says that this is normal. Technician B says that there could be an electrical drain on the battery such as a trunk light or interior light on as the last connection was being completed. Which technician is correct?

    a. A only
    b. B only
    c. Both A and B
    d. Neither A nor B

44. A starter motor is drawing too many amperes (current). Technician A says that an engine mechanical fault could be the cause. Technician B says that it could be due to a defective starter motor. Which technician is correct?

   a. A only
   b. B only
   c. Both A and B
   d. Neither A nor B

45. A fully charged 12-volt battery should indicate _____.

   a. 12.6 volts or higher
   b. a specific gravity of 1.265 or higher
   c. 12 volts
   d. both a and b

46. A starter cranks for a while, then whines. Technician A says that the starter solenoid may be bad. Technician B says that the starter drive may be bad. Which technician is correct?

   a. A only
   b. B only
   c. Both A and B
   d. Neither A nor B

47. A driver turns the ignition switch to "start" and nothing happens (the dome light remains bright). Technician A says a discharged battery could be the cause. Technician B says that an open control circuit such as a defective neutral safety switch could be the cause. Which technician is correct?

   a. A only
   b. B only
   c. Both A and B
   d. Neither A nor B

48. Slow cranking by the starter can be caused by all except _____.

   a. a low or discharged battery
   b. corroded or dirty battery cable connections
   c. engine mechanical problems
   d. an open solenoid pull-in winding

49. A starter motor turns slowly when the engine is being cranked. Technician A says that a positive battery cable with greater than 0.5 volt voltage drop could be the cause. Technician B says that a defective (high resistance) negative battery cable could be the cause. Which technician is correct?

   a. A only
   b. B only
   c. Both A and B
   d. Neither A nor B

50. All of the following could be a cause of excessive starter ampere draw except _____.

   a. a misadjusted starter pinion gear
   b. a loose starter housing
   c. armature wires separated from the commutator
   d. a bent armature

51. Any the following can cause higher-than-normal starter current draw except _____.

   a. A defective (seized) A/C compressor
   b. Worn starter brushes
   c. Field coils shorted to ground
   d. An open starter relay

52. Technician A says that high resistance in the cables or connections can cause rapid clicking of the solenoid. Technician B says that a battery must be 75% charged for accurate testing of the starting and charging systems. Which technician is correct?

   a. A only
   b. B only
   c. Both A and B
   d. Neither A nor B

53. A rebuilt starter turns but will not disengage from the flywheel. The *most likely* cause is _____.

   a. a missing solenoid plunger return spring
   b. a defective starter drive
   c. the shift fork installed backward
   d. the solenoid contact installed backward

54. Technician A says a high-scale ammeter can be used to test the current draw of a starting circuit. Technician B says a high-scale voltmeter can be used to test the current draw of a starting circuit. Which technician is correct?

   a. A only
   b. B only
   c. Both A and B
   d. Neither A nor B

55. A starter makes a grinding noise. Which is the *least likely* cause?

   a. A defective starter drive
   b. A defective flywheel
   c. Incorrect distance between the starter pinion and the flywheel
   d. Worn starter brushes

56. A technician connects one lead of a digital voltmeter to the positive (+) terminal of the battery and the other meter lead to the B terminal of the starter solenoid and then cranks the engine. During cranking, the voltmeter displays a reading of 878 mV. Technician A says that this reading indicates that the positive battery cable or cable end has too high resistance. Technician B says that this reading indicates that the starter is defective. Which technician is correct?

   a. A only
   b. B only
   c. Both A and B
   d. Neither A nor B

57. The starter does not crank the engine and the solenoid does not click. Any of these could be the fault *except* _____.

   a. an open in the neutral safety switch
   b. an open battery ground connection
   c. an open for the solenoid ground
   d. an open in the solenoid hold-in winding

58. Battery voltage reads 10.32 volts on a DMM during engine cranking. Technician A says that the battery could be weak. Technician B says the starter may be defective. Which technician is correct?

   a. A only
   b. B only
   c. Both A and B
   d. Neither A nor B

59. Technician A says that a shorted diode in an alternator can discharge a battery. Technician B says that dirt on the battery can cause it to discharge. Which technician is correct?

    a. A only
    b. B only
    c. Both A and B
    d. Neither A nor B

ELECTRICAL/ELECTRONIC SYSTEMS (A6)

CATEGORY: CHARGING SYSTEM DIAGNOSIS AND REPAIR

60. An alternator does not charge and the service technician checked for voltage at the output terminal of the alternator and the meter read zero volts. What is the *most likely* cause?

    a. An open diode inside the alternator
    b. A blown alternator maxi fuse or an open fusible link for the charging system
    c. Excessively worn alternator brushes
    d. Shorted stator winding

61. The charging voltage of 12.4 volts is the same as the battery voltage. With the engine off, 0.0 volts is measured at the BAT terminal of the alternator. Technician A says the alternator is defective. Technician B says the fusible link or alternator output fuse is blown. Which technician is correct?

    a. A only
    b. B only
    c. Both A and B
    d. Neither A nor B

62. An acceptable charging circuit voltage on a 12-volt system is _____.

    a. 13.5 to 15.0 volts
    b. 12.6 to 15.6 volts
    c. 12 to 14 volts
    d. 14.9 to 16.1 volts

63. A dead battery is being diagnosed and it was discovered that the charging voltage is 12.6 volts. Technician A says that the alternator is defective. Technician B says that the battery may be defective. Which technician is correct?

    a. A only
    b. B only
    c. Both A and B
    d. Neither A nor B

64. Technician A says that a voltage-drop test of the charging circuit should be performed when current is flowing through the circuit. Technician B says to connect the leads of a voltmeter to the positive and negative terminals of the battery to measure the voltage drop of the charging system. Which technician is correct?

    a. A only
    b. B only
    c. Both A and B
    d. Neither A nor B

65. Technician A says that a loose accessory drive belt or defective belt tensioner can cause the alternator to produce less than normal output. Technician B says that a poor ground connection on the alternator case can cause lower alternator output. Which technician is correct?

    a. A only
    b. B only
    c. Both A and B
    d. Neither A nor B

66. An alternator is producing lower than the specified charging voltage. Which is the *least likely* cause?

    a. The battery is weak or defective
    b. The engine speed is not high enough during testing
    c. The drive belt is loose or slipping
    d. Cold outside temperature

67. A technician is checking the charging system for low output. A voltage drop of 1.67 volts is found between the alternator output terminal and the battery positive terminal. Technician A says that a corroded connector could be the cause. Technician B says that a defective rectifier diode could be the cause of the voltage drop. Which technician is correct?

   a. A only
   b. B only
   c. Both A and B
   d. Neither A nor B

68. A voltmeter is connected to the charging system as shown with the engine running. The voltmeter will display what value regarding the charging system condition?

   a. Charging system voltage drop
   b. AC (ripple) voltage
   c. Charging system voltage
   d. Ignition control system voltage

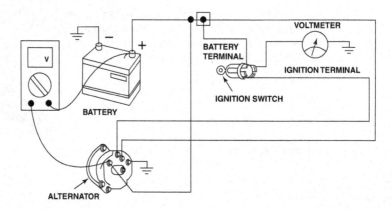

69. A fusible link between the battery and alternator is hot to the touch. The charging system voltage is 9.8 volts. What is the *most likely* cause?

   a. Overcharging
   b. Undercharging
   c. High resistance in the fusible link
   d. A poor battery ground

70. An alternator is noisy. What is the *least likely* cause?

   a. A defective or loose drive belt
   b. A defective rectifier diode
   c. A defective bearing
   d. Worn brushes

71. An alternator overrunning pulley (AOP) is being tested with the accessory drive belt removed. It is functioning correctly if _____.

   a. the pulley rotates freely in only one direction
   b. the pulley is locked in both directions
   c. the pulley is unlocked in both directions
   d. either b or c

CATEGORY: LIGHTING SYSTEMS DIAGNOSIS AND REPAIR

72. A defective brake switch could prevent proper operation of the _____.

   a. cruise control
   b. ABS brakes
   c. shift Interlock
   d. all of the above

73. When the parking lamps are on and the turn signal is flashing, the side marker lamp alternates flashes with the turn signal. What is the *most likely* cause?

   a. An open bulb
   b. An open turn signal switch
   c. A blown parking light fuse
   d. Normal operation

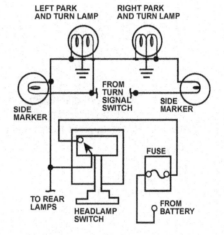

74. The left turn signal indicator light on the dash lights dimly whenever the parking or headlights are on, even though the turn signal is off. Technician A says that the most likely cause is a short circuit in the steering column. Technician B says that a common cause is a poor ground at the left front parking light. Which technician is correct?

   a. A only
   b. B only
   c. Both A and B
   d. Neither A nor B

75. A customer complains that the life of the halogen headlight bulbs is only two weeks. Several different brands have been tried with the same results. What is the *most likely* cause?

   a. Poor ground at the headlights
   b. Shorted headlight switch
   c. The new bulbs were touched with bare hands during installation
   d. The bulbs were installed backwards

76. The fuse #7 shown is blown. Technician A says that the headlights will not work. Technician B says the taillights and parking
lights will not work. Which technician is correct?

    a. A only
    b. B only
    c. Both A and B
    d. Neither A nor B

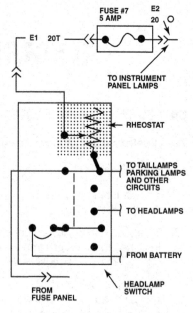

77. Two technicians are discussing a turn signal switch. Technician A says that a faulty turn signal switch
could prevent the brake lights from working. Technician B says that a faulty brake switch will prevent
the proper operation of the turn signals. Which technician is correct?

    a. A only
    b. B only
    c. Both A and B
    d. Neither A nor B

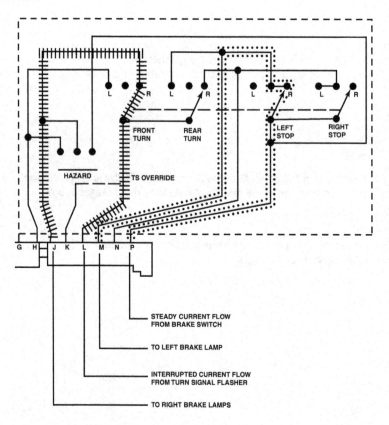

78. A corroded light socket could *most likely* cause _____.

    a. a fuse to blow in the circuit
    b. the light to be dim as a result of reduced current flow
    c. a feedback to occur to another circuit
    d. damage to occur to the bulb as a result of decreased voltage

79. The right-side high beam does not work. The other lights on the vehicle function normally. What is the *most likely* cause?

    a. A defective dimmer switch
    b. A defective headlight
    c. A defective headlight ground
    d. A discharged battery

80. A vehicle's reverse lights are always on, even in "drive." What is the *most likely* cause?

    a. A misadjusted neutral safety switch
    b. An open neutral safety switch
    c. One of the reverse lightbulbs has been installed backward
    d. The wrong bulb was installed for the reverse lights

81. When the lights are turned on, the left taillight is dim, while the right taillight is a normal brightness. When the brakes are applied, the left light totally goes out, while the right side works properly. What is the *most likely* cause?

    a. A poor ground connector at the left bulb socket
    b. A shorted left bulb
    c. A defective brake pedal switch
    d. A shorted right bulb

82. Trailer lights are spliced into the existing wiring. The turn indicator lights on the dash flash rapidly when a turn signal is activated. Technician A says that the wiring must be reversed. Technician B says that the flasher should be changed. Which technician is correct?

    a. A only
    b. B only
    c. Both A and B
    d. Neither A nor B

83. A defective taillight or front turn signal/park lightbulb could cause _____.

    a. the turn signal indicator on the dash to light when the lights are turned on
    b. the dash lights to come on when the brake lights are on
    c. the lights-on warning chime sounds if the brake pedal is depressed
    d. all of the above

84. The high beam indicator on the dash does not come on but both headlight beams work. Technician A says that the indicator bulb could be defective. Technician B says the dimmer switch could be defective. Which technician is correct?

   a. A only
   b. B only
   c. Both A and B
   d. Neither A nor B

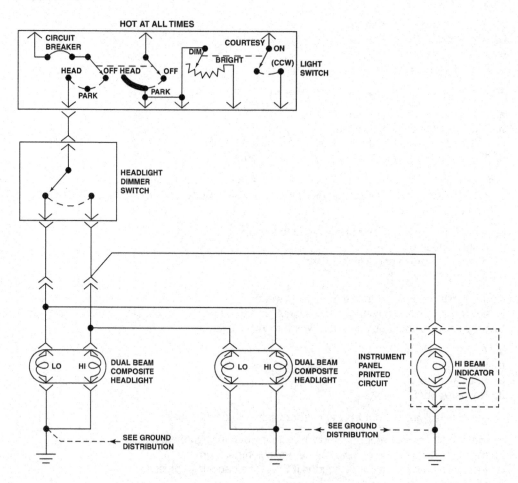

85. The headlights failed on a vehicle. A melted dimmer switch was found during a visual inspection. Technician A says that high output headlight bulbs might have been installed causing the switch to fail. Technician B says that adding auxiliary lights in parallel with the headlights could be the cause. Which technician is correct?

   a. A only
   b. B only
   c. Both A and B
   d. Neither A nor B

86. The left high beam headlight does not work and the bulb has been replaced with a known good one. Looking at the schematic, what is a possible cause?

   a. Open at ground 101
   b. Open in circuit 711 (GN/WH)
   c. Open at ground 100
   d. Open high beam relay

Headlamp Flasher

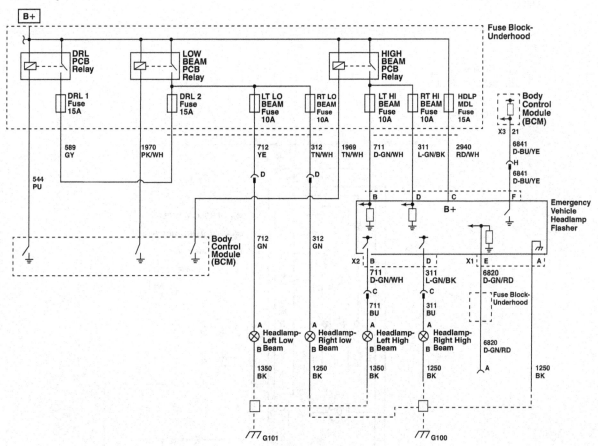

CATEGORY: INSTRUMENT CLUSTER AND DRIVER INFORMATION SYSTEMS DIAGNOSIS AND REPAIR

87. Two technicians are discussing a fuel gauge. The type of sensor used to measure the fuel level is a
_____

- **a.** rheostat
- **b.** potentiometer
- **c.** thermistor
- **d.** hall Effect sensor

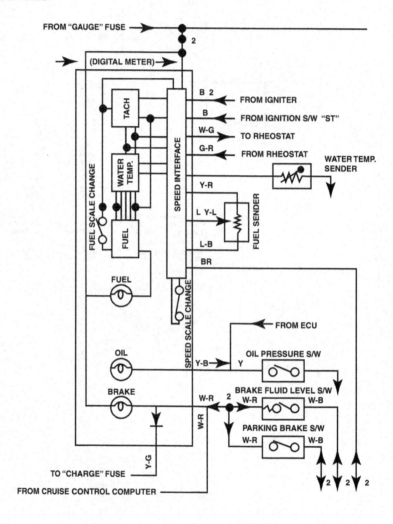

88. A brake warning lamp on the dash remains on whenever the ignition is on. If the wire to the pressure differential switch (usually a part of a combination valve or built into the master cylinder) is unplugged, the dash lamp goes out. Technician A says that this is an indication of a hydraulic brake problem. Technician B says that the problem is probably due to a stuck parking brake cable switch. Which technician is correct?

- **a.** A only
- **b.** B only
- **c.** Both A and B
- **d.** Neither A nor B

89. The charge light does not come on when the key is turned to the "run" position. What is the *most likely* cause?

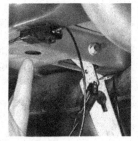

   a. A blown (melted) alternator output fusible link
   b. A burned-out bulb
   c. A defective diode in the alternator
   d. A short inside the alternator

90. The 15 A fuse #3 is blown. What could be the cause?

   a. An open at point Y
   b. A short-to-ground at X
   c. A short-to-ground at Z
   d. A short-to-ground at Y

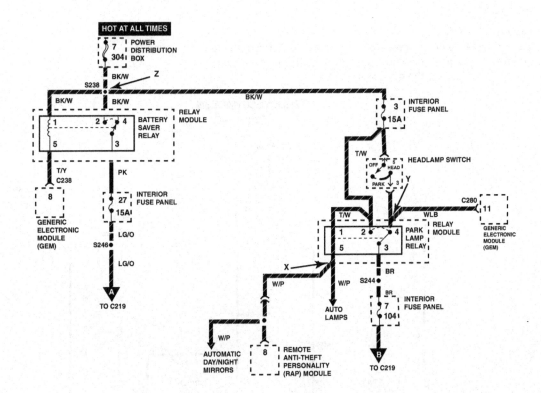

91. A vehicle comes in with a nonfunctioning gas gauge. When the sending unit wire is disconnected and grounded, the gauge reading goes to "full." Technician A says this proves that the gauge is okay. Technician B says this proves that the sending unit is bad. Which technician is correct?

   a. A only
   b. B only
   c. Both A and B
   d. Neither A nor B

92. If an oil pressure warning lamp on a vehicle is on all the time, yet the engine oil pressure is normal, what is the *most likely* cause?

   a. A defective (shorted) oil pressure sending unit (sensor)
   b. A shorted dash warning light
   c. An open wire between the sending unit (sensor) and the dash warning lamp
   d. Clogged oil pump passage(s)

93. A data circuit is being checked using an ohmmeter. Service information stares that the circuit contains two 120 ohms terminating resistors in parallel at each end to help reduce electromagnetic interference into the data lines. What resistance should, the technician observe on the ohmmeter if measuring the terminating resistors?

a. 120 ohms
b. 240 ohms
c. 60 ohms
d. Zero or close to zero ohms

94. The oil pressure warning lamp is on whenever the engine is running. The service technician measured the oil pressure using a mechanical gauge it is reads within factory specification. What is the *most likely* cause?

a. An open in the oil pressure switch
b. A short-to-ground between the pressure switch and the indicator lamp
c. An open in the ignition circuit that feeds the warning lamp
d. A blown fuse for the dash warning lights

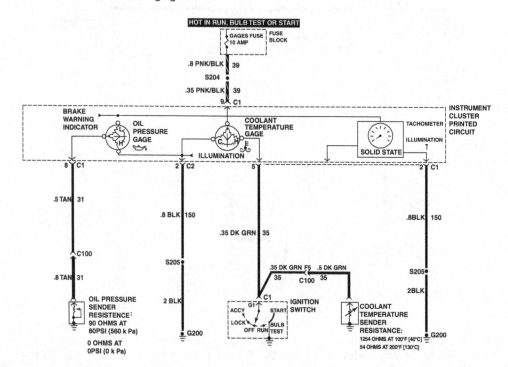

95. The left side turn signal indicator light on the dash blinks rapidly when the left side turn signals are turned on, but the right side flashes normally when the right side turn signals are turned on. What is the *most likely* cause?

a. A defective flasher unit
b. Burned out right front parking lamp bulb
c. Burned out taillight bulb on the left side
d. A shorted brake switch

CATEGORY: BODY ELECTRICAL SYSTEMS DIAGNOSIS AND REPAIR

96. A body-related diagnostic trouble code was set indicating a fault between the body control module (BCM) and the brake pedal position (BPP) sensor was retrieved. What is a possible cause?

- **a.** A short-to-ground at Y
- **b.** An open at X
- **c.** A short-to-ground at X
- **d.** Either b or c

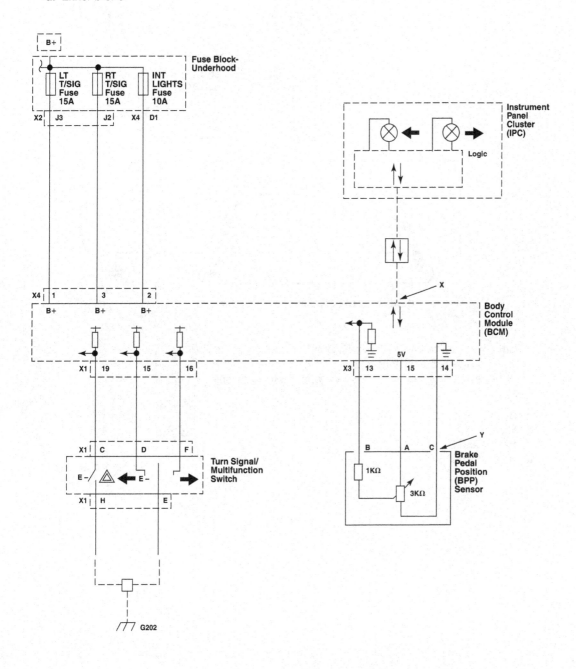

97. The indicating lightbulb burned out in the circuit shown. Technician A says that the rear defogger will not work. Technician B says that the relay will not operate without the bulb in the circuit. Which technician is correct?

    a. A only
    b. B only
    c. Both A and B
    d. Neither A nor B

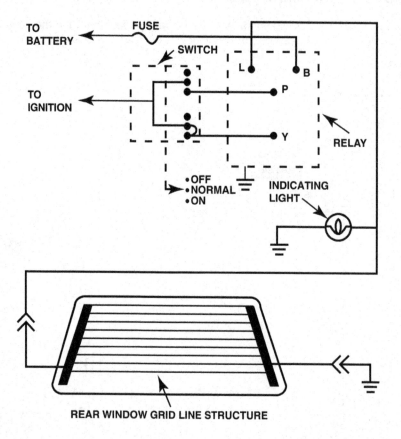

REAR WINDOW GRID LINE STRUCTURE

98. A horn relay is being checked using a DMM set to read ohms. Technician A says the relay being tested is okay. Technician B says the relay being tested is defective (open). Which technician is correct?

    a. A only
    b. B only
    c. Both A and B
    d. Neither A nor B

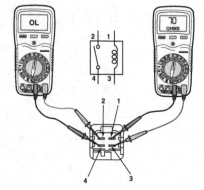

99. The horns do not operate when the horn button is depressed. During the diagnosis procedure, the technician was able to make the horns work by connecting a fused jumper wire between terminals 30 and 87 of the horn relay. What is the *most likely* cause?

    a. A horn ground connection has high resistance
    b. A failed horn relay
    c. High resistance between the horn relay and the horns
    d. A short-to-ground between the horn button and the horn relay

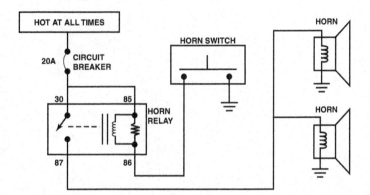

100. A horn blows all the time and cannot be shut off unless the wire(s) to the horn is removed. What is the *most likely* cause?

    a. An open horn relay
    b. The horn wire in the steering column is shorted to ground
    c. A poor ground on the horn
    d. A defective horn

101. The horn does not work but the horn relay can be heard to click whenever the horn is depressed on the steering wheel. Which is the *least likely* cause?

    a. The horn wire in the steering column is shorted to ground
    b. The relay contacts are corroded
    c. A defective horn
    d. An open horn ground connection

102. The windshield wipers work normally until the headlights or the blower motor are turned on and then the wipers slow down to about half the normal speed. What is the *most likely* cause?

    a. Worn brushes in the wiper motor
    b. A weak battery
    c. A defective wiper switch
    d. A poor body-to-engine ground

103. What is the meaning of the dotted line between the instrument panel cluster (IPC) and the Body Control module (BCM)?

   a. Bidirectional data communication lines
   b. Both power and ground for both modules
   c. Common ground connection for both modules
   d. Electrostatic protection shield

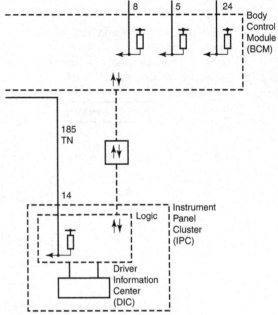

104. The wipers will not go to the park position but simply stop where they are when the switch or ignition is turned off. Technician A says a poor ground for the wipers could be the cause. Technician B says that the motor assembly may need to be replaced. Which technician is correct?

   a. A only
   b. B only
   c. Both A and B
   d. Neither A nor B

105. The engine cooling fan does not operate. Technician A says a blown fusible link could be the cause. Technician B says that a defective engine fan relay could be the cause. Which technician is correct?

   a. A only
   b. B only
   c. Both A and B
   d. Neither A nor B

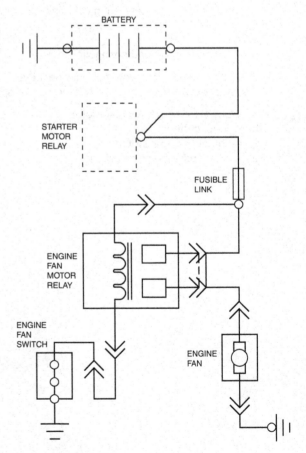

106. If an open occurred at terminal #28 of the high/low relay, what is the *most likely* result?

a. High-speed operation only
b. The wipers will not operate at any speed
c. The 15 A fuse will blow when the wipers are tuned on
d. Low-speed operation only

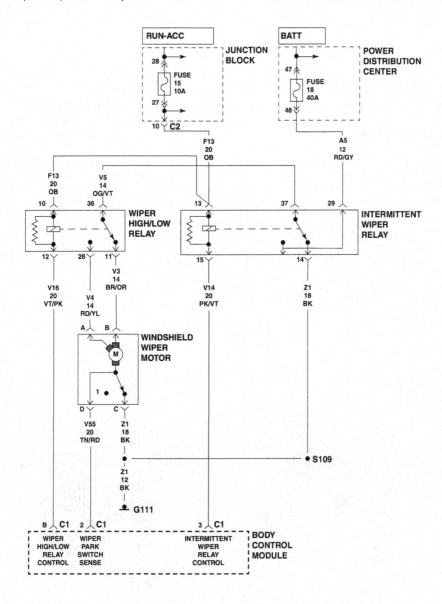

107. A radio operates normally on FM but does not receive AM signals. Which is the *least likely* cause?

a. A defective antenna
b. A defective radio
c. A high resistance in power lead wires
d. A poor ground connection on the antenna

108. The driver and passenger side airbags are being disabled as protection against the possibility of accidental deployment. The technician should look for electrical connectors that are what color?

a. Red
b. Yellow
c. Black
d. Green

109. A blower motor stopped working on all speeds. A technician tested the motor touching a jumper wire from the battery positive (+) terminal to the motor power terminal and the motor did run. Technician A says that the motor should be checked using a fused jumper lead to test for excessive current draw. Technician B says that the resistor pack and/or relay are likely to be defective. Which technician is correct?

- **a.** A only
- **b.** B only
- **c.** Both A and B
- **d.** Neither A nor B

110. A blower motor is drawing more than the specified current. Technician A says that the blower motor ground connection could be corroded. Technician B says that the blower relay is shorted. Which technician is correct?

- **a.** A only
- **b.** B only
- **c.** Both A and B
- **d.** Neither A nor B

111. The "BATT 3" (40 A) fuse is blown preventing the operation of the rear window defogger grid. What is a possible cause?

- **a.** An open circuit at "Z"
- **b.** A short-to-ground at "X"
- **c.** A short-to-ground at "Z"
- **d.** An open at "X"

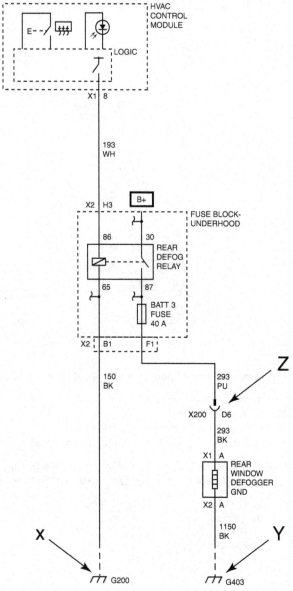

112. The A/C compressor clutch does not engage. Technician A says that an open high pressure cutout switch could be the problem. Technician B says a blown compressor clutch diode could be the cause. Which technician is correct?

    a. A only
    b. B only
    c. Both A and B
    d. Neither A nor B

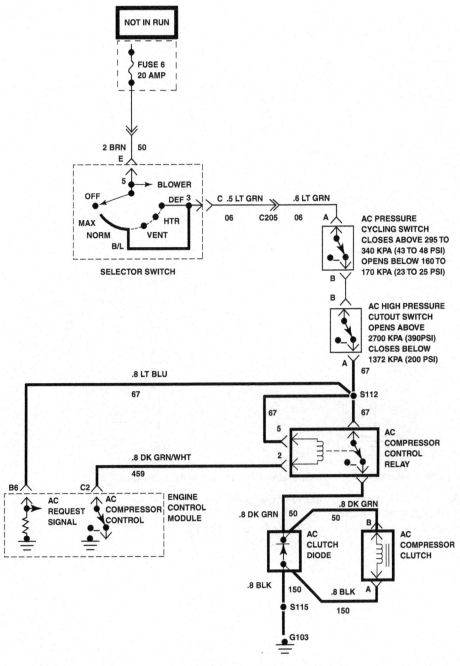

113. The cruise control stops working when the vehicle is being driven over bumpy roads but works normally on smooth roads. Technician A says that the brake switch could be misadjusted. Technician B says that this is a normal safety device to prevent the driver from speeding while traveling over bumpy roads. Which technician is correct?

    a. A only
    b. B only
    c. Both A and B
    d. Neither A nor B

114. A technician is checking a blower motor with an ammeter. It shows excessive current draw. What is the *most likely* cause?

    a. A bad ground
    b. A binding blower motor
    c. A loose connection
    d. A blown fuse

115. A blower is running slow on all speeds. What is the *most likely* cause?

    a. A blown resistor
    b. Worn/dry bearings in the motor
    c. A bad fan switch
    d. Open ignition switch

116. Technician A says that item "A" has a higher resistance than item "B". Technician says that the setup is a series-parallel circuit. Which technician is correct?

    a. A only
    b. B only
    c. Both A and B
    d. Neither A nor B

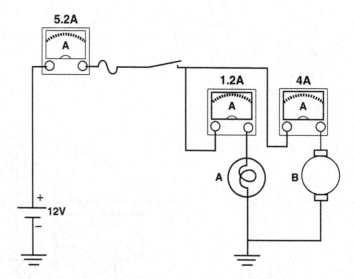

117. If only one power door lock is inoperative, what is the *most likely* cause?

    a. A poor ground connection at the power door lock relay
    b. A defective motor (or solenoid)
    c. A defective (open) circuit breaker for the power circuit
    d. A defective (open) fuse for the control circuit

118. No sound is heard from the left rear speaker. What is the *most likely* cause?

   a. A defective audio unit
   b. Poor ground at G502
   c. An open antenna lead
   d. A defective speaker

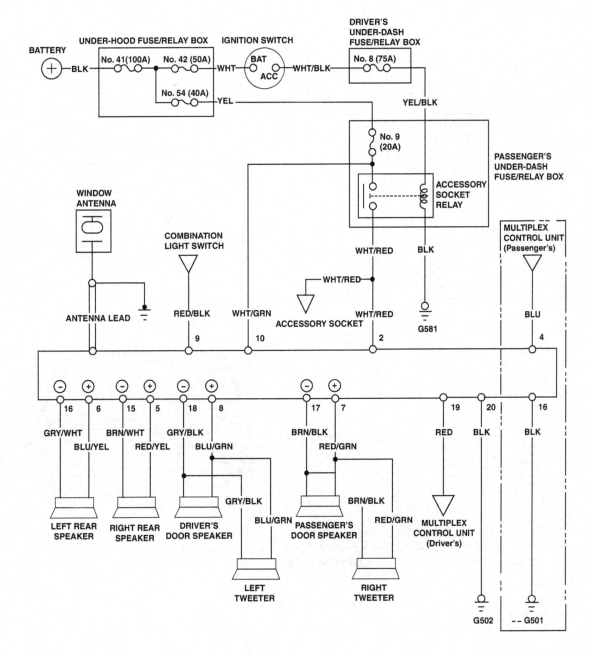

119. The trunk lid will not operate from the dash switch or the remote. Technician A says that a scan tool should be used to activate the trunk module to check whether the circuit can function. Technician B says to replace the dash switch. Which technician is correct?

   a. A only
   b. B only
   c. Both A and B
   d. Neither A nor B

120. The blower motor operates at low speed regardless of the position selected on the blower motor switch. Technician A says an open thermal limiter could be the cause. Technician B says an open at the "LO" contact of the blower motor switch could be the cause. Which technician is correct?

    a. A only
    b. B only
    c. Both A and B
    d. Neither A nor B

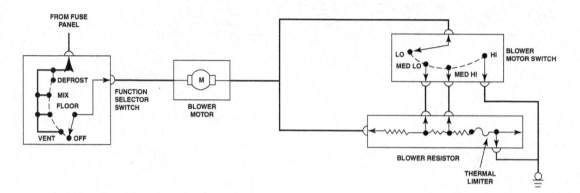

121. A rear window defogger is being tested using a DMM as shown. If the meter lead on the right is moved to the midpoint "c", what would a typical reading be for a properly operating defogger?

    a. About 12 volts
    b. About 6 volts
    c. Almost zero volts
    d. OL

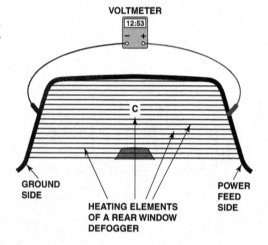

122. One horn out of the two on the vehicle does not work. Technician A says that a poor ground connection on the horn that does not work could be the cause. Technician B says that an open in the horn contact ring in the steering column could be the cause. Which technician is correct?

    a. A only
    b. B only
    c. Both A and B
    d. Neither A nor B

ELECTRICAL/ELECTRONIC SYSTEMS (A6)

CATEGORY: GENERAL ELECTRICAL/ELECTRONIC SYSTEM DIAGNOSIS

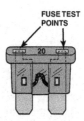

1. **The correct answer is c.** Both technicians are correct. Technician A is correct because a short to voltage will usually affect more than one circuit and depending on the resistance involved may or may not cause a fuse to blow. Technician B is correct because a short to ground involves a power side wire contacting ground, which reduces or eliminates the resistance in the circuit and will cause a fuse to blow. Answers a, b, and d are not correct because both technicians are correct.

2. **The correct answer is d.** All of the above are correct. Answer a is correct because the customer concerns could be occurring on and off. Answer b is correct because there may be other faults that the customer is not aware of that could have an effect on the electrical fault. Answer c is correct because verbal communication and terminology could be misinterpreted by the customer and/or the service advisor.

3. **The correct answer is c.** A fusible link has fireproof insulation and will not burn or even discolor if the wire inside has melted. To check a fusible link, simply pull on the ends to see if it stretches like a rubber band, which would indicate the wire inside has melted. Answer a is not correct because if the insulation has been cut, the fusible link must be replaced. Answer b is not correct because replacing a fusible link is not the proper method to use to check to see if it is blown. Answer d is not correct because a fusible link must be replaced if cut even if it was okay before the inspection.

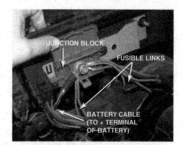

4. **The correct answer is b.** The meter reading of 0.010 k ohms is 10 ohms because on the "k" scale, a number 1 (1.000) means 1,000 and a 0.001 means 1 ohm (one-thousandth of a thousand) so 10 ohms is represented by 0.010 ohms. Answer a is not correct because 0.010 ohms is ten/thousandth of an ohm and not 10 ohms. Answer c is not correct because 0.10 M ohm is one-tenth of a million ohms or 100,000 ohms and not 10 ohms. Answer d is not correct because 10.0 k ohms is 10,000 ohms, not 10 ohms.

5. **The correct answer is c.** Both technicians are correct. Technician A is correct because a test light will provide resistance and light as long as the circuit is shorted to ground. Technician B is correct because a circuit breaker will open if the current exceeds its rating to prevent any damage to the wiring from excessive current flow. When the fault has been disconnected, the circuit breaker will not trip indicating to the technician that the location of the fault has been found. Answer d is not correct because both technicians are correct.

6. **The correct answer is b.** The meter is connected in series in the circuit and the reduced amount of current through the circuit due to the corrosion on the lamp terminal would be indicated on the meter display. Answer a is not correct because the leads are attached to two parts of the circuit and there is power applied to the circuit. To measure resistance, the circuit must be open to prevent current from flowing, which could damage an ohmmeter. Answer c is not correct because the meter should be connected across a load or part of a circuit in parallel, not in series as shown. Answer d is not correct because to measure available voltage, the meter should be connected across the load in parallel and not in series as shown.

7. **The correct answer is c.** Both technicians are correct. Technician A is correct because if the ohmmeter display shows zero or low ohms, this means that there is little if any resistance between the meter leads. The component being tested has continuity and current will flow if connected to an electrical power source. Technician B is correct because an infinity reading, such as "OL" on the display, means that there is such a high resistance between the meter leads that the meter is unable to measure on the highest setting. In other words, the component being measured lacks continuity and no current will flow if connected to an electrical power source. Answer d is not correct because both technicians are correct.

8. **The correct answer is a.** A meter reading of OL means over limit or overload and indicates an open circuit. For all practical reasons, no electrical current will flow if connected to an electrical power source. Answer b is not correct because if the component is shorted, the meter will read low or zero ohms instead of OL. Answer c is not correct because a normal circuit should have some resistance instead of being open where no current will flow. Answer d is not correct because if the circuit or component has low resistance, the meter should display the value and not show that the component or circuit is electrically open.

9. **The correct answer is b.** With the meter set to read K ohms, the reading of 0.93 means that the resistance of the component being measured has 0.93 of a K ohm or 930 ohms. Answers a, c, and d are not correct because they are not slightly less than 1000 ohms.

10. **The correct answer is a.** A millivolt is one-thousandth of a volt, or 1/1000, or 0.001. Therefore, 432 thousandths of a volt would be 0.432. Answers b, c, and d are not correct because they do not represent 432 millivolts.

11. **The correct answer is d.** A voltage drop should occur when current flows through an electrical load. If the voltage is the same on both sides of the load, such as a lightbulb, this means that no current is flowing and an open circuit ground is the cause. Answer a (open bulb) is not correct because if the bulb were electrically open, voltage would not be available on both sides. Answer b is not correct because a short to ground would cause current to flow and the voltage would drop to zero or close to zero instead of remaining the same on both sides of the bulb. Answer c is not correct because if current were flowing through the bulb, there should be a difference in voltage across the bulb and a corroded socket. This could affect the brightness of the bulb but this is not important because there is no current flow.

12. **The correct answer is d.** Neither technician is correct. Technician A is not correct because the relay could not click if the coil winding, which creates the magnetic field needed to move the armature (movable contact) of the relay, were open. Technician B is not correct because a shorted relay coil could not create a magnetic field strong enough to cause the relay to click. Answers a, b, and c are not correct because neither technician is correct.

13. **The correct answer is a.** Technician A is correct because as current flows through an electrical load, the voltage drops. In this case, all three lamps must have the same resistance because each lamp dropped the voltage by 4 volts in this series circuit. Technician B is not correct because a drop in voltage when current flows through an electrical load is normal. Answers c and d are not correct because Technician A only is correct.

14. **The correct answer is b.** If there is an open circuit at "W" then no current as flow to the blower motor except when the speed selector is turned to "5" position of the high blower more speed control. Answer a is not correct because the area at location "X" is already connected to ground so if this part was sent to ground, this would not affect the operation of the circuit. Answer c is not correct because an open at "Y" would cause the blower to not operate at any speed even high due to the open circuit. Answer d is not correct because a short-to-ground at "Z" would not affect the operation of the blower motor because the circuit is already connected to ground.

15. **The correct answer is a.** The technician should select DC (direct current) volts because most circuits in a vehicle use 12 volts and can be checked using the DC V position on the DMM. Answer b is not correct because even though DC A (amperes) can be used to check for current flow in a circuit, it is not used to check for the presence of electricity. Answer c is not correct because even though the bulb can be tested using this position to see if the filament is okay, it cannot be used to check for the presence of electricity at the socket. Answer d is not correct because lights use DC and not AC.

16. **The correct answer is d.** The voltmeter readings indicate that less than 7 volts is available to operate the motor, yet the voltage is okay up to the motor switch. This indicates that there is high resistance (high voltage drop) either in the switch or the wiring from the switch to the motor. Answer a is not correct because only 6.82 volts is available to operate the motor and this indicates a high resistance fault in the circuit. Answer b is not correct because the electrical load (motor) should create the highest voltage drop and this is the case even though the motor has less available voltage than it should for proper operation. Answer c is not correct because the meter is reading the difference in voltage between the input to the switch and the ground which shows a normal reading.

17. **The correct answer is a.** Technician A is correct because if the relay does not click, there is a fault in the control circuit that operates the coil of the relay and a defective switch could be the cause. Technician B is not correct because the relays do not operate to send electrical power to the motor. While the motor(s) could be defective, the fault is in the control circuit because the relay(s) does not click when the switch is moved. Answers c and d are not correct because Technician A only is correct.

18. **The correct answer is d.** Neither technician is correct. Technician A is not correct because the voltmeters are measuring the difference in voltage between the meter leads, which indicates that the voltage drop across each of the lamps is 4.0 volts. Technician B is not correct because the sum (total) of the voltage drop equals 12 volts indicating that there is little if any resistance in the wiring or the connection. Answer c is not correct because neither technician is correct.

19. **The correct answer is c.** A short-to-ground is the most likely cause for a fuse to blow because the electrical power will take the path of least resistance resulting in a rapid increase in the flow of current, which will blow the fuse. Answer a is not correct because high resistance results in a decrease (not an increase) in current flow and would not cause the fuse to blow. Answer b is not correct because corrosion on the electrical connector would create high resistance and a decrease (not an increase) in current flow. Answer d is not correct because a poor ground would cause resistance in the circuit and while it could cause the lighter to not function correctly, the high resistance would not cause the fuse to blow.

20. **The correct answer is c.** A short-to-ground is the most likely cause for a fuse to blow because the electrical power will take the path of least resistance resulting in a rapid increase in the flow of current, which will blow the fuse. Answer a is not correct because high resistance results in a decrease (not an increase) in current flow and would not cause the fuse to blow. Answer b is not correct because corrosion on the electrical connector would create high resistance and a decrease (not an increase) in current flow. Answer d is not correct because a poor ground would cause resistance in the circuit and while it could cause the lighter to not function correctly, the high resistance would not cause the fuse to blow.

21. **The correct answer is b.** A blown fuse will stop the flow of electrical power and therefore the wiper motor would not operate. Answers a, c, and d are not correct because each could be the cause of a windshield wiper motor operating too slowly because each would reduce the current flow through the motor.

22. **The correct answer is b.** Technician B is correct because OL (over limit) means that the resistance between the leads exceeds the meter's capability. If the meter were auto ranging or set to the highest resistance range, the OL indicates infinity resistance or an open circuit. Technician A is not correct because even though the leads could be defective, the meter display still shows an open circuit between the leads. Answers c and d are not correct because Technician B only is correct.

23. **The correct answer is b.** The voltmeter reads the difference in voltage between the two meter leads. In this case, with one meter lead connected to ground, the other meter lead will then show what voltage is available at the bulb. Answer a is not correct because if the voltmeter reads the difference in voltage between the two meter leads and with one at the positive post of the battery d the other at the bulb, all the meter will read is the difference between these two test points which would likely be less than 0.5 volt and not measure the voltage applied to the bulb. Answer c is not correct because the meter leads will measure the difference in the voltage between the leads and this setup will result in a negative reading of about –0.5 volts and will not display the voltage available at the bulb. Answer d is not correct because this arrangement of meter lead connections will display battery voltage with a negative reading due to the reversed polarity (negative to battery positive and positive (red) led to ground. This setup will not display the voltage applied to the bulb.

24. **The correct answer is a.** The connector is being checked for a voltage drop with the circuit in operation. A zero reading indicates no resistance in the connector and indicates that it has no resistance. Answer b is not correct because corroded terminals would cause a voltage drop due to the resistance and the meter would read higher than zero voltage drop across the terminals of the connector. Answer c is not correct because the circuit is operating because the lamp is on. Answer d is not correct because the battery has enough voltage to light the lamp and the meter simply displays the voltage difference between the test leads and is not measuring the battery voltage.

25. **The correct answer is d.** Neither technician is correct. Technician A is not correct because a coil of a relay, out of the vehicle, cannot be checked for voltage drop using DC volt scale because there is no applied voltage. Technician B is not correct because the relay coil should measure between 60 and 100 ohms for most relays and should not read OL (open circuit or over limit in the motor). Answers a, b, and c are not correct because neither technician is correct.

26. **The correct answer is d.** Neither technician is correct. Technician A is not correct because the meters are testing the voltage drop across the relay contacts and even though the diode may be blown, it cannot be determined by this test procedure. Technician B is not correct because there is voltage on both sides of the movable arm (contacts) of the relay, which indicates that the connector is closed without resistance and not open (infinity resistance). Answers a, b, and c are not correct because neither technician is correct.

27. **The correct answer is c.** Both technicians are correct. Technician A is correct because a test light needs to be properly grounded to allow current to flow from the test point through the test lightbulb and to ground. Technician B is correct because the taillights must be activated so that voltage can be checked at the taillight socket. Answers a, b, and d are not correct because both technicians are correct.

28. **The correct answer is b.** If the relay coil is open, no current will flow and the relay will not operate. If the relay does not operate, then the circuit it control (the lightbulb) will not work. Answer a is not correct because if the relay coil is electrically open, the relay will not operate and the circuit to the lightbulb will not operate. Answer c is not correct because the coil of the relay is what causes the arm (armature) of the relay to work and make the clicking sound. The relay coil is electrically open and therefore no current will flow through the relay coil and the relay will not click. Answer d is not correct because the open relay coil will result in no electrical current flowing through the relay and which cannot cause a fuse to blow.

29. **The correct answer is b.** Technician B only is correct because all repaired wires under the hood (or under the vehicle) must be sealed to prevent moisture from getting into a splice where it could cause corrosion. A splice sleeve that contains adhesive inside can also be used to make a weather-proof wire repair. Technician A is not correct because electrical tape will not seal the splice from water, which could lead to corrosion and high resistance in the circuit. Answers c and d are not correct because Technician B only is correct.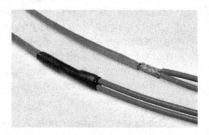

30. **The correct answer is a.** Technician A is correct because using a fuse in the jumper wire will help protect against excessive current flow through the jumper lead if one end accidentally touches metal when the other end is attached to the circuit. Technician B is not correct because a switch, which should have little or no resistance, can be safely bypassed using a jumper wire without doing any harm to the circuit. However, an electrical load should not be bypassed. Answers c and d are not correct because Technician A only is correct.

ELECTRICAL/ELECTRONIC SYSTEMS (A6)

CATEGORY: BATTERY AND STARTING SYSTEM DIAGNOSIS AND REPAIR

31. **The correct answer is d.** All of the above are probable causes of a clicking solenoid including low battery voltage (answer a), defective hold-in winding coil in the solenoid (answer b), and poor connections at the battery (answer c). Low voltage is the usual cause of a clicking solenoid and low battery voltage or loose/corroded battery terminals are the most common causes. Answers a, b, and c are not correct because all are correct.

32. **The correct answer is b.** The last connection should be to the engine block or jump start terminal of the disabled vehicle because a spark will occur and this spark should be as far away as possible from the battery so as to not ignite the escaping gases. Answer a is not correct because if the last connection were made at or near the battery, there is a chance that the spark created could ignite the escaping gases. Answer c is not correct because no harm will be done to the alternator if the proper polarity is observed and therefore, the alternators do not need to be disconnected. Answer d is not correct  because the ignition on both vehicles should be off (not on) to prevent the possible damage that could occur to electronic devices from the spark that occurs when the last connection is completed.

33. **The correct answer is a.** Technician A only is correct because at the end of a battery load test, the battery voltage should be higher than 9.6 volts at room temperature. Technician B is not correct because the battery should be loaded to one-half (rather than 2 times) the CCA rating. Answers c and d are not correct because Technician A only is correct.

34. **The correct answer is d.** All of the above are correct. Answer a is correct because a high initial charge is usually necessary to start the chemical reaction inside the cells to make the electrolyte conductive so the battery can accept a charge. Answer b is correct because a battery may not accept a charge, if totally discharged, until the electrolyte becomes conductive. Answer c is correct because temperature above 125F (hot to the touch) can warp plates inside the battery. Answers a, b, and c are not correct because all are correct.

35. **The correct answer is a.** It is normal for a vehicle to have a normal key-off battery drain of 20 to 30 mA (0.02 to 0.03 A). Answer b (2 to 3 amperes), answer c (0.2 to 0.4 A), and answer d (150 to 300 mA) are not correct because they are all much higher than the maximum allowable specification of 50 mA (0.05 A) as stated by most vehicle manufacturers.

36. **The correct answer is a.** It is normal for a vehicle to have a normal key-off battery drain of 20 to 30 mA (0.02 to 0.03 A). Answer b (2 to 3 amperes), answer c (0.2 to 0.4 A), and answer d (150 to 300 mA) are not correct because they are all much higher than the maximum allowable specification of 50 mA (0.05 A) as stated by most vehicle manufacturers.

37. **The correct answer is a.** Technician A only is correct because a key-off battery drain could be caused by many different components and circuits and removing fuses one at a time until the draw decreases to normal is the recommended method to use to locate the circuit causing the draw. Technician B is not correct because a short finder is used to locate a short-to-ground that causes enough current to flow to blow a fuse and not just enough to drain a battery. Answers c and d are not correct because Technician A only is correct.

38. **The correct answer is c.** Both technicians are correct. Technician A is correct because the computer stores learned idle speed and other engine operating parameters that will be lost when the battery is disconnected. Technician B is correct because the stored radio station presets will usually be lost if the battery is disconnected. Some anti-theft radios require that a code be entered after the battery has been reconnected to restore proper operation. Answers a, b, and d are not correct because both technicians are correct.

39. **The correct answer is b.** Technician B only is correct because an absorbed glass matt battery has low internal resistance and can be damaged if charged at voltage higher than 15 volts. Most conventional battery charges charge at a voltage level of 16 volts or higher. Therefore to safely charge an AGM battery requires a charger that is specified for AGM batteries. Technician A is not correct because using a conventional battery charger set at a high charge rate could destroy an AGM battery. Answers c and d are not correct because only Technician B is correct.

40. **The correct answer is a.** Technician A only is correct because a good battery will display a hydrometer reading within 0.050 between the highest and lowest tested cell. A variation greater than 0.050 indicates a possible faulty battery. Technician B is not correct because the maximum allowable difference between cells of a battery during a hydrometer test is 0.05, not 0.005. Answers c and d are not correct because Technician A only is correct.

41. **The correct answer is c.** Both technicians are correct. Technician A is correct because even though batteries are designed to withstand being deep cycled a few times, the constant discharge and recharge will drastically shorten the life of the battery. Technician B is correct because if the alternator is always attempting to charge a battery that is fully discharged, harm can be done to the alternator due to the constant charging without ever reaching the voltage regulator limit. Answers a, b, and d are not correct because both technicians are correct.

42. **The correct answer is a.** Technician A only is correct because while the battery cannot discharge through the plastic case, the concrete is cold and damp. If a battery is stored on concrete, the difference in temperature between the top and bottom of the cells causes the battery to self-discharge. All batteries should be stored in cool dry locations. Technician B is not correct because even though a battery may self-discharge if stored on concrete, it can be charged on concrete as long as it does not remain on the concrete floor in storage after it has been fully charged. Answers c and d are not correct because Technician A only is correct.

43. **The correct answer is c.** Both technicians are correct. Technician A is correct because an excessive key-off battery drain (parasitic draw) could cause the battery to become discharged during the weekend and be unable to crank the engine on Monday. Technician B is correct because the battery itself could have lost its ability to hold a charge or to provide enough cranking amperes to start the engine. Answers a, b, and d are not correct because both technicians are correct.

44. **The correct answer is b.** Technician B is correct because a spark indicates that an electrical load is causing current to flow from the battery as the last cable is attached. It is normal to see a small spark due to the electrical load on many small keep-alive or memory circuits, but a large spark is abnormal and the cause should be located and corrected to avoid discharging the battery. Technician A is not correct because even though a small spark is normal, a large spark indicates that an electrical device is conducting current and could discharge the battery if not corrected. Answers c and d are not correct because Technician B only is correct.

45. **The correct answer is c.** Both technicians are correct. Technician A is correct because an engine mechanical fault could cause the starter to be under a heavier-than-normal load, thereby increasing the current draw for the battery. Due to the reduced CEMF, the starter draws more than the normal amount of current from the battery. Technician B is correct because a defective starter will cause an increase in current from the battery. Answers a, b, and d are not correct because both technicians are correct.

both a and b are correct. Answer c is not correct because a fully-charged 12-volt battery will have 12.6 volts or higher.

46. **The correct answer is b.** Technician B is correct because a worn starter drive will cause the starter motor to spin and not rotate the engine flywheel. Technician A is not correct because if the starter is rotating, the solenoid has to be working because the drive pinion is forced to mesh with the flywheel before current flows through the solenoid to the starter motor. Answers c and d are not correct because Technician B only is correct.

47. **The correct answer is b.** Technician B only is correct because an open in the control circuit, such as a neutral safety or clutch switch, will prevent the flow of electrical current to the starter solenoid and therefore, no current to the starter. If no current flows to the starter, the dome light will remain bright and no sound will be heard from the starter. Technician A is not correct because even though the battery is discharged, the solenoid should at least click and the voltage (as observed by looking at the dome light) should drop. Answers c and d are not correct because Technician B only is correct.

48. **The correct answer is d.** If the solenoid hold-in winding were open, the solenoid and the starter would not crank the engine at all and therefore, could not be the cause of slow cranking. Answers a (discharged battery), b (corroded battery cable connections), and c (engine mechanical problem) can all cause slow cranking

49. **The correct answer is c.** Both technicians are correct. Technician A is correct because an excessive voltage drop (greater than 0.5 volt) can cause the starter to rotate slower than normal during engine cranking. Technician B is correct because resistance anywhere in the power side or ground return side of the cranking of the cranking circuit can cause slow engine cranking. Answers a, b, and d are not correct because both technicians are correct.

50. **The correct answer is c.** If wires were separated from the commutator of the starter armature, an open circuit would result and little if any current would flow through the starter. Answer a (misadjusted starter pinion gear) could cause the starter to drag and draw excessive current if the clearance between the flywheel and the pinion were too close. Answer b (loose starter housing) could cause excessive starter current draw if the armature becomes bound due to the misalignment of the armature bushings (bearings). Answer d (bent armature) could cause excessive starter current draw when the armature rubs against the field coils when it rotates.

51. **The correct answer is d.** An open relay means that no current will flow and as a result cannot be the cause of higher-than-normal starter current draw. Answer a is not correct because a defective (seized) A/C compressor could be the cause of excessive starter current draw. Answer b is not correct because worn starter brushes can cause higher-than-normal starter current draw. Answer c is not correct because if the field coil of the starter were shorted-to-ground, this would cause higher-than-normal starter draw.

52. **The correct answer is c.** Both technicians are correct. Technician A is correct because if the battery cables or connectors have high resistance, the starter solenoid will often click rapidly due to the engagement, releasing, and engagement of the solenoid windings. The solenoid engages when the starter is first being supplied with current, but releases when the starter draw causes the battery voltage to drop low enough to allow the solenoid windings to hold the yoke plunger in the applied position. As soon as the solenoid is released, the battery voltage again is high enough to engage the solenoid and the process repeats. Technician B is correct because if the battery is not at least 75% charged, the results of starter amperage testing may indicate that the starter is defective while the actual cause is a weak battery. Lower than normal battery voltage causes the starter to rotate slower, thereby produces less counter EMF (CEMF) and more current than normal flows from the battery to the starter. Answers a, b, and d are not correct because both technicians are correct.

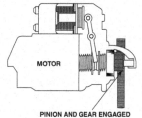

PINION AND GEAR ENGAGED

53. **The correct answer is c.** A missing solenoid return spring could cause the starter drive to remain engaged in the flywheel after the ignition switch has been released. Answer b (starter drive) is not correct because the purpose of the plunger return spring is to force the starter drive out of engagement with

54. **The correct answer is a.** A missing solenoid return spring could cause the starter drive to remain engaged in the flywheel after the ignition switch has been released. Answer b (starter drive) is not correct because the purpose of the plunger return spring is to force the starter drive out of engagement with the flywheel when the starter stops. Answer c is not correct because the most likely result of installing the shift fork backward would be less than full engagement of the drive pinion gear to the flywheel. Answer d is not correct because the solenoid contact will operate normally even if installed backward.

55. **The correct answer is a.** Technician A is correct because a high-scale ammeter is needed to test the current (amperes) draw of a starter. Technician B is not correct because a voltmeter is not required except to measure the battery voltage during the starter test and a high-scale meter is not needed. Answers c and d are not correct because Technician A only is correct.

56. **The correct answer is d.** Worn starter brushes could affect the operation of the starter but are not as likely to cause a grinding sound. Answer a (starter drive) is not correct because a defective drive or pinion gear on the drive could cause a grinding sound. Answer b (flywheel) is not correct because if the teeth are excessively worn or damaged, they can cause a grinding sound. Answer c (pinion to flywheel clearance) is not correct because if the clearance is not within specifications, a whine or grinding sound could be heard during cranking.

57. **The correct answer is a.** Technician A only is correct because a voltage drop reading of 878 mV (0.878 V) exceeds most vehicle manufacturers' maximum specifications of 0.5 volt (500 mV) and is the result of excessive resistance in the positive cable or at the connection between the cable and the battery terminal. Technician B is not correct because a voltage drop test cannot indicate the condition of a starter motor. Answers c and d are not correct because Technician A only is correct.

58. **The correct answer is d.** If the hold-in winding was open, the solenoid would still click due to the operation of the pull-in winding inside the starter solenoid. Answer a is not correct because an open in the neutral safety switch could be the cause of the starter to not operate and the solenoid to not click. Answer b is not correct because an open battery ground connection could be the cause of the starter to not operate and the solenoid to not click. Answer c is not correct because an open solenoid ground could be the cause of the starter to not operate and the solenoid to not click.

59. **The correct answer is d.** Neither technician is correct. Technician A is not correct because the voltage should be above 9.6 volts during cranking and the reading of 10.32 exceeds this maximum value. Technician B is not correct because the cranking voltage does not indicate a starter or cranking circuit fault. Answer c is not correct because neither technician is correct.

ELECTRICAL/ELECTRONIC SYSTEMS (A6)

CATEGORY: CHARGING SYSTEM DIAGNOSIS AND REPAIR

60. **The correct answer is c.** Both technicians are correct. Technician A is correct because a diode should block the flow of electricity from the battery into the alternator and if a diode were shorted, current would be drained from the battery. Technician B is correct because dirt combined with moisture in the air can cause some electric current to flow between the terminal posts of the battery. Answers a, b, and d are not correct because both technicians are correct.

61. **The correct answer is b.** If the fusible link or maxi fuse is blown between the alternator and the battery, no voltage will be measured at the output terminal of the alternator and the alternator will not be able to charge the battery. Answer a is not correct because an open diode while it can cause a charging system problem such as an alternator whine would not prevent battery voltage from being measured at the output terminal of the alternator. Answer c is not correct because excessively worn brushes could affect the output of the alternator but would not prevent battery voltage from being measured at the output terminal of the alternator. Answer d is not correct because while a shorted stator would reduce the output of the alternator, it would not prevent battery voltage from being measured at the output terminal of the alternator.

62. **The correct answer is b.** Technician B only is correct because battery voltage should be measured at the output terminal of the alternator (alternator) unless there is an open circuit. The most likely cause of an open circuit between the battery and the alternator is a blown fusible link. Technician A is not correct because even though the alternator may be defective, the test indicating 0.0 volt at the output terminal is not an indication that it is defective. Answers c and d are not correct because Technician B only is correct.

63. **The correct answer is a.** The charging system voltage should be within 13.5 to 15.0 volts according to most vehicle manufacturers' specifications. Answer b is not correct because 12.6 volts is too low and 15.6 volts is too high and could damage the battery. Answer c is not correct because 12 volts is too low a voltage to adequately charge the battery. Answer d is not correct because the voltage is too high and could damage the battery and some electrical devices in the vehicle.

64. **The correct answer is c.** Both technicians are correct. Technician A is correct because a good alternator should be able to produce at least 13.5 volts. Technician B is correct because a sulfated or defective battery could absorb all of the current produced by the alternator and not indicate the proper charging system voltage. Answers a, b, and d are not correct because both technicians are correct.

65. **The correct answer is a.** Technician A only is correct because to measure a voltage drop between two points of a circuit, current must be flowing. Technician B is not correct because by measuring voltage at the battery terminal, the meter is simply indicating the charging or battery voltage and not the voltage drop of the power side or ground side of the alternator circuit. Answers c and d are not correct because Technician A only is correct.

66. **The correct answer is c.** Both technicians are correct. Technician A is correct because a loose drive belt will slip over the alternator drive pulley and not transmit engine power to the alternator resulting in reduced or zero alternator output. Technician B is correct because a poor ground connection on the case of the alternator will create a voltage drop (resistance) in the charging circuit, which will decrease the alternator output. Answers a, b, and d are not correct because both technicians are correct.

67. **The correct answer is d.** Cold outside temperature is unlikely to cause an alternator to produce a lower than specified charging voltage and is likely to cause the voltage to be higher due to the temperature compensation factor built into the electronic voltage regulator or PCM software. Answer a (defective battery) is not correct because it can cause a lower-than-normal charging voltage because the battery could be draining all of the output attempting to achieve a full-charge state. Answer b is not correct because a low engine speed could reduce the charging voltage. Answer c is not correct because a slipping or loose drive belt could decrease the charging voltage, especially at higher engine speeds.

68. **The correct answer is a.** Technician A is correct because a corroded connector between the alternator (alternator) and the battery is the likely cause of an excessive voltage drop. Technician B is not correct because a component inside the alternator cannot cause a voltage drop in the wiring between the alternator (alternator) and the battery. Answers c and d are not correct because Technician A only is correct.

69. **The correct answer is a.** A voltmeter displays the voltage difference between the two meter leads. In this case with one meter lead connected to the output terminal of the alternator and the other lead connected to the positive terminal of the battery, the voltmeter will be reading the difference between these two points. This reading is the voltage drop. Answer b is not correct because AC ripple voltage is measured by connecting the voltmeter to the output terminal of the alternator or the positive terminal of the battery with one lead and to ground or the negative terminal of the battery with the other lead with the voltmeter set to read AC volts. Answer c is not correct  because the charging system voltage is measured with the meter leads connected to the positive and negative post of the battery or to the output terminal of the alternator and the other lead to ground. Answer d is not correct because the meter is not connected to a voltage source, the ignition or ground which is needed to measure ignition control system voltage.

70. **The correct answer is c.** High resistance in the fusible link between the alternator (alternator) and the battery will cause the wire to become hot and will reduce the voltage measured at the battery. Answer a is not correct because overcharging is unlikely to cause a lower-than-normal charging voltage. Answer b is not correct because the alternator is undercharging as a result of the high voltage drop in the fusible link and is not the cause. Answer d is not correct because a poor battery ground could cause a low voltage, but could not cause the fusible link to become hot to the touch.

71. **The correct answer is d.** Worn brushes are unlikely to cause an alternator to be noisy. Answers a, b, and c are all possible causes for a noisy alternator. Answer a (loose drive belt) can cause noise if worn or loose. Answer b (defective rectifier diodes) can cause alternator noise that is similar to a bearing noise due to the magnetic induction variation that occurs inside an alternator if one or more diodes are defective. Answer c (defective bearing) will make a growling or rumbling noise.

ELECTRICAL/ELECTRONIC SYSTEMS (A6)

CATEGORY: LIGHTING SYSTEMS DIAGNOSIS AND REPAIR

72. **The correct answer is a.** An alternator overrunning pulley uses a one-way roller clutch that allows the pulley to freely rotate in only one direction if working as designed. Answers a, b, and c are not correct because they do not indicate the proper operation for a good alternator overrunning pulley.

73. **The correct answer is d.** All of the above are correct. Answer a is correct because a defective brake switch will prevent cruise control operation. Answer b is correct because the brake pedal switch is an input to many ABS units and uses this signal to get ready to handle a possible ABS event. Without the brake pedal input, the application of the ABS operation could be delayed and/or set an ABS related diagnostic trouble code (DTC). Answer c is correct because the shifter will not be able to be moved from the park position if the shift solenoid does not receive voltage from the brake switch.

74. **The correct answer is d.** It is normal operation on many vehicles because the side marker is wired between the parking light and the turn signal circuits. Opposing voltages would cause the side marker to go out when the lights are on and the turn signal light is on at the same time. Answer a is not correct because an open bulb would not light. Answer b is not correct because an open turn signal switch would not provide electrical power to cause the turn signals to flash. Answer c is not correct because a blown fuse for the parking light circuit would prevent the operation of the parking lamps.

75. **The correct answer is b.** Technician B only is correct because the current flowing through the headlights or parking lights will flow through the turn signal indicator on the dash if the ground connection is corroded or has high resistance. Technician A is not correct because even though it is possible that a short circuit could cause this condition, it is not the most likely. Answers c and d are not correct because Technician B only is correct.

76. **The correct answer is c.** Halogen bulbs will have a shorter-than-normal service life if bare fingers touch the glass ampoule. The oils from the skin will cause the glass to expand at uneven rates leading to premature failure. Answer a is not correct because a poor ground would cause a decrease in electrical current flow through the bulbs, which could affect the operation and brightness but would unlikely decrease the life of the bulbs. Answer b is not correct because a shorted headlight switch would not be able to be turned off and while it may cause a battery drain, it would not cause the headlight bulb to have a short service life. Answer d is not correct because the bulb cannot be installed backward due to the positioning of the terminals in the electrical connector.

77. **The correct answer is d.** Neither technician is correct. The blown fuse would prevent the operation of the instrument panel lamps. Technician A is not correct because the power for the headlights is entering the headlight switch from the battery and not from the fuse, which is protecting the instrument panel lamp circuit. Technician B is not correct because the electrical power for the taillights and parking lights is entering the headlight switch from the battery and is not affected by the blown fuse for the instrument panel lamp circuit. Answer c is not correct because neither technician is correct.

78. **The correct answer is a.** Technician A is correct because the current comes from the brake switch through the turn signal switch and to the rear lights. An open in the turn signal switch could prevent the brake lights from working. Technician B is not correct because a defective brake switch, while it could prevent the brake lights from functioning, will not affect the operation of the turn signals. Answers c and d are not correct because Technician A only is correct.

79. **The correct answer is b.** A corroded light socket will cause an increase in circuit resistance causing the bulb to be dimmer than normal due to the reduced current (amperes) flow. Answer a is not correct because corrosion causes an increase, not a decrease, in circuit resistance. For a fuse to blow, there has to be a reduction in the circuit resistance, which would increase the current flow above the rating of the fuse. Answer c is not correct because even though the additional resistance in the socket could cause a main feedback concern, it is not the most likely cause. Answer d is not correct because the lower battery voltage would not cause damage to the bulb.

80. **The correct answer is b.** A defective headlight (open filament) is the most likely cause of the high beam not working on one side of the vehicle. Answer a is not correct because a defective dimmer switch would affect both high beam lamps instead of just the right side bulb. Answer c is not correct because the ground used for the high beam is the same ground used for the low beam and the low beam is functioning correctly. Answer d is not correct because a discharged battery would affect the operation of all of the lights and not just the right-side high beam.

81. **The correct answer is a.** A misadjusted neutral safety switch is the most likely cause of the backup lights remaining on all the time. Most neutral safety switches contain contacts that close when the gear selector is in reverse to send current to the backup (reverse) lights. Answer b is not correct because an open switch means that no current will flow through the switch. Answers c and d are not correct because even if the bulb were installed backward, the lights would not remain on because the power comes from the neutral safety switch.

82. **The correct answer is a.** A poor ground will cause the light to go out when additional current is applied because the connection will become hot, increasing the resistance even higher, which will reduce the current flow through the bulb enough that it appears to go out completely. Answer b is not correct because a shorted bulb would not light at all. Answer c is not correct because a defective brake switch would affect both rear brake lights and since the right brake light functions correctly, the fault has to be somewhere else. Answer d is not correct because the bulb lights are okay.

83. **The correct answer is b.** Technician B only is correct because when trailer lights are connected, more current than normal flows through the flasher, creating the rapid flashing indicating a fault to the driver. The technician should replace the flasher unit or rewire the trailer lights using a relay to avoid this problem. Technician A is not correct because even if the wiring were reversed, additional current will flow through the turn signal flasher and create the rapid flashing. Answers c and d are not correct because Technician B only is correct.

84. **The correct answers is d.** All of the above could result. Answer a is correct because the ground for the side marker light often flows through the front turn signal bulb and without this ground, the current would flow through and light the turn signal indicator lamp on the dash. Answer b is correct because a defective (shorted) brake light will create a path from the brake light circuit to the taillight circuit, which can then allow current to flow to the dash lights when the brake pedal is depressed. Answer c is correct because if the brake lightbulb was shorted to the taillight circuit, the electronics may be activated indicating that the lights are on even though they are off but the brake pedal has been depressed with the ignition key off.

85. **The correct answer is a.** Technician A only is correct because the bulb will not light if it is burned out and yet the high beam will function correctly. Technician B is not correct because the high beam functions correctly, which indicates that the dimmer switch is able to switch to the high beam position. Answers c and d are not correct because Technician A only is correct.

86. **The correct answer is c.** Both technicians are correct. Technician A is correct because a higher wattage bulb will draw more current than the standard bulb. This extra current and bulb wattage can overheat the bulb socket and burn the insulation of the wiring as well as damage the headlight and dimmer switch. Technician B is correct because adding extra lighting in parallel with the existing lights increases the current flow through the headlight and dimmer switches. Answers a, b, and d are not correct because both technicians are correct.

ELECTRICAL/ELECTRONIC SYSTEMS (A6)

CATEGORY: INSTRUMENT CLUSTER AND DRIVER INFORMATION SYSTEMS DIAGNOSIS AND REPAIR

87. **The correct answer is b.** An open in the circuit 711(GN/WH) would prevent the circuit being complete to the left high beam only. Answer a is not correct because an open at ground 101 (G101) would also affect the left side low beam which is operating normally. Answer c is not correct because an open at ground 100 (G100) would affect the right side headlights (low and high beam) and not affect the left side high beam only. Answer d is not correct because a fault with high beam relay would affect both high beams and the problem is only associated with the left side high beam headlight.

88. **The correct answer is b.** The fuel gauge shown is a potentiometer with three wires. Some use two wires and are therefore referred to as a rheostat. Answer a is not correct because this example shows three wires and is therefore a potentiometer and not a rheostat. Answer c is not correct because the sensor is not a thermistor. Answer d is not correct because while a Hall Effect sensor does usually use three wires, the unit shown shows a resistor which is not used in a Hall Effect sensor.

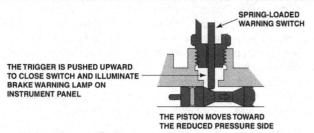

SPRING-LOADED
WARNING SWITCH

THE TRIGGER IS PUSHED UPWARD
TO CLOSE SWITCH AND ILLUMINATE
BRAKE WARNING LAMP ON
INSTRUMENT PANEL

THE PISTON MOVES TOWARD
THE REDUCED PRESSURE SIDE

89. **The correct answer is a.** Technician A only is correct because the pressure differential switch will provide the electrical ground for the red brake warning lamp if there is a difference in pressure between the two separate brake systems. When the wire was removed, the dash light went out indicating that it was in fact the pressure differential switch that was grounding the light circuit. Technician B is not correct because if the parking brake had been applied (or the switch was stuck), the red brake warning lamp would not have gone out when the wire was removed from the pressure differential switch. Answers c and d are not correct because Technician A only is correct.

90. **The correct answer is b.** A burned out bulb is the most likely cause for the charge indicator lamp to not light when the ignition is on (run) and the engine is off. Answer a is not correct because even though a blown fusible link will cause a no charge condition, it is not likely to prevent the dash warning lamp from lighting when the ignition is on and the engine is off. Answers c and d are not correct because even though a defective diode (answer c) or a short inside the alternator (answer d) could cause a no charging condition, they are unlikely to cause the red dash warning lamp to not light when the ignition is on and the engine is off.

91. **The correct answer is d.** A short to ground at point Y would cause excessive current to flow which would blow 15 A #3 fuse in the interior fuse panel the interior fuse panel when the lights were turned on. Answer a is not correct because an open at point Y would prevent current from flowing and would not cause a fuse to blow. Answer b is not correct because while a short to ground at this location would reduce the circuit resistance, because of the coil winding in the relay above point X, the fuse would not likely blow. Answer c is not correct because while it would cause the 30 A fuse blow, it would not be the cause of the 15 A fuse to blow.

92. **The correct answer is c.** Both technicians are correct. Technician A is correct because the movement of the dash gauge, when the sending unit wire was grounded, indicated that the gauge will react to changes in resistance in the circuit. Technician B is correct because the test checked that the wiring and the dash unit were able to function and react to changes in resistance in the circuit, which leaves just the tank sending unit as the most likely cause for the inoperative fuel gauge. Answers a, b, and d are not correct because both technicians are correct.

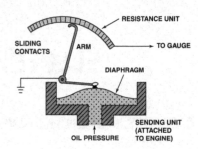

93. **The correct answer is a.** The most likely cause of the oil pressure warning lamp to be on all the time, even though the oil pressure is normal, is a defective oil pressure sending unit. Most sending units provide the ground for the warning lamp circuit and if the sending unit was shorted, the lamp would light whenever the ignition was on. Answer b is not correct because a shorted dash warning lamp would not light at all and therefore could not be the cause. Answer c is not correct because an open wire would prevent the sending unit from providing the ground necessary to complete the circuit for the warning lamp. Answer d is not correct because the oil pressure was measured to be okay and the problem is in the light circuit not with the engine.

94. **The correct answer is c.** The resistance of two equal resistors connected in parallel is half the value of each resistor. Therefore, the two 120 ohm resistors in parallel should measure 60 ohms (120/2 = 60). Answer a is not correct because while 120 ohms is the value of each resistor, there are two of them connected in parallel. This means that any current flow is split with half of the current flowing through one and half of the current flowing through the other. As a result, the total resistance presented to the current is half or 60 ohms. Answer b is not correct because the resistors are connected in parallel and not in series. If they were connected in series, the current flowing through the first resistor and then the second resistor would result in the current "seeing" a total of 240 ohms. However, these resistors are connected in parallel and the current splits reducing the value of the resistance. Answer d is not correct because the ohmmeter will be applying a voltage to the resistors and will read a resistance of the two resistors that are connected in parallel which is 60 ohms.

95. **The correct answer is b.** A ground between the dash warning light and the pressure sensor can cause the lamp to be on all the time the ignition is on even if the oil pressure is normal. This occurs because the lamp comes on when the oil pressure sensor goes to ground with no oil pressure. Answer a is not correct because an open circuit results in no current flow and therefore, the oil pressure light would not come on. Answer c is not correct because an open circuit results in no current flow and therefore, the oil pressure light would not come on.

ELECTRICAL/ELECTRONIC SYSTEMS (A6)

CATEGORY: BODY ELECTRICAL SYSTEMS DIAGNOSIS AND REPAIR

96. **The correct answer is c.** A burned out bulb on the left side is the most likely cause of a rapid turn indicator lamp blinking on one side only. The flasher unit causes the dash turn indicator lamp to blink rapidly to warn the driver that there is a fault in the system as a safety measure required of all vehicle manufacturers. Some vehicles will cause the turn indicator lamp to not flash at all if there is a fault. Answer a is not correct because a defective flasher unit would affect both sides and not just the left side turn signals. Answer b is not correct because the turn signals work as designed on the right side indicating that all of the bulbs on the right are functioning. Answer d is not correct because even though a shorted brake switch could cause the brake light to be on all the time, it is unlikely to cause a fault with only the left side turn signals.

97. **The correct answer is d.** Either b or c can be the cause of a communication error between the BPP and the BCM. The two parallel arrows indicated module communication data lines. Answer a is not correct because there is a ground at Y already so a short-to-ground at this location would not have any effect on the circuit operation.

98. **The correct answer is d.** Neither technician is correct. Technician A is not correct because the indicator light is a separate section of the circuit connected in parallel and the bulb burning out would not affect the operation of the rear window defogger. Technician B is not correct because the lightbulb does not affect the operation of the relay or the rear window defogger except that the driver will not see the indicator light come on when the defogger is turned on.

99. **The correct answer is b.** The most likely cause is the failure of the horn relay itself. Because the horns work when terminals 30 and 87 are connected, means that the horns and the ground for the horns are normal. Answer a is not correct because the horns operate normally when the relay is bypassed, which indicates that the ground connections at the horns do not have excessive resistance. Answer c is not correct because the horns operate normally when the relay is bypassed, which indicates that the electrical connection between the horn repay and the horns is not a problem. Answer d is not correct because if the circuit was normal in the relay, this would cause the horns to operate at all times and not to work when the horn button is depressed.

100. **The correct answer is b.** Most horn switches operate by grounding the circuit for the horn relay. If this switch were to fail and become grounded all the time, the horn would blow all the time. Answer a is not correct because an open in the horn relay would break the flow of current to the horns and not cause it to be energized all the time. Answer c is not correct because a poor ground would cause an increase in circuit resistance and a decrease in current flow through the horn causing the horn to sound fainter than normal and could not cause it to blow all the time. Answer d is not correct because a defective horn would not function or function poorly and could not be the cause of blowing all the time.

101. **The correct answer is a.** A shorted horn wire is the least likely cause of an inoperative horn because this fault would not cause the relay to click. Answer b is not correct because if the relay contacts were corroded, the resistance created would prevent enough current to operate the horn, yet the contacts will still move and click as the relay coil is energized. Answer c is not correct because a defective horn could allow the relay to click but not sound because of a fault within the horn itself. Answer d is not correct because an open horn ground connection would prevent the horn from working, yet the relay would still click when energized.

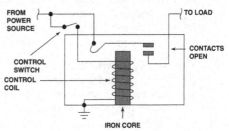

102. The correct answer is a. A shorted horn wire is the least likely cause of an inoperative horn because this fault would not cause the relay to click. Answer b is not correct because if the relay contacts were corroded, the resistance created would prevent enough current to operate the horn, yet the contacts will still move and click as the relay coil is energized. Answer c is not correct because a defective horn could allow the relay to click but not sound because of a fault within the horn itself. Answer d is not correct because an open horn ground connection would prevent the horn from working, yet the relay would still click when energized.

103. The correct answer is a. The double arrows pointing in both directions between two modules represent a data communication line such as CAN. Answer b is not correct because power (B+) is usually shown as being connected to a circuit protection device such as a fuse or circuit breaker. A ground connection is often shown with a ground symbol and or a connection to a common ground shared by more than one component. Answer c is not correct because ground connection is often shown with a ground symbol and or a connection to a common ground shared by more than one component. Answer d is not correct because it a shield is usually represented using a circle showing dotted lines around the wire or wires carrying low voltage signals.

104. The correct answer is b. Technician B is correct because the park mechanism is incorporated into the wiper motor assembly. Even though some wipers can be repaired for this fault, in most cases the entire wiper motor assembly must be replaced. Technician A is not correct because a poor ground for the wiper circuit would cause the wiper motor to operate slower than normal and is unlikely to cause the wipers to fail to park properly. Answers c and d are not correct because Technician B only is correct.

105. The correct answer is c. Both technicians are correct. Technician A is correct because a blown fusible link could prevent electrical power from reaching the blower motor. Technician B says that a defective engine fan relay could prevent power from reaching the fan motor. Answers a, b, and d are not correct because both technicians are correct.

106. The correct answer is d. If an open occurred at the relay, the current could not flow from the fuse 18 through the intermittent relay and to the low speed brush on the wiper motor. Answer a is not correct because terminal #28 affects the operation of the low speed, not the high speed because the high-speed brush is off to the side creating a lower resistance path to ground causing more current to flow resulting in a faster rotating motor. Answer b is not correct because the wiper will function correctly on low speed through terminal #11 at the relay. Answer c is not correct because an open means that there is no electrical connection and therefore no current flows, which would not cause a fuse to blow.

107. The correct answer is d. If an open occurred at the relay, the current could not flow from the fuse 18 through the intermittent relay and to the low speed brush on the wiper motor. Answer a is not correct because terminal #28 affects the operation of the low speed, not the high speed because the high-speed brush is off to the side creating a lower resistance path to ground causing more current to flow resulting in a faster rotating motor. Answer b is not correct because the wiper will function correctly on low speed through terminal #11 at the relay. Answer c is not correct because an open means that there is no electrical connection and therefore no current flows, which would not cause a fuse to blow.

108. The correct answer is b. The electrical connectors for airbags are usually yellow to help identify them. Answers a, c, and d are not correct because most airbag connectors are yellow.

109. The correct answer is c. Both technicians are correct. Technician A is correct because even though the blower motor operates, it may be drawing more than the specified current. A fused jumper lead equipped with a 20 A fuse is a commonly used method to determine if the motor is drawing more than 20 A. Technician B is correct because an open in the fan control relay or resistor pack could cause the blower motor to not operate. Answers a, b, and d are not correct because both technicians are correct.

110. The correct answer is d. Neither technician is correct. Technician A is not correct because corroded ground connections would cause an increase in circuit resistance and a decrease (rather than an increase) in current flow through the motor. Technician B is not correct because a shorted blower relay would cause the blower motor to run all the time and would not cause the motor to draw more current as would occur if the motor itself were defective. Answer c is not correct because neither technician is correct.

111. The correct answer is c. If there is a short-to-ground at "Z", excessive current will flow, which can cause the 40 amp fuse to blow. Answer a is not correct because an open at "Z", while it would prevent the operation of the rear window defogger, it would not cause the fuse to blow. Answer b is not correct because a short-to-ground at "X" would not affect the operation of the circuit because there is already a ground connection at this point. Answer d is not correct because while an open at "X" would prevent the relay coil from being energized and the rear defogger from working, this would not cause the fuse to blow.

112. The correct answer is c. If there is a short-to-ground at "Z", excessive current will flow which can cause the 40 amp fuse to blow. Answer a is not correct because an open at "Z", while it would prevent the operation of the rear window defogger, it would not cause the fuse to blow. Answer b is not correct because a short-to-ground at "X" would not affect the operation of the circuit because there is already a ground connection at this point. Answer d is not correct because while an open at "X" would prevent the relay coil from being energized and the rear defogger from working, this would not cause the fuse to blow.

113. The correct answer is c. If there is a short-to-ground at "Z", excessive current will flow which can cause the 40 amp fuse to blow. Answer a is not correct because an open at "Z", while it would prevent the operation of the rear window defogger, it would not cause the fuse to blow. Answer b is not correct because a short-to-ground at "X" would not affect the operation of the circuit because there is already a ground connection at this point. Answer d is not correct because while an open at "X" would prevent the relay coil from being energized and the rear defogger from working, this would not cause the fuse to blow.

114. The correct answer is c. If there is a short-to-ground at "Z", excessive current will flow which can cause the 40 amp fuse to blow. Answer a is not correct because an open at "Z", while it would prevent the operation of the rear window defogger, it would not cause the fuse to blow. Answer b is not correct because a short-to-ground at "X" would not affect the operation of the circuit because there is already a ground connection at this point. Answer d is not correct because while an open at "X" would prevent the relay coil from being energized and the rear defogger from working, this would not cause the fuse to blow.

115. The correct answer is c. If there is a short-to-ground at "Z", excessive current will flow which can cause the 40 amp fuse to blow. Answer a is not correct because an open at "Z", while it would prevent the operation of the rear window defogger, it would not cause the fuse to blow. Answer b is not correct because a short-to-ground at "X" would not affect the operation of the circuit because there is already a ground connection at this point. Answer d is not correct because while an open at "X" would prevent the relay coil from being energized and the rear defogger from working, this would not cause the fuse to blow.

116. The correct answer is c. If there is a short-to-ground at "Z", excessive current will flow which can cause the 40 amp fuse to blow. Answer a is not correct because an open at "Z", while it would prevent the operation of the rear window defogger, it would not cause the fuse to blow. Answer b is not correct because a short-to-ground at "X" would not affect the operation of the circuit because there is already a ground connection at this point. Answer d is not correct because while an open at "X" would prevent the relay coil from being energized and the rear defogger from working, this would not cause the fuse to blow.

117. The correct answer is c. If there is a short-to-ground at "Z", excessive current will flow which can cause the 40 amp fuse to blow. Answer a is not correct because an open at "Z", while it would prevent the operation of the rear window defogger, it would not cause the fuse to blow. Answer b is not correct because a short-to-ground at "X" would not affect the operation of the circuit because there is already a ground connection at this point. Answer d is not correct because while an open at "X" would prevent the relay coil from being energized and the rear defogger from working, this would not cause the fuse to blow.

118. The correct answer is d. The most likely cause for a speaker to not function is the speaker itself being defective. Answer a is not correct because a defective audio unit, while it could affect just one speaker if defective, is likely to cause problems with more than one speaker. Answer b is not correct because a poor ground at G502 would affect all speakers the same and not just the left rear. Answer c is not correct because an open antenna lead would affect the radio reception and affect all speakers the same and not just the left rear.

119. The correct answer is a. Technician A is correct because many devices are operated directly by an electronic module from inputs from switches. If a scan tool can operate the trunk release, then this test confirms that the module and the trunk release solenoid circuits are functional. If the scan tool cannot operate the trunk, then the technician knows that the problem could be the trunk release circuit, switches, or the control module. Technician B is not correct because even though the dash switch could be defective, it is unlikely to cause the trunk release to not function from either the switch or the remote. Answers c and d are not correct because Technician A only is correct.

120. The correct answer is d. Neither technician is correct. Technician A is not correct because an open thermal limiter would prevent the fan motor from operating at any speed, except high, and could not be the cause of the fan operating at low speed only. Technician B is not correct because an open at the "LO" contact in the switch would not affect the operation of the fan on the LO setting because no current flows through the switch when the low position is selected. Answers a, b, and c are not correct because neither technician is correct.

121. The correct answer is b. The voltage should drop as current flows through the rear window defogger grids due to the resistance of the heater wires. The power side of the grid should measure about 12 volts as shown and zero volts at the ground side. At the midpoint, the voltmeter should measure about 6 volts. Answers a, c, and d are not correct because these answers do not state the correct voltage at the midpoint.

122. The correct answer is a. Technician A is correct because a poor electrical ground connection can prevent one horn from operating, yet not affect the other horn because each horn is mounted separately to the body or frame of the vehicle. Technician B is not correct because a defect in the horn contact ring would affect both horns. Answers c and d are not correct because Technician A only is correct.

HEATING AND AIR CONDITIONING CONTENT AREAS

This ASE study guide for Heating and Air Conditioning (A7) is divided into the sub-content areas that correlate to the actual ASE certification test as follows:

CONTENT AREA	QUESTIONS IN TEST	NUMBER OF STUDY GUIDE QUESTIONS
A. A/C System Diagnosis and Repair	17	64 (1–64)
B. Refrigeration System Component Diagnosis and Repair	10	25 (65–89)
1. Compressor and Clutch (5)		
2. Evaporator, Condenser, and Related Components (5)		
C. Heating and Engine Cooling Systems Diagnosis and Repair	23	21 (90–110)
TOTAL	50	110

TIME ALLOWED TO TAKE THE TEST

The allocated time to take the Engine Repair Certification test is 75 minutes. ASE adds 10 additional questions to the test for research purposes for a total of 60 questions. These questions do not count toward your score, but they are embedded within the test and there is no way of knowing which ones do not count. As result, the technician needs to answer 60 questions in 75 minutes, or about one question per minute.

If taking the recertification A7 test, there are just 25 questions with no additional research questions included. The time allocated to take the recertification test is 30 minutes, which means about one minute per question.

BEFORE USING THIS STUDY GUIDE

Before trying to answer the questions and looking at the explanations, look over the following list of the content that ASE states will be covered in the certification test. For best results using this study guide, check service information or consult an automotive textbook for details on any of the content areas that are not familiar before trying to answer the questions. For additional information about the ASE test, visit the website at **www.ase.com**.

HEATING AND AIR CONDITIONING (A7) CERTIFICATION TEST

A. A/C SYSTEM DIAGNOSIS AND REPAIR (12 QUESTIONS)

1. Diagnose the cause of unusual operating noises of the A/C system; determine needed repairs.
2. Identify system type and conduct performance test on the A/C system; determine needed repairs.
3. Diagnose A/C system problems indicated by refrigerant flow past the sight glass (for systems using a sight glass); determine needed repairs.
4. Diagnose A/C system problems indicated by pressure gauge readings; determine needed repairs.
5. Diagnose A/C system problems indicated by sight, sound, smell, and touch procedures; determine needed repairs.
6. Leak-test A/C system; determine needed repairs.
7. Identify and recover A/C system refrigerant.
8. Evacuate A/C system.
9. Clean A/C system components and hoses.
10. Charge A/C system with refrigerant (liquid or vapor).
11. Identify lubricant type; inspect level in A/C system.

B. REFRIGERATION SYSTEM COMPONENT DIAGNOSIS AND REPAIR (10 QUESTIONS)

1. Compressor and Clutch (5 questions)

1. Diagnose A/C system problems that cause the protection devices (pressure, thermal, and control modules) to interrupt system operation; determine needed repairs.
2. Inspect, test, and replace A/C system pressure and thermal protection devices.
3. Inspect, adjust, and replace A/C compressor drive belts, pulleys, and tensioners.
4. Inspect, test, service, and replace A/C compressor clutch components or assembly.
5. Identify required lubricant type; inspect and correct level in A/C compressor.
6. Inspect, test, service, or replace A/C compressor.
7. Inspect, repair, or replace A/C compressor mountings.

2. Evaporator, Condenser, and Related Components (5 questions)

1. Inspect, repair, or replace A/C system mufflers, hoses, lines, filters, fittings, and seals.
2. Inspect A/C condenser for air flow restrictions.
3. Inspect, test, and replace A/C system condenser and mountings.
4. Inspect and replace receiver/drier or accumulator/drier.
5. Inspect, test, and replace expansion valve(s).
6. Inspect and replace orifice tube(s).
7. Inspect, test, or replace evaporator(s).
8. Inspect, clean, and repair evaporator housing, and water drain.
9. Inspect, test, and replace evaporator pressure/temperature control systems and devices.
10. Identify, inspect, and replace A/C system service valves (gauge connections).
11. Inspect and replace A/C system high pressure relief device.

C. HEATING AND ENGINE COOLING SYSTEMS DIAGNOSIS AND REPAIR (5 QUESTIONS)

1. Diagnose the cause of temperature control problems in the heater/ventilation system; determine needed repairs.
2. Diagnose window fogging problems; determine needed repairs.
3. Perform cooling system tests; determine needed repairs.
4. Inspect and replace engine cooling and heater system hoses.
5. Inspect, test, and replace radiator, pressure cap, coolant recovery system, and water pump.
6. Inspect, test, and replace thermostat, bypass, and housing.
7. Identify, inspect, and recover coolant; flush, and refill system with proper coolant.
8. Inspect, test, and replace fan (both electrical and mechanical), fan clutch, fan belts, fan shroud, and air dams.
9. Inspect, test, and replace heater coolant control valve (manual, vacuum, and electrical types).
10. Inspect, flush, and replace heater core.

D. OPERATING SYSTEMS AND RELATED CONTROLS DIAGNOSIS AND REPAIR (16 QUESTIONS)

1. Electrical (8 questions)

1. Diagnose the cause of failures in the electrical control system of heating, ventilating, and A/C systems; determine needed repairs.
2. Inspect, test, repair, and replace A/C-heater blower motors, resistors, switches, relay/modules, wiring, and protection devices.
3. Inspect, test, repair, and replace A/C compressor clutch coil, relay/modules, wiring, sensors, switches, diodes, and protection devices.
4. Inspect, test, repair, replace, and adjust A/C-related engine control systems.
5. Inspect, test, repair, replace, and adjust load-sensitive A/C compressor cutoff systems.
6. Inspect, test, repair, and replace engine cooling/condenser fan motors, relays/modules, switches, sensors, wiring, and protection devices.
7. Inspect, test, adjust, repair, and replace electric actuator motors, relays/modules, switches, sensors, wiring, and protection devices.
8. Inspect, test, service, or replace heating, ventilating, and A/C control panel assemblies.

2. Vacuum/Mechanical (4 questions)

1. Diagnose the cause of failures in the vacuum and mechanical switches and controls of the heating, ventilating, and A/C systems; determine needed repairs.
2. Inspect, test, service, or replace heating, ventilating, and A/C control panel assemblies.
3. Inspect, test, adjust, and replace heating, ventilating, and A/C control cables and linkages.
4. Inspect, test, and replace heating, ventilating, and A/C vacuum actuators (diaphragms/motors) and hoses.
5. Identify, inspect, test, and replace heating, ventilating, and A/C vacuum reservoir, check valve, and restrictors.
6. Inspect, test, adjust, repair, or replace heating, ventilating, and A/C ducts, doors, and outlets.

3. Automatic and Semiautomatic Heating, Ventilating, and A/C Systems (4 questions)

1. Diagnose temperature control system problems; determine needed repairs.
2. Diagnose blower system problems; determine needed repairs.
3. Diagnose air distribution system problems; determine needed repairs.
4. Diagnose compressor clutch control system; determine needed repairs.
5. Inspect, test, adjust, or replace climate control temperature and sun-load sensors.
6. Inspect, test, adjust, and replace temperature blend door actuator(s).
7. Inspect, test, and replace low engine coolant temperature blower control system.
8. Inspect, test, and replace heater water valve and controls.

9. Inspect, test, and replace electric and vacuum motors, solenoids, and switches.

10. Inspect, test, and replace ATC control panel.

11. Inspect, test, adjust, or replace ATC microprocessor (climate control computer/programmer).

12. Check and adjust calibration of ATC system.

E. REFRIGERANT RECOVERY, RECYCLING, HANDLING, AND RETROFIT (7 QUESTIONS)

1. Maintain and verify correct operation of certified equipment.

2. Identify and recover A/C system refrigerant.

3. Recycle or properly dispose of refrigerant.

4. Label and store refrigerant.

5. Test recycled refrigerant for non-condensable gases.

6. Follow federal and local guidelines for retrofit procedures.

HEATING AND AIR CONDITIONING (A7)

CATEGORY: HEATING, VENTILATION, A/C (HVAC) AND ENGINE COOLING SYSTEM SERVICE, DIAGNOSIS, AND REPAIR

1. A vehicle is being checked for a lack of cooling concern about two months after another shop had replaced the compressor. Technician A says that debris from the old compressor could have clogged the orifice tube. Technician B says that the system could be low on charge due to a leak in the system. Which technician is correct?

   a. A only
   b. B only
   c. Both A and B
   d. Neither A nor B

2. A vehicle came to the shop with a system that was not cooling correctly. A low refrigerant charge caused by a leaking condenser was determined to be the cause. Before the refrigerant was recovered, an identifier was used to check the refrigerant. It was determined that the refrigerant was contaminated. What should the technician do?

   a. Recover it into a separate container used for contaminated refrigerant
   b. Allow it to escape from the system so it does contaminate the recovery system
   c. Recover and recycle it
   d. Add new refrigerant to the system and do not recover

3. Two technicians are discussing leak testing of an air-conditioning system. Technician A says that the blower motor resistor pack can be removed to test the evaporator for possible leaks using a leak detector. Technician B says to check the evaporator for leaks at the condensate drain. Which technician is correct?

   a. A only
   b. B only
   c. Both A and B
   d. Neither A nor B

4. An engine runs normally until the air conditioning is engaged. Then it idles roughly and occasionally stalls. What is the *most likely* cause?

   a. A shorted ECT sensor
   b. A stuck idle air control (IAC)
   c. A clogged orifice tube
   d. The air-conditioning system is overcharged

5. The air-conditioning system seems to be functioning correctly, but it does not cool as fast or as cold as a similar model. Which is the *least likely* cause?

   a. Debris clogged condenser
   b. Low on refrigerant charge
   c. Partially clogged orifice tube
   d. Partially clogged condensate drain

6. A lack of cooling is being diagnosed. On an 80°F (27°C) day, both low and high pressure gauges read 87 psi (600 kPa). Technician A says that a clogged orifice tube is the most likely cause. Technician B says that the system is low on refrigerant charge. Which technician is correct?

   a. A only
   b. B only
   c. Both A and B
   d. Neither A nor B

7. A lack of cooling is being diagnosed after the system was retrofitted to R-134a. The high-side pressure is higher than normal and the compressor feels cool when touched. What is the *most likely* cause?

   a. A lack of oil in the system
   b. Undercharged with refrigerant
   c. Overcharged with refrigerant
   d. Clogged or restricted condenser

8. The discharge line from the compressor is hot to the touch. Technician A says that the system is low on refrigerant. Technician B says that the compressor is worn and is not compressing the refrigerant enough for proper operation of the air-conditioning system. Which technician is correct?

   a. A only
   b. B only
   c. Both A and B
   d. Neither A nor B

9. An A/C system equipped with a sight glass is being diagnosed. Bubbles (foam) are observed all of the time the system is working with the doors open and the blower fan speed set to high. Which is the *most likely* cause?

   a. The system is empty of refrigerant—just air is in the system
   b. The system is low on refrigerant
   c. The system is overcharged with refrigerant
   d. There is water in the system

10. A strong pungent odor comes out of the air-conditioning vents. Technician A says that mouthwash should be poured into the air inlet near the windshield to stop the odor. Technician B says that fungicide should be sprayed onto the evaporator to stop the odor. Which technician is correct?

   a. A only
   b. B only
   c. Both A and B
   d. Neither A nor B

11. The technician can test for trapped air (non-condensable gases) inside the refrigerant container by _____.

   a. checking the outside of the container for frost
   b. checking the pressure versus temperature of the container
   c. weighing the container
   d. sending the container to a special laboratory for analysis

12. Technician A says that the refrigerant oil removed during reclaiming should be measured. Technician B says that refrigerant oil can be disposed of with regular engine oil. Which technician is correct?

   a. A only
   b. B only
   c. Both A and B
   d. Neither A nor B

13. Refrigerant should be identified _____.

   a. after recovery, but before recycling
   b. before recovery
   c. before charging the system
   d. after charging the system, but before releasing the vehicle to the customer

14. To be sure that all of the moisture in an air-conditioning system has been boiled and removed, a vacuum of at least _____ in. Hg should be drawn on the system for at least _____ minutes.

   a. 28, 45
   b. 29, 60
   c. 30, 90
   d. 30, 120

15. After the refrigerant has been recovered and recycled, where should it be kept for long-term storage?

   a. In an EPA approved container
   b. In the recovery machine storage unit
   c. In the recycling machine storage unit
   d. In a DOT approved container

16. What should the technician do before recovering refrigerant from a vehicle?

　　a. Test it using a refrigerant identifier and a sealant identifier
　　b. Connect pressure gauges and check the high- and low-side pressures
　　c. Tighten the Schrader valves to be sure they are properly sealed
　　d. Start the engine and allow the air-conditioning system to work for several minutes

17. A technician discovers that 20% of the refrigerant in a vehicle is unknown. What service operation should the service technician perform?

　　a. Recover and recycle the refrigerant as normal
　　b. Recover the refrigerant into a container labeled unknown refrigerant
　　c. Cycle the compressor clutch until the unknown refrigerant is purged from the system
　　d. Recover the refrigerant and remove the non-condensable gases

18. A technician checked the pressure on a 30 lb. container of R-134a at 80°F (27°C) and the pressure was 101 psi (700 kPa) (see chart). Technician A says that the tank should be vented until the pressure is reduced if the identifier detected non-condensable gases (air) were in the refrigerant. Technician B says that additional refrigerant should be added to lower the pressure. Which technician is correct?

　　a. A only
　　b. B only
　　c. Both A and B
　　d. Neither A nor B

Maximum Container Pressure					
Temperature		R-12 Pressure		R-134A Pressure	
°F	°C	psi	kPa	psi	kPa
70	21.1	80	552	76	524
75	23.9	87	600	83	572
80	26.7	96	662	91	627
85	29.5	102	703	100	690
90	32.2	110	758	109	752
95	35.0	118	814	118	814
100	37.8	127	876	129	889
105	40.6	136	937	139	958
110	43.4	146	1007	151	1041

19. According to the chart, how much vacuum needs to be applied to boil water from an air-conditioning system if the temperature is 78°F (26°C)?

　　a. 0 in. Hg
　　b. 15 in. Hg
　　c. 29 in. Hg
　　d. 30 in. Hg

BOILING POINT OF WATER UNDER VACUUM		
Vacuum Reading (in. Hg)	Pounds per Square Inch Absolute Pressure (psla)	Water Boiling Point
0	14.696	212°F (100°C)
10.24	9.629	192°F (89°C)
22.05	3.865	151°F (66°C)
25.98	1.935	124°F (51°C)
27.95	0.968	101°F (38°C)
28.94	0.481	78°F (26°C)
29.53	0.192	52°F (11°C)
29.82	0.019	1°F (-17°C)
29.901	0.010	-11°F (-24°C)

20. An orifice tube-type air-conditioning system is being serviced with HFO-1234yf (R-1234yf). Which SAE standard recovery, recycling, and recharging machine should be used?

    a. J1770
    b. J2210
    c. J2843
    d. J2851

21. Both high-side pressures and low-side pressures are low with the engine running and the selector set to the air-conditioning position. Technician A says that the system is undercharged. Technician B says the cooling fan could be inoperative. Which technician is correct?

    a. A only
    b. B only
    c. Both A and B
    d. Neither A nor B

22. A lack of cooling is being diagnosed. A technician discovers that the high-pressure line is hot to the touch on both sides of the orifice tube. Technician A says that is normal operation for an orifice tube system. Technician B says that the orifice tube may be clogged. Which technician is correct?

    a. A only
    b. B only
    c. Both A and B
    d. Neither A nor B

23. Frost is observed on the line between the condenser and the receiver/drier. Technician A says that this is normal if the air conditioning were being operated on a hot and humid day. Technician B says that a restriction in the line or at the outlet of the condenser could be the cause. Which technician is correct?

    a. A only
    b. B only
    c. Both A and B
    d. Neither A nor B

24. The discharge air temperature is warm and the pressure gauges shown represent which *most likely* cause?

    a. Low on refrigerant
    b. Lack of airflow through the condenser
    c. Defective compressor
    d. Icing of the evaporator

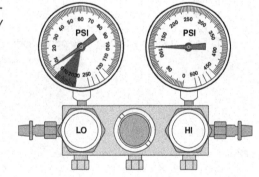

25. The airflow from the vents slows down after the vehicle has been driven for a while and the pressure gauges shown represent which *most likely* cause?

    a. Low on refrigerant
    b. Lack of airflow through the condenser
    c. Defective compressor
    d. Icing of the evaporator

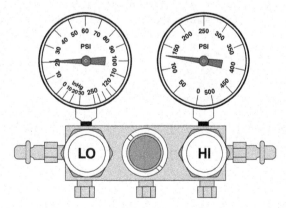

26. The discharge air temperature is warm and the pressure gauges shown represent which *most likely* cause?

   a. Overcharged with refrigerant
   b. Restricted liquid line or low on refrigerant
   c. Lack of airflow through the condenser
   d. Defective compressor

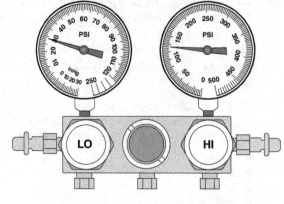

27. The discharge air temperature is cool with higher-than-normal low-side pressure along with excess high-side pressure. Which represents the *most likely* cause?

   a. Low on refrigerant
   b. Clogged condensate drain
   c. Excess refrigerant in the system
   d. Lack of airflow through the condenser

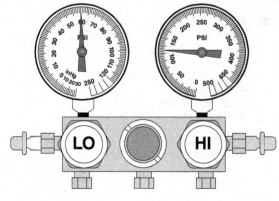

28. The discharge air temperature is warm or slightly cool. The pressure gauges shown represent which *most likely* cause?

   a. Low on refrigerant
   b. Defective compressor
   c. Excess refrigerant in the system
   d. Lack of airflow through the condenser

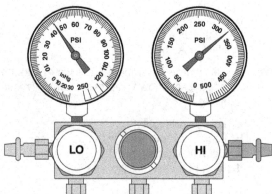

29. The owner of a vehicle equipped with an orifice tube-type air-conditioning system complains that the inside of the vehicle does not cool properly. The air-conditioning compressor clutch constantly cycles on and off whenever the air conditioning is on. Technician A says that the system is likely low on refrigerant. Technician B says that the most likely cause is an electrical short in the wiring to the air-conditioning compressor clutch. Which technician is correct?

   a. A only
   b. B only
   c. Both A and B
   d. Neither A nor B

30. Technician A says that on an air-conditioning system, the outlet temperature of the evaporator and the inlet temperature of the evaporator should be about the same if the system is fully charged. Technician B says that the outlet temperature will be colder if the system is undercharged. Which technician is correct?

a. A only
b. B only
c. Both A and B
d. Neither A nor B

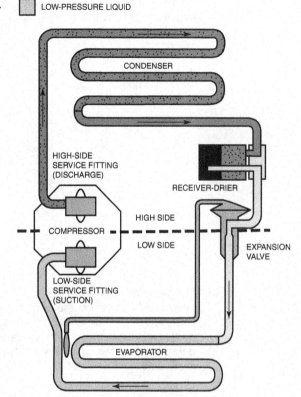

HIGH-PRESSURE VAPOR

HIGH-PRESSURE LIQUID

LOW-PRESSURE VAPOR

LOW-PRESSURE LIQUID

31. A customer states that the vehicle does not cool as well as it should. Technician A says that the system could be low on charge. Technician B says that if the electric radiator cooling fan is not functioning, this can cause a lack of cooling inside the vehicle. Which technician is correct?

a. A only
b. B only
c. Both A and B
d. Neither A nor B

32. Technician A says that some expansion valves can be tested using a CO_2 fire extinguisher to check if the cold will cause the valve to close. Technician B says that the operation of the orifice tube can be tested using a CO_2 fire extinguisher to cool the orifice tube and watching for a drop in low-side pressure. Which technician is correct?

a. A only
b. B only
c. Both A and B
d. Neither A nor B

33. An automotive air-conditioning system is being tested for a lack-of-cooling complaint. Both high and low pressures are higher than normal. Technician A says that the system is low on charge. Technician B says that the system is overcharged. Which technician is correct?

a. A only
b. B only
c. Both A and B
d. Neither A nor B

34. Technician A says that the low-side pressure of the air-conditioning system is best checked for leaks with the engine off. Technician B says that the low side of the system is best checked for leaks when the engine is on and the system is operating. Which technician is correct?

a. A only
b. B only
c. Both A and B
d. Neither A nor B

HIGH-PRESSURE VAPOR
HIGH-PRESSURE LIQUID
LOW-PRESSURE VAPOR
LOW-PRESSURE LIQUID

CONDENSER

HIGH-SIDE SERVICE FITTING (DISCHARGE)

RECEIVER-DRIER

HIGH SIDE

COMPRESSOR

LOW SIDE

EXPANSION VALVE

LOW-SIDE SERVICE FITTING (SUCTION)

EVAPORATOR

35. The high-side pressure is higher than normal. Technician A says that the compressor may be defective. Technician B says that the condenser may be clogged with leaves or other debris blocking the airflow. Which technician is correct?

a. A only
b. B only
c. Both A and B
d. Neither A nor B

36. A customer complained of a clear liquid leaking from underneath the vehicle on the passenger side after driving for a short time with the air conditioning on. The problem only occurs when the air conditioner is operating. Technician A says that the evaporator may be leaking. Technician B says that this may be normal condensed water formed on the cold evaporator coil. Which technician is correct?

a. A only
b. B only
c. Both A and B
d. Neither A nor B

37. Both the low and the high pressure are within normal ranges, yet the inside of the vehicle is not cooling. Technician A says that a partially clogged orifice tube could be the cause. Technician B says that too much refrigerant oil in the system could be the cause. Which technician is correct?

a. A only
b. B only
c. Both A and B
d. Neither A nor B

38. A technician is observing the pressure gauges when the engine is turned off and notices that the high-side and low-side pressures do not equalize quickly as they should. Technician A says that the orifice tube may be clogged. Technician B says that the desiccant may be saturated with moisture. Which technician is correct?

a. A only
b. B only
c. Both A and B
d. Neither A nor B

39. A customer states that the carpet on the floor on the passenger side is wet and noticed this when the air conditioning was first being used in the spring during damp weather. Which is the *most likely* cause?

   a. Evaporator refrigerant leak
   b. Clogged evaporator case drain
   c. Saturated desiccant in the drier
   d. Clogged screen in the accumulator

40. What two items must be installed or replaced when retrofitting a CFC-12 system to an HFC-134a system?

   a. Fitting adaptors and a label
   b. Compressor and O-rings
   c. Label and the condenser
   d. Fitting adaptors and the drier

41. A thermometer inserted into the A/C vents reads 44°F in the right and center vents, but 52°F in the left (driver) side vent. What is the *most likely* cause?

   a. Too much oil charge in the system
   b. A partially restricted orifice tube
   c. A misadjusted blend door
   d. A disconnected air discharge vent tube under the dash

42. Two technicians are discussing if a 1993 vehicle is equipped with an R-12 or an R-134a system. Technician A says that this information should be on an underhood label. Technician B says that the size and shape of the fittings can be used to help determine what refrigerant is in the system. Which technician is correct?

   a. A only
   b. B only
   c. Both A and B
   d. Neither A nor B

43. An air-conditioning performance test is being performed. All of the following should be done *except* _____.

   a. Turn blower to high speed
   b. Open the doors
   c. Set the controls for maximum cooling
   d. Place a thermometer in the inside air inlet door

44. Two technicians are discussing refrigerant oil. Technician A says that PAG oil comes in more than one viscosity and that using the wrong thickness of oil could cause damage to the compressor. Technician B says that refrigerant oil must be kept in a sealed container. Which technician is correct?

   a. A only
   b. B only
   c. Both A and B
   d. Neither A nor B

45. After the water pump was replaced and the cooling system refilled with coolant, the heater stopped providing hot air. Which is the *most likely* cause?

   a. The wrong concentration of antifreeze was installed
   b. An air pocket is trapped in the heater core
   c. A defective heater control valve
   d. A slipping water pump drive belt

46. A customer complained that the heat from the heater would come and go and vary with engine speed. What is the *most likely* cause?

   a. A defective thermostat
   b. A low coolant level
   c. A defective water (coolant) pump
   d. Incorrect antifreeze and water ratio

47. A service technician is replacing a water (coolant) pump. Technician A says that used coolant should be properly disposed of or kept for recycling. Technician B says that the used coolant should be re-used to refill the cooling system after the repair is completed. Which technician is correct?

    a. A only
    b. B only
    c. Both A and B
    d. Neither A nor B

48. A customer complained of lack of heat from the heater. A check of the cooling system shows that the upper radiator hose is not getting hot. Technician A says that the thermostat may be defective (stuck open). Technician B says that the cause could be a defective (always engaged) thermostat cooling fan. Which technician is correct?

    a. A only
    b. B only
    c. Both A and B
    d. Neither A nor B

49. A lack of heat from the heater is being diagnosed. Which is the *most likely* cause?

    a. A partially clogged radiator
    b. Hoses reversed on the heater core
    c. A partially clogged heater core
    d. A defective water pump

50. The temperature gauge approaches the red part of the temperature gauge (260°F or 127°C) if driven at slow speeds but does not overheat if driven at highway speeds. What is the *most likely* cause?

    a. Low coolant level
    b. Incorrect antifreeze/water mixture
    c. Defective water (coolant) pump
    d. Inoperative cooling fan

51. The coolant in a radiator froze when the temperature dropped to –20°F (–29°C). Technician A says that the 100% pure antifreeze in the cooling system could be the cause. Technician B says that too much water in the antifreeze could be the cause. Which technician is correct?

    a. A only
    b. B only
    c. Both A and B
    d. Neither A nor B

52. The procedure that should be used when refilling an empty cooling system includes the following: _____.

    a. determine capacity, and then fill the cooling system halfway with antifreeze and the rest of the way with water.
    b. fill completely with antifreeze, but mix a 50/50 solution for the overflow bottle.
    c. fill the block and one- half of the radiator with 100% pure antifreeze and fill the rest of the radiator with water.
    d. fill the radiator with antifreeze, start the engine, drain the radiator, and refill with a 50/50 mixture of antifreeze and water.

53. An engine coolant temperature is measured to be 210°F (100°C) even though the thermostat specification states that a 195 unit is installed in the vehicle. Technician A says the thermostat is defective. Technician B says that the radiator is clogged causing the temperature to be higher than normal. Which technician is correct?

    a. A only
    b. B only
    c. Both A and B
    d. Neither A nor B

54. Technician A says that the radiator should always be inspected for leaks and proper flow before installing a rebuilt engine. Technician B says that overheating during slow city driving can be due to a defective electric cooling fan. Which technician is correct?

   a. A only
   b. B only
   c. Both A and B
   d. Neither A nor B

55. The "hot" light on the dash is being discussed by two technicians. Technician A says that the light comes on if the cooling system temperature is too high for safe operation of the engine. Technician B says that the light comes on whenever there is a decrease (drop) in cooling system pressure. Which technician is correct?

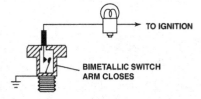

   a. A only
   b. B only
   c. Both A and B
   d. Neither A nor B

56. A customer complains that the heater works sometimes, but sometimes only cold air comes out while driving. Technician A says that the water pump is defective. Technician B says that the cooling system could be low on coolant. Which technician is correct?

   a. A only
   b. B only
   c. Both A and B
   d. Neither A nor B

57. A compressor clutch does not engage. Testing confirmed that there is 14 volts at the compressor clutch coil and a good ground connection. What is the *most likely* cause?

   a. Low refrigerant level
   b. An open pressure cycling switch
   c. A locked up compressor
   d. Excessive clutch air gap

58. A cooling system is being refilled following a repair. Technician A says to use conventional green antifreeze (ethylene glycol-based with silicate and phosphate additives) regardless of the type of coolant originally in the system. Technician B says to refill the system with the coolant specified for use by the vehicle manufacturer. Which technician is correct?

   a. A only
   b. B only
   c. Both A and B
   d. Neither A nor B

59. The windshield will not defog even though the defroster and/or the air-conditioning system seem to be functioning correctly. What is the *most likely* cause?

   a. A leaking heater core
   b. A leaking evaporator
   c. A stuck blend door
   d. Low on refrigerant charge

60. This radiator cap was discovered during routine service. Technician A says that the cooling system should be flushed and refilled with the specified coolant. Technician B says that the cap should be replaced. Which technician is correct?

   a. A only
   b. B only
   c. Both A and B
   d. Neither A nor B

61. The upper radiator hose collapses when the engine is turned off. Which is the *most likely* cause?

   a. A defective radiator cap
   b. A defective upper radiator hose
   c. A clogged radiator
   d. A low coolant level

62. A thermostatic fan clutch is leaking fluid. Technician A says that the unit should be replaced. Technician B says that it can cause the engine to overheat. Which technician is correct?

   a. A only
   b. B only
   c. Both A and B
   d. Neither A nor B

63. The water pump shown was removed from an engine that was running too hot and the impeller blades were found to be excessively worn. Technician A says that the cooling system should be flushed before being refilled with coolant. Technician B says that the specified coolant should be used to help avoid failure of the replacement pump. Which technician is correct?

   a. A only
   b. B only
   c. Both A and B
   d. Neither A nor B

64. A pressure gauge is installed on the radiator filler neck and the system pressurized to 15 psi. After a few minutes, the pressure was down to 5 psi according to the gauge on the tester. What is the *least likely* cause?

   a. A leaking water pump
   b. A leaking evaporator
   c. A leaking radiator hose
   d. A leaking heater core

HEATING AND AIR CONDITIONING (A7)

CATEGORY: REFRIGERATION SYSTEM COMPONENT DIAGNOSIS AND REPAIR

65. Both pressure gauge needles are oscillating rapidly. Which component is the *most likely* cause?

    a. The compressor (reed valves)
    b. The orifice tube (clogged)
    c. The expansion valve (stuck closed)
    d. The drier (desiccant bag is saturated with moisture)

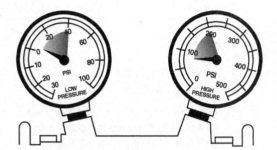

66. A noisy compressor is being discussed. Technician A says that the air-conditioning system could be low on lubricating oil. Technician B says that the system could be overcharged. Which technician is correct?

    a. A only
    b. B only
    c. Both A and B
    d. Neither A nor B

67. A front-wheel-drive vehicle has a broken condenser line. What other vehicle component may also be defective that could have caused the condenser line to break?

    a. A shock absorber
    b. An engine mount
    c. A cooling fan
    d. An air-conditioning compressor drive belt

68. Two technicians are discussing the replacement of an air-conditioning compressor clutch. Technician A says that the air gap should be adjusted. Technician B says the front compressor seal should also be replaced whenever replacing the clutch assembly. Which technician is correct?

    a. A only
    b. B only
    c. Both A and B
    d. Neither A nor B

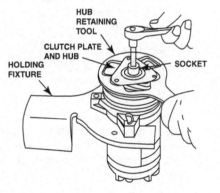

69. Technician A says that the air-conditioning compressor should operate when the controls are set to the heat position. Technician B says the air-conditioning compressor should operate when the controls are set to the defrost position. Which technician is correct?

    a. A only
    b. B only
    c. Both A and B
    d. Neither A nor B

70. The air-conditioning compressor clutch does not engage when the air-conditioning mode is selected and the engine is running. Technician A says that the system may be low on refrigerant charge. Technician B says the low-pressure switch may be electrically open. Which technician is correct?

    a. A only
    b. B only
    c. Both A and B
    d. Neither A nor B

71. An air-conditioning compressor is noisy whenever the clutch is engaged. Technician A says that the drive belt may be defective. Technician B says the compressor may be defective. Which technician is correct?

   a. A only
   b. B only
   c. Both A and B
   d. Neither A nor B

72. An oily area is discovered around the front clutch assembly of the air-conditioning compressor. Technician A says that the clutch is defective. Technician B says that the compressor seal could be leaking. Which technician is correct?

   a. A only
   b. B only
   c. Both A and B
   d. Neither A nor B

73. Technician A says that some refrigerant oil should be added to a replacement condenser to make sure that the system has the correct amount of oil. Technician B says that a specified viscosity of oil must be used to ensure proper lubrication of the compressor. Which technician is correct?

   a. A only
   b. B only
   c. Both A and B
   d. Neither A nor B

74. A condenser is being flushed. Technician A says that the old refrigerant oil can be mixed with and disposed of with used engine oil. Technician B says that refrigerant oil should be added to the new condenser in R-134a systems. Which technician is correct?

   a. A only
   b. B only
   c. Both A and B
   d. Neither A nor B

75. Technician A says that if an evaporator has been replaced, 2 or 3 ounces of refrigerant oil should be added to the system. Technician B says that the old evaporator should be drained and the oil measured to determine how much oil to add when installing the replacement evaporator. Which technician is correct?

   a. A only
   b. B only
   c. Both A and B
   d. Neither A nor B

76. Two technicians are discussing orifice tubes. Technician A says the inlet screen should be installed facing the evaporator inlet. Technician B says the inlet screen should be installed facing toward the condenser section of the system. Which technician is correct?

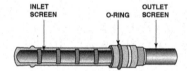

   a. A only
   b. B only
   c. Both A and B
   d. Neither A nor B

77. Technician A says that all HFC-134a systems use the same refrigerant oil. Technician B says that refrigerant oil, regardless of type, must be kept in a sealed container to keep it from absorbing moisture from the air. Which technician is correct?

   a. A only
   b. B only
   c. Both A and B
   d. Neither A nor B

78. What is being measured?

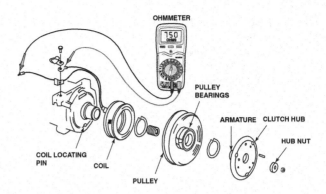

a. Available voltage at the compressor clutch
b. Voltage drop of the compressor clutch circuit
c. Capacitance of the radio suppressor
d. Resistance of the compressor clutch coil

79. What is this technician doing?

a. Installing the compressor drive pulley
b. Removing the compressor clutch assembly
c. Aligning the compressor drive pulley with the engine pulley
d. Separating the two halves of the compressor drive pulley

80. This special tool is being used to remove or install what air-conditioning component?

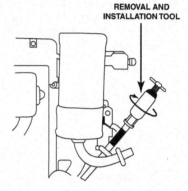

a. Low-pressure cutoff switch
b. High-pressure cutoff switch
c. Liquid line O-ring seal
d. Orifice tube

81. This special tool is used to perform what function?

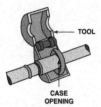

a. Install the O-rings
b. Remove the O-rings
c. Disconnect spring-lock-type couplings
d. Insert an orifice tube

82. A compressor is being replaced. Technician A says that the oil should be drained from the old compressor and measured so that the same amount of oil can be installed in the replacement compressor unless it is shipped with oil. Technician B says the drained oil should be installed in the new compressor to make sure that it is lubricated with the correct oil. Which technician is correct?

a. A only
b. B only
c. Both A and B
d. Neither A nor B

83. The capillary tube on the expansion valve has been bent shut as a result of a collision. Technician A says the expansion valve should be replaced. Technician B says that only the capillary tube needs to be replaced. Which technician is correct?

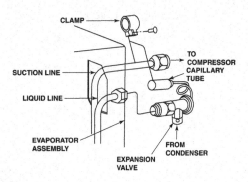

a. A only
b. B only
c. Both A and B
d. Neither A nor B

84. An automotive air-conditioning refrigerant system has been disconnected for several months and is now being returned to service. Technician A says that the receiver drier or accumulator should be replaced. Technician B says the system should be flushed and fresh refrigerant oil should be installed before evacuating and recharging the system. Which technician is correct?

a. A only
b. B only
c. Both A and B
d. Neither A nor B

85. A leaking evaporator is being replaced. Technician A says that 2 ounces or 3 ounces of refrigerant oil should be added to the new evaporator to allow for the amount that is trapped in the old evaporator. Technician B says that the condensate drain hole should be checked to see that it is open before completing the repair. Which technician is correct?

a. A only
b. B only
c. Both A and B
d. Neither A nor B

86. A compressor clutch does not engage even when a jumper wire is connected directly to the compressor connection. An ohmmeter check of the compressor clutch coil results in a reading of 14.7 kΩ. Technician A says the compressor clutch coil is okay and that the compressor itself is defective. Technician B says the compressor clutch coil is defective. Which technician is correct?

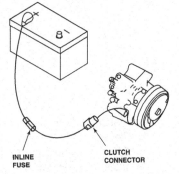

a. A only
b. B only
c. Both A and B
d. Neither A nor B

87. A replacement compressor clutch is being installed. All of the following should be checked except _____.

a. Air gap
b. Front seal leakage
c. Drive belt
d. Amount of refrigerant oil in the compressor

88. A clogged orifice tube is being replaced. Technician A says that the specified orifice tube should be used as a replacement because the orifice size can vary among the manufacturers. Technician B says that orifice tubes are sized by the outside diameter and that any orifice tube that fits will work okay. Which technician is correct?

a. A only
b. B only
c. Both A and B
d. Neither A nor B

HEATING AND AIR CONDITIONING (A7)

CATEGORY: OPERATING SYSTEMS AND RELATED CONTROLS DIAGNOSIS AND REPAIR

89. The A/C compressor clutch does not engage. Technician A says that an open high pressure cut-out switch could be the problem. Technician B says a blown compressor clutch diode could be the cause. Which technician is correct?

   a. A only
   b. B only
   c. Both A and B
   d. Neither A nor B

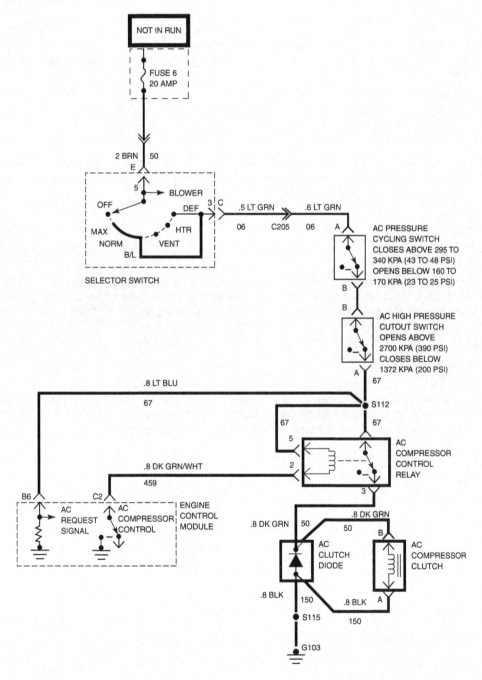

90. Technician A says that the air-conditioning compressor clutch may not engage if the steering wheel is being turned sharply and the vehicle is equipped with power steering. Technician B says that the air-conditioning compressor clutch may not engage if the refrigerant system is low on charge. Which technician is correct?

    a. A only
    b. B only
    c. Both A and B
    d. Neither A nor B

91. A "pop" is heard from the radio speakers occasionally when the defroster or air conditioning is selected. Technician A says that the compressor clutch clamping diode may be blown. Technician B says that the air-conditioning compressor clutch may have a poor electrical ground connection. Which technician is correct?

    a. A only
    b. B only
    c. Both A and B
    d. Neither A nor B

92. A reduced amount of airflow from the air-conditioning vents is being discussed. Technician A says that the evaporator could be clogged as a result of a small refrigerant leak causing oil to trap and hold dirt. Technician B says that the blower motor ground connection could have excessive voltage drop. Which technician is correct?

    a. A only
    b. B only
    c. Both A and B
    d. Neither A nor B

93. Technician A says that an electrical open in the low-pressure switch can prevent the compressor from working. Technician B says that the compressor may not operate at low outside temperatures depending on the pressure sensed by the low-pressure switch. Which technician is correct?

    a. A only
    b. B only
    c. Both A and B
    d. Neither A nor B

94. Technician A says that the voltage to the air-conditioning compressor may be turned off when some vehicles are accelerating rapidly. Technician B says that a fault in the power steering pressure switch could prevent the air-conditioning compressor from operating. Which technician is correct?

    a. A only
    b. B only
    c. Both A and B
    d. Neither A nor B

95. An automatic air-conditioning system is being diagnosed for cooler than the set temperature. Technician A says that a blocked inside air temperature sensor could be the cause. Technician B says that a blocked sun load sensor could be the cause. Which technician is correct?

    a. A only
    b. B only
    c. Both A and B
    d. Neither A nor B

96. What is the meter measuring?

    a. Resistance of the ECT sensor
    b. Voltage signal of the ECT sensor
    c. Voltage output from the PCM
    d. Resistance of the electrical connector

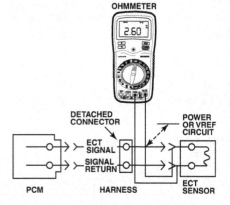

97. An HVAC relay is being checked using a DMM set to read ohms. Technician A says the relay being tested is okay. Technician B says the relay being tested is defective (open). Which technician is correct?

    a. A only
    b. B only
    c. Both A and B
    d. Neither A nor B

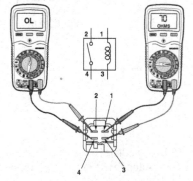

98. A blower motor stopped working on all speeds. A technician tested the motor touching a jumper wire from the battery positive (+) terminal to the motor power terminal and the motor did run. Technician A says that the motor should be checked using a fused jumper lead to test for excessive current draw. Technician B says that the resistor pack and/or relay are likely to be defective. Which technician is correct?

    a. A only
    b. B only
    c. Both A and B
    d. Neither A nor B

99. A blower motor is drawing more than the specified current. Technician A says that the blower motor ground connection could be corroded. Technician B says that the blower relay is shorted. Which technician is correct?

    a. A only
    b. B only
    c. Both A and B
    d. Neither A nor B

100. An older vehicle is being diagnosed. The airflow from the blower motor goes mostly to the defrost ducts regardless of the position of the controls. Technician A says that the recirculation door may be stuck. Technician B says that the vacuum source for the mode doors may be leaking. Which technician is correct?

    a. A only
    b. B only
    c. Both A and B
    d. Neither A nor B

101. A blower is running slowly on all speeds. What is the *most likely* cause?

    a. A blown resistor
    b. Worn/dry bearings in the motor
    c. A bad fan switch
    d. Open ignition switch

102. The blower motor operates at low speed regardless of the position selected on the blower motor switch. Technician A says an open thermal limiter could be the cause. Technician B says an open at the "LO" contact of the blower motor switch could be the cause. Which technician is correct?

a. A only
b. B only
c. Both A and B
d. Neither A nor B

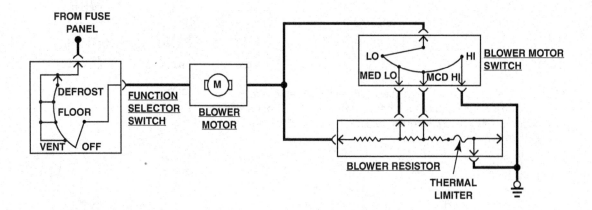

103. A vehicle equipped with automatic climate control was involved in a minor front-end collision. Afterward the system stopped cooling. What is the *most likely* cause?

a. Reduced airflow through the radiator
b. Air trapped in the refrigerant system
c. A defective blower motor resistor
d. A broken ambient air temperature sensor

104. The high-pressure electrical switch connector becomes disconnected. What is the *most likely* result?

a. The air conditioning will be cooler than the set temperature
b. The air conditioning will be warmer than the set temperature
c. The air-conditioning compressor clutch will not engage
d. The air-conditioning compressor clutch will cycle rapidly

105. Two technicians are discussing the schematic shown. Technician A says that all three switches must be closed before the air-conditioning compressor clutch will engage. Technician B says that the low-pressure switch is closed when the system pressure is very low (almost 0 psi). Which technician is correct?

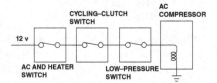

a. A only
b. B only
c. Both A and B
d. Neither A nor B

106. What service check is being performed?

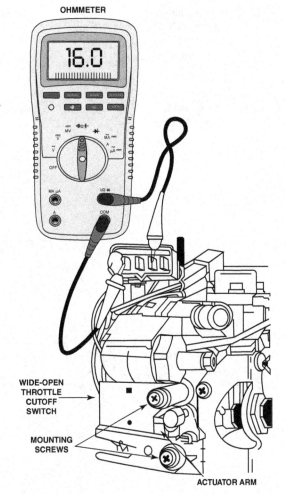

OHMMETER

16.0

WIDE-OPEN
THROTTLE
CUTOFF
SWITCH

MOUNTING
SCREWS

ACTUATOR ARM

a. Checking the voltage of the throttle switch
b. Checking the continuity of the wide-open-throttle switch
c. Measuring the current flow through the throttle cutoff switch
d. Measuring the resistance of the compressor clutch coil

107. An A/C system operating with an outside air temperature of 90°F shows a low pressure cause reading of 7 PSI and a high-side pressure reading of 108 PSI. What is the *most likely* cause?

a. An open inside temperature sensor
b. Low refrigerant level
c. A defective blend air
d. An open low pressure switch

108. An A/C system is being tested and excessive high-side pressure has been measured. Any of these could be the cause *except* _____.

a. a plugged expansion valve
b. restricted airflow through the condenser
c. an open A/C compressor diode
d. an A/C system being overcharged with refrigerant

109. In the dual climate control system shown, the temperatures for the driver and passenger are regulated by controlling which components or system?

a. Airflow through the evaporator and heater core
b. Air-conditioning pressures to the left and right side evaporator
c. Amount of coolant flowing through the heater core
d. Airflow from the outside to the left (driver's) side and right (passenger's) side

110. Two technicians are discussing the air-conditioning control circuit shown. Technician A says that the computer (ECM) controls the operation of the compressor clutch. Technician B says that the compressor clutch will not engage if the refrigerant pressure is below 8 psi or higher than 430 psi. Which technician is correct?

   a. A only
   b. B only
   c. Both A and B
   d. Neither A nor B

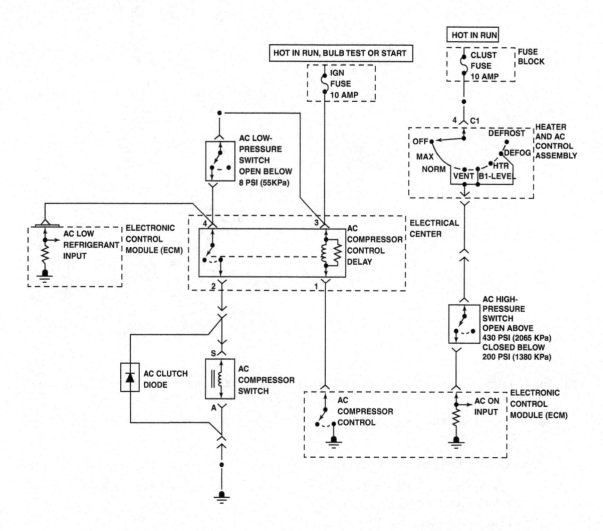

HEATING AND AIR CONDITIONING (A7)

CATEGORY: HEATING, VENTILATION, A/C (HVAC) AND ENGINE COOLING SYSTEM SERVICE, DIAGNOSIS, AND REPAIR

1. **The correct answer is c.** Both technicians are correct. Technician A is correct because debris from the old compressor can become trapped on the orifice tube causing a restriction limiting the flow of refrigerant into the evaporator. Technician B is correct because a leak would cause a lack of cooling due to less refrigerant flowing through the evaporator. Answers a, b, and d are not correct because both technicians are correct.

2. **The correct answer is a.** The contaminated refrigerant should be recovered and sent to a separate container clearly labeled to contain contaminated refrigerant. Answer b is not correct because allowing refrigerant to escape into the atmosphere is illegal. Answer c is not correct because contaminated refrigerant should never be combined with usable refrigerant (virgin or recycled) because then the contamination is expanded and affects all of the refrigerant stored together. Answer d is not correct because even though this may work, the refrigerant will leak from the system and the only proper repair is to repair the leak which requires that the refrigerant be removed from the system.

3. **The correct answer is c.** Both technicians are correct. Technician A is correct because removing the blower motor resistor pack is a very efficient method to use to get access to the evaporator for leak detection. Technician B is correct because the condensate drain is located in the bottom of the evaporator housing and would provide access to the evaporator for leak detection. Answers a, b, and d are not correct because both technicians are correct.

4. **The correct answer is b.** A stuck idle air control (IAC) will not increase the idle speed necessary to keep the engine operating correctly when the load of the air-conditioning compressor is engaged. Answer a is not correct because a shorted engine coolant temperature (ECT) sensor would most likely trigger a diagnostic trouble code and may affect engine operation but not just when the air conditioning is engaged. Answer c is not correct because a clogged orifice tube would reduce the air-conditioning system effectiveness but would not affect the idle speed of the engine. Answer d is not correct because even though an overcharged air-conditioning system would cause a greater load to be placed on the engine, it is not as likely to cause an engine idle problem as answer b.

5. **The correct answer is d.** The least likely cause of a lack of cooling is a partially blocked condensate drain. A blocked condensate drain will cause an overflow of water of the evaporator case causing the floor of the passenger side to get wet but is unlikely to reduce cooling. Answers a, b, and c are not correct because all of these could cause reduced cooling.

6. **The correct answer is d.** Neither technician is correct. Technician A is not correct because the pressure displayed on the gauges indicates that the compressor is not engaged. The pressure of R-134a at 80°F (27°C) is about 87 psi, indicating that the system has equalized and is not operating. Even though the system may have a partially clogged orifice tube, this cannot be determined by the pressure gauges because the compressor is not engaged. Technician B is not correct because even though the system may be undercharged, this condition cannot be determined because the compressor is not engaged. Answer c is not correct because neither technician is correct.

7. **The correct answer is c.** The most likely cause of a cool compressor and a higher-than-normal high-side pressure is an overcharge of refrigerant. A compressor should normally be warm to the touch. Answer a is not correct because a lack of oil in the system would tend to make the compressor operate hotter than normal rather than cool, due to the lack of lubrication. Answer b is not correct because an undercharged system results in lower-than-normal high-side pressures rather than higher than normal. Answer d is not correct because a restricted condenser would most likely cause the compressor to operate hotter than normal rather than cool to the touch.

8. **The correct answer is d.** Neither technician is correct. It is normal for the discharge line to be hot to the touch on a properly operating air-conditioning system. Technician A is not correct because a low charge would reduce the temperature of the discharge line. Technician B is not correct because a worn compressor would create less-than-normal heat and temperature of the discharge line. Answer c is not correct because neither technician is correct.

9. **The correct answer is b.** The most likely cause of bubbles (foam) in the sight glass is a low refrigerant charge. Answer a is not correct because nothing, or oil streaks, will be observed in the sight glass if the system is empty of refrigerant. Answer c is not correct because if the desiccant bags were ruptured, the sight glass will usually be clear when the system is properly charged or overcharged. Answer d is not correct because water is absorbed in the refrigerant and is not visible but will create acids, which will harm all components of the system.

10. **The correct answer is b.** Technician B is correct because a fungicide is necessary to kill fungus and mildew growth that can grow on the evaporator fins due to the moist environment. Technician A is not correct because even though most mouthwash contains alcohol, it will not be effective killing fungus and mildew. Answers c and d are not correct because Technician B only is correct.

11. **The correct answer is b.** Air is a non-condensable gas and adds pressure to the container yet it does not contribute to the cooling capacity of the refrigerant. If the pressure is higher, as shown on the chart, it contains non-condensable gases. Answer a is not correct because frost on the container is an indication that refrigerant is leaving the container causing the pressure and temperature to drop, and not an indication of the presence of air (non-condensable gases). Answer c is not correct because the weight will not indicate the pressure of air, just the amount of refrigerant that is in the container. Answer d is not correct because air can be detected by comparing the pressure inside the container to a chart, which shows what the pressure should be for a container of a certain temperature. If the pressure is higher than the chart indicates, non-condensable gases are present in the container.

Maximum Container Pressure					
Temperature		R-12 Pressure		R-134A Pressure	
°F	°C	psi	kPa	psi	kPa
70	21.1	80	552	76	524
75	23.9	87	600	83	572
80	26.7	96	662	91	627
85	29.5	102	703	100	690
90	32.2	110	758	109	752
95	35.0	118	814	118	814
100	37.8	127	876	129	889
105	40.6	136	937	139	958
110	43.4	146	1007	151	1041

12. **The correct answer is a.** Technician A is correct because any refrigerant oil that is removed from the system during the recovery process must be measured to be assured that the proper amount of oil is in the system when recharged. Technician B is not correct because the refrigerant oil might contain hydrofluorocarbons (R-134a) or chlorofluorocarbons (R-12) making the oil hazardous and unable to be recycled as conventional waste oil. Answers c and d are not correct because Technician A only is correct.

13. **The correct answer is b.** The refrigerant should be identified at the start of the A/C system service before it is recovered to guard against the possibility of contaminating the storage container or the recovery/recycling equipment with an unknown refrigerant. Answers a, c, and d are not correct because the refrigerant should be checked before any service work is performed on the system.

14. **The correct answer is a.** The refrigerant system should be evacuated to a level of 28 in. Hg or higher, for at least 45 minutes to be sure that the moisture is boiled out of the system. Answers b, c, and d are all possible and should be done, but the question asks what values are the minimum that should be achieved to be sure that the moisture is boiled out of the system before recharging with refrigerant.

15. **The correct answer is d.** Refrigerant should be stored in a container that meets Department of Transportation (DOT) standards because it will be transported. Answer a is not correct because the container has to meet DOT, not EPA standards to be able to be shipped. Answers b and c are not correct because even though refrigerant can be kept in the recovery or recycling machine, eventually it must be transferred to another storage container.

16. **The correct answer is a.** Before refrigerant is recovered, a refrigerant identifier and a sealant identifier should be used to avoid the possibility that the system has the wrong refrigerant or a mixture of refrigerants. Answer b is not correct because the wrong refrigerant could be exposed to the pressure gauges and/or equipment used to check high and low pressures. Answer c is not correct because even though the Schrader valves should be checked, it is not the first item that should be done before recovering refrigerant. Answer d is not correct because even though starting the engine and allowing the system to operate for a few minutes will not do any harm, it is not a necessary first step before refrigerant recovery.

17. **The correct answer is b.** The best answer is to recover the refrigerant into a separate container labeled unknown and to dispose of the contents of the container when full through a licensed recycler. Answer a is not correct because the unknown refrigerant can contaminate the recovery/recycling equipment. Answer c is not correct because the unknown refrigerant will not be or should not be purged from the system. Answer d is not correct because unknown refrigerant is not the same as non-condensable gases (air).

18. **The correct answer is a.** Technician A is correct because according to the chart, the container pressure should not exceed 91 psi (627 kPa) unless there is some air in the tank which contributes to the pressure but does not act as a refrigerant. The tank should be vented until the pressure is restored to normal. Technician B is not correct because additional refrigerant would not reduce the pressure in the storage container. Answers c and d are not correct because Technician A only is correct.

19. **The correct answer is c.** According to the chart, a vacuum of at least 29 in. Hg is necessary to boil moisture from the air-conditioning system at a temperature of 78°F (26°C). Answers a and b are not correct because the levels of vacuum will not be low enough to cause any trapped moisture in the system to boil. Answer d is not correct because even though 30 in. Hg will cause any moisture in the system to boil, it is not the minimum vacuum that is necessary to boil moisture out of the system.

20. **The correct answer is c.** The latest current standard machine for use with HFO-1234yf (R-1234yf) meets SAE standard J2843. Answer a is not correct because J1770 is the older standard for use with R-12 and R-134 and no longer meets the latest standards for accuracy. Answer b (J 2210) is not correct because this standard does not meet the accuracy requirements of the latest standard. Answer d (J2851) is not correct because this standard is used for R-1234yf and not for R-134a.

21. **The correct answer is a.** Technician A only is correct because a system that is undercharged (low on refrigerant) will keep the compressor from creating pressure. As a result of the low amount of refrigerant, the cooling ability is reduced. Technician B is not correct because an inoperative cooling fan will cause the discharge pressure to increase rather than decrease because the air will not be forced through the condenser, thereby not allowing the heat to be transferred from the refrigerant to the outside air. Answers c and d are not correct because Technician A only is correct.

22. **The correct answer is d.** Neither technician is correct. Technician A is not correct because the line after the orifice tube should be cool indicating that the refrigerant has passed through a restriction and is expanding. The temperature also gets cooler as the refrigerant absorbs heat to change states from a liquid to a gas. Technician B is not correct because a clogged or partially clogged orifice tube would stop the flow of refrigerant causing the tube to be hot only on one side of the orifice tube. Answers a, b, and c are not correct because neither technician is correct.

23. **The correct answer is b.** Technician B only is correct because frost indicates that the component is cold and this can be caused if a restriction forces the high-pressure gas from the condenser to expand, thereby dropping the pressure and the temperature of the refrigerant as it flows through the restricted areas. Technician A is not correct because even though hot humid weather can contribute to frost formation, it is not normal for the section between the condenser and the receiver/drier to be cold. This section of the system should be warm because the refrigerant is a high-pressure liquid in this section. Answers c and d are not correct because Technician B only is correct.

24. **The correct answer is a.** An insufficient amount of refrigerant metered into the evaporator will cause low pressure on both the low-side gauge and the high-side gauge and warmer-than-normal discharge air temperature. Answer b is not correct because a lack of airflow through the condenser will cause the high-side pressure to be higher than normal. Answer c is not correct because while a defective compressor will cause a lower-than-normal high-side pressure gauge reading, it will not cause the low-side gauge to read lower than normal. Answer d is not correct because icing on the evaporator would be the result of a fault in the system that would allow the evaporator temperature to drop below freezing creating the ice, which would block the airflow.

25. **The correct answer is d.** An icing evaporator is the most likely cause to reduce the airflow and the heat load, which causes both low- and high-side pressures to be lower than normal. A fault in the temperature control is the most likely cause for the icing of the evaporator. Answer a is not correct because even though a low refrigerant level could cause both pressure gauges to read lower than normal, it would not cause the airflow to decrease after operating for a while. Answer b is not correct because even though a lack of airflow through the condenser would cause a lack of proper cooling, this condition would create an increase, rather than a decrease in high-pressure side and could not cause a decrease in airflow through the vents inside the vehicle. Answer c is not correct because even though a defective compressor could cause lower-than-normal pressure gauge readings, it could not cause a reduction in airflow through the vents.

26. **The correct answer is b.** A restricted liquid line or a low refrigerant charge can cause this symptom and gauge readings, due to the fact that an inadequate amount of refrigerant is being metered into the evaporator. Answer a is not correct because the pressure gauge readings are too low if the system were overcharged. Answer c is not correct because the pressure gauge readings would be higher than normal, rather than lower than normal if there were a lack of proper airflow through the condenser. Answer d is not correct because a defective compressor would cause a higher-than-normal low-side pressure reading, not a reading that is lower than normal.

27. **The correct answer is c.** Excess refrigerant is the most likely cause of higher-than-normal low-side pressure gauge reading with a higher-than-normal high-side pressure reading. Too much refrigerant is being metered into the evaporator or the compressor is not pulling it out, which can occur on some systems that use a variable-displacement compressor. Answer a is not correct because a low refrigerant charge would cause the discharge air to be warm and both gauge pressure readings below normal. Answer b is not correct because a clogged condensate drain would cause water to overflow the evaporator housing and flow onto the floor of the vehicle and would not create higher-than-normal pressure on the low-side gauge. Answer d is not correct because a lack of airflow through the condenser would cause a higher-than-normal high-side pressure reading and not a higher-than-normal low-side pressure reading.

28. **The correct answer is d.** A clogged condenser coil or other obstruction that causes a lack of airflow through the condenser is the most likely cause of the warm discharge air temperature and the higher-than-normal pressures. Answer a is not correct because even though a system that is low on refrigerant will reduce cooling, the pressures would be lower, rather than higher than normal. Answer b is not correct because a defective compressor would cause the high-side pressure to be lower than normal, not higher than normal. Answer c is not correct because excess refrigerant would cause the discharge air temperature to be cool and a higher-than-normal low-side pressure and a normal high-side pressure rather than being above normal with a lack of cooling.

29. **The correct answer is a.** Technician A only is correct because a rapidly cycling compressor clutch is a common symptom of an air-conditioning system that is low on refrigerant. The compressor engages when the temperature (and pressure) rises, and then stops when the pressure is low. The low pressure is a result of a lack of refrigerant. Technician B is not correct because an electrical short would likely cause a fuse to blow and prevent the compressor clutch from operating entirely. Answers c and d are not correct because Technician A only is correct.

30. **The correct answer is a.** Technician A is correct because if the system is fully charged, the inlet of the evaporator, after the orifice tube, will be about the same temperature as the outlet of the evaporator. Technician B is not correct because the evaporator outlet temperature will be warmer than the evaporator inlet temperature if the system is low on refrigerant. Answers c and d are not correct because Technician A only is correct.

31. **The correct answer is c.** Both technicians are correct. Technician A is correct because if the system is partially charged (low on refrigerant), the cooling capacity is reduced and the system will not be able to properly cool the vehicle. Technician B is correct because if the cooling fan is not functioning, the condenser may not be able to dissipate the heat resulting in higher pressures and temperatures in the system and reduced cooling, especially in slow city-type driving conditions. Answers a, b, and d are not correct because both technicians are correct.

32. **The correct answer is a.** Technician A is correct because a cold blast from a CO_2 fire extinguisher onto the sensing bulb will cause the expansion valve to close if the sensing bulb and valve are working correctly. When the expansion valve closes, the low-side pressure gauge reading will go into a vacuum indicating that the valve closed. Technician B is not correct because an orifice tube system does not use a temperature-sensing bulb and would, therefore, be unaffected by the blast of a CO_2 fire extinguisher. Answers c and d are not correct because Technician A only is correct.

33. **The correct answer is b.** Technician B is correct because higher-than-normal pressures on both low-side and high-side gauges and warmer-than-normal vent discharge temperature are a symptom of air trapped in the system. Technician A is not correct because the pressure would be lower than normal, not higher than normal, if the system was low on refrigerant. Answers c and d are not correct because Technician B only is correct.

34. **The correct answer is a.** Technician A is correct because when the engine is off, the compressor stops and the high and low pressure in the system become equalized. This means that both the high-side pressure and the low-side pressure will be 70 psi at 70°F (21°C). Because the low-side increases (from normal of about 30 psi to 70 psi with the system off), it is more likely for leaks to be detected due to the higher pressure. Technician B is not correct because while the high side is best checked with the engine running and the system in operation, the low side is best checked with the engine off. Answers c and d are not correct because Technician A only is correct.

35. **The correct answer is b.** Technician B is correct because a partially blocked condenser will prevent air from removing the heat and create higher-than-normal high-side pressure. Technician A is not correct because a defective compressor is most likely to cause lower-than-normal high-side pressure due to its inability to compress the high temperature vapor. Answers c and d are not correct because Technician B only is correct.

36. **The correct answer is b.** Technician B is correct because when hot humid air comes in contact with the cooler evaporator coils, the moisture condenses into liquid water. This water flows out of the bottom of the evaporator housing through a small hole or opening and drips onto the ground. Technician A is not correct because if the evaporator were leaking, the refrigerant would vaporize and disappear as soon as it escaped from the sealed refrigerant system. Answers c and d are not correct because Technician B only is correct.

37. **The correct answer is b.** Technician B is correct because oil displaces refrigerant and even though the pressures are within the normal range, a lack of cooling will occur if excessive refrigerant oil has been installed in the system because the oil acts as an insulator on the inside of the evaporator and condenser. Technician A is not correct because even though a partially clogged orifice tube will likely cause the lack of proper cooling, the high-side pressure will be lower than normal (not normal as stated) due to the lack of refrigerant flow through the compressor due to the restriction. Answers c and d are not correct because Technician B only is correct.

38. **The correct answer is a.** Technician A is correct because the orifice tube connects the low and high-side pressure areas of the system. A partially clogged orifice tube is the most likely cause for a slow equalization of pressure after the engine stops. Technician B is not correct because a saturated desiccant will not cause the pressures to equalize slowly even though it could cause excessive moisture buildup to occur in the system leading to acid formation. Answers c and d are not correct because Technician A only is correct.

39. **The correct answer is b.** Water is created when warm moist air comes in contact with the cold evaporator. This water should drain out of the evaporator housing and fall onto the ground during normal air-conditioning operation unless the drain hole is clogged and the water overflows onto the floor on the passenger side of the vehicle. Answer a is not correct because an evaporator refrigerant leak would cause a discharged condition and the refrigerant would supply evaporate into the atmosphere and would not cause moisture to form on the carpet. Answer c is not correct because a saturated desiccant in the drier would allow moisture to build up inside the sealed system and would not cause water to form and drip onto the floor of the vehicle. Answer d is not correct because a clogged screen would reduce the flow of refrigerant within the system and could not cause water to drip onto the floor of the vehicle.

40. **The correct answer is a.** The gauge fittings must be unique to prevent the possibility of cross contamination between the two types of refrigerants and a label must be attached under the hood identifying the date and who did the retrofit. Answer b is not correct even though many manufacturers recommend that all of the O-rings be replaced. The compressor does not need to be replaced in most cases and therefore, it is not a required item. Answer c is not correct because even though the label must be installed, the condenser is not a required component that must be installed even though some vehicle manufacturers specify that it should be replaced. Answer d is not correct because the fittings must be replaced but the drier does not need to be replaced in all cases even though it is often recommended that it be replaced when retrofitting the system from R-12 to R-134a.

41. **The correct answer is d.** A disconnected air discharge vent tube is the most likely cause for the discharge air temperature to be greater in one vent. Answer a is not correct because too much refrigerant oil in the system would reduce the cooling for all vents and could not affect just the left side discharge vent temperature. Answer b is not correct because while a partially clogged orifice tube will cause a lack of cooling, it cannot cause a lack of cooling out of just one discharge air vent. Answer c is not correct because a blend door is used to adjust the amount of air that flows across the heater core after it has flowed through the evaporator to control the temperature of the discharge air and is not likely to cause a difference in air temperature at just one vent opening.

42. **The correct answer is c.** Both technicians are correct. Technician A is correct because the vehicle manufacturer must supply a label that identifies the type of refrigerant system and the recharge capacity. Technician B is correct because R-12 and R-134a pressure gauge fittings are unique. Answers a, b, and d are not correct because both technicians are correct.

43. **The correct answer is d.** A thermometer does not need to be placed in the inside air inlet door to perform an air-conditioning performance test because this would simply measure the temperature of the air being drawn back into the system to be cooled and would not be an important factor regarding the performance of the system. Answers a, b, and c are not correct because to perform an air-conditioning performance test, the blower should be on high (answer a), the doors should be open (answer b), and the controls set for maximum cooling (answer c).

44. **The correct answer is c.** Both technicians are correct. Technician A is correct because the oil specified by the vehicle manufacturer or the compressor manufacturer should be used to insure proper lubrication and this includes the specified type and viscosity of refrigerant oil. Technician B is correct because refrigerant oil readily absorbs moisture from the air and must be stored in an air-tight container to avoid moisture contamination. Answers a, b, and d are not correct because both technicians are correct.

45. **The correct answer is b.** Answer b is correct because if air is trapped in the heater core, the coolant cannot flow through and provide heat. This is a common problem because the heater core is usually located at the highest part of the cooling system and air always travels upwards. Answer a is not correct because even though the incorrect concentration of antifreeze in the coolant could affect the freezing protection and heat transfer ability of the coolant, it is unlikely to cause a lack of heat from the heater. Answer c is not correct because even though a defective heater control valve (stuck closed) could cause a lack of heat from the heater, it is unlikely to fail at the same time as the water pump repair and coolant replacement procedure. Answer d is not correct because even though a slipping water pump drive belt could reduce the flow of coolant through the system, it is unlikely to cause a lack of heat from the heater.

46. **The correct answer is b.** The most likely cause is a low coolant level causing coolant to flow through the heater core occasionally. Because the heater core is usually higher in the system than the engine block and the heater hoses create some resistance to coolant flow, most of the available coolant will flow through and protect the engine. Answer a is not correct because even though a defective thermostat could cause a lack of heat from the heater, it is unlikely to cause some heat at times and no heat at other times. Answer c is not correct because while a defective water pump could cause a lack of circulation, which could reduce the amount of heat from the heater, it is unlikely to cause the heat to come and go intermittently. Answer d is not correct because, while an incorrect antifreeze to water mixture could cause corrosion or other cooling system related problems, it is unlikely to cause a lack of heat concern.

47. **The correct answer is a.** Technician A is correct because used coolant contains metals that were absorbed from the engine and cooling system components during engine operation and, therefore, should be recycled by sending to an off-site recycling company or by doing it on-site using a coolant recycling machine. Technician B is not correct because most vehicle manufacturers advise against reusing coolant and usually specify that new coolant be used when refilling the cooling system. Answers c and d are not correct because Technician A only is correct.

48. **The correct answer is a.** Technician A is correct because the temperature of the coolant is regulated by the thermostat, and if it is stuck open or partially open, the coolant temperature will be lower than normal. Technician B is not correct because the fan helps remove heat from the radiator but does not regulate the coolant temperature. Answers c and d are not correct because Technician A only is correct.

49. The correct answer is c. The most likely cause of a lack of heat from the heater is a partially clogged heater core. Answer a is not correct because a clogged radiator would prevent the proper cooling of the coolant and would not cause a decrease in heater performance. Answer b is not correct because even though coolant flow could be affected slightly if the heater hoses were reversed, this condition would not prevent heat coming from the heater. Answer d is not correct because even though a defective water pump could reduce the flow of coolant through the system, it is not the most likely cause of a lack of heat concern.

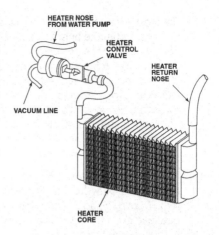

50. The correct answer is d. An inoperative cooling fan is the most likely cause of overheating at slow speeds only because at highway speeds, normal airflow permits proper heat transfer from the radiator. Answer a is not correct because even though a low coolant level could cause overheating, it is not the most likely cause of overheating only when the vehicle is being driven at slow speeds. Answer b is not correct because even though an incorrect antifreeze/water mixture could cause cooling system problems, it is unlikely to cause overheating. Answer c is not correct because even though a defective water pump could cause overheating, it is unlikely to cause overheating only when the vehicle is being driven at slow speeds.

51. The correct answer is c. Both technicians are correct. Technician A is correct because pure 100% antifreeze will freeze from –8°F to +8°F (–22°C to –13°C), unless it is mixed with water. Technician B is correct because too much water added to the coolant could raise the freezing point of the coolant. Answers a, b, and d are not correct because both technicians are correct.

52. The correct answer is a. Most vehicle manufacturers recommend that a 50/50 mix of antifreeze and water be used for the cooling system. Filling half the system with 100% antifreeze and the rest with water will result in a 50/50 mix. Answers b and c are incorrect because these methods will not result in a 50/50 antifreeze to water mix. Answer d will result in a 50/50 mix if all of the coolant can be drained from the system before refilling it with the 50/50 mix. However, this method uses more antifreeze coolant than is necessary and therefore is not the recommended method and not the best answer to this question.

53. The correct answer is d. Neither technician is correct. Technician A is not correct because 210°F is within the normal operating range of a 195°F thermostat, which starts to open at 195°F and is fully open 20° higher or by 215°F. Technician B is not correct because even though a clogged radiator can cause the engine to overheat, the temperature of the coolant is within the normal range and a clogged radiator is not likely. Answers a, b, and c are not correct because neither technician is correct.

54. The correct answer is c. Both technicians are correct. Technician A is correct because the radiator should always be checked for proper operation before using it in a vehicle with a new or rebuilt engine. Technician B is correct because overheating during slow driving could be caused by an inoperative electric cooling fan. Answers a, b, and d are not correct because both technicians are correct.

55. The correct answer is a. Technician A is correct because the HOT light (engine coolant temperature warning lamp) will come on at about 258°F (125°C) to warn the driver that the engine coolant temperature is too high for safe engine operation. Technician B is not correct because the warning light does not react to cooling system pressure, just temperature. Answers c and d are not correct because only Technician A is correct.

56. The correct answer is b. Technician B is correct because the heater will have coolant flowing through the core when the water pump is operating slowly such as during engine idle. However, when the engine speed increases, the coolant will be taking the path of lower resistance and bypass the heater core unless the coolant level is properly filled. Technician A is not correct because even though the water pump could have worn impeller blades, the most likely cause is low coolant level. Answers c and d are not correct because only Technician B is correct.

57. **The correct answer is d.** Because there is a battery voltage and a good ground at the A/C compressor clutch coil, the only possible answer to why the clutch does not engage would be an open in the coil (not one of the answers) or excessive air gap in the clutch. Answer a is not correct because even though a low refrigerant level could cause the A/C compressor to not engage, in this case there was power and ground applied indicating that all of the conditions needed for operation have been met including proper refrigerant level. Answer b is not correct because while an open pressure cycling switch could cause the A/C compressor to not engage, in this case there was power and ground applied indicating that all of the conditions needed for operation have been met including the proper operation of the pressure switch. Answer c is not correct because while a locked up compressor could keep the system from operating, it could not be the cause of the clutch not engaging.

58. **The correct answer is b.** Technician B is correct because vehicle manufacturers specify a variety of coolants based on engine design as well as the materials used in the engine and cooling system. The specified coolant should be used to ensure proper service life. Technician A is not correct because even though conventional green antifreeze can provide the necessary cooling system protection against freezing, it may contain additives that are not compatible with the material used in the engine or cooling system. Answers c and d are not correct because Technician B only is correct.

59. **The correct answer is a.** A leaking heater core will cause the fogging of the windshield due to the pressure in the cooling system forcing the coolant through a hole in the heater core and through the ducts onto the windshield. Answer b is not correct because a leak in the evaporator would allow refrigerant to escape reducing the effectiveness of the air conditioning but will not cause the windshield to become fogged. Answer c is not correct because while a stuck blend door could affect the temperature of the discharge air into the vehicle, it cannot cause fogging of the windshield. Answer d is not correct because if the air-conditioning system were low on refrigerant charge, the cooling of the interior would be reduced but would not cause the windshield to become fogged.

60. **The correct answer is c.** Both technicians are correct. Technician A is correct because the system is obviously rusty and the system should be thoroughly flushed before being refilled with the proper coolant. Technician B is correct because the deposits cannot be thoroughly cleaned from the radiator cap and therefore, it should be replaced to ensure that the cap functions correctly. Answers a, b, and d are not correct because both technicians are correct.

61. **The correct answer is a.** A defective radiator cap would prevent the coolant from flowing back into the radiator as the engine cools and the coolant contracts creating a vacuum, which can cause the upper radiator to collapse. Answer b is not correct because even though the upper hose may be defective, it is not the cause of it collapsing as the engine cools. Answer c is not correct because even though a clogged radiator can cause cooling system problems, it will not cause the upper radiator hose to collapse as the engine cools. Answer d is not correct because a low coolant level could cause overheating but not a collapsed upper radiator hose.

62. **The correct answer is c.** Both technicians are correct. Technician A is correct because the leaking viscous silicone fluid from a thermostatic fan clutch is an indication that the unit may not be able to engage when the temperature rises high enough to require the additional airflow of the fan to properly cool the radiator. The wise technician should recommend that the unit be replaced before the engine overheats due to a lack of proper airflow through the radiator. Technician B is correct because the lack of airflow through the radiator can cause the engine to overheat especially during city driving. Answers a, b, and d are not correct because both technicians are correct.

63. **The correct answer is c.** Both technicians are correct. Technician A is correct because rust or other contaminates could have caused the vanes of the pump to become corroded and flushing will clean the system to help prevent this type of reoccurring failure. Technician B is correct because some vehicle manufacturers recommend the use of antifreeze coolant that does not contain silicates that can lead to water pump wear as shown. Answers a, b, and d are not correct because both technicians are correct.

64. **The correct answer is b.** A leak in the evaporator would not cause the pressure in the cooling system to drop because it is part of the air-conditioning system and even though it is located in the same housing as the heater core, it is not part of the engine cooling system. Answers a, c, and d are not correct because a leak in any of these components would cause the pressure to drop in the cooling system.

HEATING AND AIR CONDITIONING (A7)

CATEGORY: REFRIGERATION SYSTEM COMPONENT DIAGNOSIS AND REPAIR

65. **The correct answer is a.** A defective reed valve is the most likely fault because the valves would not seal properly causing the rapid oscillations in either or both manifold gauges. Answer b is not correct because a clogged orifice tube would restrict the flow of refrigerant and reduce cooling but is not likely to cause fluctuating pressure gauge readings. Answer c is not correct because an expansion valve that is stuck closed would prevent the flow of refrigerant through the system and the low-side pressure will likely drop to zero or into a vacuum due to the action of the compressor. Answer d is not correct because if the desiccant bag were saturated with moisture, a buildup of acid could result, but it is unlikely to cause the pressure gauges to fluctuate.

66. **The correct answer is c.** Both technicians are correct. Technician A is correct because a lack of refrigerant oil can cause wear, which could lead to a noisy compressor. Technician B is correct because if the system is overcharged, some liquid refrigerant is likely to be drawn into the compressor causing noise because a liquid is not compressible. Serious damage to the reed valves and other compressor components is also possible. Answers a, b, and d are not correct because both technicians are correct.

67. **The correct answer is b.** Defective engine mounts will allow the engine to move more than normal and place stress on the lines leading from the compressor, which is mounted on the engine, and on the condenser, which is mounted to the body. Answer a is not correct because shock absorbers would not affect the movement between the condenser, which is attached to the body, and the compressor, which is attached to the engine. Answer c is not correct because even though a defective cooling fan can reduce cooling, it would not cause excessive movement to occur in the line between the compressor and the condenser. Answer d is not correct because even though a defective compressor drive belt could cause a vibration, it would not cause movement between the compressor and the condenser.

68. **The correct answer is a.** Technician A is correct. The air gap must be correctly adjusted to allow clearance when the clutch is disengaged and proper holding power when the clutch is engaged. Technician B is not correct because even though the front seal could be replaced and may be leaking, it is not necessary to replace the front seal if the clutch is being replaced. Answers c and d are not correct because Technician A only is correct.

69. **The correct answer is b.** Technician B is correct. The air-conditioning compressor should engage when the HVAC control is set to defrost because the cool evaporator will cause moisture in the air to condense into liquid water before the air is directed to the windshield, thereby reducing the chances of fogging. Technician A is not correct because even though the air is directed through the evaporator, then through the heater core, very cold air is usually dry air and the compressor does not need to be operating to cool the evaporator when the heat position is selected. Answers c and d are not correct because Technician B only is correct.

70. **The correct answer is c.** Both technicians are correct. Technician A is correct because if the system were low on refrigerant charge, the system pressure would be low keeping the low pressure switch electrically open to prevent the operation of the compressor. This low pressure switch is designed to protect the compressor because if the system is low on charge, the refrigerant oil, needed by the compressor, will not be circulating through the system, which could cause compressor damage. Technician B is correct because the low pressure switch could be open electrically either due to a fault in the switch itself or due to the fact that the pressure in the system is not high enough to cause the switch to close. The low-pressure switch is usually connected in series with the compressor clutch and an open in the switch would prevent current from reaching and operating the compressor. Answers a, b, and d are not correct because both technicians are correct.

71. **The correct answer is c.** Both technicians are correct. Technician A is correct because a defective or excessively worn drive belt can cause noise that is often confused with a bearing noise. Technician B is correct because a defective compressor will often be noisy due to worn or damaged internal parts. Answers a, b, and d are not correct because both technicians are correct.

72. **The correct answer is b.** Technician B is correct. If oil is observed near the front of the compressor, the most likely cause is a small refrigerant leak from the front seal. While the refrigerant would immediately evaporate when it leaks from the seal, the oil that is mixed with refrigerant would condense and adhere to parts near the location of the leak. Technician A is not correct because even though the clutch is attached to the front of the compressor, it is the seal and not the clutch itself that prevents refrigerant leakage from occurring around the input shaft of the compressor. Answers c and d are not correct because Technician B only is correct.

73. **The correct answer is c.** Both technicians are correct. Technician A is correct because some refrigerant oil will remain in the old condenser. To ensure that the compressor gets enough lubrication, it is important that the correct amount of refrigerant oil be in the system. Most experts recommend that 1 ounce of oil be added to the system if the condenser is flushed or replaced. Technician B is correct because the wrong viscosity (thickness) of refrigerant oil could cause excessive wear and possible premature failure of the compressor. Answers a, b, and d are not correct because both technicians are correct.

74. **The correct answer is d.** Neither technician is correct. Technician A is not correct because refrigerant oil contains traces of refrigerant and is considered to be hazardous if it contains chlorinated hydrocarbons. If this oil were to be mixed with engine oil, the entire quantity of oil has to be handled as hazardous waste. Technician B is not correct because only PAG or ester oil should be used in an R-134a system or damage to the compressor could result. Refrigerant oil does not mix with R-134a and would therefore not be circulated through the system. Answers a, b, and c are not correct because neither technician is correct.

75. **The correct answer is a.** Technician A is correct because the old evaporator has some refrigerant oil inside that cannot be drained but must be restored to ensure proper lubrication of the compressor. Most orifice tube system evaporators require 3 ounces of oil and most evaporators used on expansion valve systems require 2 ounces of oil be added to a new or flushed evaporator. Technician B is not correct because the amount of oil cannot be accurately measured if flushed or drained. Answers c and d are not correct because Technician A only is correct.

76. **The correct answer is b.** Technician B is correct because the inlet screen is designed to filter any debris that may clog the orifice tube and has a large surface area to help prevent it from restricting the flow of refrigerant. The shorter end of the tube faces the evaporator. Technician A is not correct because the inlet should face the condenser and not the evaporator. Answers c and d are not correct because Technician B only is correct.

77. **The correct answer is b.** Technician B is correct because refrigerant oil is hydroscopic and will absorb moisture from the air unless stored in a sealed container. Technician A is not correct because various types of refrigerant oils are used depending on the brand and type of compressor used in the system. Answers c and d are not correct because Technician B only is correct.

78. **The correct answer is d.** The ohmmeter is measuring the resistance of the compressor clutch coil. Answer a is not correct because the meter is set to read resistance in ohms and not voltage. Answer b is not correct because the meter is set to read resistance in ohms and not voltage. Answer c is not correct because even though an ohmmeter could be used to check a radio suppression capacitor, it cannot be used to determine its capacitance.

79. **The correct answer is b.** The tool being used is a puller and after the retaining nut and amp ring, if equipped, have been removed, the clutch assembly is pulled off of the compressor input shaft. Answer a is not correct because the puller is being used to remove, rather than install a component. Note that the jaws of the puller are gripping the housing of the compressor. Answer c is not correct because the tool is being used to remove the compressor clutch. Pulley alignment is achieved by shimming or correcting the compressor mount and not by adjusting the location of the drive pulley. Answer d is not correct because the drive pulley is one piece.

80. **The correct answer is d.** The special tool shown is being used to remove or install an orifice tube into the liquid line near the evaporator. Answers a and b are not correct because switches are not installed into the refrigerant line as shown but are accessible from the outside of the refrigerant lines using conventional tools. Answer c is not correct because even though the liquid line is being shown, the O-ring seal is installed on the outside rather than on the inside of the refrigerant line.

81. **The correct answer is c.** The special tool is used to release spring lock-type couplings used on some air-conditioning systems. Answers a and b are not correct because the tool is not needed to install O-rings. Answer d is not correct because an orifice tube is installed inside the liquid refrigerant line and is not on the outside of the line as shown.

82. **The correct answer is a.** Technician A is correct because the compressor must have enough, but not too much, lubricating oil in the system. Because the compressor holds most of the oil in the system, it is important that the quantity be accurately measured so the correct amount can be installed in the system with the replacement compressor. Technician B is not correct because old refrigerant oil should not be reused. Most refrigerant oil is hydroscopic and absorbs moisture from the air, thereby becoming contaminated. Answers c and d are not correct because Technician A only is correct.

83. **The correct answer is a.** Technician A only is correct because the capillary tube is part of the expansion valve and is serviced as an assembly. Technician B is not correct because the capillary tube is permanently attached and is part of the expansion valve and cannot be serviced separately. Answers c and d are not correct because Technician A only is correct.

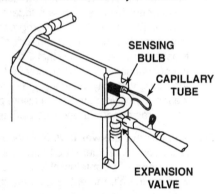

SENSING BULB

CAPILLARY TUBE

EXPANSION VALVE

84. **The correct answer is a.** Technician A is correct because the moisture in the air has caused the desiccant in the drier to become saturated and unable to provide further protection. Technician B is not correct because even though the refrigerant oil may have absorbed moisture during storage, the desiccant in the drier should be able to keep the formation of acid under control. Some vehicle manufacturers specify that the system should not be flushed because the flushing solvent remaining in the system may do more harm than if the system had not been flushed. Answers c and d are not correct because Technician A only is correct.

85. **The correct answer is c.** Both technicians are correct. Technician A is correct because an evaporator used on an orifice tube-type system typically holds 3 ounces of refrigerant oil and an evaporator used with an expansion valve holds about 2 ounces of oil. This amount of oil must be put back into the system when the evaporator is replaced to be sure that the compressor is properly lubricated during operation. Technician B is correct because a clogged condensate hole can cause water to leak onto the floor inside the vehicle or be picked up and sprayed from the AC vents in severe cases. Answers a, b, and d are not correct because both technicians are correct.

86. **The correct answer is b.** Technician B is correct because a reading of 14.7 kΩ (14,700 ohms) means that the compressor clutch coil has extremely high resistance and will not function, requiring replacement. Technician A is not correct because the resistance measurement of the clutch coil is excessively high, which would cause a lack of current flow and an inoperative compressor clutch. Answers c and d are not correct because Technician B only is correct.

87. **The correct answer is d.** The amount of refrigerant oil in the compressor does not need to be checked if just the compressor clutch is being installed. Answers a (air gap), b (front seal leakage), and c (condition of the drive belt) are not correct because they all should be checked whenever replacing the compressor clutch assembly.

88. **The correct answer is a.** Technician A is correct because each application has a specified orifice tube size and improper cooling could result if an incorrect orifice tube were to be used. Technician B is not correct because the major difference in orifice tubes is not the outside diameter but the size of the orifice hole itself, which regulates the amount of refrigerant flow into the evaporator. Answers c and d are not correct because Technician A only is correct.

HEATING AND AIR CONDITIONING (A7)

CATEGORY: OPERATING SYSTEMS AND RELATED CONTROLS DIAGNOSIS AND REPAIR

89. **The correct answer is a.** Technician A is correct because an open high-pressure cutout switch would prevent the operation of the A/C compressor clutch. Technician B is not correct because the diode is used to reduce the voltage spike that occurs when the clutch is disengaged and would not prevent the clutch from engaging. Answers c and d are not correct because Technician A only is correct.

90. **The correct answer is c.** Both technicians are correct. Technician A is correct because a power steering pressure sensor usually opens the electrical circuit to the compressor clutch when the power steering pressure rises above 300 psi (2,000 kPa) indicating that the vehicle is turning and engine power is needed to drive the power steering pump. Technician B is correct because the low-pressure switch opens the electrical circuit to the compressor if the system pressure drops below a certain point that indicates the system is low on charge to help protect the compressor, which could fail due to lack of proper lubrication if allowed to operate with little if any refrigerant in the system. Answers a, b, and d are not correct because both technicians are correct.

91. **The correct answer is a.** Technician A is correct because a defective compressor clutch clamping diode would cause the clutch to produce a high-voltage spike that will often cause the radio to pop through the speakers. Technician B is not correct because a poor ground connection would create excessive circuit resistance and would not cause the radio speakers to pop. Answers c and d are not correct because Technician A only is correct.

92. **The correct answer is c.** Both technicians are correct. Technician A is correct because airflow would be restricted if dirt clogged the evaporator. The dirt usually will build up if there is a refrigerant leak, which also allows some refrigerant oil to escape. This oil coats the fins of the evaporator and traps dirt eventually restricting the airflow through the evaporator. Technician B is correct because if the blower motor ground had excessive resistance (high voltage drop), then current flow through the blower motor is reduced causing the fan to turn slower than normal, which would reduce the airflow from the vents. Answers a, b, and d are not correct because both technicians are correct.

93. **The correct answer is c.** Both technicians are correct. Technician A is correct because an open switch means that no current will flow through the switch to the compressor clutch circuit. Technician B is correct because a low-pressure switch is electrically open when the refrigerant pressure is too low to permit safe operation of the compressor. At low temperatures, the pressure of the refrigerant is often low enough to keep the low-pressure switch open, thereby preventing the operation of the compressor clutch. Answers a, b, and d are not correct because both technicians are correct.

94. **The correct answer is c.** Both technicians are correct. Technician A is correct because many AC compressor clutches are disengaged when the accelerator pedal is depressed toward wide open throttle (WOT) either by a separate switch or by the computer responding to the signal from the throttle position (TP) sensor. Technician B is correct because many air-conditioning compressor clutches are disengaged by a power steering pressure switch when the power steering pressure rises above a certain level, usually about 300 psi (2,000 kPa). Answers a, b, and d are not correct because both technicians are correct.

95. **The correct answer is a.** Technician A is correct because if the inside air temperature sensor is blocked, the sensor will be unable to sense that cool air is being sent to the interior. As a result of this blocked sensor, the air-conditioning system will continue to deliver cool air waiting for the inside temperature sensor to react resulting in a cooler-than-normal temperature inside the vehicle. Technician B is not correct because if the sun load sensor were blocked, the temperature inside the vehicle would tend to be warmer than normal, not cooler than normal, because the system would not compensate for the heating effect of the sun inside the vehicle. Answers c and d are not correct because Technician A only is correct.

96. **The correct answer is a.** The resistance of engine coolant temperature (ECT) sensor is being measured because the sensor has been disconnected from power and the meter is set to read ohms. Answer b is not correct because the electrical connector is disconnected and the meter is not set to read voltage. Answer c is not correct because the electrical connector is disconnected and the meter is not set to read voltage. Answer d is not correct because the meter leads are touching the sensor wires and not the connector terminals.

97. **The correct answer is a.** Technician A is correct because the relay coil measures 70 ohms right in the middle of the usual reading of between 50 and 100 ohms for most relay coils. The OL reading between terminals #2 and #4 indicates that the relay contacts are open, which they should be until the coil is energized. Technician B is not correct because it is normal for the contacts to be open when the coil of the relay is not energized. Answers c and d are not correct because Technician A only is correct.

98. **The correct answer is c.** Both technicians are correct. Technician A is correct because even though the blower motor operates, it may be drawing more than the specified current. A fused jumper lead equipped with a 20 A fuse is a commonly used method to determine if the motor is drawing more than 20 A. Technician B is correct because an open in the fan control relay or resistor pack could cause the blower motor to not operate. Answers a, b, and d are not correct because both technicians are correct.

99. **The correct answer is d.** Neither technician is correct. Technician A is not correct because corroded ground connections would cause an increase in circuit resistance and a decrease (rather than an increase) in current flow through the motor. Technician B is not correct because a shorted blower relay would cause the blower motor to run all the time and would not cause the motor to draw more current as would occur if the motor itself were defective. Answer c is not correct because neither technician is correct.

100. **The correct answer is b.** Technician B is correct because the default positions for the vacuum-operated mode door is to the heat and defrost setting as a safety measure in the event of a failure. Technician A is not correct because the recirculation door simply opens the inlet to the inside or outside of the vehicle and would not affect where the air is directed. Answers c and d are not correct because Technician B only is correct.

101. **The correct answer is b.** Worn or dry bearings will cause the motor to drag and operate at a slower-than-normal speed. Answer a is not correct because a blown resistor would cause an open circuit and prevent blower motor operation. Answer c is not correct because a bad switch could create a high resistance in the circuit but would more likely fail open thereby stopping the operation of the blower motor. Answer d is not correct because an open switch will stop the flow of electrical power to the motor and the motor would not operate.

102. **The correct answer is d.** Neither technician is correct. Technician A is not correct because an open thermal limiter would prevent the fan motor from operating at any speed and could not be the cause of the fan operating at low speed only. Technician B is not correct because an open at the "LO" contact in the switch would not affect the operation of the fan on the LO setting because no current flows through the switch when the low position is selected. Answers a, b, and c are not correct because neither technician is correct.

103. **The correct answer is d.** The ambient air temperature sensor is usually located in front of the radiator on most vehicles and if the sensor were damaged, it would prevent the operation of the air-conditioning compressor clutch. If the sensor is electrically open, the air-conditioning controller (computer) would interpret the sensor reading as being very cold and would prevent the operation of the compressor clutch. Answer a (reduced airflow through the radiator) is not correct because this condition could cause the engine to operate hotter than normal and could affect the operation of the air conditioning, but is unlikely to prevent all cooling. Answer b is not correct because air trapped in

the system, while it could reduce cooling, is unlikely to occur due to a collision. Answer c is not correct because even though a defective blower motor can cause a lack of proper interim cooling, it is unlikely to cause a total lack of cooling caused by a minor collision.

104. **The correct answer is c.** If the connector became disconnected on the high-pressure switch, the electrical circuit would be broken and the compressor clutch would not engage as if the system pressure had reached an excessively high level. Answer a is not correct because the air conditioning would stop working and would not cause the temperature inside the vehicle to be cooler than normal. Answer b is not correct because even though the temperature will be warmer than normal, the most likely answer is that the air-conditioning system will stop functioning. Answer d is not correct because the air-conditioning clutch would stop working entirely and would not cycle on and off.

105. **The correct answer is a.** Technician A is correct because the schematic shows a series circuit where all three switches must be closed to provide electrical power for the clutch. Technician B is not correct because the low-pressure switch prevents the operation of the compressor clutch if the pressure drops to a low level and would therefore cause the low-pressure switch to open at low pressure, not close at low pressure. Answers c and d are not correct because Technician A only is correct.

106. **The correct answer is b.** The ohmmeter is used to check resistance and continuity (low resistance) through the wide-open throttle cutoff switch. The throttle cutoff switch opens the electrical circuit to the compressor clutch during wide-open throttle operating conditions to reduce the load on the engine so that maximum power can be applied to the drive wheels. Answer a is not correct because the meter is set to read ohms, not volts. Answer c is not correct because the meter is set to read resistance (ohms) and is not set to measure current flow (amperes). Answer d is not correct because the drawing shows the wide-open throttle cutoff switch and not the compressor clutch coil.

107. **The correct answer is b.** If the refrigerant system was low on refrigerant, then the pressures would be lower than normal as shown in this example. Answer a is not correct because while an open inside (in-vehicle) temperature sensor could be the cause of a lack of cooling, it is not possible for it to cause the lower-than-normal refrigerant pressure readings. Answer c is not correct because while a defective or broken blend door could be the cause of a lack of cooling, it is not possible for it to cause the lower-than-normal refrigerant pressure readings. Answer d is not correct because an open low pressure switch would likely cause the A/C compressor clutch to not engage and therefore the pressure reading would read the same pressure instead of low, low pressure side and low, high-pressure side readings.

108. **The correct answer is c.** An open A/C compressor diode is used as protection against high voltage spikes when the A/C clutch cycles on and off and is, therefore, NOT able to affect the high-side pressure. Answer a is not correct because a plugged expansion would very likely be a cause of excessively high high-side pressure. Answer b is not correct because if the airflow through the condenser is restricted, there will be less condensation of the refrigerant gases resulting in higher-than-normal high-side pressure. Answer d is not correct because if the A/C system is overcharged, the system pressures will be higher-than-normal.

109. **The correct answer is a.** The temperature of air directed to the driver side and passenger side is regulated by controlling the airflow through the evaporator (to cool and dehumidify the air), then through the heater core (if needed) to warm the air before being sent to the left and right side discharge vents. Answer b is not correct because even though some rear air-conditioning systems used in vans or SUVs use two evaporators, most dual-climate control systems use just one evaporator and control the airflow through the system to deliver different temperatures for the driver and passenger sides of the vehicle. Answer c is not correct because the amount of coolant flowing through the heater core is constant except during maximum cooling mode. Answer d is not correct because even though the system does use outside air, it is then passed through the evaporator and heater core to achieve the desired temperature rather than just using outside air to control the temperature.

110. **The correct answer is c.** Both technicians are correct. Technician A is correct because the actual electrical connection to ground for the compressor clutch coil relay is inside the computer. When the relay coil is grounded by the computer, the relay coil is energized and current flows from the ignition fuse through the relay contacts to the compressor clutch. Technician B is correct because the compressor clutch coil circuit opens if either the low-pressure switch or the high-pressure switch opens. Answers a, b, and d are not correct because both technicians are correct.

ENGINE PERFORMANCE TEST CONTENT AREAS

This ASE study guide for Engine Performance (A8) is divided into the sub-content areas that correlate to the actual ASE certification test as follows:

CONTENT AREA	QUESTIONS IN TEST	NUMBER OF STUDY GUIDE QUESTIONS
A. General Engine Diagnosis	12	32 (1–32)
B. Ignition System Diagnosis and Repair	8	31 (33–63)
C. Fuel, Air Induction, and Exhaust Systems Diagnosis and Repair	9	34 (64–97)
D. Emissions Control Systems Diagnosis and Repair	8	20 (98–117)
1. Positive Crankcase Ventilation (1)		
2. Exhaust Gas Recirculation (2)		
3. Secondary Air Injection (AIR) and Catalytic Converter (2)		
4. Evaporative Emissions Controls (3)		
E. Computerized Engine Controls Diagnosis and Repair (Including OBD II)	13	35 (117–152)
TOTAL	50	152

TIME ALLOWED TO TAKE THE TEST

The allocated time to take the Engine Repair Certification test is 75 minutes. ASE adds 10 additional questions to the test for research purposes for a total of 60 questions. These questions do not count toward your score, but they are embedded within the test and there is no way of knowing which ones do not count. As a result, the technician needs to answer 60 questions in 75 minutes, or about one question per minute.

If taking the recertification A8 test, there are just 25 questions with no additional research questions included. The time allocated to take the recertification test is 30 minutes, which means about one minute per question.

BEFORE USING THIS STUDY GUIDE

Before trying to answer the questions and looking at the explanations, look over the following list of the content that ASE states will be covered in the certification test. For best results using this study guide, check service information or consult an automotive textbook for details on any of the content areas that are not familiar before trying to answer the questions. For additional information about the ASE test, visit the website at **www.ase.com**.

ENGINE PERFORMANCE (A8) CERTIFICATION TEST

A. GENERAL ENGINE DIAGNOSIS (12 QUESTIONS)

1. Verify driver's complaint, perform visual inspection, and/or road-test vehicle; determine needed action.
2. Research applicable vehicle information, such as engine management system operation, vehicle service history, service precautions, and technical service bulletins.
3. Diagnose the cause of unusual engine noise and/or vibration problems; determine needed action.
4. Diagnose the cause of unusual exhaust color, odor, and sound; determine needed action.
5. Perform engine manifold vacuum or pressure tests; determine needed action.
6. Perform cylinder power balance test; determine needed action.
7. Perform cylinder cranking compression test; determine needed action.
8. Perform cylinder leakage test; determine needed action.
9. Diagnose engine mechanical, electrical, electronic, fuel, and ignition problems with an oscilloscope and/or engine analyzer; determine needed action.
10. Prepare and inspect vehicle and analyzer for exhaust gas analysis; interpret HC and CO exhaust gas readings.
11. Verify correct valve adjustment on engines with mechanical or hydraulic lifters.
12. Verify correct camshaft timing; determine needed action.
13. Verify proper engine operating temperature, check coolant level and condition, and perform cooling system pressure test; determine needed repairs.
14. Inspect, test, and replace mechanical/electrical fans, fan clutch, fan shroud/ducting, and fan control devices.

B. IGNITION SYSTEM DIAGNOSIS AND REPAIR (8 QUESTIONS)

1. Diagnose ignition-related problems such as no-starting, hard starting, engine misfire, poor drivability, spark knock, power loss, poor mileage, and emissions problems on vehicles with distributor and distributorless ignition systems; determine needed repairs.
2. Check for possible ignition system related diagnostic trouble codes (DTC).
3. Inspect, test, repair, or replace ignition primary circuit wiring and components.
4. Inspect, test, and service distributor.
5. Inspect, test, service, repair, or replace ignition system secondary circuit wiring and components.
6. Inspect, test, and replace ignition coil(s).
7. Check, and adjust if necessary, ignition system timing and timing advance/retard.
8. Inspect, test, and replace ignition system pick-up sensor or triggering devices.
9. Inspect, test, and replace ignition control module.

C. FUEL, AIR INDUCTION, AND EXHAUST SYSTEMS DIAGNOSIS AND REPAIR (9 QUESTIONS)

1. Diagnose fuel system related problems, including hot or cold no-starting, hard starting, poor drivability, incorrect idle speed, poor idle, flooding, hesitation, surging, engine misfire, power loss, stalling, poor mileage, dieseling and emissions problems on vehicles with injection-type or carburetor-type fuel systems; determine needed action.
2. Check for possible fuel or induction system related diagnostic trouble codes (DTCs).
3. Perform fuel system pressure, volume, or fuel pump current draw tests; determine needed action.
4. Inspect fuel tank, filler neck, and gas cap; inspect and replace fuel lines, fittings, and hoses; check fuel for contaminants and quality.

5. Inspect, test, and replace mechanical and electrical fuel pumps and pump control systems; inspect, service, and replace fuel filters.

6. Inspect, test, and repair or replace fuel pressure regulation system and components of injection-type fuel systems.

7. Inspect, test, adjust, and repair or replace cold enrichment, acceleration enrichment, and deceleration fuel reduction or shut-off components.

8. Remove, clean, and replace throttle body; make related adjustments.

9. Inspect, test, clean, and replace fuel injectors.

10. Inspect, service, and repair or replace air filtration system components.

11. Inspect throttle body, air induction system, intake manifold, and gaskets for vacuum leaks/unmetered air.

12. Check/adjust idle speed and fuel mixture where applicable.

13. Remove, clean, inspect, test, and repair or replace fuel system vacuum and electrical components and connections.

14. Inspect, service, and replace exhaust manifold, exhaust pipes, mufflers, resonators, catalytic converters, tail pipes, and heat shields.

15. Perform exhaust system back-pressure test; determine needed action.

16. Inspect, test, clean, and repair or replace turbocharger/supercharger and system components.

D. EMISSIONS CONTROL SYSTEMS DIAGNOSIS AND REPAIR (10 QUESTIONS)

1. Positive Crankcase Ventilation (1 question)

1. Test and diagnose emissions or drivability problems caused by positive crankcase ventilation (PCV) system.

2. Inspect, service, and replace positive crankcase ventilation (PCV) filter/breather cap, valve, tubes, orifices, and hoses.

2. Exhaust Gas Recirculation (3 questions)

1. Test and diagnose emissions or drivability problems caused by the exhaust gas recirculation (EGR) system.

2. Check for possible exhaust gas recirculation (EGR) related diagnostic trouble codes (DTCs).

3. Inspect, test, service, and replace components of the EGR system, including EGR tubing, exhaust passages, vacuum/pressure controls, filters, hoses, electrical/electronic sensors, controls, solenoids, and wiring of exhaust gas recirculation (EGR) systems.

3. Secondary Air Injection (AIR) and Catalytic Converter (2 questions)

1. Test and diagnose emissions or drivability problems caused by the secondary air injection or catalytic converter systems.

2. Check for possible secondary air injection system or catalytic converter related diagnostic trouble codes.

3. Inspect, test, service, and replace mechanical components and electrical/electronically operated components and circuits of secondary air injection systems.

4. Inspect and test the catalytic converter(s).

4. Evaporative Emissions Controls (3 questions)

1. Test and diagnose emissions or drivability problems caused by the evaporative emissions control system.

2. Check for possible evaporative emission related diagnostic trouble codes (DTCs).

3. Inspect, test, and replace mechanical and electrical components and hoses of evaporative emissions control systems.

E. COMPUTERIZED ENGINE CONTROLS DIAGNOSIS AND REPAIR (13 QUESTIONS)

1. Retrieve and record stored diagnostic trouble codes.

2. Diagnose the causes of emissions or drivability problems resulting from failure of computerized engine controls with stored diagnostic trouble codes.

3. Diagnose the causes of emissions or drivability problems resulting from failure of computerized engine controls with no stored diagnostic trouble codes.

4. Use a scan tool or digital multimeter (DMM) to inspect, test, and adjust computerized engine control system sensors, actuators, circuits, and powertrain control module (PCM).

5. Measure and interpret voltage, voltage drop, amperage, and resistance using digital multimeter (DMM) readings.

6. Test, remove, inspect, clean, service, and repair or replace power and ground distribution circuits and connections.

7. Practice recommended precautions when handling static sensitive devices and/or replacing the powertrain control module (PCM).

8. Diagnose drivability and emissions problems resulting from failures of interrelated systems (cruise control, security alarms, torque controls, suspension controls, traction controls, torque management, A/C, non-OEM installed accessories, and similar systems).

9. Diagnose the causes of emissions or drivability problems resulting from computerized spark timing controls; determine needed repairs.

10. Verify, repair, and clear diagnostic trouble codes (DTCs).

ENGINE PERFORMANCE (A8)

CATEGORY: GENERAL ENGINE DIAGNOSIS

1. Technician A says that the paper test could detect a burned valve. Technician B says that a grayish-white stain could be a coolant leak. Which technician is correct?

   a. A only
   b. B only
   c. Both A and B
   d. Neither A nor B

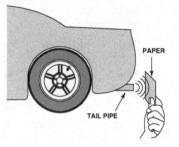

2. Two technicians are discussing oil leaks. Technician A says that an oil leak can be found using a fluorescent dye in the oil with a black light to check for leaks. Technician B says that a white spray powder can be used to locate oil leaks. Which technician is correct?

   a. A only
   b. B only
   c. Both A and B
   d. Neither A nor B

3. A good reading for a cylinder leakage test would be _____.

   a. within 20% among cylinders
   b. all cylinders below 20% leakage
   c. all cylinders above 20% leakage
   d. all cylinders above 70% leakage and within 7% of each other

4. Technician A says that during a power balance test, the cylinder that causes the biggest RPM drop is the weak cylinder. Technician B says that if one spark plug wire is grounded out and the engine speed does not drop, a weak or dead cylinder is indicated. Which technician is correct?

   a. A only
   b. B only
   c. Both A and B
   d. Neither A nor B

5. Cranking vacuum should be _____.

   a. 2.5 in. Hg or higher
   b. Over 25 in. Hg
   c. 17 to 21 in. Hg
   d. 6 to 16 in. Hg

6. Technician A says that white exhaust can be caused by a defective cylinder head gasket allowing coolant to enter the combustion chamber. Technician B says that white exhaust can be caused by the burning of automatic transmission fluid inside the engine. Which technician is correct?

   a. A only
   b. B only
   c. Both A and B
   d. Neither A nor B

7. An engine is misfiring. A power balance test indicates that when the spark to cylinder #4 is grounded, there is no change in the engine speed. Technician A says that a burned valve is a possible cause. Technician B says that a defective cylinder #4 injector or spark plug could be the cause. Which technician is correct?

    a. A only
    b. B only
    c. Both A and B
    d. Neither A nor B

8. Two technicians are discussing an engine vibration during acceleration. Technician A says that a defective (collapsed) mount can cause an engine or driveline vibration. Technician B says that some mounts are fluid filled and should be checked for leakage. Which technician is correct?

    a. A only
    b. B only
    c. Both A and B
    d. Neither A nor B

9. An engine uses an excessive amount of oil and the exhaust is blue but only at first engine start in the morning. What is the *most likely* cause?

    a. Leaking fuel injector
    b. Worn valve stem seals
    c. Leaking valve (cylinder head) cover
    d. Over-filled oil level

10. Two technicians are discussing the diagnosis of a lack-of-power problem. Technician A says that a worn (stretched) timing chain could be the cause. Technician B says that a restricted exhaust could be the cause. Which technician is correct?

    a. A only
    b. B only
    c. Both A and B
    d. Neither A nor B

11. The owner of vehicle that is equipped with a supercharger complains that lately the engine is producing lower than normal power. Which is the *most likely* cause?

    a. A stuck closed bypass valve
    b. A clogged exhaust system
    c. A plugged PCV valve
    d. Low coolant level

12. A customer was concerned about a vibration felt during acceleration only. Technician A says that a defective fuel injector could be the cause. Technician B says that a defective spark plug wire or coil on a coil-on-plug system could be the cause. Which technician is correct?

    a. A only
    b. B only
    c. Both A and B
    d. Neither A nor B

13. An engine coolant leak is being diagnosed. What color fluid could indicate a coolant leak?

    a. Green
    b. Yellow
    c. Orange
    d. Any of the above

14. A compression test gave the following results:

cylinder #1 = 155, cylinder #2 = 140, cylinder #3 = 110, cylinder #4 = 105

Technician A says that a defective (burned) valve is the most likely cause. Technician B says that a leaking head gasket could be the cause. Which technician is correct?

   a. A only
   b. B only
   c. Both A and B
   d. Neither A nor B

15. Two technicians are discussing a compression test. Technician A says that the engine should be cranked over with the pressure gauge installed for "3 puffs." Technician B says that the maximum difference between the highest-reading cylinder and the lowest-reading cylinder should be 20%. Which technician is correct?

   a. A only
   b. B only
   c. Both A and B
   d. Neither A nor B

16. Technician A says that oil should be squirted into all of the cylinders before taking a compression test. Technician B says that if the compression greatly increases when some oil is squirted into the cylinders, it indicates defective or worn piston rings. Which technician is correct?

   a. A only
   b. B only
   c. Both A and B
   d. Neither A nor B

17. During a cylinder leakage (leak-down) test, air is noticed coming out of the oil fill opening. Technician A says that the oil filter may be clogged. Technician B says that the piston rings may be worn or defective. Which technician is correct?

   a. A only
   b. B only
   c. Both A and B
   d. Neither A nor B

18. A cylinder leakage (leak-down) test indicates 30% leakage, and air is heard coming out of the air inlet. Technician A says that this is a normal reading for a slightly worn engine. Technician B says that one or more intake valves are defective. Which technician is correct?

   a. A only
   b. B only
   c. Both A and B
   d. Neither A nor B

19. Two technicians are discussing a cylinder power balance test. Technician A says the more the engine RPM drops, the weaker the cylinder. Technician B says that all cylinder RPM drops should be within 50 RPM of each other. Which technician is correct?

   a. A only
   b. B only
   c. Both A and B
   d. Neither A nor B

20. Technician A says that cranking vacuum should be the same as idle vacuum. Technician B says that a sticking valve is indicated by a floating vacuum gauge needle reading. Which technician is correct?

   a. A only
   b. B only
   c. Both A and B
   d. Neither A nor B

21. Technician A says that black exhaust smoke is an indication of a too rich air-fuel mixture. Technician B says that white smoke (steam) is an indication of coolant being burned in the engine. Which technician is correct?

   a. A only
   b. B only
   c. Both A and B
   d. Neither A nor B

22. Excessive exhaust system back pressure has been measured. Technician A says that the catalytic converter may be clogged. Technician B says that the muffler may be clogged. Which technician is correct?

   a. A only
   b. B only
   c. Both A and B
   d. Neither A nor B

23. A head gasket failure is being diagnosed. Technician A says that an exhaust analyzer can be used to check for HC when the tester probe is held above the radiator cap opening. Technician B says that a chemical-coated paper changes color in the presence of combustion gases. Which technician is correct?

   a. A only
   b. B only
   c. Both A and B
   d. Neither A nor B

24. A P0017 diagnostic trouble code (crankshaft-camshaft correlation error). What is a possible cause?

   a. Skipped timing belt
   b. Clogged VVT solenoid screen
   c. Defective variable valve timing (VVT) control solenoid
   d. Any of the above

25. A noisy valve train is being diagnosed. Technician A says that the rocker arm may be adjusted too tightly. Technician B says that the rocker arm may be adjusted too loosely or may be worn. Which technician is correct?

   a. A only
   b. B only
   c. Both A and B
   d. Neither A nor B

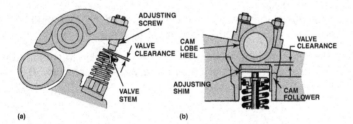

26. Two technicians are discussing the cause of low oil pressure. Technician A says that a worn oil pump could be the cause. Technician B says that worn main or rod bearings could be the cause. Which technician is correct?

   a. A only
   b. B only
   c. Both A and B
   d. Neither A nor B

27. The owner of a front-wheel-drive vehicle had the electric fan replaced due to a fault in the motor. Shortly afterward, the owner complained that the engine coolant temperature on the dash showed that the engine was running hot while driving slowly but appeared to be normal while driving at highway speeds. What is the possible cause?

   a. The fan assembly was wired backward (air blowing toward the front of the vehicle)
   b. The replacement fan is defective
   c. The fan relay is defective
   d. Any of the above

28. Using the incorrect (higher) viscosity of engine oil could cause _____.

   a. lower fuel economy
   b. oil that will turn black sooner than normal
   c. possible head gasket leakage problem
   d. lower than normal oil pressure

29. Antifreeze (except premix) should be mixed with _____.

   a. de-mineralized water
   b. clean drinking water
   c. distilled water
   d. any of the above

30. Technician A says that a worn (stretched) timing chain and worn gears will cause the valve timing to be retarded. Technician B says that if the timing chain slack is over ½ in. (13 mm), the timing chain and gears should be replaced. Which technician is correct?

   a. A only
   b. B only
   c. Both A and B
   d. Neither A nor B

31. The low oil pressure warning light usually comes on _____.

   a. whenever an oil change is required
   b. whenever oil pressure drops dangerously low (3 to 7 psi)
   c. whenever the oil filter bypass valve opens
   d. whenever the oil filter anti-drain-back valve opens

32. A smoothly operating engine depends on _____.

   a. high compression on most cylinders
   b. equal compression among cylinders
   c. cylinder compression levels above 100 psi (700 kPa) and within 70 psi (500 kPa) of each other
   d. compression levels below 100 psi (700 kPa) on most cylinders

33. An engine produces less than normal power and is slow to accelerate when the throttle is opened. Technician A says that the exhaust system could be restricted. Technician B says the valve timing may be retarded. Which technician is correct?

   a. A only
   b. B only
   c. Both A and B
   d. Neither A nor B

CATEGORY: IGNITION SYSTEM DIAGNOSIS AND REPAIR

34. An engine will not start and a check of the ignition system output indicates no spark to any of the spark plugs. Technician A says that a defective crankshaft position sensor (CKP) could be the cause. Technician B says a defective ignition switch could be the cause. Which technician is correct?

   a. A only
   b. B only
   c. Both A and B
   d. Neither A nor B

35. A flex plate is being inspected and a wide gap was seen in the sensor wheel. Technician A says that this is normal for a crankshaft position (CKP) sensor tone wheel as it helps to establish top dead center (TDC) for the PCM. Technician B says this is used by the starter motor to limit starter speed. Which technician is correct?

   a. A only
   b. B only
   c. Both A and B
   d. Neither A nor B

36. Technician A says that to check for spark by connecting a spark tester to the end of a spark plug wire. Technician B says that a regular spark plug should be connected to the end of a spark plug wire to check for spark. Which technician is correct?

   a. A only
   b. B only
   c. Both A and B
   d. Neither A nor B

37. A P0300 (random misfire detected) diagnostic trouble code (DTC) was being diagnosed and a defective (open) spark plug wire was found on a waste-spark-type ignition system. Technician A says that the companion cylinder spark plug wire should also be carefully inspected and replaced if necessary. Technician B says that the ignition coil should be replaced because the bad wire could have caused the coil to become damaged (tracked) internally. Which technician is correct?

   a. A only
   b. B only
   c. Both A and B
   d. Neither A nor B

38. Technician A says that all spark plugs should be checked for proper gap before being installed in the engine. Technician B says that platinum spark plugs should not be re-gapped after having been used in an engine. Which technician is correct?

   a. A only
   b. B only
   c. Both A and B
   d. Neither A nor B

39. What can be adjusted to set the ignition timing on a waste-spark or coil-on-plug-type ignition system?

   a. Crankshaft position (CKP) sensor
   b. Camshaft position (CMP) sensor
   c. Either a or b depending on make and model
   d. None of the above

40. An engine miss is being diagnosed. One spark plug wire measured "OL" on a digital ohmmeter set to the K Ω scale. Technician A says that the spark plug wire should be replaced. Technician B says that the spark plug wire is okay. Which technician is correct?

   a. A only
   b. B only
   c. Both A and B
   d. Neither A nor B

41. The ignition module has direct control over the firing of the coil(s) of an electronic ignition system. Which component(s) triggers (controls) the module?

   a. Pickup coil
   b. Computer
   c. Crankshaft Sensor
   d. All of the above

42. What is this part?

   a. Ignition coil
   b. Crankshaft position sensor
   c. Ignition module
   d. Camshaft position sensor

43. Technician A says that a pickup coil (pulse generator) can be tested with an ohmmeter. Technician B says that ignition coils can be tested with an ohmmeter. Which technician is correct?

   a. A only
   b. B only
   c. Both A and B
   d. Neither A nor B

44. Typical primary coil resistance specifications usually range from _____.

   a. 100 to 450 ohms
   b. 500 to 1,500 ohms
   c. 0.5 to 3 ohms
   d. 6,000 to 30,000 ohms

45. Typical secondary coil resistance specifications usually range from _____.

   a. 100 to 450 ohms
   b. 500 to 1,500 ohms
   c. 0.5 to 0.7 ohms
   d. 6,000 to 30,000 ohms

46. A compression-sensing type of ignition system_____.

   a. uses a waste-spark-type ignition system
   b. does not use a camshaft position (CMP) sensor
   c. uses a coil-on-plug type ignition system
   d. both a and b

47. Technician A says that the ignition pattern shown is okay for a distributor-type ignition. Technician B says that the coil wire could have too much resistance. Which technician is correct?

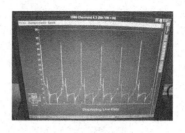

a. A only
b. B only
c. Both A and B
d. Neither A nor B

48. A spark plug wire is 2.5 feet long. If it is okay, its resistance should be less than _____.

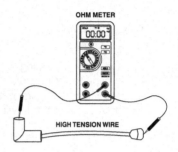

OHM METER

HIGH TENSION WIRE

a. 25 kiloohms
b. 200,000 ohms
c. 250,000 ohms
d. 2.50 kiloohms

49. Which is the *least likely* to cause a weak spark at the spark plug?

a. A partially shorted primary winding in the ignition coil
b. A 12.2-volt battery voltage
c. A high resistance spark plug wire(s)
d. A voltage drop across the ignition switch

50. Which is *most likely* to cause an engine miss on one cylinder?

a. An open spark plug wire
b. A high resistance spark plug wire
c. Excessive rotor gap
d. A clogged fuel filter

51. Just one spark plug in an engine is excessively worn. What is the *most likely* cause?

a. A high resistance in the spark plug wire
b. A shorted ignition coil
c. A loose spark plug
d. A defective ignition coil

52. A service technician should be sure to do all of the following *except* when installing spark plugs.

a. The threads should be clean and dry
b. The spark plug should be tightened, and then loosened 1/16 turn
c. A torque wrench should be used to tighten the plugs
d. The gap should be checked before installing the plugs in the engine

53. Two technicians are discussing spark plug wires. Technician A says that most spark plug wires are made with carbon impregnated nylon and should be checked with an ohmmeter for proper resistance. Technician B says that the insulation should be checked to be sure that the spark does not short-to-ground before reaching the spark plug. Which technician is correct?

a. A only
b. B only
c. Both A and B
d. Neither A nor B

54. An engine misfire was being diagnosed on a vehicle equipped with a coil-on-plug-type ignition. The technician found that the connector to one coil was damaged and the connector was replaced. What other part should be replaced?

a. Coil
b. Engine computer (PCM)
c. Spark plug
d. No part needs to be replaced

55. Low battery voltage can cause all of the following *except* _____.

a. slow engine cranking
b. damage to the ignition coil(s)
c. cause the headlights to be dimmer than normal at idle
d. cause the windshield wipers to operate slower than normal

56. A no-start condition is being diagnosed on a vehicle equipped with a distributor ignition using a remotely mounted ignition coil. The coil wire is removed from the center of the distributor cap and a spark tester is used to check for spark. There is spark out of the coil but no spark is available to any of the spark plug wires. Technician A says the rotor could be defective. Technician B says the spark plugs are fouled. Which technician is correct?

a. A only
b. B only
c. Both A and B
d. Neither A nor B

57. An engine equipped with a distributor ignition will not start when it rains. Technician A says that a replacement distributor cap and rotor will often correct this condition. Technician B says that new spark plug wires may be needed. Which technician is correct?

a. A only
b. B only
c. Both A and B
d. Neither A nor B

58. An engine miss is being diagnosed on an engine equipped with a distributor ignition. New spark plug wires helped but an engine miss still occurs. Technician A says that the distributor cap or rotor could be the cause. Technician B says that a cracked spark plug could be the cause. Which technician is correct?

a. A only
b. B only
c. Both A and B
d. Neither A nor B

59. All of the statements about spark plugs are correct *except* _____.

a. worn spark plugs decrease the voltage required to fire
b. a cracked spark plug can cause an engine miss
c. a platinum tip spark plug should not be re gapped after being used in an engine
d. spark plugs should be torqued to factory specifications when installed

60. Which of these is *least likely* to be caused by using the incorrect spark plug heat range?

a. Pinging (spark knock or detonation)
b. Poor fuel economy
c. Engine miss at idle or during acceleration
d. Slow, jerky cranking when the engine is hot

61. The scope pattern for one cylinder shows a shorter-than-normal firing line (point A to B) and a longer-than-normal spark line (Section C). Technician A says that the spark plug wire is open or has extremely high resistance. Technician B says that the spark plug is fouled. Which technician is correct?

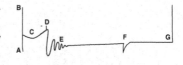

    a. A only
    b. B only
    c. Both A and B
    d. Neither A nor B

62. What should meter #1 read?

    a. Low ohms (0.5 to 3.0 ohms)
    b. 40,000 volts or more
    c. Over limit (OL)
    d. High ohms (6,000 to 30,000 ohms)

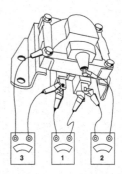

63. How should a service technician test for spark?

    a. Hold the plug wire ¼ inch from the block
    b. Use a spark tester
    c. Pull the spark plug wire away from the plug ½ inch
    d. Measure the output with a meter set to kV

ENGINE PERFORMANCE (A8)

CATEGORY: FUEL, AIR INDUCTION, AND EXHAUST SYSTEMS DIAGNOSIS AND REPAIR

64. An engine equipped with a turbocharger is burning oil (blue exhaust smoke all the time). Technician A says that a defective wastegate could be the cause. Technician B says that a clogged PCV system could be the cause. Which technician is correct?

   a. A only
   b. B only
   c. Both A and B
   d. Neither A nor B

65. An engine is idling too fast when the engine reaches operating temperature. Technician A says the engine could have a vacuum leak. Technician B says that the throttle linkage or cable could be stuck. Which technician is correct?

   a. A only
   b. B only
   c. Both A and B
   d. Neither A nor B

66. An engine stalls when slowing to a stop after being driven over 15 miles (24 km). Technician A says that a stuck torque converter clutch (TCC) solenoid could be the cause. Technician B says that a hole in the intake between the MAF sensor and the throttle plate could be the cause. Which technician is correct?

   a. A only
   b. B only
   c. Both A and B
   d. Neither A nor B

67. A vehicle equipped with a mass airflow sensor as shown will stumble or stall when in "drive" but operate normally when driven in reverse. What is the *most likely* cause?

   a. A split or crack in the air intake hose
   b. A clogged fuel filter
   c. A restricted air filter
   d. A leaking fuel injector

68. A poor fuel economy concern is being discussed. Technician A says that a pinched fuel return line could be the cause. Technician B says that a partially clogged fuel filter could be the cause. Which technician is correct?

   a. A only
   b. B only
   c. Both A and B
   d. Neither A nor B

69. An engine equipped with MAF sensor-type electronic port fuel injection is hard to start and emits black exhaust smoke when being started when hot. What is the *most likely* cause?

   a. A defective fuel pressure regulator
   b. A shorted fuel injector
   c. A clogged fuel filter
   d. A clogged air filter

70. A vehicle fails an enhanced emission test for excessive carbon monoxide (CO) emission. Which is the *most likely* cause?

   a. Clogged fuel injector(s)
   b. A stuck open fuel pressure regulator
   c. A stuck idle air control (IAC)
   d. A clogged fuel return line

71. What is the *most likely* result if the vacuum hose attached to a fuel pressure regulator is removed when the engine is running?

   a. Gasoline will flow from the regulator
   b. The fuel pressure should increase
   c. The fuel pressure should decrease
   d. No change—the hose is simply a vent

72. Technician A says that the exhaust system can be checked for restriction by using a vacuum gauge attached to manifold vacuum and operating the engine at idle speed. Technician B says the exhaust is restricted if the vacuum increases at 2,000 RPM. Which technician is correct?

   a. A only
   b. B only
   c. Both A and B
   d. Neither A nor B

73. Two technicians are discussing gasoline testing. Technician A says that water floats on top of gasoline and may stay in the tank if the fuel is drained. Technician B says that alcohol content should not exceed 10%. Which technician is correct?

   a. A only
   b. B only
   c. Both A and B
   d. Neither A nor B

74. A fuel pump should be tested for all of the following *except* _____.

   a. pressure
   b. volume
   c. current draw
   d. resistance

75. An engine idles roughly and stalls occasionally when hot. This can be caused by _____.

   a. a partially clogged air filter
   b. a partially clogged fuel filter
   c. using winter-blended gasoline in warm weather
   d. a loose gas cap

76. Technician A says that black exhaust smoke is an indication of excessive oil consumption. Technician B says that blue smoke is an indication of excessive amount of fuel being burned in the engine. Which technician is correct?

   a. A only
   b. B only
   c. Both A and B
   d. Neither A nor B

77. Excessive exhaust system back pressure has been measured. This can be caused by_____.

   a. a clogged catalytic converter
   b. a defective AIR pump diverter valve
   c. clogged EGR valve ports
   d. excessively retarded valve timing

78. Two technicians are discussing fuel filters. Technician A says that a clogged fuel filter will increase fuel pressure. Technician B says that a clogged fuel filter could cause damage to the electronic fuel pump. Which technician is correct?

    a. A only
    b. B only
    c. Both A and B
    d. Neither A nor B

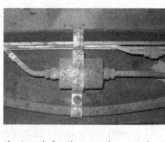

79. A fuel injected engine is hard to start hot or cold. Technician A says that a defective engine coolant temperature (ECT) sensor could cause this condition. Technician B says a leaking fuel injector could cause the problem. Which technician is correct?

    a. A only
    b. B only
    c. Both A and B
    d. Neither A nor B

80. An engine hesitates when the throttle is depressed, yet runs normally at cruise speeds. Which is the *most likely* cause?

    a. A dirty air filter
    b. A defective TP sensor
    c. A partially clogged fuel filter
    d. A dripping injector

81. Technician A says that catalytic converters should last the life of the vehicle unless damaged. Technician B says that catalytic converters wear out and should be replaced every 50,000 miles (80,000 kilometers). Which technician is correct?

    a. A only
    b. B only
    c. Both A and B
    d. Neither A nor B

82. An engine equipped with gasoline direct injection (GDI) is being discussed. Technician A says that the sound of the injectors can be louder than a typical engine equipped with port-type fuel injection and may result in customer concerns. Technician B says that excessive carbon buildup in the backside of the intake valves can occur on some GDI engines which would cause a lack of power concern. Which technician is correct?

    a. A only
    b. B only
    c. Both A and B
    d. Neither A nor B

83. An engine equipped with electronic throttle control (ETC) system runs but the engine speed is fixed at a high idle and a dash warning light is on. What is the *most likely* cause?

    a. Throttle return spring is broken
    b. System is default mode due to failure of a major component or circuit fault
    c. A broken throttle cable
    d. Stuck throttle pedal

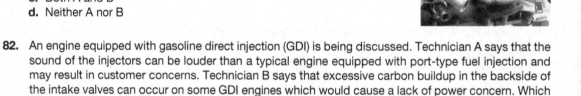

84. The fuel pressure drops rapidly when the engine is turned off. Technician A says that one or more injectors could be leaking. Technician B says that a defective check valve in the fuel pump could be the cause. Which technician is correct?

    a. A only
    b. B only
    c. Both A and B
    d. Neither A nor B

85. Gasoline used should be fresh and the octane as specified by the vehicle manufacturer. What symptoms are *most likely* to be caused by using gasoline that is old or is in a vehicle that has been stored for a while?

   a. Hard to start
   b. Rough or unstable idle
   c. Stalling
   d. All of the above

86. Which driver-controlled action is not harmful to electric fuel pumps?

   a. Operating the vehicle with a low fuel level
   b. Operating the vehicle in the city only; seldom driving at highway speeds
   c. Not replacing the fuel filter regularly
   d. Using alcohol-enhanced fuel

87. Two technicians are discussing fuel filters. Technician A says that some fuel filters are "single pass" filters used in returnless systems and are often designed to last the life of the vehicle. Technician B says that all fuel filters are located on the return line of the old fuel injection systems and could increase fuel pressure if it becomes clogged. Which technician is correct?

   a. A only
   b. B only
   c. Both A and B
   d. Neither A nor B

88. Two technicians are discussing plastic fuel lines. Technician A says that a special tool is often required to separate the connections at the fuel filter on vehicles using plastic fuel lines. Technician B says that some fuel filters use a ground strap that must be connected to a metal part of the vehicle. Which technician is correct?

   a. A only
   b. B only
   c. Both A and B
   d. Neither A nor B

89. What terminals of an ISO fuel pump relay socket should be connected using a fused jumper lead to engage the electric fuel pump?

   a. #85 and #86
   b. #30 and #87
   c. #87 and #85
   d. #85 and #30

90. Two technicians are discussing the cracked exhaust manifold shown. Technician A says that the crack could cause noise. Technician B says that the crack can cause the O_2S to read incorrectly, which could affect the engine operation. Which technician is correct?

   a. A only
   b. B only
   c. Both A and B
   d. Neither A nor B

91. A vehicle is being serviced because of a rough and unstable idle concern especially when the engine is cold yet no diagnostic trouble codes have set. The vehicle is equipped with a variable valve timing (VVT) system. Which is the *most likely* to cause the problem?

   a. An aftermarket low backpressure exhaust system
   b. Using gasoline that has been stored a long time
   c. A fault with the electronic throttle control (ETC) system
   d. A fault with the variable valve timing (VVT) system

92. The unit shown performs what function?

   a. Measures the amount of air entering the engine
   b. Filters the air
   c. Heats the incoming air to the engine
   d. Is used to diagnose engine misfires and backfires

93. A customer complains that the throttle sticks at times. Technician A says that varnish buildup around the throttle body can be the cause. Technician B says that a kinked throttle cable could be the cause. Which technician is correct?

   a. A only
   b. B only
   c. Both A and B
   d. Neither A nor B

94. A vehicle equipped with a throttle-by-wire system was being serviced and several diagnostic trouble codes (DTCs) were set during the repair. After the repair, the engine would run at idle speed only. Technician A says that the electronic throttle sensor is defective. Technician B says that the DTCs should be cleared before further testing to be sure that the computer is not preventing proper operation of the throttle. Which technician is correct?

   a. A only
   b. B only
   c. Both A and B
   d. Neither A nor B

95. A lean air-fuel mixture is being diagnosed. Technician A says that a stuck IAC could be the cause. Technician B says that a hole in the air inlet between the MAF sensor and the throttle plate could be the cause. Which technician is correct?

   a. A only
   b. B only
   c. Both A and B
   d. Neither A nor B

96. The owner of a vehicle equipped with a gasoline direct injection (GDI) system complains that the engine hesitates during acceleration, especially when the engine is cold. What is the *most likely* cause?

   a. A dirty air filter
   b. A partially clogged fuel filter
   c. Excessive fuel pump pressure
   d. Carbon deposits on the intake valves

97. The dash warning light shown means what system fault has been detected?

   a. Variable valve timing (VVT) system
   b. Electronic throttle control (ETC) system
   c. Gasoline direct injection (GDI) system
   d. Wide band oxygen sensor circuit fault

(a)

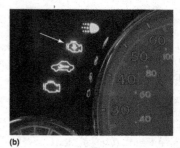
(b)

(c)

ENGINE PERFORMANCE (A8)

CATEGORY: EMISSIONS CONTROL SYSTEMS DIAGNOSIS AND REPAIR

98. This test port is used to test which system?

 a. Evaporative (EVAP)
 b. EGR
 c. PCV
 d. Catalytic converter (backpressure)

99. Two technicians are discussing positive crankcase ventilation (PCV) valves. Technician A says that if the valve rattles, it is good. Technician B says the PCV valve may still require replacement even if it rattles. Which technician is correct?

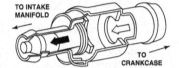

 a. A only
 b. B only
 c. Both A and B
 d. Neither A nor B

100. A vacuum-type EGR valve is being tested. Technician A says that the engine should be off to test the EGR valve. Technician B says a positive backpressure EGR valve will not hold vacuum if tested using a vacuum pump without the engine running. Which technician is correct?

 a. A only
 b. B only
 c. Both A and B
 d. Neither A nor B

101. Technician A says that a partially clogged EGR passage can cause the vehicle to fail due to excessive NO_x emissions. Technician B says the vehicle could fail for excessive CO if the EGR passage were clogged. Which technician is correct?

 a. A only
 b. B only
 c. Both A and B
 d. Neither A nor B

102. Technician A says the catalytic converter must be replaced if it rattles when tapped. Technician B says a catalytic converter can be defective and not be working yet not be clogged. Which technician is correct?

 a. A only
 b. B only
 c. Both A and B
 d. Neither A nor B

103. Used catalytic converters must be kept for possible inspection by the EPA for how long?

 a. 30 days
 b. 60 days
 c. 90 days
 d. 6 months

104. A vehicle fails an emission test for excessive NO$_x$. Which exhaust control device has the greatest effect on the amount of NO$_x$ produced by the engine?

   a. PCV
   b. Air pump
   c. Carbon (charcoal) canister
   d. EGR

105. The oxygen sensor of a vehicle has a constant voltage output of about 750 mV. Which exhaust emission control device could be damaged if the vehicle is not repaired to operate correctly?

   a. PCV
   b. Carbon (charcoal) canister
   c. Catalytic converter
   d. EGR

106. A P0304 (misfire on cylinder 4 detected) is being diagnosed. Which fault is *least likely* to be the cause?

   a. Clogged EGR passages except for cylinder #4
   b. Cracked spark plug
   c. Loose gas cap
   d. Electrically open fuel injector

107. The exhaust on one bank of a V-8 is restricted. How would this show up on a scan tool?

   a. Lean exhaust readings on both banks
   b. Negative fuel trim on one bank and positive fuel trim on the other bank
   c. Knock sensor (KS) reading high
   d. A P0420 (catalytic converter efficiency) DTC

108. A vehicle is running rich. Technician A says that overfilling the fuel tank can cause the carbon canister to become saturated with gasoline, which can cause a rich running condition. Technician B says that an exhaust leak upstream from the O$_2$S could be the cause. Which technician is correct?

   a. A only
   b. B only
   c. Both A and B
   d. Neither A nor B

109. Two technicians are discussing the evaporative control system. Technician A says that the carbon (charcoal) canister should be replaced regularly as part of routine maintenance. Technician B says the carbon (charcoal) inside of the EVAP canister can dissolve in gasoline and leave a yellow deposit in the engine when burned. Which technician is correct?

   a. A only
   b. B only
   c. Both A and B
   d. Neither A nor B

110. If this part were to fail, what is the *most likely* result?

   a. Air switching valve damage could occur
   b. The engine could start pinging (spark knock)
   c. An excessive amount of CO exhaust emissions
   d. Rough idle due to the resulting vacuum leak

111. If one of these tubes leading to the exhaust manifold were to rust through causing a hole, what is the *most likely* result?

   a. Engine miss during acceleration
   b. Exhaust noise
   c. Rough and unstable idle
   d. Stall during deceleration (coast down stall)

112. If a vehicle is driven hundreds of miles with a defective (stuck open) EVAP purge valve, what could happen?

a. A possible overheated and damaged catalytic converter
b. Poor fuel economy
c. Exhaust backpressure will increase, which could clog the EGR valve
d. Both a and b are possible

113. A catalytic converter is cherry red during engine operation. Technician A says that a rich air-fuel mixture could be the cause. Technician B says that a stuck AIR pump switch valve could be the cause. Which technician is correct?

a. A only
b. B only
c. Both A and B
d. Neither A nor B

114. An EGR valve is stuck partially open. What is the *most likely* result?

a. Pinging (spark knock)
b. Rough idle—runs normally at highway speeds
c. Fast idle
d. Lack of power at highway speeds

115. A DTC P0442 (a small evaporative leak) has been detected. Technician A says a loose gas cap could cause the problem. Technician B says a loose evaporative system hose could be the problem. Which technician is correct?

a. A only
b. B only
c. Both A and B
d. Neither A nor B

116. Technician A says that a defective one-way exhaust check valve could cause the air pump to fail. Technician B says that the airflow to the exhaust manifold when the engine is warm can cause a drivability problem. Which technician is correct?

a. A only
b. B only
c. Both A and B
d. Neither A nor B

117. This represents a waveform for _____.

a. MAF
b. BARO
c. O2S
d. TP

ENGINE PERFORMANCE (A8)

CATEGORY: COMPUTERIZED ENGINE CONTROLS DIAGNOSIS AND REPAIR

118. A vehicle equipped with gasoline direct injection (GDI), and an electronic throttle control system has a high idle speed (about 1,200 RPM) and will not accelerate any faster. This condition could be due to _____.

    a. a fault in the electronic throttle control system
    b. a fault in the low pressure in-tank electric fuel pump
    c. a fault with the high-pressure pump
    d. a fault with the fuel pressure regulator

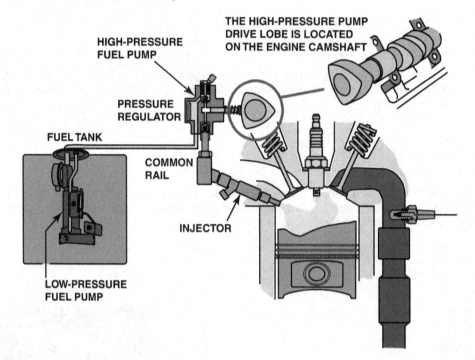

119. An oxygen sensor (O2S) is being tested and the O2S voltage is fluctuating between 800 millivolts and 200 millivolts. Technician A says the engine is operating too lean. Technician B says the engine is operating too rich. Which technician is correct?

    a. A only
    b. B only
    c. Both A and B
    d. Neither A nor B

120. An oxygen sensor in a fuel-injected engine is slow to react to changes in air-fuel mixture. Technician A says that the O2S may need to be replaced. Technician B says that driving the vehicle at highway speeds may restore proper operation of the O2S. Which technician is correct?

    a. A only
    b. B only
    c. Both A and B
    d. Neither A nor B

121. Technician A says that OBD II SAE (generic) codes are the same for all OBD II vehicles. Technician B says that the DLC is located under the hood on all OBD II vehicles. Which technician is correct?

    a. A only
    b. B only
    c. Both A and B
    d. Neither A nor B

122. The IAC counts are zero. Technician A says that the engine may have a vacuum leak or a stuck throttle cable. Technician B says the throttle plate(s) may be dirty or partially clogged. Which technician is correct?

    a. A only
    b. B only
    c. Both A and B
    d. Neither A nor B

123. An engine is operating at idle speed with all accessories off and the gear selector in park. Technician A says that a scan tool should display injector pulse width between 1.5 and 3.5 milliseconds. Technician B says that the oxygen sensor activity as displayed on a scan tool should indicate over 800 millivolts and less than 200 millivolts. Which technician is correct?

    a. A only
    b. B only
    c. Both A and B
    d. Neither A nor B

124. Two technicians are discussing fuel trim. Technician A says that oxygen sensor activity determines short-term fuel trim numbers. Technician B says that a positive (+) long-term fuel trim means that the computer is adding fuel to compensate for a lean exhaust. Which technician is correct?

    a. A only
    b. B only
    c. Both A and B
    d. Neither A nor B

125. The idle speed on a port fuel-injected engine is too high. Which defective component is the *most likely* cause?

    a. MAP
    b. O2S
    c. IAT
    d. IAC

126. A technician is looking at scan data with the engine at idle speed and in park and notices that the MAP sensor voltage reading is about 1.0 volt (18 in. Hg). Technician A says that the reading is normal. Technician B says that the reading indicates a possible MAP sensor fault. Which technician is correct?

    a. A only
    b. B only
    c. Both A and B
    d. Neither A nor B

127. The voltage output of a zirconia oxygen sensor is low (close to 0 volts). Technician A says the engine is operating too lean. Technician B says the engine is operating too rich. Which technician is correct?

    a. A only
    b. B only
    c. Both A and B
    d. Neither A nor B

128. A typical TP sensor used in electronic throttle control (ETC) systems includes _____.

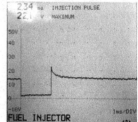

   a. one standard three-wire TP sensor
   b. two TP sensors in one with one producing an increase in voltage as the other one produces a decreasing voltage as the throttle plate moves toward wide open
   c. three TP sensors in one with two producing an increase in voltage as the other one produces a decreasing voltage as the throttle plate moves toward wide open
   d. either b or c

129. Which of the following describes acceptable oxygen sensor activity from rich to lean and lean to rich?

   a. 128 to 136 times per minute (60 seconds)
   b. 8 to 10 times per second
   c. 1 to 5 times per second
   d. 30 to 40 times per second

130. Which of the following describes acceptable oxygen sensor activity as measured with a multimeter set to read DC volts?

   a. 0.350 to 0.550 volts
   b. 0.150 to 0.950 volts
   c. 0.450 to 0.850 volts
   d. 0.450 volts and steady

131. Two technicians are discussing the diagnosis of a TP sensor voltage low fault stored diagnostic trouble code (DTC). Technician A says that if the opposite DTC (TP sensor high) can be set, the problem is the component itself. Technician B says if the opposite DTC cannot be set, the problem is with the wiring or the computer. Which technician is correct?

   a. A only
   b. B only
   c. Both A and B
   d. Neither A nor B

132. The preferred method to clear diagnostic trouble codes (DTCs) is to _____.

   a. disconnect the negative battery cable for 10 seconds
   b. use a scan tool
   c. remove the computer (PCM) power feed fuse
   d. cycle the ignition key on and off 40 times

133. Two technicians are discussing a vehicle that will not crank. Technician A says that it could be due to a fault or setting of the vehicle security system. Technician B says that it can be a defective starter motor. Which technician is correct?

   a. A only
   b. B only
   c. Both A and B
   d. Neither A nor B

134. This waveform of a fuel injector represents _____.

   a. a normal pattern
   b. a clogged injector
   c. a shorted injector
   d. neither A nor B

135. This waveform of a fuel injector represents _____.

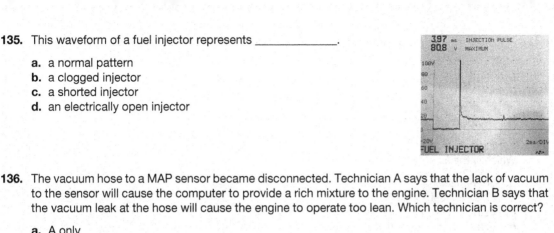

   a. a normal pattern
   b. a clogged injector
   c. a shorted injector
   d. an electrically open injector

136. The vacuum hose to a MAP sensor became disconnected. Technician A says that the lack of vacuum to the sensor will cause the computer to provide a rich mixture to the engine. Technician B says that the vacuum leak at the hose will cause the engine to operate too lean. Which technician is correct?

   a. A only
   b. B only
   c. Both A and B
   d. Neither A nor B

137. A drivability problem that does not set a DTC is being discussed by two technicians. Technician A says that a dirty MAF sensor could be the cause. Technician B says a shorted TP sensor could be the cause. Which technician is correct?

   a. A only
   b. B only
   c. Both A and B
   d. Neither A nor B

138. Which of the following scan tool data is the *least likely* reading for a proper operating engine at idle speed in park or neutral?

   a. ECT = 200°F (93°C)
   b. IAC = 56 counts
   c. TP = 0.51 V
   d. MAP = 1.01 V

139. The following scan tool data is shown to two technicians:
   ECT = 195°F (91°C)   MAP = 0.98 V
   O2S = 450 to 850 mV   MAF = 4 g/s
   TP = 0.46 V IAT = 80°F (27°C)
   Technician A says the engine is operating too rich. Technician B says that all of the scan data looks normal. Which technician is correct?

   a. A only
   b. B only
   c. Both A and B
   d. Neither A nor B

140. OBD II DTCs are retrieved by using _____.

   a. a jumper wire to short two terminals at the data link connector (DLC)
   b. a scan tool
   c. turning the ignition on, off, and back on within 5 seconds
   d. an analog voltmeter connected to the DLC

141. A vehicle fails an enhanced exhaust emission test for excessive hydrocarbon (HC) emissions. The other exhaust emissions were within state standards. Technician A says that a defective fuel pressure regulator could be the cause. Technician B says that a fault in the secondary ignition such as an open spark plug wire could be the cause. Which technician is correct?

   a. A only
   b. B only
   c. Both A and B
   d. Neither A nor B

142. A vehicle fails an enhanced exhaust emission test for excessive oxides of nitrogen (NO_x) emission. Which is the *most likely* to be the cause?

    a. A defective cooling fan
    b. Excessively high fuel pump pressure
    c. A defective AIR pump switching valve
    d. A clogged PCV valve

143. A vehicle fails an enhanced exhaust emission test for excessive carbon monoxide (CO) emission. Which is the *least likely* to be the cause?

    a. A defective fuel pressure regulator (excessive pressure)
    b. A leaking fuel injector
    c. A stuck open purge valve
    d. A stuck closed EGR valve

144. A multiport fuel-injected V-8 engine has a rough and unstable idle and the customer states that it has stalled at times. There are no stored diagnostic trouble codes. Which is the most likely cause?

    a. A bad throttle position (TP) sensor
    b. An open fuel injector winding
    c. An open oxygen sensor (O2S) lead
    d. A dirty throttle plate

145. A multiport fuel-injected engine has a knocking noise on medium to hard acceleration. Which of the following is the *most likely* cause?

    a. An excessively rich air-fuel mixture
    b. A partially clogged EGR passage
    c. An intake manifold gasket leak
    d. An open in one lead of the crankshaft position (CKP) sensor

146. A V-6 equipped with sequential port fuel injection is idling rough. Three DTCs are stored and they represent misfire codes for cylinder 1, 3, and 5. Technician A says that leaking upper injector O-rings could be the cause. Technician B says that a dirty throttle plate could be the cause. Which technician is correct?

    a. A only
    b. B only
    c. Both A and B
    d. Neither A nor B

147. The owner of a sport utility vehicle (SUV) is concerned with poor fuel economy. A check with a scan tool shows no stored DTCs and the data stream shows the following information:
HO2S = 198 to 815 mV   Injector pulse width = 3.3 ms
ECT = 100°C   TP = 0.51 V
Technician A says that the thermostat could be defective. Technician B says the engine is operating too rich. Which technician is correct?

    a. A only
    b. B only
    c. Both A and B
    d. Neither A nor B

148. Two technicians are discussing monitors. Technician A says that the monitor for each system, such as the catalytic converter monitor, has to run before a diagnostic trouble code can be set. Technician B says that the monitor status can be checked using a scan tool. Which technician is correct?

    a. A only
    b. B only
    c. Both A and B
    d. Neither A nor B

149. The injector pulse width on a port fuel injected engine is higher than normal. Technician A says that it could be caused by a vacuum leak. Technician B says that it can be caused by a clogged fuel injector. Which technician is correct?

   a. A only
   b. B only
   c. Both A and B
   d. Neither A nor B

150. An engine equipped with gasoline direct fuel injection starts and idles perfectly but lacks power when the vehicle is being driven under a heavy load. Technician A says that the high pressure pump could be not working as designed. Technician B says the intake valves may be covered with carbon reducing the airflow through the engine. Which technician is correct?

   a. A only
   b. B only
   c. Both A and B
   d. Neither A nor B

151. A customer complains of sluggish performance and poor fuel economy. A DTC for HO2S voltage low (lean exhaust) has been set. Technician A says that one or more fuel injectors could be clogged. Technician B says that the fuel return line from the regulator could be clogged. Which technician is correct?

   a. A only
   b. B only
   c. Both A and B
   d. Neither A nor B

152. An engine will not go into closed loop. Which sensor is the *most likely* to be at fault?

   a. Oxygen sensor (O2S)
   b. Intake air temperature (IAT)
   c. MAP sensor
   d. BARO sensor

ENGINE PERFORMANCE (A8)

CATEGORY: GENERAL ENGINE DIAGNOSIS

1. **The correct answer is c.** Technician A is correct because any misfire will cause paper held at the tailpipe to "puff." A burned valve will cause one cylinder to not produce as strong an exhaust stream as the others creating the uneven exhaust detected by holding the paper at the tailpipe. Technician B is correct because antifreeze tends to leave a gray/white stain on the engine where coolant has leaked and then evaporated by the engine heat. Answers a, b, and d are not correct because both technicians are correct.

2. **The correct answer is c.** Technician A is correct because a fluorescent dye can be added to the engine oil and allowed to circulate. A black light is then turned on and any leaks will show as a bright yellow-green area. This is the preferred method for locating fluid leaks. Technician B is correct because a white powder spray (such as foot spray) will show the location of leaks by turning dark where the liquid contacts the white powder. Answers a, b, and d are not correct because both technicians are correct.

3. **The correct answer is b.** A good mechanically sound engine should measure less than 20% leakage. The lower the amount of leakage, the better the engine. Answer a is not correct because all cylinders should be less than 20%, not within 20% of each other. Answer c is not correct because the leakage should be less than 20%, not more than 20%. Answer d is not correct because the leakage should be very low. A 70% leakage rate means that 70% of the air entering the cylinder is escaping past the piston rings or valves.

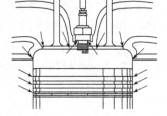

4. **The correct answer is b.** Technician B is correct because if the engine speed (RPM) drops when a cylinder is canceled (spark plug wire is grounded), the cylinder is producing power and contributing to the engine speed at idle. Technician A is not correct because the biggest drop in engine RPM is created by the strongest cylinder, not the weakest. Answers c and d are not correct because only Technician B is correct.

5. **The correct answer is a.** Vacuum measured during cranking should be at least 2.5 in. Hg. Obviously, the higher the cranking vacuum, the better the engine cylinder is sealed. Answer b is not correct because the only time that vacuum in an engine can be near 25 in. Hg. is during deceleration. Answer c is not correct because even though it is possible for some engines to produce 17 to 21 in. Hg. during cranking, it should not be considered the specification for cranking vacuum. Answer d is not correct for the same reason as given for answer c.

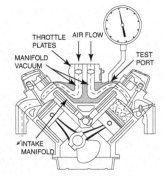

6. **The correct answer is c.** Both technicians are correct. Technician A is correct because coolant which contains about 50% water will cause steam or white exhaust especially in cold weather. Technician B is correct because automatic transmission fluid can get into the intake manifold and be burned in the combustion chamber creating white exhaust if there is a fault in the vacuum modulator used on some automatic transmissions/transaxles. Answers a, b, and d are not correct because both technicians are correct.

7. **The correct answer is c.** Both technicians are correct. Technician A is correct because a burned valve will cause the cylinder to produce less than normal power. Technician B is correct because a fault in either the injector or the spark plug can cause the cylinder to misfire. Answers a, b, and d are not correct because both technicians are correct.

8. **The correct answer is c.** Both technicians are correct. Technician A is correct because a defective engine mount can cause the engine to be out of position in the vehicle causing a vibration. Technician B is correct because a leaking mount will reduce its ability to dampen engine vibrations. Answers a, b, and d are not correct because both technicians are correct.

9. **The correct answer is b.** If the valve stem seals are worn, then oil will be drawn into the combustion chamber and burned causing the blue exhaust smoke. This is most noticeable at first engine start of the day because it allows time for the oil to flow past the guides and into the cylinders after the engine has not been run for a period of time. Answer a (leaking fuel injector) is not a likely cause of seeing blue exhaust smoke at first engine start. If the fuel injector were leaking it would likely cause black exhaust smoke out the tailpipe when the engine is first started, not blue exhaust smoke. Answer c (leaking valve cover gasket) is not a likely cause of blue exhaust even though oil on the exhaust manifold could cause some fumes to be seem but not when the engine is first started. Answer d (over-filled oil level) could not be the cause of blue exhaust smoke even though it could cause an oil leak.

10. **The correct answer is c.** Both technicians are correct. Technician A is correct because if the timing chain is stretched, the valve timing (and ignition timing) will be retarded. This causes the engine to produce less than normal power especially at low engine speeds (RPM). Technician B is correct because a restricted exhaust will increase exhaust back pressure and will cause the engine to produce less than normal power. Answers a, b, and d are not correct because both technicians are correct.

11. **The correct answer is b.** A clogged exhaust system is correct because if the exhaust system is restricted, the amount of airflow through the engine is reduced. When the amount of airflow through the engine is reduced, the amount of poster that the engine produces is reduced. Answer a is not correct because if the bypass were stuck closed then the supercharger would be able to supply full output to the engine. The only way the bypass valve could be the cause of a low power concern would be if it were stuck open (not closed). Answer c is not correct because while a plugged PCV valve could cause increased crankcase pressures, it would not cause a substantial reduction in engine output. Answer d is not correct because while a decrease in coolant level could cause the engine to run hotter than normal, it would not cause a substantial reduction in engine output.

12. **The correct answer is c.** Both technicians are correct. Technician A is correct because a clogged or defective fuel injector would result in an engine misfire that would be most noticeable during acceleration. Technician B is correct because a defective spark plug wire or coil on a coil-on-plug type of ignition system would cause a misfire that would most likely to occur and be noticeable during acceleration. Answers a, b, and c are not correct because both technicians are correct.

13. **The correct answer is d.** Any of the above colors could be a coolant. Answer a (green) can be a coolant because this is the color of old conventional inorganic acid technology (IAT) antifreeze. Answer b (yellow) is correct because some hybrid organic acid technology (HOAT) coolants are yellow in color. Answer c (orange) is correct because organic acid technology coolants such as DEX-COOL is orange in color. Answers a, b, and c are not correct because any of the above are correct.

14. **The correct answer is b.** Technician B is correct because if the head gasket were leaking between cylinder number 3 and 4, the compression on these cylinders would be lower than normal. The defective gasket would allow compression to escape to the adjacent cylinders. Technician A is not correct because a burned valve would only affect one cylinder. It would be very rare that two cylinders side-by-side would both have a burned valve and is therefore not a "likely" cause. Answers c and d are not correct because only Technician B is correct.

15. **The correct answer is b.** Technician B is correct because the maximum difference, as specified by most vehicle manufacturers, is 20%. If the highest reading is 160 psi, then the lowest cylinder compression should be greater than 128 psi (160 × 20% = 32 psi, 160 psi – 32 psi = 128 psi). Technician A is not correct because the engine should be cranked through at least four compression events or 4 to 5 "puffs" (not 3 "puffs"). Answers c and d are not correct because only Technician B is correct.

16. **The correct answer is b.** Technician B is correct because if the compression reading is greatly increased with a couple of squirts of oil in the cylinder, then when the compression test is first performed without the oil, the piston rings are worn or broken. Technician A is not correct because oil should only be squirted into those cylinders that achieved a lower than normal compression test reading to help determine the reason for the low compression. Answers c and d are not correct because only Technician B is correct.

17. **The correct answer is b.** Technician B is correct because if the piston rings were worn (or broken), compressed air could escape past the rings and flow into the crankcase. The air would then escape from the engine through the oil drain-back holes and other openings in the block and eventually be heard at the oil fill opening. Technician A is not correct because the oil filter is not being tested and the compressed air entering the combustion chamber could not get into or past the oil filter. Answers c and d are not correct because only Technician B is correct.

18. **The correct answer is b.** Technician B is correct. A leakage of 30% is excessive and if air is heard escaping from the engine air inlet, then one or more intake valves must be leaking. It is also possible that the cylinder being tested is not at TDC on the compression stroke. If the cylinder were at TDC of the exhaust stroke, both intake and exhaust valves would be open and air would also be heard coming from the tailpipe. Technician A is not correct because 30% leakage is too much for a slightly worn engine. Leakage should not exceed 20%. Answers c and d are not correct because only Technician B is correct.

19. **The correct answer is b.** Technician B only is correct. All cylinders should drop the same (within 50 RPM) when they are canceled or grounded out. This indicates that each cylinder was contributing an equal amount of the operation of the engine. If a cylinder drops the RPM less than others, the cylinder is weak. Technician A is not correct because the more the engine RPM drops when a cylinder is canceled, the more that cylinder is contributing to the operation of the engine. Answers c and d are not correct because only Technician B is correct.

20. **The correct answer is d.** Neither technician is correct. Technician A is not correct because the specification for cranking vacuum is greater than 2.5 in. Hg. Even though a sound engine with a completely closed throttle may be able to produce 17 in. Hg to 21 in. Hg vacuum (at sea level) during cranking, it is not the specification for cranking vacuum. Technician B is not correct because a floating vacuum gauge needle is an indication of an overly rich or lean air-fuel mixture, not a sticking valve. A sticking valve will cause the vacuum gauge needle to move rapidly up and down. Answer c is not correct because neither technician is correct.

21. **The correct answer is c.** Both technicians are correct. Technician A is correct because an excessively rich air-fuel mixture will create black exhaust smoke. A slightly rich engine may not emit black smoke because the catalytic converter will usually oxidize the unburned fuel (hydrocarbons) into H_2O (water) and CO_2 (carbon dioxide). Technician B is correct because white smoke or steam is an indication that coolant is getting into the combustion chamber and is being vaporized by the heat of combustion. White exhaust smoke also occurs if automatic transmission fluid (ATF) is drawn into the combustion chamber due to a fault with the vacuum modulator on an older automatic transmission. Answers a, b, and d are not correct because both technicians are correct.

22. **The correct answer is c.** Both technicians are correct. Technician A is correct because a clogged catalytic converter can be the cause of an exhaust system restriction. Technician B is correct because a clogged (or damaged) muffler can cause an exhaust system restriction. A muffler can be clogged by parts broken from the internal baffles. If the catalytic converter is replaced and the exhaust is still restricted, a clogged muffler (or resonator) could be the cause. Answers a, b, and d are not correct because both technicians are correct.

23. **The correct answer is c.** Both technicians are correct. Technician A is correct because if exhaust gases are escaping from the combustion chamber and into the coolant past a defective head gasket, HC (hydrocarbons) or CO (carbon monoxide) emissions will be able to be measured above the coolant with the engine running. Technician B is correct because chemical-coated paper that changes color when exposed to exhaust gases can also be used to verify a defective head gasket. Answers a, b, and d are not correct because both technicians are correct.

24. **The correct answer is d.** Any of the above could be the cause of a P0017 diagnostic trouble code (DTC). Answer a is correct because a skipped timing belt would cause the code to be set for a mismatch between the crank and camshaft sensors. Answer b is correct because a clogged VVT screen could prevent the proper amount of engine oil from flowing through the valve to achieve the commanded camshaft position. This lack of oil flow could set the DTC. Answer c is correct because if there is a fault in the VVT solenoid such as an electrical or mechanical fault, this could cause the camshaft to fail to achieve the commanded position and could cause the DTC to set.

25. **The correct answer is b.** Technician B is correct because noise is created by the rocker arm pounding onto the end of the valve when the clearance (lash) is greater than specified by the vehicle manufacturer. Technician A is not correct because the engine will not create noise if the valve clearance is too tight. The valves may not close all the way if the clearance is too tight which could lead to a burned valve. Answers c and d are not correct because only Technician B is correct.

26. **The correct answer is c.** Both technicians are correct. Technician A is correct because a worn oil pump can cause low oil pressure. An oil pump wears because it is the only engine part that operates on unfiltered oil. Technician B is correct because worn bearings allow an excessive amount of oil to escape and return to the oil pan resulting in a drop in oil pressure. Answers a, b, and d are not correct because both technicians are correct.

27. **The correct answer is d.** Any of the answers are possible causes of the engine running hotter than normal while driving at slow speeds. Answer a is correct because if the fan motor was wired backward, the fan would blow forward, which would reduce the airflow through the radiator and would cause the engine to run hotter than normal. At higher speeds, the fan is commanded off so the airflow from the vehicle moving forward would restore proper engine cooling. Answer b is also correct because the replacement fan could be defective preventing enough airflow to properly cool the engine at low vehicle speeds. Answer c is correct because if the fan relay were defective, it would prevent the fan motor from working and could cause the engine to run hotter than normal at slow vehicle speeds.

28. **The correct answer is a.** If engine oil that has a higher viscosity than specified such as using SAE 10W-30 instead of the specified SAE 5W-20, this could result in reduced fuel economy due to the extra drag caused by the thicker oil. Answer b is not correct because oil turns color usually due to contaminants and dirt in the oil and is not affected by its viscosity. Answer c is not correct because the pressure around a head gasket is not affected by the viscosity of the engine oil. Answer d is not correct because a higher viscosity engine oil will likely increase, not decrease, the oil pressure.

29. **The correct answer is d.** Using water that is free from chemicals or mineral is best for the cooling system and will help prevent rust and corrosion. While most experts recommend using de-mineralized (purified) water (answer a), any of the types of water can be used. Answer b is correct because many vehicle manufacturers state that good clean drinking water can be used safely. Some experts recommend the use of distilled water (answer c), because it is readily available and cost effective and does not contain any chemicals such as chlorine or minerals that could cause rust or corrosion in the cooling system.

30. **The correct answer is c.** Both technicians are correct. Technician A is correct because as the timing chain stretches, the camshaft will lag behind the rotation of the crankshaft (retarded). Technician B is correct because the timing chain and gears should all be replaced as a set if the slack is greater than factory specifications (usually less than ½ in.). Answer a, b, and d are not correct because both technicians are correct.

31. **The correct answer is b.** The oil pressure light comes on whenever the pressure drops to between 3 and 7 psi. Answer a is not correct because the oil pressure light is not the same as the amber "change oil soon" light. Answer c is not correct because there is no indication when the bypass valve opens, which often occurs when the oil is cold or the oil filter is dirty and creates a restriction. Answer d is not correct because this valve simply keeps oil from draining back into the oil pan after the engine stops running.

32. **The correct answer is b.** A smooth operating engine depends on equal compression in all cylinders. Answer a is not correct because high compression on most, but not all, cylinders could indicate a fault and will likely cause the engine to run rough. Answer c is not correct because even though all cylinders should be above 100 psi during a compression test, they should be much closer than 70 psi from the highest to the lowest cylinder. Answer d is not correct because all engines should be able to produce at least (greater than) 100 psi compression.

ENGINE PERFORMANCE (A8)

CATEGORY: IGNITION SYSTEM DIAGNOSIS AND REPAIR

33. **The correct answer is c.** Both technicians are correct. Technician A is correct because the engine would produce less than normal power if the exhaust is restricted. Technician B is correct because the engine would produce less than normal power at low speeds if the valve timing was retarded due to a worn timing chain or other fault. Answers a, b, and d are not correct because both technicians are correct.

34. **The correct answer is c.** Both technicians are correct. Technician A is correct because a no-spark condition can be caused by a faulty crankshaft position (CKP) sensor. The CKP signals the ignition module or the computer to fire the spark plug based on the CKP signal for piston position. Technician B is also correct because a defective ignition switch could allow the engine to crank yet not supply the electrical current to power the ignition coil primary circuit, which typically requires 5 A to 12 A. Answers a, b, and d are not correct because both technicians are correct.

35. **The correct answer is a.** Technician A only is correct because this tone (notched) wheel is used by the crankshaft position sensor to provide engine speed and piston position information to the Powertrain Control Module (PCM). Answer b (Technician B) is not correct because the tone wheel is not used by the starter motor even though the engine speed is being monitored by the PCM from signals produced by the CKP sensor. Answers c and d are not correct because only technician A is correct.

36. **The correct answer is a.** Technician A is correct because a spark tester should be used to check for spark and it should be attached to a spark plug wire. The spark tester clip should be attached to the engine and the engine cranked to check for spark at the tester. A spark tester requires at least 25,000 volts to fire so the ignition system is working if the spark tester fires. Technician B is not correct because a standard gap spark plug only requires about 3,000 volts outside of the engine, whereas it may require 10,000 volts or more to fire a spark plug under compression inside the engine. Answers c and d are not correct because only Technician A is correct.

37. **The correct answer is c.** Both technicians are correct. Technician A is correct because high resistance in a spark plug wire on the companion cylinder in a waste-spark system can cause a misfire to occur to on the companion cylinder. Technician B is also correct because if the high voltage spark cannot reach ground, it can arc inside the coil itself creating a low resistance path called a track, also called leakage. Answers a, b, and d are not correct because both technicians are correct.

38. **The correct answer is c.** Both technicians are correct. Technician A is correct because all spark plugs should be checked for the proper gap before installing in the engine. Most spark plugs are gapped at the factory but may not be the correct gap for the vehicle or the gap may have changed during shipping and handling. Technician B is also correct because platinum becomes brittle when used in an engine and could break off if a gapping tool is used to reset the gap after the spark plugs have been run in an engine. Answers a, b, and d are not correct because both technicians are correct.

39. **The correct answer is d.** None of the answers is correct because the ignition timing is non-adjustable on waste-spark or coil-on-plug-type ignition systems. Answer a is not correct because the crankshaft position (CKP) sensor, if movable, is simply made that way to provide proper clearance and moving; it does not affect the ignition timing. Answer b is not correct because the camshaft position (CMP) sensor is used for cylinder identification and fuel timing and will not affect or change the ignition timing if moved even if possible. Answer c is not correct because neither answer a nor b is correct.

40. **The correct answer is a.** Technician A is correct because a reading of "OL" on the display of a digital meter set to read K ohms (1,000 ohms) means that the resistance is higher than the meter is able to read. This means that the spark plug wire is electrically open (lacks continuity) and should be replaced. Technician B is not correct because the meter reading indicates a spark plug wire that has excessive resistance and should be replaced. Answers c and d are not correct because only Technician A is correct.

41. **The correct answer is d.** The ignition module can be triggered by a pickup coil (distributor-type ignition), computer, or crankshaft position sensor depending on year, make, and model of the vehicle. Service information should be checked to determine which unit is used to trigger the module if diagnosing a no-start condition. Answers a, b, and c are all correct, but the best answer is d.

42. **The correct answer is a.** The photo is a coil used on a coil-near-plug ignition system. Answers b, c, and d are not correct because the best answer is a coil assembly even though a coil-on-plug (COP) or coil-near-plug ignition coil often includes the ignition module as part of the coil assembly.

43. **The correct answer is c.** Both technicians are correct. Technician A is correct because a pickup coil can be tested using an ohmmeter to be sure the coil windings are within the resistance specifications as well as to check that it is not shorted-to-ground. Technician B is also correct because even though the output of a coil cannot be checked using an ohmmeter, both the primary and secondary windings can be checked for specified resistance. Answers a, b, and d are not correct because both technicians are correct.

44. **The correct answer is c.** The best answer is 0.5 to 3 ohms. Answers a, b, and d are not correct because they are not close to being the resistance of a typical ignition coil primary winding.

45. **The correct answer is d.** The secondary winding of most ignition coils will fall within the range from 6,000 to 30,000 ohms. Answers a, b, and c are not correct because they do not match the typical resistance of the secondary winding of an ignition coil.

46. **The correct answer is d.** Both answers and b are correct. Answer a is correct because a compression-sensing type of system uses a waste-spark-type ignition system and compares when the one of the companion cylinders fires first which is the cylinder NOT on compression stroke. Answer b is correct because by using a compression-sensing circuit, the powertrain control module (PCM) can determine which cylinder is under compression and then using data from the crankshaft position (CKP) sensor determine the cylinder location thereby eliminating the need for a camshaft position sensor. Answer c is not correct because the compression-sensing circuit requires a waste-spark type ignition and not a coil-on-plug type system to work.

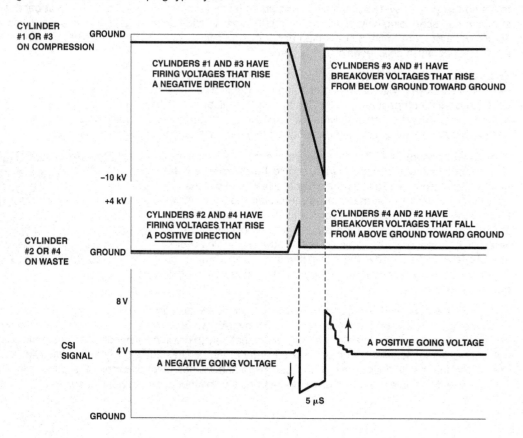

47. **The correct answer is b.** Technician B is correct because the voltage to fire the spark plugs exceeds 20,000 V (20 kV). The maximum voltage should be 15,000 V (15 kV) and the higher voltage could be caused by a defective coil wire since it affects all cylinders. Technician A is not correct because the firing voltages are too high. Answers c and d are not correct because only Technician B is correct.

48. **The correct answer is a.** A good spark plug wire should measure less than 10,000 ohms of resistance per foot of length. Therefore, a spark plug wire that is 2.5 feet long should measure less than 25,000 ohms (25 kΩ) (2.5 × 10,000 Ω = 25,000 Ω). Answers b and c are not correct because 200,000 ohms and 250,000 ohms are too high a resistance. Answer d is not correct because a wire can be greater than 2,500 ohms and be okay.

49. **The correct answer is b.** The least likely cause of a weak spark is a battery voltage of 12.2 volts. Even though a battery voltage is less than normal, it could be enough to allow the ignition coil(s) to become fully saturated and provide the correct spark to the spark plugs. Answer a is not correct because a partially shorted primary winding of the ignition coil could cause a weak spark and the question asks for which is the least likely to cause a weak spark. Answer c is not correct because a spark plug wire with high resistance could cause a weak spark. Answer d is not correct because a voltage drop across the ignition switch would reduce the current flow to the coil which could cause a weak spark.

50. **The correct answer is a.** An open spark plug wire can cause an engine to miss on one cylinder because an open wire lacks electrical continuity and no spark can reach the spark plug. Answer b is not correct because even though a high resistance spark plug wire can cause a weak spark to the spark plug, it is not the most likely to cause an engine miss. Answer c is not correct because a worn rotor would affect all cylinders, not just one. Answer d is not correct because even though a clogged fuel filter could affect engine performance, it will not cause an engine miss on one cylinder.

51. **The correct answer is c.** A loose spark plug can prevent the heat from escaping to the cylinder head thereby causing excessive wear to the center and side electrodes. Answer a is not correct because, while a high resistance spark plug wire could cause an engine miss, it would not cause the spark plug to be excessively worn. Answer b is not correct because a shorted ignition coil could cause an engine miss but would not cause the spark plug to become excessively worn. Answer d is not correct because a defective ignition coil could cause a misfire but cannot cause a spark plug to run hotter even on a coil-on-plug-type ignition system.

52. **The correct answer is b.** All spark plugs should be tightened to the vehicle manufacturer's specifications and not loosened after tightening. Answer b is the only one of the four answers which is not true and is therefore the correct answer because the question asks that all except that one should be performed. Answers a, c, and d are all incorrect because they are the correct items that should be done and are therefore not the right answer.

53. **The correct answer is c.** Both technicians are correct. Technician A is correct because spark plug wire should be checked with an ohmmeter to be certain it has the proper resistance. Technician B is also correct because the insulation should be inspected for areas where the high voltage spark could arc to ground. Answers a, b, and d are not correct because both technicians are correct.

54. **The correct answer is d.** No part needs to be replaced if the cause of the engine miss was corrected by replacing the electrical connector to the coil. If a diagnostic trouble code (DTC) was stored, it should be erased. Answers a, b, and c are not correct because no part needs to be replaced.

55. **The correct answer is b.** Damage to the ignition coil(s) will not occur if the battery voltage is low even though the output may be less than normal. Answers a, c, and d are not correct because low battery voltage can cause slow engine cranking, dim headlights, and slower than normal windshield wiper operations.

56. **The correct answer is a.** Technician A is correct because there is spark from the coil and no spark to the spark plugs, and the distributor rotor is likely defective allowing the spark to travel to the steel distributor shaft. Technician B is not correct because while fouled spark plugs could cause a no-start condition, they cannot be the cause of no spark reaching the spark plugs.

57. **The correct answer is c.** Both technicians are correct. Technician A is correct because moisture combined with dirt or crack can provide an electrical path to ground for the spark through the distributor cap or rotor. Technician B is also correct because water on spark plug wires that do not have proper insulation can cause the spark to travel to ground through the water. Answers a, b, and d are not correct because both technicians are correct.

58. **The correct answer is c.** Both technicians are correct. Technician A is correct because a defective distributor cap or rotor can cause an ignition miss if all of the sparks do not have a good electrical path to the spark plugs. Technician B is also correct because a cracked spark plug can cause an engine miss because the spark can travel through the crack to ground outside of the engine and no spark is available to burn the air-fuel mixture inside the engine.

59. **The correct answer is a.** Worn spark plugs require a higher (not a lower) voltage to fire due to the rounding of the center electrode and the increased gap. Answers b, c, and d are all correct statements about spark plugs.

60. **The correct answer is c.** Using the incorrect spark plug could cause the engine to run poorly but is least likely to cause slow jerky cranking. Answers a, b, and c can all be caused by using an incorrect spark plug heat range. If the heat range is too high (hot), then spark knock is likely, especially in warm weather and under moderate load conditions. If a too cold a heat range plug is used, a misfire due to fouling can occur which would reduce fuel economy (answer b) or cause a misfire (answer c).

61. **The correct answer is b.** Technician B is correct because a fouled spark plug allows the spark to take the path of least resistance and flow through the carbon to the steel shell of the plug and not jump across the gap between the center and the side electrodes. This results in a lower-than-normal firing voltage, yet the spark line is longer than normal because the spark energy remaining in the coil is dissipated over a longer period of time because a spark did not occur. A cracked plug could also cause this same condition. Technician A is not correct because a defective spark plug wire would cause a higher voltage (higher firing line) and a shorter-than-normal spark line. Answers c and d are not correct because Technician B only is correct.

62. **The correct answer is a.** The primary winding of a typical high-energy ignition coil should measure from 0.5 to 3.0 ohms depending on the year, make, and model of vehicle. Answers b, c, and d are not correct because these do not represent acceptable resistance ranges for the primary winding of an ignition coil.

63. **The correct answer is b.** A spark tester has a calibrated gap of about 0.75 inch (1.9 cm), which requires at least 25,000 volts (25 kV) to fire. If an ignition system is capable of firing a spark tester, then the ignition system is okay. If the spark tester does not fire or fires only intermittently, then there is an ignition system fault. Answer a is not correct because holding the spark plug wire ¼ inch away from ground is not a scientific method to check for proper spark voltage. A 0.25-inch spark requires about 10,000 volts to jump, yet it requires at least 20,000 volts to fire a spark plug under load inside the combustion chamber. Answer c is not correct for  the same reason why answer a is not correct—not an accurate way to check for proper firing voltage. Answer d is not correct because the ignition system must be loaded to register its maximum output and a meter cannot measure the short duration spark.

ENGINE PERFORMANCE (A8)

CATEGORY: FUEL, AIR INDUCTION, AND EXHAUST SYSTEMS DIAGNOSIS AND REPAIR

64. **The correct answer is b.** Technician B is correct because a clogged PCV valve can cause an increase in crankcase pressure, which can force oil into the air inlet where it then is drawn into the combustion chamber and burned creating blue exhaust smoke. Technician A is not correct because a wastegate is located on the exhaust side of the turbocharger and cannot cause the engine to burn oil. Answers c and d are not correct because only Technician B is correct.

65. **The correct answer is c.** Both technicians are correct. Technician A is correct because a vacuum leak can cause the engine speed to increase especially on those engines equipped with a speed density-type fuel injection system. Technician B is also correct because the throttle plate itself could be partially stuck open due to binding throttle linkage or cable. Answers a, b, and d are not correct because both technicians are correct.

66. **The correct answer is c.** Both technicians are correct. Technician A is correct because the engine would stall if the TCC solenoid were stuck in the applied position even if it is turned off electrically by the brake switch. Technician B is also correct because if air were able to enter the engine between the MAF sensor and the intake, it would lean the air-fuel mixture because it is not being measured. This lean mixture could cause the engine to stall. Answers a, b, and d are not correct because both technicians are correct.

67. **The correct answer is a.** A split or crack in the air in-take hose between the MAF and the throttle plate al-lows "false air" (air not measured by the MAF sensor) to enter the engine. Because this air is not measured, the resulting air-fuel mixture is leaner than normal causing the engine to stumble or stall. Answer b is not correct because a clogged fuel filter will usually affect engine performance under load and not just in drive but not reverse. Answer c is not correct because a clogged air filter will usually affect engine operation under load and not in drive only. Answer d is not correct because a leaking fuel injector will affect engine operation and fuel economy, but is not the most likely cause of a stumble and stall when in drive only.

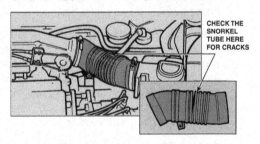

CHECK THE SNORKEL TUBE HERE FOR CRACKS

68. **The correct answer is a.** Technician A is correct because a pinched fuel return line will cause the fuel pressure to increase creating a richer air-fuel mixture and possible poor fuel economy. Technician B is not correct because a partially clogged fuel filter could affect engine operation, especially at high engine speeds and loads by restricting the flow of fuel, but it will not cause the engine to use more fuel. Answers b, c, and d are not correct because Technician A only is correct.

69. **The correct answer is a.** A defective fuel pressure regulator is the most likely cause of causing a hot restart problem. If the fuel pressure regulator has a hole in the rubber diaphragm, fuel is allowed to flow into the intake manifold flooding the intake with fuel. Then when the engine is restarted, the fuel cause an excessively rich air-fuel mixture in the cylinders which can cause the engine to be hard to start (excessive engine cranking) and the exhaust to be black when it does start due to the excessive amount of fuel in the cylinders. Answer b is not correct because a shorted fuel injector will cause excessive current to flow through the injector and while it could cause the injector to deliver fuel

sooner (more current would cause the injector pintle to open sooner), it is not likely that one shorted fuel injectors to cause a hot restart problem and excessive black exhaust smoke. Answer c is not correct because a clogged fuel filter would cause a decrease in the amount of fuel delivered to the engine and therefore not cause a rich condition at engine restart on a warm engine. Answer d is not correct because a clogged air filter would reduce the amount of air entering the engine and would reduce engine power but would not cause the engine to operate too rich at engine startup. The PCM would determine the amount of air entering the engine using the MAF sensor data and then deliver the amount of fuel that matches the amount of air entering the engine.

70. **The correct answer is d.** A clogged fuel return line will cause the fuel pressure to increase, which will likely cause the engine to operate with a richer-than-normal air-fuel ratio creating excessive CO exhaust emissions. Answer a is not correct because a clogged fuel injector would reduce the flow of fuel and would not create excessive CO exhaust emissions, which are caused by a rich air-fuel mixture. Answer b is not correct because a fuel pressure regulator that is stuck open would create a lower-than-normal fuel pressure leading to a possible drivability problem, but not a rich air-fuel mixture. Answer c is not correct because a stuck IAC can cause an idle-related problem but would not cause a richer-than-normal air-fuel mixture.

71. **The correct answer is b.** The fuel pressure should increase because the manifold vacuum applied to the diaphragm of the regulator helps compress the spring inside and lowers the pressure needed to allow fuel to flow back to the fuel tank. Answer a is not correct because gasoline should not be in the vacuum portion of the regulator unless there was a fault with the diaphragm. Answer c is not correct because the fuel pressure should increase, not decrease, when the vacuum is removed from the fuel pressure regulator. Answer d is not correct because there should be a pressure difference if the regulator is controlled by the engine load.

72. **The correct answer is d.** Technician A is not correct because while a vacuum gauge can be used to check for an exhaust restriction, the engine speed should be at 2,000 to 2,500 RPM and not at idle. Technician B is not correct because the vacuum will decrease (not increase) if there is an exhaust restriction. Answers a, b, and c are not correct because neither technician is correct.

73. **The correct answer is b.** Technician B is correct because most vehicle manufacturers recommend a maximum of 10% alcohol in the gasoline for proper engine operation. Technician A is not correct because water is heavier (more dense) than gasoline and sinks to the bottom of gasoline tanks. Answers c and d are not correct because only Technician B is correct.

74. **The correct answer is d.** The resistance is normally not measured as part of fuel pump testing. Answers a, b, and c are not correct because these three items are usually measured when testing an electric fuel pump for proper operation.

75. **The correct answer is c.** Answer c is correct because the winter-blended gas will vaporize easily so that cold-weather starting is possible, which can cause drivability concerns if the weather turns warm. Answer a is not correct because a partially clogged air filter will cause a decrease in engine power but cannot cause a drivability problem when the weather is warm. Answer b is not correct because a partially clogged fuel filter would result in a decrease in the amount of fuel delivered but would affect the operation of the engine under heavy loads or high engine speeds first and not affect engine operation at idle speed nor only when hot. Answer d is not correct because a loose gas cap can cause a evaporative emission diagnostic trouble code to set or a "check gas cap" message on the driver information display but will not cause a drivability problem when hot.

76. **The correct answer is d.** Neither technician is correct. Technician A is not correct because black smoke is created when an excessively rich air-fuel mixture is burned in the combustion chamber and not due to excessive oil usage. The cause can include leaking fuel injectors or fuel pressure regulator (return type system only). Technician B is not correct because blue smoke is created when excessive amount of oil is burned. The cause can include worn valve stem seals or worn piston rings on older vehicles. Answers a, b, and c are not correct because both technicians are not correct.

77. **The correct answer is a.** A clogged or restricted catalytic converter can cause excessive exhaust system backpressure. Answer b is not correct because a defective AIR pump diverter valve would cause airflow from the secondary air injection (SAI) system to flow to the wrong location, but would not have any effect on the flow of the exhaust through the exhaust system. Answer c is not correct because, while a clogged EGR valve exhaust port(s) could cause the exhaust gas recirculation system not to function correctly, it would not have any effect on the flow of the exhaust from the engine itself. Answer d is not correct because even though retarded valve timing could cause reduced engine performance, it would not have any effect on the flow of the exhaust gases through the exhaust system.

78. **The correct answer is b.** Technician B is correct because a clogged or partially clogged fuel filter can cause a strain on the electric fuel pump in the fuel tank, which will cause the pump motor to draw more current leading to possible overheating. Technician A is not correct because even though the pump motor may be drawing more current (amperes) with a clogged filter, the pressure itself is maintained by the fuel pressure regulator. Only if the fuel return line was clogged, would the pressure increase. Answers c and d are not correct because Technician B only is correct.

79. **The correct answer is c.** Both technicians are correct. Technician A is correct because a faulty engine coolant temperature (ECT) sensor could cause the computer to supply either a too lean or a too rich mixture. Technician B is correct because a leaking fuel injector could cause fuel to drip into the combustion chamber causing a rich air-fuel mixture that would be difficult to burn and result in hard starting. In extreme cases, the leaking fuel injector(s) can cause a hydrostatic lock, which could prevent the engine from cranking. Answers a, b, and d are not correct because both technicians are correct.

80. **The correct answer is b.** A hesitation when the throttle is depressed is most likely caused by a defective throttle position (TP) sensor. As soon as the throttle is moved, the signal from the TP sensor signals the computer to supply an extra amount of fuel by either increasing the pulse width for an instant or by pulsing the injectors on two or three times to provide the extra fuel necessary to prevent the engine from stumbling. Answer a is not correct because even though a dirty air filter can contribute to the covering of the mass air flow sensor and cause a decrease in airflow, it is not the most likely cause of a hesitation. Answer c is not correct because while a clogged fuel filter can cause a lack of power, it usually affects engine operation at wide open throttle and not just as the throttle is being opened. Answer d is not correct because a dripping injector would most likely affect fuel economy and is not likely to be the cause of a hesitation.

81. **The correct answer is a.** A catalytic converter is designed to last the life of the vehicle unless it is physically damaged or harmed by an excessively rich or lean air-fuel mixture. Technician B is not correct because the catalytic converter does not wear out because it does not enter into the chemical reaction that occurs inside the converter. Answers c and d are not correct because only Technician A is correct.

82. **The correct answer is c.** Both technicians are correct. Technician A is correct because a gasoline direct injection (GDI) system operates at a much higher pressure (500 to 2,900 psi) than a typical port fuel injection system which operates at about 30 to 60 psi. The higher pressures result in more noticeable noise when the injectors are opened but usually only with the hood open and the engine at idle speed. The injector noise is usually not noticed inside the vehicle and should not be a customer concern. Technician B is correct because many engines equipped with GDI do tend to produce carbon deposits on the backside of the intake valves especially if the vehicle is driven at slow speeds and at low engine speeds. Answers a, b, and d are not correct because both technicians are correct.

83. **The correct answer is b.** When an electronic throttle control (ETC) system detects a fault in the system, it defaults to a throttle setting of about 16% to 20%. This means that the driver will be able to move the vehicle out of the way and not cause an unsafe situation. The system fault could be with the accelerator pedal position (APP) sensor, the throttle position (TP) sensor, or the throttle body assembly. Answer a is not correct because even though some early ETC systems used a throttle cable to move the APP sensor, it is not the most likely cause of an engine operating only at a high idle speed. Answer c is not correct because most systems do not use a throttle cable, and even with the system that do, the engine speed would be limited to idle speed and not set at a high idle speed. Answer d is not correct because a stuck throttle pedal could cause the engine to operate at a high idle; it would not necessarily cause the system warning light to come on which is triggered when a fault in the system has been detected. If the throttle pedal were stuck, the system would not sense that a steady throttle is a fault and would not light the system warning lamp.

84. **The correct answer is c.** Both technicians are correct. Technician A is correct because the fuel pressure would drop if one or more fuel injectors were leaking. Technician B is correct because the fuel pressure would drop if the check valve in the outlet of the fuel pump was leaking. Answers a, b, and d are not correct because both technicians are correct.

85. **The correct answer is d.** All of the above are symptoms of using old gasoline. Answer a is correct because the "light ends" or parts of the fuel that evaporate easily are the first part that is lost when gasoline is stored. Without the light ends, getting the remaining gasoline to ignite can be a challenge. Answer b is correct because the fuel will not burn consistently and will usually cause the engine to not operate smoothly resulting in a rough or unstable idle. Answer c is correct because the fuel will not burn correctly due to the evaporation of many of the components of the fuel, and this can cause the engine to stall especially when the engine is cold.

86. **The correct answer is b.** Operating a vehicle in the city and seldom driving at highway speed will not cause harm to the fuel pump even though this type of driving may be hard on the engine oil. Answer a is not correct because operating a vehicle with a low fuel level could cause harm to the fuel pump since any water or alcohol in the tank will settle on the bottom and be drawn into the pump. Answer c is not correct because not replacing the fuel filter could cause a strain on the fuel pump and cause it to draw more current (amperes) than normal because it is trying to force fuel through a restricted filter. Answer d is not correct because using alcohol-enhanced fuel can be harmful due to its tendency to absorb any moisture in the tank and then accumulate in the bottom of the tank.

87. **The correct answer is a.** Technician A is correct because the fuel is sent to the filter after it flows through the fuel pressure regulator and is then consumed by the engine and is therefore passing through the fuel filter only once. In a return-type system, the fuel is returned to the fuel tank and therefore could flow through the filter several times before being consumed by the engine. Technician B is not correct because the fuel filter is located on the supply side of the system and will not change the fuel pressure if it becomes clogged even through the fuel valve could decrease. Answers b, c, and d are not correct because Technician A only is correct.

88. **The correct answer is c.** Both technicians are correct. Technician A is correct because plastic fuel line connectors usually require special release tools to separate the connection at the fuel filter to avoid causing damage. Technician B is correct because the ground strap needs to be grounded to prevent the buildup of static electricity that is created when gasoline flows through plastic fuel lines. Answers a, b, and d are not correct because both technicians are correct.

89. **The correct answer is b.** The terminal of a typical relay that connects to the power is terminal #30 and the load device is usually connected to terminal #87. Using a fused jumper wire between these two terminals will activate the electric fuel pump. Answer a is not correct because terminals #85 and #86 are for the relay coil and not the power and the load. Answer c is not correct because terminal #87 is the normally open (NO) terminal and #85 is the ground side for the relay coil. Answer d is not correct because terminal #85 is the ground terminal and #30 is the power input terminal. Connecting these two terminals together could blow a fuse in the fused jumper lead.

90. **The correct answer is c.** Both technicians are correct. Technician A is correct because a cracked exhaust manifold could be noisy due to the escaping exhaust gases especially when cold, even though engine noise often covers up the noise in many cases. Technician B is correct because a cracked exhaust manifold will allow outside air (oxygen) to enter the exhaust between exhaust pulses. This extra oxygen will be interpreted by the oxygen sensor as a lean exhaust. Answers a, b, and d are not correct because both technicians are correct.

91. **The correct answer is b.** Using old or stale gasoline will likely cause the engine to be hard-to-start and not run smoothly resulting in a rough or unstable idle especially when the engine is cold. Answer a is not correct because using an aftermarket exhaust system would cause an increase in exhaust nosier and maybe an issue with some older engines that use a vacuum controlled EGR valve. In these engines, the lack of the normal backpressure could prevent the EGR from opening or opening at the proper time which could result in a spark knock condition but would not cause a rough or unstable idle. Answer c is not correct because while the electronic throttle control system does control the idle speed, a fault in the system would likely cause a diagnostic trouble code to set and therefore not a likely cause in this situation. Answer d is not correct because while the variable valve timing (VVT) system does control the camshaft timing, a fault in the system would likely cause a diagnostic trouble code to set and therefore not a likely cause in this situation.

92. **The correct answer is a.** The unit shown is a mass air flow (MAF) sensor which measures the mass (weight) of the air entering the engine. Answer b is not correct because even though the unit may be equipped with a screen, it is not an air filter. Answer c is not correct because even though most MAF sensors contain an electronic circuit that keeps a wire or film hot, it is not for the purpose of heating the air, but is used to determine the mass of the air. Answer d is not correct because even though it is a major sensor, it is not used by the computer to detect engine misfires.

93. **The correct answer is c.** Both technicians are correct. Technician A is correct because the buildup of varnish on the backside (engine side) of the throttle plate can create a ridge that can cause the throttle to stick. Technician B is correct because a kinked throttle cable can cause the throttle to stick. Answers a, b, and d are not correct because both technicians are correct

94. **The correct answer is b.** Technician B is correct because the computer can be programmed to limit engine operation if a diagnostic trouble code (DTC) is set. All DTCs should be cleared after any repair and proper operation of the vehicle confirmed. Technician A is not correct because even though the electronic throttle sensor is defective, it is not likely to fail when servicing another part of the system. Answers a, c, and d are not correct because only Technician B is correct.

95. **The correct answer is b.** Technician A is not correct because the IAC controls the amount of air bypassing the throttle plate to regulate idle speed and does not create a lean air-fuel mixture. Technician B is correct because this "false air" will lean the air-fuel mixture because it bypasses the MAF sensor and is not measured by the computer.

96. **The correct answer is d.** The most likely cause of the problem is due to carbon deposits on the backside of the intake valves which is a common occurrence on engine equipped with gasoline direct injection (GDI) systems. Answer a is not correct because even though a clogged air filter could cause a drivability problem, it is not the most likely to cause a hesitation when cold only. Answer b is not correct because while a clogged fuel filter could cause a problem especially at high engine speeds and loads, it is not likely to be the cause of a hesitation when cold. Answer c is not correct because excessive fuel pressure will tend to richen the air-fuel mixture, which would tend to help eliminate or reduce a hesitation.

97. **The correct answer is b.** The dash warning light indicates lower than normal or reduced power when the electronic throttle control (ETC) system goes into the default mode when a fault has been detected. The engine speed is fixed at 16% to 20% (fast idle) so the vehicle can be moved to an area of safety but cannot be driven. Answer a is not correct because a fault in the variable valve timing (VVT) system would likely cause the malfunction indicator lamp (MIL) to light and a diagnostic trouble code to be set and not any other warning lamp. Answer c is not correct because a fault in the gasoline direct injection (GDI) system would likely cause the MIL to light and a diagnostic trouble code to be set and not any other warning lamp. Answer d is not correct because a fault in the wide band oxygen sensor circuit would likely cause the MIL to light and a diagnostic trouble code to be set and not any other warning lamp.

ENGINE PERFORMANCE (A8)

CATEGORY: EMISSIONS CONTROL SYSTEMS DIAGNOSIS AND REPAIR

98. **The correct answer is a.** The test port is used to pressurize the evaporative emission control system with an inert gas to a pressure not to exceed 1 psi. Answers b, c, and d are not correct because the test port shown is only used to test the evaporative (EVAP) control system and does not check the EGR, PCV, or catalytic converter backpressure.

99. **The correct answer is b.** The spring inside the PCV valve can lose tension due to heating and cooling cycles during normal engine operation. If the valve does not rattle, then it is defective and should be replaced, but this does not mean that it is serviceable just because it does rattle when shaken. Technician A is not correct because the valve rattles does not mean that the valve is good. The valve should be replaced when it does not rattle when shaken or whenever recommended to be replaced by the vehicle manufacturer interval. Answers c and d are not correct because Technician B only is correct.

100. **The correct answer is b.** Technician B is correct because a positive backpressure-type EGR valve requires exhaust backpressure to close a vent. Otherwise, vacuum applied to the EGR valve diaphragm will be vented and vacuum will not hold. Technician A is not correct because even though many EGR valves can be tested without the engine running, many positive and negative backpressure EGR valves require that the engine be running to get accurate test results. Answers c and d are not correct because only Technician B is correct.

101. **The correct answer is a.** Technician A is correct because the purpose of the EGR is to recirculate some (4% to 10%) of the exhaust back into the intake air-fuel mixture as inert material that does not burn to keep combustion temperatures down, which reduces the formation of oxides of nitrogen. If the EGR passages are partially clogged, this would reduce the flow of exhaust and increase the formation of NO_x. Technician B is not correct because the EGR system does not affect the formulation of CO, which is caused by an excessively rich air-fuel mixture. Answers c and d are not correct because Technician A only is correct.

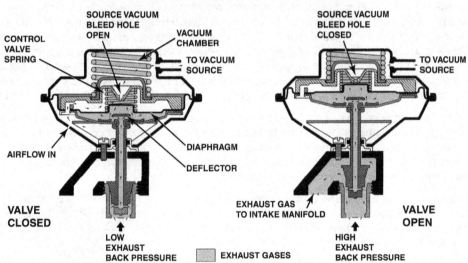

POSITIVE BACK PRESSURE EGR VALVE OPERATION

102. **The correct answer is c.** Both technicians are correct. Technician A is correct because if a catalytic converter rattles when tapped, the internal substrate is broken and the converter should be replaced. Technician B is correct because a catalytic converter can be poisoned by additives in the fuel, oil, or other contaminates and be chemically unable to function, yet not be physically clogged. Answers a, b, and d are not correct because both technicians are correct.

103. **The correct answer is b.** A used catalytic converter must be kept for 60 days to be available for inspection by state or federal agency personnel to be sure that it required replacement based on the published standards. Answers a, c, and d are not correct because they are not the specified time that the unit must be kept before being scrapped or sold for recycling.

104. **The correct answer is d.** The EGR system has the greatest amount of effect on the formulation of NO_x in an engine because burned exhaust introduced into the combustion chamber reduces the peak temperatures where nitrogen (N_2) and oxygen (O_2) combine to form NO_x. Answer a is not correct because the PCV system affects mostly CO emissions. Answer b is not correct because an air pump reduces CO and HC exhaust emissions. Answer c is not correct because the carbon canister (EVAP) system reduces HC emissions.

105. **The correct answer is c.** The air-fuel mixture must be lean at times to supply the oxygen necessary for the oxidation process to occur inside the catalytic converter and it must also be rich at times to help the converter reduce NO_x into N_2 and O_2. If the exhaust is rich all of the time, the catalytic converter can overheat and be damaged. Answers a, b, and d are not correct because these systems do not rely on the correct air-fuel mixture to be able to function correctly.

106. **The correct answer is c.** A loose gas cap will cause an EVAP diagnostic trouble code to set but will not cause a misfire on one cylinder and is therefore the least likely cause of a P0300 DTC. Answer a is not correct because if the all of the exhaust passages for the EGR were clogged except for cylinder number four, then all of the exhaust would flow into cylinder four and would likely cause a misfire. Answer b is not correct because a cracked spark plug could cause a misfire and cause a P0304 DTC to be set. Answer d is not correct because an electrically open fuel injector could cause a misfire and a P0304 DTC being set.

107. **The correct answer is b.** The fuel trim numbers will be negative on the bank that has the restricted exhaust because the PCM determines the air-fuel ratio needed for proper operation form the oxygen sensors. The oxygen sensor on the bank that has the restricted exhaust will show richer than normal and therefore a negative fuel trim value. Answer a is not correct because the restricted exhaust side will show a rich condition with negative fuel trims instead of a lean condition and positive fuel trim. Answer c is not correct because even though the engine will not run correctly, a restricted exhaust on one bank would not likely cause a high knock sensor reading. Answer d is not correct because while the engine operating with a restricted exhaust on bank will not perform correctly (low on power), the restricted exhaust would not likely cause a catalytic converter low efficiency diagnostic trouble code from being set.

108. **The correct answer is c.** Both technicians are correct. Technician A is correct because during the purge process, a vacuum is drawn on the carbon canister, which is vented to the fuel tank. If the tank has been overfilled, liquid gasoline instead of vapor is drawn into the canister and into the engine where it is burned creating a richer-than-normal air-fuel mixture. Technician B is correct because an exhaust leak upstream from the oxygen sensor allows outside air to enter the exhaust between the exhaust pulses. This air (oxygen) is sensed by the O_2S and the computer adds extra fuel creating an over rich condition. Answers a, b, and d are not correct because both technicians are correct.

109. **The correct answer is d.** Neither technician is correct. Technician A is not correct because the carbon (charcoal) canister is designed to last the life of the vehicle and does not require routine replacement or service unless there is a fault. Technician B is not correct because nothing will dissolve carbon; although liquid gasoline can harm the canister, it does not leave a yellow deposit. Answer c is not correct because neither technician is correct.

110. **The correct answer is a.** The air switching valve(s) can be damaged if the one-way check valve fails allowing exhaust gases to flow from the exhaust manifold to the valves and the air pump itself. Answer b is not correct because a defective check valve could not cause the engine to ping or spark knock, which is often caused by a lean air-fuel mixture and/or operating too hot. Answer c is not correct because excessive CO is caused by an excessively rich air-fuel mixture, which could not be caused by a faulty air pump check valve. Answer d is not correct because the check valve is located in the exhaust and cannot affect the engine operations or cause a vacuum leak.

111. **The correct answer is b.** The air pump tubes connect directly to the exhaust manifold and if a hole is created in the tube, exhaust gases would escape creating exhaust noise. Answer a is not correct because the hole in air pump tubes will not affect engine operation or cause the engine to miss unless the escaped exhaust damages a spark plug wire. Answers c and d are not correct because a hole in the air pump exhaust tubes will not affect engine operation or air-fuel mixture.

112. **The correct answer is d.** Both answers a and b are possible. Answer a is correct because raw fuel through the stuck open purge valve would cause the engine to run richer than normal. With an abnormal amount of extra fuel being supplied to the engine, it is possible that the catalytic converter could be damaged by having it flooded with too much fuel. Answer b is possible because even though the PCM through the use of the fuel trims would reduce the amount of fuel delivered to the engine through the injectors, the overall effect would likely be poorer fuel economy due to the unregulated fuel flowing through the purge valve. Answer c is not correct because unless there is an exhaust restriction, excessive backpressure is not caused by excessive fuel by itself although it could cause the converter to overheat. A restricted exhaust system would not affect the EGR valve.

113. **The correct answer is c.** Both technicians are correct. Technician A is correct because an excessively rich air-fuel mixture will cause the catalytic converter to overheat while performing the oxidation process of converting HC and CO into CO_2 and H_2O. Technician B is correct because the output of the air pump should be directed to the catalytic converter during the closed loop operation. If the switching valve were stuck and allowed the flow of air from the air pump to remain flowing to the exhaust manifold, the oxygen sensor (O_2S) would read the extra oxygen and the computer would command a richer-than-normal air-fuel mixture creating the catalytic converter overheating condition. Answers a, b, and d are not correct because both technicians are correct.

114. **The correct answer is b.** The EGR valve is usually not open at idle, and if it were partially stuck open, it would cause the entering exhaust gas to displace the air (oxygen) in the cylinder, which would likely cause a rough idle. The engine would perform normally at highway speeds because it is normal operation to have the EGR valve on and flowing exhaust gases into the combustion chamber at highway speeds. Answer a is not correct because exhaust gases entering the combustion chamber displaces mostly the oxygen (about 15 times more air by weight than gasoline) creating a richer-than-normal air-fuel mixture, whereas pinging or spark knock is usually caused by a leaner-than-normal air-fuel mixture. Answer c is not correct because the flow of exhaust into the engine at idle will likely decrease (not increase) engine speed. Answer d is not correct because it is normal operation of the EGR valve to supply some exhaust to the combustion chamber at highway speeds, so no difference in engine operation would be noticeable.

115. **The correct answer is c.** Both technicians are correct. Technician A is correct because a loose gas cap could cause enough air to escape to fail the OBD II monitor test. Technician B is correct because even a small hole can cause the OBD II monitor to fail the EVAP test. Answers a, b, and d are not correct because both technicians are correct.

116. **The correct answer is c.** Both technicians are correct. Technician A is correct because the exhaust could travel up through the defective one-way check valve and damage the air pump as well as the switching valves and hoses. Technician B is also correct because the airflow from the air pump should be switched from the exhaust manifold to the catalytic converter when the engine is operating in closed loop. If the air were to continue to flow to the exhaust manifold, the oxygen sensor would read the air from the AIR pump as being caused by a lean air-fuel mixture; then the vehicle computer would try to incorrectly enrich the mixture. Answers c and d are not correct because both Technicians A and B are correct.

117. **The correct answer is d.** A throttle position (TP) voltage waveform is shown because the voltage level starts low (closed throttle), then increases as the throttle is opened and decreases as the throttle is closed. Answer a is not correct because the output of a typical MAF sensor is a square wave with varying frequency depending on the amount of air entering the engine. Answer b is not correct because even though the voltage output of a BARO sensor changes with atmospheric pressure, the voltage waveform could not change rapidly as shown. Answer c is not correct because an oxygen sensor waveform indicates the voltage changing frequently from less than 200 mV to greater than 800 mV.

CATEGORY: COMPUTERIZED ENGINE CONTROLS DIAGNOSIS AND REPAIR

118. **The correct answer is a.** A fault in the electronic throttle control system can result in the system defaulting to the home position for the throttle plate which is usually 16% to 20% (high idle). This default position is used so the vehicle can be moved from the road yet not driven because the system may not be able to control the throttle opening due to the fault. Answer b is not correct because a fault with the low pressure pump in the fuel tank may cause an engine operating problem but could not cause the engine speed to be stuck at a fast idle. Answer c is not correct because a fault with the high-pressure pump driven by the camshaft may cause an engine operating problem but could not cause the engine speed to be stuck at a fast idle. Answer d is not correct because a fault with the fuel pressure regulator may cause an engine operating problem but could not cause the engine speed to be stuck at a fast idle.

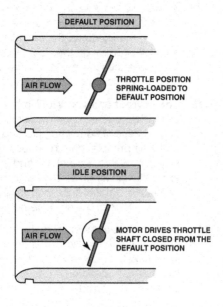

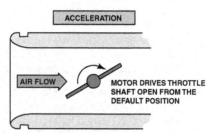

119. **The correct answer is d.** Technician A is not correct because the oxygen sensor voltage should fluctuate between 800 millivolts or higher to 200 millivolts or lower in a properly operating engine and control system. Technician B is not correct for the same reason. Answers a, b, and c are not correct because neither technician is correct.

120. **The correct answer is c.** Both technicians are correct. Technician A is correct because an oxygen sensor is slow to react to rich and lean conditions if it has deteriorated. Technician B says that the oxygen sensor may be able to be restored to proper operation by driving the vehicle at highway speeds for an extended period of time to burn off any accumulated carbon deposits that could cause the sensor to react slowly. Answers a, b, and d are not correct because both technicians are correct.

121. **The correct answer is a.** Technician A is correct because all SAE DTCs are the same for all vehicle manufacturers on vehicles that are OBD II compliant. An SAE or generic DTC is one that has a zero (0) as the first number such as P0304. Technician B is not correct because the data link connector (DLC) is located inside the vehicle either to the left or the right of the centerline of the vehicle. Answers c and d are not correct because only Technician A is correct.

122. **The correct answer is a.** Technician A is correct because a low or zero idle air control (IAC) count or percentage indicates that the engine is idling too fast and the computer is attempting to reduce the speed as much as possible. A vacuum leak will cause the engine to idle faster, especially if it is a speed density engine compared to a mass air flow engine. A stuck throttle cable could also cause the engine to idle faster than normal causing the computer to attempt to slow the engine by closing the IAC. Technician B is not correct because dirty throttle plates would reduce the airflow through the engine lowering the idle speed. The computer would then command a higher (not a lower) IAC pintle position and the IAC counts (or percentages) would be higher than normal. Normal IAC counts or percentage is 15 to 20. Answers c and d are not correct because Technician A only is correct.

123. **The correct answer is c.** Both technicians are correct. Technician A is correct because most engines should require between 1.5 and 3.5 milliseconds of injector pulse on time to supply fuel necessary to operate the engine at idle without any loads applied. Technician B is correct because the oxygen sensor should fluctuate from above 800 millivolts to below 200 millivolts if the oxygen sensor and the engine controls are operating normally. Answers a, b, and d are not correct because both technicians are correct.

124. **The correct answer is c.** Both technicians are correct. Technician A is correct because fuel trim is the correction factor for the amount of fuel delivered to the engine that is based on the oxygen sensor readings. Technician B is correct because a positive fuel trim such as +22% means that the computer is increasing the injector pulse width to bring the oxygen sensor values back into normal operating mode. Answers a, b, and d are not correct because both technicians are correct.

125. **The correct answer is d.** A defective IAC could cause excessive idle speed especially if it failed when the engine was cold and the IAC was being commanded to provide a high idle speed. A stuck pintle or open electrical wiring could prevent the PCM from operating the IAC to slow the idle speed. Answer a (MAP sensor) is not likely to cause an excessive idle speed although a defective MAP could cause other drivability concerns such as hesitation on acceleration. Answer b (O_2S) is not correct because this sensor controls the feedback for the air-fuel mixture and could not cause the idle speed to be excessive. Answer c (IAT) is not correct because the intake air temperature sensor does not control idle speed.

126. **The correct answer is a.** Technician A is correct. A heavy load on an engine causes the manifold vacuum to decrease and the voltage of the MAP sensor to increase. A reading of about 1.0 volt and 18 in. Hg represents a normal reading for a sound engine operating at or near sea level. Technician B is not correct because this is a normal reading. Answers c and d are not correct because only Technician A is correct.

127. **The correct answer is a.** Technician A is correct because a lean exhaust will cause the oxygen sensor to produce a low voltage because the difference between the oxygen content outside the sensor and inside the exhaust are similar and therefore, the sensor voltage signal is close to zero. Technician B is not correct because a low oxygen sensor voltage indicates a lean exhaust condition, not a rich exhaust condition. Answers c and d are not correct because only Technician A is correct.

128. **The correct answer is b.** A typical throttle position (TP) sensor used in an electronic throttle control (ETC) system uses two sensors which operate opposite to each other as a failsafe feature. Answers a, c, and d are not correct because they do not include two opposite reading TP sensors.

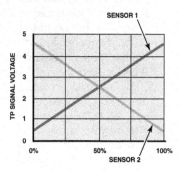

129. **The correct answer is c.** A properly operating engine control system and oxygen sensor should result in the switching from lean to rich and rich to lean about one to five times per second (1 to 5 Hz). A higher switching rate usually indicates a misfire condition. Answers a, b, and d are not correct because they are not within the acceptable range for O2S activity.

130. **The correct answer is b.** A correctly operating computer control system and oxygen sensor should produce an O2S signal voltage that fluctuates from below 200 mV (0.200 V) and above 800 mV (0.800 V). Therefore, a reading of 0.150 V (150 mV) and 0.950 V (950 mV) is the best answer. Answers a, c, and d do not represent a good operating range for the oxygen sensor.

131. **The correct answer is c.** Both technicians are correct. Technician A is correct because if the opposite code can be set, the computer itself as well as the wiring is okay. Technician B is correct because if the opposite code cannot be set, then the fault has to be in the wiring to the TP sensor or in the computer. Answers a, b, and d are not correct because both technicians are correct.

132. **The correct answer is b.** The preferred method to use to clear diagnostic trouble codes is to use a scan tool. Answer a is not correct because disconnecting the battery may not erase codes due to capacitors inside the computer being able to retain the memory. Disconnecting the battery will also cause the loss of radio presets, memory seat presets, and drivability learned values. Answer c is not correct because even though this method will clear the DTCs, it will also clear learned drivability values that could affect the way the engine operates when it is started. Answer d is not correct because it usually requires 40 warm-up cycles to clear any codes (OBD II) and not just ignition cycles.

133. **The correct answer is c.** Both technicians are correct. Technician A is correct because if the security system is activated or has a fault, the engine may not crank. Technician B is correct because a no-crank condition could be caused by a defective starter motor. More diagnosis would be required to determine the root cause. Answers a, b, and d are not correct because both technicians are correct.

134. **The correct answer is c.** The waveform represents a shorted fuel injector because the inductive kick (spike) fails to reach the 30 V minimum. Answer a is not correct because a normal injector voltage waveform should show as an inductive kick (spike) of at least 30 volts.

135. **The correct answer is a.** The injector voltage waveform is normal because it illustrates the proper voltage levels including an inductive kick (spike) that exceeds 30 volts when the injector is turned off. Answers b, c, and d are not correct because a normal injector voltage waveform is shown.

136. **The correct answer is a.** Technician A is correct because if the MAP sensor vacuum hose is disconnected, the MAP sensor signal to the computer will be a high voltage (close to 5 volts) indicating that the engine is operating under a heavy load (low vacuum). The computer will increase the fuel delivery to the engine by increasing the pulse width and the engine will operate with a richer-than-normal air-fuel mixture. Technician B is not correct because even though there will be a slight vacuum leak because the hose has been disconnected, the air-fuel mixture will be richer than normal due to the signal from the MAP sensor indicating that the engine is operating under a heavy load. Answers c and d are not correct because only Technician A is correct.

137. **The correct answer is a.** Technician A is correct because a dirty MAF sensor will not accurately measure the amount of air entering the engine, but will not set a diagnostic trouble code. Technician B is not correct because a shorted TP sensor would set a diagnostic trouble code. Answers c and d are not correct because Technician A only is correct.

138. **The correct answer is b.** The IAC counts or percentage should be about 15 to 25 if everything is operating correctly. The higher-than-normal IAC reading could mean a restricted intake or a heavier-than-normal load on the engine. Answer a is not correct because a normal operating engine will have a coolant temperature between 195° and 215° on most engines and from 180° to 200° on those engines that are equipped with a 180° thermostat. Answer c is not correct because a normal TP sensor voltage at idle is about 0.5 V. Answer d is not correct because the voltage of a MAP sensor at idle ranges from 0.88 V to 1.62 V and 1.01 V is within this range.

139. **The correct answer is a.** Technician A is correct because the O2S voltage is higher than normal indicating a richer-than-normal air-fuel mixture. It should range from below 200 mV to higher than 800 mV. Technician B is not correct because while all of the other parameters look okay, the O2S values are not correct. Answer c and d are not correct because only Technician A is correct.

140. The correct answer is b. A scan tool is required to retrieve OBD II diagnostic trouble codes. Answer a is not correct because a jumper wire should not be used to jump any terminals of the data link connector on a vehicle equipped with OBD II. Answer c is not correct because although a similar method can be used to retrieve DTCs on many Chrysler vehicles equipped with OBD, the procedure is not the same as stated in the question. Answer d is not correct because an analog voltmeter is used to retrieve OBD I Ford DTCs but cannot be used to retrieve OBD II DTCs.

141. The correct answer is b. Technician B is correct because a fault in the ignition system would prevent ignition and the unburned fuel (HC) would leave the cylinder and exit the exhaust system. Technician A is not correct because a defective fuel pressure regulator is not likely to cause excessive HC because if the regulator was stuck shut or had a restriction, the exhaust would be rich. A rich air-fuel mixture will increase carbon monoxide (CO) emissions and could increase the HC emissions as well. Because the CO level was normal, the most likely cause is ignition system related. Answer c and d are not correct because Technician B only is correct.

142. The correct answer is a. A defective cooling fan can cause the engine to operate at a temperature higher than normal creating conditions where NO_x can form inside the cylinders. It requires about 2500°F (1370°C) for the nitrogen (N) and the oxygen (O) to combine chemically. Answer b is not correct because high fuel pressure is likely to cause the air-fuel mixture to be richer than normal, which tends to reduce the combustion temperature and reduce the possibility of creating excessive NO_x. Answer c is not correct because an air pump related failure could not likely cause the combustion chamber temperature to increase and cause excessive NO_x emissions. Answer d is not correct because a clogged PCV valve would tend to cause the air-fuel to become richer. A lean or hot operating engine is needed for NOx to form inside the combustion chamber.

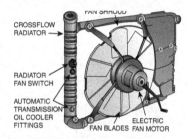

143. The correct answer is d. The EGR system is designed to provide about 6% to 10% of inert exhaust gases into the combustion chamber to reduce the formation of oxides of nitrogen. A stuck closed (no exhaust flow) EGR valve would not have a major impact on the air-fuel mixture, which must be rich to produce an excessive amount of carbon monoxide (CO). Answer a is not correct because a defective fuel pressure regulator could cause a higher-than-normal fuel pressure causing a richer-than-normal air-fuel mixture. Answer b is not correct because a leaking fuel injector can cause a rich air-fuel mixture and thereby create an excessive amount of CO exhaust emissions. Answer c is not correct because a stuck open purge valve can cause a rich air-fuel mixture by allowing engine vacuum to draw gasoline fumes from the carbon canister.

144. The correct answer is d. If the throttle plate was dirty on a multiport fuel injected engine, the airflow would be restricted and the idle could be unstable. Answer a is not correct because even though a bad TP sensor could cause an engine operation problem, it is not as likely to cause a rough or unstable idle as dirty throttle plates. Answer b is not correct because an open injector winding will cause one cylinder to miss but the idle will usually be corrected by the idle air control. Answer c is not correct because an open oxygen sensor lead will cause the engine to operate in open-loop and the idle speed should not be affected to an extent that it could cause the engine to stall.

145. The correct answer is b. A partially clogged EGR valve could cause the engine to ping or spark knock due to a lack of recirculated exhaust gases in the combustion chamber. The PCM is programmed to provide the proper amount of fuel and ignition timing for a properly functioning emission control system. Answer a is not correct because a rich air-fuel mixture is unlikely to cause the engine to ping or spark knock during acceleration. A lean, not a rich, mixture can cause spark knock. Answer c is not correct because even though an intake manifold leak could cause the engine to ping, it is usually not large enough to change the air-fuel mixture enough to cause a noticeable problem without other symptoms. Answer d is not correct because an open in the CKP sensor would cause the engine to stop running.

146. The correct answer is d. Neither technician is correct. Technician A is not correct because leaking upper O-rings would cause an external fuel leak and not a vacuum leak. Technician B is not correct because a dirty throttle plate would affect all cylinders and not just the odd numbered. Answer c is not correct because neither technician is correct.

147. The correct answer is d. Neither technician is correct. Technician A is not correct because the engine coolant temperature, as determined from the scan data, is normal for most vehicles ($100°C =$ $212°F$). Technician B is not correct because the engine seems to be operating correctly according to the HO_2S voltage reading. Answer c is not correct because neither technician is correct.

148. The correct answer is c. Both technicians are correct. Technician A is correct because if there is something that prevents the monitor from running, a DTC will not set unless all of the criteria is met to run the monitor. Technician B is correct because most global as well as enhanced and factory scan tools will display monitor status. Answers a, b, and d are not correct because both technicians are correct.

149. The correct answer is c. Both technicians are correct. Technician A is correct because a vacuum leak will cause the engine to operate a little leaner than normal which will cause the PCM to enrich the air-fuel mixture by increasing the pulse width of the injector. Technician B is correct because a clogged fuel injector would not be able to supply the needed amount of fuel and the PCM would increase the injector pulse width based on the oxygen sensor signal that the exhaust is lean. Answers a, b, and d are not correct because both technicians are correct.

150. The correct answer is c. Both technicians are correct. Technician A is correct because if the camshaft lobe that drives the high-pressure pump, the amount of fuel delivered to the engine would be reduced. If the engine fuel system is not able to supply the needed amount of fuel, the engine would not be able to achieve the desired power. Technician B is correct because if excessive carbon is on the intake valve, this would restrict the airflow through the engine and result in reduced engine power. Answers a, b, and d are not correct because both technicians are correct.

151. The correct answer is a. Technician A is correct because clogged fuel injector(s) could cause a lean exhaust because the injectors cannot flow enough fuel. Technician B is not correct because a clogged fuel return line would increase fuel pressure resulting in a richer, not a leaner, air-fuel mixture. Answers c and d are not correct because only Technician A is correct.

152. The correct answer is a. The oxygen sensor has to be about $600°F$ ($315°C$) and producing a variable voltage signal before the computer will go into closed loop if all other conditions are met. If the oxygen sensor is not producing a variable voltage signal, then the PCM will not enter closed loop operation. Answer b is not correct because the intake air temperature (IAT) sensor is used to modify the amount of fuel and spark advanced based on the temperature of the incoming air and would not prevent the engine from achieving closed loop operation. Answer c is not correct because the MAP sensor is used to measure engine load and if at fault would not likely prevent the engine from achieving closed-loop operation. Answer d is not correct because the barometric pressure sensor is simply used to control fuel delivery based on altitude or weather conditions and would not prevent closed-loop operation.

LIGHT VEHICLE DIESEL ENGINES CONTENT AREAS

This ASE study guide for Light Vehicle Diesel Engines (A9) is divided into the sub-content areas that correlate to the actual ASE certification test as follows:

CONTENT AREA	NUMBER OF QUESTIONS IN THE TEST	NUMBER OF STUDY GUIDE QUESTIONS
A. General Diagnosis	9	25 (1–25)
B. Cylinder Head and Valve Train Diagnosis and Repair	5	10 (26–35)
C. Engine Block Diagnosis and Repair	5	15 (36–50)
D. Lubrication and Cooling Systems Diagnosis and Repair	6	12 (51–62)
E. Air Induction and Exhaust Systems Diagnosis and Repair	12	24 (63–86)
F. Fuel System Diagnosis and Repair	13	33 (87–119)
Totals	**50**	**119**

TIME ALLOWED TO TAKE THE TEST

The allocated time to take the Engine Repair Certification test is 75 minutes. ASE adds 10 additional questions to the test for research purposes for a total of 60 questions. These questions do not count toward your score, but they are embedded within the test and there is no way of knowing which ones do not count. As a result, the technician needs to answer 60 questions in 75 minutes, or about one question per minute.

If taking the recertification A9 test, there are just 25 questions with no additional research questions included. The time allocated to take the recertification test is 30 minutes, which means about one minute per question.

BEFORE USING THIS STUDY GUIDE

Before trying to answer the questions and looking at the explanations, look over the following list of the content that ASE states will be covered in the certification test. For best results using this study guide, check service information or consult an automotive textbook for details on any of the content areas that are not familiar before trying to answer the questions. For additional information about the ASE test, visit the website at **www.ase.com**.

LIGHT VEHICLE DIESEL ENGINES (A9) CERTIFICATION TEST

A. GENERAL DIAGNOSIS (9 QUESTIONS)

1. Verify the complaint, and road/dyno test vehicle; review driver/customer concerns/expectations and vehicle service history (if available); determine further diagnosis.

2. Record vehicle identification number (VIN). Identify engine model, calibration, and serial numbers to research applicable vehicle and service information, service precautions, and technical service bulletins; determine needed actions.

3. Perform scan tool check and visual inspection for physical damage and missing, modified, or tampered components; determine needed actions.

4. Check and record electronic diagnostic codes, freeze frame, and/or operational data; monitor scan tool data; determine further diagnosis.

5. Clear diagnostic trouble codes (DTCs) and verify the repair.

6. Inspect engine assembly and compartment for fuel, oil, coolant, exhaust, or other leaks; determine needed repairs.

7. Inspect engine compartment wiring harness, connectors, seals, and locks; check for proper routing and condition; determine needed repairs.

8. Listen for and isolate engine noises; determine needed repairs.

9. Isolate and diagnose engine related vibration problems; determine needed actions.

10. Check engine exhaust for abnormal odor and/or smoke color and volume; determine further diagnosis.

11. Check fuel for contamination, quantity, quality, and consumption; determine needed actions.

12. Perform crankcase pressure test; determine further diagnosis.

13. Diagnose surging, rough operation, misfiring, low power, slow deceleration, slow acceleration, and shutdown problems; determine needed actions.

14. Check cooling system for freeze point, level, contamination, condition, temperature, pressure, circulation, and fan operation; determine needed repairs.

15. Check lubrication system for contamination, oil level, temperature, pressure, filtration, and oil consumption; take oil sample and obtain oil analysis if needed; determine needed repairs.

16. Diagnose no-cranking, cranks but fails to start, hard starting, and starts but does not continue to run problems; determine needed actions.

17. Diagnose engine problems caused by battery condition, connections, or excessive key-off battery drain; determine needed repairs.

18. Diagnose engine problems resulting from an electrical undercharge, overcharge, or a no-charge condition; determine needed action.

B. CYLINDER HEAD AND VALVE TRAIN DIAGNOSIS AND REPAIR (5 QUESTIONS)

1. Remove, inspect, disassemble, and clean cylinder head assembly(s).

2. Inspect threaded holes, studs, and bolts for serviceability; service/replace as needed.

3. Measure cylinder head thickness, and check mating surfaces for flatness, corrosion, warpage and surface finish; inspect for cracks/damage; check condition of passages; inspect core and gallery plugs; determine serviceability and needed repairs.

4. Inspect valves, guides, seats, springs, retainers, rotators, locks, and seals; determine serviceability and needed repairs.

5. Inspect and/or replace injector sleeves, glow plug sleeves, and seals; pressure test to verify repair (if applicable); measure injector tip, nozzle, or prechamber protrusion where specified by manufacturer.

6. Inspect and/or replace valve bridges (crossheads) and guides; adjust bridges (crossheads) if applicable.

7. Reassemble, check, and determine required cylinder head gasket thickness; install cylinder head assembly and gasket as specified by the manufacturer.

8. Inspect pushrods, rocker arms, rocker arm shafts, electronic components, wiring harness, seals; repair/replace as needed.

9. Inspect, install, and adjust cam followers, lash adjusters, and retainers; adjust valve clearance if applicable.

10. Inspect, measure, and replace/reinstall overhead camshaft and bearings; measure and adjust endplay.

11. Inspect and time drive gear train components (includes gear, chain, and belt systems).

C. ENGINE BLOCK DIAGNOSIS AND REPAIR (5 QUESTIONS)

1. Remove, inspect, service, and install pans, covers, ventilation systems, gaskets, seals, and wear rings.

2. Disassemble, clean, and inspect engine block for cracks; check mating surfaces and related components for damage or warpage and surface finish; check deck height; check condition of passages, core, and gallery plugs; inspect threaded holes, studs, dowel pins, and bolts for serviceability; service/replace as needed.

3. Inspect and measure cylinder walls for wear and damage; determine needed service.

4. Inspect in-block camshaft bearings for wear and damage; replace as needed.

5. Inspect, measure, and replace/reinstall in-block camshaft; measure and correct end play; inspect, replace/reinstall, and adjust cam followers (if applicable).

6. Clean and inspect crankshaft and journals for surface finish, cracks, and damage; check condition of oil passages; check passage plugs; measure journal diameters; check mounting surfaces; determine needed service.

7. Determine the proper select-fit components, such as pistons, connecting rod, and main bearings.

8. Inspect and replace main bearings; check cap fit and bearing clearances; check and correct crankshaft end play.

9. Inspect, replace, verify, and adjust the drive gear train components (includes gear, chain, and belt systems).

10. Inspect, measure, or replace pistons, pins, and retainers.

11. Measure piston-to-cylinder wall clearance.

12. Identify piston, connecting rod bearing, and main bearing wear patterns that indicate connecting rod and crankshaft alignment or bearing bore problems; check bearing bore and bushing condition; determine needed repairs.

13. Check ring-to-groove fit and end gaps; install rings on pistons; assemble pistons and connecting rods and install in block; check piston height/protrusion; check liner height/protrusion (if applicable); replace rod bearings and check clearances; check condition, position, and clearance of piston cooling jets (nozzles).

14. Inspect crankshaft vibration damper; determine needed repairs.

15. Inspect flywheel/flexplate and/or dual-mass flywheel (including ring gear) and mounting surfaces for cracks, wear, and runout; determine needed repairs.

D. LUBRICATION AND COOLING SYSTEMS DIAGNOSIS AND REPAIR (6 QUESTIONS)

1. Verify base engine oil pressure and check operation of pressure sensor/switch and pressure gauge; verify engine oil temperature and check operation of temperature sensor.

2. Inspect, measure, repair/replace oil pump, housing, drives, pipes, and screens; check drive gear clearance.

3. Inspect, repair/replace oil pressure regulator assembly including: housing, bore, spring, regulator valve(s), oil filter by-pass valve(s), and anti-drain back valve.

4. Inspect, clean, test, and reinstall/replace oil cooler, by-pass valve, lines, and hoses.

5. Inspect turbocharger lubrication and cooling systems; repair/replace as needed.

6. Change engine oil and filters using proper type, viscosity, and rating per manufacturer specifications.

7. Inspect and reinstall/replace pulleys, tensioners, and drive belts; adjust drive belts and check alignment.

8. Verify coolant temperature; check operation of temperature and level sensors, switches, and temperature gauge.

9. Inspect and replace thermostat(s), bypass(es), housing(s), and seal(s).

10. Flush and refill cooling system; following manufacturer's specification, add proper coolant type; bleed air from system.

11. Inspect and replace water pump(s), housing(s), hoses, and idler pulley(s) or drive gear.

12. Inspect radiator(s), pressure cap(s), and tank(s); pressure test cooling system and radiator cap(s); determine needed repairs.

13. Inspect and repair/replace cooling fan, fan hub, fan clutch, controls, and shroud(s).

E. AIR INDUCTION AND EXHAUST SYSTEMS DIAGNOSIS AND REPAIR (12 QUESTIONS)

1. Inspect and service/replace air induction piping, air cleaner, and element; determine needed actions.

2. Perform intake manifold pressure tests; inspect, test, clean, and/or replace charge air cooler and piping system; determine needed actions.

3. Inspect, test, and replace turbocharger(s) (including variable ratio/geometry VGT), pneumatic, hydraulic, vacuum, and electronic controls and actuators; inspect, test, and replace wastegate and wastegate controls.

4. Inspect, test, and replace intake manifold(s), variable intake manifold(s), gaskets, actuators, temperature and pressure sensors, and connections.

5. Perform exhaust back pressure and temperature tests; determine needed actions.

6. Inspect and repair/replace exhaust manifold(s), gaskets, piping, mufflers, and mounting hardware.

7. Inspect, test, and repair/replace preheater/inlet air heater and/or glow plug system and controls.

8. Inspect, test, and replace exhaust aftertreatment system components and controls, including diesel oxidation catalyst (DOC), selective catalyst reduction (SCR), diesel exhaust fluid (DEF), and diesel particulate filter (DPF); check regeneration system operation.

9. Inspect, test, service, and replace EGR system components including EGR valve(s), EGR cooler by-pass valve(s), EGR cooler(s), piping, electronic sensors, actuators, controls, and wiring.

10. Inspect, test, and replace airflow control (throttle) valve(s) and controls.

11. Inspect, test, and replace crankcase ventilation system components, including sensors, filters, valves, and piping.

F. FUEL SYSTEM DIAGNOSIS AND REPAIR (13 QUESTIONS)

1. Inspect, clean, test, and repair/replace fuel system tanks, vents, caps, mounts, valves, single/dual supply and return lines, and fittings.

2. Inspect, clean, test, and repair/replace fuel transfer and/or supply pump, sensors, strainers, fuel/water separators/indicators, filters, heaters, coolers, ECM cooling plates (if applicable), and mounting hardware.

3. Check fuel system for air; determine needed repairs; prime and bleed fuel system; check and repair/replace primer pump.

4. Inspect, test, and repair/replace low fuel pressure regulator supply and return systems, including low pressure switches.

5. Inspect and reinstall/replace high-pressure injection lines, fittings, transfer tubes, seals, and mounting hardware.

6. Inspect, adjust, and repair/replace electronic throttle and PTO control devices, circuits, and sensors.

7. Perform on-engine inspections, tests, and replace high pressure common rail fuel system components and electronic controls.

8. Perform on-engine inspections and tests; replace hydraulic electronic unit injector(s) (HEUI) components and electronic controls.

9. Perform on-engine inspections and tests; replace pump-line-nozzle fuel system (PLN-E) components and electronic controls.

10. Perform on-engine inspections and tests; replace electronic unit injector(s) (EUI) components and electronic controls.

11. Inspect and replace electrical connector terminals, pins, harnesses, seals, and locks.

12. Connect diagnostic scan tool to vehicle/engine; access, verify, and update software calibration settings and injector calibration codes; perform control module re-learn procedures as needed.

13. Use a diagnostic scan tool to inspect and test electronic engine control system, sensors, actuators, electronic control modules, and circuits; determine further diagnosis.

14. Measure and interpret voltage, voltage drop, amperage, and resistance readings, using a digital multimeter (DMM) or appropriate test equipment.

15. Diagnose engine problems resulting from failures of interrelated systems (for example: cruise control, security alarms/theft deterrent, transmission controls, exhaust aftertreatment systems, electronic stability control, or non-OEM installed accessories).

LIGHT VEHICLE DIESEL ENGINES (A9)

CATEGORY: GENERAL ENGINE DIAGNOSIS

1. What type engine oil rating should be used in all 2007 and newer light diesel engines?

   a. SAE
   b. API
   c. CJ-4
   d. ILSAC

2. A light diesel engine does not crank, but only if the truck has been sitting for a few days. If the truck is started and used every day, then it always starts. What test should the technician perform?

   a. A battery drain (parasitic draw) test
   b. Injector timing test
   c. Intake restriction test
   d. Exhaust backpressure test

3. When does the technician know to replace the air filter?

   a. When the filter looks dirty
   b. Every three years or every 30,000 miles
   c. When the air filter monitor indicates that it needs to be replaced
   d. When a "low power" message appears on the dash

4. The engine oil in diesel engines should be replaced _____.

   a. according to the specified number of miles the vehicle has traveled
   b. the number of months since the last oil change
   c. the number of engine running hours
   d. all of the above

5. The engine oil in a light diesel engine was checked and it was over-filled, even though it was at the correct level when it was checked after the last oil change. What is the *most likely* cause?

   a. Normal expansion of the oil due to temperature
   b. Diesel fuel has leaked into the engine oil
   c. Transmission fluid has leaked into the engine oil through the rear main seal
   d. Air has been pumped into oil from the turbocharger

6. A light diesel equipped with two batteries does not start (no crank condition) after sitting for two days. A battery drain of 0.030 amperes was measured. The vehicle owner had replaced one of the two batteries when it failed a battery load test, but did not replace the other battery because it tested as being serviceable. Technician A says that the bad battery could be draining the new battery and that the old battery should also be replaced. Technician B says that the battery drain is excessive and the source should be found and corrected to fix the problem. Which technician is correct?

   a. A only
   b. B only
   c. Both A and B
   d. Neither A nor B

7. What part or component should be removed to test cylinder compression on a diesel engine?

   a. An injector
   b. An intake valve rocker arm and stud
   c. A glow plug
   d. A glow plug or injector

8. An engine with a HEUI fuel system that is hard to start and misfire is being discussed. Technician A says this may be caused by the engine oil and filter being past their recommended service interval. Technician B says this may be caused by the use of an incorrect oil filter and the wrong type of engine oil. Which technician is correct?

   a. Technician A
   b. Technician B
   c. Both A and B
   d. Neither A nor B

9. Injector replacement on a late model diesel engine is being discussed. Technician A says the calibration code of the new injector must be programmed into the engine control module. Technician B says that the failure to use the correct calibration code may result in excessive emissions. Which technician is correct?

   a. Technician A
   b. Technician B
   c. Both A and B
   d. Neither A nor B

10. Technician A says that glow plugs are used to help start a diesel engine and are shut off as soon as the engine starts. Technician B says that the glow plugs are turned off as soon as a flame is detected in the combustion chamber. Which technician is correct?

    a. A only
    b. B only
    c. Both A and B
    d. Neither A nor B

11. The term "retarded injection timing" best refers to injection timing occurring _____.

    a. closer to TDC than normal
    b. farther away from TDC than normal
    c. at TDC
    d. at BDC

12. Lower-than-normal oil pressure could be caused by _____.

    a. a worn oil pump
    b. worn rod bearings
    c. worn main bearing
    d. all of the above

13. A late model pickup truck equipped with a common rail, light duty diesel engine is being diagnosed for excessive black smoke from the tailpipe. What could be the cause?

    a. An empty diesel exhaust fluid container
    b. A clogged air filter
    c. The incorrect engine oil used at the last oil change
    d. A stuck closed fuel injector

14. A light diesel vehicle has several diagnostic trouble codes for failure of the after treatment devices. What should the technician do first?

    a. Clear the codes
    b. Perform a visual inspection of the engine and the exhaust system
    c. Replace the air and fuel filters
    d. Check that the fuel level is above 15% and below 85%

15. When checking for a fuel leak under the hood of a light diesel vehicle, what should the technician do?

    a. Use a strong light to better see where the diesel fuel is leaking from
    b. Use cardboard to block the flow of the leak
    c. Use a hydrocarbon leak detector
    d. Use baby power and cover the area so the location of the leak can be seen

16. When checking the fuel of a light diesel vehicle, what color should the fuel be on diesel used for highway use?

   a. Purple
   b. Red
   c. Clear or amber
   d. Greenish/blue

17. The fuel specified for use for most light diesel engines is _____.

   a. #1
   b. #2
   c. #3
   d. #4

18. What is used to test the coolant on a light diesel?

   a. Hydrometer
   b. Test strip
   c. Refractometer
   d. Any of the above

19. An oil sample was drawn from a diesel engine to determine if the oil needs to be changed. The sample tested high for silicon. What does this indicate to the technician?

   a. Sealer from an oil pan gasket replacement was in the oil
   b. Sealer may be leaking from the intercooler
   c. The oil filter is clogged
   d. The oil has excessive dirt

20. One of the pair of batteries used in a pickup truck equipped with a diesel engine has been tested as being weak, but the other battery tests as being serviceable. What is considered to be "best practice"?

   a. Replace both batteries
   b. Replace the defective battery and charge the good one
   c. Replace the defective battery plus the connecting battery cables
   d. Test both batteries again and recharge the bad one as needed until is fully charged

21. The starter does not crank the diesel engine fast enough to start. What is a possible problem?

   a. Defective starter
   b. Discharged battery
   c. Excessive voltage drops in the battery cables
   d. Any of the above

22. A diesel overheats but only at highway speed. What is a likely cause?

   a. A leaking water pump
   b. A missing front air dam
   c. A defective fan clutch
   d. A collapsed heater hose

23. A defective injector needs to be replaced on a common rail diesel engine. What should the technician do?

a. After replacing the injector, recalibrate the PCM using the number etched on the side of the new injector
b. After replacing the injector, start the engine and allow it to idle for two minutes until the PCM learns the new injector
c. Make sure that the replacement injector is designed for the specific cylinder because each cylinder has its own unique calibration
d. Replace all of the injectors because they are a matched set

24. After completing a repair where there was a diagnostic trouble code set and clearing the code, what should the technician do to confirm that the problem has been successfully fixed?

a. Check that all OBD II monitors have been run and passed
b. Clear all freeze frames
c. Disconnect the battery for 30 minutes
d. Allow the diesel engine to idle for 30 minutes

25. What can be used to check the freezing point of the coolant?

a. Hydrometer
b. Test strip
c. Refractometer
d. Either a or c

LIGHT VEHICLE DIESEL ENGINES (A9)

CATEGORY: CYLINDER HEAD AND VALVE TRAIN DIAGNOSIS AND REPAIR

26. Why is it important to check the valve bridges (crossheads) when performing cylinder service on a light diesel engine?

    a. They can affect injector timing
    b. They can affect valve opening distance
    c. They affect the cylinder head height
    d. They can affect the compression ratio of the cylinder

27. In what order should the head bolts be loosened when removing a cylinder head from a light diesel engine?

    a. In the same order as shown in the head bolt tightening sequence
    b. In the opposite order as shown in the head bolt tightening sequence
    c. The order does not matter but they should be loosened slowly
    d. Removed quickly to help avoid warpage of the head from front to the rear of the engine order

28. When reassembling a diesel engine the high-pressure pump must be correctly timed if the engine is equipped with what type of cam drive arrangement?

    a. Gear
    b. Chain
    c. Belt
    d. Any of the above

29. Which of the following is the most common method for achieving consistent head gasket clamping force on today's cast iron diesel engines?

    a. Torqueing bolts starting from the outside toward the center
    b. Reusing torque-to-yield head bolts that have previously been tightened to the yield point
    c. Torqueing the bolts to final torque in one step
    d. Using MLS-type head gaskets

30. Diesel engines that use pre-combustion chambers to create velocity and promote atomization are being discussed. What type of diesel injection system uses a pre-combustion chamber?

    a. Common rail
    b. Direct
    c. High pressure
    d. Indirect

31. A valve bridge was found to be distorted. What should the technician do?

    a. Bend it straight
    b. Replace it with a new part
    c. Send to a machine shop to be re-machined straight
    d. Use a shorter pushrod for the valve that is affected

32. What type of diesel engine is there a need to check pre-chamber protrusion?

    a. All light diesels
    b. All diesel engines smaller than 7 liters in displacement
    c. Indirect injection diesel engines
    d. All common rail diesel engines

33. Why should the cylinder head gasket thickness be checked when assembling a light diesel engine?

   a. To ensure proper compression ratio
   b. To make sure that the intake matches the cylinder head
   c. To make sure that the pistons are kept to the correct distance from the injectors
   d. All of the above

34. The drive train components need to be properly timed on what type of system?

   a. Gear
   b. Chain
   c. Belt
   d. All of the above

35. What tool should be used to clean threaded holes?

   a. WD-40
   b. A thread chaser
   c. A tap
   d. Clean engine oil

LIGHT VEHICLE DIESEL ENGINES (A9)

CATEGORY: ENGINE BLOCK DIAGNOSIS AND REPAIR

36. Most diesel engines equipped with a manual transmission use what type of flywheel?

    a. Aluminum
    b. Steel
    c. Dual-mass
    d. Carbon fiber with a cast iron insert

37. Crankshaft journal diameters should be measured using _____.

    a. micrometer
    b. feeler gauge
    c. plastigage®
    d. dial indicator

38. A bearing shell is being installed in a connecting rod. The end of the bearing is slightly above the parting line. Technician A says that this is normal. Technician B says that the bearing is too big. Which technician is correct?

    a. A only
    b. B only
    c. Both A and B
    d. Neither A nor B

39. Typical piston-to-cylinder wall clearance on a diesel engine is _____.

    a. 0.0001 to 0.0003 inch
    b. 0.001 to 0.003 inch
    c. 0.010 to 0.030 inch
    d. 0.100 to 0.300 inch

40. A diesel engine was disassembled and a small diameter curved tube was found in the bottom of the oil pan. What is the *most likely* use of this now broken part?

    a. Nothing that would belong in a diesel engine uses a small tube
    b. Piston cooling jet (nozzle)
    c. Oil pump pickup tube
    d. Oil cooler tube

41. What tool or measuring device should be used to check crankshaft alignment or bearing bore problems?

    a. Dial bore gauge
    b. Telescoping gauge and micrometer
    c. Precision straight edge and a feeler gauge
    d. All of the above

42. What is needed to check bearing clearances?

    a. Plastigage
    b. Telescoping gauge and a micrometer
    c. Dial bore gauge
    d. Either a or b

43. When disassembling a diesel engine block assembly, what should the technician do that is considered to be recommended procedure (best practice)?

    a. Remove all fasteners in the reverse of the torque tightening sequence
    b. Tag and bag all small parts and fasteners so that they can be reinstalled
    c. Clean the surfaces before performing a visual inspection for cracks and other faults
    d. All of the above

44. Technician A says that the dye penetrant test method can be used to detect cracks in iron, steel, or aluminum parts. Technician B says that the dye penetrant test can only be used with aluminum parts. Which technician is correct?

   a. A only
   b. B only
   c. Both A and B
   d. Neither A nor B

45. To check a crankshaft journal for taper and out of round, the journal should be measured in at least how many locations?

   a. One
   b. Two
   c. Four
   d. Six

46. Magnetic crack inspection is a procedure that uses _____.

   a. red dye to detect cracks in aluminum
   b. black light to detect cracks in iron or aluminum engine parts
   c. fine iron powder to detect cracks in iron parts
   d. magnet to remove cracks from iron parts

47. Many cleaning methods involve chemicals that are hazardous to use and expensive to dispose of after use. The least hazardous method is generally considered to be the _____.

   a. pyrolytic oven
   b. hot vapor tank
   c. hot soak tank
   d. cold soak tank

48. Two technicians are discussing removing and installing a crankshaft vibration damper (harmonic balancer). Technician A says that a puller is often needed to remove a vibration damper. Technician B says that an installation tool is often needed to install a vibration damper. Which technician is correct?

   a. A only
   b. B only
   c. Both A and B
   d. Neither A nor B

49. The typical journal-to-bearing clearance is _____.

   a. 0.00015 to 0.00018 inch
   b. 0.0005 to 0.0025 inch
   c. 0.150 to 0.250 inch
   d. 0.020 to 0.035 inch

50. If the gauging plastic strip (Plastigage®) is wider than specified after the bearings are tightened, this results _____.

   a. in excessive oil clearance
   b. from using old, dried Plastigage®
   c. in insufficient oil clearance
   d. in a small side (thrust) clearance

LIGHT VEHICLE DIESEL ENGINES (A9)

CATEGORY: LUBRICATION AND COOLING SYSTEMS DIAGNOSIS AND REPAIR

51. Which of the following ingredients is added to the engine coolant to prevent cavitation?

    a. Nitrate
    b. Silicate
    c. Ethylene glycol
    d. Phosphate

52. Normal oil pressure at idle speed on a light diesel is _____.

    a. 100 to 140 psi
    b. 70 to 90 psi
    c. 40 to 60 psi
    d. 5 to 10 psi

53. Engine oil is leaking for the oil pressure sensor/switch. What is the proper repair?

    a. Replace the switch with a new part
    b. Change the oil and add sealer
    c. Replace the sensor/switch with a mechanical gauge
    d. Change the engine oil and add one quart (liter) less than specified

54. The proper coolant to use in a light diesel is _____.

    a. embittered green coolant
    b. coolant that is specified by the vehicle manufacturer
    c. Propylene glycol (PG) coolant
    d. distilled water and methanol

55. What should be used to pressure test cooling system?

    a. A hand-operated pump with a built-in pressure gauge
    b. A shop air-powered gun
    c. The water pump by operating the engine at a fast idle until pressure builds
    d. Using the exhaust back-pressure at the inlet to the turbocharger

56. A gooey liquid is seen from the area around the thermostatic fan clutch. What could be the cause?

    a. This is normal operation and represents condensation around the area
    b. This is a sign that the clutch needs to be replaced due to leakage of the silicone fluid
    c. The engine has overheated
    d. The drive belt has overheated due to increased friction

57. Where is the water drain located that is used to remove water from the fuel system on most light diesel vehicles?

    a. At the fuel filter
    b. At the lowest place on the fuel tank
    c. At the highest place on the fuel tank
    d. At the end of the fuel rail

58. The engine oil specified for use in 2007 and newer light diesels should be_____.

    a. ultra-low viscosity
    b. high viscosity
    c. low ash
    d. synthetic oil

59. A pressure cap is used on the radiator to _____.

    a. keep the coolant flowing through the system
    b. force the coolant into small passages in the cylinder head
    c. raise the boiling temperature of the coolant
    d. force the coolant into the intercooler

60. Which of the following causes cavitation erosion in the cooling system?

    a. The use of cylinder sleeves
    b. Using a radiator cap with too high a pressure rating
    c. Vapor bubble implosion on the cylinder wall side of the water jacket
    d. High silicate levels in the antifreeze

61. Which statement is true about thermostats?

    a. The temperature marked on the thermostat is the temperature at which the thermostat should be fully open
    b. Thermostats often cause overheating
    c. The temperature marked on the thermostat is the temperature at which the thermostat should start to open
    d. Both a and b

62. An engine oil cooler should be inspected for _____?

    a. engine oil leaks
    b. coolant leaks
    c. air leaks
    d. both a and b

LIGHT VEHICLE DIESEL ENGINES (A9)

CATEGORY: AIR INDUCTION AND EXHAUST SYSTEMS DIAGNOSIS AND REPAIR

63. The exhaust gas recirculation (EGR) system is designed to _____.

    a. increase the temperature of the intake air to improve combustion
    b. decrease the temperature of combustion in the cylinders to reduce oxides of nitrogen emissions
    c. reduce the load on the cooling system while under a heavy load
    d. pre-heat the fuel before it is injected into the cylinders for better combustion

64. A light diesel engine equipped with a variable ratio/geometry turbocharger (VGT) lacks power. The owner also complains that the exhaust brake does not work. What is the *most likely* cause?

    a. Restricted exhaust system
    b. Clogged air filter
    c. Stuck turbocharger vanes
    d. Stuck open cooling system thermostat

65. What should be done when the outside temperature is expected to drop below the freezing temperature of the diesel exhaust fluid (DEF)?

    a. Move the vehicle inside a heated space
    b. No precautions are necessary
    c. Draw out the DEF and store inside a warm space and then refill the tank before starting the engine
    d. Add DEF antifreeze to the diesel exhaust fluid storage tank

66. The fuel filler opening on a light diesel is sized so _____.

    a. diesel only fuel can be added
    b. gasoline could be added in error because the nozzle size is smaller than the diesel fuel opening
    c. E85 (85% ethanol and 15% gasoline) could be added in error
    d. either b or c

67. The replaceable fuel filter on most light diesels is located _____.

    a. between the fuel tank and the engine in the low pressure side of the fuel system
    b. between the high-pressure pump and the nozzles
    c. between the fuel filler tube and the fuel tank which is at atmospheric pressure
    d. inside the fuel tank

68. The "water-in-fuel" sensor is located where in the diesel fuel system?

    a. In the fuel tank
    b. In the fuel filter assembly
    c. In the high-pressure rail
    d. Between the fuel filler opening and the fuel tank

69. Which exhaust aftermarket emission control device requires action by the driver/owner for service to remain functional?

   a. Selective catalyst reduction (SCR)
   b. Exhaust gas recirculation (EGR)
   c. Diesel particulate filter (DPF)
   d. Diesel oxidation catalyst (DOC)

70. Diesel exhaust fluid (DEF) is _____.

   a. distilled water with some (less than 10%) urea
   b. ammonia and urea and water
   c. 32.4% urea and 67.5% de-ionized water
   d. 67.5% urea and 32.4% distilled water

71. Diesel exhaust fluid contains water so it could freeze in cold weather. What action is needed by the vehicle owner or operator when cold temperatures are approaching?

   a. Take the DEF container into a heated space until needed to keep it from freezing
   b. Allow the engine to reach operating temperature before driving
   c. No action is needed because the container is designed to expand when the fluid freezes
   d. Plug in the DEF heater to an electrical outlet

72. DEF freezes at what temperature?

   a. 32°F (0°C)
   b. 12° F (–11° C)
   c. 0° F (–18°C)
   d. –8° F (–22°C)

73. An intake restriction gauge on the air filter assembly of a diesel engine is showing a red line. The gauge reading indicates what action is needed?

   a. The air filter should be replaced and the gauge reset
   b. The air filter is okay to continue to use
   c. The air filter gauge should be reset but the air filter itself is usable
   d. The air filter housing may be leaking air indicating more diagnosis is needed

74. If regeneration of the DPF does not occur and the driver ignores the dash warning lamp, what can occur?

   a. The engine connecting rods could be bent or break due to the forces involved
   b. The engine will produce less than normal power
   c. The engine will produce a hissing sound from the intake
   d. The engine will stall at any time and will not restart

75. A wastegate used on a turbocharged light diesel engine is used to control _____.

   a. exhaust backpressure
   b. pressure build-up in the cooling system
   c. turbocharge upper limit (boost) pressure
   d. fuel injection pressure

76. Diesel exhaust fluid (DEF) is used to reduce _____.

   a. CO emissions
   b. CO_2 emissions
   c. NOx emissions
   d. HC emissions

77. The EGR cooler system on newer design diesel engines is used to _____.

   a. increase the temperature of the coolant in the cooling system
   b. assist in reducing PM emissions
   c. assist in lowering NOx emissions
   d. open the EGR valve

78. A late model diesel engine equipped with a diesel particulate filter (DPF) has a yellow DPF warning lamp illuminated and lack power. Technician A says the vehicle needs to be driven under a load at a moderate speed for 20 to 40 minutes. Technician B says to tow the vehicle to a repair facility to replace the diesel particulate filter. Which technician is correct?

   a. Technician A
   b. Technician B
   c. Both A and B
   d. Neither A nor B

79. The operation of the selective catalyst reduction (SCR) system is being discussed. Technician A says a SCR catalyst converts urea into hydrogen gas. Technician B says the urea mixes with the exhaust gases and decomposes to form ammonia, which reacts with the NO_X to separate it into nitrogen and oxygen. Who is correct?

   a. Technician A
   b. Technician B
   c. Both A and B
   d. Neither A nor B

80. A stuck variable ratio/geometry (VGT) turbocharger could cause what type of driver complaint?

   a. Excessive oil consumption
   b. Lack of power
   c. Visible white exhaust smoke
   d. Excessive black or blue exhaust smoke

81. A preheater (inlet air heater) is used to _____.

   a. warm the air to help cold starting
   b. reduce oxides of nitrogen exhaust emissions
   c. help warm the cab in cold weather
   d. any of the above depending on application

82. On some diesel engines, an airflow control (throttle) valve is used to _____.

   a. help introduce exhaust gasses into the intake as part of the EGR system
   b. control idle speed
   c. act as an engine governor to control maximum engine speed
   d. control the amount of over-boost from the turbocharger

83. Pressure sensors are used to monitor which emission control device?

   a. SCR
   b. DEF
   c. DPF
   d. DOC

84. A reductant level sensor contains a _____.

   a. heater plus three electrodes plus a ground electrode
   b. float assembly
   c. pump motor assembly
   d. pump and filter assembly

85. What sensor is used in the exhaust system in a 2007 or newer light diesel engine that is NOT likely used in the exhaust system of a similar vehicle equipped with a gasoline engine?

   a. Oxygen sensor
   b. NO$_x$ sensor
   c. Delta pressure sensors
   d. Both b and c

86. When checking to see if the air filter should be replaced during a regular service, what should the technician do?

   a. Use a trouble light to see if light can be seen through the filter
   b. Check the air filter restriction monitor located on the air filter housing
   c. Remove the filter and use shop air to clean
   d. Remove the filter assembly and clean using a water-based liquid-based cleaner

CATEGORY: FUEL SYSTEM DIAGNOSIS AND REPAIR

87. The diesel engine intake pump (lift pump) is what type of pump?

    a. Low pressure; high volume
    b. High pressure; low volume
    c. Low pressure; low volume
    d. High pressure; high volume

88. The water drain for the fuel system is usually located at the _____.

    a. fuel tank
    b. fuel filter
    c. high pressure pump
    d. fuel rail

89. After replacing the fuel filter on a light diesel vehicle, what should be performed before starting the engine?

    a. Top off the fuel tank with fresh diesel fuel
    b. Prime and bleed the system
    c. Remove the water valve
    d. Crank the engine with the injectors disconnected for 10 seconds

90. On a hydraulic electronic unit injector (HEUI) system, why is the engine condition critical to proper operation?

    a. The engine oil lubricates the high-pressure pump
    b. Some engine oil is mixed with the diesel fuel before injection
    c. Engine oil is used to operate the fuel injectors
    d. Engine oil is used to help remove exhaust soot from the exhaust

91. What do the numbers/letters on the side of a common rail fuel injector indicate?

    a. Injector calibration code
    b. Part number
    c. Cubic centimeters (cc) fuel flow rating of the injector
    d. Opening pressure of the injector

92. What unit should be selected on a digital multimeter (DMM) to measure voltage drop?

    a. ACA
    b. ACV
    c. DCV
    d. Ohms

93. What do the numbers/letters on the side of a common rail fuel injector indicate?

    a. Injector calibration code
    b. Part number
    c. Cubic centimeters (cc) fuel flow rating of the injector
    d. Opening pressure of the injector

94. After replacing an injector on the common rail light diesel engine, what tool is needed to complete the repair?

   a. A scan tool to calibrate the PCM to the new injector
   b. An O-ring sealing tool
   c. A new air filter
   d. A new fuel filter

95. Caution should be taken when working around a running light diesel common rail diesel engine because of high voltage present around the _____.

   a. dual 12-volt batteries
   b. alternator
   c. injectors
   d. turbocharger

96. The diesel engine replaceable fuel filter is usually located _____.

   a. between the fuel tank and the engine
   b. inside the fuel tank and is not a replaceable part
   c. between the turbocharger and the intercooler assembly
   d. at the inlet to the high-pressure pump

97. A light diesel is hard to start (cranks a long time before starting) in cold weather. When measuring the current draw during cranking, the amperage draw is below specifications. Technician A says that one or more glow plugs could be open. Technician B says that the starter motor is likely to be defective. Which technician is correct?

   a. A only
   b. B only
   c. Both A and B
   d. Neither A nor B

98. What size is the fuel filler opening on a light diesel?

   a. 13/16 inch (21 mm)
   b. 15/16 inch (24 mm)
   c. 1.25 or 1.5 inch (32 or 38 mm)
   d. Either b or c

99. Most common rail diesel use a small coolant cooled radiator to cool the air between the turbocharger and the intake manifold. What is the purpose of this cooler?

   a. To cool the engine oil which increases its life
   b. To help cool the engine coolant
   c. To increase engine performance
   d. To cool the exhaust

100. What is the purpose of using a cooler for the exhaust gases flowing between the exhaust manifold and the EGR valve?

   a. To keep the EGR valve from melting from the heat of the exhaust
   b. To make the exhaust gases more effective for reducing oxides of nitrogen emissions
   c. To reduce exhaust system backpressure
   d. To warm the intake for improved fuel economy

101. Diesel engines operate "un-throttled"; however, some common rails diesel are equipped with a throttle place which is used _____.

   a. as governor to prevent the engine from exceeding the maximum allowable engine speed
   b. to create a pressure drop to allow exhaust gases to flow into the intake to help the EGR system
   c. to prevent backfiring through the intake
   d. to control engine speed when the cruise control is being used

102. A common rail diesel is found covered with diesel fuel. What should be used to help locate the source of the leak?

   a. Cardboard
   b. A scan tool
   c. A digital meter
   d. A stethoscope

103. When replacing an electronic unit injector(s) (EUI), what procedure should be performed on a common rail light diesel?

   a. The PCM needs to be reflashed to the latest software
   b. The calibration code on the injector needs to be inputted to the PCM using a scan tool
   c. The fuel filter has to be replaced
   d. The air filter is required to be replaced at the same time if an injector is replaced

104. A rough idle and low performance is being diagnosed on a light diesel equipped with hydraulic electronic unit injector(s) (HEUI). Technician A says that dirty or low engine oil level could be the cause. Technician B says that low Cetane diesel fuel could be the cause. Which technician is correct?

   a. A only
   b. B only
   c. Both A and B
   d. Neither A nor B

105. A light diesel engine stalls after it starts and runs for a short time. What is a possible cause?

   a. A defective glow plug
   b. A misadjusted intake valve
   c. A clogged oil filter
   d. A leak in the suction side of the fuel line

106. A light diesel engine cranks normally but cranks for a long time before starting. What is a possible cause?

   a. High Cetane fuel
   b. Open intake heater or glow plugs
   c. One of the two batteries is discharged
   d. High resistance in the battery cables

107. A turbocharged light diesel engine is creating blue exhaust smoke and oil in the intake passages was found during a visual inspection. Based on the customer concern and the visual inspection, what is a likely cause?

   a. A defective turbocharger
   b. A fault with the high-pressure pump producing too much pressure
   c. A restricted intake
   d. A defective glow plug

108. A light diesel engine has low power. Which of these could be a possible cause?

   a. A clogged air filter
   b. A restricted fuel filter
   c. A stuck open EGR valve
   d. Any of the above

109. A fuel injector is being replaced on a common rail light diesel engine. Technician A says that the fuel line should be tightened using a torque wrench. Technician B says that the fuel injector calibration code should be programmed into the PCM using a special tool that comes with each new injector. Which technician is correct?

   a. A only
   b. B only
   c. Both A and B
   d. Neither A nor B

110. Light diesel engines built after 2007 should use diesel fuel with what level of sulfur?

   a. 15 ppm
   b. 50 ppm
   c. 150 ppm
   d. 500 ppm

111. The high-pressure fuel pump used on a common rail light diesel engine is driven by the _____.

   a. crankshaft
   b. camshaft
   c. auxiliary shaft
   d. accessory drive belt

112. What fuel system component is used in a vehicle equipped with a diesel engine that is not usually used on the same vehicle when it is equipped with a gasoline engine?

   a. Fuel filter
   b. Fuel supply line
   c. Fuel return line
   d. Water-fuel separator

113. The diesel injection pump is usually driven by a _____.

   a. gear off the camshaft
   b. belt off the crankshaft
   c. shaft drive off the crankshaft
   d. chain drive off the camshaft

114. Which diesel system supplies high-pressure diesel fuel to all of the injectors all of the time?

   a. Distributor
   b. Inline
   c. High-pressure common rail
   d. Rotary

115. Glow plugs should have high resistance when _____ and lower resistance when _____.

   a. cold/warm
   b. warm/cold
   c. wet/dry
   d. dry/wet

116. Modern common rail diesel fuel systems may use _____ to control high side fuel system pressure.

   a. an electronic solenoid valve
   b. fuel rail pressure limiting valve
   c. fuel control actuator (FCA)
   d. all of the above

117. Why are low ash oils required for current model year diesel engines?

   a. EGR system compatibility
   b. Required use of ULSD fuels
   c. EPA regulation of ash emissions
   d. Exhaust after-treatment compatibility

118. The replaceable fuel filter on most light diesels is located _____.

   a. between the fuel tank and the engine in the low pressure side of the fuel system
   b. between the high-pressure pump and the nozzles
   c. between the fuel filler tube and the fuel tank which is atmospheric pressure
   d. inside the fuel tank

119. In a pump-line-nozzle fuel system (PLN-E), why are all the fuel lines the same length?

   a. To reduce noise
   b. To ensure proper injection timing to each cylinder
   c. So that all of the lines can be interchanged
   d. To keep costs down at the factory

LIGHT VEHICLE DIESEL ENGINES (A9)

CATEGORY: GENERAL ENGINE DIAGNOSIS

1. **The correct answer is c.** The oil that must be used in a 2007 or newer diesel engine has to be rated as low ash with a rating of CF-4. Answer a is not correct because SAE is the rating system used to describe the viscosity (not the ash levels) of the oil. Answer b is not correct because API is the organization that set the standards but it does not represent the rating that is required for all 2007 and newer light diesel engines. Answer d is not correct because ILSAC is the organization that set the standards but it does not represent the rating that is required for all 2007 and newer light diesel engines.

2. **The correct answer is a.** A battery drain (parasitic) draw test should be performed because of the symptom. It appears that the batteries have been discharged over a few days period, which is not a normal condition and could be explained by having something electrical in the vehicle drawing current from the batteries. Answer b is not correct because an injector timing test would not determine what was causing the batteries from being drained over a few days of time. Answer c is not correct because while an intake restriction could be the cause of reduced engine performance and power, it is not likely to be the cause of a battery that loses its charge over a short period of time. Answer d is not correct because while an exhaust restriction could be the cause of reduced engine performance and power, it is not likely to be the cause of a battery that loses it charge over a short period of time.

3. **The correct answer is c.** The air filter monitor is the best indication that the air filter needs to be replaced because it uses the pressure drop across the filter to determine when it is restricted and need to be replaced. Answer a is not correct because an air filter for a diesel engine, not being throttled, must use a multiple layer filter to help avoid the possibility of it being cut or torn, which would allow dirt into the engine without any restriction. As a result, diesel air filters cannot be judged accurately for restriction by sight alone. Answer b is not correct because while some vehicle manufactories recommended that the air filter be replaced at time or mileage in-

tervals, the conditions under which a light diesel operates can require replacement much soon than every three years or every 30,000 miles and is therefore is not the best answer considering that one answer has the technician check the air filter monitor. Answer d is not correct because the low power warning lamp is used to indicate that an electronic throttle control (ETC) fault has been detected or an emissions control system needs to be serviced and is not used to indicate a clogged air filter.

4. **The correct answer is d.** All of the three options are correct. The engine oil should be replaced according to the specified number of miles the vehicle has traveled (answer a) or the number of months since the last oil change (answer b) or the number of engine running hours (answer c). Answers a, b, and c are not correct because the oil should be changed based on all of the factors, not just one of them.

5. **The correct answer is b.** A higher than normal engine oil level is most likely due to diesel fuel leaking into the oil from a leak in the high-pressure fuel system. Answer a is not correct because even though hot oil does tend to expand when it gets warmer, the amount is almost impossible to measure because the oil gets thinner as it gets hotter and as a result is not likely the explanation for a higher-than-normal engine oil level. Answer c is not correct because the transmission is not physically connected to the transmission, so fluid transfer from the transmission to the engine is not possible. Answer d is not correct because while the oil being fed to the turbocharger is not likely to be forced into the oil but instead if there is a fault with the turbocharger, the oil would enter the intake of the engine and be burned during the combustion process and not end up in the crankcase of the engine.

6. **The correct answer is a.** Technician A only is correct because a weak battery will draw current from the new battery in an attempt to keep the voltages of the two batteries, which are connected in parallel, the same. Technician B is not correct because the battery drain is not excessive because it does not exceed the industry standard of 0.050 amperes (50 milliamperes), and therefore, this is not the root cause of the customer concern. Answer c (both technicians A and B) and d (neither technician A nor B) are not correct because only technician A is correct.

7. **The correct answer is d.** A glow plug or an injector should be removed, but not both, to install a compression tester so a compression test can be performed. Answer a is not correct because while an injector could be removed to perform a compression test, the best answer is that either the injectors or a glow plug (answer d) could be removed. Answer b is not correct because a valve does not need to be disconnected in order to perform a compression test. Answer c is not correct because while a glow plug could be removed to perform a compression test, the best answer is that either the injectors or a glow plug (answer d) could be removed.

8. **The correct answer is c.** Both technicians are correct. Technician A is correct because old dirty engine oil usually has a higher than normal viscosity and therefore would not work well with the hydraulically operated fuel injectors used in a HEUI-type system. As a result, the injectors may not open correctly, leading to a misfire or a hard-to-start condition. Technician B is correct because using engine oil that does not have the specified viscosity would not work well with the hydraulically operated fuel injectors used in a HEUI-type system. As a result, the injectors may not open correctly, leading to a misfire or a hard-to-start condition. Answers a, b, and d are not correct because both technicians are correct.

9. **The correct answer is c.** Both technicians are correct. Technician A is correct because each injector is tested for flow rate after assembly and assigned a calibration code number that must be entered into the PCM after the injectors is installed to ensure that the proper amount of fuel is delivered to meet factory specifications and requirements. Technician B is correct because each injector is tested for flow rate to ensure that the proper amount of fuel is delivered to meet the specified emissions standards.

10. **The correct answer is d.** Neither technician is correct. Technician A is not correct because the glow plugs are usually kept working after the engine starts to help reduce exhaust emissions. Technician B is not correct because glow plugs are not capable of detecting the flame front and they are kept working after the engine starts to reduce exhaust emissions. Answers a, b, and c are not correct because neither technician is correct.

11. **The correct answer is a.** The term "retarded timing" refers to the delay in the injector timing. In normal operation, the injector is fired before the piston reaches the top of the cylinder, called before top dead center (BTDC). When the injection is retarded, this means that the firing is delayed and therefore occurs when the piston is closer to the top of the compression stroke and therefore closer to the top of the cylinder referred to as top dead center (TDC). Answer b is not correct because retarded injector timing means that the injector is occurring closer, rather than farther away from TDC. Answer c is not correct because while if the injector was fired at TDC, this would mean that it was retarded, and it can be before TDC and still be retarded. Answer d is not correct because the injector would never be fired when the piston is at the bottom (BDC) as no combustion would occur.

12. **The correct answer is d.** All of the factors could cause lower-than-normal oil pressure. Answer a is correct (worn oil pump) because this can cause lower-than-normal output which would reduce the oil pressure supplied to the engine. Answer b (worn rod bearings) is also correct because the excessive bearing clearance would cause leakage of the oil and would cause lower-than-normal oil pressure. Answer c (worn main bearings) is also correct because the excessive bearing clearance would cause leakage of the oil and would cause lower-than-normal oil pressure.

13. **The correct answer is b.** A clogged air filter will restrict the amount of air entering the engine, and while the system may be able to reduce the amount of fuel delivered to match the reduced airflow, incomplete combustion is the most likely result of black exhaust smoke. Answer a is not correct because if the DEF container was empty, the diesel control system would prevent the engine from producing power and may even prevent the engine from starting but would not cause the engine to produce black exhaust smoke. Answer c is not correct because while the incorrect oil can cause a degradation of the engine itself over time, it is unlikely to be the cause of black exhaust smoke. Answer d is not correct because a stuck closed injector would prevent the cylinder from firing and therefore could not be the cause of black exhaust smoke.

14. **The correct answer is b.** A part of most vehicle manufacturer's specified diagnostic procedure is a visual inspection and it should be the first or almost the first step that should be performed by the service technician. Answer a is not correct because codes should only be cleared when the repair has been made and confirmed that the root cause has been found and corrected. Answer c is not correct because while a fault in the after treatment system may be related to the air and fuel filters, this is not what the technician should perform first without any indication that they could be cause of the problem. Answer d is not correct because the level of the fuel in the tank is not a factor to consider when diagnosing after treatment faults with a light diesel engine.

15. **The correct answer is b.** Whenever trying to locate the source of a fuel leak in a diesel engine, cardboard should be used which will show fuel being sprayed on to it by a color change. Diesel fuel under high pressure can penetrate the skin, so cardboard should be used instead of a hand around a running diesel engine that has a fuel leak. Answer a is not correct because while a strong light may help see where the fuel is leaking from, most vehicle manufacturers recommend the use of cardboard. Answer c is not correct because while a hydrocarbon leak detector could detect hydrocarbons in the air, it is not recommended for use to locate the source of a high-pressure diesel fuel leak; this is mainly because the technician's hand would need to hold the detector close to the source to be detected and this could result in personal injury. Answer d is not correct because while baby powder may show where the leaks are, the high pressure fuel will often just blow it out of the way making the location of the leak difficult or impossible to find.

16. **The correct answer is c.** Diesel fuel should be clear or amber in color if it is taxed for highway use. Answer a is not correct because if the fuel is dyed, this means that it is for off-highway use, and purple is only used in Canada for gasoline designed for off-road use and not for diesel fuel. Answer b is not correct because if diesel fuel is dyed red, this means that it is non-taxed and should only be used for off-road. Answer d is not correct because if the fuel is dyed, this means that it is for off-highway use and while normal on-road diesel may appear to be greenish/blue, it is usually clear (no color) or amber in color for highway use (taxed)

17. **The correct answer is b.** Normal diesel fuel used for most temperatures is #2. The lighter #1 is used in extreme low temperatures areas only due to its lower BTU content and the higher numbers are not used in diesel engine that are used on the highways and are used in stationary or marine applications only. Answer a is not correct because the lighter #1 is used in extreme low temperatures areas only due to its lower BTU content. Answer c is not correct because #3 diesel fuel is not used on the highways and are used in stationary or marine applications. Answer d is not correct because #4 diesel fuel is not used on the highways and are used in stationary or marine applications.

18. **The correct answer is d.** Any of the above is the correct answer. Answer a is not correct because using a hydrometer is a tool that can used to test coolant so are the other two answers. Answer b is correct because using a test strip is a tool that can used to test coolant so are the other two answers. Answer c is also correct because using a refractometer is a tool that can used to test coolant so are the other two answers.

19. **The correct answer is d.** Silicon is dirt, whereas if the word is spelled with an "e" at the end (silicone), this means a type of sealer. Answer a is not correct because silicon is not a sealer but is instead dirt such as silicon sand. Answer b is not correct because silicon is not a sealer but is instead dirt such as silicon sand. Answer c is not correct because while a clogged oil filter could be a contributing factor of the engine having excessive silicon in the oil, there are many other reasons with the most common being a defective or incorrectly fitting air filter allowing dirt to enter the engine.

20. **The correct answer is a.** Both batteries must be replaced as a pair even if one of them is found to be weak or defective to avoid having the weak battery from taking most of the charge from the alternator. Answer b is not correct because the weak battery will affect the good battery and therefore the best practice includes replacing both batteries even if one is found to be weak or defective. Answer c is not correct because the weak battery will affect the good battery and therefore the best practice includes replacing both batteries even if one is found to be weak or defective. Answer d is not correct because the weak battery will affect the good battery and therefore the best practice includes replacing both batteries even if one is found to be weak or defective and will not be helped by recharging the weak one.

21. **The correct answer is d.** Any of the above is the correct answer. A defective starter is correct because a worn or defective starter will often not be able to supply the needed rotating torque or speed needed to start a diesel engine. A discharged battery could also be the cause preventing the starter motor from being able to supply the needed rotating speed for a diesel engine to start. Excessive voltage drop in the battery cable is also a possible reason for the starter motor to not be able to spin the diesel engine fast enough for the engine to start. A voltage drop is resistance in the cable which reduces the amount of current (amperes) that can be transferred from the batteries to the starter motor. Answers a, b, and c are not correct because any of the components could be the cause.

22. **The correct answer is b.** An air dam is used to stop air from flowing underneath the vehicle and instead is used to direct the airflow from forward movement through the radiator. If the front air dam is missing, there may not be enough airflow through the radiator to properly cool the engine at highway speed. Answer a is not correct because a leaking water pump while it could result in the amount of coolant in the system would not be a direct cause of overheating at highway speeds and not during city driving conditions. Answer c is not correct because a defective fan clutch would cause the engine to tend to overheat when the vehicle speed is low such as in city-type driving and not have a major affect at highway speed due to the airflow from the vehicle moving forward which is enough to keep the radiator temperature under control. Answer d is not correct because a collapsed heater hose while it would affect the amount of heat to the heater would not likely be the cause of an overheating condition at highway speeds only.

23. **The correct answer is a.** The technician needs to use a scan tool and enter the calibration code etched into the side of the injectors to make sure that the PCM will deliver the specified amount of fuel. Answer b is not correct because the calibration procedure has to be done using a scan tool as it will not be learned by having the engine idle. Answer c is not correct because each injector is tested for flow rate and then a calibration code is etched on the injector. They are not sorted for use in any particular cylinder. Answer d is not correct because each injector is tested and its flow rate is determined and a code is assigned for each injector instead of being matched to each other.

24. **The correct answer is a.** After a repair has been performed and before returning the vehicle to the owner, the service technician should check that all of the OBD II monitors have been performed and passed and ensure that the engine concern has been corrected. Answer b is not correct because the freeze frames will be deleted when the diagnostic trouble codes (DTCs) are cleared, which should be done after the repair but before the monitors are checked. Many monitors do not run if there are stored DTCs, so these need to be cleared before the monitor status is checked. Answer c is not correct because while disconnecting the battery will usually clear DTCs, but this will not ensure that the monitors will run and pass, which is needed to be performed to make sure that the engine performance concern has been successfully repaired. Answer d is not correct because while some monitors may run when the engine is at idle speed, many require that the vehicle be driven on the road following the drive cycle as recommended by the vehicle manufacturer and found in service information.

25. **The correct answer is d** (either a or c). Either an hydrometer (answer a) or a refractometer (answer c) can be used to check the freezing point of coolant. Answer b (test strip) cannot be used to determine the freezing temperature of the coolant. A test strip used to test the condition of the coolant and the pH but it cannot be used to test the freezing temperature. Answer a is not correct because either a hydrometer or a refractometer can be used to test the freezing temperature of the coolant. Answer c is not correct because either a refractometer or a hydrometer can be used to test the freezing temperature of the coolant.

LIGHT VEHICLE DIESEL ENGINES (A9)

CATEGORY: CYLINDER HEAD AND VALVE TRAIN DIAGNOSIS AND REPAIR

26. **The correct answer is b.** The valve crossheads (valve bridges) are used to open two valves by the use of one pushrod. This design is commonly used in diesel engines that use four valves per cylinder in an overhead valve (OHV) arrangements. If a crosshead is bent, this will cause one of the two valves to open more or less than the other valve creating performance and emission issues. Answer a is not correct because a common rail diesel does not use a pre-combustion chamber but instead the air-fuel mixture is ignited in the combustion chamber itself. Answer c is not correct because the valve bridge only affects the opening of the valve (s) and does not affect the injector operation. Answer c is not correct because the valve bridge only affects the opening of the valve (s) and does not affect the height of the cylinder head. Answer d is not correct because the valve bridge only affects the opening of the valve (s) and does not affect the compression ratio of the engine.

27. **The correct answer is b.** Whenever removing a cylinder head, the fasteners should be loosened in the opposite order of the tightening sequence. This means that the fasteners should be loosened starting at the ends and working toward the center. Answer a is not correct because by starting in the center and working toward the outside could cause the cylinder head to warp. Answer c is not correct because it does matter in what order the fasteners are loosened to relieve any built up stress in the cylinder which would be relieved by loosening the fasteners starting at the ends and moving toward the center. Answer d is not correct because the rate should be slow, not fast, and loosened from the ends to the center to help relieve any stress that may be in the cylinder head.

28. **The correct answer is d.** Any of the above is correct because the high-pressure pump must be timed regardless of the type of driver used. Answer a is not correct because while a gear type valve train needs to be correctly timed, it has to be timed if the engine is equipped with any of the other types of pump drive. Answer b is not correct because while a chain type valve train needs to be correctly timed, it has to be timed if the engine is equipped with any of the other types of pump drive. Answer c is not correct because while a belt type valve train needs to be correctly timed, it has to be timed if the engine is equipped with any of the other types of pump drive.

29. **The correct answer is d.** Using multilayer steel gaskets (MLS) is the best way to achieve consistent head gasket clamping force. Multilayer steel gaskets contain elastomer material between layers of thin steel sheets, which allows the gap between the block and the cylinder had to seal without the need for excessive tightening torque on the head bolts. Answer a is not correct because all fasteners should be tightened following the torque tightening chart as specified by the vehicle manufacturers. This procedure tightens the fasteners starting in the center and then working toward the outer part (ends) of the cylinder head and NOT from the outside toward the center. Answer b is not correct because torque-to-yield fasteners almost always must be replaced rather than reused according to most vehicle manufactures' instructions. Answer c is not correct because most vehicle manufactures specify that the head bolts be tightened in a specific sequence and at intervals such as half the full torque, then three-fourths of full torque, and then to the final torque specifications.

30. **The correct answer is d.** Pre-combustion chambers are only found on engines that use a glow plug to ignite the diesel fuel in a small chamber. When the air-fuel mixture ignites in the small chamber, the flame front expands into and ignites the air-fuel mixture in the combustion chamber. Answer a is not correct because a common rail diesel does not use a pre-combustion chamber but instead the air-fuel mixture is ignited in the combustion chamber itself. Answer b is not correct because a direct injection diesel does not use a pre-combustion chamber but instead the air-fuel mixture is ignited in the combustion chamber itself. Answer c is not correct because all diesel engines use high-pressure but only an indirect diesel engine uses a pre-combustion chamber.

31. **The correct answer is b.** A bent valve bridge should always be replaced with a new part to help insure that both valves are opened the same distance for best engine operation. Answer a is not correct because if the bridge were straightened, it would likely bend again due to the fact that it has been weakened. Replacing the bridge with a new part is considered to be the best practice. Answer c is not correct because the part has been weakened and the best procedure (best practice) is to replace it with a new part. Answer d is not correct because the best procedure (best practice)  is to replace it with a new part and not try to work around the issue by using a different length push-rod, even if that would be possible.

32. **The correct answer is c.** Pre-combustion chambers are only found on engines that use a glow plug to ignite the diesel fuel in a small chamber. When the air-fuel mixture ignites in the small chamber, the flame front expands into and ignites the air-fuel mixture in the combustion chamber. Answer a is not correct because not all light diesels use a pre-combustion chamber. Answer b is not correct because not all light diesels, regardless of size (displacement), use a pre-combustion chamber. Answer d is not correct because all common rail diesel inject the fuel into the combustion chamber directly and not into a pre-combustion chamber.

33. **The correct answer is a.** Head gasket thickness has a major effect on the compression ratio of a diesel engine, so using the specified head gaskets and following all of the engine assembly procedures as specified by the vehicle manufacturer are very important to the proper operation of the engine. Answer b is not correct because, while it is important that the intake lines up with the cylinder head on any engine, it is not as critical on a diesel engine compared to a gasoline engine and would not likely affect the operation or the emissions of a light diesel. Answer c is not correct because the clearance between the fuel injectors and the piston is great enough that this would not be the main issue compared to the proper compression ratio. Answer a is not correct because only answer a is correct which means that answer b and c and therefore d cannot be correct.

34. **The correct answer is d.** Regardless of the type of high-pressure pump drive, all have to be timed correctly. Answers a, b, and c are not correct because while has to be timed, it does not matter which type of cam drive is used as all of them require that the high-pressure pump be correctly timed.

35. **The correct answer is b.** Using a thread chaser is the recommend tool to use to clean threaded holes. Answer a is not correct because while WD-40 may be used with a thread chaser, it alone cannot do a good job of cleaning the threads in a threaded hole. Answer c is not correct because a tap can remove metal and may cause damage to the existing threads instead of cleaning the threads like a thread chaser can do.  Answer d is not correct because while engine oil may be used with a thread chaser, clean engine oil alone cannot do a good job of cleaning threads in a threaded hole.

LIGHT VEHICLE DIESEL ENGINES (A9)

CATEGORY: ENGINE BLOCK DIAGNOSIS AND REPAIR

36. **The correct answer is c.** Most light diesel engine vehicles use a dual-mass flywheel to help dampen the firing impulses of a diesel from getting into the transmission and the rest of the drivetrain. Answer a is not correct because flywheels used on diesel engine are made from cast iron and are dual-mass design. A flywheel made from aluminum would need to have a cast iron clutch friction surface and would be too light to adsorb the torsional forces produced in a diesel engine. Answer b is not correct because flywheels used on diesel engine are made from cast iron and are dual-mass design. A flywheel made from steel would need a cast iron clutch friction surface and would be too light to adsorb the torsional forces produced in a diesel engine. Answer d is not correct because made from carbon fiber would need to have a cast iron clutch friction surface and would be too light to adsorb the torsional forces produced in a diesel engine.

37. **The correct answer is a.** A micrometer is the measuring instrument that should be used to measure the crankshaft journal diameters because it can be used to measure the journal directly and in thousandths of an inch. Answer b is not correct because a feeler gauge can only be used to measure the clearance between surfaces and cannot be used to actually measure a crankshaft journal diameter. Answer c is not correct because while Plastigage® can be used to determine bearing clearance, it cannot be used to measure the crankshaft journal diameter. Answer d is not correct because while a dial indicator can be used to measure movement such as crankshaft end play, it cannot be used to measure the diameter of a crankshaft journal.

38. **The correct answer is a.** Technician A only is correct. The insert bearing should extend slightly above the bearing cap to provide the necessary crush when assembled to keep the bearing from spinning during engine operation. Answer b is not correct because the bearing size is determined by the thickness of the insert and the difference between a standard and a 0.010 in. undersize bearing (thicker shell) insert may not be visible. Answers c and d are not correct because they do not indicate that Technician A only is correct.

39. **The correct answer is b.** Typical piston-to-cylinder clearance is one to three thousandth of an inch (0.001 in. to 0.003 in.), which is the best answer. Answers b, c, and d are too great a clearance.

40. **The correct answer is b.** A small diameter tube is likely an oil piston cooling nozzle that has broken off at the oil gallery. Answer a is not correct because there are oil nozzles (squirters) used in all turbocharged light diesel engines to help keep the temperature of the piston crown under control. Answer c is not correct because an oil pickup tube uses a larger diameter tube than a piston nozzle and is not likely what the technician found in the oil pan. Answer d is not correct because the oil cooler is located outside of the engine and would not be found inside the oil pan.

41. **The correct answer is d.** All of the above are correct. Answer a (dial bore gauge) is a measuring tool that can be used to measure the crankshaft bearing bore dimension. Answer b (telescoping gauge and micrometer) can also be used to measure the crankshaft bearing bore dimension. Answer c (precision straight edge and a feeler gauge) can also be used to determine if the main bearing bores are in alignment.

42. **The correct answer is d.** Either a (Plastigage®) or b (telescoping gauge and a micrometer) can be used to check bearing clearance. Answer c (dial bore gauge) can be used to measure bearing bore size and check it for taper and out-of-round; it cannot be used to determine bearing clearance.

43. **The correct answer is d.** All of the above are correct. Answer a is correct because the tightening sequence for most parts that are attached to the block are loosened in the reverse order of the tightening sequence or in other words from the outside fasteners to the inner fasteners. Answer b is also correct because all small parts should be labeled and kept together for each component removed and the best way to achieve this is to place all of the bolts, nuts, and other small parts into a plastic bag and label the bag. Answer c is also correct because the engine components need to be clean before checking them for cracks and other faults that could affect the structural strength of the engine. Answers a, b, and c are not correct because all of the answers are correct.

44. **The correct answer is a.** Technician A is correct. Dye penetrant is primarily used to check pistons and other nonmagnetic materials for cracks, but it can be used to check iron and steel parts. Answer b is not correct because even though these are other methods that can be used to check iron and steel parts for cracks, the dye penetrant method can be used on other materials besides aluminum. Answers c and d are not correct because they do not state that Technician A only is correct.

45. **The correct answer is d.** To check for taper, the crankshaft journal has to be measured at a minimum of six locations. Answers a, b, and c are not correct because when measuring taper, there must be at least two measurements so the difference (taper) can be determined and this does not allow enough measurements to determine out-of-round. To be able to determine accurately whether or not a crankshaft journal is out-of-round or tapered, at least six measurements must be taken 120° apart.

46. **The correct answer is c.** Magnetic lines of force tend to get stronger at edges and therefore, a fine powder can be used to locate cracks in iron parts. Answer a is not correct because aluminum parts cannot be checked using a magnetic field. Answer b is not correct because a magnetic method can be used on iron, but not on aluminum parts. Answer d is not correct because the answer states that the magnet removes the cracks rather than simply detecting the cracks.

47. **The correct answer is a.** The pyrolytic oven is the least hazardous method of cleaning. Answers b, c, and d are not correct because the chemicals used in these cleaning methods represent hazards to the service technician during their use and may also create a hazardous waste problem.

48. **The correct answer is c.** Both technicians are correct. Many crankshaft vibration dampeners (harmonic balancers) are a light press fit on the end of the crankshaft, which requires the use of a puller to safely remove, and an installation tool to safely install, to prevent causing damage to the balancer. Answers a, b, and d are not correct because both technicians are correct.

49. **The correct answer is b.** Most bearing oil clearance specifications are usually close to 0.001 in. to 0.003 in. and 0.0005 in (one-half thousandth) to 0.0025 in. (two and a half thousandth) is a typical clearance specification. Answer a is too small a clearance and answers c and d represent too much clearance.

50. **The correct answer is c.** If the Plastigage® strip has been squeezed so that it is wider than specified, the oil clearance is insufficient. Answer a is not correct because a large oil clearance will not squeeze the plastic strip as much and the clearance will be larger than specified. Answer b is not correct because even though this could cause an inaccurate reading, the best answer is still c. Answer d is not correct because side clearance is not measured using Plastigage®.

LIGHT VEHICLE DIESEL ENGINES (A9)

CATEGORY: LUBRICATION AND COOLING SYSTEMS DIAGNOSIS AND REPAIR

51. **The correct answer is a.** A coolant designed for use in diesel engines usually specifies a certain level of nitrate to help protect the cylinder liners form cavitation. Answer b is not correct because it is the added nitrates and not the silicates that are used to help prevent damage from cavitation. Answer c is not correct because all coolant recommended by the vehicle manufacturers is ethylene glycol based and therefore is not used to prevent the damage caused by cavitation. Answer d is not correct because it is the added nitrates and not the phosphate that are used to help prevent damage from cavitation.

52. **The correct answer is d.** Normal oil pressure is generally 10 psi per 1000 RPM and therefore oil pressure between 5 psi and 10 psi would be the best answer. Answers a, b, and c are too high for normal oil pressure at idle speed for a light diesel engine.

53. **The correct answer is a.** If the oil pressure sensor is leaking, then the sensor needs to be replaced with a new part. Answer b is not correct because while a sealer may or may not stop a leak at the threads of an oil pressure sensor, it will not work to repair a sensor itself if it is leaking. Answer c is not correct because while a mechanical gauge would fix the leaking sensor by removing it, this is not the repair that the customer would expect and would not be the correct fix for this customer concern. Answer d is not correct because changing the engine oil would not likely stop an oil pressure sensor/switch from leaking.

54. **The correct answer is b.** The only coolant that should be used in a light diesel is the coolant recommended by the vehicle manufacturer. Answer a is not correct because while the specified coolant may be embittered, it is not a type or specification for coolant. Answer c is not correct because propylene glycol (PG) coolant is not recommend for use by any vehicle manufacturer and is instead a type of coolant marketed at parts stores as an alternative to ethylene glycol, which is the type of base coolant recommended for use in light diesel engines. Answer d is not correct because methanol (methylene alcohol) is not a recommended coolant in any engine.

55. **The correct answer is a.** A hand-operated pressure tester should be used to pressurize the cooling system to the pressure of the pressure cap and then check for leaks. Answer b is not correct because using shop compressed air could over-pressure the cooling system and harm to the components and hoses in the system. Answer c is not correct because even though pressure would increase in a closed system, using the engine water pump is not the specified procedure to follow based on vehicle manufacturers' recommendations. Answer d is not correct because using the exhaust is not the specified procedure to follow based on vehicle manufacturers' recommendations.

56. **The correct answer is b.** Any leak seen around the clutch fan indicates that the silicone fluid is leaking and the clutch fan requires replacement. Answer a is not correct because the clutch contains a silicone liquid which does not become a vapor at high temperatures and therefore would not then condense. Answer c is not correct because the leaking clutch fan is not an indication that the engine has overheated but if it did become overheated, it could be at least partially due to the failed (leaking) clutch fan. Answer d is not correct because the silicon fluid inside the clutch fan is located in the center section of the clutch fan and would not likely be affected by a slipping fan drive belt.

57. **The correct answer is a.** The location where the water drain is located is at the fuel filter assembly. Answer b is not correct because the drain is located at the fuel filter and not at the bottom of the fuel tank. Answer c is not correct because the drain is located at the fuel filter and not at the top of the fuel tank where water would never be located because water is heavier than diesel fuel. Answer d is not correct because the water drain is located at the fuel filter and not at the end of the fuel rail assembly.

58. **The correct answer is c.** The oil that must be used in 2007 and newer diesel engine is CJ-4 which has low ash. Low amount of ash in the oil is important because the diesel particulate filter (DPF) can be clogged from ash which is not burned off during regeneration like particulate matter (PM) also called soot can be so it accumulates and would eventually clog the unit. Answer a is not correct because the viscosity can vary depending on temperature and engine brand and application. Answer b is not correct because the viscosity can vary depending on temperature and engine brand and application. Answer d is not correct because the oil recommendation specified by the vehicle manufacturer include viscosity and rating and does not include whether or not the oil is made from synthetic or mineral stocks.

59. **The correct answer is c.** The pressure cap is designed to provide additional pressure on the cooling system above atmospheric to raise the boiling temperature of the coolant about that of water. Answer a is not correct because the coolant is moved through the cooling system by using the water pump and does not use the pressure that the radiator cap provides to move the coolant. Answer b is not correct because the coolant is moved through the cooling system and into all passages using the water pumps and does not use the pressure that the radiator cap provides to move the coolant. Answer d is not correct because the coolant is moved through the cooling system and into all components using the water pumps and does not use the pressure that the radiator cap provides to move the coolant.

60. **The correct answer is c.** Cavitation is the collapsing of air pockets that are found in the cooling system due to normal operation of the cylinder liners moving inward and outward during combustion and/or from a lack of pressure on the cooling system. Answer a is not correct because while cavitation can occur in a diesel engine that uses wet-cylinder sleeves, the use of sleeves is the reason for cavitation. Answer b is not correct because a pressure cap with a higher than pressure would not be the cause of cavitation because cavitation is often increased when the cooling system pressure is too low, not too high. Answer d is not correct because using a coolant with high silicate is not the reason for cavitation.

61. **The correct answer is c.** The temperature on the thermostat is the temperature that it starts to open and is fully opened about 20° higher. Answer a is not correct because the temperature on the thermostat is when it starts to open not when it is fully open. Answer b is not correct because even though thermostats can cause overheating, they most often fail in the open position causing the engine to not reach operating temperature. Answer d is not correct because it involves both answers a and b which were not correct.

62. **The correct answer is d.** Both answers a and b are correct. Any engine oil cooler should be inspected for both an engine oil leak (answer a) and coolant leak (answer b). Answer c is not correct because there is oil and coolant in the engine oil cooler and no air so an air leak would simply be seen as an oil and coolant leak.

LIGHT VEHICLE DIESEL ENGINES (A9)

CATEGORY: AIR INDUCTION AND EXHAUST SYSTEMS DIAGNOSIS AND REPAIR

63. **The correct answer is b.** The purpose of using exhaust gases and introducing them back into the intake to reduce the peak temperatures inside the combustion chamber to reduce the formation of oxides of nitrogen. Answer a is not correct because even though the exhaust gas may be at a higher temperature than the inlet air temperature, it is the fact that the exhaust gases are inert (unable to enter into a chemical reaction), which is the reason why it is used and used to reduce NO_x exhaust emissions. Answer c is not correct because the exhaust entering the intake would not reduce the heat load on the cooling system and in fact adds to the amount of heat that needs to be removed because the exhaust gases need to be cooled to be more effective at reducing NO_x emissions. Answer d is not correct because the exhaust gases are not used to warm the fuel but instead the exhaust gases are recirculated back into the intake to reduce NO_x exhaust emissions.

64. **The correct answer is c.** The most likely cause of a lack of power concern is a stuck variable ratio/geometry turbocharger vanes. The exhaust brake uses the vanes of the turbocharger to restrict the flow of the exhaust to act as an exhaust break, so this is why this is the most likely cause. Answer a is not correct because while a restricted exhaust could result in reduced power from the engine, it would be unlikely be the cause of the exhaust brake not functioning too. Answer b is not correct because while a restricted air filter could result in reduced power from the engine, it would be unlikely be the cause of the exhaust brake not functioning too. Answer d is  not correct because while a stuck open thermostat could result in reduced power from the engine, it would unlikely be the cause of the exhaust brake not functioning too.

65. **The correct answer is b.** DEF will freeze when the temperature drops to 12°F (–11°C) or lower, but the system and the container that hold the fluid are designed to withstand the freezing, so no precautions are needed for a properly operating DEF system. Answer a is not correct because there is no need to keep the vehicle above the freezing temperature of the DEF as the system is designed to function at temperatures below the freezing temperature of the diesel exhaust fluid. Answer c is not correct because there is no need to remove the fluid and store it inside the freezing temperature because the system is designed to function at temperatures below the freezing temperature of the diesel exhaust fluid. Answer d is not correct because nothing but DEF should be added to the diesel exhaust fluid storage tank because the system is designed to work at all temperatures, even those below the freezing point of DEF.

66. **The correct answer is d.** Either b or c is correct. Answers b and c are correct because the filler size used on light diesel is 15/16 inch (24 mm) and is larger than the filler used for gasoline and/or E85 which is 13/16 inch (21 mm). As a result, gasoline (answer b) or E85 (answer c) could be added to the fuel tank of diesel engine vehicle in error. Answer a is not correct because the fuel filler size is large enough to allow other types of fuel beside diesel fuel to be accidentally added to the fuel tank.

67. **The correct answer is a.** The replaceable fuel filter is located in the low pressure part of the fuel system usually founded on the frame rail between the fuel tank and the engine. Answer b is not correct because the replaceable fuel filter is located in the low pressure section of the fuel system and not in the high-pressure part. Answer c is not correct because the replaceable fuel filter is located in the low pressure side and not in or near the fuel filler tube. Answer d is not correct because the replaceable fuel filter is located in the low pressure section of the fuel system and not in the tank where the filter screen is located, but this is considered part of the fuel pump and not a replaceable fuel filter.

68. **The correct answer is b.** The water-in-fuel sensor and drain are usually combined into the fuel filter assembly. Answer a is not correct because the water-in-fuel sensor and the drain used to remove the water is located in the low pressure fuel line usually mounted to the frame rail of the vehicle for easy access. Answer c is not correct because the sensor and the fuel filter assembly are located in the low pressure, not the high pressure part of the fuel system. Answer d is not correct because the sensor and the fuel filter assembly are located in the low pressure, not near the fuel filler opening to the fuel tank.

69. **The correct answer is a.** The exhaust after treatment system that requires the owner/driver of the vehicle to perform some service is the selective catalyst reduction (SCR) which requires that the diesel exhaust fluid (DEF) be filled when low. Answer b is not correct because the exhaust gas recirculation (EGR) system does not require any routine service to keep it functioning unless it is found to be defective. Answer c is not correct because the diesel particulate filter (DPF) system does not require any routine service to keep it functioning unless it is found to be defective. Answer d is not correct because the diesel oxidation catalyst (DOC) system does not require any routine service to keep it functioning unless it is found to be defective

70. **The correct answer is c.** Diesel exhaust fluid (DEF), called Ad Blue in Europe, consists of 32.4% urea and 67.5% de-ionized water. Answer a is not correct because DEF is not distilled water and some urea. Answer b is not correct because DEF is a precise amount of urea and de-ionized water and not ammonia, urea, and water. Answer d is not correct because DEF is 32.4% urea and 67.5% de-ionized water and not 67.5% urea and 32.4% distilled water.

71. **The correct answer is c.** DEF will freeze at temperatures that may be experienced in parts of the country that get cold temperatures but the container and the system is designed to handle the resulting expansion of the container. Answer a is not correct because the DEF system is designed to handle the freezing of the fluid, so no action is required by the owner/driver of the vehicle to keep the fluid from freezing. Answer b is not correct because the DEF will freeze if exposed to low enough temperatures but the system is designed to operate correctly without having to wait for the system to thaw out before the vehicle can be driven. Answer d is not correct because the DEF system is designed to allow it to function at temperatures before the freezing temperature of the fluid and no action such as having to plug a heater into an outlet is needed.

72. **The correct answer is b.** Diesel exhaust fluid (32.4% urea and 67.5% de-ionized water freezes at 12°F (−11°C) and the system is designed to work normally at this temperature and below. Answers a (32°F (0°C), c (0°F (−18°C), and d (−8° (−22°C) are not correct because these do not state the correct freezing temperature of diesel exhaust fluid.

73. **The correct answer is a.** Answer a is correct because the gauge is used to measure the pressure drop across the air filter and the red line indicates that the pressure drop has reached the point where the air filter needs to be replaced. When the air filter is replaced, the gauge should be reset. Answer b is not correct because the red line indicates that the air filter is restricted enough to require that the air filter be replaced. If the line were green, then the air filter is not restricted enough to require replacement. Answer c is not correct because the filter is not okay to use because the gauge indicates that it is restricted. Answer d is not correct because the gauge is indicating a restriction in the airflow through the filter, so if there was a leak in the housing, the gauge would not likely show a restriction.

74. **The correct answer is b.** If the DPF warning messages are ignored, the engine will power will be reduced until a forced regeneration is performed. Answer a is not correct because while engine power will be reduced and the exhaust back pressure will increase, this increase is not likely to cause any engine damage such as bent or broken connecting rods. Answer c is not correct because while the exhaust back pressure is higher when regeneration is required, this increased back pressure is unlikely to cause a hissing sound from the intake. Answer d is not correct because while the system may cause the engine to reduce power, it is unlikely to cause the engine to stop running and not restart because this would be a safety issue and the software controlling this system would prevent this from occurring.

75. **The correct answer is c.** A wastegate is a valve that causes the exhaust to bypass the turbocharger once the boost pressure reaches or exceeds a certain level to limit boost. Answer a is not correct because while a wastegate is located in the exhaust, it is used to control the boost from a turbocharger and not to control exhaust system backpressure directly. Answer b is not correct because the wastegate is located in the exhaust system and does not have any effect on the pressure in the cooling system. Answer d is not correct because the wastegate is located in the exhaust system and does not have any effect on the pressure in the fuel injection system.

76. **The correct answer is c.** The selective catalyst reduction (SCR) system that uses diesel exhaust fluid (DEF) is designed to reduce oxides of nitrogen (NO_X) exhaust emissions. Answer a (CO), b (CO_2), and d (HC) are not correct because DEF is used to reduce NO_X exhaust emission.

77. **The correct answer is c.** The cooler the exhaust gases being recirculated back into the intake stream, the more efficient they are at reducing NO_X exhaust emissions. Answer a is not correct because the cooling system is used to reduce the temperature of the exhaust gases entering back into the intake and is not used to heat the coolant in the cooling system. Answer b is not correct because the cooler used to cool the exhaust gases are used to reduce NO_X exhaust emissions and no particulate matter (PM) emissions. Answer d is not correct because the cooler is used to cool the exhaust temperature and does not help in the opening of the EGR valve.

78. **The correct answer is a.** Technician A is correct because when the DPF warning lamp comes on, this indicates that the delta pressure sensors have detected a restriction in the DPF and the system must perform a regeneration to clean the filter. This procedure usually includes driving the vehicle for about half an hour as the system injects additional fuel into the exhaust to burn out the carbon trapped in the DPF. Answer b is not correct because there is no need to replace the diesel particulate filter unless it is totally clogged but instead, it simply needs to be cleaned during a normal regeneration cycle. Answers c and d are not correct because only technician A is correct.

79. **The correct answer is b.** Technician B only is correct because SCR catalyst converts NO_X into nitrogen and oxygen which are then expelled from the exhaust instead of harmful NO_X. Answer a (Technician A) is not correct because the urea used in the SVCR system is used to break apart NO_X into nitrogen and oxygen and does not convert the gas to hydrogen. Answers c and d are not correct because only technician B is correct.

80. **The correct answer is b.** If the variable ratio/geometry (VGT) turbocharger were to become stuck, the engine would not be able to supply normal power. Answer a is not correct because if the vanes on the turbocharger were stuck, this would not cause oil to leak into the engine intake or cause an increase in oil consumption but instead, only a decrease in power output. Answer c is not correct because if the vanes on the turbocharger were stuck, this would not create white exhaust smoke but instead, only a decrease in power output. Answer d is not correct because if the vanes on the turbocharger were stuck, this would not create black or blue exhaust smoke but instead, only a decrease in power output.

81. **The correct answer is a.** The preheater located in the air inlet on some light diesel engines is used to heat the incoming air to help the engine start when the engine is cold. Using an intake air heater eliminates the need for glow plugs at each cylinder. Answer b is not correct because the heater is used to heat the air entering the engine and is not used to reduce oxides of nitrogen exhaust emissions, which is controlled using the EGR. Answer c is not correct because the heater is used to heat the air entering the engine and is not used to heat the cabin air. Answer d is not correct because the heater is used to only heat the air entering the engine and not used for any other purpose.

82. **The correct answer is a.** The throttle valve, if used on a light diesel engine, is used to create a difference in pressure to help the exhaust gases flow from the EGR system to the combustion chamber. Answer b is not correct because the throttle plate does not control engine or idle speed like they do in a gasoline engine but only to help control the flow of exhaust gases in the intake system. Engine speed is controlled by the fuel delivery in a diesel engine. Answer c is not correct because the throttle plate is not used to control engine speed but instead is only used to help the flow of the exhaust gases from the EGR system. Engine speed is controlled  by the fuel delivery in a diesel engine. Answer d is not correct because the throttle plate is used to improve the flow of exhaust from the EGR system and is not used to control over-boost from the turbocharger which is handled by a waster gate or a variable ratio/geometry vane type turbocharger.

83. **The correct answer is c.** Pressure sensors are used to detect the difference in pressure between the inlet and the outlet of the diesel particulate filter (DPF) to help determine when it needs to be cleaned and a regeneration commended. Answers a, b, and d are not correct because pressure sensors are not used in the other systems or chemicals but only used in the DPF.

84. **The correct answer is a.** The reductant sensor is the sensor used to detect the level of diesel exhaust fluid (DEF) in the storage container in the vehicle and its function is similar to the fuel level sensor. Because the DEF can freeze and expand, the sensor uses three electrodes and a ground to determine the level of the fluid. Answer b is not correct because the DEF fluid sensor uses three electrodes and a ground to detect the fluid level instead of a float because DEF can freeze and expand causing a float to be inoperable at low temperatures. Answers c and d are not correct because the DEF level sensor uses three electrodes and a ground to detect fluid level and does not use the pump motor assembly (answer c) or the pump and filter assembly (answer d) to determine the fluid level.

85. **The correct answer is d.** Both answer b and c are correct. Answer b (NO_X sensor) is correct because it is used in diesel engine to detect oxides or nitrogen so that the SCR system can function to reduce it to specified levels and is not commonly be used in a gasoline engine exhaust system. Answer c is correct too because a delta pressure sensors are used to monitor the diesel particulate filter (DPF) system and is not used in a gasoline engine exhaust system. Answer a is not correct because an oxygen sensor is used in both a diesel engine and in a gasoline engine exhaust system.

86. **The correct answer is b.** The best way to judge the condition of an air filter used on a light diesel engine is to use the pressure differential gauge found on the air cleaning housing. When the restriction is enough to require replacement, most gauges will display a red line on the gauge. Answer a is not correct because a diesel air filter uses multiple layers of overlapping material so light cannot be seen through it using a light event when used on a new filter making this an invalid test. Answer c is not correct because using compressed air is not recommended by many vehicle manufactures because it can harm the filter material and not remove the small dirt particles that are embedded in the filter material. Answer d is not correct because cleaning a paper-type filter with any liquid is not recommended by any vehicle manufacturer and is unlikely to be effective in the removal of dirt trapped in the filter.

CATEGORY: FUEL SYSTEM DIAGNOSIS AND REPAIR

87. **The correct answer is a.** The lift pump located inside the fuel tank is designed to supply fuel to the high pressure pump and is a low pressure/high volume type of pump. Answers b, c, and d are not correct because a lift pump is designed to furnish a high volume of fuel to the high pressure pump at relatively low pressure.

88. **The correct answer is b.** The water drain is located at the fuel filter assembly which also contains a storage location for water that may be in the fuel. Answers a, c, and d are not correct because the water drain is located at the fuel filter assembly and not at the fuel tank (answer a), or at the high pressure pump (answer c), or at the fuel rail (answer d).

89. **The correct answer is b.** The fuel filter needs to be bled of any air that is likely to be in the fuel system after a fuel filter has been replaced. This is usually achieved by using the built-in prime pump that is located at the top of the fuel filter assembly. Answer a is not correct because by simply filling the tank with fresh diesel fuel will not purge any trapped air from the fuel system. Answer c is not correct because by removing the water valve will simply drain any water from the fuel filter assembly and not purge any air that is trapped in the system after replacing the fuel filter. Answer d is not correct because the engine should never be cranked or started with the injector lines loosened due to the dangers involved with high-pressure fuel.

90. **The correct answer is c.** A hydraulic electronic unit injector (HEUI) system uses engine oil at high pressure to open the injectors. Any problem with the engine oil including using the incorrect viscosity of the oil or is dirty and needs to be changed can affect the way the engine starts and runs. Answer a is not correct because even though the high-pressure pump is lubricated by the engine oil, it is the fact that this type of system uses the engine oil to open the injectors that has a major effect on how the engine runs. Answer b is not correct because engine oil does not mix with diesel fuel but instead is used to power the operation of the injector and the oil does not come in contact directly with the diesel fuel. Answer d is not correct because the engine oil is used to open the fuel injector but is not used to help remove exhaust soot from the exhaust which is the job of the diesel particulate filter (DPF).

91. **The correct answer is a.** The number/letters on the side of a fuel injector designed for a common rail diesel engine represents the calibration code that has to be placed the PCM memory when a replacement injector is installed suing a scan tool. Answers b (part number), c (cubic centimeters fuel flow rating of the injector), and d (opening pressure of the injector) are not correct because the code is the calibration that needs to be added to the PCM whenever an injector is replaced.

92. **The correct answer is c.** The correct setting for measuring voltage drops using a digital multimeter (DMM) is DC volts (DCV). Answers a, b, and d are not correct because the meter should be set to DC volts and not AC amperes (ACA) (answer a), AC volts (answer b), or ohms (answer d).

93. **The correct answer is a.** The numbers/letters on a light diesel common rail diesel engine is the calibration code that must be used along with a scan tool if an injector is ever replaced. Answer b is not correct because while it looks to be a part number, it is unique to each injector and used for calibration. Answer c is not correct because while the calibration code may indicate the flow of the injector, it is not shown in the numbers or letters but instead is a code used by the PCM to determine the pulse width needed to achieve the needed flow from the injector to meet exhaust emission standards. Answer d is not correct because it is the calibration code and used by the PCM and does not inductee the opening pressure of the injector on a common rail system.

94. **The correct answer is a.** A scan tool is needed to be used so that the calibration code can be inputted into the PCM memory so that the replacement injector will flow the correct amount of fuel. Answer b is not correct because while a special tool may be needed to install the injector, a scan tool is needed to recalibrate the PCM to the calibration code on the replacement injector Answer c is not correct because while a new air filter may be needed at the same time as the injector replacement, replacing the air filter is not needed to complete the repair after injector replacement. Answer d is not correct because while a new fuel filter may be needed at the same time as the injector replacement, replacing the fuel filter is not needed to complete the repair after injector replacement.

95. **The correct answer is c.** Diesel fuel injectors used on a common rail diesel engine use a high voltage pulse to open and therefore can be a shock hazard to the service technician who may be working around the injectors when the engine is running. Answer a is not correct because two 12-volt batteries connected in parallel represents just 12 volts of potential which is not high enough to be a shock hazard. Answer b is not correct because the alternator represents just 12 volts of potential which is not high enough to be a shock hazard. Answer d is not correct because a turbocharger is an exhaust-driven device and while it may represent a hot surface and a potential source of a burn, it does not present a shock hazard.

96. **The correct answer is a.** The replaceable fuel filter is located in the low pressure side of the fuel delivery system between the fuel tank and the engine. Answer b is not correct because while there is a filter (sock) located inside the fuel tank and attached to the lift pump assembly, it is a normally replaceable filter. Answer c is not correct because the replaceable filter is located between the fuel tank and the engine and not between the turbocharger and the intercooler assembly. Answer d is not correct because while the filter may be located near the inlet to the high pressure pump, it is usually located in the low pressure section of the fuel system between the fuel tank and the engine.

97. **The correct answer is a.** Technician A only is correct because if one or more glow plugs were open (electrically not able to function) then there would be a lack of heat in the combustion chamber which could be the cause of the hard-to-start condition. Answer b (Technician B) is not correct because while a defective starter could be the cause of a hard-to-start condition, it would not be the cause of the need to crank the engine for an extended period of time before it does start. Answers c and d are not correct because only Technician A is correct.

98. **The correct answer is d.** The fuel filler opening on a vehicle equipped with a diesel engine is either 15/15 inch (24 mm) or 1.25 or 1.5 inch (32 or 38 mm) which are commonly found at truck stops. Answers a, b, and c are not correct because either of the two larger sizes of filler tubes is to be found on vehicle equipped with a diesel engine.

99. **The correct answer is c.** The intercooler is designed to lower the temperature of the air entering the engine. A turbocharger increases the pressure and the temperature of the air and the greater engine power is achieved if this air is cooled. The engine will produce 1% more power for every 10° cooler the temperature of the air entering the engine. Answer a is not correct because this cooler is designed to cool the air entering the engine and not the engine oil which has its own cooler. Answer b is not correct because this cooler is designed to cool the air entering the engine and not the engine coolant. Answer d is not correct because the cooler is designed to cool the air entering the engine and does not cool the exhaust.

100. **The correct answer is b.** By cooling the exhaust gases before they enter the combustion chamber by way of the EGR valve, the cooled gases are more effective at reducing NO_X exhaust emissions. Answer a is not correct because the exhaust is cooled to make it more effective at reducing NO_X emissions and is not used to cool the EGR valve. Answer c is not correct because the exhaust is cooled, but this does not reduce the exhaust backpressure which is produced by the turbocharger itself plus the other systems and components in the exhaust system. Answer d is not correct because the exhaust gases are cooled to help reduce NO_X emissions and are not used for improved fuel economy even though by improving the efficiency of the EGR system, an improvement in fuel economy may be possible, but it is not the primary reason for cooling the exhaust gases used by the EGR valve.

101. **The correct answer is b.** The throttle plate is used on many diesel engines in order to create a difference in pressure to help force the exhaust gases from the EGR valve to flow into the cylinders at certain times during engine operation. The throttle valve is not used to control engine speed like it is in a gasoline engine. Answer a is not correct because it is used to help the flow of exhaust from the EGR valve to the cylinders and is not used to limit or control engine speed. Answer c is not correct because it is used to help the flow of exhaust from the EGR valve to the cylinders and is not used to prevent backfiring through the intake. Answer d is not correct because it is used to help the flow of exhaust from the EGR valve to the cylinders and is not used to control engine speed or used as a cruise control device.

102. **The correct answer is a.** Cardboard should be used when trying to locate the source of a fuel leak in a diesel engine to help prevent personal injury due to high-pressure fuel. Answer b is not correct because while a scan tool may be used to help diagnosis a diesel engine, it is not the tool for locating the source of a fuel leak in a diesel engine. Answer c is not correct because while a digital meter may be used to help diagnosis a diesel engine, it is not the tool for locating the source of a fuel leak in a diesel engine. Answer d is not correct because while a stethoscope may be used to help diagnosis a diesel engine, it is not the tool for locating the source of a fuel leak in a diesel engine.

103. **The correct answer is b.** Whenever replacing an electronic unit injector(s) (EUI), a scan tool is required to add the injector calibration code into the PCM so the correct amount of fuel can be delivered based on the injector calibration. Answer a is not correct because while a PCM may need to be re-flashed to the latest software to fix an engine operating condition, it is not needed when replacing an injector. However, a scan tool is needed to enter the injector calibrations code which is different from a software update. Answers c and d are not correct because, while replacing the air and fuel, filters may also be done at the same time as when an injector is replaced, these are not a service procedure that is required to be performed.

104. **The correct answer is a.** Technician A only is correct because a hydraulic electronic unit injector(s) (HEUI) uses engine oil to operate and if the oil is low or dirty, it can be the root cause of an engine operating fault such as a rough idle or low performance. Answer b (Technician B) is not correct because low Cetane fuel can cause hard to start and poor fuel economy concerns but is not likely to be the cause of a rough idle or low performance. Answers c and d are not correct because only Technician A is correct.

105. **The correct answer is d.** A leak in the suction side of the fuel line is the most likely cause of a diesel engine starting and then stalling after it operates for a short time. Air in the system results in the fuel not being able to be compressed by the high-pressure pump and the engine then stops due to a lack of fuel. Answer a is not correct because a defective glow plug would make the engine hard to start but could not be the cause of the engine starting and then stalling. Answer b is not correct because a misadjusted intake valve could cause the engine to run rough but it is unlikely to be the cause of the engine stalling after it is has run for a short time. Answer c is not correct because a clogged oil filter would not be noticeable to the operation of the engine because the oil would simply flow through the by-pass which is designed to allow oil to continue to lubricate the engine in the event the filter were to become clogged.

106. **The correct answer is b.** If the glow plugs or air intake heater was electrically open, this can cause the diesel engine to be hard to start due to the lack of heat in the combustion chambers. Answer a is not correct because the diesel engine would be hard to start if the Cetane rating was lower than normal (not higher than normal). Answer c is not correct because if one of the two batteries was discharged, the cranking speed of the starter motor may be lower than normal and while this could be the cause of a hard to start concern, it is not a likely cause of an engine cranking normally but is hard to start. Answer d is not correct because if there was high resistance in the battery cables, the cranking speed of the starter motor may be lower than normal and while this could be the cause of a hard-to-start concern, it is not a likely cause of an engine cranking normally but is hard to start.

107. **The correct answer is a.** A defective turbocharger can cause oil to seep into the air stream and then flow through the intake to the cylinders where the oil is burned and creates blue exhaust smoke. Answer b is not correct because a fault with the high-pressure pump would unlikely cause blue exhaust smoke except indirectly if the higher-than-normal fuel pressure could cause engine oil to be washed off the cylinder walls which could cause the engine to use oil. However, the higher pressure is monitored by the PCM and the injector pulse width is limited to help prevent this from happening, so this is not a likely cause of the blue smoke. Answer c is not correct because a restricted intake would simply cause a lack of power and would not likely be the cause of blue exhaust smoke. Answer d is not correct because a defective glow plug would likely cause the engine to be hard to start especially in cold weather but is not likely to be the cause of blue exhaust smoke.

108. **The correct answer is d.** Any of the three items could be the cause of lower-than-normal power from a light diesel engine. Answer a (a clogged air filter) could be the cause because this would restrict the amount of air that is supplied to the engine which would result in reduced power from the engine. Answer b (a clogged fuel filter) could be the cause because this would restrict the amount of fuel that is supplied to the engine which would result in reduced power from the engine. Answer c (a stuck open EGR valve) could be the cause because this would result in too much exhaust gases being introduced to the engine intake to the engine which would result in reduced power from the engine.

109. **The correct answer is a.** Technician A only is correct because all fuel lines should be tightened using a torque wrench to factory specifications to insure a proper seal. Answer b (Technician B) is not correct because while the injector calibration of the new injector needs to be programmed into the PCM, this process is achieved using a scan tool and not a special tool that comes with a new injector. Answers c and d are not corrrect because only Technician A is correct.

110. **The correct answer is a.** The amount of sulfur in ultra-low sulfur diesel (ULSD) is just 15 parts per million (PPM). Answers b (50 ppm), c (150 PPM), and d (500 PPM) are not correct because the standard is for the level of sulfur in the fuel to be less than 15 PPM.

111. **The correct answer is b.** The high-pressure pump is operated from the camshaft on light diesel engines. Answers a (crankshaft), c (auxiliary shaft), and d (accessory drive belt) are not correct because the high pressure pump is driven from the camshaft.

112. **The correct answer is d.** A water separator is used only on diesel engines and not used in vehicle that uses a gasoline engine. Answers a (fuel filter), b (fuel supply line), and c (fuel return line) are all components that are often used in vehicles that use a gasoline engine and therefore are not a component that is used only in a vehicle equipped with a diesel engine.

113. **The correct answer is a.** The diesel engine high pressure pump is usually gear driven off the camshaft. Answers b (belt off the crankshaft), c (shaft drive off the crankshaft), and d (chain drive off the camshaft) are not correct because the high-pressure pump is driven by a gear off the camshaft.

114. **The correct answer is c.** A common rail type diesel engine supplies high pressure fuel to the rail where each injector is attached. The PCM then commands the injectors to open to allow fuel delivery to each cylinder as needed. Answers a (distributor), b (inline), and d (rotary) are not correct because these types of systems supply high pressure to each injector when it is time to fire each injector in sequence.

115. **The correct answer is b.** Glow plug has high resistance when it is warm and low resistance when it is cold. This allows a lot of current to flow when the engine and the glow plugs are cold resulting in rapid heating of the glow plugs to help start a cold diesel engine. Then when the glow plugs get hot, the resistance increases thereby reducing the flow of electrical current through the glow plugs. Answers a (cold/warm), c (wet/dry), and d (dry/wet) are not correct because the resistance of the glow plugs are low when cold and high when warm.

116. **The correct answer is d.** All of the above are correct. Answers a (an electronic solenoid valve), b (fuel rail pressure limiting valve), and c (fuel control actuator (FCA)) are all terms for what is used to control the high side fuel system pressure.

117. **The correct answer is d.** Low ash oil is required for use in a 2007 and newer diesel engine because they use a diesel particulate filter (DPF) which is part of the exhaust system after treatment system and is used to trap particulate material (carbon) which can be burned off during regeneration but ask form oil cannot be burned off. Answers a (EGR system compatibility), b (required use of ULSD fuels), and c (EPA regulation of ash emissions) are not correct because the low ash requirement is needed for the proper operation of the DPF.

118. **The correct answer is a.** The replaceable fuel filter is located in the low pressure part of the fuel delivery system which is located between the fuel tank and the high-pressure pump. Answers b (between the high-pressure pump and the nozzles), c (between the fuel filler tube and the fuel tank which is atmospheric pressure), and d (inside the fuel tank) are not correct because they do not describe the location of the replaceable fuel filter used on light diesel engines.

119. **The correct answer is b.** In a pump-line-nozzle fuel system (PLN-E) system, the injector timing is affected by the time the fuel takes to flow from the pump to the injectors so as to help ensure equal injector timing, each high-pressure line is the same length. Answer a is not correct because the purpose of the equal length lines to ensure proper injector timing and does not have to do with the reduction of noise from the high-pressure system. Answer c is not correct because even though each line is the same length, they are not the same shape making them not able to be used in any other but the exact location where they are located. Answer d is not correct because while the lines being the same length may make it easier to the manufacturer, they have to be the best to fit each individual cylinder, and it is the injector timing consideration that determines the equal length and not the manufacturing of the fuel lines as the reason they are used.

AUTO MAINTENANCE AND LIGHT REPAIR CONTENT AREAS

This ASE study guide for Auto Maintenance and Light Repair (G1) is divided into the sub-content areas that correlate to the actual ASE certification test as follows:

CONTENT AREA	QUESTIONS IN THE TEST	NUMBER OF STUDY GUIDE QUESTIONS
A. Engine Systems	9	25 (1–25)
B. Automatic Transmission/Transaxle	4	8 (26–33)
C. Manual Drive Train and Axles	6	12 (34–45)
D. Suspension and Steering	13	26 (46–71)
E. Brakes	11	22 (72–93)
F. Electrical	8	16 (94–109)
G. Heating, Ventilation, and Air Conditioning	4	6 (110–115)
Totals	**55**	**115**

TIME ALLOWED TO TAKE THE TEST

The allocated time to take the Auto Maintenance and Light Repair Certification test is 90 minutes. ASE adds 10 additional questions to the test for research purposes for a total of 65 questions. These questions do not count toward your score but they are embedded within the test and there is no way of knowing which ones do not count. As a result, the technician needs to answer 60 questions in 75 minutes, or about one question per minute.

If taking the recertification G1 test, there are just 25 questions with no additional research questions included. The time allocated to take the recertification test is 30 minutes, which means about one minute per question.

BEFORE USING THIS STUDY GUIDE

Before trying to answer the questions and looking at the explanations, look over the following list of the content that ASE states will be covered in the certification test. For best results using this study guide, check service information or consult an automotive textbook for details on any of the content areas that are not familiar before trying to answer the questions. For additional information about the ASE test, visit the website at **www.ase.com**.

AUTO MAINTENANCE AND LIGHT REPAIR (G1) CERTIFICATION TEST

A. ENGINE SYSTEMS (9 QUESTIONS)

1. Verify driver's complaint and/or road-test vehicle; determine necessary action. Utilize service manuals, technical service bulletins (TSBs), and product information.
2. Inspect engine assembly for fuel, oil, coolant, and other leaks; determine necessary action.
3. Check for abnormal engine noises.
4. Inspect and replace pans and covers.
5. Change engine oil and filter; reset oil life monitor.
6. Inspect and test radiator, heater core, pressure cap, and coolant recovery system; determine needed repairs; perform cooling system pressure and dye tests.
7. Inspect, replace, and adjust drive belt(s), tensioner(s), and pulleys.
8. Inspect and replace engine cooling system and heater system hoses, pipes, and fittings.
9. Remove and replace engine thermostat and coolant bypass.
10. Inspect and test coolant; drain, flush, and refill cooling system with recommended coolant; bleed air as required.
11. Inspect and replace accessory belt–driven water pumps.
12. Confirm fan operation (both electrical and mechanical); inspect fan clutch, fan shroud, and air dams.
13. Verify operation of engine-related warning indicators.
14. Perform air induction/throttle body service.
15. Inspect, service, or replace air filter(s), filter housing(s), and air intake system components.
16. Inspect and replace crankcase ventilation system components.
17. Inspect exhaust system for leaks; check hangers, brackets, and heat shields; determine needed repairs.
18. Retrieve and record diagnostic trouble codes (DTCs).
19. Remove and replace spark plugs; inspect secondary ignition components for wear or damage.
20. Inspect fuel tank, filler neck, fuel cap, lines, fittings, and hoses; replace external fuel filter.
21. Inspect canister, lines/hoses, and mechanical and electrical components of the evaporative emissions control system (EVAP).
22. Check and refill diesel exhaust fluid (DEF).

B. AUTOMATIC TRANSMISSION/TRANSAXLE (4 QUESTIONS)

1. Road-test the vehicle to normal operation; retrieve and record diagnostic trouble codes (DTCs).
2. Determine fluid type, level, and condition.
3. Inspect transmission for leaks; replace external seals and gaskets.
4. Inspect and replace CV boots, axles, drive shafts, U-joints, drive axle joints, and seals.
5. Visually inspect condition of transmission cooling system, lines, and fittings.
6. Inspect and replace power train mounts.
7. Replace fluid and filter(s).

C. MANUAL DRIVE TRAIN AND AXLES (6 QUESTIONS)

1. Inspect, adjust, replace, and bleed external hydraulic clutch slave/release cylinder, master cylinder, lines, and hoses; clean and flush hydraulic system; refill with proper fluid.
2. Inspect and replace power train mounts.

3. Inspect, adjust, and replace transmission/transaxle external shifter assembly, shift linkages, brackets, bushings/grommets, pivots, and levers.

4. Inspect and replace external seals.

5. Check fluid level; refill with fluid.

- **Drive Shaft, Half-Shaft, and Universal Joints/Constant Velocity (CV) Joint (Front- and Rear-Wheel Drive)**

6. Road-test the vehicle to verify drive train noises and vibration.

7. Inspect, service, and replace shafts, yokes, boots, universal/CV joints; verify proper phasing.

8. Inspect, service, and replace drive shaft center support bearings.

9. Inspect, service, and replace wheel bearings, seals, and hubs, excluding press-type bearings.

- **Rear-Wheel-Drive Axle Inspection**

10. Identify fluid leakage problems.

11. Inspect, drain, and refill with lubricant.

12. Inspect and replace rear axle shaft wheel studs.

13. Inspect axle housing and vent; inspect rear axle mountings.

- **Four-Wheel/All-Wheel Drive**

14. Inspect, adjust, and repair transfer case manual shifting mechanisms, bushings, mounts, levers, and brackets.

15. Check transfer case fluid level and inspect condition; drain and refill with fluid.

16. Inspect, service, and replace front drive/propeller shaft and universal/CV joints.

17. Inspect front drive axle universal/CV joints and drive/half shafts, axle seals, and vents.

18. Inspect front wheel bearings, seals, and hubs.

19. Inspect transfer case, front differential, and axle seals and vents.

20. Inspect tires for correct size for vehicle application; check for wear.

21. Retrieve and record diagnostic trouble codes (DTCs).

22. Inspect and verify operation of 4WD/AWD system.

D. SUSPENSION AND STEERING (13 QUESTIONS)

1. Disarm airbag (SRS) system.

2. Check power steering fluid level; determine fluid type and adjust fluid level; identify system type (electric or hydraulic).

3. Inspect, adjust, and replace power steering pump belt(s), tensioners and pulleys; verify pulley alignment.

4. Identify power steering pump noises, vibration, and fluid leakage.

5. Remove and replace power steering pump; inspect pump mounting and attaching brackets; remove and replace power steering pump pulley; transfer related components.

6. Inspect and replace power steering hoses, fittings, O-rings, coolers, and filters.

7. Inspect and replace rack and pinion steering gear bellows/boots.

8. Flush, fill, and bleed power steering system.

9. Retrieve and record diagnostic trouble codes (DTCs).

10. Inspect electronic suspension components (ride height sensors, wiring, etc.).

- *Steering Linkage*

11. Inspect, adjust (where applicable), and replace pitman arm, center link (relay rod/drag link/intermediate rod), idler arm(s), and mountings.

12. Inspect, replace, and adjust tie rods, tie rod sleeves/adjusters, clamps, and tie rod ends (sockets/bushings).

13. Inspect and replace steering linkage damper(s).

- *Front Suspension*

14. Identify front suspension system noises, handling, ride height, and ride quality concerns; disable air suspension system.

15. Inspect upper and lower control arms, bushings, and shafts.

16. Inspect and replace rebound and jounce bumpers.

17. Inspect track bar, strut rods/radius arms, and related mounts and bushings.

18. Inspect upper and lower ball joints (with or without wear indicators).

19. Inspect non-independent front axle assembly for damage and misalignment.

20. Inspect front steering knuckle/spindle assemblies and steering arms.

21. Inspect front suspension system coil/air springs and spring insulators (silencers).

22. Inspect front suspension system leaf spring(s), leaf spring insulators (silencers), shackles, brackets, bushings, center pins/bolts, and mounts.

23. Inspect front suspension system torsion bars and mounts.

24. Inspect and replace front stabilizer bar (sway bar) bushings, brackets, and links.

25. Inspect front strut cartridge or assembly.

26. Inspect front strut bearing and mount.

27. Identify noise and service front wheel bearings/hub assemblies.

- *Rear Suspension*

28. Identify rear suspension system noises, handling, and ride height concerns; disable air suspension system.

29. Inspect rear suspension system coil/air springs and spring insulators (silencers).

30. Inspect rear suspension system lateral links/arms (track bars), and control (trailing) arms.

31. Inspect and replace rear stabilizer bars (sway bars), bushings, and links.

32. Inspect rear suspension system leaf spring(s), leaf spring insulators (silencers), shackles, brackets, bushings, center pins/bolts, and mounts.

33. Inspect and replace rear rebound and jounce bumpers.

34. Inspect rear strut cartridge or assembly, and upper mount assembly.

35. Inspect non-independent rear axle assembly for damage and misalignment.

36. Inspect rear ball joints.

37. Inspect and replace rear tie rod/toe linkages.

38. Inspect rear knuckle/spindle assembly.

39. Inspect and replace shock absorbers, mounts, and bushings.

40. Identify noise related concerns and service rear wheel bearings/hub assemblies.

41. Identify driver assist systems, if applicable.

- *Wheel Alignment*

42. Identify alignment-related symptoms such as vehicle wander, drift, and pull.

43. Perform pre-alignment inspection; prepare vehicle for alignment, and perform initial wheel alignment measurements.

44. Measure front and rear wheel camber; adjust as needed.

45. Measure caster; adjust as needed.

46. Measure front wheel toe; adjust as needed.

47. Center the steering wheel using mechanical methods.

48. Measure rear wheel toe; adjust as needed.

49. Measure thrust angle.

50. Calibrate steering angle sensor.

- *Wheels and Tires*

51. Identify tire wear patterns.

52. Inspect tire condition, tread depth, size, and application (load and speed ratings).

53. Check and adjust tire air pressure. Utilize vehicle tire placard and information.

54. Diagnose wheel/tire vibration, shimmy, and noise concerns; determine needed repairs.

55. Rotate tires/wheels and torque fasteners/wheel locks.

56. Dismount and mount tire on wheel.

57. Balance wheel and tire assembly.

58. Identify and test tire pressure monitoring systems (TPMS) (indirect and direct) for operation. Verify instrument panel lamps operation; conduct relearn procedure.

59. Repair tire according to tire manufacturers' standards.

E. BRAKES (11 QUESTIONS)

1. Check for poor stopping, pulling, dragging, noises, high or low pedal, and hard or spongy pedal.

2. Check the master cylinder fluid level and condition; inspect for external fluid leakage.

3. Inspect flexible brake hoses, brake lines, valves, and fittings for routing, leaks, dents, kinks, rust, cracks, or wear; inspect for loose fittings and supports; determine needed repairs.

4. Verify operation of brake warning light and ABS warning light; inspect brake system wiring damage and routing.

5. Test parking brake indicator light, switch, and wiring.

6. Bleed and/or flush hydraulic system.

7. Select, handle, store, and install proper brake fluids.

- *Drum Brakes*

8. Remove, clean, inspect, and measure brake drums; follow manufacturers' recommendations in determining need to machine or replace.

9. Machine drums according to manufacturers' procedures and specifications.

10. Using proper safety procedures, remove, clean, and inspect brake shoes/linings, springs, pins, self-adjusters, levers, clips, brake backing (support) plates, and other related brake hardware; determine needed repairs.

11. Lubricate brake shoe support pads on backing (support) plate, self-adjuster mechanisms, and other brake hardware.

12. Inspect wheel cylinder(s) for leakage, operation, and mounting; remove and replace wheel cylinder(s).

13. Install brake shoes and related hardware.

14. Adjust brake shoes and parking brake.

15. Check parking brake system operation; inspect cables and components for wear, rust, and corrosion; clean or replace components as necessary; lubricate and adjust assembly.

16. Reinstall wheel, torque lug nuts, and make final brake checks and adjustments.

- *Disc Brakes*

17. Retract integral parking brake caliper piston(s) according to manufacturers' recommendations.

18. Remove caliper assembly from mountings; inspect for leaks and damage to caliper housing.

19. Clean and inspect caliper mountings and slides/pins for wear and damage.

20. Remove, clean, and inspect pads and retaining hardware; determine needed repairs, adjustments, and replacements.

21. Clean caliper assembly; inspect external parts for wear, rust, scoring, and damage; replace any damaged or worn parts; determine the need to repair or replace caliper assembly.

22. Clean, inspect, and measure rotors with a dial indicator and a micrometer; determine the need to index, machine, or replace the rotor.

23. Remove and replace rotors.

24. Machine rotors, using on-car or off-car method.

25. Install pads, calipers, and related attaching hardware; lubricate components; bleed system.

26. Adjust calipers with integral parking brakes.

27. Fill master cylinder with recommended fluid; reset system.

28. Reinstall wheel, torque lug nuts, and make final brake checks and adjustments.

29. Road-test vehicle and burnish/break-in pads according to manufacturers' recommendations.

30. Test brake pedal free travel with and without engine running to check power booster operation.

31. Check vacuum supply (manifold or auxiliary pump) to vacuum-type power booster.

32. Inspect the vacuum-type power booster unit for operation, and vacuum leaks; inspect the check valve for proper operation.

33. Identify operation of electric-hydraulic assist system; check system for leaks and operation.

34. Identify operation of hydro-boost assist system; check system for leaks and operation.

F. ELECTRICAL (8 QUESTIONS)

1. Disarm/re-enable airbag; verify lamp operation.

2. Check voltages, grounds, and voltage drops in electrical circuits; interpret readings.

3. Check current flow in electrical circuits and components; interpret readings.

4. Check continuity and resistances in electrical circuits and components; interpret readings.

5. Perform battery tests (load and capacitance); determine needed service.

6. Maintain or restore electronic memory functions.

7. Inspect, clean, fill, or replace battery.

8. Perform slow/fast battery charge in accordance with manufacturers' recommendations.

9. Inspect, clean, and repair or replace battery cables, connectors, clamps, and hold-downs.

10. Jumpstart a vehicle with a booster battery or auxiliary power supply.

11. Perform starter current draw test; interpret readings.

12. Inspect switches, connectors, and wires of starter control circuits.

13. Remove and replace starter.

14. Perform charging system output test and identify undercharge, no-charge, or overcharge condition.

15. Inspect, adjust, and replace generator (alternator) drive belts, pulleys, and tensioners.

16. Remove, inspect, and replace generator (alternator).

17. Inspect, replace, and aim headlights/bulbs and auxiliary lights (fog lights/driving lights).

18. Inspect interior and exterior lamps and sockets; repair as needed.

19. Inspect lenses; determine needed repairs.

20. Verify instrument gauges and warning/indicator light operation; reset maintenance indicators.

21. Verify horn operation; determine needed repairs.

22. Verify wiper and washer operation; replace wiper motor, blades, washer pump, and hoses and nozzles as needed.

G. HEATING, VENTILATION, AND AIR CONDITIONING (4 QUESTIONS)

1. Verify HVAC operation (vent temperature, blower and condenser fan, compressor engagement, blend and mode door(s) operation).

2. Identify A/C refrigerant type; recover and recharge system per manufacturer's specifications.

3. Visually check A/C components for signs of leaks.

4. Inspect A/C condenser for restricted airflow.

5. Inspect and replace cabin air filter.

6. Check drive belt for wear and tension; adjust or replace as needed.

7. Inspect and clean evaporator drains.

AUTO MAINTENANCE AND
LIGHT REPAIR (G1)

CATEGORY: ENGINE SYSTEMS

1. A P0300 is what type of diagnostic trouble code?

   a. A vehicle specific (Ford, Nissan, BMW, etc.) code
   b. A generic code (same for all makes and model with that fault)
   c. A type of code that can only be retrieved by using a jumper wire to and counting the light flashes
   d. A type of code used by General Motors only

2. Coolant should be tested for _____.

   a. pH
   b. freezing/boiling point (temperature)
   c. specific gravity
   d. all of the above

3. During a cylinder leakage (leak-down) test, air is noticed coming out of the oil fill opening. Technician A says that the oil filter may be clogged. Technician B says that the piston rings may be worn or defective. Which technician is correct?

   a. A only
   b. B only
   c. Both A and B
   d. Neither A nor B

4. Leaking antifreeze can be what color?

   a. Green
   b. Orange
   c. Red
   d. Any of the above

5. What precautions are needed to be performed to help prevent air from getting trapped in the cooling system when replacing coolant?

   a. Use the proper antifreeze as specified
   b. Open bleeder valve(s) during filling
   c. Use premixed coolant
   d. Wear protective gloves

6. When replacing a water pump, be sure to _____.

   a. torque all fasteners to factory specifications
   b. use a new gasket/seal
   c. check that the accessory drive belt is properly aligned and adjusted to the proper tension
   d. all of the above

7. What tool is required to retrieve diagnostic trouble codes (DTCs) on a 1996 and newer vehicle?

   a. Test light
   b. Fused jumper wire
   c. Scan tool
   d. Any of the above

8. When replacing an external fuel filter, best practices include _____.

   a. using the same brand as the original as the replacement filter
   b. reusing the filter after cleaning
   c. relieving fuel systems pressure before removing the fuel line connections
   d. tightening fasteners as tight as possible

9. Why should the customer concern be verified by the service technician?

   a. To be able to include a charge on the work order
   b. To verify that the repair can be verified under the same conditions as when the concern was verified
   c. To make sure that a true problem exists
   d. Both b and c

10. An engine is leaking oil. Where should the technician look to locate the source of the leak?

    a. At the highest, most forward location where the fluid is seen
    b. At the lowest, most rearward location where the fluid is seen
    c. Look for where it is dry and then look upward
    d. At the lowest, most forward location where the fluid is seen

11. Engine makes a knock noise and is heard when the engine stops. What is the most likely cause?

    a. Worn main bearings
    b. A cracked or loose flexplate
    c. Worn rod bearings
    d. A cracked connecting rod

12. When replacing engine covers, what is considered to be best practice?

    a. Use an inch-pound torque wrench to tighten the fasteners to specifications
    b. Use RTV on rubber gaskets to insure a leak-free seal
    c. Always use new engine covers and never reuse old covers
    d. All of the above

13. After changing the oil and filter, what should a service technician do?

    a. Reset the oil filter life monitor (OLM)
    b. Check for leaks
    c. Verify that the oil level is correct
    d. All of the above

14. What should be performed as part of a cooling system inspection?

    a. Pressurize the system to 50 PSI (345 kPa) to check for leaks
    b. Pressure-test the radiator cap
    c. Check that the coolant has freeze protection to 0°F (−18°C)
    d. All of the above

15. When should the diesel exhaust fluid (DEF) (AdBlue) be refilled?

    a. When the dash warning message appears
    b. Usually at each scheduled oil change
    c. When the engine is overhauled
    d. Both A and B

16. If a new thermostat has a "jiggle valve," where should it be located when installing it?

   a. At the highest point (up or 12 o'clock)
   b. At 3 o'clock position
   c. At the bottom (6 o'clock) position
   d. At the 9 o'clock position

17. The air dam under the front of a vehicle is missing due to contact with a parking lot barrier. The part should be replaced because _____.

   a. it can cause overheating in city-type driving conditions
   b. it can cause overheating at highway speeds
   c. no need to replace it because it is strictly for a sporty appearance
   d. it reduces wind noise at highway speed

18. An electric cooling fan operates _____.

   a. whenever the engine is running to keep the coolant cool
   b. at highway speeds to ensure that there is enough air flowing through the radiator
   c. at low vehicle speeds
   d. only when the heater is turned on

19. Which warning lamp comes on when the ignition is first turned on as a bulb check?

   a. The "Check Engine" light—malfunction indicator lamp (MIL)
   b. Airbag warning light
   c. ABS amber warning light
   d. All of the above

20. An engine may need to have an air induction/throttle body service performed if the engine is performing how?

   a. Low power at high speed
   b. Rough unstable idle/stalling
   c. Poor fuel economy
   d. Misfires under heavy load

21. A clogged air filter will likely cause what symptom on a fuel-injected engine?

   a. Poor or reduced fuel economy
   b. Lower-than-normal power
   c. Higher-than-normal NO_x exhaust emissions
   d. All of the above

22. A defective or clogged PCV valve can _____.

   a. rough or unstable idle
   b. a lack of power
   c. an engine misfire under heavy load
   d. excessive evaporative emissions

23. Technician A says that oil should be squirted into all of the cylinders before taking a compression test. Technician B says that if the compression greatly increases when some oil is squirted into the cylinders, it indicates defective or worn piston rings. Which technician is correct?

    a. A only
    b. B only
    c. Both A and B
    d. Neither A nor B

24. What happens to the operation of a diesel engine, if the diesel exhaust fluid (DEF) is not refilled as specified?

    a. A warning light will come on but nothing else
    b. Engine may produce less-than-normal power
    c. It may require a longer-than-normal cranking time to start
    d. The glow plugs could be damaged due to the higher temperatures created

25. Two technicians are discussing a compression test. Technician A says that the engine should be cranked over with the pressure gauge installed for "4 puffs." Technician B says that the maximum difference between the highest reading cylinder and the lowest-reading cylinder should be 20%. Which technician is correct?

    a. A only
    b. B only
    c. Both A and B
    d. Neither A nor B

AUTO MAINTENANCE AND
LIGHT REPAIR (G1)

CATEGORY: AUTOMATIC TRANSMISSION/TRANSAXLE

26. Before testing a vehicle to determine if the automatic transmission is performing normally, which should be performed?

    a. Check for any stored diagnostic trouble codes
    b. Check the fluid level
    c. Check the fluid condition and color
    d. All of the above

27. Why is a scan tool needed when checking the level of automatic transmission fluid on a transmission/transaxle that is not equipped with a dipstick?

    a. To determine the fluid temperature
    b. To check for any stored diagnostic trouble codes
    c. To check which solenoids inside the transmission/transaxle are active
    d. To determine the fluid capacity

28. Before replacing the filter in an automatic transmission/transaxle, why should service information be checked first?

    a. The filter may not be replaceable unless the unit is disassembled
    b. The filter may be a spin-on-type filter
    c. The pan may be required to be removed
    d. Any of the above

29. Automatic transmission diagnostic trouble codes include what numbers such as P0XXX?

    a. 3XX
    b. 5XX
    c. 6XX
    d. 7XX

30. What type of automatic transmission fluid (ATF) should be used when replacing the fluid after transmission/transaxle service?

    a. A known brand name of the specified type
    b. A synthetic blend usually SAE 5W-30
    c. A non-friction-modified ATF to ensure that the clutches apply smoothly
    d. A highly-friction-modified ATF in all automotive transmissions/transaxles

31. The ATF cooling lines should be checked for leaks or damage. How many cooling lines are there for a typical automatic transmission/transaxle?

    a. One
    b. Two
    c. Three
    d. Four

32. What is needed to be done to replace the fluid in an automatic transmission/transaxle?

    a. Remove a drain plug
    b. Remove the pan
    c. Remove the vent plug
    d. Either a or b depending on the unit

33. Automatic transmission cooling lines are located _____.

    a. between the transmission and the radiator
    b. between the transmission and the rear axle
    c. inside the transmission or transaxle
    d. inside the HVAC module

AUTO MAINTENANCE AND
LIGHT REPAIR (G1)

CATEGORY: MANUAL DRIVE TRAIN AND AXLES

34. Powertrain mounts are made with _____.

    a. rubber
    b. fluid filled
    c. steel
    d. either a or b

35. Service information should be checked before replacing/adding manual transmission/transaxle fluid because it can be _____.

    a. Automatic transmission fluid (ATF)
    b. engine oil
    c. gear lube
    d. any of the above

36. Drive axle (differential case) fluid is usually _____.

    a. engine oil (usually SAE 5W-30 or SAE 10W-30)
    b. ATF
    c. gear lube (usually SAE 80W-90)
    d. Any of the above

37. Transfer case fluid is _____.

    a. engine oil (usually SAE 5W-30 or SAE 10W-30)
    b. ATF
    c. gear lube (usually SAE 80W-90)
    d. Any of the above are possible

38. The tires on an all-wheel-drive vehicle should all be _____.

    a. same brand and size
    b. same inflation pressure
    c. within 1/16 in. of the same tread depth
    d. all of the above

39. What type of fluid is usually specified to be used in the hydraulic clutch system?

    a. DOT 3 brake fluid
    b. SAE 80-W-90 gear oil
    c. Engine oil (usually SAE 5W-30)
    d. Ethylene glycol

40. To flush a hydraulic clutch system, what should be used?

    a. DOT 3 brake fluid or clutch fluid
    b. DOT 5 brake fluid
    c. Solvent
    d. Brake clean

41. Rust stains are seen around a universal joint. This usually _____.

    a. normal appearance when the vehicle is used in an area that uses salt on the roads
    b. a cast instead of a forged joint is used on this vehicle
    c. the joint has rusted and will normally require replacement
    d. the joint needs to be oiled

42. Why does drive shaft positions need to be marked when they are removed?

    a. To ensure that the drive shaft will be kept balanced
    b. To ensure proper phasing
    c. To ensure that the correct end of the drive shaft is installed at the correct end of the vehicle
    d. To keep the same fasters for each position

43. Where is a center support bearing usually used?

    a. In a long rear-wheel-drive vehicle that uses a two-piece drive shaft
    b. In a front-wheel-drive vehicle
    c. In a four-wheel-drive vehicle that uses a two-piece rear drive shaft
    d. Both a and c

44. Why is it important that all four tires are the same size and tread depth on an all-wheel-drive vehicle?

    a. The vehicle may suffer from a driveline bind or a vibration if unequal size tires are used
    b. The oil level may not be accurately measured if the tire size is not equal
    c. The speedometer will not read correctly
    d. All of the above

45. CV Joint boots should be carefully inspected during routine service because they are made from _____ and can be torn or ripped allowing the grease to escape.

    a. steel
    b. rubber or flexible plastic
    c. aluminum
    d. vinyl

AUTO MAINTENANCE AND LIGHT REPAIR (G1)

CATEGORY: SUSPENSION AND STEERING

46. Which step is NOT usually done when disarming an airbag system?

    a. Removing the airbag module(s) from the vehicle
    b. Removing the airbag fuse
    c. Disconnecting the electrical connector to the airbag
    d. Disconnecting the battery

47. Where is the type of power steering fluid needed found?

    a. On the reservoir fill cap
    b. In the owner's manual
    c. In service information
    d. Any of the above

48. Accessory drive belts are checked for all except _____.

    a. cracks
    b. wear
    c. length
    d. alignment

49. Which is the preferred method to bleed air from a power steering system?

    a. Raise the front wheel off the ground and turn the steering wheel lock-to-lock
    b. Start the engine and allow to idle
    c. Use a vacuum pump attached to the reservoir cap opening
    d. Use a bleeding tool

50. When replacing steering or suspension parts, which precaution is needed to be performed?

    a. Fasteners tightened to factory specifications
    b. Most parts need to be replaced in pairs (left and right side)
    c. The front wheels should be in the straight-ahead position when the final parts are tightened
    d. All of the above

51. A steering dampener looks like a _____.

    a. bump stop
    b. shock absorber
    c. pulley
    d. straight long steel rod

52. Wear indicator ball joints indicate that they are worn enough to need replacement in what location?

    a. A line near the attaching not
    b. A raised area around the grease fitting
    c. A special type of rubber grease seal
    d. Any of the above depending on manufacture

53. A coil spring is correctly installed in an SLA-type of suspension system in which _____.

    a. the two holes on the lower control arm are covered by the spring
    b. the two holes are open in the lower control arm
    c. one hole is covered and the other hole is open or just partially open
    d. the spring tip shows at the upper spring mount

54. Which statement is true about springs?

   a. Torsion bars are often adjustable to control ride height
   b. Leaf springs use a center bolt
   c. Spring can sag resulting in lower ride height
   d. All of the above

55. A scan tool is likely to be needed to perform which operation?

   a. Measure rear toe (total)
   b. Calibrate steering angle sensor
   c. Center the steering wheel
   d. All of the above

56. The specified tire inflation pressure is found _____.

   a. on the driver's side door placard
   b. on the tire sidewall
   c. in the owner's manual
   d. either a or c

57. A TPMS relearn procedure involves performing the procedure starting with which tire?

   a. Right front
   b. Right rear
   c. Left front
   d. Left rear

58. When rotating tires/wheels using a modified "X" method on a front-wheel-drive vehicle, where should the right front wheel be placed?

   a. Right front
   b. Right rear
   c. Left front
   d. Left rear

59. Some power steering systems use a long section of tubing between the steering gear and the reservoir. What is the purpose of this long section of return line?

   a. To allow the fluid to cool
   b. To prevent air from entering the power steering system
   c. To reduce pump noise
   d. To make it easier for the technician to remove the line

60. Airbag wiring connectors are what color?

   a. Yellow
   b. Orange
   c. Blue
   d. Green

61. Some electric power steering systems operate on 42 volts. If so, what color conduit is used around the wiring?

   a. Red
   b. Orange
   c. Blue or yellow
   d. Green

62. A vehicle equipped with an air suspension system needs to be disabled before hoisting the vehicles or before making repairs to the system. What is the most commonly used method to disable the system?

   a. Use a scan tool
   b. Disconnect the air pump
   c. Turn the switch off for the system
   d. Disconnect the air lines at each shock absorber

63. A replacement unit that is used to replace the strut plus the spring and upper bearing assembly is referred to as a _____.

   a. a complete strut
   b. a loaded strut
   c. a strut-spring assembly
   d. a strut-bearing assembly

64. A shackle is used in what type of suspension system?

   a. Leaf spring
   b. Coil spring
   c. McPherson strut
   d. Multi-link

65. If not equal side to side, which alignment angle is NOT a pulling angle?

   a. Caster
   b. Camber
   c. Front toe
   d. Both b and c

66. A tire is excessively worn in the center of the tread. What is the most likely cause?

   a. Excessive positive camber
   b. Overinflation
   c. Underinflation
   d. Excessive positive caster

67. Wheel lug fasteners _____.

   a. should be tightened in a star pattern (tighten one, skip one then tighten the next one, and so on)
   b. should be tightened to factory specifications
   c. should be tightened using a torque wrench or a torque limiting adapter
   d. all of the above

68. Due to environmental concerns, what type of wheel weighs should be used?

   a. Clip-on lead weights only
   b. Stick-on wheel weights only (lead or steel)
   c. Steel, zinc, or composite weights
   d. Any of the above depending on the vehicle

69. In what part of a tire can a repair be performed as long as it is small hole?

   a. In the tread area, only
   b. In the tread area or sidewall only
   c. Within 1 in. (25 mm) of the tire bead only
   d. Anywhere in the tire

70. If the jounce (bump) stops are damaged in the rear, what else should the technician check?

   a. Proper ride height
   b. Shock absorbers for leakage
   c. Worn or sagging springs
   d. All of the above

71. The TPMS warning light is on when the vehicle is being driven. This indicates _____.

   a. a fault in the tire pressure monitoring system (TPMS) has been detected
   b. one or more tires are underinflated
   c. the spare tire sensor is defective
   d. Any of the above

AUTO MAINTENANCE AND LIGHT REPAIR (G1)

CATEGORY: BRAKES

72. A vehicle pulls to the right during hard braking. What is a possible cause?

    a. Air in the lines
    b. A stuck caliper on the right front
    c. A stuck caliper on the left front
    d. Misadjusted rear drum brakes

73. Brake lines should be inspected for what faults?

    a. Leaks
    b. Kinks
    c. Rust
    d. All of the above

74. Typical lug nut torque specifications for a passenger vehicle is usually _____.

    a. 60–70 lb-ft
    b. 80–100 lb-ft
    c. 110–150 lb-ft
    d. 160–180 lb-ft

75. What should be performed before adjusting the parking brake on a vehicle using front disc brakes and rear drum brakes?

    a. Check that the thickness of the front disc brake pads is with factory specifications
    b. Check for proper adjustment of the rear drum brake shoes
    c. Check the brake fluid level
    d. All of the above

76. A disc brake caliper does not move and one of the pads is worn more than the other. What is the most likely cause?

    a. Normal for disc brakes
    b. The caliper piston is likely to be stuck
    c. The caliper sides are likely to be stuck
    d. The caliper dust shield could be leaking and causing this condition

77. Thickness variation specification for most disc brake rotors is _____.

    a. 0.0005 in.
    b. 0.005 in.
    c. 0.050 in.
    d. 0.500 in.

78. The type of brake fluid recommended for use in the master cylinder is _____.

    a. DOT 3
    b. DOT 4
    c. DOT 4+ or LV
    d. any of the above depending on the vehicle

79. What type of grease should be used to lubricate the slides on a disc brake caliper?

 a. Wheel bearing grease
 b. Chassis grease
 c. Silicone grease
 d. Any of the above

80. Why does the brake pedal need to be depressed several times after replacing the disc brake pads?

 a. To seat the pads into the caliper piston assembly
 b. To force the pistons outward so that the pads contact the rotor
 c. To bed in the brake pads
 d. To break in the new pads

81. Two technicians are discussing how to check a vacuum brake booster for proper operation. Technician A says that the brake pedal should be depressed several times, and then depressed and held down and the engine started. Technician B says that the vacuum booster is working normally if the booster is able to supply two or three assisted brake applications before becoming a hard-to-depress brake pedal. Which technician is correct?

 a. A only
 b. B only
 c. Both A and B
 d. Neither A nor B

82. What is the most likely cause of a low brake pedal after new master cylinder was installed?

 a. Overfilled master cylinder reservoir
 b. Air in the system
 c. Misadjusted rear drum brakes
 d. Incorrect adjustment of the brake pedal

83. How many drum brake shoe support pads are located on each backing plate?

 a. 6
 b. 4
 c. 2
 d. 8 or more depending on make and model of vehicle

84. A technician should not test-drive a vehicle on a public street or highway if _____.

 a. the amber ABS warning light is on
 b. the red brake warning light is on
 c. the brake fluid level is not at the maximum level
 d. any of the above

85. The parking brake will not hold a vehicle from moving and the cables are swollen. What is the most likely cause?

 a. Misadjusted rear drum brake linings
 b. Misadjusted parking brake
 c. Rusted parking brake cables
 d. Stuck parking pawl

86. How should the technician drive the vehicle in order to properly burnish/break-in new disc brake pads?

 a. Perform several light (easy) stops from highway speed
 b. Perform moderately hard braking from about 50 MPH (80 km/h) until the vehicle speed reaches 20 MPH (32 km/h) and repeat several times
 c. Perform two easy (light) stops from 20 MPH (32 km/h)
 d. Perform hard braking from highway speed just one time

87. When machining a brake drum, according to many vehicle manufacturers, how much material should be left for wear?

 a. As long as the drum is machined to the "discard" measurement, that is all that is needed
 b. Machine to the maximum ID measurement
 c. Allow 0.030 in. for wear before the "discard" measurement
 d. Any of the above depending on the make and model

88. The red brake warning light is on. Technician A says that the parking brake could be on. Technician B says that the brake fluid could be low. Which technician is correct?

   a. A only
   b. B only
   c. Both A and B
   d. Neither A nor B

89. How should brake fluid be stored?

   a. Kept in the original container with the cap secured to keep air from entering
   b. Kept in a glass jar with a screw top lid
   c. Transfer to a measuring cup and label it "brake fluid" for easy use
   d. In its original container and kept in the refrigerator to keep it cold

90. What amount of vacuum should be measured at the vacuum booster with the engine running?

   a. 5–7 inches Mercury (in. Hg.)
   b. 8–10 inches Mercury (in. Hg.)
   c. 10–14 inches Mercury (in. Hg.)
   d. At least 15 inches Mercury (in. Hg.)

91. Where is there vacuum in a vacuum brake booster with the engine running and brake pedal up (not depressed)?

   a. On the front (engine side) of the internal diaphragm
   b. At the rear (passenger compartment side) of the booster
   c. On both sides of the internal diaphragm
   d. At the brake pedal air valve, only

92. In a rear drum brake assembly, if one lining is longer than the other, the longer lining should be installed _____.

   a. toward the front of the vehicle (on the left on the right rear and on the right on the right side of the vehicle)
   b. toward the rear of the vehicle (on the right and on the right rear and on the left on the right side of the vehicle)
   c. either position is okay
   d. on the same side as where the parking brake cable enters the backing plate

93. Which statement(s) is/are true?

   a. If the red brake warning light is on, this could indicate a fault with the hydraulic system
   b. If the amber ABS warning light is on, this indicates a fault with the ABS system
   c. If the red brake warning light is on, the vehicle should not be test-driven
   d. All of the above are correct

AUTO MAINTENANCE AND
LIGHT REPAIR (G1)

CATEGORY: ELECTRICAL

94. The voltage drop is being tested on the positive (power) side of a cranking circuit. Technician A says that the voltmeter test leads need to be placed at the battery positive and the other test lead to the battery stud of the starter to measure the voltage drop on the positive part of the circuit. Technician B says that the engine has to be cranked using the starter to measure the voltage drop. Which technician is correct?

    a. A only
    b. B only
    c. Both A and B
    d. Neither A nor B

95. A technician wants to check the current flow (amperes) in a circuit. What needs to be done?

    a. The circuit has to be disconnected and the meter leads connected in series with the circuit being tested
    b. An inductive meter could be used to measure the current if attached to a wire in the circuit
    c. Set the meter to read DCA and then connect the meter leads to the positive and negative terminals of the battery
    d. Either a or b

96. When jump-starting a vehicle, the last connection from another vehicle or a jump box should be _____.

    a. the connection to a good ground on the disabled vehicle away from the battery
    b. the connection to the negative terminal of the good vehicle
    c. the connection to the positive terminal of the disabled vehicle
    d. any of the above

97. The airbag warning lamp flashes a few times when the vehicle is started and then stops flashing and goes out. This indicates _____.

    a. a fault has been detected in the airbag system
    b. normal self-test of airbag system
    c. the airbag module requires recalibration
    d. any of the above depending on make, model, and year of vehicle

98. A starter is being replaced. What precautions are needed before performing this procedure?

    a. Disconnect the negative battery cable
    b. Disconnect the positive battery cable
    c. Remove the starter fuse
    d. Disarm the driver's side airbag for safety

99. A charging system output test indicates that the alternator is not supplying the specified output. Technician A says that the drive belt could be worn and causing the lower-than-normal output. Technician B says that the drive belt tensioner could be faulty. Which technician is correct?

    a. A only
    b. B only
    c. Both A and B
    d. Neither A nor B

100. When replacing lightbulbs, a wise technician should _____.

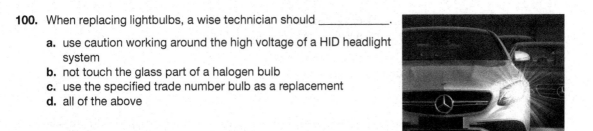

    a. use caution working around the high voltage of a HID headlight system
    b. not touch the glass part of a halogen bulb
    c. use the specified trade number bulb as a replacement
    d. all of the above

101. Technician A says that memory functions can be kept when disconnecting a battery by connecting a "memory saver" to the lighter plug on many vehicles. Technician B says that memory functions can be kept when disconnecting a battery by connecting a "memory saver" to the 16-pin diagnostic link connector (DLC) on 1996 and newer vehicles. Which technician is correct?

    a. A only
    b. B only
    c. Both A and B
    d. Neither A nor B

102. Some starters are equipped with shims. Where are these shims installed if used?

    a. Between the starter and the engine block
    b. Between the flywheel and the starter pinion gear
    c. Between the engine crankshaft and the flexplate
    d. Any of the above depending on application

103. To measure the voltage drop in an electrical circuit using a DMM, what position should the meter be set to?

    a. DCV
    b. DCA
    c. ACA
    d. ACV

104. To measure the current flow through a horn circuit using a DMM, what position should the meter be set to?

    a. DCV
    b. DCA
    c. ACA
    d. ACV

105. How is the state of charge (SOC) of a vehicle battery determined?

    a. By using a conductance tester or load tester
    b. By measuring the resistance of the battery cables
    c. By checking battery voltage with the engine running at idle speed
    d. By using a scan tool

106. What fluid should be used in the windshield washer system?

    a. Distilled water
    b. Antifreeze mixed 50/50 with demineralized water
    c. Windshield washer fluid
    d. Clean drinking water

107. The charging system voltage on most vehicles with the engine running should be _____.

    a. 11.5–12.5 volts
    b. 13–15 volts
    c. 16–18 volts
    d. above 20 volts

108. A starter is barely able to rotate the engine and it does not start. The starter current was measured and it was over 300 amperes on a V-6 engine. It could be due to_____.

    a. a worn starter motor or engine mechanical fault
    b. high resistance in the battery cables
    c. a defective alternator
    d. any of the above

109. A lightbulb is being tested using an ohmmeter and it reads 0.5 ohms between the two terminals of the bulb. This measurement indicates _____.

    a. normal resistance
    b. the bulb is shorted
    c. the bulb filament is open
    d. the filament is grounded

AUTO MAINTENANCE AND LIGHT REPAIR (G1)

CATEGORY: HEATING AND AIR CONDITIONING

110. When checking for vent temperature, where should the measurement be made?

    a. At the center outlets
    b. At the outlet on the driver's side
    c. At the defroster vents
    d. At the passenger side AC vent

111. Cabin filters _____.

    a. may be accessed from inside the vehicle on the passenger side behind the glove compartment
    b. are under the hood on the passenger side
    c. should be replaced as part of regular maintenance
    d. all of the above

112. Where is the evaporator (condensate) drain outlet usually located?

    a. Behind the glove compartment inside the vehicle
    b. Under the vehicle on the passenger side
    c. Under the hood near the AC compressor
    d. Any of the above depending on make, model, and year of vehicle

113. What is often seen at the location of a refrigerant leak?

    a. A clear liquid leaking or dripping
    b. A green mist is seen
    c. An oily area
    d. Any of the above

114. Clear water is seen dripping from under the vehicle, on the passenger side. This is an indication of _____.

    a. a leaking evaporator
    b. a leaking heater hose
    c. normal condensate
    d. a fault with the blower motor

115. The vent temperature as measured at the center vent on a vehicle with the air conditioning set to "maximum" should read _____.

    a. 30° lower than ambient
    b. 0°–15°F (–18° to –9°C)
    c. 15°–25°F (–9° to –4°C)
    d. 29°–32°F (–2° to 0°C)

AUTO MAINTENANCE AND LIGHT REPAIR (G1)

CATEGORY: ENGINE SYSTEMS

1. **The correct answer is b.** The number zero after the P (passenger car) indicates that the code is the same for all vehicles (generic). If the number had been a one or a two, then this would indicate that it is a vehicle-specific DTC. Answer a is not correct; the first number is a zero which indicates that the code is the same for all vehicles regardless of make or model. Answer c is not correct because OBDII trouble codes cannot be retrieved using a jumper wire and counting flashes, which was commonly done with some older vehicles before 1996. Answer d is not correct; the first number is a zero which indicates that the code is the same for all vehicles regardless of make or model.

2. **The correct answer is d:** All of the above are correct. Answer a is not correct by itself because while the pH can be an indication that the coolant needs to be replaced, the coolant also needs to be checked for the other factors. Answer b is not correct because while the freezing and boiling points are important, the coolant must also be checked for the other aspects to determine the true condition of the coolant. Answer c is not correct because even though the specific gravity is often used as a measure of the freezing and boiling point (percentage of ethylene glycol in the coolant), the coolant must also be checked for the other aspects to determine the true condition of the coolant.

3. **The correct answer is b.** Technician B only is correct because during a leak-down test, air under pressure is applied to the combustion chamber and when heard exiting the oil fill opening means that the piston rings are the cause of the air leak. Answer a is not correct because the air does not flow though the oil and therefore a could not cause the air to exit from the oil fill opening. Answers c and d are not correct because only technician B is correct.

4. **The correct answer is d.** Antifreeze can be colored green, orange, or red and therefore the best answer is that any of the above colors could be coolant leaking. Answers a, b, and c are not correct because the color of the coolant can be any of the colors listed.

5. **The correct answer is b.** To help prevent air from being trapped in the cooling system, the bleeder valve, located at the highest point in the cooling system, should be opened to allow the air to escape. Answer a is not correct because, while using the proper antifreeze is important, it will NOT prevent air from getting trapped in the system. Answer c is not correct because even though some vehicle manufacturers such as Honda and Toyota specify that premixed coolant be used, it will NOT prevent air from getting trapped in the system. Answer d is not correct because wearing protective gloves will not prevent air from getting trapped in the cooling system.

6. **The correct answer is d.** All of the above are correct. Answer a is correct because all fasteners should be tightened to factory specifications when installing a new water pump. Answer b is also correct because a new gasket or seal is specified to be used by the vehicle manufacturers whenever installing a new water pump. Answer c is also correct because the accessory drive belt that rotates the new water pump should be correctly installed, aligned with the proper tension. Answers a, b, and c are not correct because all of them are correct.

7. **The correct answer is c.** A scan tool is the specified tool to use to retrieve diagnostic trouble codes from OBDII (1996+) vehicles. Answer a is not correct because while a test light may be able to be used to retrieve DTCs on older (prior to 1996) vehicles, it is not possible to use to retrieve codes on OBDII vehicles. Answer b is not correct because while a test light may be able to be used to retrieve DTCs on older (prior to 1996) vehicles, it is not possible to use to retrieve codes on OBDII vehicles. Answer d is not correct because only a scan tool can be used to retrieve diagnostic trouble codes from all OBD II vehicles.

8. **The correct answer is c.** The fuel pressure should be relieved before removing a fuel filter because the fuel is under pressure on fuel-injected engines that use an electric fuel pump located inside the fuel tank. Answer a is not correct because while using the same brand as the original is often a wise choice, it does not have to be

used if the replacement filter is designed to match the physical and performance specifications of the original. Answer b is not correct because a filter cannot be cleaned. Answer d is not correct because the fasteners should be tightened to the vehicle manufacturer's specified torque and not tightened as much as possible.

9. **The correct answer is d.** Both b and c are correct. Answer b is correct because the concern has to be verified in order for the repair to be verified. Answer c is also correct because the concern has to be verified to ensure that the customer concern is a true problem and not normal operation. Answer a is not correct because while there may be a charge to the customer for diagnosis, there is seldom a charge to the customers for verifying the customer concern.

10. **The correct answer is a.** Any fluid leak will tend to fall downward due to gravity and to flow toward the rear of the vehicle during driving due to airflow. Answer b is not correct because while fluids will be seen dripping from the lowest place, the location of the leak is usually higher. Answer c is not correct because the fluid leak will be wet (not dry). Answer d is not correct because the source of the leak is the highest place (not the lowest) where the fluid is seen.

11. **The correct answer is b.** A cracked flexplate will often make noise that sound like an engine knock, if cracked or the attachment bolts are loose and is often heard when the engine stops. Answer a is not correct because worn main bearing will be heard when the engine is first started and before oil reaches the bearings and not the most likely cause of an engine know noise when the engine stops. Answer c is not correct because worn rod bearing will be heard when the engine is first started and before oil reaches the bearings and not the most likely cause of an engine know noise when the engine stops. Answer d is not correct because if a connecting rod was cracked, it would likely result in a loud noise when it broke and would not likely be the cause of a knock noise when the engine stops.

12. **The correct answer is a.** All fasteners should be tightened to the vehicle manufacturer's specifications and this may be expressed in inch-pounds (not foot-pounds). Answer b is not correct because using RTV on a rubber gasket will cause the gasket to move out of location which will likely cause a leak. Answer c is not correct because old engine covers can be reused if they are not damaged and the gasket surface is unharmed. Answer d is not correct because just answer a is correct.

13. **The correct answer is d.** All of the above are correct. Answer a is correct because the oil life monitor should be reset so it will work as designed to warn the driver when the oil needs to be changed and to clear the message. Answer b is also correct because the technician should always verify that no leaks are present after an oil change and before releasing the vehicle back to the owner. Answer c is also correct because the oil level should always be checked to make sure that is properly filled and not overfilled nor underfilled.

14. **The correct answer is b.** The pressure cap should be tested as part of any cooling system inspection to make sure that it is able to hold the specified pressure. Answer a is not correct because the cooling system should be pressurized to no higher than the pressure rating of the pressure cap and this is usually less than 17 PSI. Answer c is not correct because the freeze protection should be –34 degrees (not just zero degrees). Answer d is not correct because answers a and c are not correct.

15. **The correct answer is d.** Both a and b are correct. Answer a is correct because the fluid should be added when the warning message appears on the dash. Answer b is also correct because most vehicle manufacturer's size the DEF reservoir so that it should only need to be filled at the schedule oil change intervals, thereby making it more convenient for the vehicle owner. Answer c is not correct because the diesel exhaust fluid is consumed by the emission-control system when the engine is running and needs to be filled on a regular basis.

16. **The correct answer is a.** The "jiggle" valve is an opening in the thermostat that allows air to escape upward to the radiator where it can then leave the cooling system and not get trapped as an air pocket. This valve needs to be placed in the up position because air is lighter than the coolant and will

tend to move upward in the system. Answers b, c, and d are not correct because they do not state that the jiggle valve needs to be at the 12 o'clock position to allow any trapped air to escape.

17. **The correct answer is b.** The air dam used in the front of the vehicle is used to direct the airflow up through the radiator and not underneath the vehicle at highway speeds. Therefore, if the air dam is missing, a lack of cooling at highway speeds is the most likely cause. Answer a is not correct because during city-type driving the cooling fan is responsible for ensuing sufficient airflow through the radiator and the ram air effect is not a big factor at lower vehicle speeds. Answer c is not correct because it serves a function and while it does add a sporty look to many vehicles, this is not the purpose or function of the front air dam. Answer d is not correct because the air dam directs the air through the radiator instead of traveling underneath the vehicle and while it may reduce wind noise at highway speed, that is not the purpose and function of the air dam.

18. **The correct answer is c.** The purpose and function of an electric cooling fan is to provide airflow through the radiator at low vehicle speed. At higher vehicle speeds, normal airflow is enough to insure proper cooling and most electrical cooling fans are turned off above 35 MPH (56 km/h). Answers a and b are not correct because the electric cooling fans are usually turned off to improve fuel economy and because they are not needed to provide airflow when the vehicle is traveling above 35 MPH (56 km/h). Answer d is not correct because the water pump supplies coolant to the heater core when the engine is running and the cooling fan is only used to cool the radiator.

19. **The correct answer is d.** All of the above warning lights are turned on as a bulb check when the ignition is first turned on. Answers a, b, and c are not correct because all of the mentioned warning lights come on when the ignition is turned on as a bulb check.

20. **The correct answer is b.** A throttle body and/or air induction cleaning is most likely to help correct a rough or unstable idle condition. At idle speed, the airflow is low and slow and affected by deposits that tend to build up on the backside of the throttle plate. Answer a is not correct because the airflow above idle speed is usually not affected by the deposits on the backside of the throttle plate. Answer c is not correct; although carbon cleaning can benefit how the engine performs and may result in smoother engine operation, the deposits on the backside of the throttle plate will not have any effect on fuel economy. Answer d is not correct because under a heavy load, the throttle is opened and the engine would not be affected too much by deposits on the backside of the throttle plate or at least enough to cause a misfire.

21. **The correct answer is b.** A clogged air filter will restrict the airflow into the engine and this will reduce engine power. It is similar to having a throttle plate that does not open all the way. The engine will operate normally at idle and at low speeds but will not have normal power. Answer a is not correct because a restricted air filter does not affect the air–fuel ratio in a fuel-injected engine unlike what can occur if the engine was equipped with a carburetor. Answer c is not correct because the air–fuel ratio is not affected and therefore the exhaust emissions, including NOx emissions, would not change. Answer d is not correct because only b is correct.

22. **The correct answer is a.** A clogged or defective PCV valve will affect the idle because 20% or more of the air entering the engine at idle flows through the PCV valve. Therefore, any fault with the valve that affects airflow will affect engine operation but mostly at idle speed only. Answer b is not correct because a defective PCV valve will unlikely recue engine power because the amount of air entering the engine above idle speed is very small compared to the amount of air entering the engine through the throttle plate. Answer c is not correct because an engine misfire is unlikely to be caused by a defective PCV because the amount of air entering the engine above idle speed is very small compared to the amount of air entering the engine through the throttle plate would not cause a misfire. Answer d is not correct because a fault with the PCV valve does not affect the evaporative emission control system, which is part of the fuel system and not part of the engine vacuum.

23. **The correct answer is b.** Technician B only is correct because oil will seal the piston rings and as a result will cause the compression to increase compared to the first test when oil was not added to the cylinder. Technician A is not correct because a compression test should be performed with the engine in its normal state and then oil added only to the cylinder(s) that tested low to help determine if the fault is due to piston rings. Answers c and d are not correct because only technician B is correct.

24. **The correct answer is b.** If the DEF level becomes low, a warning message is displayed. If this message is ignored and DEF is not added, then eventually the engine power will be reduced. Answer a is not correct because eventually the engine will not start if the DEF is not filled. Answer c is not correct because while the engine power will be reduced if the warning message is ignored, the cranking of the engine is not affected. Answer d is not correct because the glow plugs are not affected by the DEF messages.

25. **The correct answer is c.** Both technicians are correct. Technician A is correct because the engine needs at least 4 puffs to get a consistent reading. Technician B is correct because all cylinders should be within 20% of each other so that each cylinder contributes equally to the power output of the engine. Answers a, b, and d are not correct because both technicians are correct.

AUTO MAINTENANCE AND
LIGHT REPAIR (G1)

CATEGORY: AUTOMATIC TRANSMISSION/TRANSAXLE

26. **The correct answer is d.** All of the above are correct. Answer a is correct because stored diagnostic trouble codes should be retrieved as many do not cause the "Check Engine" light to come on so the driver would never know there was a fault detected. Answers b and c are also correct because the level, color, and condition of the fluid are all important when diagnosing automatic transmission/transaxles concerns.

27. **The correct answer is a.** A scan tool is used to monitor the temperature of the automatic transmission fluid. Vehicle manufacturers specify that the fluid level be at a certain level at a specified temperature and the scan tool can monitor the temperature from reading provided by the fluid temperature sensor. Answer b is not correct because while it is important to check for stored diagnostic trouble codes (DTCs), the purpose of using a scan tool to check fluid level is to use the data from the fluid temperature sensor to detect the temperature of the ATF. Answer c is not correct because the operation of the solenoids is not important information to know to check the level of the transmission fluid. Answer d is not correct because a scan tool is not capable of determining the fluid capacity of the transmission or transaxle.

28. **The correct answer is d.** All of the above are correct. Answer a is correct because vehicle manufacturers specify where the filter is located as well as the recommended service procedure. Answer b is correct because vehicle manufacturers specify where the filter is located and what type of filter to use. Answer c is correct because vehicle manufacturers specify where the filter is located as well as the service procedure to follow to replace it.

29. **The correct answer is d.** The correct answer included numbers that start with a seven (7). Answer a is not correct because a DTC that is 3xxx means that it includes vehicle-related DTCs. Answer b is not correct because a DTC that is 5xxx means that it includes vehicle speed-related DTCs. Answer c is not correct because a DTC that is 6xxx means that it includes computer output-related DTCs.

30. **The correct answer is a.** The correct answer states that the specified fluid be used. It also includes that a known brand name be used to help avoid some that may not meet specifications. Answer b is not correct because engine oil is not used in automatic transmissions/transaxles. Answer c is not correct because a non-friction modified ATF would result in hash (not smooth) shifts and is not recommended except for use in older band-type units. Answer d is not correct because even though high-friction-modified ATF is used in many automatic transmissions/transaxles, it is not used in all of them.

31. **The correct answer is b.** The correct answer is two lines and this includes one from the transmission/transaxle to the radiator and the other from the radiator back to the automatic transmission/transaxle. Answer a is not correct because there are two cooler lines. Answer c is not correct because there are two cooler lines, not three. Answer d is not correct because there are two cooler lines, not four.

32. **The correct answer is d.** The correct answer includes either a drain plug, used in some units or removes the pan, used in most units. Answer a is not correct because while some units do use a drain plug, others need to have the pan removed. Answer b is not correct because while most units do require that the pan be removed, many units use a drain plug. Answer c is not correct because, while all units use a vent, it is not removed to service the unit.

33. **The correct answer is a.** Automatic transmission cooling lines are metal lines that run between the transmission or transaxle to the radiator where the ATF is cooled through a separate passage inside the radiator. Answer b is not correct because the lines do not extend rearward to the rear axle. Answer c is not correct because the cooler itself is located inside the radiator on most vehicles. Answer d is not correct because the cooling lines travel to the radiator and not to the heating, ventilation, and air conditioning (HVAC) module.

AUTO MAINTENANCE AND LIGHT REPAIR (G1)

CATEGORY: MANUAL DRIVE TRAIN AND AXLES

34. The correct answer is d. Either a or b is correct. Answer a is correct because powertrain mounts can be and are mostly made from reinforced rubber to allow some movement to absorb noise and vibrations from the engine and transmission. Answer b is also correct because many mounts are fluid filled so they can absorb noise and vibration. Answer c is not correct because, while the backing of the mount is often made from steel, the mounts themselves are rubber to so they can absorb noise and vibrations.

35. The correct answer is d. The correct answer includes ATF, engine oil, or gear lube and the specified fluids to use in manual transmissions/transaxles. Answer a is not correct because while ATF is the specified fluid to use in many units, it is not to be used in all manual transmissions/transaxles. Answer b is not correct because while engine oil is often specified in some manual transmission/transaxles, it is not specified for use in all units. Answer c is not correct because while gear lube may be specified for use in some older manual transmissions/transaxles, it is not specified to be used in all units.

36. The correct answer is c. The correct answer is gear lube because of the need for sliding friction protection offered by a gear lube that extreme pressure (EP) additive provides. Answer a is not correct because automatic transmission fluid (ATF), while used in many manual transmissions and transfer cases, is not suitable to use in a drive axle that uses hypoid gears. Answer d is not correct because only gear lube is used in a drive axle that uses hypoid gears.

37. The correct answer is d. The correct answer includes ATF, Engine oil, or gear lube and is the specified fluid to use in transfer cases depending on the year, make, and model of vehicle. Answer a is not correct because, while engine oil is often specified in some manual transmission/transaxles, it is not specified for use in all units. Answer b is not correct because while ATF is the specified fluid to use in many units, it is not to be used in all transfer cases. Answer c is not correct because while gear lube may be specified for use in some older manual transfer cases, it is not specified to be used in all units.

38. The correct answer is d. All of the above are correct. Answer a is correct because all tires should be the same brand (size can vary slightly by brand) and size. Answer b is also correct because all tires should have the same inflation pressure which would affect diameter and rolling circumference. Answer c is also correct because the tread depth should all be the same within 1/16 inch.

39. The correct answer is a. The correct answer is DOT 3 brake fluid and is the specified fluid to use in most hydraulic clutch systems. Answer b is not correct because gear lube is used in a drive axle that uses hypoid gears and is not specified for use in a hydraulic clutch system. Answer c is not correct because while engine oil may be specified for use in many manual transmissions and transfer cases, it is not suitable to use in a hydraulic clutch systems. Answer d is not correct because only brake fluid is to be used in hydraulic clutch systems.

40. **The correct answer is a.** The correct answer is either DOT 3 brake fluid or clutch fluid, which is similar to brake fluid and is the specified fluid to use in hydraulic clutches. Answer b is not correct because DOT 5 brake fluid is not specified for use in hydraulic clutches. Answer c is not correct because solvent is not specified for use in hydraulic clutches Answer d is not correct because brake clean is not specified for use in hydraulic clutches.

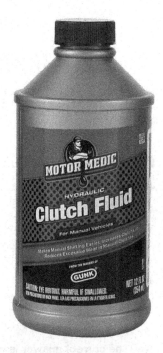

41. **The correct answer is c.** The correct answer is that rust dust is what is being seen and this means that the needle bearings inside the U-joint are rusting and small particles are being thrown outward. Answer a is not correct because while rust is frequently seen on metal parts where salt is used on the roads, a U-joint has grease inside and this joint should, while it can be rusty on the outside, not be throwing off rust particles due to surface rust. Answer b is not correct because whether the U-joint is cast or forged, this would not be the cause of the rust dust being seen thrown off by the joint. Answer d is not correct because while some U-joints have a grease fitting and should be greased, they are not to be coated with oil because the oil cannot get into the needle bearing.

42. **The correct answer is b.** The correct answer is that many joints, especially those that use a center support bearing, need to be properly phased to reduce driveline vibration so it is important to mark the position when removing a drive shaft. Answer a is not correct because the position of the U-joint would not affect the balance of the driveshaft; even though it was out-of-phase, it would cause a vibration. Answer c is not correct because while some drive shafts look the same at both ends, most have a unique U-joint which means that the drive shaft cannot be installed backward. Answer d is not correct because while some U-joints have a grease fitting and should be greased, they are not to be coated in oil because there is no need to keep the easterners in the same position as this would not affect the balance at all.

43. **The correct answer is d.** Both a and c are correct. Answer a is correct because long vehicles need to use a two-piece drive shaft in order to reduce the critical speed that can cause it to whip at high vehicle speeds. Answer c is also correct because some four-wheel drive vehicles use a two-piece driveshaft for the rear drive axle. Answer b is not correct because front wheel vehicles use shafts and therefore do not need to use a two-piece assembly.

44. **The correct answer is a.** The vehicle may suffer from a vibration or driveline bind if the tires are not the same diameter causing them to rotate at different speeds. Answer b is not correct because the oil level is not affect enough by different tire size to affect the reading. Answer c is not correct because the speedometer readings would not be affecting enough by different tire size to affect the speed. Answer d is not correct because only answer a is correct.

45. **The correct answer is b.** The correct answer is that the boots (bellows) are made from rubber or plastic. Answer a is not correct because while CV joints themselves are made from steel, the boots (bellows) are not made from steel. Answer c is not correct because CV joint boots are not made from aluminum. Answer d is not correct because CV joint boots are made from rubber or plastic and not vinyl.

AUTO MAINTENANCE AND
LIGHT REPAIR (G1)

CATEGORY: SUSPENSION AND STEERING

46. **The correct answer is a.** In this question, the correct answer is what is NOT done and that is the actual removal of the airbag module prior to working on the vehicle. Answer b is not correct because removing the airbag fuse is procedure that is often specified to be used to disable the airbag system. Answer c is not correct because disconnecting the airbag electrical connector is procedure that is often specified to be used to disable the airbag system. Answer d is not correct because disconnecting the battery is procedure that is often specified to be used to disable the airbag system.

47. **The correct answer is d.** Any of the above is correct. Answer a is correct because the specified power steering fluid is often written on the cap. Answer b is not correct because the specified fluid is included in the owner's manual. Answer c is correct because the specified fluid to use in the power steering system is also included in service information.

48. **The correct answer is c.** This question asks for what is specified except meaning that the length of an accessory drive belt is not checked when inspecting the belt during routine service. Answer a is not correct because cracks are something that should be checked for in a belt during an inspection. Answer b is not correct because wear is something that should be checked for in a belt during an inspection. Answer d is not correct because belt alignment is something that should be checked for during an inspection.

49. **The correct answer is a.** Answer a is correct because by raising the front wheels off the ground reduces the forces on the steering and this prevents the trapped air in the fluid from being broken up into small bubbles which are hard to bleed out of the system. Answer b is not correct simply starting the engine and will not likely be able to cause the fluid to move enough through the system without turning the steering wheel. Answer c is not correct because while some vehicle manufacturers specify that a vacuum be applied to the reservoir cap opening, this procedure is used in the event that normal bleeding procedures did not work and therefore is not the preferred method as specified by most vehicle manufacturers. Answer d is not correct because a special tool is not specified or needed to bleed air from a power steering system.

50. **The correct answer is d.** All of the above are correct. Answer a is correct because the specified torque should be applied to all steering and suspension fasteners. Answer b is correct because the specified procedure is to replace component in pairs even if a part on one side of the vehicle is found to be defective. Answer c is correct because the many steering and suspension parts contain rubber and rubber has a memory. If a part is installed with the front wheels pointing to one side, then the rubber in the part will tend to force the vehicle, to the side where it was installed.

51. **The correct answer is b.** The steering dampener is a shock-like device that helps prevent movement of the front wheel to the steering wheel. Answer a is not correct because a bump stop is a stationary bumper and does not help dampen steering forces. Answer c is not correct because a pulley is used to drive the power steering pump but it does not dampen the steering. Answer d is not correct because a steering dampener uses the movement of hydraulic fluid through a shock-like device to dampen steering forces and a straight steel rod would not perform this function.

52. **The correct answer is b.** The wear indicator is the area around the base of the grease fitting. The base is normally raised below the bottom of the joint and when it wears and becomes flush with the bottom of the joint, it is the indication that the joint is worn and requires replacement. Answer a is not correct because a line is not used to indicate ball joint wear. Answer c is not correct because it is the steel raised part around the grease fitting that is the wear indicator and not a rubber seal. Answer d is not correct because all wear indicator ball joints use the same raised area around the grease fitting.

53. **The correct answer is c.** When the coil spring is correctly installed, one of the holes in the lower control arm will be completely covered and the other should be open or just partially covered. If the spring was installed upside down or not seated correctly, either holes or neither hole will be covered. Answer a is not correct because only one hole should be covered. Answer b is not correct because one hole should be completely covered. Answer d is not correct because it is at the lower part of the spring that is inspected to ensure that it is in the specified location, not at the upper end of the spring.

54. **The correct answer is d.** All of the above are correct. Answer a is correct because torsion bars can be adjusted to control ride (suspension) height. Answer b is correct because leaf springs do use a center bolt to hold the leaves together. Answer c is correct because springs can and do sag over time and thus can affect the ride (suspension) height.

55. **The correct answer is b.** The steering angle sensor usually requires the use of a scan tool to calibrate the steering wheel angle sensor after an alignment has been performed. Answer a is not correct because a scan tool is not required to measure rear toe. Answer c is not correct because the front tie rod ends are used to adjust the steering wheel straight ahead and while a scan tool is then needed to calibrate the steering wheel sensor, it is not used to center the steering wheel. Answer d is not correct because only answer b is correct.

56. **The correct answer is d.** Both answers a and c are correct. Answer a is correct because the specified inflation pressure is on a placard on the driver's door or in the owner's manual (answer c). Answer b is not correct simply starting the engine and will not likely be able to cause the fluid to move enough through the system without turning the steering wheel. Answer c is not correct because the pressure on the sidewall of the it is the maximum pressure that the tire can handle is not the pressure to use when inflating a tire.

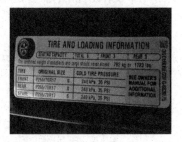

57. **The correct answer is c.** Most, if not all, vehicle manufacturers specify that the relearn procedure starts with the left front wheel and move clockwise around the vehicle. Answers a, b, and d are not correct because it is the left front wheel where the relearn process is specified to be used first.

58. **The correct answer is b.** Using the modified X method of tire rotation, the drive wheels are moved straightforward or rearward the non-drive wheels are moved forward or rearward and crossed. This means that on a front wheel drive vehicle, the right front will be moved straight back to the right rear position. Answers a, c, and d are not correct because the specified position is at the right rear.

59. **The correct answer is a.** The long length of return line is often placed in the airstream so that air flowing past the line will cool the power steering fluid. Answer b is not correct because a length of return line would not have any effect on the air entering the system because the line is closed and not open to the atmosphere. Answer c is not correct because a length of return line would not affect the pump at all and would not reduce noise. Answer d is not correct because the length of the return line may make removing the line harder rather than easier for the service technician.

60. **The correct answer is a.** Yellow is the color of electrical connectors used in airbag circuits. Answers b, c, and d are not correct because yellow, not orange (high voltage wring), blue (42 volts circuits), or green are used to indicate airbag circuit connectors.

61. **The correct answer is c.** Blue or yellow is the color of electrical conduit used in electric power steering systems that use 42 volts. Answers a (red), b (orange), and d (green) are not correct because the color of the electrical conduit is either blue or yellow depending on the make and model of vehicle that uses a 42-volt electric power steering system.

62. **The correct answer is c.** Most vehicles equipped with an air suspension have a switch, usually located in the trunk area that should be used to turn off the system if it is to be lifted on a hoist. This keeps the suspension system from letting all of the air out of the system. Answer a is not correct because while a scan tool may be able to be used to disable the system, it is not the primary way to do so for routine service operations. Answer b is not correct because while disconnecting the air pump may work, this unit is usually in a location that is difficult to get to and is not designed to be sued to disconnect the system during routine service operations. Answer d is not correct because while disconnecting the air shocks may work, this procedure is not designed to be sued to disconnect the system during routine service operations.

63. **The correct answer is b.** An assembly that contains the strut plus the upper mount and spring is called a loaded strut. Answer a is not correct because while the name is similar, the assembly is called a loaded strut and not a complete strut. Answer c is not correct because while the name is similar, the assembly is called a loaded strut and not a strut-spring assembly. Answer d is not correct because while the name is similar, the assembly is called a loaded strut and not a strut-bearing assembly.

64. **The correct answer is a.** A shackle is the part of a leaf spring system that allows the spring to become longer when the vehicle hits a bump. Answer b is not correct because a shackle is used with a leaf spring and not a coil spring. Answer c is not correct because a shackle is used with a leaf spring and not a McPherson strut suspension. Answer d is not correct because a shackle is used with a leaf spring and not a multi-link suspension system suspension.

65. **The correct answer is c.** Front toe always splits equally when the vehicle moves forward and if the toe is unequal side to the side, the steering wheel angle changes but the toe always splits equally and does not cause a pull. Answer a is not correct because caster unequal caster will cause a pull. Answer b is not correct because camber unequal caster will cause a pull. Answer d is not correct because only toe (answer c) is correct.

66. **The correct answer is b.** A tire that is overinflated will cause excessive wear to occur in the center of the tire tread. Answer a is not correct because excessive positive camber will cause the tire to wear on the outside of the tread (not in the center). Answer c is not correct because if the tire was under-inflated, the outside edges of the tire would wear more. Answer d is not correct because excessive positive caster would not cause excessive inside tire wear but instead would not wear the tires excessively or if driven in city-type conditions may show camber-type wear to both the inside and outside edges of tire.

67. **The correct answer is d.** All of the above are correct. Answer a is correct because lug nuts should always be tightened in a star pattern. Answer b is correct because lug nuts should always be tightened to factory specified torque. Answer c is correct because lug nuts should be tightened using a torque wrench or a torque absorbing adapter to insure proper tightening torque.

68. **The correct answer is c.** Wheel weights should be made from steel, zinc, or a composite to help safeguard the environment by avoiding the use of lead. Answer a is not correct because clip-on lead weights contain lead and have been outlawed in many states. Answer b is not correct because weights containing lead have been outlawed in many states. Answer d is not correct because only none-lead weights are to be used (answer c).

69. **The correct answer is a.** A tire repair should only be attempted in the tread area. Answer b is not correct because a tire repair should not be attempted in the sidewall of a tire. Answer c is not correct because a tire repair should never be attempted in the sidewall or near the bead of a tire. Answer d is not correct because a tire repair should only be attempted in the tread area.

70. **The correct answer is d.** All of the above are correct. Answer a is correct because if the ride height (suspension height) is not correct, the vehicle could be bottoming out against the jounce (bump) stops when the vehicle hits a bump in the road. Answer b is correct because if the shock absorbers are defective, they may not be able to control the movement of the vehicle when to travel over rises or dips in the road, which can cause the suspension to bottom out on the jounce (bump) stops. Answer c is correct because worn or sagging springs can cause the vehicle to have a lower-than-normal ride height and this can cause the vehicle to strike the jounce (bump) stops more often.

71. **The correct answer is b.** A tire pressure monitoring system warning light that is one and not flashing indicates that the system has detected a tire with low inflation pressure. Answer a is not correct because if there is a fault with the system, the warning lamp will flash and not stay on steady. Answer c is not correct because if there was a fault with a sensor, the warning light will be flashing and not on steady. Answer d is not correct because a tire pressure monitoring system warning light that is one and not flashing indicates that the system has detected a tire with low inflation pressure.

AUTO MAINTENANCE AND
LIGHT REPAIR (G1)

CATEGORY: BRAKES

72. **The correct answer is c.** If the caliper was stuck and not able to move on the left front, it would not be able to provide adequate braking force and therefore could be the cause of the vehicle pulling toward the right during braking. Answer a is not correct because air in the lines would cause a low brake pedal and mushy brake pedal but would not likely be the cause of a pulling condition during hard braking. Answer b is not correct because a stick caliper on the right would cause the right front brake to not work correctly and therefore would likely cause the vehicle to pull toward the left and not toward the right. Answer d is not correct because while misadjusted rear brakes can cause a low brake pedal, they would not likely be the cause of a pulling toward one side during hard braking.

73. **The correct answer is d.** All of the above are correct. Answer a is correct because brake lines should be inspected for leaks. Answer b is correct because brake lines should be inspected for brake kinks. Answer c is correct because brake lines should be inspected for rust.

74. **The correct answer is b.** The usual torque specified for passenger vehicle lug nuts is 80–100 Lb.-Ft. Answers a (60–70 Lb.-Ft.), c (110–150 Lb.-Ft.), and d (160–180 Lb.-Ft.) are not correct because they are not within the range of normal torque specifications.

75. **The correct answer is b.** On a vehicle equipped with a front disc brakes and rear drum brakes, the rear drum brakes are used as the parking brake. If the rear brakes are properly adjusted, then the parking brake will not be properly adjusted. Therefore vehicle manufacturers specify that the rear brakes be adjusted before the parking brake is adjusted. Often after adjusting the rear brakes, the parking brake works as designed without further adjustment. Answer a is not correct; even though the thickness of the front disc brake pads is important, the parking brake does not use the front disc brakes. Answer c is not correct because while the brake fluid level is important, the parking brake adjustment is not affected by the level of the brake fluid. Answer d is not correct because only answer b is correct and the others are not correct.

76. **The correct answer is c.** On a vehicle equipped with a floating or sliding caliper-type disc brakes, if the slides or guide pins do not move, then the one pad will wear more than the other (usually the inboard pad). Answer a is not correct because one pad worn more than the other is not normal even though it may be normal for the caliper to be fixed on a fixed-type caliper design. Answer b is not correct because if the caliper piston was stuck in the bore of the caliper, no braking forces would be applied to the brake pads and therefore the pads would not wear at all, let alone only on one side. Answer d is not correct because a leaking caliper dust shield may cause the brakes to grab if brake fluid got on the pads, but this could not cause the caliper to be stuck nor cause one brake pad to wear more than the other.

77. **The correct answer is a.** The maximum allowable thickness variation of a disc brake rotor is a half of one-thousandth of inch or 0.0005. Answers b, c, and d are not correct because they are not a half of a thousandth of an inch.

78. **The correct answer is d.** Any of the above is correct which depends on the make, model, and year of vehicle. Domestic and Asian brands of vehicles often specify DOT 3 brake fluid, whereas European vehicle manufacturers often specify DOT 4, DOT 4+, or DOT 4 LV (low viscosity). Answer a is correct because most domestic and Asian vehicle manufacturers specify DOT 3 brake fluid for use in their vehicles. Answer b is correct because European vehicle manufacturers often specify DOT 4 brake fluid. Answer c is correct because European vehicle manufacturers often specify DOT 4+ or DOT 4 LV brake fluid be used in their vehicles.

79. **The correct answer is c.** Most vehicle manufacturers recommend that silicone brake grease be used to lubricate disc brake caliper slides. This type of grease does not react with the rubber used in the O-rings or dust boots. Answer a is not correct because wheel bearing grease is not specified by vehicle manufacturers for use with disc brake caliper slides and it may cause swelling of the rubber used in O-rings and sealing boots. Answer b is not correct because chassis grease is not specified by vehicle manufacturers for use with disc brake caliper slides and it may cause swelling of the rubber used in O-rings and sealing boots. Answer d is not correct because only silicone brake grease is the only lubricant of those listed that is specified for use by vehicle manufacturers on disc brake guide pins.

80. **The correct answer is b.** The brake pedal should be depressed several times after replacing disc brake pads to force the pads against the rotors. Answer a is not correct because, while these may be some clearance between the piston and the back of the disc brake pad, the major reason for depressing the brake pedal is to move the pads against the rotor. Answers c and d are not correct because bedding the disc brake pads involves driving the vehicle and this is performed after the brake pedal has been depressed several times to force the pads against the rotors then the vehicle can be driven to begin the bedding (breaking in) process.

81. **The correct answer is c.** Both technicians are correct. Technician A is correct because to test a vacuum booster, the vacuum needs to be depleted from the booster which normally requires that the brake pedal be depressed several times and then the pedal depressed and held down when the engine is started. If the booster is working as designed, the brake pedal should drop when the engine is started. Technician B is correct because a working vacuum booster should be able to supply two or three assisted brake applications after the engine has stopped running. Answers a, b, and d are not correct because both technicians are correct.

82. **The correct answer is b.** The most likely cause of a low brake pedal after the installation of a replacement master cylinder is that there is still air trapped inside the master cylinder. This is why vehicle manufacturers recommend that the master cylinder be held on a bench before being installed on the vehicle to make sure that no air is trapped in the passages of the master cylinder. Answer a is not correct because overfilling the master cylinder reservoir will not have any effect on the brake application even though it may cause brake fluid to leak out of the reservoir. Answer c is not correct because, even though misadjusted rear drum brake can cause a lower-than-normal brake pedal, it is not the most likely cause of a low brake pedal after the installation of a master cylinder. Answer d is not correct because, even though misadjusted brake pedal can cause a lower-than-normal brake pedal, it is not the most likely cause of a low brake pedal after the installation of a master cylinder.

83. **The correct answer is a.** There are six brake shoe pads on each backing plate, with three for each of the two brake shoes. Answers b, c, and d are not correct because there are six and not 4 (answer b), 2 (answer c), or 8 or more (answer d).

84. **The correct answer is b.** If the red brake warning light is on, this indicates that there is a hydraulic failure in the system or the parking brake is applied. For safety, the cause of the warning light should be determined and corrected before test-driving the vehicle. Answer a is not correct because if the amber ABS warning light is on, this indicates a fault with the ABS system and therefore the base brakes should operate normally making it safe to drive the vehicle. Answer c is not correct because the red braking warning light will come on if the brake fluid is below the minimum level, not below the maximum level. Answer d is not correct because only answer b is correct.

85. **The correct answer is c.** Parking brake cables that are swollen indicates that the steel cable inside has rusted and expanded. The rust will often prevent the parking brake cable to move and therefore will require to be replaced to restore proper parking brake operation. Answer a is not correct because while misadjusted rear drum brakes can be the cause of the parking brake not holding a vehicle stationary, it would not be the cause of swollen parking brake cable. Answer b is not correct because while a misadjusted parking brake cable could be the cause of a parking brake not holding a vehicle, it would not explain why the parking brake cable is swollen. Answer d is not correct because a parking pawl is part of an automatic transmission/transaxle and not part of a parking braking system.

86. **The correct answer is b.** The burnishing in (bedding in or breaking in) of new disc brake pads includes braking moderately from about 50 MPH (80 km/h) until the vehicle speed reaches 20 MPH (32 km/h) and repeat several times. Answer a is not correct because the stops need to be moderately hard to create the heat needed to cure the pads and to produce a layer of friction material to the rotor (called the transfer layer). Answer c is not correct because the stops need to be moderately hard to create the heat needed to cure the pads. Answer d is not correct because performing just one hard braking from highway speed is not the specified method used to burnish in new disc brake pads.

87. **The correct answer is c.** Most vehicle manufacturers specify that 0.030 inch be left to allow for wear before the brake drum reaches the discard dimension. Answer a is not correct because the discard dimension is the size of the drum that requires that it be discarded and therefore it should not be used in further service. Answer b is not correct because the maximum ID measurement is the inside diameter that is allowed and therefore it should not be used in further service. Answer d is not correct because only answer c is correct.

88. **The correct answer is c.** Both technicians are correct. Technician A is correct because the red brake warning lamp will come on if the parking brake is applied. Technician B is correct because the red braking warning light will come on if the brake fluid is below the minimum level on most vehicles. Answers a, b, and d are not correct because both technicians are correct.

89. **The correct answer is a.** Brake fluid can absorb moisture directly from the air, so it is important to keep it stored in a sealed container. Answer b is not correct because, even though brake fluid can be stored in a glass container with a screw top lid, keeping it in its original container is best to help avoid contamination. Answer c is not correct because brake fluid needs to be kept in a sealed container and not left open where it could be exposed to the air. Answer d is not correct because, while it can and should be kept in its original container, it does not have to be kept in a refrigerator to keep the temperature of the fluid low.

90. **The correct answer is d.** The minimum vacuum needed for the vacuum booster to function correctly is 15 inches of mercury (in. Hg.) Answers a, b, and c are not correct because most vehicle manufacturers specify that the vacuum should be at least 15 in. Hg.

91. **The correct answer is c.** Before the brake pedal is applied, there is vacuum on both sides of the internal diaphragm. When the brake pedal is depressed, air enters the rear (passenger compartment side) of the vacuum booster where the pressure then exerts a force against the internal diaphragm. The internal diaphragm is mechanically connected to the input shaft of the master cylinder and as a result, this action reduces the driver's effort during braking. Answer a is not correct because there is vacuum applied to both sides of the internal diaphragm before the brake pedal is depressed. Answer b is not correct because there is vacuum applied to both sides of the internal diaphragm before the brake pedal is depressed. Answer d is not correct because there is vacuum applied to both sides of the internal diaphragm before the brake pedal is depressed and the air valve is used to allow outside air pressure into the rear chamber of the booster assembly.

92. **The correct answer is b.** The longer lining is the lining that does the most work and therefore is the one toward the rear on a dual (Duo) servo drum brake. Answer a is not correct because the longer lining needs to be at the rear (not front) position in order to provide the braking forces needed. Answer c is not correct because the longer lining needs to be at the rear (not front) position in order to provide the braking forces needed. Answer d is not correct because while this may apply to some drum brakes, many drum brakes use front entry and rear entry parking brake cable making this identification not accurate in all cases.

93. **The correct answer is d.** All of the above are correct. Answer a is correct because brake lines should be inspected for leaks. Answer b is correct because brake lines should be inspected for brake kinks. Answer c is correct because brake lines should be inspected for rust.

AUTO MAINTENANCE AND
LIGHT REPAIR (G1)

CATEGORY: ELECTRICAL

94. **The correct answer is c.** Both technicians are correct. Technician A is correct because to test the voltage drop of the positive battery cable, one meter lead needs to be connected to the most positive part of the circuit, which is at the positive battery terminal. Then the other meter lead needs to be attached to the battery stud of the starter. Technician B is correct because resistance (voltage drop) is only effective when current flows, so the engine needs to be cranked using the starter to measure the voltage drop of the battery-to-starter cable. Answers a, b, and d are not correct because both technicians are correct.

95. **The correct answer is d.** Either a or b is correct. Answer a is correct because to measure current flow (amperes) in a circuit, the current needs to run through the meter and this means connecting the meter leads in series in the circuit. Answer b is correct because an inductive ammeter uses a sensor built into the clamp that measures the current in the wire by measuring the strength of the magnetic field that surrounds any wire carrying a current. Answer c is not correct because the meter fuse would blow because the meter  set on DCA is a low resistance path and current would flow directly from the positive terminal to the negative terminal of the battery.

96. **The correct answer is a.** The last connection should be the on the engine itself or the body away from the battery because a spark often occurs when the last connection is made and this spark could ignite the hydrogen gas given off of the battery when the connection is made. Answers b, c, and d are not correct because the connection is close to the battery and a spark could cause the hydrogen gas to catch fire or cause the battery to explode.

97. **The correct answer is b.** It is normal for the air bag warning lamp to flash when the vehicle is started as part of the system self-test. Answer a is not correct because if there was a fault detected in the system, the air bag warning lamp would light after and stay on after the self-test. Answer c is not correct because the flashing and then going out is normal and does not indicate a fault or a need for any service procedures to be performed on the system. Answer d is not correct because the flashing of the air bag warning lamp at engine start and then going out is a normal operation for all vehicles equipped with an air bag system.

98. **The correct answer is a.** To prevent a possible spark and personal injury, the battery should be disconnected before performing any service work that requires the main battery cables be disconnected. Answer b is not correct because the negative cable, not the positive cable, should be disconnected. If a wrench were to touch the body of the vehicle when removing the positive battery cable from the battery, a spark would likely occur but a spark will not occur if the negative battery was being removed. Answer c is not correct because the starter circuit is not usually protected by a fuse. Answer d is not correct because there is no need to disconnect the air bag especially if the negative battery cable has been removed from the battery.

99. **The correct answer is c.** Both technicians are correct. Technician A is correct because if the alternator drive belt was worn, it could be slipping especially under a heavy electrical load and therefore not charge enough to meet the output specifications. Technician B is correct because if the drive belt tensioner was faulty, then the alternator drive belt could slip and cause the alternator to not be able to produce its rated output. Answers a, b, and d are not correct because both technicians are correct.

100. **The correct answer is d.** Any of the above is correct. Answer a is correct because HID headlights do use high voltage so the wise service technician should read, understand, and follow all safety instructions that pertain to this type of headlight system. Answer b is correct because the oil on your hands can cause the glass part of the bulb to expand at different rates and often cause the bulb to have a short service life. Answer c is correct because the same trade number of bulb should always be used because the trade number determines the size as well as the brightness of the bulb which match the original bulb.

101. **The correct answer is c.** Both technicians are correct. Technician A is correct because the memory can be kept alive by connecting a 9-volt or a 12-volt battery to the lighter plug on many vehicles. Then when the battery is disconnected, the battery connected to the lighter plug will be used to keep the memory functions from being lost. Technician B is correct because there is a chassis ground (terminal #4) and power (terminal #16) available to the data link connector (DLC) on all OBD II vehicles since 1996 which can be used to supply battery power to the vehicle when the vehicle's battery is disconnected. Answers a, b, and d are not correct because both technicians are correct.

102. **The correct answer is a.** Many vehicles built by General Motors use a shim between the starter and the engine block. This shim is used to match the gear tooth depth to the engine block to allow for differences when the engine block is machined at the factory. Answer b is not correct because the shim is located between the starter and the engine block and not between the flywheel and the starter. Answer c is not correct because the shim is located between the starter and the engine and not between the engine crankshaft and the flexplate. Answer d is not correct because the shim is located between the starter and the engine only.

103. **The correct answer is a.** To measure voltage drop, the meter needs to be set to read DC volts (DCV). Answer b is not correct because to measure voltage drop, the meter should be set to read voltage and not DC amperage. Answer c is not correct because to measure voltage drop, the meter should be set to read voltage and not AC amperage. Answer d is not correct because to measure voltage drop, the meter should be set to read DC voltage and not AC voltage.

104. **The correct answer is b.** To measure current flow, the meter needs to be set to read DC amperes (DCA). Answer a is not correct because to measure current, the meter should be set to read amperes and not DC voltage (DCV). Answer c is not correct because to measure current in amperes, the meter should be set to read DC amperes and not AC amperes (ACA). Answer d is not correct because to measure current, the meter should be set to read DC amperes and not AC voltage.

105. **The correct answer is a.** The state of charge (SOC) of a battery is usually determined using a hand-held electronic conductance tester or by using a load tester. Answer b is not correct because the resistance of the battery cable cannot be used to determine the SOC of a battery. Answer c is not correct because the voltage being measured with the engine running is the charging system voltage and cannot be used to determine the SOC of a battery. Answer d is not correct because while a scan tool can display the battery voltage, it cannot be used to determine the state-of-charge of the battery.

106. **The correct answer is c.** Only windshield washer fluid should be used in a windshield washer system. Typical windshield wiper fluid contains methanol alcohol to protect the fluid from freezing and also used to help clean the windshield. Answer a is not correct because using distilled water, while it will work when used in areas that do not have freezing weather, it will not help keep the windshield clean and is not recommended for use by vehicle manufacturers. Answer b is not correct because using engine antifreeze will cause smearing of the fluid on the windshield and is not recommended for use by vehicle manufacturers. Answer d is not correct because using clean drinking water, while it will work when used in areas that do not have freezing weather, it will not help keep the windshield clean and is not recommended for use by vehicle manufacturers.

107. The correct answer is b. Typical charging system voltage usually falls within 13 and 15 volts for most vehicles. Answers a, c, and d are not correct because they do not reflect the usual voltage of a charging system.

108. The correct answer is a. High amperage draw and slow starter operation are an indication of a defective starter motor or an engine mechanical fault that is causing the engine to crank slower than normal. Answer b is not correct because high resistance in the battery cable, while it would result in the starter rotating slower than normal, would also tend to decrease the current draw from the battery and not go high as in this case. Answer c is not correct because, while a defective alternator can cause the battery to have a low state-of-charge and cause a slow cranking problem, it cannot be the cause of a starter requiring higher-than-normal current draw. Answer d is not correct because only answer a is correct.

109. The correct answer is a. A light bulb filament often has a resistance, measured at room temperature, of about a 0.5 ohm. However, when the filament has current flowing through it, the resistance increases so that current flow results in a calculated resistance of about 10 times that of the resistance of a filament measured at room temperature. Answer b is not correct because the bulb filament resistance is normal and does not indicate that it is shorted to another filament or to ground. Answer c is not correct because if the filament were electrical open, the resistance would be infinity and the meter reading would show "OL" or over limit. Answer d is not correct because the filament resistance is normal and does not indicate being grounded, which would likely be a much lower resistance reading or zero or almost zero.

AUTO MAINTENANCE AND LIGHT REPAIR (G1)

CATEGORY: HEATING AND AIR CONDITIONING

110. **The correct answer is a.** Vehicle manufacturers specify that the air discharge temperature form an air-conditioning system be measured at the center vents. Answers b, c, and d are not correct because the temperature should be measured at the center vent and not at the driver's side (answer b), defroster vents (answer c), or the passenger side vent (answer d).

111. **The correct answer is d.** All of the above is correct. Answer a is correct because a cabin filter may be located behind the glove compartment inside the vehicle. Answer b is correct because a cabin air filter access may be from under the hood on the passenger side. Answer c is correct because all cabin air filters should be replaced regularly as part of routine vehicle maintenance as specified in service information.

112. **The correct answer is b.** The evaporator drain is located under the vehicle on the passenger side so that condensation due to moist air flowing through a cool evaporator will cause the moisture to condense on the evaporator and then it has a place to flow out of the housing to the ground under the vehicle. Answer a is not correct because while the evaporator case is located behind the glove compartment on the passenger side, the drain from the housing is located under the vehicle. Answer c is not correct because the drain is located at the base of the evaporator housing under the vehicle and not near the AC compressor. Answer d is not correct because the drain is always located under the vehicle on the passenger side.

113. **The correct answer is c.** When refrigerant leaks, the location can often be seen by looking for an oily spot because as the refrigerant leaves, it takes with it some refrigerant oil. The refrigerant escapes into the atmosphere but the refrigerant oil does not and is seen near the location of the leak. Answers a, b, and d are not correct because the refrigerant escapes into the atmosphere and there is nothing left except for an oily film from the refrigerant oil.

114. **The correct answer is c.** Clear water dripping from the condensate drain at the base of the evaporator housing is normal and represents condensed moisture from the air as it passed through the cool evaporator. Answer a is not correct because an evaporator contains a refrigerant and if it was leaking, the refrigerant would be escaped to the atmosphere and would not be seen dripping from the vehicle. Answer b is not correct because if the heater hose were leaking the liquid would be colored due to the antifreeze coolant in the engine cooling system and not be clear water. Answer d is not correct because a blower motor fault would not cause clear water to be seen dripping from underneath the vehicle.

115. **The correct answer is a.** While specifications do vary according to vehicle make, model, and year, most specifications specify that normal discharge air temperature should be 30 degrees lower than the outside (ambient) air temperature. Answers b, c, and d are not correct because the temperature has to be above 32°F (0°C) to prevent freezing of the moisture in the air.

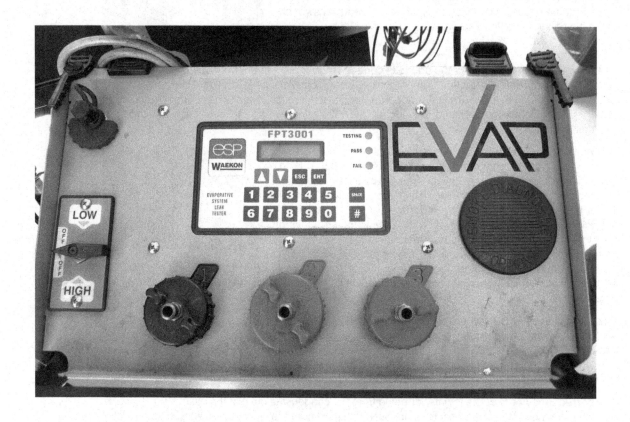

ADVANCED ENGINE PERFORMANCE SPECIALIST CONTENT AREAS

This ASE study guide for Advanced Engine Performance Specialist Test (L1) is divided into the sub-content areas that correlate to the actual ASE certification test as follows:

CONTENT AREA	QUESTIONS IN TEST	NUMBER OF STUDY GUIDE QUESTIONS
A. General Powertrain Diagnosis	6	24 (1–24)
B. Computerized Powertrain Controls Diagnosis (including OBD II)	16	41 (25–65)
C. Ignition System Diagnosis	6	24 (66–89)
D. Fuel Systems and Air Induction Systems Diagnosis	8	25 (90–114)
E. Emission Control Systems Diagnosis	8	26 (115–140)
F. I/M Failure Diagnosis	6	10 (141–150)
Totals	**50**	**150**

TIME ALLOWED TO TAKE THE TEST

The allocated time to take the Engine Repair Certification test is 130 minutes. ASE adds 10 additional questions to the test for research purposes for a total of 60 questions. These questions do not count toward your score but they are embedded within the test and there is no way of knowing which ones do not count. As a result, the technician needs to answer 60 questions in 150 minutes, or about two questions per minutes.

If taking the recertification L1 test, there are just 50 questions with no additional research questions included. The time allocated to take the recertification test is 135 minutes, which means about two minutes per question.

BEFORE USING THIS STUDY GUIDE

Before trying to answer the questions and looking at the explanations, look over the following list of the content that ASE states will be covered in the certification test. For best results using this study guide, check service information or consult an automotive textbook for details on any of the content areas that are not familiar before trying to answer the questions. For additional information about the ASE test, visit the website at **www.ase.com**.

ADVANCED ENGINE PERFORMANCE SPECIALIST (L1) CERTIFICATION TEST

A. GENERAL POWERTRAIN DIAGNOSIS (6 QUESTIONS)

1. Verify customer concern; determine if the concern is the result of a malfunction or normal system operation.
2. Inspect and test for missing, modified, inoperative, or tampered powertrain mechanical components.
3. Locate relevant service information.
4. Research system operation using technical information to determine diagnostic procedure.
5. Use appropriate diagnostic procedures based on available vehicle data and service information; determine if available information is adequate to proceed with effective diagnosis.
6. Determine the relative importance of observed vehicle data.
7. Differentiate between powertrain mechanical and electrical/electronic problems, including variable valve timing (VVT) and variable valve lift (VVL) systems.
8. Diagnose drivability problems and emission failures caused by cooling system problems.
9. Diagnose drivability problems and emission failures caused by engine mechanical problems.
10. Diagnose drivability problems and emission failures caused by problems or modifications in the transmission and final drive, or by incorrect tire size.
11. Diagnose drivability problems and emission failures caused by intake or exhaust system problems or modifications.
12. Determine root cause of failures.
13. Determine root cause of multiple component failures.
14. Determine root cause of repeated component failures.
15. Verify effectiveness of repairs.

B. COMPUTERIZED POWERTRAIN CONTROLS DIAGNOSIS—INCLUDING OBD II (16 QUESTIONS)

1. Verify customer concern; determine if the concern is the result of a malfunction or normal system operation.
2. Inspect and test for missing, modified, inoperative, or tampered computerized powertrain control components.
3. Locate relevant service information.
4. Research system operation using technical information to determine diagnostic procedure.
5. Use appropriate diagnostic procedures based on available vehicle data and service information; determine if available information is adequate to proceed with effective diagnosis.
6. Determine current version of computerized powertrain control system software and updates; perform reprogramming procedures.
7. Research OBD II system operation to determine the enable criteria for setting and clearing diagnostic trouble codes (DTCs) (including permanent DTCs) and malfunction indicator lamp (MIL) operation.
8. Interpret OBD II scan tool data stream, diagnostic trouble codes (DTCs), freeze frame data, system monitors, monitor readiness indicators, and trip and drive cycle information to determine system condition and verify repair effectiveness.
9. Determine the relative importance of displayed scan tool data.
10. Differentiate between electronic powertrain control problems and mechanical problems.
11. Diagnose no-starting, hard starting, stalling, engine misfire, poor drivability, incorrect idle speed, poor idle, hesitation, backfire, surging, spark knock, power loss, reduced fuel economy, illuminated MIL, and emission problems caused by failures of computerized powertrain controls.

12. Diagnose failures in the data communications bus network; determine needed repairs.
13. Diagnose failures in the anti-theft/immobilizer system; determine needed repairs.
14. Perform voltage drop tests on power circuits and ground circuits.
15. Perform current flow tests on system circuits.
16. Perform continuity/resistance tests on system circuits and components.
17. Test input sensor/sensor circuit using scan tool data and/or waveform analysis.
18. Test output actuator/output circuit using scan tool, scan tool data, and/or waveform analysis.
19. Confirm the accuracy of observed scan tool data by directly measuring a system, circuit, or component for the actual value.
20. Test and confirm operation of electrical/electronic circuits not displayed in scan tool data.
21. Determine root cause of failures.
22. Determine root cause of multiple component failures.
23. Determine root cause of repeated component failures.
24. Verify effectiveness of repairs.

C. IGNITION SYSTEM DIAGNOSIS (6 QUESTIONS)

1. Verify customer concern; determine if the concern is the result of a malfunction or normal system operation.
2. Inspect and test for missing, modified, inoperative, or tampered components.
3. Locate relevant service information.
4. Research system operation using technical information to determine diagnostic procedure.
5. Use appropriate diagnostic procedures based on available vehicle data and service information; determine if available information is adequate to proceed with effective diagnosis.
6. Determine the relative importance of displayed scan tool data.
7. Differentiate between ignition electrical/electronic and ignition mechanical problems.
8. Diagnose no-starting, hard starting, stalling, engine misfire, poor drivability, backfire, spark knock, power loss, reduced fuel economy, illuminated MIL, and emission problems caused by failures in the electronic ignition (EI) systems; determine needed repairs.
9. Test for ignition system failures under various engine load conditions.
10. Test ignition system component operation using waveform analysis.
11. Confirm ignition timing and/or spark timing control.
12. Determine root cause of failures.
13. Determine root cause of multiple component failures.
14. Determine root cause of repeated component failures.
15. Verify effectiveness of repairs.

D. FUEL SYSTEMS AND AIR INDUCTION SYSTEMS DIAGNOSIS (8 QUESTIONS)

1. Verify customer concern; determine if the concern is the result of a malfunction or normal system operation.
2. Inspect and test for missing, modified, inoperative, or tampered components.
3. Locate relevant service information.
4. Research system operation using technical information to determine diagnostic procedure.
5. Evaluate the relationships between fuel trim values, oxygen sensor readings, air/fuel ratio sensor readings, and other sensor data to determine fuel system control performance.
6. Use appropriate diagnostic procedures based on available vehicle data and service information; determine if available information is adequate to proceed with effective diagnosis.
7. Determine the relative importance of displayed scan tool data.
8. Differentiate between fuel system mechanical and fuel system electrical/electronic problems.
9. Differentiate between air induction system mechanical and air induction system electrical/electronic problems, including electronic throttle actuator control (TAC) systems.

10. Diagnose hot or cold no-starting, hard starting, stalling, engine misfire, spark knock, poor drivability, incorrect idle speed, poor idle, flooding, hesitation, backfire, surging, power loss, reduced fuel economy, illuminated MIL, and emission problems on vehicles equipped with multiport fuel injection and direct injection fuel systems; determine needed action.

11. Inspect fuel for quality, contamination, water content, and alcohol content; test fuel system pressure and fuel system volume.

12. Evaluate mechanical and electrical operation of fuel injectors and fuel pump (including digitally controlled fuel pump systems).

13. Determine root cause of failures.

14. Determine root cause of multiple component failures.

15. Determine root cause of repeated component failures.

16. Verify effectiveness of repairs.

E. EMISSION CONTROL SYSTEMS DIAGNOSIS (8 QUESTIONS)

1. Verify customer concern; determine if the concern is the result of a malfunction or normal system operation.

2. Inspect and test for missing, modified, inoperative, or tampered components.

3. Locate relevant service information.

4. Research system operation using technical information to determine diagnostic procedure.

5. Use appropriate diagnostic procedures based on available vehicle data and service information; determine if available information is adequate to proceed with effective diagnosis.

6. Determine the relative importance of displayed scan tool data.

7. Differentiate between emission control systems mechanical and electrical/electronic problems.

8. Differentiate between drivability or emissions problems caused by failures in emission control systems and other engine management systems.

9. Perform functional tests on emission control subsystems; determine needed repairs.

10. Determine the effect on exhaust emissions caused by a failure of an emission control component or subsystem.

11. Use exhaust gas analyzer readings to diagnose the failure of an emission control component or subsystem.

12. Diagnose hot or cold no-starting, hard starting, stalling, engine misfire, spark knock, poor drivability, incorrect idle speed, poor idle, flooding, hesitation, backfire, surging, power loss, reduced fuel economy, illuminated MIL, and emission problems caused by a failure of emission control components or subsystems.

13. Determine root cause of failures.

14. Determine root cause of multiple component failures.

15. Determine root cause of repeated component failures.

16. Verify effectiveness of repairs.

F. I/M FAILURE DIAGNOSIS (6 QUESTIONS)

1. Verify customer concern; determine if the concern is the result of a malfunction or normal system operation.

2. Inspect and test for missing, modified, inoperative, or tampered components.

3. Locate relevant service information.

4. Evaluate emission readings obtained during an I/M test to assist in emission failure diagnosis and repair.

5. Evaluate HC, CO, NO_x, CO_2, and O_2 gas readings; determine the failure relationships.

6. Use test instruments to observe, recognize, and interpret electrical/electronic signals.

7. Analyze HC, CO, NO_x, CO_2, and O_2 readings; determine diagnostic test sequence.

8. Diagnose the cause of no-load I/M test HC emission failures.

9. Diagnose the cause of no-load I/M test CO emission failures.

10. Diagnose the cause of loaded-mode I/M test HC emission failures.
11. Diagnose the cause of loaded-mode I/M test CO emission failures.
12. Diagnose the cause of loaded-mode I/M test NO_x emission failures.
13. Evaluate the MIL operation for onboard diagnostic I/M testing.
14. Evaluate monitor readiness status for onboard diagnostic I/M testing.
15. Diagnose communication failures with the vehicle during onboard diagnostic I/M testing.
16. Perform functional I/M tests (including fuel cap test).
17. Verify effectiveness of repairs.

ADVANCED ENGINE PERFORMANCE
SPECIALIST TEST (L1)

CATEGORY: GENERAL POWERTRAIN DIAGNOSIS

1. A port fuel-injected OBD-I equipped V-6 engine with an MAF sensor has a rough idle and no diagnostic trouble codes (DTCs). Technician A says that the wrong PCV valve could have been installed during a previous service. Technician B says that a missing oil filler cap could be the cause. Which technician is correct?

   a. A only
   b. B only
   c. Both A and B
   d. Neither A nor B

2. Service information is available from all of the following *except* the _____.

   a. service manual
   b. owner's manual
   c. electronic service information CDs
   d. factory Web sites

3. Which of the following data stream information is the *least likely* to be helpful during the diagnosis of a hard starting problem?

   a. O2S
   b. ECT
   c. CMP
   d. CKP

4. A DTC P0326 (knock sensor circuit range or performance) is being diagnosed. Technician A says that an engine mechanical fault such as a loose crankshaft harmonic balancer pulley could be the cause. Technician B says that an excessively lean air/fuel mixture could cause excessive knock sensor activity. Which technician is correct?

   a. A only
   b. B only
   c. Both A and B
   d. Neither A nor B

5. A vehicle is being diagnosed that overheats only during city-type driving, yet does not overheat if driven at highway speeds. Technician A says that an inoperative electric cooling fan may be the cause. Technician B says that a partially clogged radiator is the most likely cause. Which technician is correct?

   a. A only
   b. B only
   c. Both A and B
   d. Neither A nor B

6. The coolant temperature gauge on a rear-wheel-drive vehicle indicates that the engine is running hotter than normal, but only after it has been driven at highway speeds for several miles (km). The temperature gauge indicates normal coolant temperature when the vehicle is driven at lower speeds such as in city traffic. Which is the *least likely* cause?

   a. Defective fan clutch
   b. Restricted radiator
   c. Low coolant level
   d. Worn water pump impellers

7. An engine overheats and loses coolant, yet there is no evidence of an external leak. Technician A says that the cooling system should be pressure tested to help find the cause of the coolant loss. Technician B says that a 4- or 5-gas exhaust analyzer can be used to read the hydrocarbons (HC) coming from the radiator fill opening with the engine running to determine whether the head gasket is defective. Which technician is correct?

   a. A only
   b. B only
   c. Both A and B
   d. Neither A nor B

8. A vehicle failed a loaded I/M emission test for excessive NO_x and experiences spark knock (also called ping or detonation) during acceleration. Which is the *least likely* cause?

   a. Partially clogged radiator
   b. Lean air/fuel mixture
   c. Partially clogged catalytic converter
   d. Carbon deposits in the cylinder

9. The owner of a sport utility vehicle installed larger wheels and tires than specified. Technician A says that the vehicle will likely accelerate slower than before the change. Technician B says that the fuel economy (gas mileage) will be calculated as being lower than before the change. Which technician is correct?

   a. A only
   b. B only
   c. Both A and B
   d. Neither A nor B

10. The owner of a vehicle equipped with a positive backpressure-type EGR valve system installs a low restriction exhaust system. What is the *most likely* result?

   a. Reduced performance and fuel economy
   b. Possible spark knock and increased NO_x exhaust emissions
   c. Rough idle and possible excessive CO exhaust emissions
   d. Reduced performance and possible excessive HC exhaust emissions

11. The temperature gauge on a vehicle was starting to read into the red (danger) zone. An inspection of the engine indicated that the serpentine belt was loose. What is *most likely* to be the root cause of the problem?

   a. A defective belt
   b. An incorrect water pump
   c. A clogged radiator
   d. A broken belt tensioner spring

12. The air pump switching valves were discovered to have melted due to excessive heat. Which is the *most likely* root cause?

   a. A loose AIR pump drive belt
   b. A broken one-way exhaust check valve
   c. An EGR valve that is stuck open
   d. A cracked exhaust manifold

13. An engine has had repeated oil pump failures. Each time the oil pickup screen is covered with silicone sealer restricting the flow of oil. What is the *most likely* root cause of this repeated component failure?

 a. The use of the wrong RTV sealer on the gaskets
 b. The use of too much RTV sealer
 c. Defective intake manifold gaskets that are being distorted by gasoline and the parts are falling into the oil pan
 d. The use of the wrong type of engine oil, which is dissolving the RTV sealer

14. A broken valve spring is suspected. Which tests could best detect a broken valve spring?

 a. Running compression; cranking vacuum
 b. Running compression; running vacuum
 c. Cranking compression; cranking vacuum
 d. Scope firing lines; cranking vacuum

15. A restricted exhaust system could be best diagnosed by which test?

 a. Vacuum test at idle
 b. Vacuum at 2,500 RPM
 c. Cylinder leak down test
 d. Running compression test

16. An engine starts, and then stalls. If the oxygen sensor is removed, the engine will start and run. What is the *most likely* fault?

 a. Stuck open EGR valve
 b. Defective oxygen sensor
 c. Defective MAP sensor
 d. Clogged exhaust system

17. An engine is not reaching proper operating temperature. What is the *most likely* cause?

 a. A clogged radiator
 b. The cooling fan running all of the time
 c. A defective thermostat
 d. A missing fan shroud

18. An engine runs rough and usually stalls after a cold start. After a few minutes, the engine runs normally. Which is the most likely cause of poor engine operation following a cold start?

 a. A defective or stuck open EGR valve
 b. A clogged PCV valve
 c. A clogged fuel filter
 d. Deposits on the intake valves

19. Service information states that the vehicle is equipped with a thermostat rated at 195°F. The temperature reading on a scan tool indicates that the engine is operating with a coolant temperature of 210°F. Technician A says that the cooling fan is likely to be defective. Technician B says that the cooling system is low on coolant. Which technician is correct?

 a. A only
 b. B only
 c. Both A and B
 d. Neither A nor B

20. A vehicle is tested using paper held close to the tailpipe and it fluctuates at idle. Technician A says that a defective injector or spark plug wire could be the cause. Technician B says that a hole in the exhaust system could be the cause. Which technician is correct?

   a. A only
   b. B only
   c. Both A and B
   d. Neither A nor B

TAIL PIPE

PAPER

21. A vehicle fails the dipstick test (the "oil" flames up when lit). Technician A says that this can cause the engine to run too rich. Technician B says that this can cause a false lean DTC to be set because the gasoline fumes could be drawn into the engine through the PCV system. This extra fuel causes the oxygen sensor to signal the computer to lean the mixture (lean command). Which technician is correct?

   a. A only
   b. B only
   c. Both A and B
   d. Neither A nor B

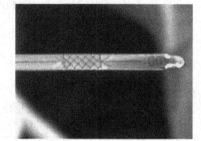

22. After an intake manifold gasket repair, a rough idle with a misfire DTC for cylinders 1, 3, and 5 (rear bank) on a V-6 engine is detected. What is the *most likely* cause?

   a. Defective fuel pressure regulator
   b. Leaking injector O-rings on cylinders 1, 3, and 5
   c. Clogged catalytic converter
   d. One shorted injector

23. An engine cranks, but will not start. Technician A says to check for spark using a spark tester. Technician B says you can check to see if the injectors are being pulsed by using a Noid light. Which technician is correct?

   a. A only
   b. B only
   c. Both A and B
   d. Neither A nor B

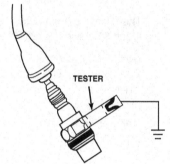

TESTER

24. A P0300 (random misfire) DTC is being diagnosed. What service information is needed to be able to perform an effective diagnosis?

   a. Spark plug wire resistance specifications
   b. VIN
   c. Engine code
   d. All of the above

ADVANCED ENGINE PERFORMANCE
SPECIALIST TEST (L1)

CATEGORY: COMPUTERIZED POWERTRAIN CONTROLS DIAGNOSIS

25. Both upstream oxygen sensors were replaced due to lack of activity (P0134 and P0140). Two weeks later, the same two DTCs were set and again, both oxygen sensors showed little response. Which is the *most likely* root cause of this repeated failure?

    a. Using regular grade instead of premium grade gasoline
    b. A weak fuel pump
    c. The use of the incorrect silicone sealer (RTV) during a previous engine repair
    d. A defective EGR valve (stuck partially open)

26. An EGR valve is being replaced. Which of the following service information items is the *least likely* to be needed to be sure the technician receives the correct replacement part?

    a. The 10th digit of the VIN
    b. The part number from the original part
    c. The 8th digit of the VIN
    d. The 1st digit of the VIN

27. Which item listed is not needed to know for an accurate diagnosis of an engine performance concern?

    a. Gasoline grade being used
    b. When and where the problem occurs
    c. The brand of oil used
    d. Stored or pending DTCs

28. The following scan data were retrieved from a vehicle that had two stored DTCs for low O2S voltage (bank #1 and bank #2). What is the most likely cause based on the following scan tool data?

    HO2S1 = 0.093 V to 0.110 V
    HO2S2 = 0.004 V to 0.209 V
    STFT = +2%
    LTFT = +24%
    MAF = 2.7 g/s
    ECT = 100°C
    IAT = 22°C
    MAP = 1.41 V

    a. A defective fuel pump
    b. A partially clogged PCV valve or hose
    c. Partially clogged EGR ports
    d. An EVAP purge valve stuck open

29. A P0740 (torque converter clutch system problem) DTC is set. The freeze frame indicated the following parameters were present when the DTC was set. What is the *most likely* cause?

Vehicle speed = 50 mph (80 km/h)
ECT = 208°F (98°C)
IAT = 75°F (24°C)
TCC = on
EGR = 43%
Injector pulse width = 8.3 ms
IAC = 67 counts
TP = 1.97 V
Brake switch = off
Transmission gear = 4th (OD)
MAP = 2.48 V
Purge duty cycle = 28%

   a. A worn (defective) torque converter clutch
   b. A defective or misadjusted TP sensor
   c. A defective thermostat
   d. Excessive EGR flow

30. Which scan tool parameter is the most important to check when diagnosing a no-start condition?

   a. ECT
   b. CKP
   c. IAT
   d. HO2S

31. Which scan tool parameter is the most important to check when diagnosing a random misfire DTC (P0300)?

   a. HO2S
   b. Misfire counter
   c. MAF
   d. MAP

32. An engine lacks power and there are no stored DTCs. Which of the following scan tool readings at idle is the *most likely* to indicate the cause?

   a. HO2S1 = 0.088 V to 0.917 V
   b. MAF = 3.8 g/s
   c. Injector pulse width = 3.3 ms
   d. MAP = 2.01 V

33. A vehicle is being diagnosed for a poor fuel economy concern and the MIL light is on. A DTC for the oxygen sensor circuit is the only stored code. Technician A says that the O2S wire connector could be unplugged. Technician B says the O2S could be contaminated. Which technician is correct?

   a. A only
   b. B only
   c. Both A and B
   d. Neither A nor B

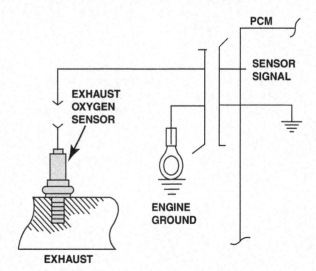

34. An engine equipped with speed density-type port fuel injection is idling faster than normal. The IAC count (%) is 0 (zero). Technician A says that the PCM is commanding the higher idle speed as a result of a signal from the power steering switch or AC compressor. Technician B says that a vacuum leak is a possible cause. Which technician is correct?

   a. A only
   b. B only
   c. Both A and B
   d. Neither A nor B

35. A rough unstable idle is being diagnosed on a port-injected engine. There are no stored DTCs and no other drivability concerns. Technician A says that a dirty throttle plate(s) could be the cause. Technician B says that a clogged fuel filter could be the cause. Which technician is correct?

   a. A only
   b. B only
   c. Both A and B
   d. Neither A nor B

36. A technician is using a DMM set to read DC volts and attaches one test lead to the negative (–) post of the battery and the other lead to the back probed ground terminal of the TP sensor with the key on, engine off. The meter reads 0.55 V. This reading indicates what condition?

   a. TP sensor signal voltage reading
   b. Excessive computer ground voltage drop
   c. A discharged battery
   d. Reference voltage from the PCM

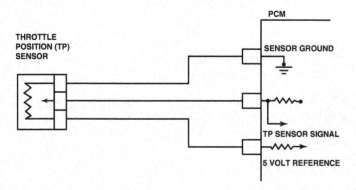

37. A fuel pump circuit is being diagnosed. The battery voltage is 12.6 volts but the voltage at the connector near the pump reads 12.4 volts. What is the *most likely* condition?

   a. A defective fuel pump relay
   b. Corrosion at the connector or wiring
   c. A defective fuel pump
   d. This is a normal reading

38. An electric fuel pump is being measured for the specified current flow. Technician A says that the measurement can be taken by removing the fuel pump relay and connecting the ammeter leads to the specified terminals. Technician B says that a higher than specified current draw could indicate a clogged fuel filter. Which technician is correct?

   a. A only
   b. B only
   c. Both A and B
   d. Neither A nor B

39. Technician A says that an oxygen sensor can be tested using a DMM set to read AC volts. Technician B says that the voltage measured at the signal wire of the oxygen sensor should change range between less than 0.200 V to greater than 0.800 V. Which technician is correct?

    a. A only
    b. B only
    c. Both A and B
    d. Neither A nor B

40. The waveform shown represents which defective sensor?

    a. MAP
    b. TP
    c. HO2S
    d. MAF

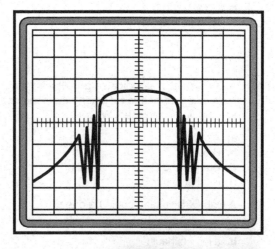

41. An idle concern is being diagnosed. Using a bi-directional scan tool, the technician increases the idle air control counts (percentage) and the idle remains unchanged. Which is the *most likely* cause?

    a. A vacuum leak
    b. A defective IAC
    c. A clogged fuel filter
    d. An inoperative EGR valve

42. A P0401 DTC (exhaust gas recirculation flow insufficient detected) is being diagnosed using a bi-directional scan tool. The technician commands the EGR valve 100% on and the engine speed drops and starts to idle roughly but does not stall. Technician A says that this test shows that the EGR system is functioning and the problem must be with the EGR flow detection sensor (MAP or O2S) circuits. Technician B says that the DTC is likely a false code and should be erased and the vehicle driven to see if the code sets again. Which technician is correct?

    a. A only
    b. B only
    c. Both A and B
    d. Neither A nor B

43. The "hot" dash warning lamp came on during driving and the technician checked the engine coolant temperature (ECT) sensor using a scan tool. The scan tool indicated a coolant temperature of 194°F (90°C). Using an infrared pyrometer, the temperature near the thermostat housing read 239°F (115°C). Technician A says that the ECT sensor is defective. Technician B says that the cooling system may be low on coolant. Which technician is correct?

    a. A only
    b. B only
    c. Both A and B
    d. Neither A nor B

44. A no-start condition is being diagnosed. All scan data with the key on, engine off, indicates all parameters are normal and engine speed is displayed during cranking. Technician A says that the fuel pump relay could be defective. Technician B says that the crankshaft position (CKP) sensor could be defective. Which technician is correct?

    a. A only
    b. B only
    c. Both A and B
    d. Neither A nor B

45. A DTC is set that indicates a fault with the intake air temperature (IAT) sensor circuit. Technician A says that parameters for setting the code should be determined. Technician B says that the IAT sensor should be replaced. Which technician is correct?

    a. A only
    b. B only
    c. Both A and B
    d. Neither A nor B

46. A high O2S voltage could be due to _____.

    a. a rich exhaust
    b. a lean exhaust
    c. a defective spark plug wire
    d. both a and c

47. A low O2S voltage could be due to _____.

    a. a rich exhaust
    b. a lean exhaust
    c. a defective spark plug wire
    d. Both b and c

48. A technician is working on a vehicle equipped with a port fuel injection. After connecting the vehicle to a scan tool, the technician finds it has a long-term fuel trim of +20%. Technician A says that an exhaust leak in front of the oxygen sensor could cause this. Technician B says that a defective plug wire could cause this. Which technician is correct?

    a. A only
    b. B only
    c. Both A and B
    d. Neither A nor B

49. A fuel-injected engine has a long-term fuel trim of +19% at idle and a long-term fuel trim of 0% at 2,500 RPM. What is the *most likely* cause?

    a. A small vacuum leak
    b. A defective MAF
    c. A defective fuel pressure regulator
    d. A faulty IAC

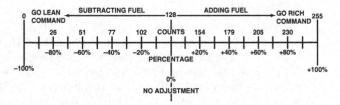

50. The O2S is being tested on a fuel-injected 4-cylinder engine. The reading is relatively steady ranging from 0.388 to 0.460 volts. Adding propane increases the voltage to 0.687 volts and creating a vacuum leak lowers the voltage to 0.312 volts. Technician A says the O2S may be defective. Technician B says there could be a crack in the exhaust manifold allowing outside air to enter the exhaust system upstream from the O2S. Which technician is correct?

  a. A only
  b. B only
  c. Both A and B
  d. Neither A nor B

51. A V-6 engine with a speed density-type fuel injection stalls occasionally. The following scan data were retrieved. Technician A says the engine is operating too lean. Technician B says that the throttle plates may be dirty restricting the amount of air into the engine at idle speed. Which technician is correct?

  a. A only
  b. B only
  c. Both A and B
  d. Neither A nor B

SCAN TOOL DATA			
Engine Coolant Temperature Sensor (EC'T) 195°F (91°C)	Intake Air Temperature Sensor (IAT) 67°F (18°C)	Manifold Absolute Pressure Sensor (MAP) 2.60 volts	Throttle Position (TP) Sensor 0.61 volts
Actual Engine 810 RPM	Desired Engine 725 RPM	Vehicle Speed Sensor (VSS) 0 mph	Battery Voltage (B+) 14.5 volts
Idle Air Control Valve (IAC) 0 Counts	Evaporative Emission Canister Solenoid (EVAP) Off	Torque Converter Clutch Solenoid (TCC) Off	EGR Valve Control Solenoid (EGR) 0%
Malfunction Indicator Lamp (MIL) Off	Diagnostic Trouble Codes None	Open/Closed Loop Closed	Heated Oxygen Sensor (HO₂S) 020-410 mV
Measured Ignition Timing (°BTDC)	Base Timing: 10°	Actual Timing: 10°	

52. A technician is checking for proper EGR valve operation by raising the engine speed to 2,500 RPM and then disconnecting the hose or electrical connector from the EGR valve. The engine speed increased. Which is the *most likely* cause?

  a. Restricted EGR passages
  b. This is normal operation
  c. A bad oxygen sensor, because idle speed should not have increased
  d. The MAP sensor is not properly responding to change in EGR flow

53. A 4-cylinder engine with speed density controlled fuel injection runs rich and the scan tool data indicates that the MAP sensor voltage varies rapidly. Technician A says that an intake manifold gasket leak could be the cause. Technician B says that a skipped timing belt could be the cause. Which technician is correct?

  a. A only
  b. B only
  c. Both A and B
  d. Neither A nor B

54. A 4-cylinder engine is fully warm and an analysis of the scan data indicates a shorter-than-normal injector pulse width and yet a fixed upstream oxygen sensor voltage above 800 mV. There are no stored DTCs. Which is the *most likely* cause?

    a. A bad MAP sensor
    b. A weak fuel pump
    c. A defective fuel pressure regulator
    d. Fouled spark plugs

55. Technician A says the meter is checking for excessive resistance of the connector. Technician B says that the resistance of the ECT sensor signal return circuit is being measured. Which technician is correct?

    a. A only
    b. B only
    c. Both A and B
    d. Neither A nor B

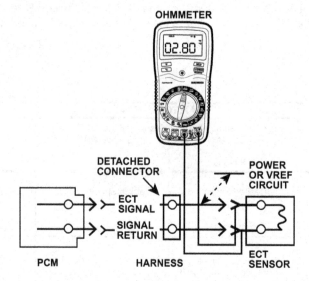

56. A PCM is inoperative and requires replacement. Technician A says that all controlled circuits should be checked for proper resistance before installing the new unit. Technician B says that the ignition key should be in the off position whenever disconnecting or reconnecting the PCM. Which technician is correct?

    a. A only
    b. B only
    c. Both A and B
    d. Neither A nor B

57. An engine equipped with electronic fuel injection and a mass air flow sensor (MAF) hesitates and runs rough while accelerating in forward gears, but accelerates normally while being driven in reverse. What is the *most likely* cause?

    a. An air leak in the air induction system between the MAF and the throttle plate
    b. A defective oxygen sensor(s)
    c. An automatic transmission pressure problem
    d. A clogged exhaust system

58. The downstream AIR one-way check valve is stuck open. Technician A says that the oxygen sensor voltage reading will be constantly low. Technician B says that the engine may be operating richer than normal. Which technician is correct?

    a. A only
    b. B only
    c. Both A and B
    d. Neither A nor B

59. A multiport V-6 engine uses the system where each bank of three injectors is wired in parallel. Each injector has a specification of 12 ohms. An ohmmeter is connected across the circuit for each bank and one bank reads 4.0 ohms and the other bank reads 2.9 ohms. What is the *most likely* cause?

  a. One open injector
  b. All injectors are shorted
  c. All injectors are OK
  d. One injector is shorted

60. The following DTC was retrieved from a vehicle: P0107 (MAP sensor low voltage). Technician A says that a short-to-ground at terminal "a" of the MAP sensor could be the cause. Technician B says that a short-to-ground at terminal #50 at the ECM could be the cause. Which technician is correct?
  You will need to refer to the L1 Composite Vehicle Reference Booklet for this question.

  a. A only
  b. B only
  c. Both A and B
  d. Neither A nor B

61. The automatic transmission will not go into reverse. The transmission works in all other gear positions. Technician A says that an open at terminal #348 could be the cause. Technician B says that a blown #40 fuse could be the cause. Which technician is correct?
  You will need to refer to the L1 Composite Vehicle Reference Booklet for this question.

  a. A only
  b. B only
  c. Both A and B
  d. Neither A nor B

62. The generator (alternator) does not charge. With the engine running, the technician used a DMM set to DC volts and tested the voltage at terminal #101 of the ECM. The voltage was 0 V DC. Technician A says the generator (alternator) is defective. Technician B says that the PCM is defective. Which technician is correct?
  You will need to refer to the L1 Composite Vehicle Reference Booklet for this question.

  a. A only
  b. B only
  c. Both A and B
  d. Neither A nor B

63. The air-conditioning system does not cool the inside of the vehicle and the MIL is on. The retrieved codes indicate that the AFR sensor 1, bank one had a heater circuit problem. Technician A says that a blown fuse #20 could be the cause. Technician B says that an open at terminal #151 could be the cause. Which technician is correct?
  You will need to refer to the L1 Composite Vehicle Reference Booklet for this question.

  a. A only
  b. B only
  c. Both A and B
  d. Neither A nor B

64. A technician is diagnosing an engine with multiple DTCs including low voltage output from the TP, MAP, and fuel tank pressure sensors. An analysis of the service information indicates that all three sensors share the same 5-volt reference from the ECM. Technician A says that the ECM may be defective. Technician B says that one of the three sensors could be shorted to ground. Which technician is correct?
  You will need to refer to the L1 Composite Vehicle Reference Booklet for this question.

  a. A only
  b. B only
  c. Both A and B
  d. Neither A nor B

65. A DTC P0300 (random misfire detected) is being diagnosed. Technician A says that a leaking intake manifold gasket could be the cause. Technician B says clogged EGR ports could be the cause. Which technician is correct?

  a. A only
  b. B only
  c. Both A and B
  d. Neither A nor B

ADVANCED ENGINE PERFORMANCE
SPECIALIST TEST (L1)

CATEGORY: IGNITION SYSTEM DIAGNOSIS

66. An engine miss is being diagnosed. One spark plug was discovered to be excessively worn and snow white while the others appear slightly worn and normal color. What is the *most likely* cause?

    a. A vacuum leak
    b. A loose spark plug
    c. A defective fuel pressure regulator
    d. A partially stuck open EGR valve

67. Where is the spark plug gap specification found on most vehicles?

    a. On the underhood decal
    b. In the owner's manual
    c. In the service manual (information)
    d. All of the above

68. Spark plugs with the incorrect heat range were accidentally installed in an engine during routine service. What is the *most likely* result?

    a. Low idle
    b. Missing or spark knock
    c. Hard starting when cold
    d. Hard starting when hot

69. A poor fuel economy concern was being diagnosed on a V-6 engine equipped with a waste-spark-type electronic ignition (EI). The service technician discovered that three of the six spark plugs had worn center electrodes and the other three had worn side electrodes. What is the *most likely* cause of this wear pattern?

    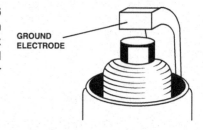

    GROUND ELECTRODE

    a. The plugs that had the worn side electrodes were not tightened enough when they were installed
    b. The plugs that had the worn center electrodes were the wrong heat range plugs
    c. The wires were installed incorrectly at the coils
    d. This is normal operation

70. An engine miss is being diagnosed on an engine equipped with a waste-spark-type electronic ignition (EI). Each plug wire is removed from the spark plug and a spark tester is installed one at a time, and then the engine is started. All but one of the cylinders fires the spark tester. Technician A says that the ignition module is the most likely cause. Technician B says that the coil is the most likely cause. Which technician is correct?

    a. A only
    b. B only
    c. Both A and B
    d. Neither A nor B

71. The spark plug wires on a waste-spark-type electronic ignition were accidentally installed on the wrong terminal of the correct coil. The wire going to cylinder number 3, for example, was accidentally placed on the coil terminal to cylinder number 6 on a V-6 engine. Which is the *most likely* result?

   a. No change in engine operation will be noticed
   b. The engine will miss and may set a misfire DTC
   c. The engine will spark knock (ping) during acceleration
   d. The engine will run smoothly, but will be sluggish and lack power

72. A lack of power concern is being diagnosed on a fuel-injected V-6 engine equipped with waste-spark electronic ignition (EI). Technician A says that the spark plugs should be checked for condition and wear. Technician B says that the spark plug wire should be checked for damage and proper resistance. Which technician is correct?

   a. A only
   b. B only
   c. Both A and B
   d. Neither A nor B

73. Spark plug wires are being checked for proper resistance using a DMM set to read kiloohms. The factory specification states that the resistance should be less than 10,000 ohms per foot of length. The wire being tested is two feet long. The digital display shows 28 kiloohms. Technician A says the spark plug wire should be replaced. Technician B says the wire is OK. Which technician is correct?

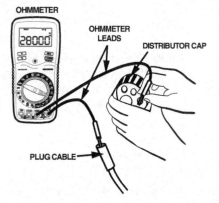

   a. A only
   b. B only
   c. Both A and B
   d. Neither A nor B

74. An open spark plug wire was discovered and replaced on an engine equipped with a distributor ignition (DI). Technician A says that the distributor rotor should be carefully inspected because the bad spark plug wire could have caused a spark to burn through to the distributor shaft. Technician B says the distributor cap should be checked for carbon tracking, which could be caused by the bad spark plug wire. Which technician is correct?

   a. A only
   b. B only
   c. Both A and B
   d. Neither A nor B

75. A no-start condition is being diagnosed on an engine that is equipped with a distributor ignition (DI). Normal spark is available out of the ignition coil, but none of the spark plugs are getting spark. Which is the *most likely* cause?

   a. A defective (open) spark plug wire
   b. A burned through rotor
   c. A tracked distributor cap
   d. Excessively worn spark plugs

76. A vehicle equipped with a distributor ignition (DI) is difficult to start in rainy or damp weather. New spark plugs were installed, yet the problem continues. Technician A says the spark plug wires may be the cause. Technician B says the distributor cap may be the cause. Which technician is correct?

   a. A only
   b. B only
   c. Both A and B
   d. Neither A nor B

77. An engine equipped with a distributor ignition misses under load. Using a regular spark plug connected to one of the spark plug wires with the shell of the plug against the cylinder head and grounded, a blue spark shows while the engine is being cranked. A spark tester was tried and no spark occurred across the electrodes when the engine was cranked. Technician A says the ignition coil could be shorted. Technician B says the problem is most likely not an ignition problem because a spark jumped across the spark plug OK. Which technician is correct?

   a. A only
   b. B only
   c. Both A and B
   d. Neither A nor B

78. A replacement distributor was installed in an engine to solve a no-start condition. The old distributor was carefully marked and the replacement installed in the exact location as the original, but the ignition timing was not checked or adjusted. Now the engine runs, but cranks slowly when the engine is hot. Technician A says the ignition timing could be retarded from specifications. Technician B says that the most likely cause is a defective starter motor. Which technician is correct?

   a. A only
   b. B only
   c. Both A and B
   d. Neither A nor B

79. The ignition timing is being checked on an engine equipped with a distributor ignition (DI). Technician A says that a connector usually needs to be disconnected before the timing can be checked or adjusted. Technician B says that a timing light pickup should be attached to the coil wire to be able to read the timing on all cylinders. Which technician is correct?

   a. A only
   b. B only
   c. Both A and B
   d. Neither A nor B

80. A miss on cylinder number 3 of an engine equipped with coil-on-plug ignition is being diagnosed. The technician selects Hertz (Hz) on a DMM and measures the primary at the coil with the engine running. The meter reads 28 Hz. What does this reading indicate?

   a. The coil is shorted
   b. The PCM is not pulsing the coil primary
   c. The PCM is pulsing the coil primary
   d. The spark plug is fouled or cracked

81. A customer comments that the engine misses when going up a hill or on hard acceleration. When viewing the distributor ignition on a scope, the technician sees that the #5 firing line is about 5 to 6 kV higher than the rest, and the spark line slants down from the firing line to the coil oscillations. What is the *most likely* cause?

   a. A fuel fouled plug on #5
   b. A plug with a closed gap on #5
   c. A high-resistance plug wire on #5
   d. A shorted ignition coil

82. A distributor ignition (DI) is being tested using an ignition scope. The spark duration is short (less than specifications), and the firing voltage is low on all cylinders. What is the *most likely* cause?

   a. The spark plugs have excessive gap
   b. The rotor to distributor air gap is too close
   c. The secondary is shorted between its windings
   d. The primary coil resistance is too low

83. Point B on the secondary ignition scope pattern shown indicates what condition?

   a. The voltage required to ionize the spark plug gap
   b. The total resistance to be overcome in the secondary circuit
   c. The voltage required to maintain the spark
   d. Both a and b

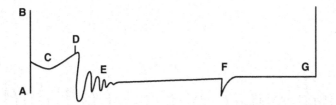

84. An engine has a rough idle condition. The technician checks the spark duration and obtains the following results: (specification = 0.85 to 2.2 ms). What is the *most likely* cause?

   Cylinder #1–0.90 ms   Cylinder #2–1.0 ms
   Cylinder #3–1.1 ms   Cylinder #4–2.4 ms

   a. Cylinder #1 plug has a wide gap
   b. Cylinder #4 plug has a wide gap
   c. Cylinder #4 plug has a narrow gap
   d. Cylinder #1 plug has a narrow gap

85. On a V-6 engine equipped with electronic ignition (waste spark) with a firing order of 123456, what is common about cylinders #6 and #3?

   a. They share the same exhaust manifold
   b. They are side-by-side in the engine
   c. They are directly opposite each other in the engine
   d. They are paired cylinders

86. Two technicians are discussing the cause of a random misfire DTC (P0300) with the scan tool data shown below representing the freeze frame of the condition present when the DTC was set. Technician A says a defective or fouled spark plug could be the cause. Technician B says a shorted ignition coil could be the case. Which technician is correct?

   a. A only
   b. B only
   c. Both A and B
   d. Neither A nor B

SCAN TOOL DATA			
Engine Coolant Temperature Sensor (ECT)	Intake Air Temperature Sensor (IAT)	Manifold Absolute Pressure Sensor (MAP)	Throttle Position (TP) Sensor
201°F (94°C)	86°F (30°C)	1.62 volts	1.45 volts
Actual Engine	Desired Engine	Vehicle Speed Sensor (VSS)	Battery Voltage (B+)
920 RPM	925 RPM	15 mph	14.7 volts
Idle Air Control Valve (IAC)	Evaporative Emission Canister Solenoid (EVAP)	Torque Converter Clutch Solenoid (TCC)	EGR Valve Control Solenoid (EGR)
36 Counts	Off	Off	10%
Malfunction Indicator Lamp (MIL)	Diagnostic Trouble Codes	Open/Closed Loop	Heated Oxygen Sensor (HO$_2$S)
On	P0300	Closed	83-957 mV
Measured Ignition Timing (°BTDC)	Base Timing: 8°		Actual Timing: 8°

87. Technician A says the waveform of the camshaft position (CMP) and crankshaft position (CKP) sensors indicate that the timing belt has been installed with the camshaft a few teeth off. Technician B says that the waveform shows a fault with the crankshaft position (CKP) sensor such as one tooth missing from the reluctor ring. Which technician is correct?

   a. A only
   b. B only
   c. Both A and B
   d. Neither A nor B

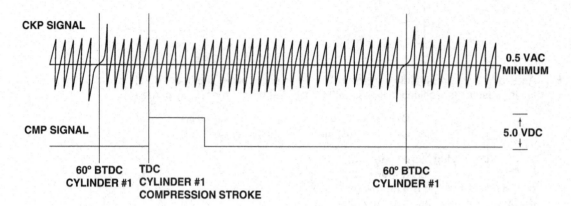

88. The MIL is flashing indicating a severe misfire has been detected by the PCM. Technician A says that a cracked spark plug could be the cause. Technician B says that an open at terminal "b" of ignition coil 6 could be the cause. Which technician is correct?

   a. A only
   b. B only
   c. Both A and B
   d. Neither A nor B

89. A no-start condition is being diagnosed. The engine cranks normally but does not start. Technician A says a short-to-ground at terminal "b" of the camshaft position sensor could be the cause. Technician B says that a blown #4 fuse could be the cause. Which technician is correct?
You will need to refer to the L1 Composite Vehicle Reference Booklet for this question.

   a. A only
   b. B only
   c. Both A and B
   d. Neither A nor B

ADVANCED ENGINE PERFORMANCE
SPECIALIST TEST (L1)

CATEGORY: FUEL SYSTEMS AND AIR INDUCTION SYSTEMS

90. A lack of power is being diagnosed. The following waveform shows the current flow through an electric fuel pump. The speed of the pump motor is 10,000 RPM and the current draw is 5 amperes (specifications are 4 to 7 amperes). Technician A says that the fuel filter may be clogged. Technician B says that the fuel pump should be replaced. Which technician is correct?

a. A only
b. B only
c. Both A and B
d. Neither A nor B

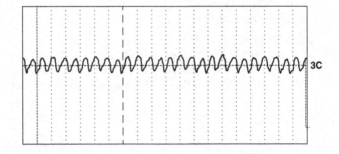

91. During routine service, it was noticed that the air filter was missing. Which other component could directly affect the engine operation as a result of the missing filter?

a. MAF sensor
b. MAP sensor
c. Oxygen sensor
d. IAT sensor

92. A customer complained that the engine spark knocks (pings) during rapid acceleration or when driving up a hill. Which is the *least likely* cause?

a. A missing air cleaner cold air hose
b. Carbon buildup in the combustion chambers
c. Lack of sufficient exhaust gas recirculation (EGR) flow
d. A pinched or restricted fuel return line

93. A lack of power is being diagnosed. The scan tool data (PID) at engine idle includes: Which is the most likely fault?

ECT = 195°F
IAT = 78°F
IAC = 20
MAF = 4.4 g/s
MAP = 1.1 volt
Injector pulse width = 4.5 ms
RPM = 750
Vehicle speed = 0 mph
HO2S1 = 198 mV to 618 mV
HO2S2 = 50 mV to 571 mV

a. Contaminated oxygen sensors
b. A clogged fuel filter or bad fuel pump
c. A bad thermostat
d. A stuck IAC

94. Long-term fuel trim is +2% at idle speed and +27% at 2,500 RPM. Which is the *most likely* cause?

a. A defective fuel pressure regulator
b. An intake manifold leak
c. A weak fuel pump
d. A partially clogged catalytic converter

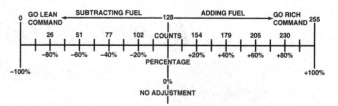

95. A P0132 (O_2 sensor circuit high voltage, bank 1 sensor 1) on a four-cylinder engine is being diagnosed. Technician A says that an intake manifold gasket leak (vacuum leak) could be the cause. Technician B says that a defective fuel pressure regulator could be the cause. Which technician is correct?

a. A only
b. B only
c. Both A and B
d. Neither A nor B

96. A DTC P0101 (MASS or volume airflow circuit range or performance problem) is being diagnosed. Technician A says that a loose connection between the MAF sensor and the throttle body could be the cause. Technician B says the MAF sensor may be defective. Which technician is correct?

a. A only
b. B only
c. Both A and B
d. Neither A nor B

97. An engine equipped with port fuel injection is difficult to start after being off for several minutes. Technician A says that the fuel pressure regulator could be defective. Technician B says that one or more fuel injectors could be leaking. Which technician is correct?

a. A only
b. B only
c. Both A and B
d. Neither A nor B

98. A port fuel injected V-6 engine stalls occasionally and has a rough unstable idle. There are no stored DTCs and there are no other drivability concerns. Which of the following is the *most likely* cause?

a. A weak fuel pump
b. A dirty throttle plate(s)
c. A partially clogged fuel filter
d. A dirty fuel injector

99. A fuel injected vehicle is achieving less-than-normal fuel economy. Which of the following would be the *least likely* cause?

a. A clogged fuel filter
b. A defective fuel pressure regulator
c. A pinched or restricted fuel return line
d. A fuel injector(s) stuck open

100. A lack of power complaint is being diagnosed. The technician attaches a fuel pressure gauge and disconnects and plugs the vacuum line to the fuel pressure regulator and rapidly accelerates the engine. The pressure drops 3 psi. Technician A says that this is normal operation. Technician B says the fuel filter could be clogged. Which technician is correct?

a. A only
b. B only
c. Both A and B
d. Neither A nor B

101. A gasoline sample is being analyzed for excessive alcohol content. A cylinder holding 9 ml of the sample gasoline and 1 ml of water is shaken. The sample turns cloudy. After allowing the sample to sit for several minutes, a line of separation between the gasoline and alcohol appears at a level 3 ml from the bottom. This test indicates what percentage of alcohol is present?

   a. 0%
   b. 10%
   c. 20%
   d. 30%

102. A customer states that premium grade gasoline (91+ octane) has been used in the vehicle instead of the recommended regular grade (87 octane). What is the *most likely* result?

   a. Excessive carbon buildup on intake valves
   b. Burned exhaust valves
   c. Rough idle and possible stall during cold weather starting
   d. Damage to oxygen sensor(s)

103. A vehicle equipped with electronic fuel injection has had three fuel pumps in the last three months. Technician A says that a clogged fuel filter could be the cause. Technician B says that contamination in the fuel tank could be the cause. Which technician is correct?

   a. A only
   b. B only
   c. Both A and B
   d. Neither A nor B

104. A vehicle equipped with TBI-type fuel injection has exhaust gas readings of:

HC = 380 PPM   CO = 0.01% CO_2 = 14.7% O_2 = 1%

What is the *most likely* fault?

   a. The catalytic converter is not working
   b. The fuel pressure regulator is defective
   c. The thermostat is too cold
   d. The IAC counts are too high

105. An engine will not start. A technician unplugs the MAF sensor and the engine starts. The *most likely* cause of the no-start condition was _____.

   a. a defective PROM
   b. a defective TP sensor
   c. a defective MAF sensor
   d. a defective MAP sensor

106. A fuel-injected engine hesitates when accelerated from a stop. Which sensor or system would be the *most likely* cause?

   a. The oxygen sensor
   b. Low cylinder compression
   c. The TP sensor
   d. Excessive exhaust back pressure

107. A fuel pressure test indicates low fuel pump pressure on a port-injected vehicle. The technician closes off the fuel return line and the pump pressure reaches normal maximum pressure. This test indicates _____.

    a. the injectors are leaking down
    b. the regulator is defective
    c. the pump is defective
    d. the oil pressure switch or fuel pump relay is defective

108. When a technician removes the vacuum hose from the fuel pressure regulator on an idling port-injected engine, what should occur?

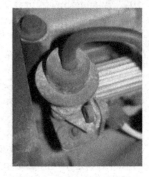

    a. The engine should stumble or stall
    b. The fuel pressure should increase
    c. The fuel pressure should decrease
    d. The engine will greatly increase in speed (RPM)

109. A customer complains of poor performance and lack of power with the following specifications. Technician A says that a weak fuel pump could be the cause. Technician B says a clogged fuel filter could be the cause. Which technician is correct?

    a. A only
    b. B only
    c. Both A and B
    d. Neither A nor B

SCAN TOOL DATA			
Engine Coolant Temperature Sensor (ECT)	Intake Air Temperature Sensor (IAT)	Manifold Absolute Pressure Sensor (MAP)	Throttle Position (TP) Sensor
201°F (94°C)	88°F (31°C)	3.81 volts	3.08 volts
Actual Engine	Desired Engine	Vehicle Speed Sensor (VSS)	Battery Voltage (B+)
1850 RPM	1850 RPM	67 mph	14.8 volts
Idle Air Control Valve (IAC)	Evaporative Emission Canister Solenoid (EVAP)	Torque Converter Clutch Solenoid (TCC)	EGR Valve Control Solenoid (EGR)
151 Counts	On	On	73%
Malfunction Indicator Lamp (MIL)	Diagnostic Trouble Codes	Open/Closed Loop	Heated Oxygen Sensor (HO₂S)
Off	None	Closed	201-654 mV
Measured Ignition Timing (°BTDC)	Base Timing: 13°		Actual Timing: 13°

110. A technician is working on an OBD-II V-8 engine equipped with port fuel injection. After connecting the vehicle to a scan tool, the technician finds it has a long-term fuel trim of + 20% on bank 1. Bank 2 shows 0% fuel trim. Technician A says that an exhaust leak in front of the oxygen sensor on bank 1 could cause this. Technician B says that a defective plug wire on a cylinder on bank 1 could cause this. Which technician is correct?

    a. A only
    b. B only
    c. Both A and B
    d. Neither A nor B

111. A fuel-injected engine has a long-term fuel trim of +18% at idle and a long-term fuel trim of 0% at 2,500 RPM. The *most likely* cause is _____.

    a. a small vacuum leak
    b. a defective MAF
    c. a defective fuel pressure regulator
    d. a faulty IAC

112. The injector pulse width is longer than normal. Technician A says that the engine may be getting extra fuel such as from the charcoal canister. Technician B says that the engine may have a cracked exhaust manifold. Which technician is correct?

    a. A only
    b. B only
    c. Both A and B
    d. Neither A nor B

113. A short-term fuel trim of –2% and a long-term fuel trim of +25% means:

    a. The engine is running lean now
    b. The engine has a history of running rich
    c. The engine has a history of running lean
    d. The engine is running rich now

114. The stock air cleaner assembly was replaced with a cold air induction (CAI) aftermarket device that uses a low restriction air filter. What is the *most likely* result of this change?

    a. A leaner-than-normal air-fuel mixture
    b. A richer-than-normal air-fuel mixture
    c. A louder noise under the hood during acceleration
    d. Both b and c

ADVANCED ENGINE PERFORMANCE
SPECIALIST TEST (L1)

CATEGORY: EMISSION CONTROL SYSTEMS DIAGNOSIS

115. A vehicle has had repeated EGR valve transducer failures. What is the *most likely* cause?

    a. A clogged catalytic converter
    b. A vacuum leak at the intake manifold gasket
    c. A partially clogged fuel injector
    d. Clogged EGR ports

116. The following scan data has been retrieved from a vehicle with a drivability problem.

LTFT = +2% @ idle
LTFT = +22% @ 2500 RPM
P0171 = bank 1 too lean
P0174 = bank 2 too lean

Which system is the *most likely* to be the cause of the problem?

    a. A fault in the exhaust system
    b. A fault in the induction system
    c. A fault in the emission control system
    d. A fault in the fuel delivery system

117. A no-start condition is being investigated. Scan tool data indicates a TP sensor voltage of 5 volts. Which is the *most likely* cause?

    a. 5-volt V ref shorted to signal wire
    b. Open signal wire between TP sensor and PCM
    c. Signal wire shorted to ground
    d. Defective TP sensor

118. A no-start condition is being diagnosed. A check of the 5-volt reference voltage from the PCM indicates 0 volts with key on, engine off. The DTCs include: P0122 (TP sensor voltage low), P0107 (MAP sensor voltage low), and P0452 (fuel tank pressure sensor voltage low). Technician A says that an open 5-volt reference circuit near the PCM could be the cause. Technician B says that a shorted fuel tank pressure sensor could be the cause. Which technician is correct?

    a. A only
    b. B only
    c. Both A and B
    d. Neither A nor B

119. A vehicle fails an enhanced I/M test for excessive NO_x emissions. Technician A says that an excessively lean air-fuel mixture being supplied to the engine could be the cause. Technician B says that a defective cooling fan could be the cause. Which technician is correct?

    a. A only
    b. B only
    c. Both A and B
    d. Neither A nor B

120. A vehicle fails for excessive NO$_x$ emissions during an enhanced I/M test. Technician A says that a clogged EGR port(s) could be the cause. Technician B says that a partially clogged radiator could be the cause. Which technician is correct?

   a. A only
   b. B only
   c. Both A and B
   d. Neither A nor B

121. A vehicle is being repaired for excessive NO$_x$ emissions. Technician A says that a partially clogged PCV valve or hose could be the cause. Technician B says that a defective spark plug wire or worn spark plug could be the cause. Which technician is correct?

   a. A only
   b. B only
   c. Both A and B
   d. Neither A nor B

122. A V-8 engine with a P0171 DTC (bank 1 O2 sensor low voltage) is being diagnosed. Which is the *most likely* cause?

   a. A defective spark plug or spark plug wire
   b. A defective fuel pressure regulator
   c. A leaking injector
   d. A contaminated MAF sensor

123. A P0132 DTC (bank 1 O2 sensor high voltage) is being diagnosed. Which is the *most likely* cause?

   a. A defective spark plug or spark plug wire
   b. A clogged injector
   c. A leaking injector
   d. A contaminated MAF sensor

124. A DTC P0442 (evaporative emission control system leak detected). Which is the *most likely* cause?

   a. A loose gas cap
   b. A clogged PCV hose
   c. A restricted carbon canister purge line
   d. A defective fuel tank pressure sensor

125. A vehicle is being diagnosed for failing an enhanced I/M emission test for excessive CO exhaust emissions. Which is the *most likely* cause?

   a. A clogged EVAP hose
   b. A lack of proper preconditioning
   c. A defective spark plug wire
   d. An inoperative EGR valve

126. Which of the following is the most likely root cause of a lean oxygen sensor signal from both upstream sensors on a V-6 engine?

   a. An open spark plug wire
   b. A contaminated MAF sensor
   c. A fouled spark plug
   d. A clogged fuel injector

127. A problem of spark knock (ping or detonation) is being diagnosed. Technician A says that plugged exhaust ports in the EGR system could be the cause. Technician B says that an empty (gutted) catalytic converter could be the cause. Which technician is correct?

    a. A only
    b. B only
    c. Both A and B
    d. Neither A nor B

128. Two technicians are discussing catalytic converters. Technician A says that a nonworking (chemically poisoned) catalytic converter will test as being clogged during a vacuum or back pressure test. Technician B says that the temperature of the inlet and outlet of the converter can detect if it is working okay. Which technician is correct?

    a. A only
    b. B only
    c. Both A and B
    d. Neither A nor B

129. The engine idle is rough and unstable with the following scan tool data. Technician A says that a partially stuck open EGR valve could be the cause. Technician B says that a defective (stuck open) AIR switching valve could be the cause. Which technician is correct?

    a. A only
    b. B only
    c. Both A and B
    d. Neither A nor B

SCAN TOOL DATA			
Engine Coolant Temperature Sensor (ECT) 212°F (100°C)	Intake Air Temperature Sensor (IAT) 86°F (30°C)	Manifold Absolute Pressure Sensor (MAP) 2.0 volts	Throttle Position (TP) Sensor 0.45 volts
Actual Engine 760 RPM	Desired Engine 790 RPM	Vehicle Speed Sensor (VSS) 0 mph	Battery Voltage (B+) 14.7 volts
Idle Air Control Valve (IAC) 55 Counts	Evaporative Emission Canister Solenoid (EVAP) Off	Torque Converter Clutch Solenoid (TCC) Off	EGR Valve Control Solenoid (EGR) 0.0%
Malfunction Indicator Lamp (MIL) Off	Diagnostic Trouble Codes None	Open/Closed Loop Closed	Heated Oxygen Sensor (HO$_2$S) 401-930 mV
Measured Ignition Timing (°BTDC) Base Timing: 12°		Actual Timing: 12°	

130. A customer complains of poor fuel economy with the following scan tool data. Technician A says that the EGR valve may be stuck partially open. Technician B says that the canister purge diaphragm may have a leak. Which technician is correct?

   a. A only
   b. B only
   c. Both A and B
   d. Neither A nor B

SCAN TOOL DATA			
Engine Coolant Temperature Sensor (ECT) 181°F (83°C)	Intake Air Temperature Sensor (IAT) 100°F (38°C)	Manifold Absolute Pressure Sensor (MAP) 3.80 volts	Throttle Position (TP) Sensor 2.86 volts
Actual Engine 2500 RPM	Desired Engine 2500 RPM	Vehicle Speed Sensor (VSS) 55 mph	Battery Voltage (B+) 14.7 volts
Idle Air Control Valve (IAC) 102 Counts	Evaporative Emission Canister Solenoid (EVAP) On	Torque Converter Clutch Solenoid (TCC) On	EGR Valve Control Solenoid (EGR) 88%
Malfunction Indicator Lamp (MIL) Off	Diagnostic Trouble Codes None	Open/Closed Loop Closed	Heated Oxygen Sensor (HO_2S) 760-950 mV
Measured Ignition Timing (°BTDC)	Base Timing: 10°		Actual Timing: 10°

131. Two technicians are discussing positive crankcase ventilation (PCV) valves. Technician A says that if the valve does not rattle, it is bad. Technician B says the PCV valve may still require replacement even if it does rattle. Which technician is correct?

   a. A only
   b. B only
   c. Both A and B
   d. Neither A nor B

132. Technician A says that a defective one-way exhaust check valve could cause the air pump to fail. Technician B says that the airflow should stop flowing to the exhaust manifold when the engine is warm (closed loop operation). Which technician is correct?

   a. A only
   b. B only
   c. Both A and B
   d. Neither A nor B

133. Technician A says that overfilling the fuel tank can cause the carbon canister to become saturated with gasoline. Technician B says that nitrogen under 14 inches of water pressure is usually applied to the EVAP system during I/M testing or leak testing. Which technician is correct?

   a. A only
   b. B only
   c. Both A and B
   d. Neither A nor B

134. Technician A says that electronic EGR valves can often be opened using a scan tool. Technician B says a positive backpressure-type EGR valve should be tested using a vacuum pump with the engine running. Which technician is correct?

a. A only
b. B only
c. Both A and B
d. Neither A nor B

135. Technician A says that a partially clogged EGR passage can cause the vehicle to fail due to excessive NO_x emissions. Technician B says the vehicle could fail for excessive CO if the EGR passages were clogged. Which technician is correct?

a. A only
b. B only
c. Both A and B
d. Neither A nor B

136. Technician A says the catalytic converter must be replaced if it rattles when tapped. Technician B says a catalytic converter can be defective and not be working yet not be clogged. Which technician is correct?

a. A only
b. B only
c. Both A and B
d. Neither A nor B

137. Used catalytic converters must be kept for possible inspection by the EPA for how long?

a. 30 days
b. 60 days
c. 90 days
d. 6 months

138. Which exhaust emission control device reduces the amount of NO_x produced by the engine?

a. PCV
b. Air pump
c. Charcoal canister
d. EGR

139. Which exhaust control device requires that the air-fuel mixture being supplied to the engine alternate between rich and lean?

a. PCV
b. Carbon (charcoal) canister
c. Catalytic converter
d. EGR

140. Two technicians are discussing a vehicle problem of a rough idle. Technician A says that a fault in the PCV system could be the cause. Technician B says that a partially open EGR valve could be the cause. Which technician is correct?

a. A only
b. B only
c. Both A and B
d. Neither A nor B

ADVANCED ENGINE PERFORMANCE
SPECIALIST TEST (L1)

CATEGORY: I/M FAILURE DIAGNOSIS

141. An engine has been diagnosed with a defective cooling system thermostat because it never gets up to operating temperature. Technician A says that this will result in excessive HC exhaust emissions. Technician B says that this means that there will be excessive NO_X exhaust emissions. Which technician is correct?

    a. A only
    b. B only
    c. Both A and B
    d. Neither A nor B

142. Two technicians are discussing the results of an exhaust emission test. While all of the gases were below the maximum allowed, it was noticed that the CO and O_2 readings were the same. Technician A says that this means that the engine is operating too rich. Technician B says that this means that there may be an ignition misfire fault. Which technician is correct?

    a. A only
    b. B only
    c. Both A and B
    d. Neither A nor B

143. A vehicle failed an exhaust emissions test due to excessive NO_X emissions. All of the other exhaust gases were normal. What is the *most likely* cause?

    a. A fault with the EGR system
    b. Rich air-fuel mixture
    c. An ignition misfire
    d. A clogged catalytic converter

144. A vehicle failed an exhaust emissions test due to excessive CO emissions. All of the other exhaust gases were normal. What is the *most likely* cause?

    a. A fault with the EGR system
    b. Rich air-fuel mixture
    c. An ignition misfire
    d. A partially clogged catalytic converter

145. A vehicle failed an emission test for excessive HC and CO. What is the *most likely* cause?

    a. A fault with the EGR system
    b. Rich air-fuel mixture
    c. An ignition misfire
    d. A partially clogged catalytic converter

146. A vehicle failed an exhaust emission test for excessive HC emissions. The exhaust readings for CO and CO_2 are lower than normal and the readings for O_2 and HC are higher than normal. What is the *most likely* cause?

    a. Lean misfire
    b. Rich exhaust
    c. Clogged EGR ports
    d. Partially clogged air filter

147. A vehicle failed an exhaust emissions test due to excessive HC emissions. All of the other exhaust gases were normal. What is the *most likely* cause?

   a. Rich air-fuel mixture
   b. Lean air-fuel mixture
   c. An ignition misfire
   d. A clogged catalytic converter

148. An inspection and maintenance (I/M) program includes_____.

   a. a check of the exhaust gases
   b. an inspection of the gas cap
   c. a visual check to insure that all emission control devices are in place and not disabled
   d. all of the above

149. The following exhaust emissions were measured during a loaded-mode I/M test:

HC: 15 ppm
CO: 1.3 %
NO_X: 55 ppm
CO_2: 12.7%
O_2: 0.3%

Technician A says that this indicates excessive HC exhaust emissions. Technician B says that this means that there are excessive NO_X exhaust emissions. Which technician is correct?

   a. A only
   b. B only
   c. Both A and B
   d. Neither A nor B

150. An exhaust emission test results showed excessively high O_2 readings yet passed for all gases that were regulated. What is the *most likely* cause of the excessively high O_2 reading?

   a. A missing air filter
   b. A fouled spark plug
   c. A hole in the exhaust
   d. A stuck open fuel injector

ADVANCED ENGINE PERFORMANCE
SPECIALIST TEST (L1)

CATEGORY: GENERAL POWERTRAIN DIAGNOSIS

1. **The correct answer is c.** Both technicians are correct. Technician A is correct because if the wrong PCV valve is used, too much or too little air will be drawn through the crankcase ventilation system resulting in an incorrect or variable air-fuel mixture. About 20% of the air needed by the engine flows through the PCV system. Oxygen sensor input and fuel trim is often not a correcting factor on many vehicles equipped with OBD-I. Technician B is correct because the extra air being drawn into the closed system through the open oil filler cap is air not being measured by the MAF sensor and will, therefore, cause the air-fuel mixture to be too lean for normal engine operation. Answers a, b, and d are not correct because both technicians are correct.

2. **The correct answer is b.** This is an "except"-type of question and service information is available from all except the owner's manual, even though it may contain some specifications and other important information. Answer a is not correct because the service manual is the primary source of service information for many vehicles. Answer c is not correct because electronic information is a major source of service information for many vehicles. Answer d is not correct because many vehicle manufacturers now have service information on secure Web sites.

3. **The correct answer is a.** The oxygen sensor is not an effective input sensor until the engine has been running long enough to heat the sensor to about 600°F (315°C) and is therefore not likely to be the cause of hard starting problems. Answer b is not correct because the engine coolant temperature (ECT) is a major input as to the fuel mixture needed by the engine during a cold start. Answer c is not correct because the camshaft position (CMP) sensor is used by the PCM to trigger the fuel injection pulses on many engines and is therefore important for the normal starting of a fuel-injected engine. Answer d is not correct because the crankshaft position  (CKP) sensor is a major input to the PCM during cranking and represents engine speed (RPM). A fault with this sensor will definitely cause a starting problem. Answers b, c, and d are not correct because all of these sensors are important and could affect the starting of the engine.

4. **The correct answer is c.** Both technicians are correct. Technician A is correct because a loose harmonic balancer pulley could create a vibration that is interpreted by the PCM as engine detonation. The knock sensor would signal the PCM to retard ignition timing, but because the vibration is not actually caused by detonation, the vibration continues and thereby triggers the KS DTC. Technician B is correct because an excessively lean air-fuel mixture can cause engine detonation, and even though the ignition timing would be retarded, it may not be enough to reduce the detonation and thereby trigger the knock sensor DTC. Answers a, b, and d are not correct because both technicians are correct.

5. **The correct answer is a.** Technician A only is correct because the vehicle only overheats during slow speed driving when airflow through the radiator is reduced. At higher vehicle speeds, there is enough airflow through the radiator to provide for proper engine cooling. Answer b is not correct because a partially clogged radiator is more likely to cause the engine to overheat while driving at highway speed where greater coolant flow is occurring due to increased engine speed. Answers c and d are not correct because only Technician A is correct.

6. **The correct answer is a.** The least likely cause of overheating at highway speeds only would be a defective fan clutch. Airflow through the radiator at highway speeds should be enough to provide for sufficient cooling. Answers b, c, and d are not correct because all three could be reasons why the engine can overheat at highway speeds when coolant flow is higher than during slow speed driving.

7. **The correct answer is c.** Both technicians are correct. Technician A is correct because a pressure test can often locate engine coolant leaks that are overlooked or cannot be observed during a routine visual inspection. Technician B is correct because if unburned hydrocarbons (HC) are measured from the radiator fill opening, combustion gases must be getting into the cooling system. A defective head gasket is the most likely cause. Answers a, b, and d are not correct because both technicians are correct.

8. **The correct answer is c.** A partially clogged catalytic converter is not likely to cause excessive NO_x exhaust emissions because the increased backpressure would tend to decrease engine vacuum, which in turn would tend to enrich the air-fuel mixture, thereby reducing the tendency to create excessive NO_x exhaust emissions. Excessive NO_x emissions are usually caused by a hot or lean running engine. Answer a is not correct because a partially clogged radiator could cause the engine to run hotter than normal and therefore be likely to create excessive NO_x exhaust emissions. Answer b is not correct because a lean air-fuel mixture tends to burn hotter than normal and is likely to cause excessive NO_x exhaust emissions. Answer d is not correct because carbon deposits in the cylinder have the effect of increasing the compression, thereby increasing the possibility of creating excessive NO_x exhaust emissions.

9. **The correct answer is c.** Both technicians are correct. Technician A is correct because the larger wheels and tires will travel farther with each revolution, requiring more torque from the engine, thereby reducing the acceleration rate compared to the same vehicle equipped with stock size wheels and tires. Technician B is correct because even though the engine will be rotating slower at a particular vehicle speed, the odometer will register fewer miles than the actual distance. When the amount of gasoline is divided into the lower number of miles traveled, the result is a lower-than-normal calculated miles per gallon figure. Answers a, b, and d are not correct because both technicians are correct.

10. **The correct answer is b.** The low restriction exhaust system reduces backpressure. Exhaust system backpressure is needed to close a vent valve in a positive-backpressure-type EGR valve. Reduced backpressure, therefore, can prevent the EGR from opening properly, increasing the chances of spark knock (pinging) and creating excessive NO_x exhaust emissions. Answer a is not correct because a low restriction exhaust usually increases performance and fuel economy even though the opposite can occur. Answer c is not correct because if the EGR does not open, it is unlikely to be the cause of a rough idle. Excessive CO exhaust emission is usually caused by a rich air-fuel mixture and the installation of a low restriction exhaust would tend to cause the mixture to be leaner (not richer). Answer d is not correct because the low restriction exhaust is likely to increase performance and is unlikely to cause an increase in HC exhaust emission, which is the result of incomplete combustion or lack of proper ignition of the air-fuel mixture.

11. **The correct answer is d.** The most likely cause of a loose serpentine accessory drive belt is a broken tensioner spring. Answer a is not correct because even though a defective belt could be the cause, it is not the most likely cause of loose belt tension. Answer b is not correct because even though an incorrect water pump could cause the engine to overheat, it is doubtful that it could cause the drive belt to be loose unless the replacement pump came equipped with an undersized pulley. Answer c is not correct because even though a clogged radiator could cause the engine to overheat, it cannot cause the serpentine accessory drive belt to be loose.

12. **The correct answer is b.** A broken one-way exhaust check valve is the most likely cause of excessive heat destroying the air pump switching valves. The valves are designed to allow air to flow from the AIR pump to the exhaust manifold and to block the flow of hot exhaust gases back up into the hoses and switches in the system. Answer a is not correct because a loose AIR pump belt, while it could cause noise and prevent the pump from working correctly, would be unlikely to cause the switching valves to fail due to heat. Answer c is not correct because a stuck open EGR valve would drastically affect engine operation, but would not  create a problem where exhaust gases could get to the AIR switching valves. Answer d is not correct because while a cracked exhaust manifold could cause some exhaust to leak out, it is unlikely that the crack would align with and melt the AIR switching valves which are usually located near the AIR pump at the front of the engine.

13. **The correct answer is b.** The use of too much RTV sealer will result in some of the extra material dropping off of the oil pan/block rail and falling into the oil pan where it is picked up and clogs the oil pump screen. Answer a is not correct because even though the wrong type of RTV sealer could damage oxygen sensors, it is the use of too much rather than the type of sealer used that has caused the repeated problem. Answer c is not correct because it is unlikely to be the cause of repeated failure and the intake manifold gaskets are designed to withstand the effects of gasoline and gasoline additives. Answer d is not correct because oil cannot dissolve RTV sealer regardless of the type, brand, or viscosity.

14. **The correct answer is b.** A broken vacuum spring will likely prevent the valve from closing properly; therefore, it could be best detected during a vacuum test at idle (fluctuating vacuum reading) and when performing a compression test at idle speed (all spark wires are connected except for the cylinder being tested). A lower than average reading on a running compression test usually indicates a valve train-related problem. Answer a is not correct because a cranking vacuum test would be unlikely to determine a fault with a broken valve spring due to the slow engine speed during cranking, which allows time for the valve to close completely even if the spring was broken. Answer c is not correct because, again, cranking vacuum is not a good test to detect a broken valve spring. Answer d is not correct because even though the scope firing lines could be used to detect a problem, the vacuum test during cranking would not be a good test to detect a broken valve spring.

15. **The correct answer is b.** If the exhaust system is partially restricted, the vacuum will drop if the engine speed is increased to about 2500 RPM. The exhaust starts to back up at the restriction until some exhaust still remains in the cylinder at the end of the exhaust stroke, which occupies space in the cylinder and prevents some of the intake charge from entering during the intake stroke thereby lowering the vacuum reading. Answer a is not correct because the exhaust produced at idle speed may not back up into the cylinder as would more likely occur if the engine speed were increased. Answer c is not correct be-  cause a cylinder leak down test is used to check for any leakage escaping the cylinder with the piston at top dead center and would not test for a restricted exhaust system. Answer d is not correct because a running compression test is performed to check that the valves open fully and would not indicate whether the exhaust system is restricted.

16. **The correct answer is d.** Because the engine starts and runs after the oxygen sensor was removed, this is an indication that the exhaust system was clogged and that the small opening for the oxygen sensor provided enough exhaust flow to allow the engine to run. Answer a is not correct because even though a stuck open EGR valve could cause a drivability concern and could cause the engine to stall, it is not the most likely cause of the no-start condition. Answer b is not correct because the engine started when the oxygen sensor was removed allowing exhaust to flow out of the opening. The oxygen sensor could be defective, but this would not cause the engine to not start or start when removed. Answer c is not correct because even though a defective MAP sensor could affect engine operation and could even cause a start/stall condition, it is unlikely to be the reason why the engine will start when the oxygen sensor was removed. The excessive backpressure created by the clogged exhaust would affect the MAP sensor, but a defective MAP sensor is not the most likely cause.

17. **The correct answer is c.** A defective thermostat (stuck open) is about the only reason why an engine cannot reach normal operating temperature. Answer a is not correct because a clogged radiator would cause the engine to run hotter than normal rather than not being able to reach normal operating temperature. Answer b is not correct because the cooling fan, while it will keep the radiator cool, will not keep the temperature below the opening temperature of the thermostat. Answer d is not correct because a missing fan shroud will allow the cooling fan to recirculate underhood air rather than draw cooler outside air from in front of the radiator and could cause the engine to operate hotter than normal, not cooler than normal.

18. **The correct answer is d.** Carbon deposits on the intake valve absorb gasoline as the air-fuel mixture flows past the valve resulting in a leaner-than-normal mixture, which causes the engine to run rough or stall after a cold start. After a short time, after the deposits are saturated with fuel, the engine runs OK. When the engine is turned off, the fuel in the deposits evaporates. Answer a is not correct because a defective or stuck open EGR valve would affect engine operation mostly when the engine is warm and not just after a cold start. Answer b is not correct because a clogged PCV valve, while it will affect the operation of the engine at idle speed, is unlikely to cause poor engine operation only after a cold start. Answer c is not correct because a clogged fuel filter is most likely to cause a lack of power rather than cause the engine to stall after a cold start.

19. **The correct answer is d.** Neither technician is correct. Technician A is not correct because a thermostat rated at 195°F will not be fully open until about 20° higher or until the coolant temperature reaches 215°F. Technician B is not correct because the 210°F coolant temperature reading is normal and does not represent a cooling system problem. Answers a, b, and c are not correct because neither technician is correct.

20. **The correct answer is c.** Both technicians are correct. Technician A is correct because an engine miss caused by a defective fuel injector or spark plug wire will cause the exhaust to be uneven. Technician B is correct because a hole in the exhaust system will cause the paper held at the tailpipe to fluctuate because some of the exhaust gases escape from the hole. Answers a, b, and d are not correct because both technicians are correct.

21. **The correct answer is a.** Technician A is correct because engine oil contaminated with gasoline will cause the engine to run richer than normal. The gasoline fumes are drawn into the intake manifold through the PCV system. Technician B is not correct because, even though the fumes will be drawn into the system and the richer mixture is detected by the oxygen sensor, the computer will not overcompensate and supply a leaner-than-normal mixture nor will it set a lean DTC. Answers c and d are not correct because only Technician A is correct.

22. **The correct answer is b.** If the lower O-rings around the fuel injectors were leaking, a small vacuum leak would result in a leaner-than-normal mixture being supplied to the affected cylinder resulting in a misfire DTC. Answer a is not correct because, while a defective fuel pressure regulator could affect certain cylinders if the diaphragm had a hole allowing gasoline to flow into the intake manifold and create a richer-than-normal mixture for those cylinders, it is not likely to occur after an intake manifold gasket replacement. Answer c is not correct because a clogged catalytic converter would affect all cylinders and not just the rear bank. Answer d is not likely because the misfire DTC affected three cylinders, not just one.

23. **The correct answer is c.** Both technicians are correct. Technician A is correct because spark should be checked using a spark tester, which loads the secondary ignition enough for it to produce at least 25,000 V (25 kV), whereas a conventional spark plug fired in outside air only requires about 3 kV to jump the gap. Technician B is correct because a Noid light replaces the fuel injector electronically and allows the service technician to observe the pulsing on and off of the injector by the PCM. Answers a, b, and d are not correct because both technicians are correct.

24. **The correct answer is d.** All of the above are correct. Answer a is correct because a defective spark plug wire could cause a misfire and knowing the resistance specification is needed. Answer b is correct because the vehicle identification number (VIN) is needed for TSBs and other service information regarding computer updates and other reasons that could relate to a random misfire DTC. Answer c is correct because the engine code is needed to correctly identify the correct TSB or test procedure to follow.

ADVANCED ENGINE PERFORMANCE
SPECIALIST TEST (L1)

CATEGORY: COMPUTERIZED POWERTRAIN CONTROLS DIAGNOSIS

25. **The correct answer is c.** The use of the wrong type of silicone sealer, which uses acetic acid as a curing agent, could cause damage to the oxygen sensors. Answer a is not correct because the grade of gasoline, even though it can affect the operation of the engine, will not cause repeated oxygen sensor failures unless contaminated. Answer b is not correct because a weak fuel pump may cause a leaner-than-normal air-fuel mixture but is unlikely to cause damage to the oxygen sensors. Answer d is not correct because, even though a partially open EGR valve can cause idle-related problems, it is not likely to cause damage to the oxygen sensor.

26. **The correct answer is d.** The first digit of the vehicle identification number represents the country where the vehicle was assembled and is not usually needed to properly identify the vehicle. Answer a is not correct because the 10th digit indicates the model year, and this is a very important information. Answer b is not correct because there are often numerous different part numbers of a component such as an EGR valve that could be used on the same vehicle depending on the emission calibration. Answer c is not correct because the 6th digit represents the engine code and is important to order the correct parts.

27. **The correct answer is c.** The brand of oil is not needed although knowing the viscosity of the oil used may be helpful. If too thick an oil is used (SAE 10W-30 instead of the specified SAE 5W-30), the hydraulic lifters may not be able to bleed down fast enough and keep the valve(s) open, causing a misfire. Answer a is not correct because the grade (regular or premium) may be helpful to know especially if there is an engine spark knock concern or a knock sensor related DTC. Answer b is not correct because when and where the problem occurs needs to be known so that the same condition can be duplicated to verify that the root cause has been found and corrected. Answer d is not correct because a pending or stored DTC can lead the service technician to the area where the problem has occurred.

28. **The correct answer is a.** A defective fuel pump is the most likely cause for both upstream oxygen sensors to read low (lean exhaust). A lack of proper pressure or volume would cause less fuel to be injected into the engine. As noted by the short-term fuel trim (STFT) and long-term fuel trim (LTFT), the fuel is being added in an attempt to compensate for the resulting lean exhaust. Answer b is not correct because a clogged PCV valve or hose would tend to cause the engine to operate slightly richer (not leaner) than normal because about 20% of the air needed by the engine at idle flows through the PCV system. Answer c is not correct because clogged EGR ports would reduce the amount of exhaust gases being added to the air-fuel mixture and would tend to displace oxygen and cause the resulting mixture to have less (not more) oxygen in the exhaust. Answer d is not correct because if the EVAP purge valve was stuck open, the extra fuel would be entering the engine driving the mixture richer, not leaner.

29. **The correct answer is a.** A worn clutch inside the torque converter could cause slippage, which would result in a difference in the specified speed between the input and output of the transmission/transaxle and trigger a DTC. All of the engine parameters are within normal operating range and do not indicate an engine operation concern. Answer b is not correct because the TP sensor voltage is reasonable for a vehicle in overdrive gear and traveling at 50 MPH. Answer c is not correct because the scan tool data seem to indicate normal readings because if the engine were equipped with a 195°F thermostat, it is fully open 20° higher or at 215°F. Therefore, 208°F is within a reasonable engine operating temperature range. Answer d is not correct because the EGR flow percentage is a commanded, rather than an actual value and does represent a normal reading at steady cruise speeds and loads.

30. **The correct answer is b.** The crankshaft position (CKP) is the most important sensor for starting because it is the signal used by the PCM to determine engine speed. If engine speed is not detected, the PCM will not fire the fuel injectors. Answer a is not correct because, even though the engine coolant temperature (ECT) sensor is a high authority sensor at engine start, it is not as critical as the crankshaft position sensor. If poor running when cold is the symptom, then the ECT would be the most important sensor. Answer c is not correct because the intake air temperature (IAT) sensor is a low authority sensor and information from this sensor modifies the amount of calculated fuel needed by the engine that is first determined by the ECT sensor. A fault in the IAT sensor would not cause a no-start condition. Answer d is not correct because the oxygen sensor (HO_2S) does not produce usable voltage signals to the PCM until after it reaches a temperature of about 600°F (315°C) and therefore could not be the cause of a no-start condition.

31. **The correct answer is b.** The misfire counter display on a scan tool will show which cylinder or cylinders are misfiring, and therefore, can help the technician locate and correct the root cause of the DTC. Answer a is not correct because, even though rapidly changing oxygen sensor voltage can indicate a misfire, this data will not help determine which cylinder or cylinders are the cause. Answer c is not correct because the mass air flow (MAF) sensor information would not help the technician determine the root cause of a random cylinder misfire DTC. Answer d is not correct because, even though the MAP  sensor voltage will change during a misfire event, the data from this sensor are not likely to be helpful in determining the root cause of the misfire.

32. **The correct answer is d.** The MAP sensor voltage should be about 1 volt and the voltage increases as the vacuum decreases. Therefore, a reading of slightly more than 2 volts indicates a lower-than-normal vacuum reading at idle, which could be caused by retarded valve timing or other engine faults. Answer a is not correct because the oxygen sensor voltage is OK ranging from below 100 mV to over 900 mV. Answer b is not correct because the MAF sensor output of 3.8 grams per second is within the normal range of 3 to 7 grams per second for most engines at idle speed. Answer c is not correct because the injector pulse width of 3.3 ms is within the normal range of 1.5 to 3.5 ms for most engines at idle speed.

33. **The correct answer is c.** Both technicians are correct. Technician A is correct because an oxygen sensor DTC will likely be set if the connector is unplugged. Technician B is correct because a contaminated oxygen sensor will often set a DTC because of reduced activity. Answers a, b, and d are not correct because both technicians are correct.

34. **The correct answer is b.** Technician B is correct because extra air is being drawn into the engine through the vacuum leak causing the MAP sensor to read a lower-than-normal vacuum in the intake manifold. With the extra air and fuel commanded by the PCM due to the decreased vacuum, the idle speed increases. The PCM commanded the IAC to slow the engine speed by reducing the counts, but at zero counts, the IAC could no longer lower the engine speed. Technician A is not correct because the IAC counts are zero indicating that the PCM is commanding a lower, not a higher, idle speed. Answers c and d are not correct because only Technician B is correct.

35. **The correct answer is a.** Technician A is correct because a dirty throttle plate(s) could restrict the amount of air entering the engine at idle speed, yet not set a DTC or affect engine operation in any other way. Technician B is not correct because a clogged fuel filter would most likely result in reduced engine power and would be unlikely to affect the idle. Answers c and d are not correct because only Technician A is correct.

36. **The correct answer is b.** A reading between the TP sensor ground and the battery negative terminal should not exceed 0.2 V (200 mV). The reading of 0.55 V represents excessive voltage drop between the TP sensor, through the PCM, and to the PCM ground connection. Further voltage drop testing would be needed to determine the exact location of the excessive resistance (voltage drop) in the circuit. Answer a is not correct because the reading is taken at the ground of the TP sensor and not at the signal wire. Answer c is not correct because the two meter leads are measuring the difference in voltage between two ground locations, which indicate a voltage drop and not the available battery voltage. Answer d is not correct because the meter lead was attached to the ground terminal of the TP sensor and not to the reference voltage (V-ref) terminal of the TP sensor.

37. **The correct answer is d.** It is normal for a difference in voltage (voltage drop) between the battery and the fuel pump to be 0.2 volt due to the resistance in the wires and connectors. Most vehicle manufacturers specify a maximum voltage drop of 0.5 V in the fuel pump circuit. Answer a is not correct because the difference in voltage does not indicate a problem with the power side of the fuel pump circuit, including the fuel pump relay. Answer b is not correct because the test indicated that there was no excessive resistance in the power side of the fuel pump circuit, even though there could be a problem with the ground side, which was not discussed in this question. Answer c is not correct because even though the fuel pump could be defective, the test being performed indicates no problem with the power side of the fuel pump circuit.

38. **The correct answer is c.** Both technicians are correct. Technician A is correct because attaching the meter leads in series in the fuel pump circuit at the relay socket will allow the service technician to measure the current flow (amperes) required by the fuel pump. Technician B is correct because a reading higher than specified could indicate that the pump is operating under a heavier-than-normal load such as trying to pump fuel through a partially clogged fuel filter. Answers a, b, and d are not correct because both technicians are correct.

39. **The correct answer is b.** Technician B is correct because an engine in fuel control with a properly operating oxygen sensor should read between at least as low as 200 mV (0.200 V) and at least as high as 800 mV (0.800 V). Technician A is not correct because the meter should be set to read direct current (DC) volts and not alternating current (AC) volts. Answers c and d are not correct because only Technician B is correct.

40. **The correct answer is b.** The waveform shows a throttle position (TP) sensor that is momentarily shorting to ground during a sweep test. The downward voltage spikes indicate the voltage shorting to ground and the upward voltage spikes occur when signal dropout opens the circuit. Answer a is not correct because a typical MAP sensor will be a straight horizontal line, which moves upward or downward depending on engine load or a square wave whose frequency changes with load. Answer c is not correct because the ends of the waveform indicate that the signal is starting and ending at a low voltage, which best indicates the TP sensor. Answer d is not correct because an MAF sensor waveform is usually a square wave whose frequency changes with airflow through the engine.

41. **The correct answer is b.** If the idle speed does not change when the IAC is being commanded, there is a problem with the IAC or the IAC circuit. Answer a is not correct because while a vacuum leak could cause an idle-related problem, it would be unlikely to prevent the engine speed to increase as the IAC commanded position is being changed. Answer c is not correct because a clogged fuel filter would most likely affect the operation of the engine under load and is unlikely to prevent the engine speed from changing when the IAC is being commanded. Answer d is not correct because the EGR system usually opens when the engine speed is above idle and is used to control excessive NO_X exhaust emission. An inoperative EGR is unlikely to prevent the engine idle speed from changing when the IAC is being commanded.

42. **The correct answer is d.** Neither technician is correct. Technician A is not correct because the engine should stall when the engine is warm and operating at idle speed when the EGR valve is opened. Because the engine speed decreased only, some exhaust gases entered the cylinder(s), but not enough to control NOX emissions. The lack of flow DTC is often detected by the PCM commanding the EGR on during deceleration and checking for a given change in engine vacuum or fuel trim as measured by the MAP or O_2S sensors. Technician B is not correct because there is usually a reason why the DTC was set. Answer c is not correct because neither technician is correct.

	DTC P0401 Exhaust Gas Recirculation (EGR) Flow Insufficient			
Step	Action	Value(s)	Yes	No
1	Was the Powertrain on Board Diagnostic System Check performed?	—	Go to Step 2	Go to A Powertrain On Board Diagnostic (OBD) System Check
2	1. Inspect the exhaust system for modification of original installed parts or leaks. 2. If a problem was found, repair exhaust system as necessary. Was a condition present that required repair?	—	Go to Step 5	Go to Step 3
3	1. Remove the EGR valve. 2. Visually and physically inspect the following items: • Pintle, valve passages and the adapter for excessive deposits or any kind of a restriction. • EGR valve gasket and pipes for leaks. 3. If a problem is found, clean or replace EGR system components as necessary. Was a condition present that required repair?	—	Go to Step 5	Go to Step 4
4	1. Remove the EGR inlet and outlet pipes from the exhaust manifold and the intake manifold. 2. Inspect the manifold EGR ports and the EGR inlet and outlet pipes for a blockage caused by excessive deposits, casting flashing or other damage. 3. If a problem is found, correct the condition as necessary. Was a condition present that required repair?	—	Go to Step 5	Go to Diagnostic Aids
5	1. Review and record the scan tool Fail Records data. 2. Clear DTC and monitor EGR Test Count display on the scan tool while operating the vehicle as specified in Diagnostic Aids. 3. Continue operating the vehicle EGR Test Count until 9 – 12 test sample have been taken. 4. Select scan tool Specific DTC information for DTC P0401. Note test result does scan tool indicate DTC P0401 Test Ran and Passed?	—	System OK	Go to Step 2

43. **The correct answer is b.** Technician B only is correct. The temperature displayed on the scan tool represents the temperature of the engine coolant temperature (ECT) sensor. The dash "hot" light is obviously triggered from a separate sensor and the temperature reading from the infrared pyrometer both indicate that the engine is operating hotter than normal. Technician A is not correct because while the ECT sensor could be defective, the most likely reason for the sensor not to register the true coolant temperatures is due to an air pocket caused by low coolant level. Low coolant level could cause the engine to operate hotter than normal and would keep the ECT from indicating the true temperature if an air pocket was trapped around the sensor. Answers a, c, and d are not correct because only Technician B is correct.

44. **The correct answer is a.** Technician A is correct because a no-start condition can be caused by a defective fuel pump relay. The PCM should have energized the fuel pump relay because an engine speed (RPM) signal is present. Technician B is not correct because the engine speed (RPM) is received from the crankshaft position (CKP) sensor and even though it could be giving a weaker-than-normal signal, at least the sensor is working and is therefore unlikely to be the cause of a no-start condition. Answers c and d are not correct because only Technician A is correct.

45. **The correct answer is a.** Technician A is correct because before the root cause of a problem can be determined, it is important to know what events most occur before the DTC is set. This is also important to know to verify that the root cause has been corrected and that the DTC will not set again. Technician B is not correct because there are many other possible causes for an IAT DTC besides the sensor itself, even though through testing the cause might be the sensor. Answers c and d are not correct because only Technician A is correct.

46. **The correct answer is a.** A high oxygen sensor voltage is present when there is little oxygen content in the exhaust such as when a rich exhaust is present. Answer b is not correct because a lean exhaust indicates that there is a lot of oxygen near the oxygen sensor, which produces a low, not a high signal voltage. Answers c and d are not correct because the oxygen sensor is an oxygen sensor and not a hydrocarbon sensor. When an ignition misfire occurs, unburned hydrocarbons pass the oxygen sensor plus 21% oxygen from the air-fuel mixture that was not burned. This oxygen in the exhaust results in a low-voltage (not a high-voltage) signal from the oxygen sensor.

47. **The correct answer is d.** Both b and c are correct. Answer b is correct because a lean exhaust indicates that there is a lot of oxygen near the oxygen sensor, which produces a low signal voltage. Answer c is correct because the oxygen sensor is an oxygen sensor and not a hydrocarbon sensor. When an ignition misfire occurs, unburned hydrocarbons pass the oxygen sensor plus 21% oxygen from the air-fuel mixture that was not burned. This oxygen in the exhaust results in a low-voltage signal from the oxygen sensor. Answer a is not correct because a rich exhaust will result in a high voltage (above 450 mV from the oxygen sensor), not a low voltage.

48. **The correct answer is c.** Both technicians are correct. Technician A is correct because an exhaust leak upstream from the oxygen sensor will draw outside air in through the leak and the oxygen sensor will interpret it as being caused by a lean air-fuel mixture. The PCM will richen the air-fuel mixture using short-term and long-term fuel trim in an attempt to correct for this false lean condition. Technician B is correct because an ignition misfire caused by a defective spark plug wire will also be interpreted by the oxygen sensor as being a lean exhaust because the unburned air-fuel mixture contains 21% oxygen that was exhausted past the oxygen sensor. Answers a, b, and d are not correct because both technicians are correct.

49. **The correct answer is a.** A small vacuum leak could cause the PCM to add fuel at idle, but due to the fact that the leak represents a very small portion of the intake air needed at 2500 RPM, the air-fuel mixture would be unaffected. Answer b is not correct because a defective MAF sensor would be unlikely to only affect the air-fuel at idle speed and not affect it at higher engine speeds. Answer c is not correct because if the regulator were leaking, the fuel trim would be negative (not positive as stated in the question). If the regulator was defective and supplying a higher-than-normal pressure, it is unlikely to affect the engine air-fuel mixture at idle only. Answer d is not correct because an IAC is used for idle speed control and does not affect the air-fuel mixture.

50. **The correct answer is a.** Technician A is correct because by adding propane, a good oxygen sensor should produce a voltage of at least 800 mV (0.800 V). When a vacuum leak is created, a good sensor should produce a voltage of less than 200 mV (0.200V). As an oxygen sensor degrades, the voltage range of the sensor decreases just as in this case. Technician B is not correct because an exhaust leak upstream of the oxygen sensor should result in an output voltage lower than normal, but the sensor should have responded with a higher high and a lower low voltage when tested. Answers c and d are not correct because only Technician A is correct.

51. **The correct answer is a.** Technician A is correct because an analysis of the scan tool data indicates a lower-than-normal oxygen sensor voltage range, indicating a lean air-fuel mixture, as well as zero IAC counts, indicating a vacuum leak on a speed density-type fuel injection system. Technician B is not correct because, even though dirty throttle plates could cause idle problems, most of the scan data indicate a vacuum leak causing a lean air-fuel mixture as the cause. Answers c and d are not correct because only Technician A is correct.

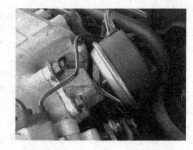

52. **The correct answer is b.** It is normal operation of the EGR system to provide 6% to 10% of the exhaust back into the intake stream to limit combustion temperatures and reduce the formation of NO_x exhaust emissions. When the EGR valve was disconnected, the flow of exhaust gases stopped flowing into the cylinders, resulting in a normal increase in engine speed. Answer a is not correct because restricted EGR ports would reduce the flow of exhaust gases into the cylinders and would result in less of an increase in engine speed when the EGR valve is disabled. Answer c is not correct because even though there was a change in the mixture in the cylinder, the reason for the increase in speed could not be the result of a bad oxygen sensor. In fact, the oxygen sensor was a major reason why the engine increased in speed when the EGR valve was disabled. Answer d is not correct because the MAP sensor responds to intake manifold pressure, not to the flow of exhaust gases in the EGR system.

53. **The correct answer is a.** Technician A is correct because an intake manifold gasket leak would cause the vacuum to be lower when the cylinder closest to the leak is on the intake stroke. When other cylinders are on the intake stroke, the intake manifold vacuum would be steady. This change in vacuum is picked up by the MAP sensor as a lower and rapidly changing vacuum causing the PCM to richen the air-fuel mixture. Technician B is not correct because, although a skipped or incorrectly installed timing belt will reduce the vacuum causing a richer-than-normal air-fuel mixture, it is unlikely to cause the MAP sensor voltage to vary rapidly. The incorrect valve timing would affect all cylinders equally. Answers c and d are not correct because only Technician A is correct.

54. **The correct answer is c.** A defective fuel pressure regulator either leaking or stuck at higher-than-normal pressure would cause the engine to operate richer than normal. The oxygen sensor voltage indicates that the exhaust is rich and the PCM is commanding a reduced injector pulse width in an attempt to restore proper operation. Answer a is not correct because while a defective MAP sensor could be the cause of an excessively rich mixture, it is not the most likely cause. Answer b is not correct because a weak fuel pump would tend to cause a leaner-than-normal air-fuel mixture, not a richer mixture as indicated by the high oxygen sensor voltage and resulting shorter injector pulse width. Answer d is not correct because failed spark plugs would cause the oxygen sensor to send lower-than-normal oxygen sensor voltage due to the unburned oxygen in the air-fuel mixture that passed by the sensor on the exhaust stroke.

55. **The correct answer is d.** Neither technician is correct. Technician A is not correct because the ohmmeter leads are connected to the ECT sensor terminals and not the connector. Technician B is not correct because the meter leads are attached to the sensor itself and not to the signal return circuit. Answer c is not correct because neither technician is correct.

56. **The correct answer is c.** Both technicians are correct. Technician A is correct because if an output device such as a solenoid had less than the specified resistance, excessive current flow through the unit could cause damage to the replacement PCM and could have been the root cause of the failure of the original PCM. Technician B is correct because with the ignition switch in the off position, all ignition-controlled circuits are de-energized and therefore will be unlikely to create a spark when the PCM is disconnected or connected. Answers a, b, and d are not correct because both technicians are correct.

57. **The correct answer is a.** A leak in the air inlet between the MAF sensor and the throttle body is the most likely cause of rough running when in forward drive gear and yet running OK when in reverse. When in forward gear, the engine torque tends to move the engine on its mounts away from the MAF sensor. If there is a tear or opening in the hose, this allows unmetered air into the engine. Because this extra air bypasses the MAF, the computer does not supply enough fuel for this extra "false" air. When the vehicle is driven in reverse, the engine torque tends to close any openings in the air inlet, thereby reducing or stopping the entry of extra air and the engine would operate correctly in reverse. Answer b is not correct because a defective oxygen sensor, while it could affect engine operation, is unlikely to make the engine run well only in reverse. Answer c is not correct because when the transmission is in reverse, the line pressure increases, but this would be unlikely to cause the engine to operate correctly while in reverse, but not OK when in forward gears. Answer d is not correct because a clogged exhaust system would affect engine operation in all gears, especially at higher speeds, rather than just in forward gears.

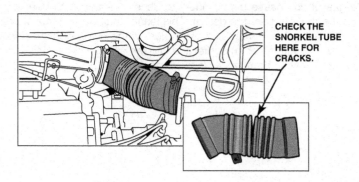

CHECK THE
SNORKEL TUBE
HERE FOR
CRACKS.

58. **The correct answer is c.** Both technicians are correct. Technician A is correct because if AIR pump is being supplied to the exhaust manifold at all times due to a stuck open one-way check valve, the oxygen sensor will read low voltage all of the time. Technician B is correct because the low oxygen voltage will be interpreted by the PCM as being a lean air-fuel mixture and it will command that the injector pulse width be increased in an attempt to get the oxygen sensor voltage higher, resulting in a richer-than-normal condition. Answers a, b, and d are not correct because both technicians are correct.

59. **The correct answer is d.** The most likely cause is that one of the three injectors on the bank that reads 2.9 ohms is shorted. Three 12-ohm injectors should measure 4 ohms if they are connected in parallel (total resistance equals the value of equal resistance connected in parallel divided by the number) 12 ÷ 3 = 4 ohms. Answer a is not correct because one open injector would create a resistance reading of 6 ohms (2 good injectors of 12 ohms each divided by 2 equals 6 ohms). Answer b is not correct because one bank of injectors is definitely OK (4 ohms bank). Answer c is not correct because both banks should measure the same resistance.

60. **The correct answer is a.** Technician A only is correct because if there is a short-to-ground at terminal "a," the 5-volt reference voltage going to the MAP sensor would be zero, triggering the low voltage DTCs. Technician B is not correct because terminal #50 is a ground connection and if the wire touched ground (short-to-ground), then no harm or fault will occur because both represent zero voltage. Answers c and d are not correct because only Technician A is correct.

61. **The correct answer is d.** Neither technician is correct. Technician A is not correct because an open at terminal #348 would prevent the operation of any gear selection and not just reverse. Technician B is not correct because a blown fuse #40 would prevent the operation of the entire transmission range plus many other circuits and would therefore not be the cause of just an inoperative reverse gear selection. Answers a, b, and c are not correct because neither technician is correct.

62. **The correct answer is a.** Technician A only is correct because there should be a voltage on terminal #101 from the terminal of the generator (alternator). The PCM applies a variable-duty cycle signal to ground the field winding of the generator without the use of a separate voltage regulator. Technician B is not correct because the PCM pulses the voltage from the generator to ground and because there is no voltage at terminal #101. This means that there is likely a fault in the generator or wiring and not necessarily the PCM.

63. **The correct answer is a.** Technician A only is correct. Technician A is correct because terminal #151 is a ground for the air–fuel ratio (AFR) heater. Technician B is not correct because fuse #20 feeds power to all of the oxygen sensors, so it is unlikely that this would set a DTC for only one of the four oxygen sensor heaters. The fuse also feeds the A/C on/off request switch which is likely the reason that the A/C did not work. Answers c and d are not correct because only Technician A is correct.

64. **The correct answer is c.** Both technicians are correct. Technician A is correct because the 5-volt reference signal comes from the ECM, so a fault with this circuit could cause all three sensors that use the 5-volt reference to produce a low (zero) voltage output signal. Technician B is correct because if one of the sensors was electrically shorted, the 5-volt reference voltage would go to ground through the shorted sensor and would cause all the sensors to read low (zero volts). Answers a, b, and d are not correct because both technicians are correct.

65. **The correct answer is c.** Both technicians are correct. Technician A is correct because a leak at the intake manifold gasket can cause the cylinders to become leaner than normal due to the extra air being drawn into the cylinder past the gasket. This leaner-than-normal mixture can cause the cylinders to misfire. Technician B is correct because if most of the EGR ports are clogged, then too much exhaust gas will flow through the open port(s) and into the cylinder(s) causing a misfire. Answers a, b, and d are not correct because both technicians are correct.

ADVANCED ENGINE PERFORMANCE
SPECIALIST TEST (L1)

CATEGORY: IGNITION SYSTEM DIAGNOSIS

66. **The correct answer is b.** A loose spark plug runs hotter than normal because heat cannot travel to the cylinder head if the spark plug is not properly tightened. Answer a is not correct because while a vacuum leak can cause a leaner-than-normal air-fuel mixture and cause a spark plug to appear white, it is unlikely to affect just one cylinder. Answer c is not correct because even though a fuel pressure regulator could be the cause of lower-than-normal fuel pressure, leading to a lean air-fuel mixture, it is unlikely to be the cause of only one white (overheated) spark plug. Answer d is not correct because a partially open EGR valve will cause rough engine operation, but is unlikely to cause one spark plug to be overheated.

67. **The correct answer is d.** Spark plug information, including the specified gap dimensions, is usually found on the underhood decal and in the owner's manual, as well as in the service manual or electronic service information. Answers a, b, and c are not correct because all are correct.

68. **The correct answer is b.** If too cold a heat range spark plugs were installed, carbon deposits would likely form causing a misfire. If too hot a heat range plugs were installed, spark knock (ping or detonation) would be likely. Answer a is not correct because while a low idle could occur, especially with colder-than-specified heat range plugs, this is not as likely as answer b. Answer c is not correct because the heat range of spark plugs has little, if any, effect on the cold starting of the engine unless, of course, they were fouled. Answer d is not correct because the heat range of the plugs has little effect on the starting of the engine.

69. **The correct answer is d.** It is normal for waste-spark ignition systems to fire one plug with straight polarity current and the other paired cylinder reversed. The polarity of the spark depends on the direction (clockwise or counterclockwise) the coil is wound and this cannot be changed by the technician. Straight polarity means that the spark jumps from the center electrode and reverse polarity means that the spark jumps from the side electrode. Answer a is not correct because even though loose spark plugs can cause excessive wear, this would not explain why three of the six plugs wore the opposite electrode from the other three. Answer b is not correct because even though the plugs with the worn center electrodes could have been the wrong heat range, it would not explain why the other three plugs had worn side electrodes. Answer c is not correct because even if the plug wires were installed backwards on the same coil, the same situation would occur, but only backwards. Each coil fires two spark plugs at the same time and the ignition system does not know or care which cylinder is receiving the straight or the reverse polarity. Most waste-spark ignition systems fire the odd number cylinders (1, 3, and 5) with straight polarity and even-numbered cylinders (2, 4, and 6) with reverse polarity.

70. **The correct answer is b.** Technician B is correct because each coil of a waste-spark electronic ignition fires two spark plugs at the same time. If only one of the spark plugs fires, then the ignition coil must be at fault because the module was able to fire the coil. The usual reason for this condition is a shorted coil that only has enough energy to fire the one plug. If one end of the coil is shorted to ground, the same thing will occur. The coil would then act just like a conventional ignition coil as is used on a distributor ignition. Technician A is not correct because the module has to be functioning because it was able to fire the coil. Answers c and d are not correct because only Technician B is correct.

71. **The correct answer is a.** No change will be noticed because the coil fires both spark plugs at the same time. Answer b is not correct because the coil will fire both spark plugs at the same time and there is no reason why a misfire would occur unless one or both spark plug wires were defective. Answer c is not correct because the ignition timing (when the spark occurs relative to piston position) is not changed when the wires were reversed. Answer d is not correct because the ignition timing and all other computer functions would be unaffected by the change in switching the two spark plugs on the same coil because both plugs would fire at the same time.

72. **The correct answer is c.** Both technicians are correct. Technician A is correct because a wise service technician should always perform a thorough visual inspection and the spark plugs are a major item that should be checked. Technician B is correct because defective spark plug wire(s) could be the cause of a lack-of-power concern and the wise technician should check them for proper resistance and visually for damage. Answers a, b, and d are not correct because both technicians are correct.

73. **The correct answer is a.** Technician A is correct because the meter reading indicates that the spark plug wire has 28,000 ohms (28 kΩ), which is well above the upper limit maximum of 20,000 ohms according to the factory specification (10,000 ohms per foot times 2 feet = 20,000 ohms). Technician B is not correct because even though the spark plug wire may not need to be replaced based on other factors, such as broken insulation, it is not within factory specifications for resistance and it should be replaced based on the ohmmeter test. Answers c and d are not correct because only Technician A is correct.

74. **The correct answer is c.** Both technicians are correct. Technician A is correct because an open spark plug wire could cause the spark to "find ground" through the plastic distributor rotor to the stud distributor shaft. Technician B is correct because the spark could arc across the terminals of the distributor shaft causing a carbon track if a spark plug wire was defective (open). Answers a, b, and d are not correct because both technicians are correct.

75. **The correct answer is b.** A burned through rotor that allows the spark energy from the coil to arc to ground (distributor shaft) rather than to the spark plugs is the most likely cause. Answer a is not correct because even though a defective spark plug wire could have been the reason for the failed rotor, it could not be the reason why none of the spark plugs are getting spark. Answer c is not correct because even though a tracked cap could cause a drivability problem, it is unlikely to cause a lack of spark to all of the spark plugs. Answer d is not correct because worn spark plugs may cause starting and drivability problems but will not cause a lack of spark to all plugs.

76. **The correct answer is c.** Both technicians are correct. Technician A is correct because spark plug wires with poor insulation can cause the engine to be hard to start during moist weather conditions because the water tends to provide a parallel path for the spark energy, thereby reducing the energy available at the spark plug. Technician B is correct because moisture or dirt on a distributor cap tends to increase the capacitance of the secondary ignition circuit and therefore, increases the voltage needed to fire the spark plugs. This is one reason why many vehicle manufacturers cover the distributor caps and wiring with plastic protective shields. Answers a, b, and d are not correct because both technicians are correct.

77. **The correct answer is a.** Technician A is correct because the ignition system was capable of producing a spark across a spark plug gap, but not enough voltage was available to jump a spark tester. It requires about 3,000 to 4,000 volts to jump a spark plug in open air, whereas it requires at least 25,000 volts to jump a typical spark tester designed for electronic-type ignition systems. A weak or shorted coil would be a logical reason why a low voltage spark was possible, but not a spark cable of firing a spark tester. Technician B is not correct because a spark plug in an engine requires from 5,000 to 15,000 volts or more to fire under compression and the fact that the spark was able to jump a spark plug in open air was not a valid test of the condition of the ignition system. Answers c and d are not correct because only Technician A is correct.

78. **The correct answer is d.** Neither technician is correct. Technician A is not correct because slow cranking, especially when the engine is hot, is a symptom of an over advanced spark timing condition, not a retarded timing condition. Technician B is not correct because even though the starter may not be operating correctly, the problem occurred immediately after the distributor was replaced; therefore, the most likely reason for the slow cranking of the engine is the incorrect ignition timing. Answers a, b, and c are not correct because neither technician is correct.

79. **The correct answer is a.** Technician A is correct because the computer-controlled spark advance must be removed before the base timing can be correctly set. Technician B is not correct because the timing light pickup has to be connected to number one cylinder on most engines because the timing is usually set using the one cylinder. All of the others will also be correctly set because of the mechanical distributor. Answers c and d are not correct because Technician A only is correct.

80. **The correct answer is c.** The PCM pulses the primary of the coil on coil-on-plug ignitions and the frequency (Hertz) reading indicates that the PCM is in fact able to pulse the coil. The coil, spark plug, and other components could still be defective but at least the technician knows that the PCM is pulsing the coil. Answer a is not correct because the coil is being pulsed and even though the coil may be shorted, this test did not test the coil for being shorted. Answer b is not correct because the frequency reading (Hertz) does indicate that the coil was being pulsed by the PCM. Answer d is not correct because even though the spark plug could be fouled or cracked, the test being performed only indicated that the coil was being pulsed. Further inspection would be necessary to determine whether the spark plug was defective or fouled.

81. **The correct answer is c.** High resistance in the spark plug wire would require higher voltage from the ignition coil as observed on the scope. The engine would miss when the required voltage needed to fire the spark plug under load exceeds the available voltage. Answer a is not correct because a fuel-fouled spark plug requires lower voltage to fire, not higher voltage. Answer b is not correct because a closed gap requires less voltage to fire rather than increased voltage even though a closed gap spark plug could cause an engine miss. Answer d is not correct because a shorted ignition coil would cause all cylinders to misfire and could not be the cause of one cylinder requiring a higher-than-normal voltage to fire the spark plug.

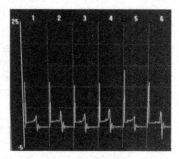

82. **The correct answer is c.** All ignition systems should be capable of supplying enough energy to jump across the spark plug electron and provide for a spark duration long enough to ensure proper ignition (1 to 2 ms). Because both the firing voltage and the spark duration were lower than normal, this indicates that the energy from the coil is lower than normal. A shorted coil secondary winding would be the only explanation that would indicate a reduction in coil energy. Answer a is not correct because wide spark plug gaps would reduce the spark duration, but the wide gaps would increase, rather than decrease the firing voltages. Answer b is not correct because a narrow gap would use less energy, rather than more energy from the coil and would not cause a problem. Answer d is not correct because low primary coil resistance would result in greater primary current flow and while this could be the cause of low spark energy, it is not the most likely because magnetic field strength is measured in ampere-turns. Increased current flow, even if some of the primary windings were shorted, could still create about the same magnetic field strength.

83. **The correct answer is d.** Both answer a and b are correct. Answer a is correct because the voltage at the tip of the spark plug must be high enough to cause the molecular bond of the oxygen (O_2) and hydrogen (H_2) in the air to ionize into atoms of oxygen and hydrogen, so the mixture becomes electrically conductive. Answer b is also correct because the height of the firing line represents the voltage needed to arc across the spark plug gap meaning that all of the resistance in the secondary ignition such as spark plug wires, distributor rotor air gap, etc. must be overcome to achieve the spark. Answer c is not correct because the voltage needed to maintain the spark is represented by the horizontal spark line (section c on the drawing). Answers a and b are not correct because both answers are correct.

84. **The correct answer is c.** A narrow spark plug gap is indicated because the spark duration is longer than specified. A charged ignition coil has a certain amount of stored energy. If the spark plug gap is small, less energy is needed to overcome the secondary circuit resistance and more is available to provide for a longer spark duration. Answer a is not correct because even though the duration is barely within specifications and could be the result of a wider-than-normal spark plug gap, the most likely cause is answer c because the duration is out of the specified range. Answer b is not correct because a wide gap would require more voltage to fire leaving less coil energy for spark duration. Because the cylinder #4 has a longer than specified duration, a wide plug gap is not a likely cause. Answer d is not correct because the short duration of cylinder #1 spark plug would indicate that the plug gap is wider, rather than narrower.

85. **The correct answer is d.** Cylinders #6 and #3 are paired meaning that when the waste-spark ignition system fires cylinder #6, it also fires cylinder #3 and vice-versa. To determine paired cylinders, underline the firing order and then draw a vertical line at halfway between numbers 3 and 4. Now place the numbers on the right under the numbers on the left. The numbers above each other represent the cylinder that is paired. When one of the paired cylinders is at top dead center (TDC) on the compression stroke, the paired cylinder is on TDC of the exhaust stroke. Answer a is not correct because the cylinder numbers indicate position and, in most cases, the even-numbered cylinders and odd-numbered cylinders share the same exhaust manifold, not cylinders #3 and #6. Answer b is not correct because the cylinders are on opposite banks of the V-6 engine. Answer c is not correct because even though the two cylinders are on opposite banks, they are not directly opposite each other.

86. **The correct answer is c.** Both technicians are correct. Technician A is correct because a random misfire DTC could be caused by a cracked spark plug. The scan tool data (freeze frame) show that all parameters are within normal range. Technician B is correct because a shorted ignition coil could also result in a misfire because of the reduced spark energy available. Answers a, b, and d are not correct because both technicians are correct.

87. **The correct answer is d.** Neither technician is correct. Technician A is not correct because the relationship between the crankshaft and camshaft are correct. Technician B is not correct because the missing tooth is normal and is the method used to allow the PCM to determine top dead center. Answers a, b, and c are not correct because neither technician is correct.

88. **The correct answer is c.** Both technicians are correct. Technician A is correct because a cracked spark plug could cause a steady misfire to occur on one cylinder, which may be enough of a misfire to trigger a catalyst damaging condition and a flashing MIL. Technician B is correct because an open at terminal b of ignition coil 6 would prevent the coil from firing causing a misfire. Answers a, b, and d are not correct because both technicians are correct.

89. **The correct answer is b.** Technician B is correct because a blown fuse #4 would prevent the operation of many components, including all of the ignition coils thereby causing a no-start condition. Technician A is not correct because a short to ground at terminal b of the camshaft position sensor would not prevent the sensor from functioning because that terminal is normally electrically connected to ground. Answers c and d are not correct because only Technician B is correct.

ADVANCED ENGINE PERFORMANCE
SPECIALIST TEST (L1)

CATEGORY: FUEL SYSTEMS AND AIR INDUCTION SYSTEMS

90. **The correct answer is d.** Neither technician is correct. Technician A is not correct because, even though the fuel filter may be partially clogged, the test results stated do not indicate that this is a problem. If the fuel filter were clogged, the current draw would be higher than specified and/or the pump motor speed would be low (less than 3,000 to 3,500 RPM). Technician B is not correct because the test results do not indicate a fault with the pump. Answers a, b, and c are not correct because neither technician is correct.

91. **The correct answer is a.** The mass air flow (MAF) sensor is the unit that would be most directly affected because dirty air can coat the sensing wire or film used to measure the mass of the air entering the engine. Answer b is not correct because even though excessive engine wear caused by operating without an air filter could reduce engine vacuum and affect the MAP sensor readings, it is not the component that is most likely to be directly affected. Answer c is not correct because even though dirty air could contaminate the oxygen sensor eventually, it is not the sensor that is the most likely to be affected directly. Answer d is not correct because even though the intake air temperature (IAT) is in the air stream and could become contaminated by dirt, it is not as high an authority sensor as the MAF and is, therefore, less likely to affect engine operation.

92. **The correct answer is d.** A restricted fuel return line would increase fuel pressure and cause the engine to receive a richer-than-normal air-fuel mixture. A richer-than-normal mixture is unlikely to cause spark knock, which usually occurs if the engine is operating too hot or too lean. Answer a is not correct because a missing air cleaner cold air hose could cause the engine spark knock because hot air from under the hood would be drawn into the engine rather than colder air drawn from outside of the engine compartment. Answer b is not correct because carbon buildup in the combustion chamber would increase compression, thereby increasing the possibility that the engine will spark knock during acceleration. Answer c is not correct because, if the proper calibrated amount of exhaust gases is not flowing back into the intake, the spark knock is likely.

93. **The correct answer is b.** The scan data indicate a lean air-fuel condition is being compensated for by the PCM by providing a longer-than-normal injector pulse width of 4.5 ms bypassed to a normal reading of 1.5 to 3.5 ms. The oxygen sensor(s) also show a lower-than-normal voltage range indicating a lean exhaust condition. Answer a is not correct because, while a contaminated oxygen sensor could affect engine operation, the contamination usually coats the sensor and keeps it from reacting to the oxygen in the exhaust stream, leading to a higher-than-normal voltage output rather than lower than normal. Answer c is not correct because it appears from the scan data that the engine coolant temperature is within the normal range (195°F to 215°F if equipped with a 195°F thermostat, and 180°F to 200°F if equipped with a 180°F thermostat). Answer d is not correct because while the IAC could be stuck, the IAC counts (20) are normal for most engines at idle (15 to 20) and if defective, would affect the idle speed of the engine and would not cause a lean air-fuel mixture.

94. **The correct answer is c.** A weak fuel pump is a likely cause for creating a lean condition at 2,500 RPM, yet be OK at idle speed. The fuel trim indicates that little correction is needed at idle but that the oxygen sensor(s) is indicating a need for additional fuel at 2,500 RPM because the LTFT is indicating that an additional 27% more fuel than usual is needed at the higher engine speed. Answer a is not correct because even though a defective fuel pressure regulator could cause the need for additional fuel, if it was not supplying high enough fuel pressure, it is unlikely to cause the engine to need more correction at higher engine speeds. Answer b is not correct because an intake manifold leak would tend to increase fuel trim more at idle speed and less at higher engine speeds. Answer d is not correct because a clogged catalytic converter would tend to keep some exhaust gases trapped in the cylinder diluting the air-fuel mixture with exhaust gases that contain little oxygen. The oxygen sensor(s) would then tend to read higher (rather than lower) and the fuel trim numbers are most likely to be negative (subtracting fuel) rather than positive (adding fuel).

95. **The correct answer is b.** Technician B is correct because a defective fuel pressure regulator can cause the fuel pressure to be higher than normal leading to a richer-than-normal air-fuel ratio. The O_2 sensor circuit high voltage DTC indicates that the air-fuel mixture is rich or some other reason that keeps the voltage too high for too long a time. Technician A is not correct because a vacuum leak would tend to lean the air-fuel mixture with a lower-than-normal oxygen sensor voltage rather than higher than normal. Answers c and d are not correct because Technician B only is correct.

96. **The correct answer is c.** Both technicians are correct. Technician A is correct because a loose connection between the MAF sensor and the throttle body can cause unmetered air (called false air) to enter the engine, thereby changing the actual air-fuel mixture compared to the calculated air-fuel ratio based on the MAF sensor reading. Technician B is correct because the MAF sensor itself can be defective or dirty, thereby preventing it from producing the proper signal to the PCM. Answers a, b, and d are not correct because both technicians are correct.

97. **The correct answer is c.** Both technicians are correct. Technician A is correct because a leaking fuel pressure regulator will allow fuel to flow into the intake manifold through the vacuum hose connector to the regulator causing an excessive amount of gasoline in the intake manifold making starting difficult. Technician B is correct because a leaking fuel injector would cause gasoline to enter the intake manifold and create a richer-than-normal air-fuel mixture when the engine is started. This extremely rich mixture in a warm engine makes starting difficult. Answers a, b, and d are not correct because both technicians are correct.

98. **The correct answer is b.** A dirty throttle plate or air intake on a port-injected engine can cause turbulence in the air stream entering the engine resulting in an unstable idle. Answer a is not correct because a weak fuel pump, while it may affect engine operation, is not likely to be the cause of an idle-only concern. Answer c is not correct because a partially clogged fuel filter is most likely to cause a lack of power concern and is unlikely to be the cause of an idle-only concern. Answer d is not correct because a dirty fuel injector could cause a reduction in the flow of fuel to one cylinder, but is unlikely to cause the idle to be rough and unstable without triggering a DTC or other fault.

99. **The correct answer is a.** A clogged fuel filter is not likely to cause an increase in fuel usage and a reduction in fuel economy because it would more likely cause a lack of power concern. Answer b is not correct because if a fuel pressure regulator is defective, it could be leaking fuel through a hole in the diaphragm directly into the intake manifold or could be providing higher-than-normal fuel pressure, both of which could cause a reduction in fuel economy. Answer c is not correct because a pinched or restricted fuel return line would cause an increase in fuel pressure and could cause a decrease in fuel economy. Answer d is not correct because, if a fuel injector was stuck open, fuel would be entering the cylinder all of the time decreasing fuel economy.

100. **The correct answer is b.** Technician B is correct because a clean fuel filter and good fuel pump should be able to supply fuel to the engine during acceleration without dropping more than 2 psi. If the pressure drops more than 2 psi, most experts feel that the fuel filter should be replaced and the test repeated. If the pressure again drops more than 2 psi, the pump should be replaced. Technician A is not correct because it is not normal operation for the fuel pressure to drop 3 psi when the engine is accelerated and does represent a fault in the fuel delivery system. Answers c and d are not correct because only Technician B is correct.

101. **The correct answer is c.** When water is added to fuel containing alcohol, the water combines with the alcohol and sinks to the bottom of the container. Because the phase separation line is 3 ml from the bottom, there is 20% alcohol (2 ml) plus the 1 ml of water added as part of the test. Answer a is not correct because the added water combines with the alcohol in the fuel to form the phase separation line above the 1 ml mark. Answer b is not correct because if 10% alcohol was in the gasoline, the phase separation line would be at 2 ml, not 3 ml. Answer d is not correct because the phase separation line was at the 3 ml mark (out of 10), but 1 ml must be subtracted from the reading because 1 ml of water was added to the sample.

102. **The correct answer is c.** The volatility of premium grade gasoline is different from regular grade gasoline and this change most often affects cold weather starting. Answer a is not correct because carbon can still build up on intake valves regardless of the octane rating of the gasoline. Deposit-control additives are added to all grades, especially higher octane fuels, helping to reduce rather than increase intake valve deposits. Answer b is not correct because a burned valve is usually caused by excessive heat in the combustion chamber or a fault that prevents the valve(s) from properly closing completely. The grade of gasoline would have little, if any, effect on the condition of the valves. Answer d is not correct because the grade of gasoline has no effect on the oxygen sensor(s).

103. **The correct answer is c.** Both technicians are correct. Technician A is correct because a clogged fuel filter can cause stress on the fuel pump leading to premature failure. Technician B is correct because fuel pumps draw fuel from the bottom of the fuel tank where water, alcohol, rust, and dirt accumulate. If any of the material is drawn through the pump, excessive wear or damage can occur. Answers a, b, and d are not correct because both technicians are correct.

104. **The correct answer is c.** Exhaust hydrocarbon (HC) exhaust emissions are due to a fault in the ignition system or a fault in the cooling system that allows the cylinder to be cooler than normal. The result of cool cylinders is that the fuel vapors in the combustion chamber condense into liquid gasoline, which cannot be burned because it lacks the necessary oxygen around the fuel to ignite. Answer a is not correct because the EGR system is used to reduced NO_x exhaust emissions, which would be higher if the EGR valve was stuck closed, but this would not cause an increase in HC emissions. Because only high HC exhaust emissions are present, a defective regulator, answer b, is not a likely cause. Answer d is not correct because high IAC counts indicate that the PCM is commanding a higher idle speed. The IAC does not affect the air-fuel mixture and is therefore unlikely to be the cause of high HC exhaust emissions.

105. **The correct answer is c.** A defective MAF sensor, that when unplugged would cause the engine to start, is the most likely cause of the no-start condition. The MAF sensor is a high authority sensor and if it were defective and sending incorrect data to the PCM, the PCM would process the incorrect information on the amount of air entering the engine and command the incorrect amount of fuel resulting in a no-start condition. When the MAF sensor is unplugged, the PCM then looks at other sensors to try to determine the amount of fuel needed including the engine coolant temperature (ECT) and engine speed data. With this backup information, the PCM will command the amount of fuel that, while it may not be exactly suitable for best performance and lowest emissions, will result in the engine starting and running. Answer a is not correct because even though a defective PROM (programmable read only memory) chip could cause a no-start condition, it would not be affected by the unplugging of the MAF sensor. Answer b is not correct because, while a defective TP (throttle position) sensor could cause a no-start condition if the signal wire was shorted to the 5-volt reference, it would not be affected by the unplugging of the MAF sensor. Answer d is not correct because a MAP (manifold absolute pressure) sensor when used on an engine equipped with a MAF is used as a backup for the MAF sensor and as a diagnostic sensor to test the EGR system on most OBD-II-equipped vehicles. A defective MAP would not cause a no-start condition.

106. The correct answer is c. A defective TP (throttle position) sensor is the most likely cause of a hesitation during acceleration. When the throttle is depressed by the driver, the TP sensor voltage increases. This increase in voltage is used by the PCM to supply additional fuel to help prevent a hesitation. If the TP sensor is not functioning, the PCM will not be able to sense that the throttle is being depressed, resulting in a hesitation. Answer a is not correct because a defective oxygen sensor, while it could affect engine operation, is not a likely cause of a hesitation problem. Answer b is not correct because low engine compression would likely cause the engine vacuum to be lower than normal resulting in a richer-than-normal air-fuel mixture being supplied to the engine due to MAP sensor readings and would be unlikely to cause the engine to hesitate when accelerated. Answer d is not correct because, even though excessive exhaust system backpressure would reduce engine performance, it is unlikely to cause the engine to hesitate when accelerating from a stop.

107. The correct answer is b. The fuel pressure regulator is located on the fuel return line. The low fuel pressure must have been caused by an open or partially open fuel pressure regulator because when the return line was closed, normal fuel pressure was restored indicating that the fuel pump itself was functioning correctly. Answer a is not correct because the pressure would not return to normal if the injectors were leaking and the fuel return line was closed. Answer c is not correct because when the fuel return line was closed, the fuel pressure was restored to normal indicating that the fuel pump was functioning correctly. Answer d is not correct because the oil pressure switch and/or the fuel pump relay could not be the cause because the fuel pump was functioning with the only problem being fuel pressure related.

108. The correct answer is b. The vacuum hose attached to the fuel pressure regulator on most fuel pressure regulators (except returnless designs) is meant to provide a vacuum assist to the regulator spring when the engine is under light load conditions, resulting in lower fuel pressure. When the engine is operating under high loads, the manifold vacuum decreases causing an increase in fuel pressure so that, regardless of engine operation, the same difference in pressure is exerted across the fuel injector. When the line is removed from the regulator, the fuel pressure should increase the same as would occur if the engine were under a heavy load. Answer a is not correct because when the hose is removed, the fuel pressure increases and would be unlikely to cause the engine to stumble or stall. Answer c is not correct because the fuel pressure would increase, not decrease. Answer d is not correct because, even though the fuel pressure would increase, normal engine controls such as the IAC would still control the speed of the engine.

109. The correct answer is c. Both technicians are correct. All of the scan tool data look normal for a vehicle traveling at 67 mph (108 km/h) except the oxygen sensor reading, which is lower than usual, not exceeding 654 mV. This tends to indicate that the engine is operating too lean. Technician A is correct because a weak fuel pump could cause the lean condition. Technician B is correct because a clogged fuel filter could cause a lean condition. Answers a, b, and d are not correct because both technicians are correct.

110. The correct answer is c. Both technicians are correct. Fuel trim numbers result from oxygen sensor readings and a +20% fuel trim number indicates that the oxygen levels in the exhaust are higher than normal and the PCM is commanding that an addition 20% fuel be injected into the cylinder to try to compensate for the lean operating condition. Technician A is correct because an exhaust leak upstream (such as a cracked exhaust manifold) could cause outside oxygen to enter the exhaust which would cause the oxygen sensor to read lower (leaner) than normal. Technician B is correct because a defective spark plug wire would cause a misfire and the unburned fuel and oxygen would be forced by the oxygen sensor. The sensor does not detect the unburned fuel but does detect the oxygen, and the voltage of the oxygen sensor would be lower than normal. Answers a, b, and d are not correct because both technicians are correct.

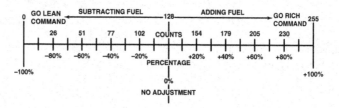

111. **The correct answer is a.** A small vacuum leak would cause a leaner-than-normal air-fuel mixture and the PCM would then compensate for this by increasing the fuel. A small vacuum (air) leak at idle represents a high percentage of the air entering the engine compared to when the engine is operating at 2,500 RPM where the small leak would not have any effect on engine operation. Answer b is not correct because even though a defective or skewed MAF sensor could be the cause of the fuel trim issue, it would be unlikely to affect the air-fuel mixture only at idle speed. Answer c is not correct because, even though a defective fuel pressure regulator can cause an air-fuel ratio problem, it is unlikely to affect the engine at idle speed only. Answer d is not correct because the IAC controls idle speed and is not used to control nor does it affect the air-fuel ratio.

112. **The correct answer is b.** Technician B is correct because a longer-than-normal injector pulse width would be commanded by the PCM if the oxygen sensor detected a lean exhaust condition. A cracked exhaust manifold would allow outside air containing 21% oxygen into the exhaust stream and past the oxygen sensor. This would cause the oxygen sensor voltage to be lower than normal and the PCM would then increase the injector pulse width with fuel trim values. Technician A is not correct because a longer (higher) than normal injector pulse width would result in more fuel being injected, which would cause the engine to operate richer. If the engine were getting fuel due to a fault with the charcoal canister (EVAP) system, the added fuel would make it richer rather than providing a leaner (lower) pulse width to compensate for the added fuel. Answers c and d are not correct because Technician B only is correct.

113. **The correct answer is c.** Fuel trim values are used to correct for a rich or lean condition as detected by the oxygen sensor(s). The short-term fuel trim (STFT) can make fast but limited changes to the air-fuel ratio, whereas the long-term fuel trim (LTFT) reacts slower but can add or subtract more fuel as necessary up to a limit. Fuel trim numbers ±10% or less are generally considered normal and do not represent a fault. In this case, the LTFT is +25%, which indicates that for whatever reason, the PCM is reacting to a lean exhaust condition by increasing the injector pulse width to compensate. When the compensation has occurred, then the exhaust should be OK, meaning that the air-fuel mixture is now correct. Answer a is not correct because, even though the engine was running lean, the fuel trim has compensated for the condition by adding fuel resulting in the engine operating correctly at this time. Answers b and d are not correct because the fuel trim number indicates that the exhaust has been lean, not rich, and is compensating by adding fuel resulting in a properly operating engine.

114. **The correct answer is c.** The most likely result of a low restriction intake air system is that the sound reduction passages will be eliminated, thereby increasing noise, especially during rapid acceleration. Answers a and b are not correct because the amount of air will be measured either by the MAF sensor or calculated based on MAP sensor readings so the proper air-fuel mixture should be maintained. More airflow is likely to result, but additional fuel will be available thereby increasing horsepower and torque even if only slightly. The only exception may occur during open loop conditions, but even then, fuel trim should cause the mixture to be close to the same as before the cold air induction system was installed. Answer d is not correct because even though answer c is correct, answer b is not correct.

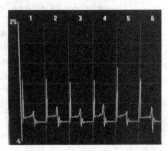

ADVANCED ENGINE PERFORMANCE
SPECIALIST TEST (L1)

CATEGORY: EMISSION CONTROL SYSTEMS DIAGNOSIS

115. **The correct answer is a.** A clogged catalytic converter would create excessive exhaust system backpressure, causing the EGR valve area to become hotter than normal. This excessive heat buildup could cause the EGR valve transducer to fail and if the restricted exhaust system problem is not corrected, another repeated failure could occur. Answer b is not correct because even though a vacuum leak at the intake manifold gasket could cause a drivability concern, it is unlikely to be the root cause of a repeated EGR valve transducer failure because resulting engine miss or incorrect air-fuel mixture could not cause excessive heat near the EGR valve. Answer c is not correct because a partially clogged injector, while it could cause a drivability problem, would not cause stress to the EGR valve or transducer. Answer d is not correct because while clogged EGR ports would likely cause engine spark knock and excessive NO_x exhaust emission, the condition is not likely to cause stress to the EGR valve transducer.

116. **The correct answer is d.** Both engine banks are lean and the fuel trim numbers indicate that fuel is being added to help compensate for a lean exhaust. The most likely fault would be in the fuel delivery system such as fuel pump and fuel filter because all cylinders are being affected. Answer a is not correct because a fault in the exhaust system, while it could cause a drivability problem, is unlikely to be the cause of a lean exhaust condition. Answer b is not correct because, even though a restriction or leak in the induction system could cause a drivability problem, it is not as likely to be the cause of a lean exhaust compared to a fault in the fuel delivery system. Answer c is not correct because, even though a fault in any of the emission control devices could cause a drivability problem, it is not as likely as the fuel delivery system to cause a lean air-fuel mixture.

117. **The correct answer is a.** A TP sensor signal wire shorted to the 5-volt reference is the most likely cause of a no-start condition because the PCM would enter the clear flood mode and command little, if any, fuel from the injectors. Answer b is not correct because an open TP sensor signal wire would not trigger the clear flood mode even though it may set a DTC. Answer c is not correct because if the TP sensor signal wire were shorted to ground, the PCM will likely set a DTC, but will not enter the clear flood mode. Answer d is not correct because while a defective TP sensor could be the cause, it would have to be that the 5-volt reference is shorted internally to the signal wire as stated in a. A defective TP sensor that is electrically open would not be the cause of a no-start condition.

118. **The correct answer is c.** Both technicians are correct. Technician A is correct because an open in the 5-volt reference to the three sensors would cause the low sensor output DTCs. Technician B is correct because if one of the sensors becomes shorted to ground, the 5-volt reference voltage would be zero or close to zero, resulting in all three sensors showing low voltage output. Answers a, b, and d are not correct because both technicians are correct.

119. **The correct answer is c.** Both technicians are correct because excessive NO_x emissions are caused by the engine operating either too hot or too lean. Technician A is correct because excessive NO_x exhaust emissions can be the result of a lean air-fuel mixture. Technician B is correct because a defective cooling fan would tend to cause the engine to operate hotter than normal, which would increase the formation of NO_x exhaust emissions. Answers a, b, and d are not correct because both technicians are correct.

120. **The correct answer is c.** Both technicians are correct. Technician A is correct because a lack of the proper amount of exhaust gases being recirculated into the air-fuel mixture due to clogged EGR ports is a common reason for excessive NO_x exhaust emissions. Technician B is correct because a lack of proper cooling can cause excessive NO_x exhaust emissions such as would occur if the radiator were partially clogged. Answers a, b, and d are not correct because both technicians are correct.

121. **The correct answer is d.** Neither technician is correct. Technician A is not correct because a partially clogged PCV valve or hose would most likely cause an increase in carbon monoxide (CO) exhaust emissions and not likely to cause an increase in NO_x exhaust emissions. Technician B is not correct because a fault in the ignition system would most likely cause excessive hydrocarbon (HC) exhaust emissions and not cause an increase in NO_x exhaust emissions. Answers a, b, and c are not correct because neither technician is correct.

122. **The correct answer is a.** A fault in the ignition system would cause a misfire. The unburned fuel and air are then exhausted past the oxygen sensor where the oxygen is interpreted by the oxygen sensor as being caused by a lean exhaust, resulting in a low sensor voltage. Answer b is not correct because a defective fuel pressure regulator, while it could be the cause of a lean air-fuel mixture, is not likely to be the cause for just bank one, but rather would affect both banks of cylinders. Answer c is not correct because a leaking fuel injector would tend to make the exhaust richer than normal rather than leaner than normal. Answer d is not correct because even though a contaminated MAF sensor can cause a lean air-fuel mixture, it is unlikely to be the cause of a lean condition on only one bank of cylinders.

123. **The correct answer is c.** A leaking fuel injector is the most likely cause of a high oxygen sensor voltage DTC because the exhaust would be richer than normal. Answer a is not correct because a fault in the secondary ignition system would create a misfire resulting in unburned fuel and air passing the oxygen sensor. The oxygen sensor would read lower than normal voltage rather than higher than normal voltage because the sensor reacts to the excessive oxygen in the exhaust rather than to the unburned fuel in the exhaust. Answer b is not correct because a clogged injector would cause the exhaust to be leaner than normal resulting in an oxygen sensor voltage being lower, rather than higher, than normal. Answer d is not correct because a contaminated MAF sensor, while it could cause a richer-than-normal air-fuel mixture, is unlikely to cause one bank of cylinders only to be richer than normal.

124. **The correct answer is a.** A loose gas cap is the most likely cause of an EVAP system leak DTC because the cap must be properly tightened after refueling to be able to pass the leak detection self-test. Answer b is not correct because the PCV system is not tested as part of the EVAP leak detection test procedure and would, therefore, not be a possible cause of the DTC. Answer c is not correct because while a restricted purge line may set an EVAP DTC, it is not likely to set a leak detection DTC. Answer d is not correct because, while a fault with the fuel tank pressure sensor could be the cause of a leak detection DTC, it is not as likely as a loose gas cap.

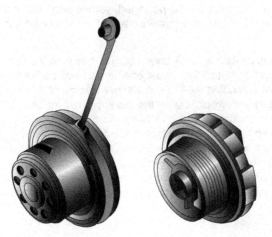

125. **The correct answer is b.** Excessive carbon monoxide (CO) exhaust emissions are usually due to a rich exhaust. If the engine has not reached normal operating temperature, it is likely that the exhaust will be richer than if the vehicle had been driven long enough to become fully warm. This process is called preconditioning. Answer a is not correct because a clogged EVAP hose, while it could set a DTC, is unlikely to cause the engine to be richer than normal. Answer c is not correct because a defective spark plug wire will cause a misfire, but because no spark occurred, the fuel and air did not burn, and therefore, no CO was produced (just unburned hydrocarbons and oxygen/nitrogen from the air). Answer d is not correct because an inoperative EGR valve would cause an increase in NO_x exhaust emissions and would not increase CO exhaust emissions.

126. **The correct answer is b.** A contaminated MAF sensor may not be able to measure accurately all of the air entering the engine. As a result of this error, all cylinders would receive more than the calculated amount of fuel. The PCM supplied just enough fuel for the measured amount of air and the result is that all cylinders would run leaner than normal. Lean exhaust readings cause the oxygen sensor to produce a lower (lean) voltage signal. Answer a is not correct because an open spark plug wire will prevent the air-fuel mixture in the cylinders from igniting. During the exhaust stroke, this unburned gasoline and air is released into the exhaust system where it passes the oxygen sensor. The oxygen sensor will produce a lower voltage due to the oxygen in the air-fuel mixture but only on the same bank as the cylinder with the bad plug wire. One cylinder misfire would not affect both oxygen sensors. Answer c is not correct because a fouled spark plug would likely cause a misfire, which could cause the oxygen sensor to read low voltage but only on the same bank as the fouled plug and would not affect the opposite bank. The oxygen sensor reacts to the oxygen in the exhaust stream, not the hydrocarbons. Answer d is not correct because, while a clogged fuel injector could cause a lean exhaust with lower than normal oxygen sensor voltage, it would only affect the oxygen sensor on the same bank of cylinders as the defective injector and not the oxygen sensors on both banks.

127. **The correct answer is c.** Both technicians are correct. Technician A is correct because, if the EGR ports are clogged, less than specified amounts of exhaust gases will be included in the air-fuel mixture and is likely to result in spark knock. Technician B is correct because a gutted catalytic converter would present less than normal exhaust system backpressure, which is needed to allow many EGR valves to open. If the EGR valve cannot open properly, spark knock and excessive NO_x exhaust emissions are likely. Answers a, b, and d are not correct because both technicians are correct.

128. **The correct answer is b.** Technician B only is correct because a catalytic converter is used to help a chemical reaction by removing the oxygen from the nitrogen in the case of NO_x exhaust emissions and to oxidize CO and HC into CO_2 and H_2O. During these chemical reactions, heat is produced. Therefore, the temperature at the outlet of a catalytic converter should be hotter than the inlet if it is functioning chemically. This test will not, however, test the efficiency of the converter. Technician A is not correct because the catalyst can be poisoned, yet the substrate not melted or damaged, which is the cause of a clogged converter. Answers c and d are not correct because Technician B only is correct.

129. **The correct answer is a.** Technician A only is correct because the idle air control counts are higher than normal (55 instead of 15 to 25 for most engines) as well as the oxygen sensor reading indicating a higher-than-normal reading (400 mV to 900 mV instead of 200 mV to 800 mV). The EGR being partially open at idle speed would cause the displacement of oxygen in the air-fuel mixture plus reduced engine power requiring that the PCM increase the IAC counts to maintain the specified idle speed. The EGR diluted air-fuel mixture also affected the oxygen sensor reading. Technician B is not correct because a stuck open AIR switch valve would cause air flow from the pump to be directed to the exhaust manifold where the added oxygen would cause the oxygen sensor voltage to drop and cause the PCM to richen the air-fuel mixture. The scan tool does not show low oxygen sensor voltage. Answers c and d are not correct because Technician A only is correct.

130. **The correct answer is b.** Technician B only is correct because all of the scan tool data look normal except for the oxygen sensor reading, which indicates that the exhaust is rich. A hole in the canister purge diaphragm would allow gasoline to flow directly into the intake manifold making the mixture richer than normal and increasing fuel consumption. Technician A is not correct because, even if the EGR valve was partially open, it is normal for it to be open at highway speeds, and therefore, there should be no difference in engine operation except at idle speed where the stuck EGR valve would cause a rough idle. Answers c and d are not correct because Technician B only is correct.

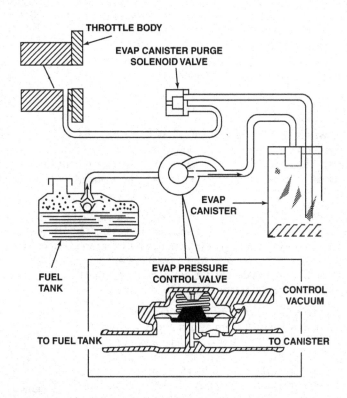

131. **The correct answer is c.** Both technicians are correct. Technician A is correct because if a PCV valve does not rattle, it is definitely bad. Technician B is correct because even though a PCV rattles when shaken, normal engine heat could have changed the spring calibration, requiring that the valve be replaced in order to restore proper crankcase ventilation. Answers a, b, and d are not correct because both technicians are correct.

132. **The correct answer is c.** Both technicians are correct. Technician A is correct because if the one-way exhaust check valve fails, hot exhaust gases would be able to flow into and cause damage to the air pump. Technician B is correct because the airflow from the air pump should be directed to the catalytic converter as soon as the engine achieves closed loop status because the extra air would prevent the proper monitoring of the exhaust gas oxygen control by the oxygen sensor. Answers a, b, and d are not correct because both technicians are correct.

133. **The correct answer is c.** Both technicians are correct. Technician A is correct because the EVAP system is designed to draw fumes from the fuel tank into the charcoal canister. If the tank is overfilled, liquid gasoline would be drawn into the canister and it would become saturated. Technician B is correct because leaks in the system can be detected by pressurizing the system with nitrogen using a low pressure of just 14 inches of water, which is about 0.5 psi. Answers a, b, and d are not correct because both technicians are correct.

134. **The correct answer is c.** Both technicians are correct. Technician A is correct because both solenoid-operated and stepper motor-operated electronic EGR valves can be operated by using the proper software and bi-directional-capable scan tool. Technician B is correct because some exhaust backpressure must be present to close the vent valve in the EGR valve to allow vacuum to open it. Answers a, b, and d are not correct because both technicians are correct.

135. **The correct answer is a.** Technician A only is correct because NOx exhaust emissions are reduced by introducing exhaust gases, which are chemically inactive (called inert) and lower the temperature of the burning air-fuel mixture enough to prevent the nitrogen (N_2) and the oxygen (O_2) from combining to form NO and NO_2 (NOx). Answer b is not correct because excessive CO exhaust emissions are caused by a richer-than-normal air-fuel ratio and would not be affected if the EGR passages were clogged. Answers c and d are not correct because Technician A only is correct.

136. **The correct answer is c.** Both technicians are correct. Technician A is correct because if a catalytic converter rattles, it is physically damaged and must be replaced. Technician B is correct because a catalytic converter can be poisoned by sulfur from the fuel or other chemicals, yet not be physically melted or clogged. Answers a, b, and d are not correct because both technicians are correct.

137. **The correct answer is b.** All catalytic converters that have been replaced must be kept for 60 days for possible inspection by authorities that would be checking that the converter was replaced for the proper reasons and that the cause of failure was reported to the customer. Answers a, c, and d are not correct because catalytic converters that have been replaced must be kept for possible inspection for 60 days.

138. **The correct answer is d.** The EGR system is the exhaust emission control device used to primarily control NOx emissions by reducing peak combustion chamber temperatures. Answer a is not correct because the PCV system is primarily used to reduce hydrocarbon (HC) emission from the crankcase. Answer b is not correct because the air pump (AIR) system is primarily used to reduce carbon monoxide (CO) exhaust emissions. Answer c is not correct because the charcoal canister (EVAP) system is primarily designed to reduce hydrocarbon (HC) emissions.

139. **The correct answer is c.** The catalytic converter must have both a rich exhaust to help reduce NO_x emissions and a lean exhaust to help reduce HC and CO emissions. Answer a is not correct because a PCV valve system is passive and while it does affect the air-fuel mixture, especially at idle, it does not need a varying mixture to function properly. Answer b is not correct because the charcoal canister system is passive and simply absorbs and releases gasoline fumes to help reduce hydrocarbon (HC) emissions. Answer d is not correct because the EGR system is used to reduce NOx exhaust emissions and does not need a varying air-fuel mixture to operate.

140. **The correct answer is c.** Both technicians are correct. Technician A is correct because about 20% of the air needed by the engine at idle speed flows through the positive crankcase ventilation (PCV) system. Any change in the flow through the system could affect the operation of the engine at idle speed. Technician B is correct because except for very controlled situations, the EGR valve on most vehicles is closed at idle speed because it is not needed to control combustion chamber temperature, which can produce NO_x exhaust emissions. If the EGR valve were open at idle, the exhaust gases entering the combustion chamber would displace oxygen and cause a rough engine idle. Answers a, b, and d are not correct because both technicians are correct.

ADVANCED ENGINE PERFORMANCE
SPECIALIST TEST (L1)

CATEGORY: I/M FAILURE DIAGNOSIS

141. **The correct answer is a.** Technician A only is correct. If the engine never reached normal operating temperature, the most likely result is excessive unburned hydrocarbon exhaust emissions. When the cylinder walls are cooler than normal, the air-fuel mixture inside the cylinder will likely condense on the cylinder walls preventing the hydrocarbons being ignited. Then when the piston moves upward on the exhaust stroke, this unburned fuel is pushed out of the cylinder and into the exhaust system. Technician B is not correct because excessive NO_X emission requires high heat and pressure which is not present when the thermostat is stuck open. Answers c and d are not correct because only Technician A is correct.

142. **The correct answer is d.** Nether technician is correct. Technician A is not correct because both CO and O_2 should be low and equal if the air-fuel ratio is correct at 14.7:1. If the CO was high, this indicates a rich mixture, whereas if the O_2 is high, a lean air-fuel ratio is indicated. Technician B is not correct because if there was an ignition misfire event occurring, the HC emissions would be higher than normal due to the unburned fuel, or hydrocarbons (HC) in the cylinder. Answers a, b, and c are not correct because neither technician is correct.

143. **The correct answer is a.** If there is a fault with the exhaust gas recirculation (EGR) system, then excessively high temperatures will occur inside the combustion chamber creating excessive amounts of NO_X. If the engine is equipped with a variable valve (cam) timing system instead of a an EGR valve, a fault in this system can result in less overlap of the intake and exhaust valves and again could be the root cause of excessive NO_X exhaust emissions. Answer b is not correct because a rich air-fuel mixture will not cause excessive heat during combustion due to the cooling effect of the excessive amount of fuel in the cylinders. Answer c is not correct because an ignition misfire would result in the unburned air-fuel to enter the exhaust system and not NO_X. Answer d is not correct because while a clogged catalytic converter could result in higher-than-normal exhaust emissions, it is unlikely to be the cause of excessive NO_X only emissions.

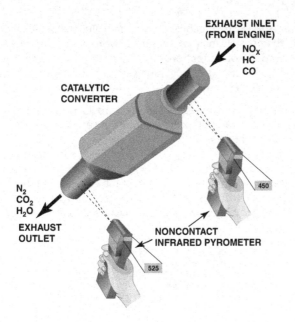

144. **The correct answer is b.** A rich air-fuel mixture is most likely to cause excessive CO exhaust emissions because there is not enough air to convert the fuel (HC) into CO_2 which is an indicator of combustion efficiency. Answer a is not correct because a fault in the EGR system would most likely cause an increase in NO_X exhaust envisions and not higher-than-normal CO emissions. Answer c is not correct because an ignition misfire would result in the unburned air-fuel mixture (HC) but because no combustion occurred, little, if any CO emissions. Answer d is not correct because while a clogged catalytic converter could result in higher-than-normal exhaust emissions, it is unlikely to be the cause of excessive CO only emissions.

145. **The correct answer is b.** When both unburned hydrocarbons (HC) and carbon monoxide (CO) are excessive, this is an indication of an air-fuel mixture that is richer than normal. Answer a is not correct because a fault with the EGR system would likely cause excessive NO_X exhaust emissions and not excessive HC and CO emissions. Answer c is not correct because an ignition misfire, while it would result in excessive HC emissions, would not be the cause of excessive CO emissions too. Answer d is not correct because a partially clogged catalytic converter would likely still be functioning even though at a reduced efficiency and could contribute to excessive HC and CO emissions; however, because these gases are normally very low from a properly operating engine, this is not a likely cause.

146. **The correct answer is a.** A lean air-fuel mixture that is too lean to burn will cause the engine to produce higher-than-normal unburned hydrocarbons (HC) and oxygen (O_2) because combustion did not occur. Answer b is not correct because while a rich mixture will cause excessive HC emissions, a rich mixture will also cause the CO levels to be higher, which is not true in this case. Answer c is not correct because if the EGR ports were clogged, the result would be excessive NO_X exhaust emissions and not excessive hydrocarbon (HC) emissions. Answer d is not correct because a partially clogged air filter on a computer-controlled engine simply reduces engine power and does not change the air-fuel ratio or the emission level.

147. **The correct answer is c.** An ignition misfire caused by a fault in either the primary or secondary ignition system, such as a cracked spark plug, would cause the unburned air-fuel mixture to be exhausted from the cylinder and detected as excessive HC emissions. Answer a is not correct because while a rich mixture will create higher-than-normal HC emissions, it will also cause an increase in CO emissions. Because CO reading was within normal limits, the fault has to be caused by something that affected unburned fuel by itself. Answer b is not correct because even though a lean air-fuel mixture could cause a misfire (lean misfire), this would also result in higher-than-normal levels of O_2. Because the O_2 levels were within the normal range, the most likely cause is answer c. Answer d is not correct because a clogged catalytic converter may not be functioning correctly and therefore would most likely cause a higher-than-normal reading for all measured emission gases, such as HC, CO, and NO_X and not just HC.

148. **The correct answer is d.** An IM program should include a check of the exhaust gases plus an inspection of the gas cap and a visual check to ensure that all emission control devices are in place and not disabled. Answers a, b, and c are not correct because an IM program should include a check of all of the items listed.

149. **The correct answer is D.** Neither technician is correct. Technician A is not correct because 15 ppm of HC is well within the normal limits for unburned hydrocarbons (HC) according to most emissions standards. Technician B is not correct because 55 ppm of NO_X is well within the normal limits for oxides of nitrogen (NO_X) according to most emissions standards. Answers a, b, and c are not correct because neither technician is correct.

150. **The correct answer is c.** A hole in the exhaust system would allow outside air (21% oxygen) to enter the exhaust system and be measured as O_2. The air enters the exhaust system during a low pressure period after each exhaust "pulse" when there is a slightly lower pressure. Answer a is not correct because while a missing air filter would cause dirt to enter the engine, it would not be the cause of excessive O_2 in the exhaust. Answer b is not correct because a fouled spark plug would likely result in a misfire causing higher-than-normal levels of HC and O_2 to exit from the exhaust, not just higher than normal levels of O_2. Answer d is not correct because a stuck open fuel injector would cause an excessive amount of fuel to enter the combustion chamber causing excessive CO and HC emissions and very low levels of O_2.